Anonymous

The Dramatic Works Of The Right Honourable Richard Brinsley Sheridan

With A Memoir Of His Life

—

Anonymous

The Dramatic Works Of The Right Honourable Richard Brinsley Sheridan
With A Memoir Of His Life

ISBN/EAN: 9783348010597

Printed in Europe, USA, Canada, Australia, Japan

Cover: Foto ©ninafisch / pixelio.de

More available books at **www.hansebooks.com**

THE

DRAMATIC WORKS

OF THE

RIGHT HONOURABLE

RICHARD BRINSLEY SHERIDAN,

WITH A

MEMOIR OF HIS LIFE,

LONDON:
BELL & DALDY, YORK STREET, COVENT GARDEN.
1869.

PREFACE.

A Memoir prefixed to the present edition of Sheridan's Dramatic Works contains the most striking circumstances that marked the eventful life of the author. These are necessarily condensed, and such only recorded as are based upon unimpeachable testimony; the numerous apocryphal anecdotes which have found their way into circulation having been intentionally rejected. The object of the editor has been to place before the public, in a single volume, both the Memoirs and the Plays in as authentic a form as existing materials permit. The difficulties attendant upon such a task may be inferred from the facts hereinafter narrated.

G. G. S.

CONTENTS.

BIOGRAPHICAL MEMOIR.

DRAMATIC WORKS.

THE LIFE

OF

THE RIGHT HONOURABLE

RICHARD BRINSLEY SHERIDAN.

SCARCELY anything remains at the present hour to attest
the superiority of Richard Brinsley Sheridan over the great
men of the times just passed away, but his contributions to the
dramatic literature of the country, yet was he acknowledged
to be at one period of his existence the most gifted genius of
his age. Unfortunately for his memory, his last and least
happy moments are those best remembered. He has been
judged of when the decay of his intellect, the carelessness,
nay, even the recklessness of his conduct, and the perplexi-
ties in which he was involved, had changed the character of
the man. He has been regarded as the dissipated thoughtless butterfly that passed through an ephemeral existence;
as one who was merely a brilliant ornament of society, or the
boon companion of an idle hour. Far superior, however, was
he to almost all those great personages who figured with him
on the stage of existence in those qualities which are most
highly prized in the busy section of the world.

His life is a romance. Even those who are wont to receive with incredulity the narrative of the biographer, believing him either a panegyrist labouring to exalt the hero
who has excited his fancy, or the promulgator of some visionary doctrine, must acknowledge that the incidents which
marked the career of Sheridan are too singular not to be recorded, and that they are of sufficient importance to be narrated by different individuals according to the respective
views they entertain of the many events in which, from his

position in the world, he was necessarily involved. If genius of the highest order in literature, if the eloquence that enchants, rivets the attention, and likewise touches the human heart, if the mingling in every question that agitates an empire, and produces an influence upon it, if splendid success followed by the sad vicissitudes of Fate are ever objects of our curiosity, they are in no one instance more singularly exemplified than in Sheridan.

He lived in an age of excitement, of which those who are now in the meridian of their days can, from the repose which they have enjoyed, form but a feeble idea. He was one of the most active, the most intelligent, the most fascinating of those who have stamped their names upon that singular page of history. There was no event in which he was not a leader, there was no great question, whether foreign or domestic, that he did not investigate and pronounce an opinion upon, which was listened to with respect and admiration by a large portion of the nation. His voice was the guide of a great and influential party; he was the attached friend of a band of patriots; and through good and evil repute supported, with manly ardour, a cause which did not bring with it the emoluments of the world, nor did he leave the camp when it was unguarded by some, and almost betrayed by others.

Professor Smyth thus speaks of him:—" There were three others that flourished at the same time with him, the great minister and splendid debater, Mr. Pitt, the great philanthropist and orator, Mr. Fox, the great philosopher and enlightened statesman, Mr. Burke; but he who to a certain degree might be said to unite the powers of all was Mr. Sheridan. He had not in such high superiority the distinguishing qualities of each—he had not the lofty tone and imposing declamation of Pitt—he had not the persuasive vehemence of Fox—he had not the inexhaustible literature and ready philosophy of Burke; but when he spoke on a great occasion, and prepared himself with all the necessary knowledge, nothing appeared wanting to the perfect orator. Grace of manner, charm of fluency of language, and above all a brilliancy of sarcasm, a wit and a humour, and again a felicity of statement made him the delight of every audience, and that excited the admiration of his opponents themselves."

The panegyric pronounced upon him by Lord Byron in

now somewhat trite, but it is most true : "Whatever Sheridan has done or chosen to do, has been, *par excellence*, always the best of its kind. He has written the best comedy, 'The School for Scandal;' the best opera, 'The Duenna'—in my mind far before that St. Giles' lampoon, the 'Beggar's Opera;' —the best farce, 'The Critic;' it is only too good for an afterpiece; and the best address, 'The Monologue on Garrick;' and to crown all, delivered the very best oration, the famous Begum speech, ever conceived or heard in this country." These, however, are but a portion of the claims which he has to the highest consideration; for scarcely had he attainèd the foremost rank amongst the comic writers of the age, when he astonished and delighted the statesmen who surrounded him with the clearness of his political views, developed with all the power and splendour of eloquence. His friends had but just marvelled at the dexterity with which he gained an influence over the heir apparent to the throne, and were canvassing the merits of the advice which guided that prince through paths of considerable difficulty, when even his opponents were unanimously praising him in the loudest language for the exhibition of the purest patriotism, and admiring the conduct that he pursued during one of the most perilous moments that ever occurred in the annals of England —the Mutiny at the Nore.

The circumstances that are detailed in the following pages will, we think, plead an apology for many of the errors that have been strongly condemned; it will be found that a large portion of his pecuniary embarrassments did not originally spring from improvidence, but from the peculiar sources of his means, and from the unexpected position in which, at the very outset of his life, he found himself. He was placed, in an unaccountable manner, at the head of a great establishment, which seemed to yield unceasing means of expenditure, from whose treasury he was enabled to draw almost without acknowledgment; it appeared to offer endless wealth—the very purse of the Fortunatus of his childish days was in his hands. It was not only the inexhaustible vein of daily treasure that enabled him to multiply his means; to create new shares, to issue debentures, and to follow the thousand devices of the skilful financier was, for a length of time, as easy as to draw a cheque upon his banker. It afforded him a marriage settlement, or a new edifice, hence the mind became vitiated, false, and factitious views of property took possession of it; all was however paper money, based upon no solid means, it lured the credulous victim on, until he expected at every step more gold—he found at last that his wealth was visionary, and when compelled to acknowledge the melancholy truth, it was too late to recede. Harassed at every step, he had recourse to deception till it became systematic, he lost his caste in society, he sought relief in dissipation, and when his home was invaded by his angry creditors, he rushed to places where he gradually learnt habits that undermined his constitution and weakened his intellect. If, however, Sheridan was to be blamed, how much more so were his friends! how much more the public! It is a deep reflection upon the morals and upon the character of the country that such a man was allowed to suffer distress and misery; the selfishness of the great, the heartlessness of society, the mammon worship of the many was never more conspicuous than in its treatment of its devoted servant.

In this country virtue and talents may be respected by the few—wealth by all—he who loses the one may in vain possess the other, his welcome in that world which hung upon his shadow is past; the good that he has done is forgotten. Such was the fate of Sheridan; those who had been the warmest admirers of his splendid talents, were at first amused with the narratives of his cleverness in eluding the vigilance of his numerous creditors, but gradually they spoke of his imprudence, and then learnt to treat him with contempt. He had to stoop to the meanest subterfuges to escape from present embarrassment, or to degrade himself by the vilest cunning for a momentary supply of funds. How humiliating to his own mind must have been the comparison of the days when listening senates were hushed when he spoke!—how fearful to him must have been the remembrance of those brilliant hours of his youth, when he was the theme of general observation! Consider him, however, in what light we may, still did he maintain some superiority over all those by whom he was surrounded, and in almost every scene of his eventful life he was an actor who obtained and excited the wonder, if not the admiration of his contemporaries.

Even the romantic incidents attending upon his private life

are such only as occur to men unlike the ordinary class of our fellow-beings. The celebrated object of his choice, the clever manner in which he contrived to outwit his rivals in love, becoming not only the theme of conversation in a fashionable watering-place, but of newspaper controversy, drew upon him at an early age the general attention; from that period every circumstance of his life became public property, indeed it was then evident that his lot could not be cast in obscurity, but that he had that within him, which, when duly exercised, would lead to his filling a distinguished position in society. How, too, did the bold daring with which he undertook the management of a great theatrical establishment tell upon the public mind, for all knew that he must be dependent on his own abilities for his financial resources ! Surrounded at an early age by men of the highest talent, he was quickly re-marked amongst them for the brilliancy of his conversation, his flashes of wit, and the ease and elegance of his manner. These qualifications which made him so delightful in society, are too apt to render their possessor self-indulgent, vain and careless, nor was Sheridan on these points unlike the rest of his fellow-beings, gradually faults began to ripen into vices, the feebleness with which he resisted the first inroads upon his original sense of honour and of virtue, led to a reck-lessness and sensuality which eventually were remembered, when his brighter qualities were somewhat dimmed. As the generation passed away in which his nobler characteristics had been developed they were almost forgotten, and those who were rising in the world saw only that state which was, in comparison, one of degradation, and hence they estimated him less than those who had been dazzled by the early lustre of his career.

Valuable, doubtless, would be considered the moral lessons deducible from a scrutiny into his errors and defects ; but sufficient for us is it in our sketch to relate the prominent circumstances of his life, to delineate him with that fair and honest colouring which is required for truth, more consonant would it be with our feelings to throw a veil over his follies and inconsistencies rather than to scan them too deeply, the brilliancy of his talents, and the severity of his misfortunes, command for the thoughtlessness of Richard Brinsley Sheri-dan, oblivion—for his sorrows, respect.

He has found two biographers, both of whom have entered with some degree of warmth into his political career. The first, Dr. Watkins, was a Tory of the old school, the other, a Whig, of equally uncompromising caste. They have seen through glasses which operate on every subject of their examination with power of a totally different kind; the same topic is magnified or diminished according to the respective instrument that each holds. Much is to be said in praise of the diligence with which Dr. Watkins has investigated the numerous great questions which engaged the attention of Sheridan, but his strong bias shines forth on all occasions. He views everything as a good consistent follower of Pitt would naturally do, he thinks only of the heaven-born minister, he insinuates that his opponents were actuated by malevolence, were besotted in ignorance, and were worthy condign punishment. His detestation of the French Revolution was only surpassed by his terror lest parliamentary reform should ever be brought about in England. From so decided a partisan there was little to be expected, and he has throughout evinced too much of the politician, of the humblest grade, to be the judge of one who had any pretension to rank amongst statesmen. Of his private life he has drawn but a feeble sketch, whatever he knew and gave was derived from Mr. Samuel Whyte, who had for a short period been Sheridan's teacher.

Moore's life has greater claims to our consideration; although it has the internal evidence of its being a laboured panegyric upon the great Whig statesman, Fox, it furnishes us with a consistent narrative of the most remarkable events in which Sheridan became a partaker, still they are more or less tinted with the colouring which, as a decided Whig, Moore was likely to make use of. The private life is of a most poetic character. It is the work of a rich fancy, rendering everything it touches more beautiful than nature in her sweet simplicity usually attempts. He sought from the immediate family and friends materials for his publication, and of course received from them only such as were likely to embellish his narrative, and produce the most favourable effect. It is not to be supposed that truth has ever been wantonly sacrificed, but much has been suppressed, and much has been overcharged; so that a picture somewhat gaudy, but bearing the general character, has been produced. Mrs Lefanu, the youngest sister of Sheridan, communicated the romantic details of the love affair in which Sheridan was so early in life involved, and they are necessarily tinctured with the feeling which an affectionate relation would naturally wish should be experienced by all those who would read the memoirs. The great advantage which Moore had was free access to all the manuscripts that Sheridan left behind him; of these he has admirably availed himself; he has shown us the gradual development of the School for Scandal from the first germ; he has exhibited to us that it was the slow and laborious effort of long consideration; that it reached by a gradual process that perfection to which it ultimately attained. From the evident study bestowed upon this and his other plays, Moore has attempted to deduce, and his opinion has been followed by others, that Sheridan was not a man of quick ideas, of rapid and vigorous fancy, but that all he did was carefully and slowly prepared, patiently digested and long paused upon before it was made public. That this may have been the case in his early career, and that in his latter days he may have had recourse to his memory rather than to his imagination may be granted, but no man was possessed of greater readiness in his best days, and few have exhibited, more quickly, unpremeditated wit, bursts of genius, and glow of fancy.

A most interesting narrative has been drawn up by the distinguished Professor of History at Cambridge, who lived under the roof of Sheridan, as the tutor of his son Thomas, and has been read by a few; it is eloquent, as everything must be from that ornament of our literature, Professor Smyth.

We have also a slight sketch by the hand of Leigh Hunt. The modesty with which he has given it, would forbid any attempt to find fault with it, but when we remember the position he holds, as a poet and a critic, that "nihil non tetigit quod non ornavit," we must be excused from expressing our regret that he has so cursorily glanced at the dramatic works of Sheridan, and so heedlessly admitted, as facts, the wanton assertions of those who have pretended to be acquainted with the circumstances of his life. The few observations on the education of Sheridan are erroneous, for although he gave little or no attention to classical knowledge, he was not so thoroughly incapable as he has described him to have been; nor ought the epithets, applied to the gentleman who fought two duels with Sheridan, to have been given without some inquiry as to the propriety of their adoption. There is, however, such polish and so much fancy in the little brochure, that it will be perused with infinite pleasure.

Sheridan was born in Dublin, in the year 1751. His family boasted on both sides genius. His grandfather, Dr. Sheridan, was the friend, nay it is said the instructor, of Swift, and was not only distinguished for his classic attainments, but "for such a ready wit and flow of humour, that it was impossible for any, even the most splenetic man, not to be cheerful in his company." He was not a fortunate man, and by no means a careful one. He lost his appointment as one of the Court Chaplains by a somewhat ludicrous incident. He was called upon to preach before the Lord Lieutenant, and as he had not prepared himself for such an event, he hastily snatched up a sermon, innocent enough of politics, but the text of which was, "Sufficient unto the day is the evil thereof;" unfortunately for him the day on which he delivered a discourse, so headed, was the first of August, the anniversary of the accession to the throne of George the First, an occasion on which every species of flattery to the powers in authority would have been much more acceptable. He was, therefore, suspected of Jacobinism, and lost all chance of rising in his profession. Thomas, the third son of Dr. Sheridan, and the father of Richard Brinsley Sheridan, was distinguished as an actor, a teacher of elocution, and as the author of a pronouncing dictionary, that has, from its first appearance, been generally received as a useful addition to our literature. Although an unsuccessful person on the great stage of life, he played his part with much energy, and his name has descended to posterity amongst those who have been useful in their generation.

It is one of the pet theories of the day, that men of genius have had on the female side a parent much above the ordinary class of women in intellectual power, and certainly Sheridan is one of the instances that may be adduced. The authoress of so many works of merit deserves a niche in the Temple of Fame; it is, however, not to be forgotten, that one of her plays, "The Dupe," was condemned for some passages that were considered as offensive to the laws of decorum "The Discovery" was more fortunate, it was hailed as a "moral, sentimental, yet entertaining performance;" but the length and languor of its scenes became somewhat insupportable. Garrick, it was, who bore the whole onus of the play, and performed a pedantic character, considered to be quite unsuited to him, in such a way as to elicit infinite entertainment; he seemed entirely to have relinquished his natural ability, and to have assumed an air of unutterable dulness; the younger Colman says, "he made the twin stars which nature had stuck in his head, look like two coddled gooseberries." Her "Memoirs of Sidney Biddulph" have been much admired, not only for their power of awakening our sympathy for the sorrows of man upon this transitory globe, but for the beautiful language in which they point out the blissful rewards of a hereafter to those who. by their conduct, may deserve them.

Amongst other productions of her pen Nourjahad is particularly distinguished alike for the development of the story and the gracefulness of its diction, and even to the present hour it enjoys a high degree of popularity amongst youthful readers, who, if they are not able to detect the moral of a tale that shows that the gifts of perpetual youth and of endless riches, if not properly estimated, will produce sensuality and brutality, are at any rate delighted with the beautiful pictures of oriental manners that she has so admirably delineated.

In his seventh year Sheridan was placed, together with his brother, under the tuition of Mr. Samuel Whyte of Dublin; they were the first two pupils he had; their mother, in giving them to his care, made use of an expression which has been oftentimes repeated as if it had been applied to Sheridan in the latter days of his boyhood. She pointed out to Mr. Whyte that in the profession he had undertaken patience was absolutely necessary. "These boys will be your tutors in that respect. I have hitherto been their only instructor, they have sufficiently exercised mine, for two such impenetrable dunces I never met with;" from such an expression, at such an age, it would be most unfair to form an opinion of the intellectual capabilities of a child.

On his parents settling in England, which was in the year 1762, Harrow was selected as the best school for his educa tion, here he exhibited none of that superior intellect for which his future life was to be distinguished. Dr. Parr has given evidence as to his deficiency in those studies which were the pride of that seminary, but observes, "He was a favourite amongst his schoolfellows, mischievous, and his pranks were accompanied by a sort of vivacity and cheerfulness; he was a great reader of English poetry, but was careless about literary fame; he appears to have been removed too early from school." He, however, in after life was, according to the same testimony, given to classic reading, and was well acquainted with the orations of Cicero and of Demosthenes, and impressed Dr. Parr with an idea that he was possessed of considerable classic attainments. Mr. Roderic, Dr. Sumner's assistant during the time that Sheridan was at Harrow, says, "that he was a shrewd, artful, and supercilious boy, without any shining accomplishments or superior learning."

During his residence at Harrow he lost his excellent and amiable mother who died at Blois, where the family had for some time resided, in the year 1766.

Whilst at Harrow he formed an intimacy with a fellow pupil Mr. Halhed, with whom he entered into a literary partnership, which was not dissolved by their both quitting their school, the one for Oxford, the other for Bath. Together they laboured upon a farce in three acts, called "Jupiter," from which they anticipated to reap a sum of no less than £200, but they were doomed to disappointment, for it never was brought before the public, and whatever of merit it may have possessed, we are unable to judge; for, with the exception of some extracts which Moore has given, we are not in possession of any remains of a burlesque which has been supposed to have remained long on the memory of Sheridan, and to have been the model on which the " Critic" was founded. A miscellany was projected by the friends, but it did not live beyond one number; this was but poor, if we may be allowed to form a judgment from the short specimen that has been preserved. A collection of occasional poems, and a volume of crazy tales, were amongst the dreams that flitted across the imaginations of the enthusiasts, but beyond fancy's first sketch it would appear that they were not allowed to proceed.

One, however, of the united productions of these aspirants to literary fame was actually committed to the press, and has reached us; it has been the means of exhibiting positive proof that they were indifferent judges of that which was likely to impress the public with a favourable opinion of their merits. They selected a Greek author, but little known, Aristænetus, and rendered his Greek prose into English verse. The facetious Tom Brown had previously translated, or rather imitated, some select pieces from the epistles of this author, but the young poets thought that he had failed in giving the elegance and the wit of the original. They stated that "their object was not so much to bring to light the merits of an undistinguished author, as to endeavour to introduce into the language a species of poetry not frequently attempted, and but very seldom with success, that species which has been called the 'simplex munditiis' in writing, where the thoughts are spirited and fanciful without quaintness, and the style simple, yet not inelegant." There is a great variation of the metres employed, and each epistle has its own particular measure, and it would be difficult to point out upon what particular species of poetry they relied for their claim to success. The epistles of Aristænetus are altogether unknown, and what could have tempted young and cultivated minds to bestow a thought upon a writer who had neither a name amongst classical authors, nor a single recommendation from a modern critic, we are utterly at a loss to imagine. We can only ascribe it to an enthusiastic taste for compositions which occasionally captivate youth, and for which we are doubtless indebted for Moore's translation of Anacreon, and for his juvenile poems which are admired at the commencement of our career in life. They were compelled to soften many passages which were indelicate in the original, and to suppress others as indecent, the preface to which the initials H. S. are added is concluded by a passage informing us that the original is divided into two parts, the present essay containing only the first, by its success must the fate of the second be determined. Carefully did they watch the impression made on the public by their labours, they saw that they were unsuccessful, and they wisely attempted no more. There is but one Epistle "The Garden of Phyllion," that possesses much merit, and this is spoilt by the introduction, not only of language somewhat too glowing, but of libertinism totally uncalled for in a descriptive pastoral. The

Tenth Epistle has some striking passages ; but with every wish to view the first productions of youth with kindness and lenity, we cannot but express our gratification that the second part never appeared, and that the first has been but little read. One of the reviews of the period has very justly said, " We have been idly employed in reading it, and our readers will in proportion lose their time in perusing this article."

In the year 1771 Sheridan's father took his young family to Bath, there to reside whilst he was fulfilling his theatrical engagements elsewhere. No place could have been more unfortunately selected for the début in life of a young man ; for whatever may have been the charm of society there, nothing could by possibility be more destructive to habits of industry and the exercise of the higher qualities of the mind and the heart, than the unvarying monotony of indolence and selfishness in which the visitors of that once fashionable watering-place constantly indulged themselves. The lounge in the pump room and in the streets of Bath may have furnished young Sheridan with sketches of those characters which have rendered his dramas the admiration of those who are initiated into society, but it was the very worst school for the education of a man whose destiny was forcibly urging him on to figure as one of the most prominent men in public life. From all quarters of the globe congregated not only the invalid to gain health from the thermal springs, but the idle, the dissipated, and also the lovers of the arts. Bilious East Indians, Irish fortune-hunters, gouty statesmen, ladies of rank, "chiefly remarkable for the delicacy of their reputation," went there to seek relief from ennui. To furnish relief for them, there was an admirable theatre, time out of mind the nursery for the London stage, and concerts, such as were not to be outrivalled in Europe, and private parties of every description, where music, dancing, or poetry, was the ruling passion. Every aspirant to fame wrote poetry, in some guise, nor was Sheridan the last amongst those who sought for a laurel from the reigning Queen of Bath, Lady Miller. This lady, so admirably described to us by Horace Walpole and by Madame D'Arblay, held at her house at Bath Easton, every Thursday, a "fair of Parnassus." We are told by the latter lady "that, notwithstanding Bath Easton is so much laughed at in London, nothing is here more tonish than to visit Lady Miller, who is extremely curious in her company. admitting few people who are not of rank or fame, and excluding of those all who are not people of character very un blemished." Horace Walpole says, "All the flux of quality contended for prizes gained for rhymes and themes; a Roman vase, dressed with pink ribbons and myrtle, received the poetry which was drawn out at every festival. Six judges of these Olympic Games retired and selected the brightest composition, which was rewarded by permission for the author to kneel and kiss the hands of Lady Miller, who crowned the victor with myrtle." This Lady Miller, whose reputation had spread far and wide, as the ruling star of Bath, was a round, coarse, plump looking dame, whose aim it was to appear a woman of fashion, and succeeded only in having the appearance of an ordinary woman in very common life with fine clothes on. Her manners were bustling, her air mock important, and appearance very inelegant. She was, however, extremely good humoured, and remarkably civil.

Many are the pieces of poetry which Sheridan, scarcely then in his twentieth year, produced; amongst them the exquisite stanzas—

> " Dry be that tear, my gentlest love,
> Be hushed that struggling sigh,
> Nor seasons, day, nor fate shall prove
> More fix'd, more true than I.
> Hush'd be that sigh, be dry that tear,
> Cease boding doubt, cease anxious fear.
> Dry be that tear.

> ' Ask'st thou how long my love will stay,
> When all that's new is past?
> How long, ah Delia, can I say
> How long my life will last?
> Dry be that tear, be hush'd that sigh,
> At least I'll love thee till I die.
> Hushed be that sigh.

> " And does that thought affect thee too,
> The thought of Sylvio's death,
> That he who only breath'd for you,
> Must yield that faithful breath?

> Hushed be that sigh, be dry that tear,
> Nor let us lose our Heaven here
>   Dry be that tear."

In a poem addressed to Lady Margaret Fordyce are those lines which have been so universally admired—

> ". . . . Marked you her cheek of rosy hue?
> Marked you her eye of sparkling blue?
> That eye, in liquid circles moving;
> That cheek abashed at Man's approving
> The one, Love's arrows darting round;
> The other, blushing at the wound:
> Did she not speak, did she not move,
> Now Pallas—now the Queen of Love!"

The rest of the poem is very indifferent, and it appears strange that lines of such singular beauty should have been introduced. Amongst the light trifles published one is to be noticed as exhibiting his varied talent, it was written on the occasion of the opening of that splendid pile of buildings, the Upper Assembly Rooms, Sept. 30th, 1771. It is entitled "An Epistle from Timothy Screw to his Brother Henry, Waiter at Almack's," of which the following is an extract.

> "Two rooms were first opened—the long and the round one,
> (These Hogstyegon names only serve to confound one,)
> Both splendidly lit with the new chandeliers,
> With drops hanging down like the bobs at Peg's ears:
> While jewels of paste reflected the rays,
> And Bristol-stone diamonds gave strength to the blaze:
> So that it was doubtful, to view the bright clusters,
> Which sent the most light out, the ear-rings or lustres.
> *   *   *   *   *   *
> Nor less among you was the medley, ye fair!
> I believe there were some beside quality there.
> Miss Spiggot, Miss Brussels, Miss Tape, and Miss Socket,
> Miss Trinket, and aunt, with her leathern pocket,
> With good Mrs. Soaker, who made her old chin go,
> Four hours, hobnobbing with Mrs. Syringo:
> Had Tib staid at home, I b'lieve none would have miss d
>   her,
> Or pretty Peg Runt, with her tight little sister," &c. &c

The allusions are to the splendid ball room and to the octagon room, two of the most perfect specimens of domestic architecture which we possess. The chandeliers, which still remain, were once considered perfect models, and as chef-d'œuvres of the art of glass making. They have been so thoroughly surpassed by modern productions, as to excite our wonder that they should still be retained.

Besides the motley group that lounged in the Crescent, the Circus or the Parades, there were many individuals of great talent with whom Sheridan had the opportunity of mixing. He, however, to judge from his letters, had no wish to be intimate with any of them, and speaks of Mr. Wyndham and Mr. Luttrel, a brother of the colonel, as the only acquaintance he had made. Amongst those who were there was the pious and clever Hannah More; the lively Mrs. Thrale; Fanny and Harriott Bowdler, both blue stockings of the deepest dye; Anstey, the author of the "Bath Guide" "with an air, look, and manner, mighty heavy and unfavourable;" Mrs. Dobson, the translator of Petrarch; Mr. Melmoth, the Pliny Melmoth, "thinking nobody half so great as himself, therefore, playing first violin without further ceremony;" Cumberland "so querulous, so dissatisfied, so determined to like nobody and nothing, but himself;" Dr. Harrington, "dry, comic, and very agreeable," and a whole host of people who have been celebrated in their day, but whose memory alas has faded away.

But the great and ruling passion at Bath was music. The public concerts were delightful recreations, they were the first in England; the private concerts were as detestable, although first rate talent was engaged, and there were amateurs of high consideration. There was Jerningham, the poet; "a mighty gentleman, who looks to be painted, and is all daintification in manner, speech, and dress, singing to his own accompaniment on the harp, whilst he looks the gentlest of all dying Corydons." Miss Latouche singing "not in your Italian style, no, that she hates, and holds very cheap; but all about Daphne and Chloe, Damon and Phyllis;" but the parties in which they sung, were usually all "confusion, worse confounded." "There were quartettos and overtures by gentlemen performers whose names and faces I never knew: such was the never ceasing battling and noise of the card

room, that a general humming of musical sounds, and now
and then a twang, was all I heard," says Madame D'Arblay.
The concerts, however, in the great Assembly Room, were
of the highest character.   Here the works of such composers as Rauzzini, Jackson, the Linleys, and Dr. Harrington, were for the first time produced in a style that had
never yet been equalled; here talent of this kind found its
devoted admirers.   Miss Guest, afterwards the celebrated
Mrs. Miles, and her father, were heard with rapture, and
many of those artists whose talents have commanded the
admiration of Europe.

Amongst those who sang, not only at the oratorios at Bath,
but who had gained a high reputation in all musical circles,
was Miss Linley, the daughter of the eminent composer,
upon whom Nature seems to have lavished her richest treasures, and Art to have nobly seconded her.

This young lady was destined to have a lasting influence
upon the conduct, the talents, and the happiness of young
Sheridan.   Various are the versions of the love tale, and difficult, most difficult, is it to arrive at the real truth of the affair.
At lovers' perjuries they say Jove laughs; and there were,
and there are, many who look upon the whole of this singular event as a tissue of absurd longings after notoriety on
the part of more than one of the individuals engaged in it.
Miss Linley was, beyond a doubt, one of the most accom
plished, as well as beautiful, young women ever seen.

At the early age of sixteen she was surrounded by a host
of admirers, and there is but little doubt that she was one of
the most decided coquettes that ever existed, but beyond this
pretty piece of female folly we sincerely believe that there
was no indiscretion; though a letter written by herself, ad
dressed to Miss Saunders, would almost lead us to imagine
even something beyond it, if that letter be genuine.   She
was admitted to be a model of personal beauty, and the
charms of the fair Maid of Bath were universally acknowledged.   As a public singer, she, was naturally exposed to al-
lurements and temptations, and was very probably obliged to
listen to offers which, in her heart, she might disdain.   The
catalogue of her lovers is somewhat long.   Halhed, the poetic
partner of Sheridan, was not only one, but even Sheridan's
own brother Charles entertained a passion for her.   Norris

who was supposed to have sung himself into her affections: Mr. Watts, a gentleman commoner of Oxford; Mr. Long, a man of large fortune; Sir Thomas Clarges, and several others less known to fame, swelled up a long list. But every student at Oxford, where she sang at the oratorios, was enchanted with this beautiful girl, to whom the title of the divine St. Cecilia was unanimously given. Nothing seemed to fright the University from its propriety so much as a rumour that was industriously circulated that one youth, happier than the rest, had found the soft hour when she had listened, and had consented to accompany him to Scotland, and that a splendid fortune was the result of this matrimonial adventure.

Whatever may have been the merits of these candidates for her love, neither poetry in the shape of Halhed, music in that of Norris, nor wealth in others, had power to move her. Whatever may have been the earlier fancies of her heart—and there seems, from her own confession, to have been some—Richard Brinsley Sheridan had silently, and unsuspiciously, succeeded in winning her affections, and in wooing her for his bride; he contrived, for all is fair in love, to mystify Halhed, to blind his brother Charles, to make the man she fancied that she loved actually odious in her eyes, and by dint of some persuasive power, which lovers only understand, wove a web around her from which there was no possibility of escaping, and eventually carried her off in spite of parents and of lovers, of threats and of swords.

Amongst the characteristics of the ancient city of King Bladud is a lively curiosity, and an innate love of becoming intimately acquainted with the particularities of every body and of every thing, which furnishes forth rich food for constant prattle. Any thing connected with an individual so gifted as Miss Linley, naturally excited the peculiarly inquisitive thirst after subjects for conversation, and soon there arose this matter of a singularly gratifying description for them, of which they failed not to avail themselves; and their appetites were richly tickled by a series of occurrences that involved Miss Linley, Sheridan, and Mr. Matthews; a gentleman of fortune, as principals; and as accessories, the master of ceremonies, Capt. Wade, Capt. Paumier, and several men moving in the highest circles; and they were commented

c

on in the "Bath Herald," conducted by Meyler, a man of considerable ability, and in the "Bath Chronicle" under the direction of Richard Crutwell.

Captain Matthews was the possessor of a large property in Wales, and usually passed the season at Bath in the enjoyment of those gratifications which the fashionable city afforded. He was not altogether, what Leigh Hunt has designated him, a married blackguard, but a man of elegant exterior, and whatever may have been his folly, with regard to Miss Linley, of kindly disposition, of lively manners, and of agreeable conversation, nor was he deficient in intellectual power; and had he bestowed as much time on the cultivation of any of the arts or sciences as he did upon whist, he might have become a useful member of society: but to this game his life was devoted, and the treatise, for a long period the whist player's grammar, which he wrote upon it, evinces that he did not consider it as a means of passing an idle hour, but as a study requiring observation, memory, and the powers of calculation. When the events, about to be narrated, were almost forgotten, and the obloquy, which had been heaped upon him in certain circles, was somewhat washed away by the healing hand of time, Captain Matthews became the centre of a circle, every member of which entertained a strong regard for him, and listened with respect and confidence to his own relation of all the facts, which were much at variance with those detailed by Moore, in his life of Sheridan, and by those who were, from their connection with Sheridan, inclined to believe the statement which from the beginning he had made. Led away by the opinion that prevailed at that period that every female who came prominently before the public was open to the attentions of any man of sufficient fortune to make a handsome settlement, Captain Matthews became a professed admirer of Miss Linley. Admitted into the bosom of the family, he, according to the assertion of Sheridan and of Miss Linley, forgot his own position as a married man, and with more than the usual licence of the times persevered in offers, which, at any rate, were received at first with love and affection, but afterwards with indignation and with expressions of abhorrence. In public he was her constant shadow, and appeared determined to prevent any other man from approaching her too nearly, and this it was said arose from u wish on his part to make it appear that he had succeeded in the lawless object of his incessant desire, and that having failed to make any impression upon her by entreaties, by presents, by threats of the committal of suicide, he sought to accomplish his wishes by the ruin of her character, and the dissemination of the vilest calumnies, which would for ever blast her reputation. To her father she dared not breathe a syllable against this individual, for he was courted and respected by her family; but at length she was determined to disclose to Sheridan, who had already gained her heart, the painful position in which she was placed. After a consultation with his sister, the singular step of a flight to the continent was resolved upon, an elopement took place, and a marriage at a village in the neighbourhood of Calais was the consequence; but as it was deemed right to keep the ceremony a secret, she afterwards went to a convent at Lisle, there to remain till such time as Sheridan might publicly claim her as his wife.

Miss Linley's extraordinary letter, which has fortunately been preserved, will best explain her share in these events.

"Bath, May 2, 1772.

"After so long a silence, and after the many unfavourable reports which must, I dare say, have prejudiced my dear friend against me, how shall I endeavour to vindicate a conduct which has but too much deserved her censure? But if my dear friend will suspend her judgment till I have made her acquainted with my real motives, I flatter myself she will rather be induced to pity than condemn me.

"At the time I wrote last, my mind was in a state of distraction not to be conceived; but I little thought, then, I should ever be forced to the cruel necessity of leaving my friends, and becoming an exile from every thing I hold dear.

"In your answer to that letter, you hinted that you thought I loved Mr. R——, and that that was the cause of my uneasiness; but in that you, as well as many others, have been deceived. I confess myself greatly to blame in my behaviour to him; but I cannot explain myself on this subject, without acquainting you with the first cause of every uneasiness and indiscretion I have since been guilty of. Let me, then, my

c 2

dear girl, beg your patience; for, though my story is long, and not very enlivening, yet such is the affection I have for you, that I cannot bear to think it possible, by the various reports which are so industriously propagated, I may entirely lose your good opinion and esteem—a thing of all others I should most regret. Excuse my being tedious; and when you know the motive which induced me to take this last step, I flatter myself you will once more restore me to your friendship.

   " At the age of twelve years, I was brought from the country, where I had been all my life, and introduced into public, with a heart capable of receiving the softest impressions, and too sincere ever to suspect deceit in another. I was led into scenes of dissipation, when reason and experience were not allowed to assist me in the many temptations which ever surrounded a young girl in such a situation. But, though my credulity often made me feel for the pretended distresses of others, yet my heart was entirely free from love, nor could I be seduced by flattery and compliments; I always considered them as words of course; and never looked upon those people as my friends who made too much use of them.

   " In an evil hour my father was introduced to Mr. Matthews, as one who wished to serve him. My father, who is, like me, too apt to believe every one his friend who professes himself so, gladly embraced the opportunity of gaining the friendship of a man who had it in his power to be of service to him in his business: little did he think he was seeking the serpent who was designed to sting his heart. Mr. Matthews, from the first moment he saw me, resolved to make me his prey, and (child as I then was) left no means untried to make himself master of my affections, thinking but too justly that an impression fixed so early in life could not easily be removed. If it were possible to describe the many arts he made use of to effect this end, you would, I am sure, at once excuse me; but as these are not to be conceived by any one but those who are capable of acting so basely, I must still rely on your goodness.

   " For three years he never ceased his assiduities to me; and though at times my conscience would upbraid me, yet by his respectful behaviour, his counterfeit distress, and by averring sentiments foreign to his heart, he made me, instead of flying from him, not only pity him, but promise him my friendship.

This was my first fault; he saw too plainly that he was not indifferent to me, and made use of every artifice to increase my regard.

"About this time the people began to take notice of his particular behaviour to me, and my friends all spoke to my father to hinder my seeing him; but my father, thinking that my youth was a sufficient safeguard for me, and unwilling to lose, as he thought, a good friend, took no notice of this first alarm. I then began to feel myself, for the first time, wretchedly involved in an unhappy passion for a man whom (though I thought him equally to be pitied) yet it was criminal in me even to think of. When he went into the country for the summer, I resolved, whatever it cost me, to tear him from my heart, and when he returned, to avoid him everywhere. With these resolutions I consoled myself till winter. When he returned, he had not been in town a week before we had repeated invitations to his house. Conscious that I could never forget him, if I was always to be exposed to his solicitations, I informed my mother of every thing he had said to me, and, at the same time, told her how far he had gained my heart.

"Oh, my dear friend, had my mother but then acted properly, I had now been happy; but she, too much attached to interest, laughed at my uneasiness, and told me that novels had turned my head; and that I fancied, if any one was civil to me, he must certainly be in love. She desired I would put such thoughts out of my head; for no man could think seriously of such a child. Thus was I again led into temptation, and exposed to all the artifices of a man whom I already loved but too well, and who was but too sensible of it. I could not fly from the danger; after my first reproof, I was ashamed to mention it again to my mother, and I had every thing to fear from my father's violent temper.

"For another year we went on in the same manner; till, at last, finding it impossible to conquer my inclinations, he soon brought me to a confession of my weakness, which has been the cause of all my distress. That obstacle removed, many others fell of course, and the next season he prevailed on me to meet him at the house of a friend, as we were not permitted to talk together in public. During this time I had many offers of marriage very much to my advantage; but I refused them all. So far had he gained my love, that I resolved never to marry.

"About this time, Mr. Long addressed me. You know by what means I was induced to suffer his visits, though you do not know likewise that another great motive was the hope of forgetting Matthews, and retiring into solitude. After I had consented to receive Mr. Long's visits, I forbade Matthews ever to speak to me; to the consequences of which you yourself were witness. He immediately pretended to be dying, and by that artifice very nearly made me really so. You know how ill I was for a long time. At last he wrote me word, that he must see me once more; that he would then take a final leave of me, and quit the kingdom directly; but he could not resolve to go without seeing me. I was weak enough to comply with his request, as I thought it would be the last time.

"Some way or other, my mother was told of it, when she taxed me with it. I immediately confessed every thing that had passed since I first acquainted her with his behaviour. She was at first greatly enraged; but on my telling her how unexceptionably he had behaved, she was pacified, and consented to conceal it from my father. And indeed, my dear, had any impartial person been present at our meeting, they would have thought Matthews the most unhappy but amiable man in the world; his behaviour was always consistent with the strictest honour; nor did he ever, in the smallest degree, give me any reason to think he had any intentions that were in the least alarming to my virtue. Deceived by such conduct, his merit shone more conspicuous: nor did I wish to get the better of my passion for one whom I thought every way so worthy of it. I considered myself as the cause of all his wretchedness, and thought it would be the height of cruelty if I did not endeavour to alleviate it. But to proceed; my mother resolved to see Matthews herself, and therefore insisted that I should write, and desire to see him again that evening. I did so, and my mother went in my place. You may imagine he was very much surprised at seeing her. She went with a full resolution to upbraid him; yet so far did his arts prevail, that he not only made her forgive but pity him, and promise that this should never make any alteration in our behaviour to him ; and we would still continue our visits and intimacy with him. He promised, however, that he never would for the future attempt to see me.

" About this time my marriage with Mr. Long broke off, and my father went to London to commence a law-suit. During the time he was absent, I went on a visit to Mr. and Mrs. Norton, where you saw me. She had been informed by un-doubted authority that my father would not only lose his suit, but that I should be exposed to the public court; as Mr Long had been informed of my meeting Matthews, and in-tended to make use of that as a plea in court. This being told me suddenly, and at a time when my spirits were greatly distressed, flung me into a high fever. I lost my senses some time, and when I recovered was so weak, and had such strong symptoms of a rapid decline, that, when my father returned, I was sent to the Wells to drink the waters. While I was there, I was told that Matthews, during my illness, had spoken disrespectfully of me in public, and had boasted it was owing to my love for him I was so ill. This behaviour from one for whom I had suffered so much shocked me greatly, and I resolved in my first heat of passion that he should not have it in his power to triumph over my weakness. The resentment I felt was of service to me, as it roused me from a state of stupid despondence, which perhaps would have occasioned my death. It was then that you received my first letter, which must have shown you in what a wretched state of mind I was.

" When I had so far recovered my spirits and health as to be able to walk and ride, I became acquainted with Mr. R——, who, from the first time he saw me, was particular in his behaviour to me. I did not at first observe it, and, as I thought him an agreeable man, and one who I was told bore an unexceptionable character, I did not avoid him so much as I certainly ought. I wished, likewise, by turning my at-tention to him, to eradicate every impression of Matthews; but, though Mr. R. behaved with the greatest delicacy, I found it impossible for me to love him. I went on in this manner some time, and by Mr. R.'s attention to me incurred the ill will of all the ladies, who did not spare to censure my conduct; but as I was conscious in my own heart of no ill, and wished to convince Matthews he had not so much reason to boast of his conquest, I paid very little attention to the envy of the women.

"Mr. R—— had not, as yet, made any professions; but one day he confessed to me that he loved me, but that it was not in his power to marry publicly, as he was entirely dependent on his father, except a pension which he had; but, at the same time, begged me to consent to marry him privately, and to go off with him to any part of the world, till his father died; when he said he would marry me again in the face of the world. This proposal, had I loved him, I should certainly have rejected; but, in the state of mind I then was, I was very angry, and refused seeing him for a great while.

"At this time, Mr. and Mrs. Norton came over to be with me, as they had heard of R——. Through his means, Mr. R—— entreated me to forgive him, and permit him to be on the footing of a friend, and assured me I never should have farther cause to be offended with him. As Mr. Norton, under whose protection I then was, had no objection, and as I really had an esteem for Mr. R——, and thought him a good young man, I consented, and we continued to walk and ride together, but never without Mr. Norton. I was thus situated when Matthews came to the Wells in his road to Wales. He had been extremely ill at Bath, and when I saw him in the public walk at the Wells I could scarce keep myself from fainting. There was such an alteration in his person that I could not believe it possible. He spoke to me once in the walk, and asked me if I resolved to be his death, declared his illness proceeded from the accounts he had heard of me and R——, and that he was now going into the country to die. You may be sure I was greatly affected with his words; but, as I had suffered so much in my reputation by being seen with him, I would not stay to explain myself, or upbraid him with his behaviour to me; I merely told him that the only way to convince me of his sincerity was to leave me, and never see me more. I left him immediately, and went home where, soon after, a lady informed me he had fainted in the Long Room, and that his friends had taken him to Wales, given over by all. This news made me relapse, and had very nearly cost me my life, till I heard again that he was well, and in good spirits, laughing at my distress, and exulting in the success of his scheme. This once more raised my resentment, and I was resolved to encourage Mr. R——; and though I could not consent to go off with him, I told him, (with my father's consent,) that when it was in his power, if he still retained his love for me, and I was free from any other engagements, I would marry him. When I returned to Bath, he followed me, but, as he was very much talked of, I would not suffer him to be so particular. When he was going to D——, he begged me to give him a letter to you, that he might, by you, sometimes hear from me; as I refused to correspond with him. As I wished to have my dear girl's opinion of him, I was not unwilling to trust him with a letter, in which I mentioned something relative to my misfortunes; but luckily mentioned no names, nor could he, if he had read it, understand whom or what it meant. He wrote to me that he was in D——, but never mentioned your name, which I was surprised at, and as I had not heard any thing from you, was a good deal hurt, thinking you would not keep your word with me. In answer to his letter, I desired to know if he had seen you, and begged to be informed of some other circumstances in his letter, which made me uneasy. To this I received no answer, and the account you gave me afterwards, convinced me that he was like all other men—deceitful. I then gave him entirely up, and contented myself with thinking how unworthy all men were of a woman's affection!

"I was in this state of mind when Matthews returned; when, in spite of all I could do or say, I was obliged to visit them, and scarcely a day passed without my having some conversation with him. In these conversations he cleared himself of the imputations alleged against him, and set my conduct in such a point of view, that he made me appear the criminal, and himself the injured person. This and being constantly with him, joined to his engaging behaviour, soon regained him that love which had never been quite extinguished. That gained, I was soon prevailed on to see him; but this did not hinder him from behaving so particular in public, that at last everybody talked of it, and many people spoke to my father.

"I was one night going to bed, when I heard my father and mother talking very loud, and my name and Matthews's were repeated very often; this induced me to listen, and I heard my mother tell my father that I was miserable, and that

Matthews was equally wretched; that we had loved one another for these some years, and that she was sure it would be my death. My father seemed sometimes to pity and sometimes to condemn me, but at last he resolved I should never see him again. In the morning, when I came to breakfast, my spirits were low, and I could not refrain from tears; this soon brought on an explanation with my father, to whom I confessed every thing that had passed; his behaviour was tender to a degree, and by that method he gained more upon me than if he had treated me harshly. Anger I can withstand, but tenderness I never could. My father, after many arguments, wherein he convinced me of the folly, if not wickedness, of such a connection, made me promise never to see him more, and told me he would break off all intercourse with the family immediately. In the afternoon of this day Mrs. Sheridan called, by Matthews's desire, to know the reason why they had not seen me that day.

"Old Mr. Sheridan (who is now in Dublin) is my father's particular friend. When they came to settle in Bath, the strictest intimacy commenced between our families. Miss Sheridan is the only-person (besides yourself) that I would place any confidence in; she is one of the worthiest girls breathing, and we have been always united in the strictest friendship. The same connection subsists between our two younger sisters. There are two brothers, who, on our first acquaintance, both professed to love me; but, though I had the greatest esteem for them, I never gave either of them the least hope that I should ever look on them in any other light than as the brothers of my friend; I own I preferred the youngest, as he is by far the most agreeable in person, understanding, and accomplishments. He is a very amiable young man, beloved by every one, and greatly respected by all the better sort of people in Bath. He became acquainted with Matthews, and was at first deceived in him, but he soon discovered the depravity of his heart, under tho specious appearance of virtue, which he at times assumed; but, perceiving the attachment between us, he resolved to make use of a little art to endeavour if he could to save me from such a villain. For this purpose, he disguised his real sentiments, and became the most intimate friend of Matthews, who at last entrusted him with all his designs in regard to me, and boasted to him how cleverly he had deceived me; for that I believed him to be an angel.

"Excuse my being thus tedious, but it was necessary to let you so far into my connection with the Sheridans, before I could account for my behaviour latterly.

"When Mr. Sheridan came to me in the evening, I only told him something had happened to make me uneasy; but bid him tell Matthews I would write to him. I accordingly wrote, and told him every circumstance that had happened, showed him how impossible it was for us to continue any such connection, and begged (for still I thought him worthy) that he would write to tell me he was convinced by my arguments, and that we might part friends, though unhappy ones. He wrote to me, and comforted me greatly by assuring me of his approbation of my conduct, and that he was ready to acquiesce in any thing to make me happy, as he was unwilling to see my father. Mr. Sheridan was appointed to settle every thing; he accordingly came to my father, and told him what Matthews had said, and that he intended to write to my father and bind himself in the most solemn manner never to see me again. My father was satisfied with this, and pitied Matthews greatly. He kept his word, and my father was happy that he had settled every thing so amicably.

"Mr. Sheridan was with me every day, and did every thing in his power to make me happy. He said if Matthews ever broke his word to my father, he never would be seen with him again; as he had engaged him in the affair, he was resolved to act the part of a man of honour. I applauded his sentiments, but said I thought it impossible that Matthews ever should;—the next day convinced me how cruelly I had deceived myself. I received a letter from Matthews, wherein he told me he was going to London, but would return in less than two months, and if I did not consent to see him sometimes, he would shoot himself that instant. He said my answer would 'determine his fate. This letter flung me into fits, as I must either break my word to my father, or consent to the death of the man, on whose life my own depended. At last I wrote and expostulated with him once more on the baseness of such a proceeding. This letter, instead of having the wished effect, produced another still more alarming; in this he flung off the tender behaviour for which I always loved him, and put on the language of a tyrant—told me he would see me, that no father on earth should hinder him, and if I would not consent, he would take me off by force. I answered this with some warmth, as I began to see I had been deceived in him. I then insisted he should never write to me again; but he contrived to make me read a letter directed in another hand, wherein he told me we had both been deceived through some mistake; said he had something to communicate of the utmost consequence to my future happiness; and if I would indulge him with ten minutes' conversation, he never after would desire to see me again; but if I refused this last request, I must expect the worst.

"Terrified as I was, with no friend to advise me, I at last consented, and appointed an hour, but the moment he saw me, he locked the door, and drawing a pistol from his pocket uttered the most horrid imprecations; and swore if I would not bind myself by the most solemn oaths to see him again on his return from London, he would shoot himself before my face. Think, my dear girl, on my cruel situation; what could I do? Half distracted, I told him I would do any thing rather than see him commit so rash an action. This was Saturday, and I promised him (if I was alive) to see him on Wednesday evening during the concert. On this condition he let me go.

"I was to spend the day with Miss Sheridan, who was ill with the tooth-ache. All the time I was with her, I was resolving in my own mind what way I was to act. To break my word with my father was impossible. If I did not see Matthews, I expected worse to ensue. What resource was there left? At length (I tremble while I write) I came to the horrid resolution of destroying my own wretched being, as the only means to prevent my becoming still more guilty, and saving my parents from still more distress. With these horrid thoughts, I searched Miss Sheridan's room for some laudanum, which I knew she had for the tooth-ache; I found a small bottle full, and put it in my pocket.

"The next day (Sunday), after church, I left my mother and sisters walking. I sat down, made my will, and wrote a letter to my father, and one to Matthews. While I was about it, Mr. Sheridan came in; he had observed me taking the laudanum, and when he saw me writing, he seemed very much alarmed. At last, after swearing him to secrecy, I told him what I intended to do, and begged him to take charge of the letters. He used every argument in the world to dissuade me from it; but finding them all useless, he entreated me at least not to take it till the afternoon, as he then would tell me something which he was sure would make me lay aside such thoughts entirely. Fearful of his betraying me, I consented; but the moment he was gone took half the quantity, and after dinner, finding it had no effect, I took the rest. My fears were true. He had gone to Dr. Harrington and Dr. W., and begged of them for God's sake to go to our house that night, in case I should have taken it before he returned in the evening. When he came I was on the settee in a state of lethargy. He immediately ran for the doctors; but before they could give me any assistance, I dropped down, as they thought, dead. I lay for some time in that dreadful state, till by force they opened my teeth, and poured something down my throat, which made me bring up a great deal of the poison.

"To describe the distress of my family at this time is impossible; but such a scene by all accounts cannot be conceived or imagined. It was happy for me that I was insensible of it, as it would certainly have had a severer effect upon me than all the poison.

"After I had taken every thing that was proper, I was put to bed, where I passed the night in the most dreadful agonies of mind, at the thoughts of what would be the consequence of this affair.

"Monday evening, Sheridan came to me. He expostulated with me with the greatest tenderness, and showed me the dreadful crime I had been about to commit, and for one who was every way unworthy of my least consideration. He then told me every circumstance relative to myself, which Matthews had told him. He showed me letters he had received from him, and wherein his villany was fully explained.

"Judge what must be my feelings, on finding the man, for whom I had sacrificed life, fortune, reputation, every thing that was dear, the most abandoned wretch that ever existed In his last letter to Sheridan he had told him that I had given him so much trouble, that he had the greatest inclination to give me up, but his vanity would not let him do that without having gained his point. He therefore said he was

resolved the next time I met him to throw off the mask, and
if I would not consent to make myself still more infamous, to
force me, and then leave me to repent at leisure. He then
told how he had acted on Saturday; and that I had promised
to see him on Wednesday. He then said he would sufficiently revenge himself for all the trouble I had given him;
but if I changed my mind, and would not see him, he was resolved to carry me off by force. The moment I read this
horrid letter I fainted, and it was some time before I could
recover my senses sufficiently to thank Mr. Sheridan for his
opening my eyes. He said he had made Matthews believe
he was equally infamous, that he might the sooner know his
designs; but he said it was not in his power to appear on a
friendly footing any longer with such a villain. Mr. Sheridan
then asked me what I designed to do. I told him my mind
was in such a state of distraction, between anger, remorse,
and fear, that I did not know what I should do; but as
Matthews had declared he would ruin my reputation, I was
resolved never to stay in Bath. He then first proposed my
going to France, and entering a convent, where he said I
should be safe from all kind of danger, and in time I might
recover my peace and tranquillity of mind; his sister would
give me letters of recommendation to St. Quintin, where she
had been four years, and he would go with me to protect me;
and after he had seen me settled, he would return to England, and place my conduct in such a light that the world
would applaud and not condemn me

"You may be assured I gladly embraced his offer, as I had
the highest opinion of him. He accordingly settled every
thing; so that we resolved to go on that fatal Wednesday
which was to determine my fate. Miss Sheridan came to
me, approved the scheme, and helped me in putting up my
clothes. I kept up my spirits very well till the day came,
and then I thought I should go distracted. To add to my
affliction, my mother miscarried the day before, owing to the
fright of Sunday. the being obliged to leave her in such a
situation, with the thoughts of the distress in which my whole
family would be involved, made me almost give up my resolution; but, on the other hand, so many circumstances con-
curred to make it absolutely necessary, that I was, in short,
almost distracted.

"At last Sheridan came with two chairs, and having put me half fainting into one, and my trunks into the other, I was carried to a coach that waited in Walcot Street. Sheridan had engaged the wife of one of his servants to go with me as a maid without my knowledge. You may imagine how pleased I was with his delicate behaviour Before he could follow the chairs he met Matthews, who was going to our house, as I had not undeceived him for fear of the consequence. Sheridan framed some excuse, and after telling him that my mother had miscarried, and that the house was in such confusion it was impossible for him to go in, begged he would go to his sister's, and wait there till he sent for him, as he had an affair of honour on his hands, and perhaps should want his assistance; by this means he got rid of him.

"We arrived in London about nine o'clock the next morning. From London we went to Dunkirk by sea, where we were recommended to an English family, who treated me very politely. I changed my name to Harley, as I thought my own rather too public. From thence we proceeded to Lisle, where by chance Sheridan met with an old schoolfellow, who immediately introduced us to an English family, with whom he boarded. They were very amiable people, and recommended us to a convent, which we resolved to accept without going farther.

"Adieu! my dear girl, and believe me yours,
"E. LINLEY."

Miss Linley was at that time but eighteen years of age, and was under articles of apprenticeship to her father until the age of twenty-one, but she was in possession of £3000, which she had obtained under singular circumstances. Mr. Long, a man of fortune, had wooed her for his wife, but she had avowed to him that, if obliged to marry him, she could never bestow her affections on him; he not only resigned himself to his disappointment, but actually took it upon himself to be the responsible cause of the breaking off the match, and paid the sum mentioned as an indemnity for the breach of covenant. Mr. Linley went to Lisle, and, after an explanation with Sheridan, it was resolved that his daughter should fulfil her engagement to him, and they returned together to England.

Scarcely had the elopement become known in Bath, than Matthews, breathing nothing but fury and rage, inserted an advertisement in the " Bath Chronicle," in which he stated that Mr. Richard Sheridan had left behind him a letter "to account for his scandalous method of running away from the place by insinuations derogatory to his character, and that of a young lady innocent as far as relates to him or to his knowledge ; " and then bestows on him the most scurrilous epithets, and denounces " some malevolent incendiaries concerned in the propagation of this infamous lie," whom he threatens to chastise in the most public manner. Sheridan having read these accusations in France, and received letters containing the most abusive threats from Matthews, he determined to meet his opponent face to face, and declared that he would not lie down to sleep until he had obtained an ample apology. The details of the first duel are of the most extraordinary character, and reflect no honour either upon the principals or their seconds, and the long war of words subsequent to it is scarcely intelligible.

Their first meeting in Hyde Park was a most ridiculous rencontre ending in nothing ; and, fearful of observations, they thence retired to a coffee-house ; and the scene that ensued, of which we have a minute description furnished in a published letter of Sheridan, is one over which the biographer may as well draw a veil, as so much of mystification exists that it would be difficult to arrive at a fair conclusion. The most favourable inference is, that Sheridan, unacquainted with the law of duelling—he could not be of fencing—for he had been a pupil of Angelo's, rushed in upon Matthews's guard somewhat unseasonably, and at the point of the sword obtained an apology. Be the circumstances what they may, the partizans of each of the duellists were busily occupied in relating the affair according to their own views ; each insinuating that much was withheld by the other. The apology, however, was ample. Matthews retracted what he had said, and begged pardon for the advertisement in the " Chronicle." A second duel was determined on, according to Moore's version of the tale, in consequence of the coolness with which Matthews found himself received in Wales, and the interference of a Mr. Barnett; whose duelling propensities were to be gratified, whilst the mortification of his principal was to be thus relieved · but those who read even Sheridan's own statement must acknowledge that the first duel was, to the duellists of that day, little more than a disgraceful scuffle, and that the fact of Sheridan's breaking his adversary's sword was quite enough to justify a second meeting. The following letter addressed to Captain Knight must be read.

"Sir,—On the evening preceding my last meeting with Mr. Matthews, Mr. Barnett * produced a paper to me, written by Mr. Matthews, containing an account of our former meetings in London. As I had before frequently heard of Mr. Matthews's relation of that affair, without interesting myself much in contradicting it, I should certainly have treated this in the same manner, had it not been seemingly authenticated by Mr. Knight's name being subscribed to it. My asserting that the paper contains much misrepresentation, equivocation, and falsity, might make it appear strange that I should apply to you in this manner for information on the subject: but, as it likewise contradicts what I have been told were Mr. Knight's sentiments and assertions on that affair, I think I owe it to his credit, as well as my own justification, first, to be satisfied from himself whether he really subscribed and will support the truth of the account shown by Mr. Matthews. Give me leave previously to relate what I have affirmed to have been a real state of our meeting in London, and which I am now ready to support on my honour, or my oath, as the best account I can give of Mr. Matthews's relation is, that it is almost directly opposite to mine.

"Mr. Ewart accompanied me to Hyde Park, about six in the evening, where we met you and Mr. Matthews, and we walked together to the ring. Mr. Matthews refusing to make any other acknowledgment than he had done, I observed that we were come to the ground: Mr. Matthews objected to the spot, and appealed to you. We proceeded to the back of a building on the other side of the ring, the ground was there perfectly level I called on him, and drew my sword (he having previously declined pistols). Mr. Ewart observed a sentinel on the other side of the building; we advanced to another part of the park. I stopped again at a

---

* The friend of Matthews in the second duel.

D

seemingly convenient place: Mr. Matthews objected to the observation of some people at a great distance, and proposed to retire to the Hercules' Pillars till the park should be clear: we did so. In a little time we returned. I again drew my sword; Mr. Matthews again objected to the observation of a person who seemed to watch us. Mr. Ewart observed that the chance was equal, and engaged that no one should stop him, should it be necessary for him to retire to the gate, where we had a chaise and four, which was equally at his service. Mr. Matthews declared that he would not engage while any one was within sight, and proposed to defer it till next morning. I turned to you and said that 'this was trifling work,' that I could not admit of any delay, and engaged to remove the gentleman (who proved to be an officer, and who, on my going up to him, and assuring him that any interposition would be ill timed, politely retired). Mr. Matthews, in the mean time, had returned towards the gate : Mr. Ewart and I called to you, and followed. We returned to the Hercules' Pillars, and went from thence, by agreement, to the Bedford Coffee House, where, the master being alarmed, you came and conducted us to Mr. Matthews at the Castle Tavern, Henrietta Street. Mr. Ewart took lights up in his hand, and almost immediately on our entering the room we engaged. I struck Mr. Matthews's point so much out of the line, that I stepped up and caught hold of his wrist, or the hilt of his sword, while the point of mine was at his breast. You ran in and caught hold of my arm, exclaiming, 'Don't kill him.' I struggled to disengage my arm, and said his sword was in my power. Mr. Matthews called out twice or thrice, 'I beg my life'—We were parted. You immediately said, 'There, he has begged his life, and now there is an end of it;' and on Mr. Ewart's saying that when his sword was in my power, as I attempted no more, you should not have interfered, you replied that you were wrong, but that you had done it hastily and to prevent mischief—or words to that effect. Mr. Matthews then hinted that I was rather obliged to your interposition for the advantage; you declared that 'before you did so, both the swords were in Mr. Sheridan's power.' Mr. Matthews still seemed resolved to give it another turn, and observed that he had never quitted his sword. Provoked at this, I then swore (with two much heat, perhaps) that he should either give up his sword and I would break it, or go to his guard again. He refused—but, on my persisting, either gave it into my hand, or flung it on the table, or the ground (which, I will not absolutely affirm). I broke it, and flung the hilt to the other end of the room. He exclaimed at this. I took a mourning sword from Mr. Ewart, and presenting him with mine, gave my honour that what had passed should never be mentioned by me, and he might now right himself again. He replied that he ' would never draw a sword against the man who had given him his life:'—but, on his still exclaiming against the indignity of breaking his sword, (which he had brought upon himself,) Mr. Ewart offered him the pistols, and some altercation passed between them. Mr. Matthews said, that he could never show his face if it were known how his sword was broke—that such a thing had never been done—that it cancelled all obligations, &c., &c. You seemed to think it was wrong, and we both proposed, that if he never misrepresented the affair, it should not be mentioned by us. This was settled. I then asked Mr. Matthews, whether (as he had expressed himself sensible of, and shocked at the injustice and indignity he had done me in his advertisement) it did not occur to him that he owed me another satisfaction; and that, as it was now in his power to do it without discredit, I supposed he would not hesitate. This he absolutely refused, unless conditionally: I insisted on it, and said I would not leave the room till it was settled. After much altercation, and with much ill-grace, he gave the apology, which afterwards appeared. We parted, and I returned immediately to Bath. I there, to Colonel Gould, Captain Wade, Mr. Creaser, and others, mentioned the affair to Mr. Matthews's credit—said that chance had given me the advantage. Mr. Matthews had consented to that apology, and mentioned nothing of the sword. Mr. Matthews came down, and in two days I found the whole affair had been stated in a different light, and insinuations given out to the same purpose as in the paper, which has occasioned this trouble. I had undoubted authority that these accounts proceeded from Mr Matthews, and likewise that Mr. Knight had never had any share in them. I then thought I no longer owed Mr. Mat-

thews the compliment to conceal any circumstance, and **I**
related the affair to several gentlemen exactly as above.

"Now, Sir, as I have put down nothing in this account but
upon the most assured recollection, and as Mr. Matthews's
paper either directly or equivocally contradicts almost every
article of it, and as your name is subscribed to that paper, I
flatter myself that I have a right to expect your answer to
the following questions.   First,

"Is there any falsity or misrepresentation in what I have
advanced above?

"With regard to Mr. Matthews's paper—did I, in the
park, seem in the smallest article inclined to enter into conversation with Mr. Matthews?   He insinuates that I did.

"Did Mr. Matthews not beg his life?   He affirms he did
not.

"Did I break his sword without warning?   He affirms I
did it without warning, on his laying it on the table.

"Did I not offer him mine?   He omits it.

"Did Mr. Matthews give me the apology, as a point of
generosity, on my desisting to demand it?   He affirms he
did.

"I shall now give my reasons for doubting your having
authenticated this paper.

"1. Because I think it full of falsehood and misrepresentation, and Mr. Knight has the character of a man of truth
and honour.

"2. When you were at Bath, I was informed that you had
never expressed any such sentiments.

"3 I have been told that, in Wales, Mr. Matthews never
told his story in the presence of Mr. Knight, who had never
there insinuated any thing to my disadvantage.

"4. The paper shown me by Mr. Barnett contains (if **my**
memory does not deceive me) three separate sheets of **writ-
ing-paper**.   Mr. Knight's evidence is annexed to the **last**,
which contains chiefly a copy of our first proposed advertisements, which Mr. Matthews had, in Mr. Knight's presence.
agreed should be destroyed as totally void; and which (in a
letter to Colonel Gould, by whom I had insisted on it) **he**
declared upon his honour he knew nothing about, nor should
ever make the least use of.

" These, Sir, are my reasons for applying to yourself, in preference to any appeal to Mr. Ewart, my second on that occasion, which is what I would wish to avoid. As for Mr. Matthews's assertions, I shall never be concerned at them I have ever avoided any verbal altercation with that gentleman, and he has now secured himself from any other.

" I am your very humble servant,

"R. B. SHERIDAN."

The second duel took place near Bath : there is something exceedingly ludicrous in the descriptions which have appeared of this ferocious rencontre. Captain Matthews was anxious to have recourse to pistols, fearful that Sheridan, if the sword was employed, would again rush in upon him, and that an ungentlemanly scuffle would be the consequence ; he was, however, overruled, not by any arguments or by any decision, but by Sheridan drawing his sword and advancing upon Matthews in a vaunting manner ; according to the " St. James's Chronicle" of July 4th, " Both their swords breaking upon the first lunge they threw each other down, and with the broken pieces hacked at each other rolling upon the ground, the seconds standing by quiet spectators." The newspapers teemed with the marvellous deeds of valour of both parties, but the favourite was young Sheridan. The letter of Mr. Barnett, the second of Matthews, descriptive of the scene, was not so satisfactory, however, to this hero of the drama as might be expected ; for he declared that Mr. Matthews discovered as much genuine cool and intrepid resolution as man could do, and that Sheridan's wounds, which were proclaimed to be of a most terrific character, were but skin deep, and that the fist or the hilt of the sword, was as likely to have produced them as the weapons used.

Certain it is that the second duel was received as a most apocryphal proof of the gallantry of Sheridan ; and it is an undeniable fact that Matthews's version of the story was essentially different. There are many now resident in Bath who remember to have heard him repeat his tale, in a consistent manner, and who imagine that Moore was made acquainted with it.

Matthews, who, even in his days of wrath, looked upon Sheridan as an exceedingly delightful companion, and as a lover of practical jokes, always spoke of the duel as a specimen of the exhibition of these qualifications. He stated that a friendly communication actually passed between them on the night previous to the duel, amounting to an invitation from Sheridan to sup with him and the seconds; that Sheridan remained at table drinking claret until the time of appointment; that when he quitted it, he walked up Milsom Street, and observing Captain Matthews's chaise waiting at the door to take him to the spot, he reeled into it himself, and insisted upon his seconds following his example; he then desired the driver to proceed to the ground, which Matthews could not have reached in time, had not the carriage of Captain Paumier taken him there. He found Sheridan in a high state of excitement from potations deep. The duel soon commenced, and, as described by Barnett, Sheridan rushed upon him and tried to wrest his sword out of his grasp; he succeeded in breaking it, and then fell down dragging Matthews upon him; a few slight wounds were made, but the blood, of which so much had been spoken, was, in fact, the claret discharged from the stomach of Sheridan. It would be impossible to arrive at any just conclusion from the statement of both parties. The reply of Sheridan to the injurious reports in several papers was so long delayed that it was at last forgotten. He had requested Woodfall to print, in the "Morning Advertiser," the articles that reflected upon his own conduct, promising to send his refutation; unfortunately, his request was complied with, and the statements of his opponents were more largely promulgated, whilst his defence, from his indolence, was never to be read. Sheridan, however, became the theme of conversation and of curiosity: thus his first step in life led to notoriety, and in the minds of many to reputation, which he fortunately was capable of maintaining.

Immediately after the public announcement of their marriage, the young couple lived for a short time in retirement at East Burnham, and it was soon generally promulgated that the fair siren had retired from the musical world; the cause was by some said to be her own dislike of appearing before large audiences, by others, the delicacy of feeling on the part of young Sheridan. The reputation which her talents had acquired, the curiosity which her adventures had excited, led every one to be anxious that Mrs. Sheridan should continue a profession which she had so much ornamented. She was, indeed, under an engagement to sing at the Triennial Festival at Worcester, and the remuneration to which she would have been entitled was one thousand pounds for twelve nights, and this not for one year only, but for several seasons; besides which, it was averaged that a large sum would be produced by a benefit; but notwithstanding the assistance of Lord North, at that time Chancellor of the University of Oxford, who was called into the negotiation, that she might sing at the meeting, the determination was inflexibly adhered to, and Sheridan would not listen to any proposal that would lead to her reappearance. The stern moralist, Dr. Johnson, spoke of this resolution to Boswell with expressions of approbation, when he learnt that a young man without a shilling would not permit his wife to become the public gaze.

From this time forward, it would appear that Sheridan had made up his mind to depend upon his own mental resources for his success in life, and to strain every nerve to acquire wealth, although, alas! for his own peace of mind and happiness, he knew little of the art by which, when once gained, it is to be kept. The first great result of this resolution was the production of one of the best comedies ever penned, and which, in spite of many deserving claimants to public approbation, has outlived the greater number of its successors.

The "Rivals" was first performed at Covent Garden, the 17th of January, 1775, and on that eventful night was proclaimed a failure. It was scarcely borne with, and all Sheridan's fond anticipations were nearly overthrown. The unfavourable reception was attributed to its being double the length of any acting comedy; to Sir Lucius O'Trigger, as being a national reflection, and likewise to the representative of Sir Lucius O'Trigger, Mr. Lee, for in this he so miserably acted as to call down shouts of disapprobation. Fortunately, on the following night, Mr. Clinch was his substitute; and so well did he satisfy Sheridan, that he prepared for Mr. Clinch's benefit the humorous farce of "St. Patrick's Day," or the "Scheming Lieutenant," which was brought out successfully in the following May. It, however, wanted any great claim to favour, and must be considered rather as a piece written for a particular occasion, than as a dramatic effort. Not so with the "Rivals;"

this was a master-piece of art on which young Sheridan had bestowed time and labour.

The comedy was brought out with all the strength of the company; Shuter was the representative of the impetuous and boisterous Sir Anthony Absolute; Quick was the Acres Lewis, Falkland; and Mrs. Green, Mrs. Malaprop; a prologue written by Sheridan was spoken by Woodward and Quick, under the characters of a Sergeant-at-Law and an Attorney; Woodward presents himself as counsel for the poet; but notwithstanding he stated that he never faced a milder jury, the storm of disapprobation commenced so early as to justify the observation afterwards made by Sheridan in his preface, that much of it must have arisen from virulence of malice rather than severity of criticism. On the tenth night Sheridan produced another prologue, which was admirably delivered by Mrs. Bulkley, whose Julia appears to have been a marked favourite with the audience. Both of the prologues are well written, and though they are not peculiarly adapted for the particular play which they ushered in, but might belong to any comedy for which the favour of an audience is to be solicited, they show that Sheridan had capacity which stood in lieu of experience, and that he had the judgment which prevented the natural vanity of a young author from becoming offensive. The epilogue was also spoken by Mrs. Bulkley, and deserves to be preserved as one of those lively and clever specimens of a style in which Sheridan would have excelled, had he bestowed some portion of time on its cultivation. It is an epigrammatic, terse, and well turned compliment to the gentler sex. The moral of his comedy is, that on the world's great stage woman rules:

> "One moral's plain, without more fuss,
> Man's social happiness all rests on us:
> Through all the drama, whether damned or not,
> Love gilds the scene, and women guide the plot."

Mrs. Sheridan's family ascribed this epilogue to her, so highly did they estimate her abilities; however, no doubt exists but that Sheridan himself composed it; he had the gratification to find his play gradually grow in public estimation, and it was received in the provinces with great enthusiasm

Of course, in Bath it was speedily produced, and as the theatrical tribunal in that city was looked up to as of the highest order, its success there gave the greatest satisfaction. Mr. Dimond, afterwards the proprietor of the theatre, produced a great impression; Keaseberry, the Acres, was an admirable comic performer, and, as acting manager, bestowed great pains upon it. At Bristol, Mrs. Canning was much admired in Julia. During the popularity of the "Rivals," Sheridan's father, who had for some years been estranged from Brinsley, and who obstinately refused a reconciliation, went to the theatre, accompanied by his daughters, to judge for himself of its merits; his son placed himself at the side scene opposite his parent, and continued throughout the performance to gaze at him with tenderness and affection. On his return home he was overpowered with emotion, and in reply to some inquiries from Mrs. Sheridan as to the cause of his apparent agitation, observed that he painfully felt that his father and sisters should sit before him, and he be unable to join them.

It would be a task of no small difficulty at this time of day to criticise the "Rivals," to hold up to admiration the scenes which are most deserving praise, or to point out the delicate touches which distinguish each character. We cannot, however refrain from making an observation in reply to those who have studied the beautiful imaginings of Sheridan, and have found several of those defects, which certainly may exist in the most carefully digested works. They have pointed out that every individual who appears on the scene is a wit of his kind, and that the humblest personage, be he a coachman, a usurer, a valet, or an humble friend, is a humourist in his way, and occasionally much too clever for his situation. To a certain extent this may be correct; but we shall never find a single smart saying, a jest, or a sneer, put into the mouth not adapted for it. Not one single phrase is misplaced; if it came from any one person but the one for whom it was written, it would appear like a daub upon a picture. Not one of his personages but is perfectly distinct in his conversation from his neighbour; a clever thing becomes doubly so, if appropriate to the situation of him who speaks it, and this is precisely the case with these dramas. Nobody else could utter the things which the Coachman or Fag says in the first scene; neither Acres nor Sir Lucius O'Trigger, could be borne with, if they had not each their own sly hits and extravagant observations, adapted with admirable judgment to their respective positions, and the characteristics by which they are distinguished. Mrs. Malaprop has been censured by critics as an outrageous caricature; but there are those in Bath to whom it has been handed down that there was an original from whom a tolerably well drawn portrait was taken, and that a lady who distinguished herself as a minuet dancer, was as remarkable for the singular "choice of epitaphs," as the She Dragon whom Sheridan has given to the world. We must confess we find it much more difficult to discover the history of his marriage, and the duel in which he was involved, in the drama. It is true that he has laid the scene in Bath, with which he was familiar; and where such persons as an Irish fortune hunter, a booby squire, a female matrimonial adventurer with a marriageable niece, an irritable country gentleman, and a love sick youth, were likely to rendezvous, but why on this account it should be found to correspond with his own romantic adventures, we cannot imagine. The clever touches at the state of society in that fashionable town, its lounges, its early hours, its circulating libraries, its abbey thickly peopled with the dead, are the natural results of the observation which even a superficial stranger might make, without it being attributed to him that a love of scandal and of satire, was predominant in him. The least interesting of his delineations, Falkland and Julia, partake of the same talent; and although they have been objected to as unnecessary to the general action of the comedy, yet they exhibit an intimate acquaintance with the springs that guide the lover's heart, and the peculiar form of jealousy which is held up to reprobation is one that required castigation. The language which the lovers express themselves in has been considered to exhibit false finery, by one who has himself given to the world much more elaborate ornament, and much more of false taste, than any other author of our age.

The youth of Sheridan must be borne in mind when we pass any critical remarks upon the "Rivals," and we then shall be disposed to view it as the production of natural genius. At the age of twenty-three, a comedy remarkable for its wit, its ingenuity, and its knowledge of the world, must be the result of innate powers. There had been no time for deep observation, reflection, and the study of human nature. There must have been a quick perception of character, a power of adaptation, and a rapid insight into the effects produced upon an audience by dramatic skill. We find individuals brought before us whom we recognise as the fair objects of legitimate comedy, their peculiarities, their foibles presented to us so as to excite our laughter, without any of that harshness or asperity which demands severe chastisement. In the midst of all their extravagances they have some redeeming good qualities, which make us pleased that they sufficiently suffer by the exposure of their follies, and the same holds good with his more matured comedy, "The School for Scandal." If the "Rivals" does not abound with the same sparkle, if there be less polish in the dialogue, if the turn of satircal wit be less epigrammatic, there is much more of the character of common life about it, there is more ingenuity in the several contrivances, the peculiarities of each individual lead to more decided ends, and are more skilfully combined to produce an effect. It is more like the usual comedies of the stage, and there are more of those conventional personages to whom time has reconciled us, and given to them its acknowledged sanction. We have had most of them placed before us by other comic writers, but they have not been so dexterously managed, nor have they appeared in so vivid a light, or been so cleverly brought together. The materials are of a very slight texture, yet the whole is woven into a solid fabric well suited to the ordinary taste. We are told that Sir Anthony Absolute and Mrs. Malaprop remind us of honest Matthew Bramble and his sister Tabitha, and that Acres is a distinct descendant of Sir Andrew Aguecheek. Granted that it is so; the greater the praise due to Sheridan in having placed in so ingenious a form before us our old favourites; and as much right have we to complain of the want of variety in the lovely flowers that are created by the hand of nature, because the petals of some of them are distinguishable in shape only by very slight apparent variations, and yet when we examine them we find they possess colouring totally distinct, and qualities quite at variance. The Irish fortune hunter, the romantic loving girl, the poltroon, and the dictatorial father, are subjects with whom we daily meet in novels and in plays; but it cannot detract from the originality of Sheridan that he

has ingeniously introduced them into a drama, made them **act**
and react upon each other, until they produce a most agreeable impression upon the mind, and give us rational amusement by the display of the singularities which it is the peculiar province of the dramatist to depict.}

The "Duenna" was brought out on the 21st of November, 1775, and immediately became a favourite with the public; it had, at the outset, a much longer career than the Beggars' Opera, which was looked upon as the most successful drama of its class ever placed upon the stage; for the progress of the composition, dramatic, poetic, and musical, a reference must be made to Moore, who has given the letters which passed between Sheridan and Linley previous to its performance. We believe that the popularity of this opera has never been exceeded, and even to this hour the common quotations from its songs prove how much they were in the thoughts of every one. Many sayings which have become proverbial, and whose origin is altogether forgotten, have their source from this old favourite of our forefathers, to which they listened with rapture, and from which it was at one period considered fashionable to repeat lines. Indeed, independently of the conversation, which is of no ordinary cast, there are so many beautiful expressions in the songs, that we cannot be surprised at their reception, nor that many should be committed to memory. We are astonished at the many comments which have been made as to the direct violation of probability in the plot of the "Duenna." It is contended that no Spanish nobleman would allow his daughter to marry a Jew recently baptized, and that it is inconsistent that Seville, the very seat of the Inquisition, should be laid down as the scene of the adventure described. So far from a recently converted Jew being an object of either suspicion or dislike, every favour was shown in Spain to those who abandoned the faith of their fathers from conviction, and they became persons of weight and respectability. Nor do we see the force of the objection that a man hackneyed in the world should marry an old duenna instead of a young and lovely girl, whose description indeed he had just heard; but the person who had drawn the picture was the parent, and naturally enough might have been supposed to have viewed his own offspring with a father's predilection, whilst the sordid lover thought only of the wealth he was to obtain, and to him the want of beauty was a secondary consideration. Whatever may be the objections which have been raised, the "Duenna" has maintained a high reputation; and should we ever again have to boast upon the stage the talents and the powers of Leoni or Braham, it will again be brought forward, its dialogue be listened to with delight, its airs refresh the memories of the old, and kindle enthusiasm in the young.

Neither prologue nor epilogue seems to have been thought necessary for an Opera, but a playful poetic finale sung by the various characters on the stage brings it to a happy conclusion. It appears that it was first printed in 1794; but upon what authority we cannot trace, for Sheridan himself disavowed ever having revised any edition. In 1807, we learn from Kelly that he performed the part, in the "Duenna," of Ferdinand. It was customary with him, when he played at night, to read his part over in the morning, in order to refresh his memory; one morning after reading the part of Ferdinand, he left the printed play of the "Duenna," as then acted, on the table. On his return home he found Sheridan reading it, and with pen and ink before him correcting it. He said to him, "Do you act the part of Ferdinand from this printed copy?" To this Kelly replied in the affirmative, and added that he had done so for twenty years. Then said he, "You have been acting great nonsense." He examined every sentence, and corrected it all through before he left him. The corrections Kelly preserved in Sheridan's own hand writing; but he observes, what could prove his negligence more than correcting an opera which he had written in 1775, in the year 1807, and then abusing the manner in which it was printed. Kelly, however, had many more opportunities of becoming acquainted with Sheridan's sins of omission, which he does not fail to communicate to his readers in those reminiscences which he has written to the great satisfaction of the lovers of music and the drama. Whatever may have been the carelessness with which the dialogue of the "Duenna" may have been produced, such was not the case either with the poetry or the music; they both of them are exquisite of their kind, and the airs were borrowed from Linley, Rauzzini, and Dr. Harrington. The letters, which are preserved, of all the parties interested in the success of the opera show that no pains were spared; in those of Sheridan, which are given by Moore, we see that he was laborious, anxious, and painstaking. We are let almost too much behind the scenes, for we find that Sunday was fixed for a musical rehearsal, and we learn how much was done for the individuals who happened at that time to take a prominent lead; thus the fondness of Leoni for a flourish, in which he was followed by Braham, was to be indulged in; Miss Brown was to show off her execution, and as Mr. " Simpson's hautboy is to cut a figure, Echo, who is always allowed to play her part, is lugged in." Linley, upon whom all the music rested, seems to have amply fulfilled the expectations of his son-in-law, and to have taken up his ideas with great quickness. The finale to the first act, so generally admired, in which Isaac and Donna Louisa sing a duet, and after Don Carlos has sung the beautiful air, " Gentle Maid," join with him in a glee, is the idea of Sheridan carried out by Linley. Don Jerome's song, " Oh the days when I was young," once in the mouth of every boy in the street, is another of Sheridan's hints. That beautiful air, " By him we love offended, how soon our anger flies," was originally composed by that celebrated Master, Rauzzini, " Fuggiamo de questo loco in piena liberta." When we compare the trash usually composed for English operas with the exquisite specimens of taste with which Sheridan has adorned the " Duenna," we cannot but express our surprise that there should be found audiences to tolerate the vile nonsense. " Had I a heart for falsehood famed;" " Oh had my love ne'er smiled on me;" " How oft, Louisa, hast thou told;" " I ne'er could any lustre see," may vie with any compositions of a similar character; they are delicate, polished, and refined; they are full of tenderness of expression, and awaken the gentlest emotions. Nor are the livelier songs to be passed over, for they are animated and full of joyous feelings.

The " Duenna," like the " Rivals," was produced at Covent Garden. We find, however, that Mr. Linley was most anxious to direct the attention of Garrick to his son-in-law, and to prepare the way for his being amongst those who offered their incense at the shrine over which he presided; and he seems gradually to have paved the road for his success at Drury Lane Theatre. There is a letter, amongst the mass of those collected in the Garrick correspondence, from Linley to Dr. Hoadley, and another also from him to Mr. Garrick. In the former he says, " I have engaged to assist my son-in-law, Sheridan, in composing an opera which he is to bring out at Covent Garden this winter. I am a good deal distressed that from some misunderstanding between him and Mr. Garrick, that he is not connected with Drury Lane House, for though I believe they are now on very good terms, yet Sheridan thinks that he has been so honourably treated by Mr. Harris, that he ought not to keep any thing that he has written from him. However, I hope Mr. Garrick will not take any thing amiss in my assisting him on this occasion, for it is a matter of absolute necessity that he should endeavour to get money by this means, as he will not be prevailed on to let his wife sing." To Garrick he says, " I have promised to assist Sheridan in compiling—I believe this is the properest term—an opera, which I understand from him he has engaged to produce at Covent Garden this season. I have already set some airs which he has given me, and he intends writing new words to some other tunes of mine. My son has likewise written some tunes for him, and I understand he is to have some others from Mr. Jackson of Exeter. This is a mode of proceeding in regard to his composition which I by no means approve of. I think he ought first to have finished his opera with the songs he intends to introduce in it, and have got it entirely new set. No musician can set a song properly, unless he understands the character and knows the performer who is to exhibit it. For my part, I shall be very unwilling for either my own name or my son's to appear in this business, and it is my present resolution to forbid it; for I have great reason to be diffident of my own abilities and genius, and my son has not had experience in theatrical compositions, though I think well of his invention and musical skill. I would not have been concerned in this business at all, but that I know there is an absolute necessity for him to endeavour to get some money by this means, as he will not be prevailed upon to let his wife sing, and indeed at present she is incapable, and nature will not permit me to be indifferent to his success. You are deservedly at that point of fame which few of the great geniuses the world has produced have arrived at—above the reach of envy—and are the protector of dramatic merit, in what place or shape soever you find it, and I look up to you as the patron and director of both theatres, virtually, if not officially. I hope Sheridan has done nothing to forfeit the protection you have hitherto shown him." These appeals to the generous and liberal feelings of the great Roscius were not in vain. Not only did he, wherever his influence extended, assist Sheridan in his way into literary society, but when the time was fully come, placed him on a pinnacle where he should have established himself, without being dazzled with the "ignes fatui" that played before his sight.

From these letters we may fairly conclude that Linley did not then sufficiently appreciate the value of his son-in-law, that he was hardly satisfied with his determination to prevent his daughter again appearing before the public, and that he was an unwilling labourer with him in the vineyard which was to produce such a valuable harvest. It must indeed have been gratifying to him to find that the "Duenna" was hailed with such rapturous delight, and that it maintained a position on the stage for so many years. Much is undoubtedly owing to the judgment and musical talent of Linley, some of the airs he introduced will ever be heard with delight. The air with Sheridan's touching words, "By him we love offended," the production of the well known Rauzzini, was a favourite in the musical world throughout Europe. It was the production of that great master to whom England is so deeply indebted for some of the first vocalists we have had; for, together with his own instruction, he instilled into the minds of his pupils, amongst whom Braham is the last, to visit Italy, to study at Rome under Latilla, or at Naples under Monopoli, Finerolli, or Porpori, at that time the most distinguished of music masters. Rauzzini himself, however, was unequalled as a musician; from his rich stores much has been gleaned up to the present hour. His career was a singular one. He was a native of Rome, and from the exquisite sweetness of his voice had been selected, in compliance with the miserable taste of that age, to be rendered fit for singing in a style then much admired, but which modern judgment has rejected. He performed the parts of the principal female, as no woman was allowed upon the stage in the Holy City. His singular beauty became the theme of general conversation; he was courted and flattered everywhere. On his visit to Munich, a distinguished personage evinced such admiration, and heaped such caresses upon him, that the ruling prince gave him a delicate hint, to which he was compelled to pay attention, that the time had arrived when his talent had ceased to be attractive. Rauzzini with some indignation resented the want of hospitality, and serious results were apprehended, when an invitation to England induced him to undertake an engagement at the Italian Opera; for the *furore* had spread to London, and his acting, his singing, and his compositions were at once fashionable. Garrick pronounced his " Pyramus" "the finest piece of representation he had ever witnessed on the Italian stage;" but alas! a change came over the "spirit of the dream ;" the climate affected his voice, and he never perfectly recovered from its effects. He settled in Bath, where for years he continued to teach, to compose, and preside at the pianoforte at all the great musical festivals. Beloved by every one, he was the centre of a most accomplished circle, comprising all the taste and talent of Bath. At Christmas Eve, Billington, Storace, Mora, Braham, and all the first-rate musicians of the day, assembled ; a concert, consisting of the Messiah, was given to the public, from which Rauzzini drew a portion of his income. This alas! never equalled his expenditure ; the consequence of which was the embitterment of his latter days; but to the last he maintained a splendid establishment, and was looked up to as one of those to whom Bath was indebted for its popularity. Whenever the venerable old man took his accustomed seat in the orchestra, tokens of regard and respect awaited him, and to the last he preserved beauty of countenance of a striking character.

In the year 1775 Garrick decided to quit the scene of his many triumphs, and to retire from the theatre, which he had for so long a period managed with singular felicity. He had just then attained the sixtieth year of his age ; and although whenever he appeared before the public he met with an enthusiastic reception, he resolved to resign his position, and to place in other hands the power he had so long wielded. He had very lately gone to considerable expense for various improvements in Drury Lane Theatre, hence his determination appeared somewhat sudden, and produced considerable surprise. When it was whispered who the individual was into whose guidance he was likely to commit the management, much conversation was naturally excited. Although it was known that Garrick had always most favourably expressed himself of the talent and character of the youthful author, and had specially introduced him to the first literary men of the day, it was likewise borne in mind that Sheridan's father had never been on good terms with Roscius, and that, on several occasions, he had expressed himself with considerable animosity against him, and had shown a degree of haughtiness in his demeanour towards him, that was likely to alienate the kind feelings which actuated Garrick, who when, according to Davies, he spoke to a publisher of Mrs. Sheridan's comedy, "*The Discovery*," eulogized it in language of the most favourable character, and even went so far as to say that the play was one of the best that he had ever read, and that money would be well laid out in its purchase. It is true that from the elder Sheridan there was little of rivalry to be dreaded by Garrick, although he was occasionally thrust forward as his equal. As a speaker and declaimer few were to be compared with him; but his monotonous tones, his pedantic manner, and his studied action, came but badly into competition with the impassioned tones and the naturally expressed feelings of Garrick. However much the theatrical world was surprised at the predilection which the veteran master of the stage exhibited for the youthful aspirant, no one doubted that the choice had fallen upon one fully equal to the task he had undertaken. He had already shown a thorough knowledge of the stage, and had brought forward the labour of his intellect, with considerable acquaintance of the points which tell with an audience. He had evinced much skill in placing before the public the "Duenna;" he had contrived to unite the dialogue and the music in a more pleasing way than usual, and his assiduity peculiarly touched the fancy of Garrick, who would not listen to numerous applicants, who no sooner heard of the probable change than they stood forward in hopes of becoming his successor. Colman would have willingly been the purchaser, but was desirous of being the sole proprietor, and as this could not be arranged, he abandoned a negotiation which he had commenced. Most probably Sheridan would not have been his

successor, had not Garrick anticipated from the kind manner, and the thoughtlessness of his young friend, that he
himself would continue to direct the theatre, and to maintain
an influence which he felt loath at once to abandon. In the
month of June a contract was entered into by which Sheridan
came into possession of two-fourteenths, Mr. Linley the same,
and Dr. Ford three-fourteenths, making, for the purchase of
Garrick's share, the total sum of thirty-five thousand pounds:
the letters which passed between Sheridan and Linley on the
subject were placed in the hands of Moore, and were published by him in his biography.

Every one who looked on this transaction was astonished
at the speculative disposition of Sheridan; they marvelled at
the whole of this singular transition from nothingness to
the possession of an immense property. Unaccustomed as
they were in those days to the bold operations of which the
present age affords such numerous instances, of purchases
made without one single sixpence of money being advanced,
all looked with an eye of wonder and suspicion at the sudden
acquisition. It was already whispered that the young author
lived far beyond his means; that he was associating with the
great and the wealthy; that he ventured to entertain upon a
liberal scale, and that there were no visible funds from which
his wealth was drawn. Various have been the explanations
offered, and many channels have been pointed at, as those
from which he was enabled to meet the demands which were
made upon him. There is, however, little doubt that he was
advised by some able financier at his first outset, and that
from Garrick he experienced the most generous consideration; but with whatever assistance he was furnished, it was
not sufficient, as the embarrassments which gradually grew
upon him fully proved. From this period may be traced the
commencement of those difficulties which harassed him in
after life, and that carelessness which ended in a recklessness
that almost became proverbial. The embarrassments which
he had to encounter, and which he fought off with adroitness,
with wit, with practical jokes, and with every species of cunning, have been the theme of the humourist for many a day,
and anecdotes, which sprang out of them, have been repeated
from father to son till they became the standing jest of families. His first commencement as a manager was not of that

E 2

brilliant kind to give any promise of great improvement in
the conduct of the theatre. An alteration of Vanburgh's play
the "Relapse" was the first production, under the name of a
"Trip to Scarborough;" it was brought out February 24th,
1777. This was an unfortunate commencement; neither the
public nor the actors were satisfied. On the second night
there was a decided opposition to its performance, but the
actors were taught that, whatever opinion they might themselves form of the merits of a piece, it was their duty to
perform their parts with propriety and with energy. The
"Tempest" was also brought forward; parts of Dryden's version were given, which, together with some songs by Thomas
Linley, served for a short time to fill up the night; but still
there was a general feeling that the public had lost by the
exchange of managers, when the town was astonished and
delighted by the production of a comedy that has deservedly
gained for its author an undying reputation, the "School
for Scandal."

On the 8th of May, 1777, that inimitable comedy, which
has become a standard play wherever the English language
is spoken, the "School for Scandal," was first brought forward. There was no doubt from the earliest moment that it
was listened to, that it was one of those brilliant and captivating productions of the human mind that are to be classed
amongst the results of that inspiration of real genius with
which some individuals, more fortunate than the rest of our
race, are occasionally gifted. It was felt throughout its performance that there were those qualities in it which excite
our admiration, and leave behind the happiest impression.
It is neither from the artifice of the plot, the delineation of
character, nor the exhibition of those strong emotions of the
heart, which either astonish us or awaken sympathy, that we
derive so much pleasure. It is from the correct adaptation
of such person to the scene, and from the happy management
of incidents, which, though few in number, always occur at
the right moment, whilst the light, airy, sparkling dialogue
suits the understanding of every auditor. It may safely be
pronounced the genuine effusion of an imagination alive to
conversational power and beauty, and to the effect of striking
contrasts. Moore was enabled, through his influence with the
remaining relations of Sheridan, to lay before the public a

large portion of the manuscripts which were originally drawn up by the author. He has shewn us how gradually, from two distinct plays, he was led to produce a perfect one, and to incorporate in that the leading ideas, which he had intended to work up into two separate pieces. It altogether forms a literary curiosity, and exhibits to us by what repeated efforts, by what lengthened process an author gradually weaves one beautiful piece of workmanship out of the various raw materials placed in his hands; and we draw the inference that the powers of man are very limited, and that time, labour, and unceasing exertion are necessary for a work which, at first sight, appears easy of construction, and simple in its development. We do not, perhaps, feel that it adds to the interest we take in the author; we are disappointed to find that the bright sparks which we fancied were struck off by a moment's collision are the effects of slow hammering; that a sparkling expression, seemingly so instantaneous and happy, has been at first a dull, dry remark, gradually elaborated into the shape in which it appears. The slow transformation of Solomon Teazle, a widower, having had five children, talking over his wife's extravagance with his butler, into the elegant, high-minded, disappointed Sir Peter Teazle; of Plausible into Joseph Surface; of a silly country girl, ill-bred, and impertinent, into the lively, elegant, fashionable, but thoughtless Lady Teazle, is interesting amongst the curiosities of literature, but by no means impresses us with that feeling of admiration for him whom we find so much an artist. We feel that we have been admitted behind the scenes, where lately we have seen a spectacle of gorgeous splendour, and the gaudy trappings, the false jewels, and the sparkling tinsel from which the magnificence of the decorations was produced, present us with a contrast somewhat too forcible to be pleasing. Much, therefore, as we feel indebted to the biographer who has ransacked every escritoir which might contain a memorandum of his hero, we almost wish that he had not shown us every erasure, every superfluity, every blot that could be seen. As no man, let his position be the highest, can conceal from those immediately around him his peculiarities and his defects, so none can bear the inquisitive examination of those who trace literary history for perfection; Minerva springs armed from the head of no one but Jupiter. The only advantage in the general view of Sheridan's character to be gained by this exhibition is, that he was neither careless nor indolent, as was generally supposed, but that he laboured with assiduity and constant diligence, and that although he might be desirous to astonish with the rapidity of his productions, he was indebted for their perfection as much to art and laborious consideration, as he was to nature and his own genius.

It is evident that there were two different sketches drawn up by Sheridan, which he afterwards blended. One of them was more properly the "School for Scandal," the other a two act Comedy for the Teazles. The following were the dramatis personæ of the latter :—

Sir Rowland Harpur.   Old Teazle.
—— Plausible.
Capt. H. Plausible.   Mrs. Teazle
Freeman.   Maria.

and the following was the opening scene :—

"ACT I

" SCENE I.—OLD TEAZLE, *alone.*

" In the year 44, I married my first wife; the wedding was at the end of the year—ay, 'twas in December; yet, before Ann. Dom. 45, I repented. A month before, we swore we preferred each other to the whole world—perhaps we spoke truth; but, when we came to promise to love each other till death, there I am sure we lied. Well, Fortune owed me a good turn; in 48 she died. Ah, silly Solomon, in 52 I find thee married again! Here, too, is a catalogue of ills—Thomas, born February 12; Jane, born Jan. 6; so they go on to the number of five. However, by death I stand credited but by one. Well, Margery, rest her soul! was a queer creature; when she was gone, I felt awkward at first, and being sensible that wishes availed nothing, I often wished for her return. For ten years more I kept my senses and lived single. Oh, blockhead, dolt Solomon! Within this twelvemonth thou art married again—married to a woman thirty years younger than thyself; a fashionable woman. Yet I took her with caution; she had been educated in the country:

but now she has more extravagance than the daughter of an Earl, more levity than a Countess. What a defect it is in our laws, that a man who has once been branded in the fore·head should be hanged for the second offence.

" *Enter* JARVIS.

" *Teaz.* Who 's there?   Well, Jarvis?

" *Jarv.* Sir, there are a number of my mistress's tradesmen without, clamorous for their money.

" *Teaz.* Are those their bills in your hand?

" *Jarv.* Something about a twentieth part, sir.

" *Teaz.* What! have you expended the hundred pounds I gave you for her use.

" *Jarv.* Long ago, sir, as you may judge by some of the items :—' Paid the coachmaker for lowering the front seat of the coach.'

" *Teaz.* What the deuce was the matter with the seat ?

" *Jarv.* Oh Lord, the carriage was too low for her by a foot when she was dressed—so that it must have been so, or have had a tub at top like a hat-case on a travelling trunk.   Well, sir, (*reads,*) ' Paid her two footmen half a year's wages, £50.

" *Teaz.* 'Sdeath and fury! does she give her footmen a hundred a year?

" *Jarv.* Yes, sir, and I think, indeed, she has rather made a good bargain, for they find their own bags and bouquets.

" *Teaz.* Bags and bouquets for footmen!—halters and bastinadoes !

Jarv. ' Paid for my lady's own nosegays, 50*l.* '

" *Teaz.* Fifty pounds for flowers! enough to turn the Pantheon into a green-house, and give a Fête Champêtre at Christmas.

" *Lady Teaz.* Lord, Sir Peter, I wonder you should grudge me the most innocent articles in dress—and then, for the expense—flowers cannot be cheaper in winter—you should find fault with the climate, and not with me.   I am sure I wish with all my heart that it was spring all the year round, and roses grew under one's feet.

" *Sir P.* Nay, but, madam, then you would not wear them; but try snow-balls, and icicles.   But tell me, madam, how can you feel any satisfaction in wearing these, when you might reflect that one of the rose-buds would have furnished a poor family with a dinner?

" *Lady T.* Upon my word, Sir Peter, begging your pardon, that is a very absurd way of arguing. By that rule, why do you indulge in the least superfluity? I dare swear a beggar might dine tolerably on your greatcoat, or sup off your laced waistcoat—nay, I dare say, he wouldn't eat your gold-headed cane in a week. Indeed, if you would reserve nothing but necessaries, you should give the first poor man you meet your wig, and walk the streets in your night-cap, which, you know, becomes you very much.

" *Sir P.* Well, go on to the articles.

" *Jarv.* (*reading.*) 'Fruit for my lady's monkey, £5 per week.'

" *Sir P.* Five pounds for the monkey!—why 'tis a dessert for an alderman!

" *Lady T.* Why, Sir Peter, would you starve the poor animal? I dare swear he lives as reasonably as other monkeys do.

" *Sir P.* Well, well, go on.

" *Jarv.* 'China for ditto'——

" *Sir P.* What, does he eat out of china?

" *Lady T.* Repairing china that he breaks—and I am sure no monkey breaks less.

" *Jarv.* 'Paid Mr. Warren for perfumes—milk of roses, 30*l.*'

" *Lady T.* Very reasonable.

" *Sir P.* 'Sdeath, madam, if you had been born to these expenses I should not have been so much amazed; but I took you, madam, an honest country squire's daughter——

" *Lady T.* Oh, filthy; don't name it. Well, heaven forgive my mother, but I do believe my father must have been a man of quality.

" *Sir P.* Yes, madam, when first I saw you, you were drest in a pretty figured linen gown, with a bunch of keys by your side; your occupations, madam, to superintend the poultry; your accomplishments, a complete knowledge of the family receipt-book—then you sat in a room hung round with fruit in worsted of your own working; your amusements were to play country-dances on an old spinet to your father while he went asleep after a fox-chase—to read Tillotson's Sermons to your aunt Deborah. These, madam, were your recreations, and these the accomplishments that captivated me. Now, forsooth, you must have two footmen to your chair, and a pair of white dogs in a phaeton; you forget when you used to ride double behind the butler on a docked bay coach-horse. . . . . Now you must have a French hair-dresser; do you think you did not look as well when you had your hair combed smooth over a roller? . . . . . . Then you could be content to sit with me, or walk by the side of the Ha! ha!

"*Lady T.* True, I did; and, when you asked me if I could love an old fellow, who would deny me nothing, I simpered and said, ' 'Till death.'

"*Sir P.* Why did you say so?

"*Lady T.* Shall I tell you the truth?

"*Sir P.* If it is not too great a favour.

"*Lady T.* Why, then, the truth is, I was heartily tired of all these agreeable recreations you have so well remembered, and having a spirit to spend and enjoy fortune, I was determined to marry the first fool I should meet with . . . . you made me a wife, for which I am much obliged to you, and if you have a wish to make me more grateful still, make me a widow."

* * * * * * * * *

"*Sir P.* Then, you never had a desire to please me, or add to my happiness?

"*Lady T.* Sincerely, I never thought about you; did you imagine that age was catching? I think you have been overpaid for all you could bestow on me. Here am I surrounded by half a hundred lovers, not one of whom but would buy a single smile by a thousand such baubles as you grudge me.

"*Sir P.* Then you wish me dead?

"*Lady T.* You know I do not, for you have made no settlement on me.

* * * * · * * * *

"*Sir P.* I am but middle-aged.

"*Lady T.* There's the misfortune; put yourself on, or back, twenty years, and either way I should like you the better.

* * * * * * * * *

Yes, sir, and then your behaviour too was different; you would dress, and smile, and bow; fly to fetch me any thing I wanted; praise every thing I did or said; fatigue your stiff face with an eternal grin; nay, you even committed poetry, and muffled your harsh tones into a lover's whisper to sing it yourself, so that even my mother said you were the

smartest old bachelor she ever saw—a billet-doux engrossed
on buckram ! !! ! !!

*   *   *   *   *   *   *   *   *

Let girls take my advice and never marry an old bachelor.
He must be so either because he could find nothing to love in
women, or because women could find nothing to love in him."

The scene, now so admirably elaborated into the screen
scene, was thus in the author's imagination, to judge from the
first draught.

" *Scene—*YOUNG PLIANT'S *Room.*

"*Young P.* I wonder her ladyship is not here ; she promised me to call this morning.   I have a hard game to play
here, to pursue my designs on Maria.   I have brought myself into a scrape with the mother-in-law.   However, I think
we have taken care to ruin my brother's character with my
uncle, should he come to-morrow.   Frank has not an ill
quality in his nature ; yet, a neglect of forms, and of the
opinion of the world, has hurt him in the estimation of all
his graver friends.   I have profited by his errors, and contrived to gain a character, which now serves me as a mask to
lie under.

" *Enter* LADY TEAZLE.

"*Lady T.* What, musing, or thinking of me ?

"*Young P.* I was thinking unkindly of you ; do you know
now that you must repay me for all this delay, or I must be
coaxed into good humour ?

"*Lady T.* Nay, in faith you should pity me—this old cur-
mudgeon of late is grown so jealous, that I dare scarce go
out, till I know he is secure for some time.

"*Young P.* I am afraid the insinuations we have had spread
about Frank have operated too strongly on him—we meant
only to direct his suspicions to a wrong object.

"*Lady T.* Oh, hang him ! I have told him plainly that
if he continues to be so suspicious, I 'll leave him entirely, and
make him allow me a separate maintenance.

Young P But, my charmer, if ever that should be the case,
you see before you the man who will ever be attached to you.
But you must not let matters come to extremities ; you can
never be revenged so well by leaving him, as by living with him,
and let my sincere affection make amends for his brutality.

" *Lady T.* But how shall I be sure now that you are sin cere? I have sometimes suspected, that you loved my niece.

" *Young P.* Oh, hang her! a puling idiot, without sense or spirit.

" *Lady T.* But what proofs have I of your love to me, for I have still so much of my country prejudices left, that if I were to do a foolish thing (and I think I can't promise) it shall be for a man who would risk every thing for me alone. How shall I be sure you love me?

" *Young P.* I have dreamed of you every night this week past.

" *Lady T.* That's a sign you have slept every night for this week past; for my part. I would not give a pin for a lover who could not wake for a month in absence.

" *Young P.* I have written verses on you out of number.

" *Lady T.* I never saw any

" *Young P.* No—they did not please me, and so I tore them.

" *Lady T.* Then it seems you wrote them only to divert yourself.

" *Young P.* Am I doomed for ever to suspense?

" *Lady T.* I don't know—if I was convinced——

" *Young P.* Then let me on my knees——

" *Lady T.* Nay, nay, I will have no raptures either. This much I can tell you, that if I am to be seduced to do wrong, I am not to be taken by storm, but by deliberate capitulation, and that only where my reason or my heart is convinced.

" *Young P.* Then, to say it at once—the world gives itself liberties——

" *Lady T.* Nay, I am sure without cause; for I am as yet unconscious of any ill, though I know not what I may be forced to.

" *Young P.* The fact is, my dear Lady Teazle, that your extreme innocence is the very cause of your danger; it is the integrity of your heart that makes you run into a thousand imprudences which a full consciousness of error would make you guard against. Now, in that case, you can't conceive how much more circumspect you would be.

" *Lady T.* Do you think so?

" *Young P.* Most certainly. Your character is like a per son in a plethora, absolutely dying of too much health.

"*Lady T.* So then you would have me sin in my own de fence, and part with my virtue to preserve my reputation.

"*Young P.* Exactly so, upon my credit, ma'am."

*   *   *   *   *   *

We may see, in the following extract, the first germ of one of the most striking passages of the play as it now exists.

"*Spat.* O Lud, ma'am, I'll undertake to ruin the character of the primmest prude in London with half as much. Ha! ha! Did your ladyship never hear how poor Miss Shepherd lost her lover and her character last summer at Scarborough? —this was the whole of it. One evening at Lady ——'s the conversation happened to turn on the difficulty of breeding Nova Scotia sheep in England. 'I have known instances,' says Miss ——, 'for last spring a friend of mine, Miss Shepherd of Ramsgate, had a Nova Scotia sheep that produced her twins.'—'What!' cries the old deaf dowager Lady Bowlwell, 'has Miss Shepherd of Ramsgate been brought to-bed of twins?' This mistake, as you may suppose, set the company a laughing. However, the next day, Miss Verjuice Amarilla Lonely, who had been of the party, talking of Lady Bowlwell's deafness, began to tell what had happened; but, unluckily, forgetting to say a word of the sheep, it was understood by the company, and, in every circle, many believed, that Miss Shepherd of Ramsgate had actually been brought to-bed of a fine boy and girl; and, in less than a fortnight, there were people who could name the father, and the farmhouse where the babes were put out to nurse."

The production of the "School for Scandal" was accompanied by one of the most exquisite poetic eulogiums ever penned. Sheridan presented the beautiful Mrs. Crewe with a revised copy of his drama, together with a poem, to which he attached the title of a portrait; there does not exist in the English language a more perfect model of elegant flattery clothed in suitable language, neither fulsome nor overstrained; he has most carefully avoided those hyperbolic expressions which are found in the dedications of the dramatic writers who preceded him, and has cleverly shunned the errors into which they were usually betrayed. The dread of ridicule taught him to eschew those bolder flights in which they indulged, and he has contrived to surround the object of his admiration with those attributes, which, even if they be painted in somewhat an exaggerated form, cannot fail to be looked upon with a partial eye. There is a sincerity of expression, and a chivalrous boldness in the ebullition of so much approbation, that we should be carried away by the high colouring used, even had we been inclined to censure it as somewhat too gaudy. Garrick wrote a prologue, not certainly in his best style, but well suited to the taste of the day; he alludes to Sheridan as a bard "too young to think that he

> Can stop the full spring tide of calumny;

and

> Proud of your smiles, once lavishly bestowed,
> Again our young Don Quixote takes the road
> To show his gratitude he draws his pen,
> And seeks this hydra Scandal in his den.
> For your applause all perils he would through,
> He 'll fight—that 's write—a cavalliero true
> Till every drop of blood—that 's ink—is spilt for you."

The epilogue was written by Colman, and was committed to the care of Mrs. Abingdon as Lady Teazle; it has remained a favourite, and, though only spoken occasionally on the provincial stage, has much merit. The parody on the beautiful lines in " Othello "—" Farewell the tranquil mind "—has been much admired, and the author has cleverly enough adapted the glorious circumstances of war to those of fashionable life, and we hear that Lady Teazle's occupation is o'er, if not with the same deep sympathy that we do the pathetic adieu from the lips of " Othello," it is with the feeling that both personages have, in their respective ways, added to the common stock of enjoyment. We unfortunately possess no printed copy of this play authenticated by its author; some incorrect editions have been printed. The one which appeared in Ireland in the year 1788 has been usually followed, and although pronounced incorrect, it has greater pretension to be " authority" than any we possess, for it is taken from the manuscript which Sheridan forwarded to his sister for the use of the manager of the Dublin Theatre, who gave her one hundred guineas and free admission for her family for the privilege of performing it. Sheridan had made an arrangement with Ridgway of Piccadilly for the purchase of the copyright, but when he was urged to furnish the manuscript, his answer was, "that he had been nineteen years endeavouring to satisfy himself with the style of the 'School for Scandal,' but had not succeeded." It is a well known fact that the last act of "Pizarro" was in an unfinished state on the very night of its first representation, and upon good authority it is affirmed, that notwithstanding the incessant labour which Sheridan had bestowed for a considerable length of time, the "School for Scandal" was announced for representation before the actors had received copies of their respective parts. Moore, on a reference to the original manuscript, found that the last five scenes bore evident marks of the haste in which they were finished, there being but one rough draught of them scribbled upon detached pieces of paper, whilst of all the preceding acts there were numerous manuscripts. On the last leaf appears in his own handwriting, "*Finished at last, thank God,*" to which the prompter has added "Amen, W. Hopkins." Great attention was bestowed on the production of the comedy, each was desirous of supporting the new manager. Garrick, as we learn from Murphy, was never known on any former occasion to be more anxious for a favourite piece; he was proud of the new manager, and in a triumphant manner boasted of the genius to whom he had consigned the conduct of the theatre. Amongst the praise which he bestowed upon Sheridan, a ready reply to a gentleman who wished to exalt the Roscius, at the expense of the new candidate for fame, has been recorded. "This is but a single play," observed the critic, "and in the long run will be but a slender help to support the theatre. To you Mr. Garrick, I must say the Atlas that propped the stage has left his station." "Has he?" said Garrick; "if that be the case he has found another Hercules to succeed him." Isaac Reed has, in the "Biographia Dramatica," very slightly alluded to an assertion that has been made that the plan was taken from a manuscript which had been previously delivered at Drury Lane by a young lady, who afterwards died of a pectoral disease; he observes that this is probably mere scandal, founded on envy of the great success of the piece. Dr. Watkins has somewhat laboriously expatiated on this report, and drawn upon himself the severe censure of Moore, who was enabled to detect the falsehood, and to show how utterly unfounded was the stupid rumour; not content with borrowing this idea from Isaac Reed, and setting it off with as much ingenuity as he could muster, Dr Watkins throws out a surmise that Mrs. Sheridan was the person to whom the rank of the first dramatic writer of the day ought to have been assigned. He indulges too in some hypercritical remarks, which are only worthy of notice, as exhibiting the anxiety of the biographer to scrape up from every source some material for his labour, regardless both of the useless information he was bestowing. and the nothingness of the detraction to which he was giving circulation. In spite of all that has been written, from the first night of its performance up to the present hour, the "School for Scandal" has maintained its position, and even when indifferently brought forward proves an unceasing attraction. Its uninterrupted run, its certainty of producing money to the treasury, its collecting together all the playgoers, are the best proofs of the estimation in which it is held; its intrinsic merit carries every thing before it. Cumberland, the irritable opponent of all merit but his own, has praised the judicious introduction of the screen; but there is an anecdote on record that he was with his young family at an early performance of the "School for Scandal;" they were seated in the stage box, the little children screamed with delight, but the less easily pleased fretful author pinched them, exclaiming, "What are you laughing at, my dear little folks? you should not laugh, my angels, there is nothing to laugh at!" and then in an under tone, "keep still, you little dunces." When Sheridan was told of this, he said "it was ungrateful of Cumberland to have been displeased with his children for laughing at my comedy, for when I went to see his tragedy I laughed from beginning to end."

There is another version of the story extant; for the friends of Sheridan were most anxious to find a reason for the hostile feelings which he was supposed to bear towards Cumberland, and which induced him to use such an unmerciful rod of flagellation in the "Critic." It is, that Sheridan being most anxious to collect the opinions of the acknowledged judges of dramatic merit, earnestly asked what Mr. Cumberland had said on the first night of the performance; "not a syllable," was the answer. "But did he seem amused?" "Why, faith, he might have been hung up beside Uncle Oliver's picture. He had the damned disinheriting countenance, like the ladies and gentlemen on the walls, he never moved a muscle.'

"Devilish ungrateful that," said Sheridan, "for I sat out his tragedy last week, and laughed from beginning to end." Cumberland, however, most strenuously denied that he was present when the "School for Scandal" was first performed. The tragedy alluded to is said to be the "Carmelites," which was the theme of ridicule of Sheridan's friends; in the "Rolliad" they heap upon it the most extravagant and ludicrous praise, calling Cumberland "the most exalted genius of the present age," and in describing this tragedy, say, "the beauties of which we will venture confidently to assert will be admired and felt when those of Shakspeare, Dryden, Otway, Southerne and Rowe shall no longer be held in estimation." Again, "Our readers, we trust, will pardon our having been diverted from the task we have undertaken, by the satisfaction of dwelling upon a few of the many beauties of this justly popular and universally admired tragedy, which, in our humble opinion, infinitely surpasses every other theatrical composition, being in truth an assemblage of every possible dramatic excellence; nor do we believe that any production, whether of ancient or modern date, can exhibit a more uncommon and peculiar selection of language, a greater variety of surprising incidents, a more rapid succession of extraordinary discoveries, a more curious collection of descriptions, similes, metaphors, images, storms, shipwrecks, challenges and visions; or a more miscellaneous and striking picture of the contending passions of love, hatred, pity, madness, rage, jealousy, remorse and anger, than this unparalleled performance presents to the admiration of the enraptured spectator. Mr. Cumberland has been represented, perhaps unjustly, as particularly jealous of the fame of his cotemporaries, but we are persuaded he will not be offended when, in the rank of modern writers, we place him second only to the inimitable author of the Rolliad." Such at any rate was the feeling which took possession of Sheridan's mind, that he gladly sought the opportunity of holding him up to public ridicule; whenever the occasion offered, his name was dragged forth. It was also alleged that every piece presented at Drury Lane, by Cumberland, met with a decided refusal; and the newspapers seemed willing to support the disappointed author. Criticisms, ill-natured, were hurled against the "School for Scandal," and comparisons were drawn between the moral tendency of the plays that issued from the prolific pen of Cumberland, and those which Sheridan had furnished to the world. This only continued to aggravate the quarrel, and led to further jealousies, which soon exhibited themselves in the production of Cumberland upon the stage, as Sir Fretful Plagiary.

It would be hypercriticism to descant upon the beauties and defects of a play that has undergone, from its very first appearance up to the present moment, investigation the most severe; that has been the theme of every dramatic censor who has examined into its construction, or pointed to it as a fair subject of comparison with the works of those who have either preceded or succeeded its author. The too constant sparkle of the dialogue, the want of connection of the scandalous college with the plot of the play, the imitation of Fielding's Blifil and Tom Jones, the investment of such a libertine as Charles with qualities that make us forget his vices, and a vast number of incongruities have been very wisely and very learnedly pointed out, and have been descanted upon with very commendable severity; but, after all, we are so charmed with the ingenuity, with the endless richness of the dialogue, that we are never tired with reading it, or with seeing it on the stage. We admire Sir Peter Teazle in spite of his uxoriousness, his old bachelor ideas; in the hand of any other dramatist he would have been ridiculous, but he is invested with a certain dignity, a tenderness of feeling, and a sense of honour, that although we must laugh at him when his unenviable position is discovered, we are glad to find that he is likely to become a happy husband after all his mortifications. We are just on the point of thinking that Lady Teazle must become the victim of her taste for extravagance and shining in scandalous society, whilst we feel she deserves a better fate, when we gladly find that she is rescued from her false position. Even Joseph Surface is delightful to us; the duplicity of his conduct, the sentimental hypocrisy of his heart are so thoroughly laid open to us, that we are convinced that he cannot be ultimately successful; we are not so anxious for even-handed justice being done to him, as we are to the dramatic villain of a novel, and we are perfectly satisfied with the punishment he meets in the exposure of his schemes. Charles's irregularities do not shock or disgust us they are punished by the reproaches which he has to encounter from

F

ever/ one. We are happy in the conclusion that every thing
that annoyed the different parties is amicably arranged; it is
this that reconciles us to the fifth act, for at the end of the
fourth act the denouément has taken place, the fall of the
screen in a common play would have been the be all and end
all, and, as occurs in the " Merchant of Venice," the act after
the condemnation of the principal character, however beautiful is the poetry, the interest would altogether have ceased.
Yet after this exciting scene we are pleased that there is
another act to wind up the story, and to tell us how everybody has got out of the scrape. Of the original acting we
have heard much. That Garrick was delighted with it, we
may conclude not only from Murphy's observations in his
life of the great actor, but from a letter from him which
has been preserved, in which he makes some remarks upon
the length of time the characters on the stage stood after
the falling of the screen; he observes " that they should be
astonished, a little petrified, yet it may be carried to too
great a length." The conventional points, which have been
handed down to us, are not many in number, but such as they
are they show that the manner of acting was carefully studied,
and, therefore, are strictly preserved. The acting of the late
Matthews in Sir Peter Teazle is said to have been in strict
conformity with the early stage directions; the pointing to the
screen with the thumb, the leer and the movements of the
elbows were precisely the same as practised by King, and as
they usually convulsed the audience with laughter, we have
a right to suppose that man, in different generations, expresses his feelings much in the same way. It has, however,
been said that Sheridan was himself never satisfied; he requested permission to read the part over to Matthews, with
whose delineation he expressed himself by no means pleased.
The personation of Lady Teazle has been supposed to be
one of extreme delicacy, and although we seldom find an
actress of a certain grade who does not think herself fully
equal to the task, yet the fastidious lover of good acting is
very apt to require a lady of personal attractions, of good
judgment, and of elegant manners, and he repudiates the
flippant attempts which have occasionally been made to
introduce her as a being made up of levity, imprudence,
and assumption. There is to be found in " Blackwood's Maga

zine" for the year 1826, a remarkably well written essay, "On Cant in Criticism," elicited by some letters which appeared from Miss Kelly to the stage manager of Drury Lane Theatre, in consequence of an ill-natured censure in which one of the newspapers indulged upon the occasion of Miss Kelly's performance of Lady Teazle. Of the high intellectual powers of Miss Kelly no doubt can exist, of her capability of sustaining some of the most difficult characters in a particular department of the drama no one who has ever seen her inimitable personations could express an hesitation, but that she does not possess the necessary qualifications for Lady Teazle the letters we have mentioned are an indisputable proof, and bear out the remark that we are compelled to make, that the many remarkable traits which are to be clearly painted to the audience are beyond the power of many an otherwise gifted actress. That Miss Kelly's reading of the character should lead her to give an air of rusticity to Lady Teazle, to assert that there is not a single line in the whole play which describes her either as a beautiful or an elegant woman, but, on the contrary, as having been six months before a girl of limited education and of the most homely habits, are singularly opposed to the author's ideas, and to those which have been entertained by all who have been considered judges of pure and genuine comedy. The invariable reading of the part has assigned to Lady Teazle the graces and the manners of a woman of fashion, of one who, with the quick perception of the female character, has been enabled rapidly to assume all the refinement and all the manners of the haut ton. The first complaint urged against her by Sir Peter Teazle, is that, though wholly bred in the country, " She plays her part in all the extravagant foppery of the fashion and the town with as ready a grace as if she had never seen a bush or a grass plot out of Grosvenor Square ;" "then the charming air with which she contradicts him ;" the great satisfaction he has in quarrelling with her, as " she never appears to such advantage, as when she is doing every thing in her power to plague him ;" his sarcasms on having made her " a woman of fashion, her elegant expenses, her luxuries ;" and after the exposure in Joseph Surface's library, the spontaneous burst of admiration with which he rushes to a reconciliation, on seeing her in another room, " She looks this way—what a remarkably elegant turn of the heads he has—Rowley, I 'll go to her," are all evidences that she possessed those charms which belong only to a superior woman, who had, if they were not natural to her, rapidly acquired the graces which fascinate mankind. There is, too, throughout an unmistakable lady-like bearing, there is a choice of language, a quick appreciation of the defects of others, much less bordering on ill nature than is perceptible in any of the scandalous school, and a purer sense of honour, after the almost fatal error into which she had fallen, expressed in the determined tone of contrition, with a knowledge of the worldly views of man, which must impress us with the conviction of her being endowed with the perception of what was most appreciated in society, and with a tact of the highest order.

Probably there never was a dramatist who more thoroughly understood the exact province of comedy than did Sheridan, no one could excite in us more cheerfulness and mirth at the follies and inconsistencies of human nature, no one could portray them better, and certainly no one has ever interested us more, even in the imperfections and immoralities of his personages. Whatever faults and vices they may exhibit, they are portrayed so as to instruct our understanding, but not to shock our feelings. His object has been to amuse, even where he censures, and the punishment which he inflicts, is that ridicule and exposure which are more mortifying than any indignation or anger. It is not only a picture of the manners of the day in which he lived, but the general features are those which will be perceptible in all ages and all times, as long as there shall be a privileged class in society, distinguished from the others by social and domestic differences. There will always be uxorious husbands, confiding women, irascible fathers, careless spendthrifts, romantic girls, hypocrites, and slanderers; such characters, modified by circumstances, and by national habits, will exist in every age and in every clime. He has not slightly sketched these characters, but has displayed them in all their full vigour; he has made them by the skill of his dialogue their own painters; each betrays his own obliquities; there is no forced effort to deceive the audience; until the development of the plot is brought about, incidents follow one upon another which explain the position of each actor in the drama, and we are gradually led on to take a warm interest in the success of each, even when we find that we are bordering on dislike of the selfishness and immoral tendency which are beginning to show themselves. It is not only the inventive and creative faculty that we admire in the fable, but the light play of wit with which the conversation abounds; we feel that we are in good company, that every man is striving to be clever and entertaining to his neighbour, and there is nothing so flattering to our vanity as to find that the amusing persons, amongst whom we chance to be mingling, are exerting themselves to please us, that they are unloading the stores of their intellect for the purpose of making us satisfied with ourselves. There is a disposition to heighten the effect by the sallies of a sportive wit, but there is no caricature, no exaggeration. There is nothing improbable, nothing but what may have occurred, every thing is perspicuous and easily developed. We have neither our hopes nor our fears painfully excited, but every thing that passes before us inspires us with the confidence that we have nothing to do, but to laugh at the exposure of the follies of the world, the mistaken views of men, the rogueries of some, the foibles of others, and that these are often blended together in such a manner as to excite our mirth and our good feeling, and to dispel the gloom which the realities of life are too often calculated to collect.

In the same volume of the "Edinburgh Review," which contains an examination into the merits of Moore as the biographer of Sheridan, there is an essay on the works of Machiavelli, by Macauley, which has been much admired for its depth of thought and its terseness of expression; a few sentences have been often quoted from it on the subject of Sheridan's plays, and Leigh Hunt, in his brief but brilliant sketch of Sheridan, has placed them in juxtaposition with an extract from one of Hazlitt's lectures on the comic writers. We have thus the bane and antidote before us. To the comedies of Machiavelli, the reviewer apportions the correct and vigorous delineation of human nature, and considers that this is the highest kind of excellence. He believes that comedy is corrupted by wit. To Congreve and to Sheridan he imputes their having deeply injured the comedy of England. He admits that they were men of splendid wit and of polished taste, but that their indiscriminate prodigality of sparkling language produces a dazzling glare, and that they unhappily

made all their characters in their own likeness. We must
confess that we cannot assent to the axiom laid down that the
real object of the drama is the exhibition of the human character. We would rather look to the comedy as not only
a representation of what is amusing in character, and in the
contrast of situations and combinations, but as a picture of
the manners, the feelings, and the language of the class of
persons who are painted. Most of Shakspeare's comedies are
romantic love tales, there is no attempt at a skilful plot,
they are made up of slight materials, the incidents are few,
the conclusions are brought about in a very arbitrary way,
probabilities overlooked, plots scarcely wound up, characters
broadly delineated, and they are altogether compositions of
an extraordinary kind, produced before the rules of art had
yet " cabined, cribbed, confined" the human imagination.
In the age in which Shakspeare lived, the lively, elegant
and sparkling dialogue would have been less understood
than quaint expressions, play upon words, and logical dis-
quisitions. In the earlier stages of society nature had her
freshness yet unaltered, and those who painted her met with
those who could appreciate her beauties. As man changed
by cultivation, by refinement, he began to admire art, and
although he can still love the first early impression that was
made upon his youthful heart, he looks to those artificial
ornaments by which he has been surrounded as the chief
source of his delight. Congreve, Wycherley, Farquhar had
prepared the audiences, before whom Sheridan's plays were
produced, to enjoy his brilliancy of wit and repartee. These
did not corrupt the taste, they were adapted to it, they were
precisely the food on which the public were anxious to live,
they were the delicacies best suited to their already pampered
appetites. They have continued to delight the rising generation for whom in vain has been prepared other luxurious
viands. After the exciting melodramas of the German school,
their exaggerated sentimentality, their mawkish sensibility,
after the light intrigue of the French comedy, its good
natured gaiety, and its enticing sensuality, we still can turn
with redoubled pleasure to the epigrammatic points, the sparkling dialogues, the pungent satire of Sheridan. All may
be too highly wrought, too elaborate, too ornamental, still
are we delighted ; we feel whilst we pry into the follies and

foibles of our brethren that they are exhibited in their richest point of view; and even the hypocrisy of a Joseph, or the cowardice of an Acres, whilst we abhor them, are laughed at, because they are genuine, and whilst they seem to belong to human nature are the best of their kind.

No one is more likely to become "laudator temporis acti" than the theatrical amateur; the first impressions of life, the earliest illusions strike so forcibly upon the imagination, that they are recollected at subsequent periods with all their freshness, and with a large proportion of the pleasure they first excited. Judgment has had but little to do with the verdict our senses have early pronounced, and when in later days we make comparisons, we naturally forget that we have, from the course of events, grown fastidious; that objects which surprised and delighted us have become familiar, and have therefore lost that which was their principal charm—their originality. We are apt to fancy that the actors of the present day are far inferior to those who formerly delighted us; we are alive to their defects, and are not struck with their peculiar merits. There can, however, be but little doubt that when the "School for Scandal" was originally produced, there was upon the boards of Drury Lane Theatre, as complete a company as ever was collected together; and that though some of the characters may have been filled at different periods by individuals of equal merit to them, yet that the play was performed in a most masterly manner, and worthy the school of the never dying Garrick. The Sir Peter Teazle was intrusted to King, who has been traditionally spoken of as one of the most perfect performers in his department, which was, however, somewhat limited. He had distinguished himself as Lord Ogleby, a character that Garrick had originally intended for himself, and which, with the assistance of Colman had been rendered admirably adapted for the great master of his art; but he excused himself on the plea that he was unwilling to study a new part. In fact, in his own farce, "Lethe," the character of Lord Chalkstone was sufficiently like to prevent his having any great desire to undertake the new one. No one could deliver such dialogue, as is found in Lord Ogleby, and in Sir Peter Teazle, with greater point than Mr. King. He excelled in a quiet, sententious mode of expressing feeling and sentiment. There was

an epigrammatic style in every thing he uttered ; for although
he could, when occasion required, give rapid utterance to his
thoughts, he seemed generally to dwell upon his words, and
then make all the happy points tersely and cleverly; his
voice was musical, his action slow, his countenance expressive
of benignity, and yet of firmness.   He had the reputation of
speaking prologues and epilogues better than any actor of the
day, rendering them, when written with spirit, little dramas
perfect in themselves; his delivery of the couplet was in the
true spirit of poetry, and, without any mixture of buffoonery
or mimicry, he painted the ludicrous and the gay with great
felicity and tact.

He continued to perform the character at Drury Lane
until his retirement, occasionally lending his aid at the other
theatres where his Sir Peter was duly estimated.   In this
he took leave of the public on the 24th of May, 1802, after
fifty-four years of unremitting zeal.   Although he had on
other occasions shown that memory is not tenacious in old age
of that with which it was once most strongly impressed, he,
for the last time, displayed, to the great admiration of those
who love the scenic art, his admirable delineation of the disappointed, anxious old bachelor.   His face, which was from
an early period strongly marked, was furrowed with age; his
eye had still some lustre, but there was much feebleness in
his step; there was, however, sufficient to teach the young
actor how great had been the veterans of Garrick's day.
With trembling lips and faltering voice he delivered an address, written by Cumberland, of which the following lines
are a specimen :—

> " Patrons, farewell !
> Though you still kindly my defects would spare,
> Constant indulgence who would wish to bear?
> Who that retains the sense of brighter days,
> Can sue for pardon, whilst he pants for praise ?
> On well-earned fame the mind with pride reflects,
> But pity sinks the man whom it protects.
> Your fathers had my strength, my only claim
> Was zeal ; their favour was my only fame."

Amidst shouts of applause the venerable old man made his
bow, and retired to the green room, where an affectionate
compliment awaited him from his dramatic brethren, in the

shape of a handsome silver cup, with an engraved motto from "Henry the Fifth," happily adapted to the occasion :—

> "If he be not fellow with the best king,
> Thou shalt find him the best king of good fellows."

From this cup his health was drunk, and he returned the compliment almost overpowered with the intensity of his feelings, for as yet these marks of admiration and of approbation had not become common, they were the spontaneous tributes of high and honourable affection; as such they were offered, as such accepted. The lavish manner in which stage compliments are now distributed, the hackneyed offerings, behind and before the curtain, which managers, actors, and audiences bestow in so many shapes, have rendered all such expressions so ludicrous that they are rather to be avoided than courted. With him it was naturally said that Sir Peter had quitted the stage. We have, however, seen many representatives who have delighted us. It is true that, at the present moment, Farren is the only actor who will leave behind him the impression of greatness, he deserves to be recorded as one worthy to be ranked with any of his predecessors.

Palmer's Joseph Surface seems to have been perfectly unapproachable by any competitor. So admirable a hypocrite has never·yet been seen; his manners, his deportment, his address, combined to render him the very man he desired to paint. His performance on the stage bore a very strong similarity to that he was famous for in private life; he was plausible, of pleasing address, of much politeness, and even of great grace. He was fond of pleasure, which he pursued with so much avidity as to be generally very careless of his theatrical duties, but when he had committed some gross absurdity, or had been, through complete neglect of his duties, on the verge of hearing a loud shout of disapprobation, "he threw up his eyes with an expression of astonishment, or cast them down as if in penitent humility, drew out his eternal white handkerchief to smother his errors, and bowed himself out of his scrapes." His plausibility and insidious arts shone forth in Joseph. Palmer opened the Royalty Theatre in 1787, in Wellclose Square, Goodman's Fields, in opposition to his former friends at Drury Lane Theatre, and attempting to perform plays he was served with a threatening notice from the proprietors of Drury Lane, Covent Garden, and the Haymarket, which obliged him to abandon his undertaking. He therefore changed his plan, but being ultimately unsuccessful he was compelled to return to Drury Lane; he was received before the curtain with the sincerest demonstrations of welcome; he felt that he was surrounded by his friends, and received the applause with all his usual mute expressions of gratitude, but the difficulty was to reconcile the manager. The meeting between the two men of address—Sheridan and Palmer—was, as Boaden narrates it, expected to produce something remarkable. Palmer, making a profound bow, approached the author of the "School for Scandal" with an air of penitent humility; his head declined; the whites of his eyes turned upwards; his hands clasped together, and his whole air exactly that of Joseph Surface before Sir Peter Teazle. He began thus: "My dear Mr. Sheridan, if you could but know what I feel at this moment HERE," *laying one hand upon his heart.* Sheridan, with inimitable readiness stopped him, "Why, Jack, you forgot *I wrote it.*" Palmer, in telling the story himself, added, "that the manager's wit cost him something, for I made him add three pounds per week to the salary I had before my desertion." There is one story related by Boaden which shows that Palmer was even superior to the manager. A friend complimenting him one day upon his address, he disclaimed any remarkable possession of the quality. "No," said he, " I really don't give myself the credit of being so irresistible as you have fancied me; there is, however, one thing in the way of address that I think I am able to do. Whenever I am arrested I think I can always persuade the sheriffs' officers to bail me." This feat, however, has been surpassed by a more modern actor of considerable talent, who not only persuaded the keeper of a spunging-house to be his bail, but to lend him two guineas to pay the attention of the servants of the establishment, whom he declared he knew not how sufficiently to recompense they were so full of civility and sympathy; he actually paid them out of the loan with three shillings, pocketing the surplus for a future occasion, and not forgetting to drink the health of the lender, as a man who ought to be encouraged as a good master and an honest friend, having no confined notions.

On an occasion when a new play was to be produced at

Drury Lane, and the greatest anxiety prevailed that it should be well brought out, it was pretty evident, at the rehearsal, that Palmer knew not one line of his part; but it was expected that as he was aware that great anticipation had been formed of its success that he would study it, more particularly as it was one that would do him much credit, and with which he had appeared more than usually pleased. The house was sure to be crowded, for the boxes were fully taken, and the night for the performance had been for some time fixed. At three o'clock on the eventful day arrived however, at the stage door, a letter; it was presented by Powell, the prompter, in the presence of Michael Kelly, to Sheridan in due form. He perused it; it was from John Palmer, announcing, as a deplorable fact, that he was taken dangerously ill, and that his appearance that night might be fatal to him. Sheridan knowing his man tolerably well, said, "I'll lay my life this is a trick of Plausible Jack, and that there is nothing the matter with him, except indeed not knowing a line of the part he has to act to-night. Let you and I call upon him," turning to Kelly, "and I am sure we shall find him as well as ever." They went to Lisle Street, where Palmer lived, but Kelly managed to slip away, and act the good natured part of preparing Palmer for the visit. He found him in the enjoyment of good health, a good dinner, and his social circle. He gave him the hint to clear away the table, and to do all he could to mystify Sheridan, who never would forgive him for postponing the play. Palmer seized the moment, swore endless gratitude for the kindness received from Kelly; rushed into his bedroom, was quickly enveloped in a dressing gown, with a large woollen nightcap on, and a face of the most becoming length; at first he could not make up his mind as to the nature of the dangerous illness with which he was to be afflicted—a dreadful and most·excruciating toothache at last presented itself to his mind. His face was immediately swollen; a handkerchief tied to his jaw, and lamentable groans issued from the agonized sufferer. Sheridan arrived; he gazed with pity and with sympathy upon the admirable actor, who, with his hand upon the usual place, and with a white handkerchief at his eyes, assured the anxious manager that his suffering corporeal was not equal to his mental, in consequence of his conviction that it was injuring the establishment. Sheridan was completely taken in ; kindly suggested the extraction of the tooth, and then to study the part and get perfect in the new play, and never had the slightest idea of the trick played upon him. One of the happy excuses which Palmer played forth on every occasion was the accouchement of his wife. He would postpone an engagement by sighing forth, with his white handkerchief to his eyes, "My best of friends, this is the most awful period of my life; I cannot be with you, my beloved wife, the partner of my sorrows and my joys, is just confined." He was engaged to act at Reading for the benefit of a poor actor, and at the very moment of expectation, a letter was despatched by Palmer instead of himself, announcing such an occurrence just to have taken place. It was read to the audience, who, of course, felt the deepest sympathy with him on such an interesting domestic occurrence, and all opposition was silenced. He merely smiled with his usual bland benignity when congratulated by Kelly upon the happiness of having a wife who, at least, once in two months rendered him a contented father.

During the period that Palmer attempted to perform at Goodman's Fields, the magistrates summoned him to appear before them, and calling upon him to show the licence by which he acted, threatened instantaneous committal unless it was produced. He bowed with excessive humility, and lamenting very much that he did not know that it was their wish that it should be laid before them, entreated their indulgence whilst he went home, which was but a short distance, for the important document. After some discussion this was assented to; Palmer's gratitude for this indulgence knew no bounds, he called upon heaven to bless them for their kindness, laying his hand as usual upon that part of the chest where he supposed he had a heart, respectfully bowed, and departed upon his errand. The magistrates waited for a considerable length of time in the room at the tavern, discussing the weather and the political topics of the day, until at length their patience was exhausted, they rang the bell to order the waiter to go to Mr. Palmer's lodgings, and desire him to say they could wait no longer. The waiter on trying to open the door, to learn the pleasure of the quorum assembled, found that it was locked, and requested the party within to open it, and they then learnt that they were fairly locked in ; for Mr.

Palmer, fully aware that there was no such document in existence, and fearing that the magistrates would, as they had the power, actually commit him, had, on shutting the door. quietly turned the key in the lock, pocketed it, and had gone his way to follow his business, as "every man hath business," and was careful to attend to nothing but that, and to be seen by nobody until the storm had blown over. A more specious representative of Joseph Surface was not to be found, nor has any one ever won such laurels. He played the part naturally ; indeed, study was always out of the question with him. It is a fact that on the occasion of the production of Hayley's tragedy of "Lord Russell," he was completely incapable of giving effect to the character of Lord Russell, as he had as usual neglected to study it ; but as he knew the tragedy of the "Earl of Essex," and that there was some similarity in the fate of the two heroes, he very dexterously recited passages from that play, contriving to fit them in, so that the audience never discovered his incapacity. With all his faults—and they were many—he was one of the greatest favourites of the public ; he was always hailed with loud approbation ; he appeared to have been made for the profession, and trod the stage as no other man could do. There was something in his departure from the great scene of life that created considerable sensation. He was performing at Liverpool the character of the Stranger, and had just pronounced the words, "there is another and a better world," when he was seized with a paroxysm, from which he never recovered. It does not appear that, as has generally been received, he died instantaneously ; but from the moment of his fall upon the stage there were but feeble indications of existence.

Charles Surface fell to the lot of William Smith, who has been characterized by Churchill in the "Rosciad," as "Smith the genteel, the airy, and the smart." All agree that he was one of the most elegant men of the day, his acquirements were of no ordinary kind. He had received a first-rate education, and had completed his studies with much credit to himself at Cambridge. He was admitted into the highest circles of society, and was particularly remarkable for the elegance of his manners. He had many of those qualifications which enabled him to perform respectably in tragedy, but he never attained-any thing like excellence in that walk. In comedy, however, as the fine gentleman, his powers were universally acknowledged. The graces of his person, the elegance of his manners, and the dignity of his deportment, admirably qualified him for that character. The style of the man moving in good society, it must be remembered, was essentially different from what it now is. The dress, the distinctions, the acquirements necessary, were so unlike any thing which we now see, that we can form but an indifferent idea of the qualifications demanded for the accomplished actor in this walk. There was more stage effect then even in private life; the powdered hair, the folding hat, the sword, the short breeches with buckles, the embroidered coat, the ruffles, and all the accessories of dress, served to distinguish the class; dancing a minuet, fencing, and fashionable raillery were amongst the indispensable accomplishments. To portray upon the stage a man of the true school of gentility required pretensions of no ordinary kind, and Smith possessed these in a singular degree, and he gave to Charles Surface all that finish for which he was remarkable. He had acquired the sobriquet of Gentleman Smith from his unvarying exhibition of an air of distinction without any false assumption. He had made it an indispensable article of his agreement with managers that his face was never to be blackened, and that he was never to be lowered through a stage door. He retired from the stage in 1787. The house was enormously crowded; and such had been the desire to be present amongst the fashionable admirers of Smith, that the pit was for the occasion converted into boxes, but there was not room for the accommodation of all; he took his farewell, he said, after having served thirty-five campaigns under the ablest generals, Garrick and Barry, and now resigned the youthful gaiety of Charles Surface to younger blood. The modern style of fine gentleman is so distinct from that of the day in which the "School for Scandal" was produced, that we cannot attempt to picture what then fascinated the audience, but the opinion of the playgoers of the day was, that "the Charles of the School for Scandal died with Smith;" but that for this "we are to blame the alteration of our dress, and the consequent familiarity of our manners." In a subsequent year he once again appeared, when his old friend King bade farewell to the stage; he was then living in retirement, surrounded by all the comforts of life;

still, anxious to assist a brother veteran upon whom fortune had not so kindly bestowed her blessings, he played Charles with great spirit, and gave an admirable picture of the gentleman of the old school, and although associations, ideas, and habits were much altered from what they had been when he was in his zenith, his audience caught the spirit of his acting, and their applause urged him on to exhibit a high flow of spirits. He concluded with some lines written for the occasion.

> " At friendship's call, ne'er to be heard in vain,
> My spirits rise—Richard's himself again."

The two scandal-mongers, uncle and nephew, each having his characteristic line of tattle, of censoriousness, and slander, fell into the hands of two excellent comedians, Dodd and Parsons, they eagerly contributed to the amusement of the public; Dodd was the most perfect fopling ever placed upon the stage, he was the most exquisite coxcomb, the most ridiculous chatterer ever seen, he took his snuff, or applied the quintessence of roses to his nose, with an air of complacent superiority, such as won the hearts of all conversant with that style of affectation. His walk upon the boards bespoke the sweet effeminacy of the person, the pink heels, the muslin of his cravat and frills are dwelt upon by the amateurs of the day as specimens of his understanding the range of his art. He is spoken of as " the prince of pink heels, and the soul of empty eminence." Parsons was the Crabtree, and was a perfect old detractor and crabbed calumniator; he was an actor of great merit too, but he never appeared to greater advantage than he did in the " Critic;" he was the original Sir Fretful Plagiary, and from his delineation most of our modern actors have borrowed their idea: it was his last performance on the 29th of January, 1795, and on the fifth of February he died. A compliment paid to his memory, on the opening of the Haymarket Theatre, in the summer, was caught at by the audience with loud expressions of their concurrence in the sentiment. A prelude was written by Colman, entitled " New Hay at the Old Market;" the audience was supposed to be made acquainted with the wants of the concern, and a dialogue between Prompter and Carpenter occurs, during which the following expressions were used

"*Carpenter.* We want a new scaffold for the Surrender of Calais.

"*Prompter.* Ah! where shall we get such another hangman? Poor fellow, poor Parsons! the old cause of our mirth is now the cause of our melancholy; he who so often made us forget our cares may well claim a sigh to his memory.

"*Carpenter.* He was one of the comicalest fellows I ever see.

"*Prompter.* Ay, and one of the honestest, Master Carpenter. When an individual has combined private worth with public talent, he quits the bustling scene of life with twofold applause, and we doubly deplore his exit."

The allusion here was to the play of the "Surrender of Calais," in which Parsons performed the chief workman at the gallows erected for the patriots who were to be hung by the decree of King Edward. The scene was an imitation of the grave diggers in "Hamlet." On an occasion when the king, George the Third, had commanded the play, Parsons, instead of saying the words set down for him, "So the king is coming: an the king like not my scaffold, I am no true man," gave a new reading, which, as it was expressed with peculiar humour, and a saucy assumption of independence, excited great laughter, more especially from the monarch. Parsons exclaimed, "An the king were here, and did not admire my scaffold, I would say da—n't he has no taste." Such a liberty in the present day would most probably cause any thing but a shout of approbation; the actors in those times were a privileged class, for whom the public at large entertained a kind of affection, which they now and then gladly evinced. These two clever performers supported each other in the scandalous school with wonderful effect; the dry sarcasm of Parsons had additional sting given to it by the thoughtless and impertinent volubility of Dodd; youth and age each had their privileged sneer and jest; the total insensibility to the wounds they were inflicting seemed, in the one instance, to arise from reckless folly, in the other, from cold, calculating ill-nature. As they are generally given at the present day, there is a want of unity in the two performers, each seems totally independent of the other, and they express their villanous fancies without that force and vigour which would arise from a mutual good understanding. The two characters are by no means so easily delineated as may be imagined, and considerable study is required to satisfy those who are neither pleased with buffoonery nor burlesque.

Baddeley is not to be forgotten as Moses. He had taken infinite pains to study the characteristics by which the Jews are distinguished from other nations, and was particularly happy in expressing them. He was to have appeared at Drury Lane, on the 20th of November, in this character, but whilst dressing for it was seized with a fit, and expired on the following day. He was originally a cook, and was employed by Foote, with whom he quarrelled, and challenging him to fight, the great comedian declined, saying, "Here is a pretty fellow! I allowed him to take my spit from the rack, and stick it by his side, and now he wants to stick me with it." His bequest of a cake and wine for the green room, on twelfth night, has tended to keep his memory alive. Lamash was an actor too of considerable experience and of much merit, and was, as the coxcombical valet, and underbred fine gentleman, a great favourite.

Nothing could exceed the mismanagement which, at this time, marked every thing that was attempted at Drury Lane Theatre; numerous were the letters addressed to Garrick. Mrs. Clive, the original Nell in the "Devil to Pay," once so great a favourite with the public, then residing in quiet tranquillity at Twickenham, yet anxiously turning her eyes to her favourite haunts of old, wrote to her old friend, " Everybody is raving against Sheridan for his supineness, there never was in nature such a contrast as Garrick and Sheridan; what have you given him that he keeps so?" But a letter from Hopkins, the prompter, will show what a change had taken place in a short time after the retirement of the great actor and manager. "We played last night 'Much Ado about Nothing,' and had to make an apology for three principal parts. About twelve o'clock Mr. Henderson sent word that he was not able to play. We got Mr. Lewis from Covent Garden, who supplied the part of Benedick. Soon after, Mr. Parsons sent word he could not play, Mr. Moody supplied the part of Dogberry; and about four in the afternoon Mr. Vernon sent word he could not play, Mr. Mattocks supplied his part of Balthazar. I thought myself very happy in getting these wide gaps so well stopped. In

G

the middle of the first act a message was brought me that Mr. Lamash, who was to play the part of Borachio, was not come to the house. I had nobody there that would go on for it, so I was obliged to cut his scenes in the first and second act entirely out, and get Mr. Wrighton to go on for the remainder of the part. At length we got the play over without the audience finding it out. We had a very bad house. Mr. Parsons is not able to play in the "School for Scandal" to-morrow night; do not know how we shall be able to settle that. I hope the pantomime may prove successful, and relieve us from this dreadful situation." All these communications could not fail to be distressing to Garrick, who, independent of the large pecuniary interest he had at stake, felt very great anxiety for the welfare of Sheridan and his colleagues: he ends a correspondence between himself and Mr. T. King, " Poor Old Drury, I feel that it will very soon be in the hands of the Philistines." The complaints against Sheridan were strongly urged; he neglected to open his letters; they were collected into an indiscriminate heap, and oftentimes, when their accumulation rather alarmed the manager, they were consigned to the flames, and frequently communications of considerable importance were thus sacrificed. Authors not only complained of the loss or neglect of their manuscripts, but boldly asserted that their plots, their incidents, and their conversations were pilfered and brought out in such shapes that the parent only recognised his offspring by some unmistakeable feature. Sheridan had occasionally to pay for this heedlessness, and under the name of gratuity, or the expression of admiration of a play not quite suited for the stage, was compelled to silence some urgent claimant with money. Occasionally this obtained for him the name of liberality; but he soon found that more were ready to take advantage of his good nature than had any real claims upon it.

The year 1788 was remarkable in the life of Mr. Sheridan from the circumstance of his becoming still further committed to the speculation at Drury Lane Theatre, for he purchased Mr. Willoughby Lacy's interests, and for the introduction on the stage of a musical entertainment entitled the "Camp." It now appears that it was the work of his brother-in law, Tickell, and what could have induced Sheridan to lend the lustre of his reputation to so worthless a piece of nonsense it is difficult to imagine. Tate Wilkinson has rescued him from the discredit of the authorship, and, therefore, it is unnecessary to say a word more than that this, together with the carelessness with which the theatre was managed, under the father of Sheridan, excited some degree of displeasure amongst the habitués of Drury Lane; nor did the monody which he wrote on the death of Garrick, and which, with a musical accompaniment, was given the next year, please the public. There seemed to be a tendency to reaction in the theatrical world, and the playgoers were apparently preparing themselves for an outbreak against their newly established friend, when he succeeded in amusing the town with that which seldom fails to please—a caricature of an author whose irritability was the source of much ridicule, and a satire which travestied the dramatic compositions of the day with great humour and fidelity.

The farce called the "Critic" was brought out on the 30th of October, and was the last dramatic effort of this great genius; for "Pizarro" is only an adaptation to the English stage of a play of Kotzebue, and the larger proportion a complete translation. The period, however, at which it was placed upon the stage, whilst a species of enthusiastic loyalty to the king, a detestation of the ruler of France, and a host of concomitant events, together with the acting of Kemble, of Mrs. Siddons, of Mrs. Jordan, gave a popularity to it which probably has never been equalled

The "Critic" has remained a favourite, even after the causes that gave rise to its being thoroughly appreciated have ceased. During the lifetime of Cumberland, a satire such as this was certain to please; nor do we agree with one of his admirers, who some time since prophesied " that the works of Cumberland will delight and edify remote generations, when the attempt to render him contemptible, on account of some little infirmity in his temper, shall have lost its point and be forgotten." So far from being realized is this, that the author of the "West Indian," and of the "Jew," is almost unknown to fame. His plays are rarely acted, and then rather for the exhibition of some favourite actor; whilst the "Critic," although the parties at whom the sarcasms were levelled are not even thought of, and although the passages which are ridiculed are scarcely known to exist, proves attractive, and mirth and merriment are called forth by every scene of a burlesque which has neither plot, nor character, nor moral to develop The audience troubles itself not for a single instant to comprehend the hidden meaning with which each scene is pregnant; it enters into a joke which one would imagine would only be intelligible to those who study dramatic lore; for the "Critic" is as much a satire upon the plays of the present day, as it was upon those of the generation just passed away.

That Cumberland was the Sir Fretful Plagiary there cannot be the slightest doubt, and that Sheridan hit his peculiarities off in the happiest manner is equally true. There is a letter from Cumberland in the Garrick correspondence tendering a piece, probably the "Battle of Hastings," which had been rejected at Covent Garden. so much like what Sir Fretful would have written, that it is enough to stamp the similitude of the two: there is another from him to Garrick complaining of Sheridan exactly like the man. "I read the tragedy in the ears of the performers on Friday morning, I was highly flattered by the audience, but your successor in management is not a representative of your polite attention to authors on such occasions, for he came in yawning at the fifth act, with no other apology than having sat up two nights running. It gave me not the slightest offence, as I put it all to the habit of dissipation and indolence, but I fear his office will suffer from want of due attention, and the present drop upon the theatre justifies my apprehension." His letters exhibit his character, there is flattery of Garrick, self-conceit, insinuations against every one. Garrick endorsed upon the back of those he sent to him upon the subject of his tragedy. the "Battle of Hastings," "a true picture of the man." Of his inflicting upon his friends the horrors of listening to the reading of his plays, there are many stories on record; none, however, are better told than by Michael Kelly, who relates what occurred to himself and Banister, who were invited to partake Cumberland's hospitality at Tunbridge Wells, but were condemned to hear him go through a manuscript play, entitled "Tiberius:" his sensitiveness upon the subject of his writings may have been excusable, but his envy of the success of any other dramatist, and his inveterate dislike to Sheridan, are sufficient grounds for his being held up to ridicule

Vaughan was the person portrayed under the name of
Dangle, he was always busied in the progress of the dramatic
world, and exceedingly anxious to be considered as possessing
great power with the press and with managers. He had occupied himself about the Richmond Theatre, and had written
some letters in the "Morning Post." He was fairly characterized as a theatrical Quidnunc, and a mock Mecænas. Colman
had launched some shafts of ridicule against him in a perio-
dical paper which he brought out under the title of Genius
where Vaughan figured as Dapper. The stupid nonsense so
often quoted from Dr. Watkins, that the exposure of these
foolish individuals to public ridicule is an offence to humanity,
is scarcely worth refutation. These persons had made themselves public property, their talents were never called in question; but those offensive foibles, which led them to depreciate
all but themselves, were held up as fair objects for merriment,
the castigation they received was in proportion to their offences, and has served as an example to those who would
thrust themselves impertinently forward without duly regard-
ing the claims of others.

Some have supposed that there are sundry sly hits at
Woodfall, who was the theatrical critic in the " Morning Chronicle," to which allusion is made, but the well-known independence of character of that excellent man shields him from
any attack; he was fully capable of asserting the rights of
the press, and of maintaining that high position which, as a
critic, he had taken up. His admirable letters to Garrick in
the year 1776 show that, however willing to acknowledge
the claims of genius, he would inflexibly maintain a straightforward integrity in the conduct of his journal, and that he
would steadily adhere to truth.

Such was the impression left upon the public mind by the
"Critic," so strongly were its points felt, that no tragedy could
be offered to the managers for a long time after its production.
Every author saw the ridicule which must attend a repetition
of those turgid, incongruous, unnatural attempts, which had
so long usurped the place of tragedy. Zorayda was brought
out, but was borne with for eight nights only; its author was
a man of considerable genius, had distinguished himself at
Cambridge, having gained the Seatonian prize, but his heroine was found to be forestalled in Tilburina, and vain was

the effort to restore to the stage any of those rhapsodies which Sheridan had thus banished. It would not be difficult for any one in the habit of reading the plays of the period to show the different passages that are burlesqued. Holcroft had at one time an idea of publishing a key to the Critic; such has been done for the Rehearsal.

Parsons, as Sir Fretful Plagiary, quickly won the kindest interpretation of his peculiar view of the character, though he did not altogether please Sheridan. Miss Pope, as Tilburina, was hailed with great rapture; every one, in a moment, recognised the heroine they had been accustomed to see whining, raving, and killing herself and her lover, in the last act of every tragedy that had been produced for a quarter of a century. Her entrance in white satin, stark mad, according to custom, was the signal for a loud and long burst of applause; " nobody could ever desire to see any body madder." She mangled her metre in the most approved fashion of the day. Bannister supported her with great tact, as Don Ferolo Whiskerandos; his whimsical situation, his combat with the captain, "Am I a beef-eater now?" furnished him with admirable opportunities for burlesque acting, of which he availed himself. Short as is the part, it has always been a favourite with the public. The refusal to " stay dying all night," which was an impromptu expression of weariness the first night of dress rehearsal was seized upon by Sheridan, and immediately introduced. Indeed, several of the points were instantaneously struck off on that occasion. Mr. Waldron, as Sir Christopher Hatton, was more popular in that short and insignificant character than in any that he performed. It was said by Sheridan, that he made more points by his toes than by his brains. The "Critic" loses nothing of its value by frequent repetition. Farren has in modern times been received as a skilful delineator of Sir Fretful Plagiary, and has deservedly been admired.

It is a well-authenticated fact, that two days before the " Critic" was announced to be played Sheridan had not finished the last scene. Every body was anxious and nervous; Mr. Linley and Dr. Ford were in no enviable state— they were joint managers, and responsible. The performers looked at each other with dread and dismay. King, who had the part of Puff to sustain, was the stage manager; it was his especial duty to find out Sheridan, and to weary him with remonstrances on the backward state of things; but matters went on much as usual; Sheridan came to the theatre, made the customary promise that he was just going home to finish it; that in fact it was completed, and only wanted an additional line or two. His father-in-law, Linley, knew the only spur to his industry and his genius; he therefore ordered a night rehearsal, and invited Sheridan to dine with him, gave him a capital dinner, proposed a lounge to Drury Lane whilst the supper was preparing; Sheridan assented, and they sauntered together up and down the stage previous to the rehearsal, when King stepped up to Sheridan, requested a moment's audience, and went with him into the small green-room, where there was a comfortable fire, a good arm chair, a table furnished with pens, ink, and paper, two bottles of claret, a tempting dish of anchovy sandwiches, and the prompter's unfinished copy of the " Critic." King, immediately Sheridan entered the room, popped out, locked the door, when Ford and Linley made their pleasure known to him, that he was to finish the wine and the farce, but not to be allowed to stir out of the room until they were both at an end. Sheridan laughed heartily at the joke, sat to in good earnest, and finished the work to the great delight of all parties.

This last act contains an inimitable scene, almost unknown to the theatrical world, as it is rarely, if ever, performed; it boasts some of the most genuine hits at the winding up of dramas and novels that have ever appeared. The family recognition of the Justice, and the wife of the highwayman, is admirable. It is a supposed hit at the tumid language of Home, the author of "Douglas," in the " Fatal Discovery," a tragedy of bombast and nonsense, which, singularly enough, was warmly patronized by Garrick, who had repudiated the popular play of " Douglas" as unfitted for the stage. We have had occasion to observe that there exists no copy of the " School for Scandal," excepting the Dublin edition, nor of the " Duenna," authorized by Sheridan himself; but, fortunately, we possess something like circumstantial evidence that the " Critic" was given in such a shape to the world as he could approve of; for, in the library of Mr. Henry Bohn, there exists a presentation copy to one of the Duke of Marlborough's family, with the undoubted autograph of the author. From this treasure we are enabled to produce an authentic version. It is a thin octavo volume, with a frontispiece beautifully engraved, having the masks of tragedy and comedy admirably executed, printed for T. Beckett, Adelphi, Strand, 1781. There are no very striking differences in the text, from that which has been usually received as genuine; indeed, it is only in the stage directions, and in the printing of the dialogue, that there is much perceptible variation. Such, however, as is the original version, we have taken care that it should be preserved in the present volume. One or two of the passages, as they appear there, are rendered somewhat striking by the introduction of italics and capitals; thus, the accusation that Sheridan plagiarized from his fellow labourers, who sent their plays for acceptance at Drury Lane Theatre, is unhesitatingly met, and sneered at, in the following dialogue, which is thus printed :—

" *Dangle.* Sir Fretful, have you sent your play to the managers yet? or can I be of any service to you?

" *Sir Fretful.* No, no, I thank you; I believe the piece had sufficient recommendation with it. I thank you, though I sent it to the manager of COVENT GARDEN THEATRE this morning.

" *Sneer.* I should have thought now that it might have been cast (as the actors call it) better at DRURY LANE.

" *Sir Fretful.* O lud, no!—never send a play there while I live, harkee! [*Whispers Sneerwell.*]

" *Sneer. Writes himself! I know he does!*"

" *Sir Fretful.* I say nothing—I take away from no man's merit—am hurt at no man's good fortune—I say nothing, but this I say—through all my knowledge of life I have observed that there is not a passion so strongly rooted in the human heart as envy.

" *Sneer.* I believe you have reason for what you say, indeed.

" *Sir Fretful.* Besides—I can tell you it is not always so safe to leave a play in the hands of those who write themselves.

" *Sneer.* What! they may steal from them, my dear Plagiary.

" *Sir Fretful.* Steal! to be sure they may, and egad! serve your best thoughts as gypsies do stolen children, disfigure them to make them pass for their own

" *Sneer.* But your present work is a sacrifice to Melpomene, and HE, you know, never ——

" *Sir Fretful.* That's no security—a dexterous plagiarist may do anything. Why, Sir, for aught I know, he might take out some of the best things in my tragedy, and put them into his own comedy."

From the same stores that were opened for the use of Moore, and from which he has collected a vast quantity of amusing information as to the early career of Sheridan in the dramatic and literary world, have been collected proofs that many things were commenced by him which were never thoroughly carried out; several unfinished pieces attest his labours and his talents. He had meditated over many designs, of which slight sketches were drawn, the outlines of characters delineated, and heads of conversation prepared, all of which never arrived at that degree of perfection which would warrant their being given to the public in any other character than as literary curiosities, these, from the eminence of the author, are well worth preserving. The memorandums of a comedy entitled "Affectation," three acts of a drama, fragments of epilogues, of poems, lead us to regret that so early in life he abandoned, for political strife, the Muses, who were so willing to hover around him, and lend him their influence.

About the year 1780 a change came over the spirit of his dream. "That year a dissolution of Parliament took place; he felt 'aspiring passions;' he bade adieu to the triumphs which a theatrical auditory had afforded him, and sought a new scene for the exhibition of talents which doubtless he felt that he possessed, and wanted only an opportunity for their display. Amongst his manuscripts are to be found indications that, even whilst he was busy in the theatrical world, he had bestowed some portion of his time and attention to politics. A paper on absenteeism, embracing some views of the cruelty practised by England upon the sister isle, by restraining her commercial freedom, and other proofs exist that he did not entirely yield himself up to the fascinations of the theatre.

The neglect, however, which necessarily followed upon his new career was soon felt at Drury Lane Theatre; and it is to be inferred that, about this time, those embarrassments com-

menced which haunted and embittered his future life. Murmurs began to be heard as to the payment of certain salaries
—whispers which gradually grew into loud complaints—that
there was no regular system followed in the management,
and no regard paid to economy. The father of Sheridan directed the affairs of Drury Lane with great difficulty; and
at last so many obstacles were thrown in his way by one set
of persons, and so little apparent wish to support him by
those who had most interest in his management, that he was
compelled to relinquish the undertaking. Sheridan himself
seemed altogether careless; invited into society by those who
were delighted with his gaiety and his talent, he plunged into
expenses for entertaining others, which very rapidly absorbed
large sums of money, whilst the facility of drawing from the
treasury led him to forget that it was only by persevering
economy fortunes are to be realized, and those we love rendered independent of the pressure of want. Light-hearted,
amiable, open to flattery, caressed for his talents by all who had
any claim to public fame, he launched into the bustle of life.
At the age of twenty-nine he had achieved a brilliant reputation, had gained an immense property, and was apparently
master of large resources, but he rushed upon an ambitious
career which dazzled him; he abandoned that of which he was
certain for that which was yet unknown. He neglected the
business of that concern by which he could have gained, as
Garrick had done before him, a splendid fortune, left it almost
without management, content to be called the kind-hearted
proprietor, and to draw money from it. An epilogue to Miss
Hannah Moore's play of "Fatal Falsehood," from his pen,
and a pantomime, "Robinson Crusoe, or Harlequin Friday,"
attributed to him, seem, for a time, to have been all that he
considered necessary for him to do for the theatre.

The biographer, who is endowed with Spurzheim's organ
comparison, would feel some difficulty in assigning to Sheridan
his proper rank as a statesman, if he sought to elucidate the
circumstances of his political career by drawing a parallel between his position and that of any of the distinguished men who
at the present moment sway the public mind. Indeed, events
are of so different a character, that another race of individuals has sprung up, who would most probably have been little
thought of had they attempted to bring themselves into

notice at an earlier period. The eloquence which was required in the stormier moments of a nation's existence would now be of little avail; the passions are no longer to be aroused—the reason is to be addressed. Men have time leisurely to reflect upon the nightly debates; these are occupied with subjects which require facts, statistic details, and knowledge of business; assiduity and practical information are more looked to than brilliancy of language or beautiful imagery. The representative of a manufacturing district, or a railway proprietor who can stutter forth his own conviction, commands more attention than the chaste speaker, or the acute logician; such, however, was not the case when Sheridan won the admiration of his country.

Politics were then more universally discussed; all ranks of society engaged in public affairs; the spirit of party ran high; matters of the deepest happiness to the human race were boldly investigated; the attempt by one set of men to stifle the expression of the general voice had engendered a rankling hatred in the bosom of others, and kindled the passions that were sought to be extinguished; these, however, have now died away. In England, since the secession from active exertion for the party of the people, of their last great leader, Sir Francis Burdett, there has been little of that enthusiasm which once animated the whole kingdom and led society to rank itself under two great sections, which, whatever might have been their subdivisions, represented, on one hand, the love of power, on the other, that of liberty. From the commencement of the great American War, until the overthrow of Napoleon, there was a constant excitement in the public mind; the mightiest changes were going forward, and opportunities offered themselves, to men to distinguish themselves, more by their power of influencing others by personal ability and their more apparent qualifications, than by their research, their inventions, or their discoveries. Above all, eloquence, which addresses itself at once to the senses, and leads them onwards, was worshipped, and brought to its possessor. not only admiration, but, beyond that, the actual affection of its auditors. No one more successfully obtained this than did Sheridan.

He was listened to, even by such a man as Professor Smyth, " as a being that belonged to another sphere, as one to whom no ordinary mortal was for a moment to be brought into likeness or comparison;" such was the wondrous power of Sheridan, that his vehement and affecting torrents of eloquence left an impression upon the mind that no subsequent series of events could ever efface; if, indeed, all that his eulogists have said of him be true, those who once listened to him have had a greater enjoyment than has fallen to the lot of the most enthusiastic admirer of public speaking. Yet, when Sheridan entered upon his career, he by no means gave promise of becoming so splendid an orator. There were, twenty years ago, at Bath, many who remembered him there as a young man walking about in a cocked hat and scarlet waistcoat, with his pockets most deplorably empty, trying various means of filling them and amusing himself. Amongst other thoughts that crossed his mind was a private play, but in rehearsal he was found incapable of filling any prominent position.

When, in 1780, Sheridan made his first address upon the subject of his return to Parliament for Stafford, in answer to a petition against his election, he was listened to with great attention, the House being uncommonly still while he was speaking, for his reputation had prepared for him a willing audience; he made, however, but little impression—it appeared, to those who were anxious to judge of his real capabilities, that nature never intended him for an orator; his enunciation was evidently very imperfect; he spoke as if his tongue was too thick for the due action of the muscles which close the teeth upon it; there was an indistinctness, of which indeed he never got rid, so that his mental powers appeared to be very far superior to his physical qualifications. He was himself agitated during the delivery of his speech, and upon its conclusion he went into the gallery where Woodfall was reporting, and with much evident anxiety tried to obtain from him his opinion of the probability of his ultimate success. With his usual frankness, Woodfall told him that he candidly advised him to stick to his former pursuits, for he had now got out of his depth; Sheridan, however, felt that within him which urged him on to future fame, and, resting his head upon his hand, exclaimed, "I know that it is in me, and out it shall come!" Woodfall was nearly right; Sheridan became, with as much labour as Demosthenes had employed, a great orator, and mind overcame the deficiencies of the earthly frame; but even to the latest moments he had occasion ally a defect which, for a short time, impeded the power of producing an impression; but when carried away by his subject all minor thoughts were dissipated by the excitement of his language, the fervour of his manner, and the woudrous lustre and expression of his eye; so that, when he ceased, all seemed to wait with the hope of something more.

This first attempt made by Sheridan to address the House naturally excited great interest. He was heard with particular attention and unusual silence; he replied to a complaint against his election for Stafford, by means of bribery and corruption; he defended his constituents from an accusation made by the lowest and most unprincipled voters. He thought it a great hardship, and wished that some adequate penalties should be inflicted on those who traduced and stigmatized a respectable body of men. Mr. Rigby did not allow these observations to pass unnoticed, but ridiculed the idea of any member being concerned for the character of his constituents. Mr. Fox threw his shield over the young member, and made some sarcastic remarks on the ministerial members, who chiefly robbed and plundered their constituents, and afterwards affected to despise them. Sheridan, himself, took the opportunity, on the next occasion of his addressing the House, which was a few evenings after, when he spoke on the Vote of Thanks to Earl Cornwallis and General Sir Henry Clinton, for their conduct in America, to show that he was not likely tamely to submit to the taunts of Mr. Rigby. He apologized to him for not answering some things that had fallen from him, in the same ludicrous strain in which he chose to view every thing, excepting what related to his own immediate interest. He acknowledged the gentleman had a kind of drollery and humour, but he liked his ingenuity, his humour and his counsels, better than his political arguments.

Sheridan's next speech, which occurred on the second reading of the bill for "The better Regulation of his Majesty's Civil List," was the first indication that he gave of his readiness of reply, and of the happy tact with which he could seize on the observations of an adversary, and turn the weapons of ridicule upon the practised debater. Mr. Courtenay, instead of discussing a serious and grave question, which involved the characters of the ministry for retaining several useless, expensive, and inconvenient places, and diverting the money of the public from its proper channels into the purse of individuals, attacked the opposition members, and observed that Oh, liberty! Oh, virtue! Oh, my country! had been the incessant, pathetic, but fallacious cry of former oppositions. The present he was sure acted on purer motives. They wept over their bleeding country; yet the patriot " eye, in a fine frenzy rolling," deigned to cast a wishful squint on riches and honour enjoyed by the minister and his venal supporters. He compared their conduct to the sentimental alderman in Hogarth's print, who, when his daughter is dying, wears a face of parental grief and solicitude; but it is to secure a diamond ring which he is drawing off her finger. He proceeded, in a ludicrous strain, to point out the anxious wish of the opposition to breathe a fresh air, but implored them not to put the drag chain upon a rising state. Mr. Sheridan, after reproving Mr. Courtenay for the unsuitable manner in which he had introduced his opinion, observed that, if they could not act with dignity, they ought to debate with decency; that he would not attempt seriously to reply to that which had an infusion of ridicule in every part; but two of his similes he must take notice of. The one was that the opposition was envious of those who basked in court sunshine, and were desirous only of getting into their places. To this insinuation he would reply, that though the sun afforded a genial warmth, it also occasioned an intemperate heat that tainted and infected every thing that it reflected on; that this excessive heat tended to corrupt, as well as to cherish, to putrefy, as well as to animate, to dry and soak up the wholesome juices of the body politic, and to turn the whole into one mass of corruption. If those, therefore, who sat near him did not enjoy so genial a warmth as the honourable gentleman, and those who, like him, kept near the nobleman in the blue riband (Lord North), he was certain that they breathed a purer air, an air less infected and less corrupt. The drag chain, of the gentleman's allusion, was never applied but when a machine was going down hill, and then it was applied wisely. He concluded a felicitous speech by assuring the honourable gentleman that the most serious part of his argument appeared the most ludicrous.

It was on the 5th of March that the first parliamentary effort, demanding talent and judgment, was made by Sheridan, and the universal opinion expressed in favour both of the matter and manner of his speech gave him a decided position in the political world. Mr. Sheridan had previously given notice of his intention to bring forward a motion for the better regulation of the police of Westminster, and he took the opportunity of coming before the house with a well-digested view of the circumstances which had presented themselves during the month of June, in the past year, when the metropolis was left for several days at the mercy of an ignorant and fanatic mob. His motions were :—

" 1. That the military force intrusted to his Majesty by parliament cannot justifiably be applied to the dispersing illegal and tumultuous assemblies of the people, without waiting for directions from the civil magistrates, but where the outrages have broke forth with such violence that all civil authority is overborne, and the immediate subversion of all legal government directly threatened "

" 2. That the necessity of issuing that unprecedented order to the military, on the 7th of June last, to act without waiting for directions from the civil magistrates, affords a strong presumption of the defective state of the magistracy of Westminster, where the riots began."

" 3. That a committee be appointed to inquire into the conduct of the magistracy and civil power of the city of Westminster, with respect to the riots in June last; and to examine and report to the House the present state of the magistracy and government of the said city."

The language he employed was not peculiarly striking, but it was to the point.

On the 13th of May, and on the 17th, the readiness of Sheridan excited much amusement in the House. On the first occasion he made some observations on lotteries, and concluded with observing, that " As the learned gentleman (the Solicitor General) who brought in the bill had already on one occasion stood forward, not only as the *censor morum*, but as the *arbiter elegantiarum*, at once the Cato and the Petronius of the age, he hoped he would be active in his new character, and join in putting a stop to lottery gaming, by bringing in a bill to abolish all the present lottery offices, and preventing the opening of any new ones in future."

On the other, on the bill for preventing desertion, Sheridan

pithily observed, " That the honourable gentleman (Mr. Pen·
ton) had·omitted to take notice of one objection adduced by
Mr. Dunning, which was, that when sailors, suspected to
be deserters, were brought before a justice of the peace by
virtue of this act, though the suspicion turned out to be
groundless, they might nevertheless, by authority of former
statutes, be impressed.   He ironically complimented the
board of Admiralty for the high sense they seemed here to
entertain of the honour of British sailors;—it might be illustrated by a very trite anecdote of Julius Cæsar; for, like his
wife, the character of our seamen must be as clear of suspicion
as of impeachment; they not only must not be deserters.
but not suspected to be so."

A few words upon the bill to amend and explain the mar·
riage act, brought in by Mr. Fox, gave that great leader of the
opposition an opportunity of complimenting, somewhat insidiously, his friend Mr. Sheridan, who opposed Mr. Fox's favourite
views. " He said his honourable friend (Mr. Fox), who brought
in the bill, appeared not to be aware that, if he carried the
clause enabling girls to marry at sixteen, he would do an
injury to that liberty of which he had always shown himself
the friend, and promote domestic tyranny, which he could
consider only as little less intolerable than public tyranny.
If girls were allowed to marry at sixteen, they would, he conceived, be abridged of that happy freedom of intercourse.
which modern custom had introduced between the youth of
both sexes; and which was, in his opinion, the best nursery
of happy marriages.   Guardians would, in that case, look on
their wards with a jealous eye, from a fear that footmen and
those about them might take advantage of their tender years
and immature judgment, and persuade them into marriage as
soon as they attained the age of sixteen.   In like manner.
young men, when mere boys, in a moment of passion, how·
ever ill directed, or perhaps in a moment of intoxication,
might be prevailed upon to make an imprudent match, and
probably be united to a common prostitute."

Fox's reply to this was, " that his honourable friend, Mr.
Sheridan, had so much ingenuity of mind, that he could con·
trive to give an argument what turn he pleased; he considered not, therefore, when what he said was really in support of domestic tyranny, he should ground it on a wish to

preserve liberty." This terminated all that fell from Sheridan during his first session.

The second session was marked by no striking proof of his senatorial ability. He seemed to wait his opportunity, and to examine carefully the opinions and strength of parties He once took occasion to reproach his former antagonist, Mr. Rigby, for the contemptuous manner in which he spoke of his constituents, when that gentleman, attempting to reply to a forcible speech of Mr. Fox on the prosecution of the American war, animadverted on the doctrine of taking counsel from their constituents, which he proclaimed unconstitutional. if not illegal. On one occasion Sheridan commented with much energy on some expressions which fell from Lord North, "that many of our best officers were unemployed and disgusted;" for it by no means appeared they had not just cause for their disgust; but the only speech worthy of being recorded is one upon a motion, made by Lord John Cavendish, of censure on Lord North. Here he had another opportunity of attacking Mr. Rigby, the paymaster of the forces. "Mr. Sheridan meant to speak to the purpose; but he wished not to be judged by the test laid down by the right honourable gentleman (Mr. Rigby), for he meant to give no offence in what he should say, though, it was true, the rule had been proposed from high authority; for undoubtedly, if the degree of offence which speeches gave was to be considered as the criterion of eloquence, the right honourable gentleman must be looked up to as the Demosthenes of that assembly. He had acted, however, in that day's debate perfectly consistent; he had assured the House that he thought the noble lord ought to resign his offices; and yet he would give his vote for his remaining in it. The honourable gentleman had long declared that he thought the American war ought to be abandoned; but he had uniformly given his vote for its continuance. He did not mean, however, to insinuate any motives for such conduct—he believed the right honourable gentleman to have been sincere; he believed that, as a member of parliament, as a privy-councillor, as a private gentleman, he had always detested the American war as much as any man, but that he had never been able to persuade the paymaster that it was a bad war: and, unfortunately, in whatever character he spoke, it was the paymaster who always voted in that House. His attacks on the noble lord, he said, appeared only an ingenious method of supporting him; it was figurative; but *ay* and *no* were speeches that did not admit of a trope." Mr. Sheridan then attacked the language used by that honourable gentleman, on all occasions, when the constituents of that House were mentioned. "His manner of treating the late petitions on the American war was highly indecent, and at that time extremely impolitic. The people began to be sufficiently irritated; gentlemen should be careful to drop no expressions of contempt towards them in that House; they had borne a great deal; and it might be imprudent to treat their patience with insult. The way to prevent the interference of the people—the way to destroy those associations and petitions, which seemed so offensive to the right honourable gentleman, was to endeavour to make Parliament respectable. Let that House show itself independent; let it show itself consistent; and the people will never think of interfering; but, if Parliament became contemptible in the eyes of the nation, the people would interfere, and neither threats nor influence would prevent them."

Sheridan was now fairly launched upon the troubled sea of politics; he had displayed that kind of talent which naturally made him an acquisition to either of the parties which sought to direct the affairs of this great empire. His eloquence, his tact, his elegance of manner, his brilliant conversation, all led to his being recognised as one who had a claim to rank amongst the leading men of the age; but it was evident that he was much better adapted to become an independent chieftain than a partisan. Although he followed the footsteps of the Whigs, he occasionally deviated from their line of march; and it was soon evident that he would act, think, and speak for himself, and that, though he was bound in strict ties of regard and of friendship to the great and good leader of the party, he would even combat him, and, when the occasion required it, would assert his own views in opposition to the man who, from his position, was entitled to express the opinions of a numerous body. The period was one of great excitement, men's minds were directed with unusual energy towards the solution of a great difficulty. A struggle carried on between the mother-country and her excited offspring had tended to awaken, in England and in the United States, the spirit of liberty, and a hatred to despotic sway. Lord North, as the ostensible minister of the crown, had accumulated upon himself the uncompromising hatred of a large portion of the people; they had been urged on by the violent declamations of Charles Fox, of Lord John Cavendish, of Edmund Burke, and of the great leaders of the Whig party. Sheridan took but little interest in this inexhaustible theme for parliamentary eloquence; and, notwithstanding the inducements he met with to exert himself, he appears to have remained almost an indifferent spectator of the struggle. There is, however, a rumour " coming," as Moore says, " from an authority worthy in every respect of the most implicit belief, that the government of the United States made him an offer of £20,000 as a mark of the high estimation in which his talents were held, but that Sheridan would not accept it." " With respect to the credibility of the transaction," continues Moore, "it is far less easy to believe that the Americans had so much money to give, than that Mr. Sheridan should have been sufficiently high-minded to have refused it."

He seemed at this period to be intent on learning the tone and temper of the House. When he spoke, it was with conciseness, and without any ambitious desire to win approbation; he felt the difficulties of his new position, and was determined to surmount them; his judgment and good taste drew upon him the notice and admiration of Charles Fox, who already, charmed with his talents, had bestowed upon him his warmest friendship.

Lord North's administration now drew to a close; the general murmuring against the war at last acted upon the supporters of the premier. On an address being moved by General Conway for a discontinuance of hostilities with America, Lord North's majority had dwindled down to a bare unit; on a similar resolution being again brought forward, he was left in a minority of nine. Mr. Sheridan made a speech on this occasion, in ridicule of Sir William Dolben, who intimated his intention of voting against the motion, although he had voted in its favour a few evenings before; this speech, which has not been recorded, is said to have been an admirable piece of satire. A few nights afterwards, Lord North announced that his administration had ceased to exist. Sheridan seems to have contented himself with general censure of the administration, but did not so virulently declaim against it as did others of the party into whose hands the reins of government now fell.

Such was, however, the respect in which Sheridan was held by his party, that when Lord North's ministry was overthrown, and the Marquis of Rockingham formed a new one, from which the country anticipated great results, he was appointed one of the under secretaries of state, a post which he had then reason to believe would be a permanent one, but in this he was doomed to disappointment. There were seeds of dissolution in that administration, which very rapidly sprung up and quickly choked the promising growth of the tree of Whiggism: but one short speech has been recorded to have been delivered by him in his new official position, and that upon a point which failed to interest the public; but he spoke briefly on another occasion, memorable in the annals of reform, when a young man, destined to rule the destinies of a mighty empire, and afterwards to oppose with all his strength the doctrines which he at first supported with zeal and enthusiasm—William Pitt—moved for a committee to inquire into the state of the representation.

The death of the Marquis of Rockingham led to such disunion, that after a short existence of four months this administration was dissolved, and made way for that coalition which was execrated by the politicians of the day, and at this hour is looked upon as having so far shaken all confidence in the integrity of public men, as to have laid the foundation for the formation of a party of the people, the principle of whose political creed was the distrust of both Whig and Tory.

Lord North and his opponent Charles Fox, antagonists in every public measure that had ever been agitated, listening to the tone of the charmers who sang of the sweets of office, of the mutability of the people, and of the smiles from the throne, threw aside every idea of the moral strength of public opinion, and fraternized. It is universally allowed that on this occasion Sheridan upheld the dignity of the statesman's character, that he boldly proclaimed his dissent from this sacrifice of character, and that he held an interview with Fox, during which he vainly attempted to change his decision; it was terminated by the remarkable expression of the great Whig leader, "It is as fixed as the Hanover succession "

Once only did Sheridan make any allusion to this coalition. The debate in which it occurred, on the preliminary articles of peace, is more remarkable from its bringing him into collision with Mr. Pitt, and his triumphant reply to some sarcasms, which the future prime minister indulged in. . The following portions of their speeches are amongst the reports of the House of Commons. " No man," observed Mr. Pitt, "admired more than he did the abilities of that right honourable gentleman, the elegant sallies of his thought, the gay effusions of his fancy, his dramatic turns, and his epigrammatic points; and, if they were reserved for a proper stage, they would, no doubt, receive what the honourable gentleman's abilities always did receive, the plaudits of the audience; and it would be his fortune ' *sui plausu gaudere theatri.*' But this was not the proper scene for the exhibition of these elegancies." To this Sheridan's instantaneous reply was: " On that particular sort of personality which the right honourable gentleman had thought proper to introduce, I need make no comment—the propriety, the taste, the gentlemanly point of it, must have been obvious to the House. But let me assure the right honourable gentleman, that I do now, and will at any time when he chooses, meet it with the most sincere good humour. Nay, I will say more, flattered and encouraged by the right honourable gentleman's panegyric on my talents, if I ever again engage in the compositions he alludes to, I may be tempted to an act of presumption, to attempt an improvement on one of Ben Jonson's best characters, the character of the Angry Boy in the 'Alchymist.'"

During this unnatural coalition, Mr. Sheridan became secretary of the treasury, his coadjutor, Richard Burke, was the brother of Edmund. Of the business-like manner in which he discharged the duties which devolved upon him, his warmest friends are necessarily silent; but his opponents speak of a laughable *affiche* which was found upon the doors of the treasury : " No applications can be received here on Sundays, nor any business done here during the remainder of the week." This was the first proof of his inaptitude to the discharge of public duty. Mr. Sheridan attempted, as did his colleagues, to justify their conduct in associating with that ministry, whose chief they had not only loudly denounced as dangerous, but actually declared their intention of impeaching for unconstitutional conduct. His speech was clever, was ingenious, but failed to convince; he, in common with the rest of his party, lost caste by this inconsistent union. The only debate which he enlivened with his wit was the threatened taxation of tombstones, actually proposed by Mr. Coke of Norfolk, as one which could meet with no objections. To which Sheridan replied, " that the only reason why the proposed tax could not be objected to was, because those out of whose property it was to be paid would know nothing of the matter, as they must be dead before the demand could be made; but then, after all, who knows but that it may not be rendered unpopular in being represented as a tax upon persons, who, having paid the debt of nature, must prove that they have done so, by having the receipt engraved upon their tombs?"

The great struggle between parties took place on the celebrated India Bill, which has been universally acknowledged to have been a measure, introduced for the government of India, that would have given to the existing ministry such patronage, and such power, as to have rendered it independent both of the sovereign and the people. The advocates of Whiggism pronounce it a master-stroke of policy, for they hold that, as their doctrines are the only true principles upon which government should be carried on, they admire the minister who could have devised means which would have given their promulgators means of perpetuating themselves in office. These views were not satisfactory to the British people, who enthusiastically received the intelligence, that the monarch had so influenced the House of Lords that the measures were rejected. The ministry that had been received with indignation was dismissed amidst expressions of triumph. Although Sheridan took no conspicuous part in the debates, he shared the odium of his party: he momentarily ceased to be a favourite with the people, who could not admire the fidelity with which he adhered to his friends, and who learnt with regret that he lent his aid in the concoction of the obnoxious measure. Once again he was to be seen in the ranks of the opposition, leading a determined attack upon the young minister, Mr. Pitt, who by a fortuitous occurrence of events was hailed as the leader of a party, at once supported by the king and the people. Sheridan was amongst the bitterest of his opponents; he lost no opportunity of assailing him with taunts and invectives. "How shuffling," exclaimed he, "is this conduct of a young minister, unhackneyed in the ways of man! This is an instance of duplicity scarcely to be paralleled by the most hoary hypocrite that ever guided the principles of a great nation. If, in the very onset, this young minister thus tramples on the constitution, what may you not expect from the audacity of his riper years?" Nor was such a style of language disliked by the House of Commons, to whom Sheridan had rendered his eloquence not only tolerable, but almost necessary.

The determined energy of the king's conduct inspired Mr. Pitt with resolution; in spite of the hostility of the House of Commons, he continued to pursue his policy until a dissolution of Parliament would allow him to take the sense of the country; for he felt assured that, whenever this occurred, he should be enabled to command a majority, for the clamour was loud, and the conduct of the coalition had shown too much of the old leaven of corruption, instead of the promised reform so long proclaimed. Sheridan, more fortunate than many of his co-mates, found himself in Parliament after a dissolution. Stafford, faithful to him, had returned him once again, and had shown a greater sympathy with their representative than many a borough that had vaunted its love of liberty and its disinterestedness. The next two sessions were not marked by any vigorous display of Sheridan's abilities. He made no bold attacks upon the minister, and in this conduct he was borne out by Fox, who almost absented himself from the field, and rarely made his appearance at all. Sheridan acted as a guerilla chief, occasionally hanging on the flanks of his enemy, making a bold excursion, showing his capability of injuring, but rarely committing himself to any thing in the shape of a regular attack. The Westminster scrutiny, now a subject forgotten by all, was the one in which Sheridan most distinguished himself. Upon the general election, Lord Hood was declared duly elected; but there was a doubt raised by Sir Cecil Wray, who, together with Mr. Fox, were the other candidates. A scrutiny was demanded, as to the legality of the majority of 235, which the latter claimed, to which the high bailiff assented. The opposition in the House of Commons sought to censure the high bailiff's conduct, and a long battle of words, renewed during the two subsequent sessions of Parliament, gave rise to two very clever speeches from Sheridan. He was also eloquent upon various reform questions; upon taxation; and upon questions connected with India. Throughout the whole of the period, he gained upon the nation by his temperate zeal, and, singular to say, by his apparent acquaintance with financial measures, and rose into consideration amongst the calculating politicians of the day for the soundness of his views and the carefulness with which he promulgated them; on one or two occasions he spoke with great deference of the prime minister, congratulating the country in rather an insidious way upon the consistency of his conduct as a parliamentary reformer. On one occasion he came into collision with Mr. Rolle, the member for Devonshire, afterwards known as Lord Rolle, and exhibited his usual tact in answering his charges, and denying his co-operation with those who had attacked him in the " Rolliad."

No ephemeral production ever produced a greater sensation than the " Rolliad;" it was hailed with rapturous shouts of laughter; impression after impression issued from the press; not even the " Antijacobin," nor "The Rejected Addresses," was read by the whole nation with greater avidity. Though now slumbering in peaceful quiet, and completely forgotten, it will amply repay the lovers of genuine mirth by its happy vein of ridicule, its playfulness, its allusions to classic literature, and its sparkling satire. The name of Rolle is scarcely known to the present generation; the only occasion on which it has come of late before the public was when, on the coronation of her Majesty, the venerable peer, the hero of the " Rolliad," stumbled on approaching to do homage to the Queen. It was forgotten that he had ever been apostrophized thus :—

> " Illustrious Rolle, O may thy honour'd name
> Roll down distinguished on the rolls of fame ;
> Still first be found on Devon's county polls,
> Still future senates boast their future Rolles,
> Since of all Rolls, which in this world we see,
> The world has ne'er produced a roll like thee."

The work purports to be criticisms on a poem supposed to have been written upon the actions of Rollo, Duke of Normandy, from whom Mr. Rolle had imprudently boasted his descent; the quotations, the subject of the pretended exertion of the critic's art, alluded to the general supporters of the minister, who were handled with caustic severity, and ludicrous animadversions; to this was added a series of political eclogues, in which Mr. Rose, Mr. Banks, Lord Liverpool, Jekyll, and other prominent characters, were chastised with no measured hand for their political principles. The same volume contains some inimitable burlesque compositions, pretended to be written by candidates for the laureateship, vacant by the death of William Whitehead. They are supposed to be such odes as are written by the laureate on such an occasion as a birthday by a number of candidates for the post. The persons selected for this medium of holding them up to ridicule were the most remarkable men of the day, all of whom were treated with much humour, and with that species of lashing which has always been considered fair in political warfare. Sheridan's brother-in-law, Tickell, General Fitzpatrick, George Ellis, Dr. French Laurence, and Joseph Richardson, took a very active portion of these publications upon themselves, and were the authors. They formed themselves into a club, and continued to exercise their ingenuity in tormenting their public opponents. The relationship in which Sheridan stood with one of those who were most actively employed, and his well-known mental resources, led to the suspicion that he was a member of the coterie, and that he gave to their united efforts his own acknowledged powers; and those who will bestow some little time on the perusal of the criticisms may fancy that they can detect " the fine old Roman hand."

Sheridan went considerably out of his way to clear himself from the suspicion of being one of the tormentors of Mr. Rolle, and took a very early opportunity of denying in the House his connection with the critics. He had spent some part of the previous summer in Lancashire, and had paid so much attention to the state of the Manchester manufacturers, as to have excited some foolish jealousy in the minds of Mr. Pitt's followers; and when Mr. Pitt brought in a bill to amend the acts for imposing a duty by excise on certain cotton manufacturers—Mr. Fox seconding the motion—an animated discussion sprung up, during which Mr. Pitt somewhat incautiously threw out an imputation on the evidence given before a committee of the House by some of the manufacturers. Mr. Sheridan warmly replied to him, "declaring that he had most unjustly aspersed those parties, whose conduct had been most laudable, and whose evidence was unquestionable." Upon this Mr. Rolle rose up, and with great warmth charged Sheridan with having made an inflammatory speech in the country, with a view to excite alarm and discontent. He said he would not mention the member who had gone down to Lancashire to stir up the manufacturers, to set them against the taxes, and to promote tumults and discontent; neither would he say who it was that distributed, or caused to be distributed, seditious and inflammatory handbills, and had them circulated, all round the country; but the fact was so, and, if he could bring the proof home to the party, he would take the proper steps to have his head stuck upon Temple Bar. He went on in a similar strain, charging Fox and Sheridan with declaring in favour of Mr. Pitt, nay, even of seconding his motion, and then voting against it, and stigmatized them as abandoning and deserting ground once taken in a most shameful manner. After Mr. Fox had replied to the empty threat of having heads stuck upon Temple Bar, and to the folly of supposing that circulating handbills was a capital offence, Mr. Sheridan rose, and denied any participation in the handbills, but said, he was not surprised at the soreness evinced by him about publications. The handbills were not the compositions that hurt him, but compositions less prosaic, but more popular, he was afraid had made Mr. Rolle so sore. This allusion was quickly taken up by the House, and received with loud laughter. He continued by saying that he was aware that the honourable gentleman had suspected that he was either the author of these compositions, or in some other way concerned in them. He did assure him, upon his honour, he was not, nor had he ever seen a line of them till they were in print in the newspaper. Mr. Rolle was not very courteous upon this manly avowal, but continued his assertions of doing all within his power to punish the author of these seditious publications. With regard to the "Rolliad," he said that he held the author of those compositions in sovereign contempt as well as his works; but as the cap fitted the right honourable gentleman he was welcome to wear it. Sheridan again replied, and in a firm and manly tone assured the right honourable gentleman that whilst he talked at random he should not notice him; but, if he charged him with being concerned in circulating any seditious handbills, he would answer him both there and elsewhere very plainly and very coarsely. This language was of course unmistakeable, and completely silenced Mr. Rolle, who bore it unmoved—

> " Here to the ferule Rolle his hand resigned,
> Here to the rod he bared the parts behind,
> But him no strifes subdued—and him no fear
> Of menaced wrath, in future more severe."

Mr. Sheridan next distinguished himself in a speech of great vigour and power upon the propositions made by the government to give commercial freedom to Ireland. Of the soundness of his views there must be considerable question, and although he was supported by the liberal party in Ireland, and by the English manufacturers, his opposition to the ministry, rather than his patriotism, must have led him to the expression of opinions, which, however plausible, are inconsistent with the principles which regulate trade, and upon which the commercial prosperity of a nation must depend. Animated and forcible were the doctrines in the style of their delivery, but futile and inconsistent in themselves; the principal ground on which Sheridan rested his opposition to the measure brought forward was, that the Parliament of Great Britain was about to extend its power, and to legislate for Ireland; that the Irish Parliament had neither hinted at, nor alluded to a proposal that the laws for regulating trade and navigation should be the same in both countries.

In the following session Mr. Pitt introduced a measure for effectually providing for the security of his majesty's dockyards at Plymouth and at Portsmouth by a permanent system of fortification, for enabling the fleet to act with full vigour and effect for the protection of commerce, the support of our distant possessions, and the prosecution of offensive operations. Mr. Sheridan, in opposing the motion, seized upon the argument that had been advanced, that a system of defence by fortification would diminish the number of troops, and therefore would give less cause for the constitutional jealousy of the power of the crown.

A question of a most extraordinary character now arose, which gave Sheridan an admirable opportunity of exhibiting to the whole empire the ability, the genius, and the eloquence

which had already acquired for him a high reputation.   The
impeachment of Warren Hastings, before the House of Lords,
afforded to his accusers an opportunity of appealing to the
high sense of honour, to the feelings, to the judgment of the
nation.   It was neither to the political nor to the fashionable
circles they had to address themselves, but to an enlightened
people, who for the first time heard that the most distin
guished rulers of nations could be brought, by legitimate authority, before the tribunal of public opinion, and could be
subjected to bitter accusations, and to the most inquisitorial
treatment.   They were astonished to behold a man, to whom
power over nations had been delegated, arraigned as a culprit
and denounced as a villain.   That Warren Hastings had been
guilty of the most daring acts of tyranny and of oppression
there can be little doubt; but that the peculiarity of his position, the extraordinary nature of the government he held, the
ignorance of those principles which are now the guides of our
conduct, are in a great measure to plead as a justification,
is almost as generally acknowledged.   Like Pizarro in Peru,
Cortes in Mexico, or his predecessor in India, Lord Clive,
he was compelled to have recourse to measures as bold as
they are dangerous, and which are incompatible with that
state of civilization best understood by European nations.
Hurried onward by the anxious desire to retain power, he
left the straightforward path that prudence keeps, and involved himself in mazes of deceit, which led to the grossest
violations of national faith and honour.   His delinquencies,
however, would have most probably passed unknown, had they
not been dragged into daylight by men who themselves were
endowed with singular powers, and had the mightiest energies
of mind to direct them.   The grandeur of the question, and
the necessity for its solution, seem to have acted on those
who were engaged upon it, and urged them on with irresistible ardour in their attack.   Posterity has derived a noble
lesson from their labours.   The delegated governors over a
feeble people have learnt that they dare not trample upon
the laws and the privileges which have existed; they have
seen that the pride of an oppressor has been humbled by
individuals, and that, even where criminality cannot be proved,
the suspicion of its existence is sufficient to excite attention
and to call for inquiry

The good sense of the present age has taught us, however, that it is altogether unfair to judge of a man, filling a high position in former days, by the standard which we now pronounce to be the guide of conduct. The Governor General of India was, at the period at which Warren Hastings was called to the station, the chief of a handful of conquerors over millions whom he was led to consider of an inferior race; he fancied that he should acquit himself of the charge committed to his care, if he extended widely the dominion of a company of merchants in England; and that, if he remitted wealth to them, he was at liberty to have recourse to such means as the people, over whom he ruled, had been accustomed to. He therefore employed artifice to encounter artifice; resolute boldness and an arm of strength, to dismay and overrule those who had submitted to the first who dared to conquer. He looked upon himself as a stranger, suddenly introduced into the midst of nations, timid and anxious to be relieved from the last batch of tyrants who were placed over them. The monarchs who nominally ruled were shadows, under whose pretended sway ministers, more powerful than themselves, exacted all that they chose to demand, and whose despotism none dared to resist. Warren Hastings was called upon to divide and to conquer his enemies, to look upon the whole system of government as a machine to be guided by the will of the person who chose, either by daring or by intrigue, to seize the helm; and all those who held power, as tools which were to be used as best might suit the views of the chief of the moment. It never crossed the mind of Warren Hastings that England was anxious to bestow the blessings of a paternal government upon the nations of Asia, or that the time would ever arrive that she would seek to be beloved instead of feared; that she should ever dream of making the natives venerate, admire, and love her laws and her institutions. He sought to avail himself of the system he found in existence, not because it was contrary to the wishes of the mother country, and opposed to the best interests of the people, but because it allowed no one but himself to exact, and to enrich themselves. The only opposition he had to encounter was from the members of the Council; the stand they took was unfortunately upon personal, not upon moral grounds; there was too much of bitterness in their animosity to act upon a mind constituted as his was, and too much of cabal to produce an influence upon the British residents in India.

The observations made by that great advocate Erskine are perhaps the best palliation for the line of conduct pursued by Hastings—they are founded upon the great truth, that he who gives authority is responsible for its due exercise. Whilst the charges against Warren Hastings were published by the House of Commons, Mr. Logie, a clergyman of the church of Scotland, wrote a pamphlet, in which they were investigated with considerable warmth and energy. On the 15th of February Mr. Fox moved in the House that a pamphlet, entitled "A Review of the principal Charges against Warren Hastings," contains matter disrespectful to his Majesty, and scandalous and indecent paragraphs reflecting on the motives which induced this House to impeach Warren Hastings, Esq., of high crimes and misdemeanors." The principal passage from which this charge sprung is—" Such an exertion of public virtue (the impeachment of Mr. Hastings)—if to public virtue it shall be referred—is, indeed, above all Greek, all Roman fame, and will furnish a memorable example to future times, that no abilities, however splendid, no services, however beneficial or meritorious, that even not the smile of the sovereign, nor the voice of the people, can protect a British subject from impeachment, and a public delinquent from punishment, if found guilty. For the future, when any officer shall return home from a situation of responsibility, his only hope must be in joining a powerful faction; for his services, let them be ever so high, or his loyalty, be it ever so exemplary, would be insufficient for his security." Mr. Pitt moved as an amendment that the words "his Majesty" be omitted. Mr. Sheridan observed that the passage insinuated that an impeachment was a mode of prosecution which leaves the sovereign no power of extending mercy after conviction, and, in reply to an observation of the Chancellor of Exchequer, who spoke of Mr. Hastings' position as a person impeached as not a very exalted one, remarked, that till he was convicted the station of Mr. Hastings was not in the eye of the law, reason, or common sense, to be considered one of degradation. Mr. Fox at length moved that "An address be presented to his Majesty, most humbly to desire that he will be graciously pleased to give directions to his Majesty's Attorney General to prosecute." The motion was unanimously agreed to. On the 9th December, 1789, Mr. John Stockdale, the printer, was tried on a criminal information, filed by the Attorney General. It was the lot of Erskine, the noble defender of the helpless, to plead for him. The speech is a perfect model of eloquence, and exhibits that style of devotion to the cause of him whom he supported which gave such peculiar interest to all he said. He did not plead for another in the cold dispassionate manner of the hireling, he rushed into the very midst of the peril which surrounded his client, he felt with him, he thought with him, he proclaimed that he acted as he himself would have done, and, with that generous zeal which belonged to his character, he would have shared his punishment if despotism and tyranny would have dared to inflict it. Not content with clearly showing the innocence of Stockdale, he threw his shield over Hastings, and with impetuous ardour and elegant words he spoke of the charges against him. He boldly expatiated on the striking absurdity exhibited by a power, itself the author of all the rapine and the oppression, in presuming to sit in judgment upon those to whom it had delegated its authority, and by whom its own tyranny had been exercised. He dwelt upon the ridiculous conduct of the nation that proceeded onwards in the most iniquitous career of plunder and rapacity, and then suddenly saying to the subordinate instruments of its usurpation, "Thus far shalt thou go, and no further. The nation was responsible for the violation of human happiness in the exercise of her Eastern dominion." With that happy power of seizing every incident that occurred, observing some slight appearance of approbation of what he had said in one or two of the jurymen, he concluded the topic thus: "Gentlemen, you are touched by the way of considering the subject, and I can acccount for it: I have been talking of man, and his nature, not as they are seen through the cold medium of books, but as I have seen them in climes reluctantly submitting to our authority. I have seen an indignant savage chief surrounded by his subjects, and holding in his hand a bundle of sticks, the notes of his untutored eloquence. 'Who is it, 'said the jealous ruler of a forest, encroached upon by the restless foot of the English adventurer,—'who is it that causes the mountains to lift up their lofty heads? Who raises the winds of the winter, and calms them again in the summer?' 'The same Being who gave to you a country on your side of the water, and ours to us on this.'" Of this, the most perfect speech ever pronounced by Erskine, the result was the triumph of Stockdale, of Warren Hastings, and of liberty over that party which ought to have disdained to prosecute for libel an individual who was nobly fighting intellectually against power, dominion, and a mighty array of talent.

Warren Hastings, as Governor of India, found from his masters at home that money was the chief object which they required from their delegate. He, too anxious to fulfil their commands, was regardless of the means he employed; and, though he himself was neither sordid nor rapacious, he lent all the faculties of his mind to the plunder and the rapine which rendered India a scene of desolation and of misery. The iniquities of his government were excusable in his eyes, for they were the result of stern necessity; there could be no check to his despotism, no limit to his avarice, but the helplessness to which he had reduced nations, and the poverty to which he exposed them. Edmund Burke was the great leader who undertook to hold up to public detestation, and to condign punishment, the individual whom he believed to be guilty of the greatest enormities, and to have trampled with unscrupulous cruelty upon the helpless beings with whom he was thrown into contact. He was supported by Sheridan, by Wyndham, and men whose names belong to the history of their country; but by no one more enthusiastically, or more powerfully, than by Sheridan.

It is deeply to be deplored that we possess such mutilated remains of his speech, which created throughout the whole of the country such an extraordinary sensation, that was listened to by the House with the most profound admiration, that elicited even from his adversaries expressions of their wonder at the mighty powers he displayed. Of the speech of February 7th, 1787, before the House of Commons, a feeble outline only has been handed down to us. All the records of that day speak of it as one of the most magnificent displays of human intellect that had ever been exhibited. For five hours and a half he commanded the universal attention of a crowded House. When he had concluded a speech which had riveted his audience, a loud and long-continued burst of enthusiastic applause seemed to echo simultaneously from all quarters; the usual decorum was forgotten, all seemed carried away by the impulse they had received. " Burke declared it to be the most astonishing burst of eloquence, argument, and wit united, of which there was any record or tradition." Fox pronounced an eulogium, and declared "all that he ever heard, all that he had ever read, when compared with it, dwindled into nothing, and vanished like vapour before the sun." The debate was suspended, and after a short expression of the opinion of several members, who declared that, though they came prepossessed in favour of Hastings, a miracle had been wrought upon their minds, whilst others wished time to cool before they were called to vote, the House adjourned, with the concurrence of Sheridan's great adversary, Pitt, who acknowledged that the speech surpassed all the eloquence of ancient or modern times, and possessed every thing that genius or art could furnish to agitate and control the human mind.

Mr. Burke spoke of his address thus : " Of all the various speeches of oratory, of every kind of eloquence that had been heard either in ancient or modern times, whatever the acuteness of the bar, the dignity of the senate, or the morality of the pulpits could furnish, had not been equal to what that House had that day heard in Westminster Hall. No holy religionist, no man of any description as a literary character, could have come up in the one instance to the pure sentiments of morality, or, in the other, to the variety of knowledge, force of imagination, propriety and vivacity of allusion, beauty and elegance of diction, and strength of expression to which they had this day listened. From poetry up to eloquence, there was not a species of composition of which a complete and perfect specimen might not have been culled from one part or other of the speech to which he alluded, and which he was persuaded had left too strong an impression on the minds of that House to be easily obliterated." We learn from Moore, that there exists a copy of this speech, taken in short hand by Mr. Gurney, which was some time in the possession of the Duke of Norfolk, then in the hands of Sheridan, and afterwards in those of Moore himself. He has furnished us with some extracts, but it is a matter of regret that the public has

x

not an opportunity of seeing it. We are now dependent upon that which has been published in the debates, from which, of course, we can form but a superficial idea of its merits. Sheridan commenced by showing that "In truth, the prosecution was not begotten in prejudice, or nursed in error. It was founded in the clearest conviction of the wrongs which the natives of Hindostan had suffered through the mal-administration of those in whose hands the country had placed extensive powers, which ought to have been exercised for the benefit of the governed, but which had been used by the prisoner at the bar for the shameful purposes of oppression.

" To convince their lordships that the British government —which ought to have been a blessing to the powers in India connected with it—had been a scourge to the natives, and the cause of desolation to the most flourishing provinces in Hindostan, he had only to read a letter that had been received not long since from Lord Cornwallis, the present Governor-General of Bengal. In that letter the noble lord stated he had been received by the Nabob Visier with every mark of friendship and respect; but the honours he received at the court of Lucknow had not prevented him from seeing the desolation that overspread the face of the country, the sight of which had shocked his very soul. He spoke to the nabob on the subject, and earnestly recommended it to him to adopt some system of government that might restore the prosperity of his kingdom, and make his people happy. The nabob's answer was strikingly remarkable. That degraded prince said to his lordship, that as long as the demands of the English government upon the revenue of Oude should remain unlimited, he (the nabob) could have no interest in establishing any system of economy; and, whilst the English should continue to interfere in the internal government of his country, it would be in vain for him to attempt any salutary reform; for his subjects knew he was only a cypher in his own dominions, and therefore laughed at and despised his authority and that of his ministers."

He then observes, that it ought to be shown that the ruling powers at home will not countenance future delinquents. " In looking round for an object fit to be held out to the world as an example of national justice, their lordships must necessarily fix their eyes upon Mr. Hastings. He was the great cause of the degradation of our character in India, and of the oppression of its devoted inhabitants; and he was the only victim that could atone for the calamities he had occasioned.

"But, whilst he pointed out the prisoner at the bar as a proper object of punishment, he begged leave to observe, that he did not wish to turn the sword of justice against that man, merely because an example ought to be made; such a wish was as far from his heart as it was incompatible with equity and justice. If he called for punishment upon Mr. Hastings, it was because he thought him a great delinquent, and the greatest of all those who, by their rapacity and oppression, had brought ruin on the natives of India, and disgrace upon the inhabitants of Great Britain.

"Whilst he called for justice upon the prisoner, he could wish also to do him justice. He would be sorry that the weight and consequence of the Commons of Great Britain, in whose name the prosecution had been set on foot, should operate to his prejudice. Indeed, whilst he had such upright judges as their lordships, it was impossible that any thing could injure him but the clearest and most unequivocal proofs of guilt."—"It is not the peering suspicion of apprehending guilt—it is not any popular abhorrence of its wide-spread consequences—it is not the secret consciousness in the bosom of the judge, which can excite the vengeance of the law, and authorize its infliction! No: in this good land, as high as it is happy, because as just as it is free, all is definite, equitable, and exact; the laws must be satisfied before infliction ensues, and ere a hair of the head can be plucked LEGAL GUILT must be established by LEGAL PROOF!"

He dwelt upon the enormity of the attack upon the princesses. "Having alluded to the different defences made by the prisoner, Mr. Sheridan next adverted to the allegations in the second charge that had been supported in evidence. He said, that the managers had proved the high birth and great rank of the Begums, or Princesses of Oude; they had also proved from the evidence of Sir Elijah Impey, Mr. Middleton, Mr. Goring, and others, how sacred was the residence of women in India. A threat, therefore, to force that residence, and violate its purity by sending armed men into it, was a species of torture, the cruelty of which could not be conceived by those who were unacquainted with the customs and notions of the inhabitants of Hindostan. A knowledge of the customs and manners of the Mussulmen of Turkey would not enable one to judge of those of Mussulmen in India: in the former, ladies went abroad veiled, and, though not so free as those in Christian countries, still they were not so closely shut up as were the ladies professing the same religion in Hindostan. The confinement of the Turkish ladies was in a great measure to be ascribed to the jealousy of their husbands; in Hindostan the ladies were confined, because they thought it contrary to decorum that persons of their sex should be seen abroad : they were not the victims of jealousy in the men; on the contrary, their sequestration from the world was voluntary; they liked retirement, because they thought it best suited to the dignity of their sex and situation : they were shut up from liberty, it was true ; but liberty, so far from having any charms for them, was derogatory to their feelings; they were enshrined rather than immured; they professed a greater purity of pious prejudice than the Mahomedan ladies of Europe and other countries, and more zealously and religiously practised a more holy system of superstition. Such was their sense of delicacy, that to them the sight of man was pollution; and the piety of the nation rendered their residence a sanctuary. What, then, would their lordships think of the tyranny of the man who could act in open defiance of those prejudices, which were so interwoven with the very existence of ladies in that country, that they could not be removed but by death? What, he asked, would their lordships think of the man who could threaten to profane and violate the sanctuary of the highest description of ladies in Oude, by saying that he would storm it with his troops, and remove the inhabitants from it by force ?"

" Mr. Sheridan showed next, that there was a very good ground for presuming that the treasures possessed by the Begum were the property of that princess; she had endeared herself to her husband, the late nabob, by flying to him in the moment of his distress, after his defeat at Buxar, and carrying with her to his relief the jewels with which, in happier days, his fondness for her had enriched her : upon these she loaned him a large supply. When the political generosity of the country restored him afterwards to his throne, his gratitude to his wife knew no bounds · her ascendancy over him was such, that she prevailed upon him to appoint his son, by her, his successor.

" The present nabob, as had appeared from a passage in a letter written by Mr. Hastings to him, and since proved in evidence, owed to her not only his birth and succession to the crown, but also the preservation of his life; for one day, his savage father in a rage attempting to cut him down with his scimitar, the Begum rushed between her husband and her son, and saved the latter through the loss of some of her own blood ; for she was wounded by the blow that was not aimed at her. A son so befriended and so preserved, Mr. Hastings had armed against such a mother : he invaded the rights of that prince, that he might compel him to violate the laws of nature by plundering his parent; and he made him a slave, that he might afterwards make him a monster. Mr. Hastings was bound to be the protector of the Begum, instead of her plunderer; for her husband, on his death-bed, bequeathed her to his friendship ; and Mr. Hastings had always called that husband his brother: but no consideration could make him discharge the duties of any obligation that could set bounds to his rapacity."

He next adverts to the conduct of Sir Elijah Impey. " The transactions in which Sir Elijah Impey bore a share, and the tenor of his evidence, were the next objects of Mr. Sheridan's animadversion. The late chief-justice of Bengal, he remarked, had repeatedly stated that Mr. Hastings had left Calcutta with two resources in his view—those of Benares and of Oude. It appeared, however, from every circumstance, that the latter resource was never in his contemplation, until the insurrection in Benares, terminating in the capture of Bedjegur, had destroyed all his hopes in that province. At that instant the mind of Mr. Hastings, fertile in resources, fixed itself on the treasures of the Begums, and Sir Elijah Impey was despatched to collect materials for their crimination. ' But I have ever thought,' said Mr. Sheridan, ' the selection of such a personage, for such a purpose, one of the greatest aggravations of the guilt of Mr. Hastings.' That he, the purity of whose character should have influenced his conduct, even in his most domestic retirements—that he, who, if consulting the dignity of British justice, should have remained as stationary as his court in Calcutta—that such a man should be called to travel 500 miles for the transactions of such a business, was a deviation without a plea, and a degradation without example. This, however, was in some degree a question to be abstracted for the consideration of those who adorned and illumined the seats of justice in Britain, and the purity of whose character precluded the necessity of any further observations on so different a conduct."

" ' This giddy chief-justice,' said Mr. Sheridan, ' disregards business. He wants to see the country: like some innocent school-boy, he takes the primrose path, and amuses himself as he goes : he thinks not that his errand is on danger and death ; and that his party of pleasure ends in loading others with irons.' When at Lucknow, he never mentions the affidavits to the nabob;—no, he is too polite ;—he never talks of them to Mr. Hastings—out of politeness too. A master of ceremonies in justice ! When examined at the bar, he said, —he imagines there must have been a sworn interpreter, from the looks of the manager. How I looked, Heaven knows, said Mr. Sheridan, but such a physiognomist there is no escaping. He sees a sworn interpreter in my looks;—he sees the manner of taking an oath in my looks !—he sees the Bason and the Ganges in my looks ! As for himself, he only looks at the tops and bottoms of affidavits ! In seven years he takes care never to look at these swearings ; and then goes home one night, and undoes the whole ; though, when he has seen them, Sir Elijah seems to know less about them than when he had not."

 The termination of this speech has been most admired. " But justice is not this halt and miserable object ! it is not the ineffective bauble of an Indian pagod !—it is not the portentous phantom of despair ;—it is not like any fabled monster, formed in the eclipse of reason, and found in some unhallowed grove of superstitious darkness and political dismay ! No, my lords !

 " In the happy reverse of all these, I turn from this disgusting caricature to the real image ! Justice I have now before me, august and pure ; the abstract idea of all that would be perfect in the spirits and the aspirings of men !—where the mind rises, where the heart expands—where the countenance is ever placid and benign—where her favourite attitude is to stoop to the unfortunate—to hear their cry and to help them, to rescue and relieve, to succour and save :—majestic from its mercy ; venerable from its utility ; uplifted without pride ; firm without obduracy ; beneficent in each preference ; lovely, though in her frown !

" On that justice I rely ; deliberate and sure, abstracted from all party purpose and political speculations ! not in words, but on facts ! You, my lords, who hear me, I conjure by those rights it is your best privilege to preserve ; by that fame it is your best pleasure to inherit ; by all those feelings which refer to the first term in the series of existence, the original compact of our nature—our controlling rank in the creation. This is the call on all to administer to truth and equity, as they would satisfy the laws and satisfy themselves, with the most exalted bliss possible, or conceivable for our nature,— the self-approving consciousness of virtue, when the condemnation we look for will be one of the most ample mercies accomplished for mankind since the creation of the world !

" My lords, I have done."

On the following day, the House of Commons resolved that a Committee should be appointed to prepare articles of impeachment against Warren Hastings.

Edmund Burke.	Welbore Ellis, Esq.
Right Hon. C. J. Fox.	Right Hon. F. Montague.
R. B. Sheridan, Esq.	Sir Grey Cooper.
Sir James Erskine.	Phillip Francis, Esq.
Right Hon. T. Pelham.	Sir Gilbert Elliott.
Right Hon. W. Wyndham.	Dudley Long, Esq.
Right Hon. And. St. John.	Viscount Maitland.
J. Anstruther, Esq.	Hon. G. A. North
Wm. Adam, Esq.	General Burgoyne.
M. A. Taylor, Esq.	Charles Grey, Esq.

A division took place upon the nomination of Mr. Francis, who had been a member of counsel in India, had fought a duel with Hastings, and had been personally at variance with Hastings ; he was rejected by a majority of 96 to 44. On the 25th of April, there were laid upon the table the articles of impeachment which had been prepared by the Committee ; they were read a first time, and ordered to be taken into consideration on the 9th of May. On that day a division took place on the question whether the report should be received. Mr.

Pitt, the Prime Minister, and his friends, either convinced of
the necessity of yielding to the reiterated demands of the
opposition, or unwilling to expose himself to the unpopularity
of shielding Hastings, or, as it has been stated, jealous of the
favour bestowed upon him by the king, joined the ranks of
those to whom they were habitually opposed, and, by a ma
jority of 175 to 89, the report was read a second time.   Mr
Burke then rose and moved, " That Warren Hastings, Esq.
be impeached of high crimes and misdemeanours upon the said
articles."   Mr. Frederic Montague next rose, and moved that
" Mr. Burke, in the name of the House of Commons, and of
all the Commons of England, do go to the bar of the House
of Lords and impeach Warren Hastings, Esq., late Governor-
General of Bengal, of high crimes and misdemeanours, and
do acquaint the Lords that the Commons will, with all convenient speed, exhibit articles against him, and make good
the same."   The motion being agreed to, Mr. Burke, attended
by the members of the House of Commons, appeared before
the Lords at their bar, and solemnly impeached Mr. Hastings.
A day was named, and, on Mr. Burke's report to the House of
Commons, he moved that the Committee already named be
appointed managers of the trial, and that the House of Commons attend as a Committee of the whole House ; assent to
these motions was given. and each party prepared for the trial
    On the 13th of February commenced, in Westminster Hall,
this remarkable trial.   Macaulay has, with singular felicity,
given us a graphic sketch of the scene ; he has associated with
it the best historical recollections, and mingled them with
the leading characters of the day.   The author of " Evelina,"
who was present on the occasion, has described to us her own
sensations, and furnished us even with the chit-chat of " the
ingenious, the chivalrous, the high-souled" Wyndham, as
well as of Burke, and of many principal actors in the scene.
She has, in less poetic language, placed before our eyes all
that struck her fancy.   We find her shuddering and drawing
involuntarily back, when Burke, the head of the committee,
made his solemn entry, holding a scroll in his hands, walking
alone, his brow knit with corroding care and deep-labouring
thought; trembling when Hastings was brought to the bar, and
summoned by a loud voice, " Warren Hastings, come forth,
answer to the charges brought against you, save your bail, or

forfeit your recognizances." There stood the late Governor-General of Bengal ; he moved on slowly, he made a low bow to the chancellor and to the court, he bowed again, and then advancing to the bar he leant his hands upon it, and dropped upon his knees ; but a voice, in the same moment, proclaiming he had leave to rise, he stood up almost instantaneously, and a third time profoundly bowed to the court. What an awful moment this for such a man—a man fallen from such height of power to a situation so humiliating—from the most unlimited command of so large a portion of the Eastern World, to be cast at the feet of his enemies, of the great tribunal of his country, and of the nation at large, assembled thus in a body to try and to judge him."

In the striking words of Macaulay, we may say "that neither the culprit nor his advocates attracted so much attention as his accusers. In the midst of the blaze of red drapery a space had been fitted up with green benches and tables for the Commons. The managers, with Burke at their head, appeared in full dress. The collectors of gossip did not fail to remark that even Fox, generally so regardless of his appearance, had paid to the illustrious tribunal the compliment of wearing a bag and sword. The box in which the managers stood contained an array of speakers such as perhaps had not appeared together since the great age of Athenian eloquence. There were Fox and Sheridan, the English Demosthenes and the English Hyperides. There was Burke, ignorant indeed or negligent of the art of adapting his reasonings and his style to the capacity and taste of his hearers, but in amplitude of comprehension, and richness of imagination, superior to every orator, ancient or modern." He proceeds, in a splendid passage, which it would be criminal to mutilate by extracts, to delineate two of the master minds of their age, Wyndham and Earl Grey. The first day was passed in reading the charges against Hastings ; this was done in so monotonous a tone that little interest was taken in the proceedings. From Madame D'Arblay we may draw our conclusion that, amongst the auditory assembled, there were many who looked upon the accused with eyes of pity and of respect, and that at the commencement of the trial he was rather the object of commiseration than of dislike. It was on the third day that Burke opened the charges ; and during the four following days he occupied the attention of the House of Lords with what may be considered to be a general outline of the charges brought against Hastings. He delivered an eloquent address, such as might be expected from one who had for months studied his subject with the utmost care; who had brooded over the wrongs which nations had endured; who deeply felt, and had ample means of giving expression to his feelings. He was listened to with the profoundest attention; and as he painted the manners, the habits, and the government of the nations of Asia, and portrayed the wrongs inflicted by Hastings, torrents of fervid eloquence were poured forth which touched the hearts of his enraptured auditory. " When he narrated, he was easy, flowing, natural; when he declaimed, energetic, warm, and brilliant. The sentiments he interspersed were as nobly conceived as they were highly coloured; the wild and sudden flights of his fancy burst forth from his creative imagination, fluent, forcible, and vivid."

Fox was the next of the accusers; his speech occupied a space of five hours. The impression produced by both these speeches upon Madame D'Arblay is worthy to be remembered, particularly as it is well known that her report was listened to with the deepest interest by the queen, and that, from that high quarter, it reached his majesty, who, during the whole of the early portion of the trial, exhibited the greatest anxiety. She states " that Burke's opening struck me with the highest admiration of his powers, from the eloquence, the fire, the diversity of expression, and the ready flow of language with which he seemed gifted. When he came to his two narratives, when he related the particulars of those dreadful murders, he interested, he engaged, he at last overpowered me. I felt my cause lost. I could hardly keep my seat. My eyes dreaded a single glance towards so accused a man as Mr. Hastings, I wanted to sink on the floor, that they might be saved from so fearful a sight. I had no hope he could clear himself, not another wish in his favour remained; but when, from this narration, Mr. Burke proceeded to his own comments and declamation, when the charges of rapacity, cruelty, and tyranny were general, and made with all the violence of personal detestation, and continued and aggravated without any further fact, or illustration, then there appeared more of study than of truth, more of invective than of justice, and, in short, so little of proof to so much of passion, that, in a very short time, I began to lift my head; my seat was no longer uneasy, my eyes were indifferent which way they looked, or what object caught them, and before I was aware of the declension of Mr. Burke's power over my feelings, I found myself a mere spectator in a public place, and looking all around me, with my opera-glass in my hand."

She says, " Mr. Fox spoke with a violence which had a sort of monotony, that seemed to result from its being fac titious; he looked all good humour and negligent care the instant before he began a speech of uninterrupted passion and vehemence; and he wore the same careless and disengaged air the very instant he had finished. A display of talents, in which the inward man took so little share, could have no powers of persuasion to those who saw them in that light, and, therefore, however brilliant they might be, they were useless to their cause, for they left the mind of the hearers in the same state that they found it."

The eagerness displayed by the public to hear Burke and Fox was even surpassed on the third of June, when it was known that upon that day the task of continuing the accusation devolved upon Sheridan. His speech in the House of Commons still vibrated on the ears of his audience; and the press had been busy in drawing comparisons between what had been heard in the House of Commons, and before the Lords. Westminster Hall presented a most extraordinary sight; on no one day had there been such an array of talent, of beauty, or of rank. As early as eight o'clock the avenues leading to the Hall were thronged, the passages through Old and New Palace Yard are described as having been crowded with persons of the first distinction; many of them peeresses in full dress, who stood in the open air upwards of an hour before the gates were opened. The exertions made in pressing forward to get convenient seats had nearly proved fatal to many. It seemed as if the eyes of the whole kingdom was on that day fixed on Sheridan. The eager quidnuncs in the country, who were not so speedily gratified with the intelligence of the day as they now are, had made every exertion to obtain the earliest report of the speech; every printing press was called into use, and every means used to forward it to the country. The usual forms of opening the business of the day, even the procession of the Lords, previously so attractive, seemed tedious, and the impatient auditory could scarcely wait the hour of twelve, when the peers took their places. Large sums were offered and declined for tickets, or for privilege; even fifty guineas it has been said was refused. When Sheridan entered the manager's box every eye was turned towards him. When the Lord Chancellor signified that the assembly was prepared to hear him, he rose, and commenced a speech which was continued on four several occasions. On one of these he was so completely exhausted as to be compelled to retire, and the House adjourned the court; on his recovery, three days afterwards, he again warmed into his subject, and completed his masterly address. With his great display of eloquence, it may be said that the interest of the drama ceased. The trial, it was true, proceeded, but it dragged slowly on; all the enthusiasm which had been excited seemed, after Sheridan had delivered his address, to have died away. It was scarcely to be expected that a second speech would strike the minds of the public with the same success as the first. The freshness of the materials was over; the feelings were not to be roused by a second edition, as they had been by the first impression. Fox, it has been said, strenuously recommended that the speech should only be the echo of the one that had excited such boundless admiration. This opinion was not in unison with that of Sheridan, who felt that he could draw upon his own genius for new resources. He boldly dared and succeeded. He was listened to with delight, and again won the applause of his country.

Sheridan appears to have made himself intimately acquainted with every fact that had occurred in India, and with every individual who had been in communication with Hastings. He had deeply studied the characters of all the parties implicated, had sought out the motives of their actions, and commented upon them with masterly discrimination. He clearly saw that Warren Hastings, with a view of supplying the wants of the Indian treasury, had cast a longing eye upon the sacred city of Benares, and had marked it out as a legitimate object of plunder. Here he expected to draw resources for his army, and remittances for his employers at home. Cheyte Sing, the ruling prince, had annually paid a rich tribute; but it was imagined that he had accumulated from his large revenues considerable treasures; demand upon demand was made upon him. In order to soothe Hastings a bribe of twenty thousand pounds was offered, and received; the transaction was for a time concealed, but after some delay the money was paid over to the company; and then not only were the previous contributions required, but fines were demanded for the delay, and a requisition was made that the unfortunate ruler should keep a body of cavalry for the service of the company. After every species of humiliating treatment, Hastings went himself to Benares, and demanded half a million; "determined to make Cheyte Sing pay largely for his pardon, or to exact a severe vengeance for past delinquency." The prince, notwithstanding every attempt to conciliate the Governor, was made prisoner in his own capital; his subjects rushed to arms, released him, and so hemmed in Hastings, that he was in the utmost peril. At one moment the people of the whole province were in commotion; an army was raised, which almost threatened the annihilation of the English, but discipline and valour soon put it to the rout. Cheyte Sing fled, the dominions passed away from him. Hastings annexed them to the British possessions; but he was grievously disappointed, not only that the amount of the treasure was far inferior to the calculations that had been made, but that the army claimed it as conquerors. To Oude he next looked; but he was well aware that the reigning vizier was too poor to assist him; that from him he could not look for that money which became every moment of greater importance to him. The two chieftains, however, met, each having his own views. Hastings, desirous of some pretext to lay an impost, Asaph ul Dowlah ruminating how he was to avoid payment of what he already owed. In whose mind the tempter first created the suggestion of their uniting to pillage a third party, we cannot surmise; but upon that point they both agreed, and the two sagacious statesmen, without appearing to have much repugnance, determined that they should confiscate the wealth of the mother and the grandmother of one of the parties. These two princesses, known under the title of the Begums of Oude, had succeeded to the revenues of the last nabob, and possessed his treasures, which were estimated at three millions. The son had at different periods made attacks upon his mother's property, and had extorted money from her. She had turned with the utmost anxiety to the English Government to protect her and a treaty under its auspices had been drawn up, in which, under the condition of certain subsidies being paid to her son, he undertook never again to molest her.

Disgraceful as is the fact, the Government that had stood forward as a mediatory power, and as a guarantee that no further extortions should occur, became a partner in an atrocious robbery; and, in the most discreditable manner, plundered and abused the helpless princesses. Under the pretext that these aged ladies had instigated the rebellion at Benares, it was resolved that their entire possessions should be taken from them, and that this wholesale spoliation should be regarded as a set-off against the debt due from the vizier of Oude to Hastings. The palace in which these ladies resided was stormed. The company's troops took possession, and, shameful to relate, the princesses were almost starved into giving up twelve hundred thousand pounds; whilst two unfortunate beings, who acted as their prime ministers, were thrown into prison, and actually put to the torture. Of the influence of Hastings over the authorities in India, there can be no stronger proof than that the chief judge, Sir Elijah Impey, anxious to partake the infamy of the deed, left his judicial seat at Calcutta to obtain any thing in the shape of evidence by which to criminate the Begums, rushed to Lucknow, administered oaths to any one ready to swear, and tarnish the purity of his ermine. Here, then, was ample material for the impassioned eloquence of Sheridan. How much is it to be deplored that we have but a meagre outline of that splendid harangue which astonished his contemporaries. A few extracts will show the style in which he treated the subject.

Of the character of Hastings he spoke in the following words:—"After having stated his complicated infamy in terms of the severest reprehension, Mr. Sheridan proceeded to observe, that he recollected to have heard it advanced by some of those admirers of Mr. Hastings who were not so explicit as to give unqualified applause to his crimes, that they found an apology for the atrocity of them in the greatness of his mind. To estimate the solidity of such a defence, it would be sufficient merely to consider in what consisted this prepossessing distinction, this captivating characteristic of greatness of mind. Is it not solely to be traced in great actions directed to great ends? In them, and them alone, we are to search for true estimable magnanimity. To them only can we justly affix the splendid title and honours of real greatness. There was indeed another species of greatness, which displayed itself in boldly conceiving a bad measure, and undauntedly pursuing it to its accomplishment. But had Mr. Hastings the merit of exhibiting either of these descriptions of greatness—even of the latter?—He saw nothing great—nothing magnanimous—nothing open—nothing direct in his measures or in his mind;—on the contrary, he had too often pursued the worst objects by the worst means. His course was an eternal deviation from rectitude. He either tyrannized or deceived; and was by turns a Dionysius and a Scapin. As well might the writhing obliquity of the serpent be compared to the swift directness of the arrow, as the duplicity of Mr. Hastings's ambition to the simple steadiness of genuine magnanimity. In his mind all was shuffling, ambiguous, dark, insidious, and little: nothing simple, nothing unmixed: all affected plainness, and actual dissimulation;—a heterogeneous mass of contradictory qualities; with nothing great but his crimes; and even those contrasted by the littleness of his motives, which at once denoted both his baseness and his meanness, and marked him for a traitor and a trickster. Nay, in his style and writing there was the same mixture of vicious contrarieties;—the most grovelling ideas were conveyed in the most inflated language; giving mock consequence to low cavils, and uttering quibbles in heroics; so that his compositions disgusted the mind's taste, as much as his actions excited the soul's abhorrence. Indeed this mixture of character seemed by some unaccountable, but inherent quality, to be appropriated, though in inferior degrees, to every thing that concerned his employers. He remembered to have heard an honourable and learned gentleman (Mr Dundas) remark, that there was something in the first frame and constitution of the company, which extended the sordid principles of their origin over all their successive operations; connecting with their civil policy, and even with their boldest achievements, the meanness of a pedlar, and the profligacy of pirates. Alike in the political and the military line could be observed auctioneering ambassadors and trading generals;

—and thus we saw a revolution brought about by affidavits; an army employed in executing an arrest; a town besieged on a note of hand; a prince dethroned for the balance of an account. Thus it was they exhibited a government which united the mock majesty of a bloody sceptre and the little traffic of a merchant's counting-house, wielding a truncheon with one hand, and picking a pocket with the other."

The speech, on the 2nd of April, on the acceptance of various bribes, by Hastings, went to prove that corruption had been the leading principle of all his actions in India; and attempted to overthrow the prevailing opinion, that as he did not amass treasures for his own use, he was not corrupt for interested purposes—that he was not mercenary.

" Mr. Sheridan declared he had been among those, who, at one time, conceived that Mr. Hastings was not stimulated in his conduct, as Governor-General, by any view to his own emolument; and that his fortune was trifling, compared with the advantages which fell within his power. But the more close and minute investigation which it was his duty to apply to the facts contained in the charge had completely altered his opinion; and he scarcely harboured even the slightest doubt of being able to satisfy the committee that Mr. Hastings had all along governed his conduct by corruption, as gross and determined, as his oppression and injustice had proved severe and galling. In reviewing his conduct, he had found it to spring from a wild, eccentric, and irregular mind. He had been everything by fits and starts. Now proud and lofty; now mean and insidious; now generous; now just; now artful; now open; now deceitful; now decided;—in pride, in passion, in everything changeable, except in corruption. In corruption he had proved uniform, systematic, and methodical;—his revenge a tempest, a tornado, blackening, in gusts of pride, the horizon of his dominion, and carrying all before it."

It was on the fourth day that, in the presence of the great historian Gibbon, he exclaimed, " I do say, that if you search the history of the world, you will not find an act of tyranny and fraud to surpass this! If you read all past histories, peruse the annals of Tacitus, read the luminous page of Gibbon, and all the ancient or modern writers that have searched into the depravity of former ages, to draw a lesson for the present, you will not find an act of treacherous, deliberate, cool cruelty that could exceed this!" Gibbon delighted with this compliment—spoke of it in his memoirs. He says: "Before my departure from England, I was present at the august spectacle of Mr. Hastings' trial in Westminster Hall. It is not my province to absolve or condemn the Governor of India, but Mr. Sheridan's eloquence demanded my applause; nor could I hear without emotion the personal compliment that he paid me in the presence of the British nation." Little did the innocent man dream that the ever ready wit of Sheridan had neutralized this elegant encomium; for some one asking him how he could bestow the epithet luminous on Gibbon's work, in a half whisper, he said, " I called it voluminous."

It is true that Miss Sheridan's partiality for her brother may have given a bias to her judgment, but she has expressed herself on the occasion of having heard the principal speakers on the trial. "And last, not least," says she, " I heard my brother. I cannot express to you the sensation of pleasure and of pride that filled my heart the moment that he rose. Had I never seen or heard his name before, I should have conceived him the first man among them at once. There is a dignity and grace in his countenance and deportment very striking, at the same time that one cannot trace the smallest degree of coxcomb superiority in his manner. His voice, too, appeared to me ex-extremely fine." There are letters, too, extant from Mrs. Sheridan, in which she speaks of her husband's success with all the natural triumph of an attached woman; her exultation springs from the heart. Burke seems occasionally to have written to her, when he was anxious to have an impression made upon the memory of Sheridan. In a letter, he says to her, " I know that his mind is seldom unemployed, but then, like all such great and vigorous minds, it takes an eagle's flight by itself, and we can hardly bring it to rustle along the ground with us birds of meaner wing in covey. I only beg that you will prevail on Mr. Sheridan to be with us this day. at half after three, in the committee. Mr. Wombell, the paymaster of Oude, is to be examined there to-day; Oude is Mr. Sheridan's particular province, and I do most seriously ask that he would favour us with his assistance. What will come of the examination I know not, but without him I do not expect a great deal from it; with him I fancy we may get out something material." It appears that this beautiful and highly-gifted woman rendered every assistance to her husband in his pursuit of information. Amongst his papers there exist ample proofs that she wrote out, with diligence and assiduity, pages of importance to him; she copied pamphlets, and collected from various sources memorandums bearing upon any subject that occupied his attention; these she pasted together, or by some contrivance of her own made easy of reference.

His triumph has been thus acknowledged by Lord Byron ·

> " When the loud cry of trampled Hindostan :
> Arose to Heaven in her appeal to Man,   •
> His was the thunder, his the avenging rod,
> The wrath—the delegated voice of God,
> Which shook the nations through his lips, and blazed,
> Till vanquished senates trembled as they praised."

An event, of a nature calculated to excite the most lively interest in the nation, now occurred, and demanded from each individual taking a lead in the direction of the public mind the utmost anxiety and reflection. Early in the month of July, 1788, a visible alteration took place in the health of the king. The physicians in attendance recommended that his majesty should go to Cheltenham to try the effects of the mineral waters there, as some tendency to excitement had been observed. It was resolved that the journey should be taken without the usual pomp and ceremony; the party, therefore, was the smallest possible, without guards or state; still the loyalty of the people would not allow the monarch to pass, without exhibiting affectionate homage. "Every town seemed all face, filled with people, as closely fastened to one another as they appear in the the pit of the playhouse." To this journey, which was undertaken as a change from the monotony of Windsor, and as likely to divert the attention of the king, and to the life at Cheltenham, has been ascribed the direction which this malady now took. Early in the month of October the royal household saw, with unspeakable alarm, the gradual advance of a mental disorder.

Amongst the most interesting narratives of the day is that which the authoress of our classic novels, Cecilia and Evelina, has furnished us with in her memoirs, published not long since under the name of her diary and letters. Miss Burney was in immediate attendance on the queen, and hence, has been enabled to describe to us with the utmost fidelity the commencement, progress, and termination of the disease. We are let into the inmost recesses of the royal palace; we have graphically described the state of alarm and anxiety felt by all, and are taught to look with veneration and admiration at the tenderness and solicitude of the afflicted queen. Such a work is invaluable; and if it be not quite equal in interest to that melancholy but interesting narration which Clery has given us of his attendance upon Louis XVI when in the Temple, it is only because from the different catastrophes our feelings are not so deeply impressed with sympathy and terror. No one could more faithfully delineate the first approach of one species of frenzy than Miss Burney has done. She thus speaks: "I had a sort of conference with his Majesty, or rather I was the object to whom he spoke, with a manner so uncommon, that a high fever could alone account for it: a rapidity, a hoarseness of voice, a volubility, an earnestness, a vehemence rather—it startled me inexpressibly—yet with a graciousness exceeding even all I met with before—it was almost kindness. The following day," she goes on with her diary, telling us, "I met him in the passage from the Queen's room, he stopped me, and conversed upon his health near half an hour; still with the extreme quickness of speech and manner that belongs to fever; and he hardly sleeps, he tells me, one minute all night; indeed, if he recovers not his rest, a most delirious fever seems to threaten him. He is all agitation, all emotion, yet all benevolence and goodness, even to a degree that makes it touching to hear him speak. He assures every body of his health, he seems only fearful to give uneasiness to others." November 1st, we find her describing him with a hoarse and altered countenance. "Nor can I ever forget him in what passed this night; when I came to the queen's dressing-room he was still with her. He was begging her not to speak to him when he got to his room, that he might fall asleep, as he felt great want of that refreshment. He repeated his desire at least a hundred times, though far enough from needing it,—the poor queen never uttered one syllable. He then applied to me, saying he was really very well, except in that one particular, that he could not sleep."

As we peruse these and similar passages in her diary, we are strongly reminded of the interview between Hamlet and Ophelia in the play-scene; and are struck with admiration of the knowledge which Shakespeare must have possessed of the workings of the mind under the first approaches of mental derangement. She proceeds to describe the deep distress of the queen, her solitary anguish, overpowered with terror, lest she should betray her feelings, and express the inevitable danger towards which she saw the king was gradually verging. Harassed by his state—believing it unknown to any but herself and her household—she at length found that a whispering of the infirmity of the king had commenced; and then read in the "Morning Herald" some anecdote which she was desirous that the editor should retract, and answer, at his peril, any further such treasonable paragraph. On the 5th of November a terrible scene occurred, which rendered all further hesitation as to the nature of his malady impossible. The king in the afternoon went out in his chaise with the princess royal for an airing; he was all smiling benignity, but gave so many orders to the postillions, and got in and out of the carriage twice, with such agitation, as to excite Miss Burney's alarm. Retiring in her own room, she was struck in the evening with the uncommon stillness that reigned throughout the palace; nobody stirred, not a voice was heard, not a step, not a motion, there seemed a strangeness in the house most extraordinary—the equerries then passed to and fro with unusual gravity, whisperings only were exchanged, all was mysterious horror; at length the news was told her, that the king at dinner had broken forth into positive delirium, which had long been apprehended by all who saw him most closely : the queen was so overpowered as to fall into violent hysterics; all the princesses were in misery, and the Prince of Wales burst into tears.

The night that followed was a fearful one. Miss Burney was called upon to attend her Majesty. "My poor royal mistress, never can I forget her countenance—pale, ghastly pale, she was seated to be undressed, and attended by Lady Elizabeth Waldegrave and Miss Goldsworthy; her whole frame was disordered, yet she was still and quiet; these two ladies assisted me to undress her, or rather I assisted them, for they were firmer from being longer present; my shaking hands and blinded eyes could scarce be of any use. The king, at the instance of Sir George Baker, had consented to sleep in the next apartment; in the middle of the night, the king insisted upon seeing if the queen was not removed from the house, and he had come into the room with a candle in his hand, and satisfied himself she was there; he stayed a full half-hour, and the depth of that terror during that time no words can paint." The confirmation of the worst fears that had been apprehended gave now no pretence for keeping from the nation the sad change that·had occurred in a monarch who had gradually become popular, and for whom the tenderest solicitude was from that period displayed. The earlier days of the king's reign had not been propitious, and he had incurred displeasure from his obstinate adherence to his own preconceived views; but now all was forgotten, all was anxious affection, and, amid hopes and fears, the nation turned to Parliament to learn from its deliberations what would be the steps which, in consonance with the spirit of the constitution. would be taken: various were the surmises which were afloat, as to the placing the power in the hands of the heir apparent to the throne, and to whose custody would be committed the person of the afflicted monarch. Upon the first assembling of Parliament, it was resolved that an adjournment should take place for a fortnight, and on the 4th of November a report of the Privy Council was laid on the table, and another adjournment took place till the 8th of December.

The Prince of Wales had, from the previous circumstances of his career, become the centre around which the opposition of the time revolved; its members looked forward to the day when he should be in possession of power as that on which their triumph would be secured, and they therefore displayed the greatest anxiety that he should be proclaimed unrestricted regent; and the doctrines they upheld were that he at once had a right to assume the royal authority. To these pretensions the administration of the day, headed by Mr. Pitt, was strenuously opposed, and the feelings of the great mass of the people were also decidedly hostile to them. It unfortunately happened that the taste and morals of the party desirous of seeing his Royal Highness at the head of affairs were most questionable. Mr. Fox, its leader, however highly gifted with intellectual power, and loved for his generous and affectionate temper, was too much addicted to those social pleasures which border on folly to be generally esteemed. Sheridan's prudence had begun to be more than doubted, and reports were widely disseminated of the recklessness of those who frequented Carlton House. Hence the slow and protracted steps which were taken by the House of Commons, the caution exercised, and the apparent wisdom of deep reflection, (whilst in fact intrigue of every description was going forward in various sections of the parties,) were quite in consonance with public opinion.

Mr. Fox was sent for from Italy; and when Mr. Pitt came forward to propose that a committee be appointed to examine the journals of the House, and report precedents of such authority as may have been had in cases of the personal exercise of the royal authority being prevented or interrupted by infancy, sickness, infirmity, or otherwise, with a view to provide for the same, Mr. Fox at once took up the position, " That whenever the sovereign, from sickness, infirmity, or other incapacity, was unable to exercise the functions of his high office, the heir apparent, being of full age and capacity, had as clear and express a right to assume the reins of government, and exercise the power of sovereignty, as in the case of his majesty's demise." Mr. Pitt's reply kindled a fire throughout the country. In the collection made of the works and the correspondence of Dr. Parr, is to be found a letter upon the subject of the king's illness from Mrs. Sheridan, in which she says, " An unlucky word about right, made use of by Charles Fox in the House, has made some little confusion in the heads of a few old Parliamentaries, who did not understand him, and Pitt has taken advantage of this, and means to move a question about it on Tuesday, which our friends wish to avoid by moving the previous question, thinking Pitt's motion mischievous and quite unnecessary." Mr. Pitt said, " That the very announcement of a claim of right rendered an inquiry into precedent and history of the greater consequence, for if such an authority should be discovered, all further debate in that House would be unnecessary; but he boldly said, that the assertion of such a right in the Prince of Wales, or any one else, was little short of treason against the constitution of the country. He pledged himself to prove that in the case of the interruption of the personal exercise of the royal authority, without the existence of any lawful provision being previously made for carrying on the government, it belonged to the other branches of the nation at large to provide, according to their discretion, for the temporary exercise of the regal functions in the name and behalf of the sovereign, as they should deem requisite, and that the Prince of Wales had no more right of himself, without their decision, to assume the government than any other individual in the country." This great constitutional doctrine was generally assented to; neither the replies of Mr. Fox, nor the invectives of Mr. Burk could shake it.

Upon the assertions of the two heads of parties, it was impossible for Sheridan, who was looked upon in the House as the personal friend of his Royal Highness, to be silent; yet his situation was one of the utmost delicacy. He had, in a letter which still exists, given the most judicious advice to that illustrious personage. He had stated "That it would greatly advance his Royal Highness's credit, and lay the strongest grounds to baffle every attempt at opposition to what he considered the just claims and rights of his Royal Highness, that the language of those who may be in any sort suspected of knowing his wishes and feelings should be of great moderation in disclaiming all party views, and avowing the utmost readiness to acquiesce in any reasonable delay."

When Mr. Pitt moved that the House will, on Tuesday next, resolve itself into a committee to take into consideration the state of the nation, Sheridan began a temperate and cautious speech. He said, "That he felt it his duty to contend against the propriety and expediency of putting the abstract proposition of the right of the Prince of Wales. It could not conciliate, but, on the contrary, it might create dissension and animosities, and therefore he insisted it would be unwise, as it was obviously unnecessary, to agitate it, or to press the House to come to any vote on it." The next sentence called down a long and continued *hear, hear,* from both sides of the House; by both parties it was hailed as indiscreet at first, but after reflection it was considered to be called for by the circumstances of the case. "He begged leave to remind the right *honourable Gentleman* of the danger of provoking that claim to be asserted (*a loud cry of Hear! hear!*), which he observed had not yet been preferred. (*Another cry of hear! hear!*) He then repeated the words, and asked, "Would the right honourable gentleman choose to have his own proposition put upon the journals, to have it recorded as his opinion, that the Prince of Wales had no more right to exercise the royal authority, during the incapacity of the king, than any other individual?" If he would not, why would he press an abstract proposition that must throw the nation into anarchy and confusion? Mr. Pitt replied to this somewhat insidiously, by saying "That he trusted the House would do their duty in spite of any threat, however high the authority from which it might proceed." Mr. Sheridan then denied that his language could be construed into a threat, he had only spoken of the danger which might arise if the prince should be provoked to assert a claim which he had not yet referred, and the discussion of which he must continue to think as mischievous in its tendency as it was absolutely unnecessary. Resolutions were carried on the 22nd December, on the motion of Mr. Pitt, which virtually brought the matter to a formal decision, taking from the Prince of Wales any claim, as a right, which he might wish to establish of acting as regent of the kingdom. The House indeed divided, but the resolutions were carried by a majority of 93; 158 voting on an amendment—251 against it.

The readiness, the quickness with which Mr. Pitt seized every word uttered by his adversaries, to aid his arguments, either by ridiculing any accidental blunder, exposing some doctrine incautiously advanced, or dexterously leading them into some glaring avowal of opinions inconsistent with the principles of Whiggery, have been generally acknowledged. When Mr. Fox used the rash and unadvised words to which we have alluded, a smile irradiated the usual gloomy and haughty face of the Prime Minister; and when the sentence was concluded, he slapped his thigh with exultation, and turning to the member who was seated near him, triumphantly exclaimed, "I'll unwhig the gentleman for the rest of his life!" and certainly, during the whole of the debates that followed, he took up a doctrine before unknown to a party that asserted the right divine of kings, and laid down an axiom, somewhat inconsistent with their usual creed, that the voice and the sense of the people, through their constituents, were to be consulted in the choice of a substitute for kingly power. Having carried the essential point, that the Lords spiritual and temporal and the Commons of Great Britain now assembled, and lawfully, fully, and freely representing all the estates of the people of this realm, have the right, and are in duty bound, to provide the means of supplying the defect of the personal exercise of the royal authority arising from his Majesty's indisposition, Mr. Pitt, on the 16th of January, moved " That it was expedient that his Royal Highness the Prince of Wales should be empowered to exercise and administer the royal authority under the style and title of regent of the kingdom ; " and then brought forward a series of resolutions as restrictions upon his power. A debate of great interest ensued, during which Sheridan exhibited considerable tact and readiness. Lord Belgrave having concluded a complimentary speech in favour of the minister, with a quotation from Demosthenes, Sheridan promptly rose and immediately pointed out the misapplication of the lines, and, in defence of his party, uttered an eulogium, certainly called for by the insinuations of his adversaries, that the prince would be surrounded by bad advisers.

" The right honourable gentleman had more than once wantonly attacked that side of the House as containing a political party. As for himself, (Mr. Sheridan added,) he made no scruple to declare he thought it the glory and honour of his life to belong to that party. He who knew the character of that party, knew it was an honour which any man might covet. Was it a disgrace to have been formed under the Marquis of Rockingham ; and under his banners to have combated on behalf of the people with success? Was it a disgrace to be connected with the Duke of Portland, a nobleman who, swayed by no mean motives of interest, nor influenced by any ambitious designs to grasp at power, nor with a view to any other purpose than the welfare of the country, dedicated his mornings unremittingly to the promotion of the public good? Mr. Sheridan remarked, he could not advert to his right honourable friend (Mr. Fox) without declaring it was the characteristic distinction of his heart to compel the most submissive devotion of mind and affection from all those who came under the observation of it; and force them, by the most powerful and amiable of all influence, to become the inseparable associates of his fortune.   With respect to his talents, he would not speak of them; they would derive no support from any man's attestation, nor from the most flattering panegyric of the most enlightened of his friends.   Thus much he would only observe, with regard to the abilities of his honourable friend, that it was the utmost effort of any other man's talents, and the best proof of their existence, that he was able to understand the extent, and comprehend the superiority of them.   It was the pride and glory of his life to enjoy the happiness and honour of his friendship; and he desired to be told whether the Duke of Portland and Mr.' Fox were less worthy of the confidence of their country, or more unfit to become ministers, because an arrogant individual chose presumptuously to load them with calumny? .Were he an independent man, standing aloof from party, and wholly unconnected with it, he could not, with patience, hear the right honourable gentleman's insulting language; but, as a party man, boasting himself to be one, how did the right honourable gentleman imagine he should receive his reflections but with that scorn and disdain which became a man conscious of the worth and value of those with whom he was connected?"

His observations on the patronage reserved. were—" He reprobated the idea of reserving the patronage of the royal household, and adverted to the right honourable gentleman's having charged his right honourable friend (when on a former occasion he quitted office) with having left a fortress behind him.   The charge was true; he admitted that his right honourable friend had done so; but then, like a coarse, clumsy workman, he had built his plan in open day, and retired with his friends, who served without pay, though their services had been long continued.   Not so the right honourable gentleman over the way; like a more crafty mason, he had collected his materials with greater caution, and worked them up with abundantly more art.   Perhaps he had taken the advice of the noble duke, famous for fortification, and, with the aid of that able engineer, had provided a corps of royal military artificers, and thrown up impregnable ramparts to secure himself and his garrison.   Upon this occasion the king's arms doubtless might be seen flying as a banner on the top of his fortress, and powerful indeed must prove the effect of the right honourable gentleman's thundering eloquence from without, and the support of the royal artificers from within, against his political adversaries. Mr. Sheridan reprobated the person, whoever it might be, that advised her Majesty to lend her name to such a proposition as that which was then made to the committee; and declared that were the one ground of suspicion of the bad advisers of the regent to be taken away, the right honourable gentleman could not be said to have produced a single argument in support of his system. He described the power that the ex-minister would derive from retaining the patronage of the king's household; and contended that the pretext that his Majesty's feelings would be shocked when he recovered and found his household changed, was ridiculous." He then added, " To talk, therefore, of his Majesty's feelings, when he should recover and find his household changed, was to suppose that he would be less shocked to learn that the constitution of his country was changed, part of his dominions ceded to foreign potentates, and other essential and important calamities and disgraces entailed on his country, which was like a man, who having been entrusted with the mansion-house of a person during his incapacity to take care of it, should suffer it to go to ruin, and the winds of heaven to blow through almost every part of it, the inclosures to be broken down, the flocks of sheep to be shorn and exposed to the storms, and all left to ruin and decay. except a few looking-glasses and old worthless gilt lumber. that were locked up in an old-fashioned drawing-room. Mr. Sheridan represented the ex-minister coming down to the House in state, with the cap of liberty on the end of a white staff, a retinue of black and white sticks attending him, and an army of beef-eaters (whom the master of the horse, the lord steward, and lord chamberlain, were to be employed in marshalling) to clear his way through the lobby."

During the long protracted debates Mr. Sheridan assiduously attended the House; made many useful observations upon the various stages of the Restriction Bill. The occasions on which he distinguished himself were many, evincing throughout a great anxiety to serve his Royal Highness, and to preserve the royal prerogative intact.

That which most tended to give the public a bad opinion of Fox, of Burke, and even of Sheridan, was the somewhat indecorous manner in which they treated the malady of the king; the too visible worship of the rising sun, and, above all, the party spirit with which they treated all public questions. Even the physicians were treated as partisans; their evidence handled with levity, sarcasm, or flat denial, just as it pleased those who addressed the House. The admirable prognostics of Dr. Willis, who was thoroughly conversant with mental maladies, were made the theme of abuse; whilst the attainments of Dr. Warren (whose practical skill, notwithstanding his reputation as a scholar, was generally questioned) were lauded to the skies; because the one was ready, and somewhat talkative, whereas the other, a slow-thinking man, was silent, reserved, and only expressed his opinions when called upon to do so. That Dr. Warren's hastily-formed judgment should have been put into competition with Dr. Willis's long-continued study is to be regretted, because it misled the party, and induced Sheridan to make a most unsuitable speech in the House, and to boldly accuse Dr. Willis of prevarication and evasion, to call him a hasty decider, and a random speaker; to say that the physic he administered "reminded him of those nostrums which were to cure this and that malady, and also disappointments in love, and long sea-voyages."

Of the letter which was addressed to Mr. Pitt, and attributed to Mr. Sheridan, so widely circulated and generally admired, the evidence of Sir James Mackintosh has settled the doubted question of its authorship; and to Mr. Burke is due, whatever of merit it may exhibit. The rumour that was so generally prevalent that Sheridan had written it plainly shows that every literary production of merit was supposed to be derived from his pen. It is unnecessary to pursue the course which was followed by Sheridan throughout the long discussions which this interesting subject provoked. Whatever of good feeling he may have gained in the bosom of the prince and his royal brothers, he must have offended the queen by the whole drift of his arguments on the clauses which gave her Majesty the custody of the royal sufferer.

Among the thirty-two clauses which constituted the Regency Bill, was a clause that provided against the regent marrying a Papist. Mr. Rolle, with considerable indelicacy, renewed the discussion which had once been opened on the subject of the supposed alliance of the Prince of Wales with Mrs. Fitzherbert, by moving that the words "or who is or should be married in law or in fact to a Papist," be inserted. Lord North, Mr. Gray, and Mr. Courtenay replied in somewhat strong language. In the course of the debate Sheridan alluded to Mr. Pitt having, on several occasions, signified his departure from office.

"Mr. Pitt said, the honourable gentleman had indulged himself in imputing words to him which he had never spoken, and applying arguments which he had never uttered. The honourable gentleman contended that he had not signified his departure from office. Surely the honourable gentleman had a perverse memory. His successors had been named to him, but he had never yet heard of the least circumstance which authorized him to declare that he was about to quit his place. When he did hear anything like it, he should have much to say to that House, to express his acknowledgments for the support he had received, to confess his obligations to them, and to declare his hopes, that he should not quit his situation avowing principles less worthy of their regard and esteem than he brought with him into office."

"Mr. Sheridan observed that the right honourable gentleman, he did not doubt, would make a fine speech at his exit from office; or, according to the vulgar expression, an excellent delivery of his last dying words and confession."

These lengthened debates were drawn to a conclusion by the announcement that his Majesty was restored to his usual state. The news was received with unbounded joy by the people, who were thoroughly wearied of the procrastination of the Ministry. Tedious, however, as may have been the discussions, they have been of deep value, and have furnished us with one of the landmarks by which the nature of the British constitution may be judged of.

The health of his father, Thomas Sheridan, had gradually declined. He for some time resided at Margate, and from thence, if he should find no amendment, he intended to proceed to Lisbon; his complaints, however, did not diminish, and on the 14th of August, 1788, he expired. He had, for some short time, retired from the stage, and had given public readings at Freemason's Hall, at Hickford's Rooms, and Coachmakers

Hall. His works, with the exception of "the Loyal Subject," "Romeo and Juliet," and "Coriolanus," which he altered and produced whilst manager of the Dublin stage, and a life of Dean Swift, were principally devoted to the elements of language. They are "A Discourse delivered in the Theatre at Oxford, and in the Senate House at Cambridge;" "A Dissertation on the Causes of the Difficulties which occur in learning the English Language;' "A Course of Lectures on Elocution;" "A Plan of Education for the Young Nobility and Gentry of Great Britain;" "Lectures on the Art of Reading;" "A General Dictionary of the English Language;" "Elements. of English." A likeness, said to be exceedingly good, is prefixed to the second edition of his Dictionary. Although at one period of his life the father was estranged from the son, and always seemed to give a preference to the elder brother, a reconciliation had taken place, in consequence of efforts repeatedly made, and oftentimes spurned by the father. Sheridan, however, paid unremitting attention to him in his last illness, and evinced for him the sincerest filial affection. His eldest sister, referring to the existence of those differences, which she lamented, says in a letter, "and yet it was that son, and not the object of his partial fondness, who at last closed his eyes." Dr. Parr wrote, at the request of Sheridan, a tribute to his memory, which, however, was not inscribed upon the cenotaph, intended by the son for St. Peter's Church, Margate It is, however, worthy to be recorded. "This monument, A. D. 1824, was, by subscription, erected to the memory of Thomas Sheridan, Esq., who died in the neighbouring parish of St. John, August 14th, 1788, in the 69th year of his age, and according to his own request was there buried. He was grandson to Dr. Thomas Sheridan, the brother of Dr. William; a conscientious nonjuror, who in 1691 was deprived of the bishopric of Kilmore. He was the son of Dr. Thomas Sheridan; a profound scholar and eminent schoolmaster, intimately connected with Dean Swift and other illustrious writers in the reign of Queen Anne. He was husband to the ingenious and amiable author of "Sidney Biddulph," and several dramatic pieces favourably received. He was the father of the celebrated orator and dramatist, Richard Brinsley Sheridan. He had been the schoolfellow, and through life was the companion of the amiable Archbishop of Mark ham. He was the friend of the learned Dr. Sumner, master of Harrow school, and the well-known Dr. Parr. He took his first academical degree in the University of Dublin, about 1736. He was honoured in the University of Oxford with the degree of A.M. in 1758, and in 1759 he obtained the same distinction at Cambridge. He for many years presided over the theatre of Dublin, and at Drury Lane; he in public estimation stood next to David Garrick. In the literary world he was distinguished by numerous and useful writings on the pronunciation of the English language. Through some of his opinions ran a vein of singularity mingled with the rich ore of genius. In his manners there was dignified ease, in his spirit invincible firmness, and in his habits and principles unsullied integrity."

This elegant summary of the principal characteristics of the life of a man who had used indefatigable exertions, but unsuccessfully, to promote the cause of education, is one of those productions of the classic pen whose judgment in the selection of ideas and of words to express them has been unequalled. There now is a plain monument raised to the memory of Mr. Thomas Sheridan, in St. Peter's, Margate, by a friend of Mr. Jarvis, who attended him professionally during his illness.

The great movements which occurred in France began to excite the attention of the people of England, and caused them to watch each event which sprung up, and to turn with anxious eye to the views taken of them by the parties who most deeply interested themselves in the direction of the public mind. The great Revolution of France, it must ever be borne in recollection, commenced with moderation, displaying only a determination to obtain by simple means a constitution worthy a free people, but innumerable difficulties presented themselves; a disastrous series of occurrences led to the ruin of all established forms; unquiet and ambitious minds were opposed to capriciousness and to feebleness; horror followed upon horror, until Europe, dismayed with the frightful scenes enacted upon the stage, shrunk back with loathing from the contemplation. All at first was anticipation of good; but the end was shame and destruction. It first appeared as the gentle breeze which refreshes as it passes along; but soon became the whirlwind, destroying as it swept by. Many of those who at first beheld a nation attempting to contribute to the increase of the happiness of human nature by the establishment of a government which should lead to freedom, to public order and security, were pleased to see the overthrow of a tyranny which arbitrarily pressed upon the humbler classes of society. They were prepared for a bold struggle, carried on by daring and determined innovators; but they did not expect the eccentric course which they took. They did not anticipate the violence that arose, nor the murders that were committed; the transition state is always one of prodigious effort, during which none can foresee its results. For those who had to encounter the dreadful position of society consequent upon the thorough overthrow of all that existed in royalty and in aristocracy, it must, indeed, have been fearful; but that which has been obtained from the rude shocks—is liberty, social order, and contentment. The perils that have been gone through could only have been borne and supported by the insane; but another race enjoys the benefits, and feels the harmony that has arisen out of discord, the mildness which was wrung from tyranny and oppression.

Sheridan was amongst those who gazed with unspeakable satisfaction at the earliest struggles of the manacled slave to unbind his fetters, to raise himself from the ground, and draw in the free breath of heaven: with him were associated men who were deeply imbued with the love of a pure, free, and mild constitution, who saw in the government of France corruption, imbecility, cupidity, and all those crimes which a long indulgence in despotism engenders and fosters. They were delighted to find a people rousing themselves from their slumber, proclaiming their rights with an irresistible and an omnipotent voice, seeking that which justice entitled them to, and determined to obtain it. They could not foresee all that arose out of this patriotic energy; and, as events occurred, their minds were often reconciled to circumstances which cooler reflection might not have sanctioned. The distrust which those who governed in France brought upon themselves shook the loyalty of those who would have supported them, and eventually led to their own destruction. It is impossible for those who merely read the page of history to form any just idea of the impressions produced by these events upon the people of England; the changes were so various they followed so rapidly one upon the other, that all reasoning was set at defiance. The fears of men were so worked upon, too, that no one became a dispassionate witness of the occurrences. Rank and power were annihilated in one country, and those who possessed them in England began to dread that their time was fully come; they prepared themselves for the struggle, and the champion of free institutions had but little chance against odds most discouraging. Sheridan, and those with whom he acted, boldly proclaimed opinions unpalatable to them, and a war of words, mingled with hatred and with fear, soon sprang up.

At this period Sheridan gave incessant labour to the duties of the House; he was a frequent speaker, selected points of interest to the community, and brought assiduity and labour to assist his natural abilities. Had the indefatigable industry with which he pursued the various subjects of discussion been exhibited by an individual connected with the administration, he would soon have filled a most distinguished post; but all his zeal, all his efforts, were directed against the system pursued by Mr. Pitt. His investigations of the public revenue, his statement of the resources and of the expenditure of the empire, led him to perceive many of the fallacious views, to combat, expose, and ridicule them. His lengthened speeches on the appointment of a Committee of Finance upon the Tobacco Regulation Bills proved to the country that he was neither indolent nor superficial; but that he diligently inquired, and clothed the result of his examination in eloquence, such as rendered abstruse questions interesting and intelligible. He sometimes met with abuse from the press; but what man, who stands prominently before the public, can escape the calumnies, the gibes, and the scoffs of those who are opposed to him? And if on the one side he is loaded with censure, he is certain on the other to meet with flattery and adulation. On one occasion he was rather carried away by too anxious a desire to defend himself, and he introduced a notice of the feelings that some entertained towards himself. He said that "Uncommon pains had been taken, in the public prints, to defame all those who had taken any part in endeavouring to procure a repeal of the Tobacco Act; and no one had been more distinguished on the occasion than himself. He begged leave to apologize for speaking concerning himself; he at all times disliked egotisms, and more so on the present occasion,

L

when the attention of the committee was to be taken up with the consideration of important subjects; but still, as it was the part which he had taken in this business that had drawn upon him the ill-will of those who had traduced him, and as they had connected his personal character with the important business in which he was then engaged, he hoped that the committee would suffer him to trespass, for some few minutes, on their patience, whilst he should proceed to a few remarks upon the attacks that had been made upon him. Those who made those attacks had gone out of the common path, and instead of pursuing the old sober staple of abuse had descended to the lowest scurrilities, and fallen without mercy, not only upon his public conduct, but also on his private life. They had made charges of a singular nature, and endeavoured to rob him of the esteem and friendship of those whom he valued most in society. Fortunately, however, their charges were as void of truth as they were fraught with malice. He had, hitherto, treated them with contemptuous silence, and would have continued in this disposition to the present day, if he had not felt some reason to think, which reason he had not heard till a few hours ago, that some of those charges were considered as founded in truth. What he more particularly alluded to were whispers or reports of jealousies among some of his dearest friends, and of a certain opposition affirmed to have been made by a noble duke (Portland) against some views or expectations which he (Mr. Sheridan) was said to have entertained; concerning such whispers and reports, he could truly declare that there was not in them one grain of truth. The opinion which they ascribed to the noble duke had never been entertained by him. Mr. Sheridan observed, that he would not venture to state to the committee the opinion that the noble duke was pleased to entertain of him, lest he should be accused of vanity in publishing what he might deem highly flattering; all, therefore, that he would assert on this occasion was, that if he had it in his power to make the man whose good opinion he should most highly prize think flatteringly of him, he would have that man to think of him precisely as the noble duke did; and then his wish on that subject would be most amply gratified.

" The jealousies to which he was described as having given occasion existed only in the brain of the traducers; they did not, they could not, exist anywhere else. He was, therefore, perfectly at his ease whilst the traducers were propagating their calumnies. He defied any man to charge him with any one act which could be tortured into a violation of any engagement founded in honour and integrity. If he could be charged, in truth, with any dishonourable, mean, or unmanly act, he should feel very differently indeed; his mind, in that case, would sting him more than the most bitter reproaches of his most calumniating enemies. As to any pretensions which might be ascribed to him, to situations far beyond his natural weight in the community, he would only observe, that it was the peculiar excellence of the British constitution, that a man could push forward into notice and distinction the talents or abilities, whatever they might be, with which Providence had endowed him."

Occasionally happy thoughts, sparkling allusions, and playful raillery enliven his dullest speeches; but it would be the height of injustice to quote them, for they are so incorporated with the rest of the matter that they would lose all their value were they to be extracted and placed alone before the reader's eye. When the Session terminated, which it did amidst the complaints of Sheridan of the procrastination of public business, the Parliament was dissolved; he hastened down to Stafford and secured his election, but not without difficulty and expense. He then returned to London to lend his aid to Charles Fox, who stood for Westminster. Here he had to meet one of the most unflinching politicians of the day, Horne Tooke; no one dared to express his sentiments more freely; no one had more sarcastic power. No man better understood the art of carrying with him the working classes, and the humbler orders of society; ready in wit, quick in apprehension, his sallies, his repartees, neither delicate nor fashioned to any but those he addressed, were listened to with delight. As a candidate for Westminster, no one but the great and good Sir Francis Burdett better knew his supporters. It was understood that Sheridan had been anxious to try his power in Westminster, and in a letter from Mrs. Sheridan to him, whilst on his canvass at Stafford, this passage occurs. "I am half sorry you have any thing to do with them, and more than ever regret you did not stand for Westminster with Charles."

Horne Tooke, instead of finding a proposer and seconder,

L 2

boldly came forward, and put himself in nomination; and—saying that the two candidates should have been ashamed to have sat and heard such ill-deserved praise bestowed upon them by their respective proposers and seconders—offered himself. He told the crowd that, as so many of these fine qualities and virtues had never done them the least good, they might as well now choose a candidate without them."

Various are the sallies which are recorded, as marking the sarcastic vein of the man; but there was one so personal to Sheridan that he never forgave it, and although at one period some degree of intimacy had existed between them, it ceased. Charles Fox, who was seldom listened to with patience by the surrounding crowd, left the hustings; while Sheridan, whose good humoured stories, and lively wit, were rather in favour, remained. Tooke observed upon this, "that it was usual with the quack doctor, when he quitted the stage, to leave his jack-pudding behind him." His ready answer to a partizan of Charles Fox has been recorded; who, addressing him, said, "Well, Mr. Tooke, as this is Monday you are sure to have all the blackguards with you." "I am delighted to hear it, sir," was the reply, "more especially when it comes from such good authority." Sheridan found himself quite unequal to cope with his virulent antagonist; the personalities, the invectives he had to encounter were not at all to his taste. He winced under the merciless infliction of the scourge; he felt how much more potent was his adversary, and was not sorry when Tooke was defeated.

The first session of the new Parliament saw Sheridan an active opponent of the administration: little, however, is worthy of notice, except the still further widening of the breach between Burke on the one side, and Fox and Sheridan on the other. Mr. Burke's work, "Reflections on the French Revolution," had attracted the deepest attention; it had produced an effect upon the followers of the Whig school, though the great leaders remained unchanged and unchangeable. The party was nearly broken up; the spirit of loyalty, which was maintained throughout the work, overpowered, in many instances, the newly-awakened feeling for liberty. The doctrines of equality, of fraternization, had alarmed the privileged classes; and they hailed the book as the manifesto of those who loved royalty, and would uphold the church in opposition to that which they so much dreaded. On the 6th of May, the House of Commons was witness to an unequalled display of passion on one side, and tenderness on another. Burke with violence and impetuosity severed the ties of friendship that so long had bound the two great men together. Burke's warning voice against the danger of trying new theories, his wish to cherish the British constitution, and to save it from the influence of French philosophy, passed by unheeded; but when Fox whispered that there would be no loss of friendship, Burke repudiated the idea, " Yes there was a loss of friendship—he knew the price of his conduct—he had done his duty at the price of his friend—their friendship was at an end." Here Fox betrayed an amiable weakness, tears coursed each other down his cheek, as he rose to reply. The House was visibly affected; not a sound was heard. It was felt that men of noble nature, long deeply attached, were torn from each other by a high sense of honour, by a sacred feeling of duty, and the love of their native land. Although the greater part of those with whom Sheridan usually acted saw without apprehension the commencement of the conflict in France, there was one master spirit of the age who feared danger in the struggle, and left the old companions of his political views. Burke, with whom Sheridan had lived on terms of intimacy, who had fought the battle against Hastings so nobly with him, who had cheered him on, and who had received him fainting in his arms, after his great effort in the House of Lords, from the earliest moment expressed his dissent from his former friend, and by his writings and speeches attempted to counteract his opinions. On the 9th of February came on the discussion on the Army Estimates; the Session had been opened on the 1st of February, and as early as the 5th, Mr. Fox had taken an opportunity, whilst discussing the reduction of the army, to observe that the army in Paris had, by its refusal to obey the court, set a glorious example, and shown that men by becoming soldiers had not ceased to be citizens; and, therefore, one of his great objections to a standing army had been removed. Mr. Burke, after some eloquently expressed compliments on Mr. Fox, deprecated the effects which such language was likely to produce; and said " that so strongly was he opposed to any the least tendency towards the means of introducing a democracy like that of the French, as well as to the end itself, that, much as it would afflict him if such a thing should be attempted, and that any friend of his should concur in such measures—he was far, very far, from believing they could—he would abandon his best friends, and join with his worst enemies to oppose either the means or the end." This declaration called forth from Fox one of the most beautiful eulogiums ever pronounced by one friend upon another. After stating the value he placed upon his friendship, he thus spoke of the splendid powers of that great orator :—" If he were to put all the political information which he had learned from books, all which he had gained from science, and all which any knowledge of the world, and in affairs, into one scale, and the improvement which he had derived from his right honourable friend's instruction and conversation were placed in the other, he should be at a loss to decide to which to give the preference." Burke was evidently pleased with these explanations, and rose to express his satisfaction ; but Sheridan was not so easily acted upon. He uttered "some warm compliments to Mr. Burke's general principles; but said that he could not conceive how it was possible for a person of such principles, or for any man who valued our own constitution, and revered the Revolution that obtained it for us, to unite with such feelings an indignant and unqualified abhorrence of all the proceedings of the patriotic party in France.

" He conceived theirs to be as just a revolution as our own, proceeding upon as sound a principle and a greater provocation. He vehemently defended the general views and conduct of the national assembly. He could not even understand what was meant by the charge against them of having overturned the laws, the justice, and the revenues of their country. What were their laws? The arbitrary mandates of capricious despotism. What their justice? The partial adjudications of venal magistrates. What their revenues? National bankruptcy. This he thought the fundamental error of the right honourable gentleman's argument, that he accused the national assembly of creating the evils which they had found existing in full deformity at the first hour of their meeting. The public creditor had been defrauded ; the manufacturer was out of employ ; trade was languishing; famine clung upon the poor; despair on all. In this situation, the wisdom and feelings of the nation were appealed to by the government; and was it to be wondered at by *Englishmen*, that a people, so circumstanced, should search for the cause and source of all their calamities; or that they should find them in the arbitrary constitution of their government, and in the prodigal and corrupt administration of their revenues? For such an evil, when proved, what remedy could be resorted to, but a radical amendment of the frame and fabric of the constitution itself? This change was not the object and wish of the national assembly only, it was the claim and cry of all France, united as one man for one purpose. He joined with Mr. Burke in abhorring the cruelties that had been committed; but what was the striking lesson, the awful moral that was to be gathered from the outrages of the populace? What, but a superior abhorrence of that accursed system of despotic government which had so deformed and corrupted human nature, as to make its subjects capable of such acts; a government that sets at nought the property, the liberty, and lives of the subjects; a government that deals in extortion, dungeons, and tortures; sets an example of depravity to the slaves it rules over; and, if a day of power comes to the wretched populace, it is not to be wondered at, however it is to be regretted, that they act without those feelings of justice and humanity which the principles and the practice of their governors have stripped them of. At the same time if there were any persons who, for the purposes of their own private and personal ambition, had instigated those outrages, they, whatever their rank, birth, or fortune, deserved the execration of mankind. Justice, however, required that no credit should be given to mere rumours on such a subject."

Mr. Burke replied that he most sincerely lamented over the inevitable necessity of now publicly declaring that, henceforth, he and his honourable friend were separated in politics. He complained "that he had not represented his arguments fairly; it was not what he expected in the moment of departed friendship. On the contrary, was it not evident that the honourable gentleman had made a sacrifice of his friendship for the sake of catching some momentary popularity?—all the applause which he could gain from clubs was scarcely worthy the sacrifice which he had chosen to make for such an acqui-

sition." Attempts were in vain made to heal the breach thus
made between two men who had so often fought together
mighty battles against power, against corruption and tyranny.
A meeting took place at Burlington House, according to a
previous arrangement; it lasted from ten o'clock at night
until three in the morning; and never was there a more remarkable display of talent on both sides.   Burke was, however, implacable; all communication ceased between them;
and though Sheridan spoke of him, in the House of Commons, as one for whose talents and personal virtue he had
the highest esteem, veneration, and regard, all was in vain.
Burke spoke of him with asperity from that time forward;
and attributed to his unwarrantable interference his own
secession from his former party.

It was alleged that Sheridan had hastened on this separa-
tion by his imprudent speeches, and that this was the result of
jealousy, and an anxious desire to fill the place in Charles Fox's
esteem that for a quarter of a century Burke had enjoyed.
Of the littleness that could invent this calumny we may
speak with contempt; but of the eagerness to diffuse the venom
we think with disgust. It is not unlikely that Sheridan should
have urged on this explanation of the differences which existed in that great party, whose chief end and aim was declared to be the love of a pure and well-defined constitution,
which, whilst it guarded the liberties of a people, acknowledged frankly the great principles of royalty, and of a House
of Lords.

A speech made by Sheridan on a motion of Mr. Grey,
against any interference in the war between Russia and the
Porte, is well worthy of perusal, as illustrating the information, and likewise the discretion and tact with which he could
handle a subject of difficulty.   It is remarkable for the avowal
of a doctrine that the prerogative of the crown to declare war
might prove obnoxious to the House, and that there existed
an ancient, constitutional, and most useful function of a British House of Commons to advise the Crown, and by a due application of their preventive wisdom to save the country from
that expense and calamity into which they might otherwise
be plunged, either by the terror of ministers, their imprudence, their neglect, or their corruption.

Mr. Sheridan retired, in the month of April, from the busi

ness of the House; during this period there are no records of speeches to be met with, no traces of his occupation. In fact, his mind was harassed by many conflicting thoughts; Mrs. Sheridan's state of health excited the deepest apprehension. She was compelled to seek change of air at Clifton. The state of Drury Lane Theatre, too, was such as to be a source of much anxiety to him; it had been pronounced by competent persons to be unfit to receive large audiences, and that it was necessary that it should be rebuilt. The circumstances attending such a determination could not fail to require all the attention of Mr. Sheridan; his time and mind were devoted to the completion of the plans that were now devised, and from which hopes were entertained that ultimate advantages would accrue. These hopes were not destined to be fulfilled; and we may look to this period of this great man's life as the one from which sprang all the ultimate misfortunes that gradually overpowered him. He had now attained the zenith of his reputation. His popularity, his talents, and his exertions were all the theme of general eulogy. Though some slight embarrassments had occurred, they had passed away like the fleeting clouds across the summer sun; but he was now destined to fall from the giddy height, and to feel how transitory are all the gifts of fortune. He had, it would seem, three establishments, and his style of living was such as became a man mingling in the richer class of society, and enjoying all that luxury can give. To build the theatre seemed an easy task; all that was required was one hundred and fifty thousand pounds. This was raised with the utmost facility in three hundred debentures of five hundred pounds each; but the difficulty of paying the interest of that large sum was scarcely calculated upon. Three instalments were to be paid up, and as soon as one was paid all was prepared. On the 4th of June, his Majesty's birthday, Old Drury Lane, the scene of so many extraordinary circumstances, closed for ever; the company went to the Opera House, and from thence, when the musical season commenced, to the Haymarket, where they played at advanced prices. On the 4th of September the first stone of the new theatre was laid. Unforeseen difficulties, fresh expenses, vexatious negotiations, combined to retard the completion of the new theatre; and during this interval a sad calamity occurred.

It was in the year 1792 that Sheridan had to mourn over the grave of his beautiful and affectionate wife. She was only thirty-eight years of age, when a pulmonary disease bereft him of the cherished partner of his happiest days; from that moment a blight fell upon him—he soon became an altered man. There was no one who was ever admitted into her presence that did not feel there was a divinity about her. Jackson, the great composer, said, "that to see her, as she stood singing beside him at the pianoforte, was like looking into the face of an angel." The Bishop of Norwich was wont! to say, that she seemed to him "the connecting link between woman and angel;" even the licentious and coarse John Wilkes was fascinated into respect and admiration: he pronounced her the most beautiful flower that ever grew in nature's garden. "This beautiful mother of a beautiful race" united so many charms, was so gifted by art as well by nature, as to surpass the ordinary beings of the earth. The incense that was offered at her shrine doubtless produced some influence upon her mind, which from her earliest years had been accustomed to the sweetest sounds of flattery. She was taught by a host of admirers that she was the theme of general adoration; she listened to the voice of the charmer, and the ill nature of the world, which never brooks superiority in an individual, accused her of coquetry, of levity, nay, of forgetfulness of the high duties which women are called upon to perform, when they would be held up as examples to their sex. Still she was a ministering angel to Sheridan; and whatever may have been the occasional sources of their disunion, she entered into all his cares and anxieties with the devotion of an attached and affectionate woman. Her letters breathe a spirit of tender love, of pride in the man of her choice, of deep anxiety and solicitude for his success in each of his undertakings. She assisted him in all the varieties of public character he was called on to assume; the dramatist, the manager of a playhouse, the statesman, found in her one fully capable of appreciating his powers, of embellishing them, of drawing them out. She was an admirable judge of poesy—herself a poet; she was a useful critic of the drama; she was skilled in electioneering; and everything that to him was an object of importance became for her a source of inquiry. Probably most of the readers of "Moore's Life of Sheridan" have felt that the chapter dedicated to the death of Mrs. Sheridan is one of the most perfect of all that have appeared; and to that we must refer for an insight into the character of this most interesting woman. He has collected together a number of letters that exhibit, in their full charms, all the bright virtues with which she was adorned, and sufficiently account for the deep grief which her loss inflicted upon her husband. Whatever may have been those imperfections which she, in common with the rest of mankind, inherited, they of course were forgotten, and quickly buried in oblivion; whilst memory loved to cherish the remembrance of those fascinations which charmed all who approached her. Sheridan mourned over his sad loss, and turned with hope to a child in whom he thought, perhaps, he might see her mother's virtues, and her mother's charms reflected. Of this consolation, however, he was deprived; she died under circumstances which must have poignantly added to his grief. " A large party was assembled at Sheridan's to spend a joyous evening in dancing, all were in the height of merriment; he himself remarkably cheerful, and partaking of the amusement, when the alarm was given that the dear little angel was dying. It is impossible to describe the confusion and horror of the scene." His affliction was severe. The child, in death, was so like her mother that every one was struck with the resemblance; for four or five days Sheridan lingered over the remains. His sense then taught him to bear up against the affliction, which had bent him down, and he became resigned to the loss of his cherished hopes.

Kelly says, " I never beheld more poignant grief than Mr. Sheridan felt for the loss of his beloved wife; and, although the world, which knew him only as a public man, will perhaps scarcely credit the fact, I have seen him night after night sit and cry like a child, while I sang to him, at his desire, a pathetic little song of my composition—

"'They bore her to a grassy grave.'"

On the 13th of December the House assembled; during the vacation the aspect of affairs had gradually become more serious. The speech from the throne announced the necessity of calling out the militia; that there existed a design to attempt the overthrow of the constitution, evidently pursued in connection and concert with persons in foreign countries; that the utmost efforts had been made to observe a strict neutrality in the war on the continent, and to avoid any interference in the internal affairs of France. But there existed strong and increasing indications there of a determination to excite disturbance in other countries, to disregard the rights of neutral nations, to extend its limits by conquest, as well as to adopt, towards other states, general measures not conformable with the laws of nations or existing treaties It was incumbent on Parliament to take steps to augment the naval and military force, and to maintain internal tranquillity. The speech concluded.

The address was moved by Sir James Sanderson, the Lord Mayor of London, and seconded by Mr. Wallace. An amendment was moved by Mr. Fox, who, looking upon it as the production of the ministry, felt that he had a right to deny the assertions contained in the speech; he did not believe in the existence of an insurrection, nor any desire to excite one; that the alarm only existed in the artful designs and practices of the ministry; there never was at home a greater spirit of loyalty; and as for those who were fighting for liberty in France, he wished them success. His amendment was, " that the House should enter into an immediate examination of the facts which were stated in the speech, and had been the cause of thus summoning Parliament." An animated debate ensued; in which, on one side, the opinions of Burke, of Wyndham, and of Dundas, were given; on the other, those of Grey, of Erskine, and of Sheridan.

Wyndham expressed his regret that he was compelled to oppose his former friends, but was satisfied that the nation was in peril; and though there might be tranquillity on the surface, there was beneath confusion and tumult.

Sheridan's speech was concise, but admirably to the point. " He believed the formidable band of republicans which had been mentioned to exist in this country to be men in buckram." " Such was his idea of the character of Englishmen, that he would take upon him to assert, that were but one French soldier to land upon our coast, under the idea of effecting any change in our government, every hand and heart in the country would be roused by the indignity, and unite to oppose so insulting an attempt." " As to the question of war, he should vote that English ministers be impeached who should enter into a war for the purpose of re-establishing the former despotism in France; who should dare in such a cause to spend one guinea, or shed one drop of blood."

The amendment was negatived. The majority of the minister had, by the desertion of so many from the Whig party, largely increased; 200 voted with him, 50 against him. Mr. Fox, still desirous that peace should be maintained, moved, on the following day, an amendment—"Trusting that your Majesty will employ every species of negotiation, to prevent the calamities of war, that may be deemed consistent with the honour and dignity of the British nation." He was seconded by Sheridan. "Peace he wished for, by all means peace;" but, he added, "if it could not be obtained, he should vote for vigorous war—not a war of shifts and scraps, of timid operation or protracted effort, but a war conducted with such energy as shall evince to the world that the nation was fighting for its dearest and most invaluable privileges" The motion was negatived; but undismayed by defeat, desirous that the nation should not plunge into that long and fearful train of calamities which war brings with it, Fox, even on the following day, proposed that a minister should be sent to France to treat with the provisional committee. Burke observed, "that he thought the debate should not proceed during the unavoidable absence of Mr. Pitt, who was absent at Cambridge, for the university of which he was canvassing." Sheridan replied : " He must be excused for paying no respect whatever to the observation of a right honourable gentleman (Mr. Burke), that it was improper to bring forward these discussions in the absence of his Majesty's first minister ! This was a tender respect to the dignity of office in that right honourable gentleman; but he must be permitted to say, that the representation of the country was indeed placed in a degraded light, if it was to be maintained that the great council of the nation was not, in this momentous crisis, a competent court to discuss the dearest interests of the people, unless the presence of a certain minister of the crown sanctioned their deliberations. But on what ground did they regret the absence of the treasury leader? Had there appeared any want of numbers or ability to compensate for this loss? What exertion that he could have furnished had been unsupplied? Had there been any want of splendid and sonorous declamation to cover a meagreness of argument? Any

want of virulence of invective to supply the place of proof
in accusation? Any want of inflammatory appeals to the
passions where reason and judgment were unsafe to be resorted to? Unquestionably, in all these respects, the Chancellor of the Exchequer had not been missed; in one article
indeed they might be justified in regretting his absence.
They had been pressed to prove the facts asserted in the
king's speech and in the proclamation; not an atom of information could any present member of the government
furnish; doubtless, therefore, the insurrection was a secret
deposited in the breast of the Chancellor of the Exchequer;
and he had taken in his pocket all the proofs of the plot to
assist his election at Cambridge." He then touched upon
what is now universally acknowledged, that the French nation
was maddened by the interference of foreign powers; that to
them all the horrors that stained that glorious desire to be
free, which marked the first onset of the Revolution, are
owing. He asked, " Were the free and generous people of
England ready to subscribe to the Duke of Brunswick's manifesto? that hateful outrage on the rights and feelings of
human nature; that wretched tissue of impotent pride, folly
and inhumanity; that proclamation which had steeled the
heart and maddened the brain of all France; which had provoked those it had devoted to practise all the cruelties it had
impotently threatened to inflict; which had sharpened the
daggers of the assassins of the 2nd of September; which had
whetted the axe now suspended over the unfortunate monarch;
—was the nation ready to subscribe to this absurd and detestable rhapsody? An honourable officer (Sir James Murray) had
attempted to defend his performance—but how? By deny
ing that it intended what it professed and threatened. From
a British officer of his character and understanding a different
defence might be expected; the honourable baronet had given
instances where the conduct of the Prussian army contradicted
the spirit of their manifesto;—what instances on the contrary
side might be adduced he would not then discuss. One case
alone had been sufficient to decide him as to the true spirit
of the league — the brutal rigour with which La Fayette
had been treated: whatever else he was, he was a brave man,
and he was in their power. The use they had made of
that power sufficiently showed how they would have treated

others whom they might well consider as entitled to tenfold enmity." This speech was, indeed, worthy the occasion, and was amongst his happiest efforts in defence of his feelings and his opinions.

Goaded on to madness by the injudicious interference of foreign powers, feeling that they could place no reliance on royal promises, that all was hollowness and subterfuge, the French nation committed a mighty crime which separated it from the rest of Europe. A feeble yet good king—the very original from whom Shakspere might have drawn his Henry the Sixth—was sacrificed; the apprehension of such a catastrophe had for some time haunted the imagination of those who were most eager for that temperate reform of abuses to which they trusted that the French Revolution would have gradually led. No one can read the speech which Sheridan next made in the House, whilst yet the fearful tribunal was sitting, which might commit an act of inhuman cruelty, without feeling that he was actuated by the sincerest love of his country, and the hope that the furious spirit raging in Paris might be allayed. It was on the 20th of December, when Mr. Hobart brought up a report from the committee of supply granting 25,000 men for the service of the year, that he expressed sentiments which even his adversaries, with the exception of him who was called " the Renegade" Burke, applauded. He stated "that he was most willing, should the hateful necessity arise, to join in the unanimous support of the House to every proposition tending to give vigour and effect to the war; still he thought that there existed in France a sincere disposition to listen to and respect the opinion of the British nation; he in his soul and conscience believed that there was not one man of any party or description who did not deprecate, and who would not deplore the fate of those persecuted and unfortunate victims, should the apprehended catastrophe take place; amongst those whose hearts would be most revolted and disgusted, would be those who had been foremost in rejoicing at the destruction of the old despotism in France, and who had eagerly hoped, that, to whatever extremes, as to principles of government, a momentary enthusiasm might lead a people new to the light of liberty, that however wild their theories might be, yet there would have appeared in the quiet, deliberate acts of their conduct those inseparable characteristics of real liberty, and of true valour, justice, magnanimity, and mercy." Burke rose and reprobated the use of such words. "The truth was, the king was in the hands of assassins, who were both his accusers and his judges, and his destruction was inevitable." He launched out into misrepresentations, to which Sheridan replied, observing, "he would not attribute them to any ill purpose, or any ill motive, but to ill temper, that had so run away with him, that he scarcely knew what he meant, or what he said." Events rapidly succeeded each other, scarcely a day intervened without some new shock to public feeling by the impetuous progress of the Revolution. The execution of the king decided many who had previously wavered in their opinions; the Whig party in Parliament dwindled to the smallest span, the great mass of the people were awe-struck by the daring act, and listened to the approach of war with less repugnance than was expected; nay, they even doubted the sagacity of Pitt, who seemed to hesitate, until he was urged on by his new associates. At length, on the 12th of February, the message came from the throne, announcing that a declaration of war had been made; an address was moved, assuring his Majesty that he might rely on the firm and effectual support of the representatives of the people in the prosecution of a just and necessary war Mr. Fox's amendment still led to the expression of a hope that a pacification should be the means followed. Burke opposed him in language totally uncalled for; he laid great stress upon the fact that the healths of Fox and of Sheridan had been received with great enthusiasm in Paris. He dwelt upon the impiety of the French, their open avowal of Atheism, and was bitter upon his former friends, exulting at the diminution of their numbers, and designating them as a phalanx.

Sheridan greatly distinguished himself by his memorable reply: he brought the full force of his eloquence into play, mingling retort, ridicule, and argument in the most forcible manner. He said that he was provoked to rise by the insinuations and charges of Mr. Burke against his honourable friend Fox. Never before had he indulged himself in such a latitude of ungoverned bitterness and spleen towards the man he still occasionally professed to respect. His ridicule of the smallness of the number of friends left to the object of his persecution, ill became him, of all mankind; but he trusted, however small that number was, there ever would be found among them men not afraid, upon such a subject, to oppose truth and temper to passion and declamation, however eloquently urged or clamorously applauded. He made a bold attack on the different set of principles he had at different times urged, and taunted him with his own changes of views, which ought to forbid his allusion to the change of opinion in others. "A book was produced, and he was proceeding to read a former speech of his (Mr. Fox's), as if he had ever once retracted his opinion on this subject. When the Speaker called him to order, the honourable gentleman did not seem to take the interruption kindly, though certainly he ought to have been grateful for it; for never, sure, was there a man who had a greater interest in discouraging the practice of contrasting the past and present speeches, principles and professions of any public man. Was the hon. gentleman ready to invite such a discussion respecting himself? If he were, and his consistency could be matter of regular question in that House, he did not scruple to assert that there was scarcely an iota of his new principles to which there was not a recorded contradiction in his former professions. Let a set of his works be produced, one member might read, paragraph by paragraph, his present doctrines, and another should refute every syllable of them out of the preceding ones; it was a consolation to those who differed from his new principles to know where to resort for the best antidote to them."

His invectives against Burke were concluded by a bitter attack upon the Allies then marching on France; he preferred seeing England fight single-handed against France. He feared the enemy less than the Ally; he disliked the cause of war, but abhorred the company we were to fight in still more. He denounced the conduct of the Allies in the Polish Revolution, as having massacred the fairest offspring of virtue —truth, and valour. "Could the right honourable gentleman palliate these things? No! But had he ever arraigned them? Why had he never come to brandish in that House a Russian dagger, red in the heart's blood of the free constitution of Poland? No; not a word, not a sigh, not an ejaculation for the destruction of all he had held up to the world as a model for reverence and imitation! In his heart is a record of brass for every error and excess of liberty, but on his

M

tongue a sponge to blot out the foulest crimes and blackest
treacheries of despotism." This allusion to the fact, that on
one occasion Burke went to the House of Commons, and with
prodigious attempt at stage effect, brandished a dagger which
his fancy or bewildered imagination led him to believe was
precisely similar to one which must be used in the French
Revolution, told with great effect upon the House.

Mr. Sheridan gave notice of his intention to bring forward
a motion relative to the existence of seditious practices in the
country; and, with a view of obtaining a full attendance, a call
of the House was ordered for the 4th of March, but when
the motion was to be brought forward after the ordinary business, no Mr. Sheridan made his appearance. Mr. Lambton
apologized; Mr. Thornton moved an adjournment; Mr. Fox
hoped every body would be punctual; Sir Henry Houghton
thought that a minister ought to be waited for; Mr. Pitt said
he was always anxious to be punctual; and everything was
said that could be said to gain time, and to allay the murmurs which began to rise, and the many little anecdotes
which were whispered about Sheridan never being punctual,
when at last he appeared, with a very proper apology in his
mouth, and one of his best speeches. He laughed at the supposed sedition, the lurking treason, and the panic; of the
latter he gave a good picture, and placed his late friends,
Wyndham and Burke, in the foreground. "This panic had
already had a great effect; and, indeed, it was much too general an impression to proceed from real danger; a general
panic was always created by phantoms and imaginary evils.
It had been always so in the panics of armies; for instance,
he believed that there was not once to be found in history an
instance in which the panic of an army had proceeded from
real danger; it always proceeded either from accident or some
stratagem of the enemy. Indeed the thing bore evidence for
itself; had the danger been real, there must have been a
difference of opinion as to the amount of it; for while there
was a difference in the size and character of the understand-
ings of men, there must be a difference in their opinions;
but those who believed anything upon the tales of sedition,
which he had before alluded to, believed everything that was
said about it, and that of itself proved its fallacy. There were
numerous instances recorded, both in prose and verse, where

nations had been misled, and had acted upon such false alarms.
There were many instances in which a panic had been communicated by one class of men to the other.

> ' ———— Sic quisque pavendo
> Dat vires famæ: nulloque auctore malorum,
> Quæ finxere timent. Nec solum vulgus inani
> Percussum terrore pavet: Sed curia, et ipsi
> Sedibus exiluere patres, invisaque belli
> Consulibus fugiens mandat decreta senatus.'

"His friend (Mr. Wyndham) had been panic-struck, and now
strengthened the hand of government, who, last session, agreeable to a vulgar adage, ' Rolled his Majesty's ministers in
the dirt.' At that period he pulled off the mask of perfidy,
and declaimed loudly against that implicit confidence which
some had argued ought to be placed in ministers. He now
thought such arguments were impolitic, and no man was more
strenuous for that confidence which he had before with so
much warmth reprobated. Another friend (Mr. Burke), to
whose doctrines Mr. Wyndham had become a convert, had
also been panic-struck. He had been so affected that he saw
nothing but a black and clouded sky; a bleak opposition,
where there was not a shrub or bush to shelter him from the
gloomy aspect of public affairs; but he had taken refuge in
the ministerial gaberdine, where he hoped for security from
the approaching storm."

It was in this speech that the motto of the *Sun* newspaper
afforded him one of his happiest hits. The lines selected by
the original proprietor of the journal were—

> ———"Solem quis dicere falsum
> Audeat?"

It was also on this occasion that he taunted Burke as hav
ing quitted the camp, but of returning to it as a spy.

A few nights afterwards Pitt took the House by surprise,
by a most eloquent speech, when stating the ways and means
for the ensuing year; he recommended unanimity and liberality in the supplies, but at the same time to watch with vigilance and even jealousy. Sheridan spoke in reply with great
readiness. "He said he gave the minister credit for the fairness
of some of his observations; but he must frankly say he had
felt the jealousy recommended much awakened by the very
extraordinary and sudden appeal to the passions of the House.

There was little novelty in it, excepting the novelty of introducing, in a day devoted to figures, all the arts of declamation He had suddenly laid down his pencil and slate, as it were, and grasping the truncheon, had finished with an harangue, more calculated for the general of an army going to storm a French redoubt, than a minister of finance discussing accounts, in a sober hour of calculation, with the stewards and attorneys of a burdened people."

The debates on the Traitorous Correspondence Bill furnished him with several opportunities of expressing his opinion upon the fallacious views entertained of the existence of treason. Lord Auckland's memorial to the States General, and the Sheffield Petition for Parliamentary Reform, both engaged his attention. He had several opportunities of coming into collision with Burke, and seemed rather to court them; he contrived to praise his eloquence, but to stigmatize his opinions. On one occasion, after his usual compliments to his wit, mirth and humour, he said he generally employed them on subjects which did not call for either; but wars, treasons, murders, or massacres. In alluding to Burke's praise of the King of Prussia, he compared the king's conduct in Dantzic with that of France—no act of hers was more desperate or more infamous. The party robbed cared not whether he was plundered by a man with a white feather, or one with a nightcap on his head; but a head with a crown, and a head with a nightcap totally altered the moral quality of the action —death inflicted by a hand wielding a pike was murder, swaying a sceptre was innocent.

The session of this year was opened on the 24th of January. The address from the throne stated that upon the issue of the contest in which the nation was engaged depended the maintenance of the constitution, laws, religion, and the security of civil society; it dwelt upon the advantages obtained. by the allied forces, and the necessity of prosecuting the war with energy and vigour; it stated that the internal discontent and confusion in France were produced by a system which violated every restraint of justice, humanity, and religion; that the principles which were promulgated in France, tended to destroy all property, to subvert the laws and the religion of every civilized nation, and to introduce universally that wild and destructive system of rapine, anarchy, and impiety—the effects of which, as manifested in France, furnished a dreadful but useful lesson to the present age and posterity. The speech was of considerable length, and called upon the nation— in what is now considered a hackneyed style, though then admired as original—to exert itself to pay for all the expenses of the war.

Lord Mornington, after the mover and the seconder had gone through the usual routine of saying a vast deal about nothing in the ordinary form of eloquence, commenced an elaborate speech to prove that, as long as the French maintained the principles they had adopted, the war should not be relinquished. "Mr. Sheridan began with observing, that the noble lord who had just sat down had divided a speech, more remarkable for its ability than its brevity, into two parts: the first, a detail of all the atrocities that had been committed during the whole course of the Revolution in France; the second a kind of posthumous arraignment of the offences of Brissot and his associates. As he did not perceive any noble or learned member inclined to rise on behalf of the accused, so he conceived the pleadings on the part of the prosecution to be closed; and as the Speaker was evidently not proceeding to sum up the evidence, he hoped he might be permitted to recall the attention of the House to the real object of that day's consideration. He admired the emphasis of the noble lord in reading his voluminous extracts from his various French documents; he admired, too, the ingenuity he had displayed in his observations upon those extracts; but he could not help farther expressing his admiration, that the noble lord should have thought proper to have taken up so many hours in quoting passages in which not one word in ten was to the purpose; and often where they did apply to the question, they directly overset the principles they were brought forward to support." He then delivered a speech which has been handed down to us corrected by himself; hence are we enabled to form some opinion of the readiness with which he could answer an opponent, the immense mass of matter connected with the politics of Europe that he had thoroughly digested, and the soundness of the views of the party he represented. Had this speech only remained for the judgment of posterity of the general principles maintained, and the soundness of the policy pursued by the advocates for peace, it would have been enough. The frenzy, folly, rashness of individuals in France had been roused by the surrounding nations, their fears had been excited, great and dreadful enormities had been committed at which the heart shuddered, and which not merely wounded every feeling of humanity, but disgusted and sickened the soul—all this was most true; but what did it prove?—what but that eternal and unalterable truth which had always presented itself to his mind. A few days afterwards Sheridan took occasion to explain to the minister, who in his simplicity and innocence seemed to be ignorant of its meaning, the nature of a ministerial job; and he gave a curious list of persons who had received money for services not performed, observing that he was only influenced by motives of good-will to the persons Mr. Pitt very injudiciously asked, if he made that assertion, could any member of the House credit it. Mr. Sheridan was about to rise, when he was interrupted by Mr. Fox declaring that in his opinion, founded upon experience, Mr. Sheridan had as much personal credit in that House as Mr. Pitt. Sheridan rose: "Whether," said he, "if I repeat my assertion, any member of the House will doubt it, or not, I cannot say; but I believe that it is in this House alone that the right honourable gentleman will venture to tell me so." The subject, however, dropped, after some remarks from Mr. Hanley and Mr. Yorke on the impropriety of personalities during the serious business of the House. Mr. Sheridan spoke this session ably on several subjects which have now lost their interest; such as on the naval force at that period; on the defensive state of Halifax; on a petition from Fyscho Palmer suffering from imprisonment; on a judgment of the court of session in Scotland upon the introduction of foreign troops into the country; on voluntary aid for raising troops without the consent of Parliament; and on taxing placemen upon the suspension of the Habeas Corpus Act.

At length Drury Lane was rebuilt; heavy had been the expenses and the disappointments; and, above all, the law had been appealed to. On the 10th of March, a grand concert, formed of selections from Handel, collected together a large audience, and on the 21st of April the first dramatic performance took place. The play was "Macbeth," the afterpiece, "The Virgin Unmasked." The prologue on the occasion was by General Fitzpatrick. The house was found generally well adapted for performances, and gave great satisfaction. There was a tribute to the memory of the old house, which was universally approved of; a plank of the stage, which Garrick had so often trod, was preserved, and formed a part of the new flooring. In a short time a little piece was brought out by Sheridan in honour of Lord Howe's victory; it was called the "First of June."

On the 30th of December, parliament met for the despatch of business; Sheridan was at his post, still maintaining the same opinions, still fighting against his great adversary. A speech of his upon the repeal of the Bill for suspending the Habeas Corpus Act gave him an opportunity, of which he fully availed himself, of showing that it was uncalled for by the state of the country; he expatiated on the detestable sys-tem of spies and informers, of the charges of sedition, of levying war, of trials, and solemnly asked Mr. Pitt, what would be the state of the country which would restore to British freemen the most glorious bulwark of their freedom. Upon Mr. Fox's motion for a committee on the state of the nation he spoke with great ability; the two friends, backed by a small minority, still continued to express with freedom those opinions which were entertained by a large body of men in England, who, satisfied with the security which the laws gave them, wished for no other change but such as would give to the people at large more ample opportunity of expressing their wishes through their representatives, and whose desire was such a reform in the House of Commons, as might take from the proprietors of boroughs the preponderating influence they held.

On the 1st of June, Mr. Anstruther, Solicitor General to the Prince of Wales, as Duke of Cornwall, acquainted the House that his Royal Highness had authorized him to assure the House that he was anxious that some regulation should be adopted for the purpose of establishing order and regu-larity in the expenditure of his income, and to prevent the incurring of debt in future, and further, to appropriate such a part of his income for the liquidation of his debts as might seem proper to the House. The prince was no longer on terms of intimacy with the leading Whigs, nor did they feel any wish to renew their homage to him. Mr. Grey, although he would vote for his having an income sufficient to support him in his position, would not pay his debts from the money of the people. Mr. Fox asked if he was well advised to apply to the House after the promise in 1787. Mr. Sheridan thought the prince's debts ought to be paid, but his Majesty should set the example. He accused those who had given him advice. By the plan now proposed, the prince had not the grace of suggesting retrenchments, nor the checks upon his future conduct. His past misconduct was exhibited in the harshest point of view; he was set in a gilded pillory, sent to do public penance in an embroidered sheet. He was left in possession of too much income to exempt him from envy, and too little to exempt him from scorn. To pay the debts something ought to be given by the king. He afterwards proposed that the estates belonging to the Duchy of Cornwall should be sold to assist in the liquidation of the debts. Mr. Sheridan continued to make remarks on the king. In the course of the debates he repudiated having received any reward, as had been insinuated, from the Prince of Wales, and positively asserted in the face of the Parliament and the country that he had not even been presented with a horse or a picture, and that he was independent in his views and opinions of the Royal Prince.

Whenever the opportunity presented itself, Sheridan pursued his former friend, Burke, with the same determination he had done in the previous session; but some of the allusions are now almost unintelligible sarcasms. Ill-natured observations abounded on both sides. A quotation from a convivial writer of the day, Captain Morris, whose songs are almost now forgotten, was hailed from Burke with great cheers by his party, and responded to by Sheridan's friends, when he had with great felicity quoted also from the same author. On the occasion of the Volunteer Bill, Mr. Francis expressed his regret that all freedom of debate was lost by confining every discussion to three or four persons. That if it were the object of eloquence to weary and deaden the attention of an unhappy audience, to exhaust all patience, to stupify rather than convince, then, indeed, the gentlemen he alluded to were supremely eloquent. Mr. Burke said he should take the hint which was drawn from a writer of very high authority with the gentleman opposite.

"Solid men of Boston, make no long potations,
Solid men of Boston, make no long orations,
      Bow, wow, wow."

Sheridan observed that the injunction against long orations was not the only moral precept in that system of ethics alluded to. He would remind him of another passage :—

" He went to Daddy Jenky, by Trimmer Hall attended,
In such good company! good lack! how his morals must be mended."

Mr. Burke complained of the attack upon his morals. Sheridan answered—"He had supposed him to have a superabundance, and he might spare some to the gentlemen that surrounded him." Once again was Sheridan called upon to appear in Wesminster Hall as an accuser of Warren Hastings. On the 14th of May, he replied to the evidence and arguments offered by the counsel for Mr. Hastings, in answer to the Begum charge. It was customary for a brother manager to accompany the manager who was to speak, with a bag containing whatever minutes might be referred to. Michael Angelo Taylor was the individual upon whom this duty devolved; and he requested Sheridan to give him the bag and papers. Sheridan's answer was "he had none, and he must get on as well as he could without them." "He would abuse Ned Law, afterwards Lord Ellenborough, ridicule Plumer's long speech, make the court laugh, please the women, and, in short, with Taylor's aid, would get triumphantly through his task." The case was opened, and he got on very well for some time, but the chancellor asked for a minute to which he was referring; Sheridan said his friend Taylor would read it. Mr. Taylor despatched a messenger for the bag, whilst Sheridan requested permission in the mean time to proceed. But soon again the chancellor wished to see the minutes; a great outcry was raised for the bag; the blame was laid on the solicitor's clerk; another messenger was sent off to Sheridan's house. On went Sheridan brilliantly and cleverly; and when the chancellor a third time anxiously required the minute, Sheridan, with great coolness and dignity, said: "On the part of the Commons, and as a manager of the impeachment, I shall conduct my case as I think proper. I mean to be correct, and your lordships, having the printed minutes before you, will afterwards see whether I am right or wrong." Fox, who was in the manager's room, ran eagerly to the Hall, and, fearing that Sheridan would suffer inconvenience from the want of the bag, asked Taylor what could be done; he, hiding his mouth with his hand, whispered him, as Moore says, in a tone of which they alone who have heard the gentleman relate the anecdote can feel the full humour, "The man has no bag." The speech itself is so poor, when contrasted with his former efforts upon the same subject, that it is not surprising that it has been universally condemned; and the introduction of some observations on woman, her fortitude, her power of bearing suffering, which have been much applauded, was altogether in worse taste than Sheridan usually exhibited. He had, however, upon the two former occasions, exhausted every source of interest; and spoke unprepared and almost forgetful of the subject of his former triumphs.

The session of 1795 commenced untowardly. The people of the humbler class in London were doubtless much irritated at the constant suspicions of disloyalty which the ministers so loudly proclaimed; their irritation was excessive; they disliked the repeal of the Habeas Corpus Act, which they had been taught to believe was the palladium of their liberty. The line of conduct pursued by Mr. Pitt was too evidently in favour of rank and wealth, and of those classes that enjoyed privileges which were denied to them. There was no outlet for the expression of their feelings; the press was gagged; for prosecutions for libel, whilst they only pretended to prevent sedition, were most unwisely urged against the free expression of thoughts very generally entertained by those whom neither corruption nor power could intimidate. The hatred of the system showed itself on the occasion of his Majesty's progress to Parliament, for the purpose of opening the session.

On the 29th of October the king went, with the usual pomp, to the house of peers; an opportunity which the people of London usually embrace to receive the monarch with the expression of the loyalty which animates their hearts. It is not only curiosity which collects so many together; but there is always an anxiety to know how the sovereign will be received. The park was on this day thronged; but instead of loud acclamations from a contented people, there were loud murmurs, groans, and threatening words. The carriage was surrounded by persons loudly demanding " the dismissal of Mr. Pitt; peace;" and even the expression "down with the king" was heard. As it approached the Horse Guards, stones were thrown at the king's carriage. In passing through Palace Yard a window was broken; and it was asserted that this had been done by an air gun. His Majesty, with great calmness and composure, proceeded to execute the function for which the day was to be remarked—the delivery of the speech from the throne—and then returned to Buckingham Palace. But the infuriated populace had increased in numbers, in daring, and in violence; and with considerable difficulty did the royal cortège proceed from St. James's to Buckingham Palace. The speech was, in every sense of the word, unsatisfactory. Sheridan was exceedingly happy in his comments upon it. It commenced with "It is a great satisfaction to me to reflect that, notwithstanding the many unfavourable events:" he observed, "He would venture to say, if any person could have previously known the speech, and had written to any part of England or Scotland, they would not have found a single man who would not have been surprised at the first noun substantive being satisfaction; or at that substantive being used in any other part of the speech. It was said to be the mark of a resigned and religious temper to be easily satisfied. If that were true, there never were ministers of more meek and primitive piety than the present; for what they had been satisfied he knew not.". He then took a view of affairs foreign and domestic, and expressed his astonishment that ministers could suffer the king, when he passed through his starving and oppressed people—and, sorry was he to hear, irritated and clamorous people—to come down to the House and express his satisfaction. He spoke of the wretched and miserable expedition to Quiberon, where it was true the blood of French emigrants only had flowed; it was not British blood, but British honour that bled at every vein. He believed that all the efforts made were to restore the House of Bourbon—a race always inimical to England as far as he could judge of the spirit of their intentions; from their prevarications he thought they were simply watching for an opportunity of effecting a counter revolution for the establishment of monarchy, and placing Louis XVIII. upon the throne.

The violent conduct of the people had now given to the administration the pretence which they had so long wanted. They could no longer be told that disaffection existed in their own imaginations, that the plots were of their own begetting, that their spies and their informers had concocted the tales which alarmed the timid, and imposed upon the credulous. "The King of England had," said they, " encountered a reception, such as the regicides of Paris had given to their king." The Lords and the Commons addressed the king after evidence had been taken of the outrage of the day. A Bill was brought into the House of Commons for securing the king's person and government against treasonable and seditious practices, and several days were occupied in its consideration. Sheridan took a prominent part in the discussion, and his speeches were full of vigour, thought, and wit. During one of the debates he related a curious anecdote respecting himself, in consequence of some observations of Mr. Hardinge on the licence of the stage; showing that the restrictions were in principle moral, and not political. " The origin of the licence was in order to repress indecencies and abuses, such as a man must want common decorum to introduce. As a proof that the licence was sometimes abused, on the night before the first appearance of the " School for Scandal," he was informed that it could not be performed, as a licence was refused. It happened at this time there was the famous city contest between Wilkes and Hopkins; the latter had been charged with some practices, similar to those of Moses the Jew, in lending money to young men under age, and it was supposed that the character of the play was levelled at him, in order to injure him in his contest, in which he was supported by the ministerial interest. In the warmth of a contested election the piece was represented as a factious and seditious opposition to a court candidate. Sheridan, however, went to Lord Hertford, then Lord Chamberlain, who laughed at the affair, and gave the licence. For his own part he deemed a theatre no fit place for politics; nor would he think much of the principles or taste of the man who should wish to introduce them into stage representation." On the 23rd of November, Mr. Stuart brought up a petition against the Bill from the London Corresponding Society. He produced a work, attributed to Mr. Reeves, the framer and president of several associations against republicans and levellers, in which a doctrine was asserted "that the government of England was a monarchy; but the monarch was the ancient stock, from which have sprung those goodly branches of the legislature—the Lords and Commons; that these, however, were still only branches, and that they might be lopped off, and the tree be a tree still, shorn, indeed, of its honours, but not, like them, cast into the fire." The pamphlet was read. Sheridan moved "that the said pamphlet is a malicious, scandalous, and seditious libel, containing matter tending to create jealousies and divisions amongst his Majesty's subjects; to alienate the affection from our present form of government, and subvert the true principles of our free constitution, and that the said pamphlet is a high breach of the privileges of this House." He made several speeches, and concluded by moving, "that the books be burnt by the common hangman." This punishment was all he proposed; he peremptorily objected to a prosecution. Ministers, however, preferred a trial, as they thought some of its odium would naturally fall on the Whigs, and they did not object to their willingness to increase the list of libellers. Sheridan said that he never recommended prosecutions for libels, because ministers had taken such matters into their own hands; he read a list of fifty or sixty persons who in the last three years had been prosecuted. He knew, that if Mr. Reeves were found guilty, he would be called a convicted innocent, as others had been called acquitted felons. The trial, however, was resolved on; Sheridan having been induced no longer to oppose it, of course an acquittal took place, in a case where neither party took any interest in the trial.

The incidents attendant upon Sheridan's first marriage excited some surprise, and if those which marked the second hymen are not altogether as wondrous, they are sufficient to show that he had not forgotten his powers over the female heart, and that, when he chose, he could successfully exert it. He was at the mature age of forty-four, when the charms of Miss Esther Jane Ogle, daughter of the Dean of Winchester, and grand-daughter of the former Bishop of Winchester, by the mother's side, appeared so irresistible, that he was determined, in spite of any obstacle, to become her affianced husband. The first interview of the two personages was any thing but flattering to the vanity of Sheridan, and leads us to form an inference that nothing but his determination to conquer, and his firm reliance upon his own resolves, would have ultimately led to a consummation of his hopes. At a fête given at Devonshire House sat Miss Ogle, where Sheridan for the first time saw her; he was walking before her; he heard her exclamation, "fright! terrible creature!" and other names of similar unmistakable import, applied to himself; for this elegant young lady it seems, with bewitching frankness, was in the habit of openly giving epithets which she thought appropriate to men and things. Sheridan's countenance had, at this period of his life, lost much of the manly beauty it might once have had; little remained but the brilliancy of his eye; intemperance had stamped her marks upon his features in legible characters; the purple cheek, the fiery nose, its common offsprings, were too strongly developed not to be discerned by the quick glance of woman; indeed they had already begun to be subjects of public comment, and served for the merriment of a hustings mob, where allusions often, in his latter day more especially, were made to his being able to light a fire by the glare of his nose. Whether Sheridan felt that the young lady's reproach might be true or not, he was at any rate determined that, notwithstanding the visible defects of his outward form, he would, by the fascinations of his mind, efface the first impression; certain it is that he exerted himself to please, and succeeded. Even his first advances produced some slight civility, the next meeting a little attention, another, a declaration from her that, although he was a monster, he was very clever; she subsequently found that though he was very ugly, he was very agreeable. Gradually there was a little emotion experienced at his presence, at length her heart was irresistibly attracted, and then altogether lost. He was, indeed, the only man with whom she could live: mutual vows of love and fidelity were exchanged. The dean, her father, was consulted; any hint from him at the disparity of their years was unheeded; he in vain hesitated—they urged. He learnt enough of the private affairs of Sheridan to convince him that it would be what the world terms a bad match; he thought that he had found out a decent excuse to prevent the ill-assorted marriage, which was, to say that he would not give his consent to his daughter's union with any man who could not put down fifteen thousand pounds in addition to five which he himself would give for a settlement upon his daughter; this he flattered himself would bring the affair to a conclusion, for where Sheridan was to find such a sum no ordinary mind could have imagined. But such were the admirable financial contrivances of his future son-in-law, that the dean found the money safely lodged in the banker's hands, to his own confusion, and the astonishment even of the most enthusiastic admirer of the skill of Sheridan. There was no deceit about it, shares were sold in Drury Lane Theatre, an estate called Polesden, at Leatherhead in Surrey, was purchased; it was carefully settled upon Mrs. Sheridan and her children; the trustees to this settlement being the late Lord Grey and Mr. Whitbread. The young lady, charming and desperately in love, was quickly united to the man of her choice, and they went to Southampton to enjoy the honeymoon, enraptured in each other's society—such was the progress of the love-match.

Sheridan of course reflected that he must take an early opportunity of imparting the information of his intended marriage to his son Tom, who was at that moment supposed to be deeply immersed in study, under the care of his tutor, Mr. Smyth, at Bognor, where they had been staying for two or three months without having received the slightest communication; the long silence was at length interrupted by the arrival of a letter, whilst they were at the breakfast table.

"My dear Tom,—Meet me at dinner, at six o'clock on Wednesday next, at Guildford; I forget the inn; I want to see you.—Ever your affectionate father, R. B. S."

This note startled Tom, who marvelled what his father could have to say; a discussion sprung up between pupil and tutor as to the possible cause of this sudden invitation;—was it to propose a seat in Parliament? could it be to point out a good marriage? was it anything to do with Drury Lane Theatre? Sundry conjectures occupied their minds until the eventful Wednesday arrived, when, followed by his groom, off rode Tom. Mr. Smyth was left alone to ruminate until his pupil's return, which he naturally must have expected on the following day; but the Thursday rolled on without his appearance; Friday, Saturday, and Sunday, not a line from either father or son. At length, on Monday, came a letter to this effect:—

"My dear Mr. Smyth,—Here I am, have been, and am

likely to be; my father I have never seen, and all that I can hear of him is, that instead of dining with me on Wednesday last, he passed through Guildford on his way to town, with four horses and lamps, about 12. I have written to him letter after letter to beg he will send me his orders, and at all events some money, for I have only a few shillings, having paid the turnpikes faithfully, and I am so bored and wearied out with waiting here, and seeing neither father nor money, nor any thing but the stable and the street, that I almost begin to wish myself with you and the books again.

" Your dutiful pupil,   T. S."

It must at any rate have been some relief to Mr. Smyth's mind to have read a note acknowledging his pupil's whereabout; but what must have been the state of nervous anxiety in which he was kept for the next ten or twelve weeks, during which he had to pace the beach at Bognor, hoping that every succeeding day might bring with it some solution to this strange enigma? At length came a frank from Sheridan, inclosing an epistle from Tom, which, in some measure, threw a light upon the mysterious occurrences which had naturally excited such singular conduct, both from father and son. He learned from it the step, which he characterizes as one of extreme folly and vanity on both sides, which Sheridan and Miss Ogle were about to take. He could find some excuse for the lady, who was doubtless dazzled by the reputation and fascinated by the conversation of the man, but none for one who had arrived at a period of life when prudence, if he ever possessed any, was called for, and the exertion of his intellects for more useful purposes in life. The answer was to this effect :—

" My dear Mr. Smyth,—It is not I that am to be married, nor you. Set your heart at rest, it is my father himself; the lady, a Miss Ogle, who lives at Winchester; and that is the history of the Guildford business. About my own age—better me to marry her, you will say. I am not of that opinion. My father talked to me two hours last night, and made out to me that it was the most sensible thing he could do. Was not this very clever of him? Well, my dear Mr. S——, you should have been tutor to him, you see. I am incomparably the most rational of the two, and now and ever

" Yours very truly and affectionately,   T. S."

Sheridan, who wanted Wanstead "for his hymeneal doves," was desirous to drive thence his volatile son and his amiable tutor, and determined that they should go to Cambridge. Mr. Smyth, who had received, for his attention to Tom, nothing in the shape of salary, and who saw that, though treated personally with the greatest respect and attention, he was left on every occasion to shift for himself, wrote a strong letter to Sheridan; receiving no answer, he posted to town, determined to tender his resignation. "Never did minister," says he, " enter a royal apartment more full of rage and indignation at the abominable behaviour of his sovereign master than I did the drawing room of Mr. Sheridan. I have since often thought of the interview that passed; of the skill with which Sheridan conducted himself; the patience with which he listened to my complaints, and the concern which he seemed to express by his countenance when I intimated to him that though I had rather serve him for nothing, than the best nobleman in the land for the best salary he could give me, still that my family were in ruin about me, and that it was impossible ——; and that he had used me, since his intended marriage, so unceremoniously, and outraged me in a variety of ways so intolerably, that neither with proper prudence nor proper pride could I continue with him any longer; nor would I sanction, by staying with his son, any measure so contrary to my opinion and so pregnant with ruin, as the one now resolved upon, his going to Cambridge." Sheridan listened with great attention, offering little or no resistance. At last, he began: " All this ruin and folly, which I entirely confess," said he, " originates in this one source, this marriage of mine with Miss Ogle; but you know, my dear Smyth," patting him on the shoulder, " no one is very wise on such subjects. I have no place to put her in but Wanstead. I did not consult you about Tom's going to Cambridge, for I knew you would be quite against it. The boy is totally ruined if you do not accompany him. It will be impossible for any one else to have any chance with him, nor should I be satisfied with any one else. I can not put him in the army, as you suppose, the ministers really make such blundering expeditions. To crown all, the theatre is out of order; our last new piece, the " Iron Chest," that should have been a golden one, is really iron. And the result of my folly—my madness if you please—is that I am worried

N

and tormented to death; and if you, at this moment, desert me and join this general combination of circumstances against me, I know not what is to become of me, and in short, you must give me further trial, and let me see if I cannot redeem myself and make you some amends for your kindness and consideration for me. I do not deserve it, I fully admit."

It may well be imagined that a young and confiding spirit, such as that possessed by Mr. Smyth, was soon soothed and flattered by similar expressions of confidence and regard from a man whose genius had been his charm and delight, and who was looked to, even then, with all his faults, as one of the greatest men of the day. He gradually yielded, and, " at last, like the month of March in the Calendar," says he, " I came into the room like a lion, and went out like a lamb;" " I recovered myself," continues he, " a little as I went down stairs. What a clever fellow this is, I thought to myself as I went out of the door; and, after a few paces down the street, I made one discovery more—what a fool am I!" But the most characteristic incident occurred just at the conclusion of the interview. " I wrote you a letter," said Smyth, " it was but an angry one, you will be so good as to think no more of it." " Oh, certainly not, my dear Smyth!" replied Sheridan, " I shall never think of what you have said in it, be assured." Putting his hand in his pocket, " Here it is," giving it up to Smyth; who was glad enough to get hold of it, and threw it into the fire. " Lo and behold, I saw that it had never been opened." The attachment of Sheridan to his son was of the most affectionate character; his anxiety was constantly shown at school, and whilst he was under the tuition of Mr. Smyth. On one occasion, Sheridan sent for him in the greatest haste from Warwickshire, where he was under the tuition of Dr. Parr, having dreamt that he had seen Tom fall from a high tree, the consequence of which had been a broken neck. It is singular that a man of so much common sense should have been so superstitious; but to his dreams he was wont to give implicit confidence; and another curious fact is that he would neither travel on a Friday, nor allow a new play to be brought out upon that which he considered an unlucky day. If Tom was upon the ice on a frosty day, if he were out shooting, if he were doing anything that Sheridan considered to be attended with danger, there was no peace until he had abandoned it. So much tenderness seems hardly reconcilable with the general conduct of Sheridan; such, however, was it that it could not but tend to render Mr Smyth's charge by no means a pleasant one. Attached, however, to the public character of the father, and pleased with the frank genuine disposition of the son, he seems to have borne, with true philosophy, the awkward position in which he was placed, until no longer human nature could endure it. The younger Sheridan seems to have possessed social qualities of a high order, and to have been endowed with many excellent intellectual qualifications. He had naturally a good voice and a taste for music. Though he returned his father's affection, he was not blind to his faults; he used frequently to lament his indolence and want of regularity, and at times, though proud of his great abilities, was unable to refrain from indulging in sarcasm at his father's expense.

Tom Sheridan was the idol of the young men at Cambridge, who pronounced him the cleverest fellow in the place, as in point of humour and fun he certainly was. His father once said to him, what really was the case, "Tom, you have genius enough to get a dinner every day in the week at the first tables in London, and that is something, but that is all, you can go no further." They thoroughly understood each other; the son was equally complimentary to the father, as many well-known anecdotes testify. On one occasion, Tom Sheridan complained, over the bottle, to him, that his pockets were empty. "Try the highway," was the father's answer. "I have," said Tom, "but I made a bad hit, I stopped a caravan full of passengers who assured me they had not a farthing, for they all belonged to Drury Lane Theatre and could not get a single penny of their salary." Kelly tells a somewhat similar story. He says that father and son were supping with him one night after the Opera, at a period when Tom expected to get into Parliament; "I think, father," says he, "that many men who are called great patriots in the House of Commons are great humbugs. For my own part, if I get into Parliament, I will pledge myself to no party but write upon my forehead, in legible characters, to be let." "And under that, Tom," said his father, "unfurnished." Tom took the joke, but was even with him upon another occasion. Mr. Sheridan had a cottage, about half a mile from Hounslow Heath: Tom, being very short of cash, asked his father to let him have some money; "I have none," was the reply. "Be the consequence what it may, money I must have," said Tom. "If that is the case," said the affectionate parent, "you will find a case of loaded pistols up stairs, and a horse ready saddled in the stable: the night is dark, and you are within half a mile of Hounslow Heath." "I understand what you mean," said Tom, "but I tried that last night, I unluckily stopped Peake, your treasurer, who told me that you had been beforehand with him, and had robbed him of every sixpence in the world."

The session of this year was not distinguished at its commencement by any striking feature. Sheridan had manfully expressed his opinions and his feelings upon the great points which had been agitated; the minor questions which were now brought forward, and were principally to enable the government to carry on the war into which they had entered, engrossed but little of his attention; he carefully abstained from throwing any impediments in the way: he simply pointed out the steps which he thought should be pursued, and supported Mr. Fox on every occasion when he thought that support necessary. After a very brilliant speech from that gentleman, on a motion which he made to censure the ministers for advancing money to the Emperor of Austria without the consent of Parliament, Sheridan made an admirable address to the House, which concluded with a contest between Lord Chatham and Mr. Pitt. A motion made by General Fitzpatrick, to obtain the release of La Fayette, through the intercession of his Majesty with the Emperor of Germany, called forth from Sheridan some well expressed opinions on the infamy of the detention of that great man in the prison of Olmutz. He expressed the highest veneration for his character, and believed that he might vie with the brightest characters in English History. To the spirit of a Hampden he united the loyalty of a Falkland.

On the 26th of February, the ministry was compelled to take a step, which alarmed the times, and seemed to hold forth the dread of an impending calamity. An order was issued by the Privy Council, prohibiting the directors of the Bank of England from issuing any cash payments till the sense of Parliament could be taken, and proper measures adopted to support the public and commercial credit of the kingdom. On the following day a message was sent to the House of Commons, recommending the subject to their immediate and serious attention. The debates were long and arduous, they were frequent and monotonous, yet did Sheridan give unwearying attention to them, and night after night exhibit the same energy and industry of which his adversaries have doubted. The annals of the country show how well he fought her battles, and how sincere he then was, in his bold attacks upon the corruption and profligacy of the system he opposed; occasionally he introduced some happy hits, even upon the driest subjects. Thus, during the debate on the stoppage of cash payments, he made a fanciful allusion to the Bank, "an elderly lady in the city, of great credit and long standing, who had lately made a faux pas, which was not altogether inexcusable. She had unfortunately fallen into bad company, and contracted too great an intimacy and connection at the St. James's end of the town. The young gentleman, however, who had employed all his arts of soft persuasion to seduce the old lady, had so far shown his designs, that by timely cutting and breaking off the connection there might be hopes of the old gentlewoman once more regaining her credit and injured reputation." Mr. Harrison's motion for the reduction of useless places gave him an opportunity of making a short but useful appeal to those who were at that time battening upon the public spoil; he more particularly alluded to Mr. Rose, whose name he publicly gave, as one holding several sinecures and situations which amounted to £10,000 annually, so that he did not spare those whom he condemned, and pointed out those whom he accused of corruption. If during the early part of the spring the nation had been somewhat alarmed at the state of its credit, it had now reason to feel the utmost anxiety. A mutiny was announced to have broken out in the Channel fleet; the dismay with which the intelligence was received was unequalled by any terror which the disasters of those times had occasioned. The stoutest hearts quailed, the kingdom was agitated from one end to the other, men looked at each other as they dreaded that there was something more to be told, and that at last the downfall of the British empire was at hand.

The particular subjects to which Sheridan devoted his attention during the remainder of the session were, an expedition to the West Indies, and that to Quiberon Bay, he still continued to enliven the House by his reading, and his sallies of wit and his humour; there are several speeches extant, from which extracts unfortunately cannot be made, which show that he possessed that readiness of reply, and quickness of thought, which some have denied to him. The dissolution of Parliament, which took place on the 20th of May, sent him back to his constituents at Stafford, who welcomed him there with every mark of respect, and returned him unopposed to the next Parliament. Mr. Sheridan now became mixed up in one of those singular literary disputes, which at the time of their occurrence excite the deepest interest, but are soon consigned like every other marvel to oblivion, excepting amongst those who love the curiosities of literature. William John Ireland was the son of a gentleman well known amongst the well-informed writers of the day. He had published some illustrations of Hogarth which had pleased the public, and he had likewise given to the world other works—"A Picturesque Tour through Holland;" "Picturesque Views on the Rivers Thames and Medway." Young Ireland had received a good education, had early imbibed a love of the drama, and one of his earliest recollections was that he had been delighted by a private play performed at Sheridan's residence in Bruton Street. At the early age of eighteen he wrote a tragedy, but, instead of bringing it before the public under his own name, he conceived the singular idea of producing it as a work of Shakspeare's which had accidentally come to light after a long lapse of years. He told his father that a grand discovery had accidentally been made at the house of a gentleman of property, that among a quantity of family papers the contracts between Lowin, Condell, and Shakspeare, and the lease granted by him and Herring to Michael Fraser, had been found; that soon afterwards the deed of gift to William Henry Ireland, described as the friend of Shakspeare, in consequence of having saved his life on the Thames when in extreme danger of being drowned, and also the deed of trust to John Heminge, had been discovered; that in pursuing the search he had been so fortunate as to find some deeds establishing beyond all controversy the title of this gentleman to a considerable property, deeds of which the gentleman was as ignorant as of his having in possession any of the MS. of Shakspeare; that in return for this service, in addition to the remarkable circumstance of the young man bearing the same name and arms with the person who saved Shakspeare's life, the gentleman promised him every thing relative to the subject, which had been or should be found either in town or at his house in the country. He then produced some MS. It is singular that the father should have lent so credulous an ear to the tale of his son, and should have become his tool; still more so, that so many men of high character and acknowledged talent should not have been able to discover the deception. It seems, from the young man's confession after the discovery, that he learnt to imitate the signature of Shakspeare, from the fac-simile in Steevens' edition, and by the assistance of a book written in the days of Elizabeth he was enabled to produce something which bore the resemblance to a play written about that period. It is to be regretted that he did not bestow his ingenuity and his assiduity upon a better cause. Had he done so, he would not have been characterized as a forger, but as a man of high talent. A worthy magistrate for London had once said that hanging a man for forgery is an infringement of the privilege of writing; Ireland thought the privilege of writing in imitation of those who are dead was no infringement upon the rights of any one. Men of the highest condition crowded to Norfolk Street, all were in raptures at what they saw; Dr. Parr fell on his knees to thank Heaven he had lived to see the autograph of Shakspeare, Dr. Warton and others were equally pleased. The commentators on the great bard, however, were not so easily duped—Malone, Steevens, and Boaden pronounced the documents forgeries.

A goodly folio appeared at the price of £4 4s., containing miscellaneous papers and legal instruments, under the hand and seal of William Shakspeare, including the tragedy of "King Lear," and a small fragment of "Hamlet," from the original MS. Malone wrote a letter to Lord Charlemont, proclaiming these forgeries. An original play, entitled "Vertigern," was taken to Sheridan, who, like the late Lord Byron, was not so enthusiastic in his admiration of the great dramatist as have been all the leading men of literature for the

last two centuries; that, however, he was well acquainted
with the writings of the bard, may be judged by an observation which he made whilst perusing it, upon coming to one
line—"This is strange, for, though you are acquainted with
my opinion of Shakspeare, he always wrote poetry." On
reading a little further he laid down the play, observing,
"There are certainly some bold ideas, but they are crude and
undigested. It is very odd, one would think that Shakspeare
must have been very young when he wrote the play. As to
the doubting whether it be really his or not, who can possibly
look at the papers and not believe them ancient?" The
general excitement on the subject fully justified Sheridan in
determining to bring out the play at Drury Lane; and a
negotiation was entered into for its purchase, which was at
length concluded by the payment to Ireland of three hundred
pounds, and an agreement to divide the profits of the performances for sixty nights. An immense assemblage was collected
on the 2nd of April, expectation was on the tiptoe, a hand-
bill was circulated at the entrance doors, complaining of a
violent and malevolent attack upon the MS., promising to
produce an answer to the most illiberal and unfounded assertions in Malone's Inquiry, and "requesting that the play of
'Vortigern' may be heard with that candour that has ever
distinguished a British audience." The appeal was not in
vain. The prologue, which gave Shakspeare as the author of
the play, was read by Mr. Whitfield, who was too flurried to
speak it. Kemble appeared any thing but satisfied with his
part; he, however, went through it until the audience, provoked by the poverty of the play, began to express loudly its
dissatisfaction. Kemble came forward, about the beginning
of the fourth act, begging for a candid hearing. This was
granted, until he pronounced some bombastic lines, which he
seemed himself to feel to be ludicrous. The house bore it no
longer; Mr. Barrymore attempted in vain to give "Vortigern"
out for repetition; its fate was sealed, and the stamp of ridicule
was attached to all those who had signed a document expressive
of their confidence in the genuineness of the forgery, at the
head and front of which stood forth the name of Samuel Parr.

During the greater part of this session the leaders of the
liberal party took little or no interest in the proceedings of
the House of Commons; they found that with their small

minority it was useless to attempt to oppose the ministerial measures, and that the country was sufficiently alive to pass ing events without having their attention directed to them On the 14th of December Sheridan and Fox were for the first time present, and were received with an ironical speech from Mr. Yorke. It was briefly noticed by Sheridan, in a speech in opposition to a motion of Mr. Pitt's, that the bill for raising a sum for the supplies of the year, by an increased assessment of taxes, be read a second time; finding the minority only 50, and the majority 175, he retired from further discussion for the session.

The following session was not allowed to pass by without the display of his varied knowledge and of his political principles. On the 4th of January he delivered an address worthy his great talents. It is ingenious, classical, worthy a statesman; the views on the condition of France and of England show that he had allowed none of the great occurrences of the day to pass without anxious examination and reflection. Some observations on libels were delivered by him on the 4th of April, which breathe much sound constitutional doctrine, and in which he states that the rights and liberties of the people owed more to Erskine than any lawyer; but on the 24th of April he made a great impression by the avowal of his dread of French ambition, by an eager desire to show that he was no longer an advocate of that government. A message was brought down from his Majesty stating that he had received information that great preparations were making for the invasion of England, and that the enemy was encouraged by correspondence and communication with traitorous and disaffected persons. He dwelt upon the dangers which threatened the country as of no ordinary magnitude, and wished to rouse and stimulate the nation into exertion—to provide every means of resistance to the insolent menaces and attempts of the enemy. The same evening he expressed his entire disapprobation of a bill, brought into the house by Mr. Pitt, to suspend again the Habeas Corpus Act. He considered the nation's great and best privilege was trial by jury. Any successful attempt to check its attributes or diminish its virtues, he regarded as the death-blow to the vitality of constitutional liberty.

No one who reads these speeches can for a moment doubt the

genuine patriotism which animated the speaker: it is manly, just, and virtuous, when danger from a foreign foe threaten the subversion of our native land, to forget how great may be the differences of opinion which may exist between parties; to think only of opposing peril, but not wantonly to suspend the liberties of the people, because suspicion is engendered, and doubts as to the honesty of some few may exist. Sheridan's opinions were hailed with delight by the great mass, and though, amongst those with whom he acted, the doctrines he promulgated were not so favourably received, and indeed shook his influence with many, he gained a higher degree of popularity than he had ever reached. He had carefully watched the tide of events, and had trimmed his bark in so skilful a manner as to have escaped the rocks and quicksands which threatened his brother Whigs. On the 18th of June he again made a brilliant speech; the subject was one admirably adapted to his powers—"The state of Ireland;" with this concluded his efforts during this exciting period. The following year he principally devoted his energies to oppose the means which were taken to bring about the abolition of the Irish Parliament under the specious name of a Union. His principal object was to have the free consent and approbation of the two parliaments then sitting, and to prevent the Government using either corruption or intimidation to obtain its appearance. Vain were his efforts, and nearly half a century's experience has shown to us how fallacious were the hopes and promises held out; the evils that then afflicted Ireland have not diminished, and Sheridan's arguments are to this day unanswered — unanswerable. His absence from the general business of the House drew down upon him some censure, on occasion of his seconding a motion of Sir Francis Burdett, relative to the state of Cold Bath Fields Prison; he observed in reply that nothing would satisfy gentlemen with regard to him; they blamed him for absenting himself, and took care never to bid him welcome when he came; but whenever he saw public principle abandoned or humanity outraged, and especially when he saw iniquity protected by the names and authority of members of that House, and the House called upon to give its sanction to such conduct, he would come forward. He then ably supported the liberal Baronet, whose noble conduct on the occasion of the disclosures at the prison gained for him that public respect which he enjoyed to the last hour of his highly valuable life.

He made an elaborate speech this session on the failure of the expedition to Holland, and others of some historical interest on the overtures made by Napoleon Bonaparte for peace; but it began to be evident that he was more careless both in the matter and the manner of his speeches, and in 1801 he spoke but once, and that somewhat feebly.

The session of 1802 was commenced with an incident which excited considerable amusement. The Prime Minister and Mr. Sheridan, entering the House at the same moment, walked up to the table, and took the oath at the same time. The Premier, who was almost as careless in pecuniary matters as his great opponent, fumbled about in his pockets for two shillings, usually paid, but found nothing. He turned round to Sheridan, who, by some extraordinary freak of fortune, had money, and was actually able to be a lender and not a borrower: this gave rise to many witticisms. One of the morning papers contained the following paragraph:—"Something is certainly on the carpet at present between the ministry and opposition, for we assert, from undoubted authority, that yesterday a loan was negotiated between Mr. Pitt and Mr. Sheridan." On the 14th of May he showed that, however careless he might have grown, he still retained a vigorous fancy, power of sarcasm, and consummate skill in party politics. Mr. Pitt had ceased to be Minister of Great Britain; he had allowed Mr. Addington to seize the reins of government until it might suit him to resume them, and Sheridan took the occasion to speak of the state of parties.

December the 8th he made an admirable speech which separated him still further from Fox, who, having been nobly received by Bonaparte, had conceived a high opinion of him, and designated him as an instrument in the hands of Providence to restore Switzerland to happiness, and to elevate Italy to splendour and importance; whilst Sheridan pronounced him "an instrument in the hands of Providence to make the English love their constitution better, to cling to it with more fondness, to hang round it with true tenderness." It is impossible by means of extracts to do justice to the beauties contained in this admirable specimen of parliamentary eloquence. It made a deep and lasting impression on the House.

try, and did more to urge the nation on to resist the power of the ruler of France than any of the laboured harangues of any of the statesmen of the day.

An offer of the place of Registrar to the High Court of Malta was offered for the acceptance of Tom Sheridan by Lord St. Vincent, but was with a high tone of feeling declined by his father, who, determined to avoid giving to his enemies any opportunity of assailing his political character, preferred making a pecuniary sacrifice of no little importance. The subject of the Prince of Wales's establishment was the only one on which he exerted his talents—a humorous description of what majesty would be without its externals, exemplified in the appearance that would be presented, were the Speaker and the House to be deprived of their trappings, was the only feature worthy recording. A report was prevalent that Sheridan was prepared to form a coalition with Mr. Addington—his defence of Lord St. Vincent rather led to this idea; but the return of Mr. Pitt to power put a stop to any further thought of this alliance. Sheridan resumed his position. Some speeches made by him on the increase of the military establishments of the country, will be perused, even now that the circumstances with which they were accompanied have lost their interest, with the best results, giving, as they do, incontestable proofs of his parliamentary ability, and his knowledge of the true principles upon which the freedom of a nation is based. Sheridan was now gratified by the recollection of the services which he had rendered the Prince of Wales; he was installed in the office of Receiver-General of the Duchy of Cornwall, the nobleman holding that position being in India; he was to fill it until his return in the year 1808: however, it became permanently his own, in consequence of the death of Lord Lake. Upon the death of Mr. Pitt, and the formation of a short-lived administration of the Whig party, Sheridan was appointed Treasurer of the Navy, a situation far beneath his expectation and the talent he had displayed. His want of industry, his known habits of life, took from him the chance of a higher post; nor whilst he filled the one for which he was selected did he show any of his usual ability. The death of Mr. Fox soon drove him from the brief taste of the sweets of office; from that period the instances of his parliamentary exertions are but rare.

On the 24th February occurred the most serious calamity which could have befallen Sheridan; the Theatre Royal, Drury Lane, whose erection had so lately as 1794 been accomplished at so vast expense, was on that day totally de stroyed by fire. It happened that there was no performance on that evening; that whilst Sheridan was in attendance in the House of Commons, on the occasion of Mr. Ponsonby's motion on the conduct of the war in Spain, the principal actors and officers of the theatre were enjoying the hospitality of Mr. Richard Wilson at his house in Lincoln's Inn Fields; all was mirth and glee there; a bumper, Success and pro sperity to Drury Lane Theatre, was just pledged around, and the glass raised to the lips, when the youngest daughter of the host rushed into the room, screaming out that Drury Lane Theatre was on fire. All rushed into the square: the fire raged with tremendous fury, the whole horizon was illumi nated; no doubt could exist as to the sad truth. Messrs. Peake and Dunn, the treasurers, Kelly, the acting manager, rushed to the spot, dashed up stairs, and at the hazard of their lives succeeded in saving the iron chest, which contained documents of great importance. The House of Commons was speedily made acquainted with the fearful event—indeed the interior of the House was illuminated by such blazes of light that there could be no doubt that some catastrophe was taking place. Every eye was turned to Sheridan, who sat in respect ful silence, whilst that assembly, with due regard to its ac complished member, entertained a motion that the House should be adjourned; but with great composure he said, "that whatever might be the extent of the private calamity, he hoped it would not interfere with the public business of the country." Kelly, the acting manager, states that with Roman fortitude he remained at his post whilst his play house was burning, and this really appears to have been the case. The ordinary version, as told by Moore, is not only that he left the House, proceeded to Drury Lane, witnessed, with a fortitude which strongly interested all who observed him, the entire destruction of his property, but gives cur rency to an anecdote which he does not evidently believe. " It is said, that as he sat at the Piazza Coffee House, dur ing the fire, taking some refreshment, a friend of his having remarked on the philosophic calmness with which he bore his misfortune, Sheridan answered, 'A man may surely be allowed to take a glass of wine by his own fireside.' Without vouching for the authenticity or novelty of this anecdote," adds Moore, " which may have been, for aught I know, like the wandering Jew, a regular attendant upon all fires since the time of Hierocles, I give it as I heard it."

The following day the actors assembled to dine with Mr. Wroughton, the stage manager, and Sheridan was requested to meet them, which he did with unusual punctuality. He spoke after dinner in a most feeling and honourable manner, gaining the approbation of all who heard him by the soundness of his advice, and the good taste with which it was given. He strongly inculcated upon the minds of the leading actors the necessity of adhering to each other. He said that he was aware that many of the principal performers might get profitable engagements at the different provincial theatres, but what would then become of the inferior ones, some of whom had large families? " Heaven forbid," he added, " that they should be deserted. No! I most earnestly recommend and entreat that every individual belonging to the concern should be taken care of. Elect yourselves into a committee, but keep in your remembrance even the poor sweepers of the stage, who, with their children, must starve, if not protected by your fostering care." Such were the sentiments of one who himself stood in the greatest need of consolation, who lost every thing, even the pianoforte that belonged to her whom most he had loved to hear sing in harmony to its notes. It was a most embarrassing position in which to be placed, all hopes of rebuilding the house seemed to be at an end. A casual conversation which Sheridan held with Mr. Whitbread led to an arrangement by which an act of Parliament was obtained for reconstructing it by subscription. It was agreed on that Sheridan was to receive £24,000 for his ......ty of the property, £4000 for the property of the fruit ...... and reversion of boxes and shares, and that Thomas, his son, was to receive for his quarter £12,000; but he was to have no concern or connection of any kind whatever with the new undertaking, nor was he to be paid until the theatre was built. Cruel, bitterly cruel were these stipulations, harshly were they enforced by Whitbread; and those who read the ...... letters of Sheridan, and the matter-of-fact ones of

Whitbread as given by Moore, will readily see that the eclipse of the greatest genius of England is to be attributed to his coming into contact with one of the coldest pieces of organization that ever moved in any orbit. Sheridan had no money to secure his re-election at Stafford, he was now a broken man, left to the mercy of strangers, a melancholy example of the vanity of trusting to those who usurp the name of friends.

In 1812, for the last time, was heard in the House of Commons that voice which had so frequently been listened to with respect and admiration; its richness was somewhat diminished, its tones were not so musical, nor was there any attempt to dazzle or to delight. The younger members looked upon George Canning as having already surpassed the favourite of their predecessors. Sheridan seemed conscious that his opponents and his former friends paid less attention to him; and one evening, in somewhat of a splenetic mood, he observed, " I am now run over by these young ones, I am like an old clock thrust behind the door."—"Very true," said a brother wit, Dudley North, "it 's all tick, tick, tick, with you now." He, however, closed his career with a speech worthy of his mighty talent, on the overtures made by France for peace; he characterized Napoleon as rapacious, insatiable, and treacherous, as one with whom it was impossible to negotiate on an honourable basis: he concluded an animated address thus:—" If after the general subjugation and ruin of Europe there should ever exist an impartial historian to record the awful events that produced this universal calamity, let that historian have to say Britain fell, and with her fell all the best securities for the charities of human life, for the power, the honour, the fame, the glory and the liberties, not only of herself, but of the whole civilized world." This speech was in opposition to the opinions of those with whom he usually acted, for they would have unhesitatingly accepted the propositions which were made; whilst he, firmly believing that no faith was to be kept with Napoleon, protested against them, and declared them to be a wretched manœuvre to cloke his designs upon Russia. Whatever may have been the views of his party, Sheridan's were the most popular with the nation. Happily for the repose of mankind his voice was listened to amidst the many who thought with him. He must be looked

upon as a true patriot, who, laying aside all party considerations, and preferring the interests of his country to all others,
boldly proclaims his opinions when founded upon honest conviction. Sheridan had the gratification of seeing the overthrow of the man whom he had ever held up to light as an
enemy to true freedom, and of seeing the realization of his
long entertained hopes. His political career was now closed.
On a dissolution of Parliament he found that Stafford was
not prepared to return him, he had no money, he had no
offices to give to the independent electors. They had not
the noble spirit to recollect that he had been the ornament
of the country, and that he conferred honour upon them,
of which their children might be proud to the latest generation, by accepting the post of their representative.

Sheridan usually held his levee in a most extraordinary
manner; his visitors were distributed in various rooms according to their station, their intimacy, or their business with
him. Some had access to his private room, others lounged
about in the library, looking at the paintings, which had the
appearance of being covered with dust and dirt; another
party occupied the well-worn chairs of the parlours. Up and
down paced, with fury in his eye—a determination to speak
his mind, and no longer to be wheedled out of his money—
some infuriated creditor who for days had in vain beset the
avenues of Drury Lane Theatre with the hope of seeing the
deeply indebted proprietor. In the butler's room were the
equally anxious tradespeople; there was a vast deal of grumbling every where; each person had some want which must be
instantaneously supplied. At every sound each eye was directed to a particular door from which it was expected that,
unless the great man stole out quietly and unnoticed, he
would at one time or other make his appearance. At length
it was opened, a sweet-toned voice was heard uttering something which seemed to please the listener, if a gentle laugh
could enable the stander by to form a judgment—Sheridan
then came out. There was something in his appearance that,
even in the days of his intemperance, at once captivated all
who saw him. There was in the shape and form of his head,
as John Kemble was wont to say, something eminently Shaks-
pearian; at any rate the prints of the immortal bard bore some

resemblance His eye was strikingly brilliant; his hair, powdered in the fashion of the day, softened down the ruddy tints of certain portions of his features; his smile was winning; he was in the elegant costume of the hour, with sufficient attention to his toilette to show that he did not disdain those additions which add to personal appearance. He walked through the crowd of suitors with an easy, unembarrassed air, bowing courteously to each, and to each he had something kind to say; and, as Boden tells us, so cordial were his manners, his glance so masterly, and his address so captivating, that the people, for the most part, seemed to forget what they actually wanted, and went away as if they had come only to look at him. 'It has been observed by Mr. Adolphus, in his life of that first-rate comedian, John Bannister, that, although the committee appointed for Drury Lane, in which Mr. Whitbread took an active part, was composed of men known to be conversant with business and punctual in their dealings, yet they were unable to raise funds more promptly or inspire more confidence in the public than Sheridan had done. There was in the gracious and winning manner of Sheridan something which animated hope in defiance of probability, and inspired confidence without the sanction of judgment. In trusting him, men were aware that they must catch an inspiration from his enthusiasm, and they sought it. In following out the plans of the more methodical committee, they became calculators, arithmeticians, accountants ; while they considered the certainty of expenditure, and the bare possibilities of gain, they were never animated with a cheering spirit, or impelled by a vigorous feeling.

That which irresistibly gained upon the heart of every one was the peculiarly modest demeanour of Sheridan. Those who knew him by the splendour only of his reputation were at once delighted with the suavity, the courtesy, and the unpretending manner with which he listened to every one, and the promptitude with which he seemed not only to comprehend the feelings of others, but to enter into them, to sympathize with them, and thoroughly to appreciate them. His whole mind seemed for the moment to be engrossed with the subject that was placed before him; and on no occasion did an unfeeling expression escape from him. He might say the most bitter thing, but the brilliancy of the idea made every

o

one forget it; and even when he was most sarcastic it was as if he was compelled to become so. Over his creditors he seemed, as long as he had any personal intercourse with them, to have an absolute control. The most unrelenting seemed to yield to the very happy method of placing the state of his affairs before them: Michael Kelly had an admirable opportunity of judging on many occasions; but on none more strikingly than when he was arrested for a debt which he had incurred as acting manager for Drury Lane Theatre. He was asked, by one of the tradesmen who supplied the establishment, for his opinion upon some furniture which Sheridan had ordered for it, and innocently enough pronounced it, according to the best of his judgment; the circumstance slipt entirely from his memory until it was, singularly enough, somewhat unpleasantly recalled to it, by his being compelled to accompany a sheriff's officer to a spunging house, whilst he was fulfilling a theatrical engagement at Liverpool. Fortunately for him, a friend relieved him from the unpleasant predicament. He immediately despatched a servant to London with a letter to Sheridan, telling him the situation he had been placed in by the forgetfulness on his part to make the payment at the proper time, and giving him a full, true, and particular account of the unhandsome treatment to which he had been subjected. Sheridan, with great promptitude, sent for the hard-hearted creditor, Henderson, remonstrated with him on the great cruelty of which he had been guilty, reasoned with him on the hardship of the law of imprisonment for debt, made him feel that shutting a man up in a prison was a most unchristian deed, pointed out to him that he had acted arbitrarily, unjustly, until the heart of this most determined creditor was not only thoroughly softened, but his mind led to the conviction that he had done very wrong, and at last his purse was actually offered to Mr. Sheridan, from which, after much unwillingness and decent hesitation on his side and great perseverance on the other, he consented, with considerable reluctance, to draw a sum. Before the interview was concluded, Sheridan had contrived to borrow two hundred pounds from Henderson, and to render him the happiest man alive by condescending to accept such a loan. All, it is true, were not equally fortunate in gaining an interview with him.

A gentleman who was one day waiting, as he had been the day before, by appointment, in the parlour, observed a gentleman walking about, and, in a sort of attempt to be civil to him, unfortunately said to him, " A fine day this—I had the pleasure of seeing you here yesterday."—" Yesterday, sir ! Yes, sir, and so you might the day before, and any day for the last six weeks ; and, if I have walked one yard, I have walked fifty miles on this damned carpet." This he said, grinding his teeth, his fist clenched, and pacing to and fro with much the appearance of a maniac.

On his first election at Stafford the general voice was all in Sheridan's favour ; his manners were so elegant, his liberality so unbounded, his promises so free, and, what was more rare, they were uniformly kept. Each voter who wanted a place, to his great delight, had one given to him ; not one who asked it but was gratified with an offer either at Drury Lane Theatre or the Opera House, to which he immediately repaired and found that he was unhesitatingly installed in his new berth. This generosity gained Sheridan his election, his return was triumphant ; and he had the good fortune always to be enabled to oblige new friends, for most of those who occupied posts quickly resigned them, as their salaries were only promises to pay, which were realized, if at all, at such a distance of time as to wear out the patience of ordinary men. Much of the inconvenience to which Sheridan was subjected arose from his procrastination : whether it was a deed that he had to sign or a letter to frank, he would still put off doing it. Nothing was ever done in time or place Letters containing money, or bearing intelligence of importance, remained unopened. Whether private or official business demanded his attention, still was there the same indolence, the same unwillingness to apply, which eventually led to the most serious results.

Professor Smyth was waiting one morning for him in his ante-room, and happened to cast his eyes on a table that stood in the middle of the room covered with manuscripts, plays, pamphlets, and papers of every description. As he proceeded to tumble them over and look at their superscriptions, he observed that the letters were most of them unopened, and that some of them had coronets on the seal. He remarked to Mr. Westley, the treasurer of Drury Lane,

who was sitting by the fire, having also for a long time
danced attendance, that Mr. Sheridan treated all alike, wafer
or coronet, pauper or peer, the letters seemed equally un
opened. "Just so," was the treasurer's reply; "indeed, last
winter I was occupying myself much as you are doing, and
for the same reason, and what should I see among these
letters but one from myself, unopened like the rest—a letter
that I knew contained a 10*l.* note within it. The history, Sir,
was that I had received a note from Mr. Sheridan, dated
Bath, and headed with the words 'Money bound,' and entreating me to send the first 10*l.* I could lay my hands upon
This I did. In the meantime I suppose some one had given
him a cast in his carriage up to town, and his application to
me had never more been thought of; and, therefore, there lay
my letter, and would have continued to lie till the housemaid
had swept it with the rest into the fire, if I had not accidentally seen it."

Mr. Smyth could not help, on going down stairs, telling
the story to his valet, Edwards, suggesting to him to look after
the letters; to which he replied—"What can I do for such a
master? The other morning I went to settle his room after
he had gone out, and, on throwing open the windows, found
them stuffed up with paper of different kinds, and amongst
them bank-notes; there had been a high wind in the night,
the windows, I suppose, had rattled; he had come in quite
intoxicated, and in the dark, for want of something better,
stuffed the bank-notes into the casement; and, as he never
knows what he has in his pocket or what he has not, they
were never afterwards missed."

The following is a characteristic specimen of his correspondence with the treasurer of Drury Lane Theatre, when
in want of money or any assistance which was to be obtained
through that channel :—

(Feb. 3rd, 1814. Biggleswade Post-mark.)
"Southhill, Friday.

"Dr. Ward,—Beg, borrow, steal, forge 10*l.* for me, and
send by return of Post, then I am with you.

"Yours truly.

"What do you think of Kean? I am glad he is to play
Richard. And note of post, how is Brinsley?"

(Post-mark, 1814, Feb. 18th, Biggleswade.   Not 'ranked.)

" (Private.)   Southhill, Thursday.

" Dr. Ward,—Thou art a trusty man, and when I write to
you I get an answer and the thing done if it can be ; and you
don't write or want to receive *love letters*, which are my horror.   I have been very ill with a violent attack of bile, kept
my bed three days ; *but don't say this to a soul*, it always does
harm in my situation.   I am now quite well, and the better
for it ; pray let two or three theatre chaps, or their connections, put up a little scaffolding in my hall that may serve
to wash the walls and whitewash the ceiling as soon as you receive this.   I will explain my motive when I arrive on Sunday.
As I suppose I have replaced the last 10*l.* you stole for me, I
trust you may reputably renew the theft; when I arrive,
should it again be wanted, as I greatly fear it will.   I have
had a very civil letter from Hudson, from whom I have great
resources coming.   There are *political* events (*home*) brewing.
One letter more will catch me here.   Ever yours, R. B. S.

" Charles Ward, Esq.,
     " Secretary's Office, Theatre, Drury Lane."

Although no man ever made a greater impression in a
social circle, in his better days, than did Sheridan, yet, in
the later period of his life, he was generally taciturn for the
greater part of the evening, and towards his close he not
unfrequently annoyed the party by a species of raillery which
was sometimes not at all understood, and was even occasionally offensive.   He would, after playing the accomplished
listener with the utmost deference to each individual, begin
recapitulating all that had passed, repeating, with sundry
observations interspersed with his own anecdotes, every remark that had been made, exhibiting great shrewdness and a
wit of a peculiar character.   He was very fond of a butt, and
nobody ever came in his way of whom he made a better use
than the good-hearted Michael Kelly, a warm Irishman, whom
he loved to represent as an eternal maker of genuine newly
imported blunders.   No man had in those days furnished the
stage with more popular songs than Michael Kelly, but they
all had the reputation of being plagiarisms from the conti-

nental composers. Kelly, finding the world wag slowly on
with him, had an idea of adding to his occupations as stage-
manager and music-seller that of wine-merchant, in consequence of there being such good vaults at the Opera House,
close to his warehouse. He consulted Sheridan, who said—
" My dear fellow, write over your door, ' Michael Kelly, composer of wines and importer of music.' " Kelly has, in his
" Reminiscences," a version of his own, and adds, as his own
repartee, " I will take the hint, Sir, and be a composer of all
wines except old Sherry; for that is so notorious for its in-
toxicating and pernicious qualities, that I should be afraid of
poisoning my customers."

Kelly, on another occasion, said a very happy thing to him,
according to his own account. One evening that their Majesties honoured Drury Lane with their presence, the play, by
royal command, was the School for Scandal. When Mr.
Sheridan was in attendance to light their Majesties to their
carriage, the King said to him—" I am much pleased with
your comedy of the School for Scandal, but I am still more
so with your play of the Rivals; that is my favourite, and I
will never give it up." His Majesty at the same time said—
" When, Mr. Sheridan, shall we have another play from your
masterly pen?" He replied, that he was writing a comedy,
which he expected very shortly to finish. " I was told of
this," says Kelly, " and the next day, walking along Piccadilly, I asked him if he had told the Queen that he was
writing a play. He said he had, and he was actually about
one. ' Not you,' said I to him, ' you will never write again,
you are afraid to write.' ' Of whom am I afraid ?' said he,
fixing his penetrating eye on me. I said—' You are afraid of
the author of the School for Scandal.' " There is an anecdote
of this sort that has been ascribed to Garrick, when he heard
that Sheridan would bring out the School for Scandal. " He
has," said he, " great things against pleasing the town."
" What are they?" was the question. " His powerful Rivals."
One of Sheridan's jests against Kelly was, that, on arriving
together at Kemble's house on one occasion, Kelly went up
the steps of the house, and begged Sheridan, who was scraping
his own shoes, to scrape for him whilst he would knock at the
door.

Another blunder, which Sheridan vouched for with perfect gravity, was that Kelly, on peeping through the hole in the stage curtain, exclaimed—"By Jesus, you can't stick a pin's head into any part of the house, it is literally choke-full; but how much fuller will it be to-morrow night when the King comes!" Some of these, although told by Michael Kelly with great good humour, are a little too bad of their kind, such as that on the first night when Lodoiska was got up, with great attention to the scenery; but during the storming of the castle, in the last scene, an accident occurred which might have proved fatal to Kelly and to Mrs. Crouch. Sheridan related all the circumstances, in his usual style, to the Duchess of Devonshire, and concluded by saying that Kelly had put a very puzzling question to him, which was—" Suppose, Mr. Sheridan, I had been killed by the fall, who would have maintained me for the rest of my life ?"

But certainly the best practical joke that Sheridan played upon Kelly was told by him with the greatest naïveté. On the 2nd of July, a musical piece, called "The Glorious First of June," was brought out with unusual pomp. There was a prologue spoken by John Kemble himself, a grand sea-fight, a splendid fête, and every thing was done to give it effect, as it was for the benefit of the widows of those who fell on that memorable occasion. It was brought out in three days; Kelly had been active in getting up the music, and had little time for the study of a part; he therefore went to Sheridan, and entreated him to make his speeches as short as possible, and to give him as little as he could to do. Sheridan received the request with his usual benignity of manner, and gave Kelly his assurance that he would comply with his wish. Kelly had to come on early in the piece to sing a song—" When in war on the ocean we meet the proud foe." There was a cottage in the distance, and Frederic (Kelly) was desired by the stage directions to look earnestly for a moment or two at the cottage, and to exclaim—" There stands my Louisa's cottage, she must be either in it or out of it," he then was to begin his song, and not one other word was there in the whole part. The audience quickly took up the joke, and this sublime and solitary speech produced the loudest laughter. At the conclusion of the entertainment, Sheridan went into the green

room, and with the most perfect gravity complimented Kelly
on the quickness he had displayed, and at his being so very
perfect in the part which he had taken so much pains to write
for him; and, considering the short time he had to study it,
it was truly astonishing. All these jokes only served to
amuse; for, as Kelly himself has said, that during the five-
and-twenty years through which he enjoyed his friendship, he
never heard him say a single word that could wound the feelings of a single individual.

The new theatre at Drury Lane was at length finished,
and under the direction of a committee it was opened,
on the 10th of October, with Hamlet and the Devil to
Pay; but Sheridan was not present; and although a resolution had been passed by the committee,*offering the use
of a box to Mrs. Sheridan, as a gratifying mark of attention
to him through her, and the offer had been twice announced
by letter from Mr. Whitbread, he studiously avoided entering
it for three years; at the end of that time he was persuaded
by that excellent-hearted nobleman, the Earl of Essex, to dine
with him and accompany him to see Kean, whom he had
once only heard in private read Othello, and of whom he
had formed a very high opinion. Once there, he found again
the spirit of the past. He had left the box, as Lord Essex
imagined, to return home, but he found him in the old classic
haunt, the green-room, where, surrounded by a happy group
of those who under his banners had reaped many a glorious
laurel, he was welcomed to a festive scene with the warmest
rejoicings; and, as they filled bumpers to his health, he once
again felt his hopes revive within him, and the remembrance
of the days that were past, nor did he forget his conversational talent when occasion presented itself to display it.

When dining at the house of Mr. Rogers, with Lord Byron

* There was something irresistibly ludicrous in the first step taken by
this body, " with due modesty and with the true spirit of tradesmen they
advertised for the best poetical addresses, to be sealed and delivered within
a certain number of days, folded and directed in a given form, in short,—
like the tender of a public contract;" forty-three persons contended for the
prize, but all were rejected, and a composition of Lord Byron's was substi-
tuted; the only advantage which the public derived was the publication or
one of the most successful series of parodies, under the name of the Rejected
Addresses, that has ever appeared.

and Moore, the conversation turned upon the addresses which had been sent to the Committee of Drury Lane Theatre for selection. Amongst others who had become competitors was Mr. Whitbread; his, like the others, in allusion to the New Drury rising out of the fire, had some verses about the phœnix; but Sheridan said that Whitbread made more of this bird than any of them—he entered into particulars, and described its wings, beak, tail,—in short it was a poulterer's description of a phœnix.

Misery now rapidly accumulated on him; his creditors hoped, by cruelty exercised on his person, to draw from the pockets of his family and his friends the money which they held dearer than those virtues which Christian charity teaches. At length they seized him, after having taken possession of all that he had; his books, his jewels, his pictures, even that of his first wife, were become the property of others. He was taken to a spunging-house! So much was he affected, that, upon his release, bitter tears flowed rapidly down his cheek; sensitive of personal honour, he deeply felt the humiliation to which he had been exposed, and ever afterwards spoke with bitterness of that which he called the profanation of his person.

Whatever may have been his distresses owing to his reck lessness and his carelessness, both friends and enemies have expressed their belief that Sheridan possessed as anxious a desire to do his duty to his creditors as any man of the nicest sense of honour could do; but that the untoward events which crowded on him—the fire at Drury Lane—the loss of his seat in Parliament—prevented his carrying out his views. The struggles he had to encounter were those of an honest man hoping to be able to pay, not of a dishonest one anxious to evade his just debts. Had he lived in these more commercial days, he would have escaped much of the obloquy that was heaped upon him.

So much has been urged against his Majesty George the Fourth for his desertion of Sheridan—so anxiously has it been attempted to impress upon the public mind that, forgetful of the earnest devotion, of the unceasing exercise of his talents in behalf of his Royal Master, he was allowed to linger on in penury and embarrassment without obtaining the slightest notice—that it has become a byeword and a blot upon

the memory of the monarch.   The pen of Moore was dipped
in the bitterest gall when he wrote his well-known "Lines on
the death of Sheridan," which hand down to posterity the
opinions of Sheridan's friends on the conduct of the Sovereign.

Still it would be unjust to pass over in silence those circumstances which, though derived from private sources,
deserve to be known, and tend to rescue the character of the
King from the charges of neglect and ingratitude.   There is
no one who does not admit one fact, that when Sheridan lost
his seat for Stafford, when " he was excluded both from the
theatre and from Parliament—the two anchors by which he
held in life were gone, and he was left a lonely and helpless
wreck upon the waves," that his Royal Highness offered, at
his own expense, to find a seat for him in the House of Commons, that he stepped forward to shield him from the threats
of arrest and imprisonment which began to harass him.
Writers in the Westminster and Quarterly Reviews have
stated that he actually presented him with four thousand
pounds for this purpose; from this statement Mr. Moore
withheld his belief, but the Edinburgh Review, in its admirable discussion of that author's Life of Sheridan, thus
gives the actual case;—" With regard to the alleged gift of
4000l. by his Majesty, we have the most sincere pleasure in
saying that we have every reason to believe that the Illustrious Person is fully entitled to the credit of that act of
munificence, though, according to our information, its unhappy
object did not derive from it the benefit which was intended.
The sum, which we have heard was about 3000l., was by his
Royal Highness's order placed in the hands of an attorney
for Sheridan's benefit, but was there either attached by his
creditors, or otherwise dissipated in such a manner that very
little of it actually reached its destination.   Nor is it to be
forgotten that, however desirous his Royal Highness might
have been to assist Sheridan, he was himself an embarrassed
man; he had been careless of his own expenditure, and there
was not in his treasury the means adequate to afford the relief
he might have felt an inclination to give.   Every portion of
the Prince's revenue was apportioned long before it was
received; and though there was a sum annually devoted to
objects of charity, and to works of benevolence, there was

little left for the casual instances which presented themselves. But it was not royal munificence that was required, it was the assistance of his own immediate family that was denied him; the whole of his debts did not amount to five thousand pounds, and Mrs. Sheridan's settlement had been fifteen thousand, and, however kind her conduct was towards him from the first moment of his malady, she does not seem to have influenced her friends to step forward to his pecuniary relief : all that has been affirmed of his forlorn situation at the hour of his death is borne out by the testimony of those who saw the utter destitution in which he was ; a neglected house—the most deplorable want of the common necessaries of life, of decent control over the servants, whose careless-ness, even of the physician's prescriptions, was remarked—do not speak of a wife's domestic management, however pure and sincere may have been her affection."

Professor Smyth has most graphically described what he observed on the melancholy occasion. He was in Kent when he heard that Sheridan was dangerously ill—he immediately went to his house in Saville Row—he was told by one of the old servants that his master was upon his death-bed. Nothing could be more deplorable than the appearance of every thing : there were strange-looking people in the hall ; the parlour seemed dismantled ; on the table lay a bit of paper, thrown carelessly and neglected—it was a prescription—it was a strong cordial. He sent up his card to Mrs. Sheridan, to whose room he was summoned. Collecting all the firmness he could, for he was unprepared for such a meeting, he found Mrs. Sheridan displaying the virtues of her sex with a greater dignity and calmness than he had expected from her. She went to Sheridan for him, who sent by her a kind mes-sage to say, if he would wait, he would get ready and see him ; but, after waiting, a bell was rung, and an announce-ment came, to say that he was unequal to the interview. "You have come from the country," said Mrs. Sheridan, "you must have something to eat ;" on his declining it, "You think," said she, "that our poor house can furnish nothing, I do believe we can ; let me try," and she rang the bell. He thanked her, but excused himself, telling her he would return the next day. The next day, however, Sheridan was no better : he talked with his wife, but his sensibility prevented his speaking much; she told him that she had sent for her friend Dr. Howley, the Bishop of London, who had instantly come up from Oxfordshire to pray by him.   On Mr. Smyth's venturing to ask after Mr. Sheridan, her reply was, " I never saw such awe as there was painted in his countenance—I shall never forget it." Thus passed away this great man, to whom was intrusted one of the finest minds, and originally one of the best hearts.

Melancholy was the close of his existence.   Early in the year 1816 symptoms of severe illness gradually exhibited themselves; his habits of life enfeebled his powers of digestion—his anxieties preyed upon his mind—until at length he sank beneath a load of misery.   A diseased state of the stomach developed itself, with symptoms of a harassing nature. There was, however, in him a natural tone and vigour of constitution which would have enabled him, with adequate attention to himself, to have withstood the inroads that were making upon his constitution ; but he had throughout life suffered but little, and therefore had not a monitor within him to advise a total change of his habits of life, nor to point out the necessity of obtaining medical aid, until at length Dr. Bain, to whose professional assistance his family usually had recourse, felt it his duty to warn him that his life was in danger.   The first public notice of his illness was his absence from a dinner in honour of St. Patrick's Day, on which occasion the Duke of Kent presided, and announced the afflicting cause of Sheridan's absence.   The intelligence was received with marks of sympathy and affection, but these were but empty tokens of respect, which, too, would speedily have been forgotten, had not an article appeared in the Morning Post calculated to rouse his friends from their apathy, and to point out the state in which he, who was once a public favourite, was now situated.—"Oh, delay not to draw aside the curtain within which that proud spirit hides its suffering.   Prefer ministering in the chamber of sickness to mustering at the splendid sorrows that adorn the hearse.   I say, ' Life and succour" against 'Westminster Abbey and a funeral.' "   This appeal, which was made without the name of the sufferer being mentioned, is ascribed by Moore to one who, though on no very cordial terms with him, forgot every other feeling in a generous pity for his fate, and in honest indignation against those who now deserted him. It was quickly responded to ; at his door the names of those who stand high in the ranks of the aristocracy, who had been the friends of his prosperity. were left as visitors. This was mockery. These great and rich personages came too late. They should have shown their feeling for him before. Already had his death-bed been brutally and shamefully outraged; a sheriff's officer had arrested him—such were the laws of England—even in those fearful agonies when the soul is about to quit this mortal frame, had prepared to carry him in his blankets to a vile spunging-house, and would have perpetrated the horrid act which would have disgraced the country, had not his physician threatened the man of law with the responsibility which he would incur if the prisoner died upon his road,—an event of which there was every probability.

On Sunday, July 7th, 1816, Sheridan expired. He was then in the sixty-fifth year of his age. The feelings of the public received a shock from an unfounded report, that even his corpse was dishonoured, and that it had been arrested Such an insult upon the morals of a people—such an abuse of the laws of the country—fortunately did not occur, and the rumour has been traced to have arisen out of the circum stance of the body being removed to the house of his attached friend, Mr. Peter Moore, in Great George Street, Westminster, from the residence of Sheridan, in Saville Row, as the distance to the Abbey would render a walking funeral from the shorter distance more convenient. On the following Saturday the last tribute of respect, empty as it was, was paid him by a royal and noble train, who followed the funeral pomp with the usual trappings of outward woe. There were two royal brothers—the Duke of York and the Duke of Sussex. There were noble pall-bearers—the Duke of Bedford, the Earl of Lauderdale, Earl Mulgrave, the Lord Bishop of London, Lord Holland and Lord Spencer. Mr. Charles Brinsley Sheridan was the chief mourner. Amongst the titled phalanx was the Duke of Argyle, the Marquises of Anglesey and of Tavistock, several earls, lords, viscounts ; amongst the least were the two men, " walking humbly side by side," who were the only real friends who soothed his dying hours—the author of the Pleasures of Memory, Samuel Rogers, and the excellent physician, Dr. Bain. It

was with great difficulty that an unoccupied spot could be
found in the Poet's Corner for the remains; but at last, close
to his great patron and attached friend, the immortal Garrick,
they found their resting-place, and a plain flat stone tells the
passer by that there is to be found—

RICHARD BRINSLEY SHERIDAN,

Born 1751,

Died 7th July, 1816.

This marble is the tribute of an attached friend,

Peter Moore.

THE RIVALS.

A COMEDY.

PREFACE

A PREFACE to a play seems generally to be considered as a kind of closet-prologue, in which—if his piece has been successful—the author solicits that indulgence from the reader which he had before experienced from the audience: but as the scope and immediate object of a play is to please a mixed assembly in *representation* (whose judgment in the theatre at least is decisive), its degree of reputation is usually as determined as public, before it can be prepared for the cooler tribunal of the study. Thus any farther solicitude on the part of the writer becomes unnecessary at least, if not an intrusion: and if the piece has been condemned in the performance, I fear an address to the closet, like an appeal to posterity, is constantly regarded as the procrastination of a suit, from a consciousness of the weakness of the cause. From these considerations, the following comedy would certainly have been submitted to the reader, without any farther introduction than what it had in the representation, but that its success has probably been founded on a circumstance which the author is informed has not before attended a theatrical trial, and which consequently ought not to pass unnoticed.

I need scarcely add, that the circumstance alluded to was the withdrawing of the piece, to remove those imperfections in the first representation which were too obvious to escape reprehension, and too numerous to admit of a hasty correction. There are few writers, I believe, who, even in the fullest consciousness of error, do not wish to palliate the faults which they acknowledge; and, however, trifling the performance, to second their confession of its deficiencies, by whatever plea seems least disgraceful to their ability. In the present instance, it cannot be said to amount either to candour or modesty in me, to acknowledge an extreme inexperience and want of judgment on matters, in which, without guidance from practice, or spur from success, a young man should scarcely boast of being an adept. If it be said, that under such disadvantages no one should attempt to write a play, I must beg leave to dissent from the position, while the first point of experience that I have gained on the subject is, a knowledge of the candour and judgment with which an impartial public distinguishes between the errors of inexperience and incapacity, and the indulgence which it shows even to a disposition to remedy the defects of either.

It were unnecessary to enter into any farther extenuation of what was thought exceptionable in this play, but that it has been said, that the managers should have prevented some of the defects before its appearance to the public—and in particular the uncommon length of the piece as represented

the first night. It were an ill return for the most liberal and gentlemanly
conduct on their side, to suffer any censure to rest where none was deserved.
Hurry in writing has long been exploded as an excuse for an author;—however, in the dramatic line, it may happen, that both an author and a manager
may wish to fill a chasm in the entertainment of the public with a hastiness
not altogether culpable. The season was advanced when I first put the play
into Mr. Harris's hands: it was at that time at least double the length of
any acting comedy. I profited by his judgment and experience in the cur-
tailing of it—till, I believe, his feeling for the vanity of a young author got
the better of his desire for correctness, and he left many excrescences remaining, because he had assisted in pruning so many more. Hence, though I
was not uninformed that the acts were still too long, I flattered myself that,
after the first trial, I might with safer judgment proceed to remove what
should appear to have been most dissatisfactory. Many other errors there
were, which might in part have arisen from my being by no means conversant with plays in general, either in reading or at the theatre. Yet I own
that, in one respect, I did not regret my ignorance: for as my first wish in
attempting a play was to avoid every appearance of plagiary, I thought I
should stand a better chance of effecting this from being in a walk which I
had not frequented, and where, consequently, the progress of invention was
less likely to be interrupted by starts of recollection : for on subjects on which
the mind has been much informed, invention is slow of exerting itself. Faded
ideas float in the fancy like half-forgotten dreams ; and the imagination in its
fullest enjoyments becomes suspicious of its offspring, and doubts whether it
has created or adopted.

With regard to some particular passages which on the first night's representation seemed generally disliked, I confess, that if I felt any emotion of
surprise at the disapprobation, it was not that they were disapproved of, but
that I had not before perceived that they deserved it. As some part of the
attack on the piece was begun too early to pass for the sentence of *judgment*,
which is ever tardy in condemning, it has been suggested to me, that much
of the disapprobation must have arisen from virulence of malice, rather than
severity of criticism : but as I was more apprehensive of there being just
grounds to excite the latter than conscious of having deserved the former, I
continue not to believe that probable, which I am sure must have been unprovoked. However, if it was so, and I could even mark the quarter from
whence it came, it would be ungenerous to retort: for no passion suffers
more than malice from disappointment. For my own part, I see no reason
why the author of a play should not regard a first night's audience as a candid
and judicious friend attending, in behalf of the public, at his last rehearsal. If he can dispense with flattery, he is sure at least of sincerity, and
even though the annotation be rude, he may rely upon the justness of the comment. Considered in this light, that audience, whose *fiat* is essential to the
poet's claim, whether his object be fame or profit, has surely a right to expect some deference to its opinion, from principles of politeness at least, if not
from gratitude.

As for the little puny critics, who scatter their peevish strictures in private
circles, and scribble at every author who has the eminence of being unconnected
with them, as they are usually spleen-swoln from a vain idea of increasing
their consequence, there will always be found a petulance and illiberality in

their remarks, which should place them as far beneath the notice of a gentleman, as their original dulness had sunk them from the level of the most unsuccessful author.

It is not without pleasure that I catch at an opportunity of justifying myself from the charge of intending any national reflection in the character of Sir Lucius O'Trigger. If any gentleman opposed the piece from that idea, I thank them sincerely for their opposition; and if the condemnation of this comedy (however misconceived the provocation) could have added one spark to the decaying flame of national attachment to the country supposed to be reflected on, I should have been happy in its fate; and might with truth have boasted, that it had done more real service in its failure, than the successful morality of a thousand stage-novels will ever effect.

It is usual, I believe, to thank the performers in a new play, for the exertion of their several abilities. But where (as in this instance) their merit has been so striking and uncontroverted, as to call for the warmest and truest applause from a number of judicious audiences, the poet's after-praise comes like the feeble acclamation of a child to close the shouts of a multitude. The conduct, however, of the principals in a theatre cannot be so apparent to the public. I think it therefore but justice to declare, that from this theatre (the only one I can speak of from experience) those writers who wish to try the dramatic line will meet with that candour and liberal attention, which are generally allowed to be better calculated to lead genius into excellence, than either the precepts of judgment, or the guidance of experience.

THE AUTHOR.

- · ---------

DRAMATIS PERSONÆ,

AS ORIGINALLY ACTED AT COVENT-GARDEN THEATRE IN 1775.

Sir Anthony Absolute . . }	*Mr. Shuter.*
Captain Absolute	*Mr. Woodward.*
Faulkland . . .	*Mr. Lewis.*
Acres	*Mr. Quick.*
Sir Lucius O'Trigger . . . }	*Mr. Lee.*
Fag	*Mr. Lee Lewes.*
David	*Mr. Dunstal.*
Thomas . . .	*Mr. Fearon.*
Mrs. Malaprop	*Mrs. Green.*
Lydia Languish	*Miss Barsanti*
Julia	*Mrs. Bulkley.*
Lucy . . .	{ *Mrs. Lessingham.*

Maid, Boy, Servants, &c.

SCENE—BATH.

Time of Action—Five Hours

PROLOGUE.

BY THE AUTHOR.

SPOKEN BY MR. WOODWARD AND MR. QUICK.

Enter SERJEANT-AT-LAW, *and* ATTORNEY *following, and giving a paper.*

Serj. WHAT 's here !—a vile cramp hand ! I cannot see
Without my spectacles.

Att.   He means his fee.
Nay, Mr. Serjeant, good sir, try again.   [*Gives money*
Serj. The scrawl improves ! [*more*] O come, 'tis pretty plain
Hey ! how 's this ? Dibble !—sure it cannot be !
A poet's brief ! a poet and a fee !

Att. Yes, sir ! though you without reward, I know,
Would gladly plead the Muse's cause.

Serj.   So !—so !

Att. And if the fee offends, your wrath should fall
On me.

Serj.   Dear Dibble, no offence at all.

Att. Some sons of Phœbus in the courts we meet,

Serj. And fifty sons of Phœbus in the Fleet !

Att. Nor pleads he worse, who with a decent sprig
Of bays adorns his legal waste of wig.

Serj. Full-bottom'd heroes thus, on signs, unfurl
A leaf of laurel in a grove of curl !
Yet tell your client, that, in adverse days,
This wig is warmer than a bush of bays.

Att. Do you, then, sir, my client's place supply,
Profuse of robe, and prodigal of tie——
Do you, with all those blushing powers of face,
And wonted bashful hesitating grace,
Rise in the court, and flourish on the case.   [*Exit*

Serj. For practice then suppose—this brief will show it,—
Me, Serjeant Woodward,—counsel for the poet.
Used to the ground, I know 'tis hard to deal
With this dread court, from whence there 's no appeal ;
No tricking here, to blunt the edge of law,
Or, damn'd in equity, escape by flaw :
But judgment given, your sentence must remain ;
No writ of error lies—to Drury-lane !

Yet when so kind you seem, 'tis past dispute
We gain some favour, if not costs of suit.
No spleen is here! I see no hoarded fury;—
I think I never faced a milder jury!
Sad else our plight! where frowns are transportation,
A hiss the gallows, and a groan damnation!
But such the public candour, without fear
My client waves all right of challenge here.
No newsman from our session is dismiss'd,
Nor wit nor critic we scratch off the list;
His faults can never hurt another's ease,
His crime, at worst, a bad attempt to please:
Thus, all respecting, he appeals to all,
And by the general voice will stand or fall.

PROLOGUE.

BY THE AUTHOR.

SPOKEN ON THE TENTH NIGHT, BY MRS. BULKLEY.

GRANTED our cause, our suit and trial o'er,
The worthy serjeant need appear no more ;
In pleasing I a different client choose,
He served the Poet—I would serve the Muse
Like him, I 'll try to merit your applause,
A female counsel in a female's cause.
  Look on this form*,—where humour, quaint and sly,
Dimples the cheek, and points the beaming eye;
Where gay invention seems to boast its wiles
In amorous hint, and half-triumphant smiles;
While her light mask or covers satire's strokes,
Or hides the conscious blush her wit provokes.
Look on her well—does she seem form'd to teach?
Should you expect to hear this lady preach?
Is grey experience suited to her youth?
Do solemn sentiments become that mouth?
Bid her be grave, those lips should rebel prove
To every theme that slanders mirth or love.
  Yet, thus adorn'd with every graceful art
To charm the fancy and yet reach the heart——

Pointing to the figure of Comedy.

P 2

Must we displace her? And instead advance
The goddess of the woful countenance—
The sentimental Muse!—Her emblems view,
The Pilgrim's Progress, and a sprig of rue!
View her—too chaste to look like flesh and blood—
Primly portray'd on emblematic wood!
There, fix'd in usurpation, should she stand,
She 'll snatch the dagger from her sister's hand:
And having made her votaries weep a flood,
Good heaven! she 'll end her comedies in blood—
Bid Harry Woodward break poor Dunstal's crown!
Imprison Quick, and knock Ned Shuter down;
While sad Barsanti, weeping o'er the scene,
Shall stab herself—or poison Mrs. Green.

    Such dire encroachments to prevent in time,
Demands the critic's voice—the poet's rhyme.
Can our light scenes add strength to holy laws!
Such puny patronage but hurts the cause:
Fair virtue scorns our feeble aid to ask;
And moral truth disdains the trickster's mask
For here their favourite stands*, whose brow severe
And sad, claims youth's respect, and pity's tear;
Who, when oppress'd by foes her worth creates,
Can point a poniard at the guilt she hates.

ACT I.

Scene I.—A Street.

Enter THOMAS; *he crosses the Stage;* FAG *follows, looking after him.*

Fag. What! Thomas! sure 'tis he?—What! Thomas! Thomas!

Thos. Hey!—Odd's life! Mr. Fag!—give us your hand, my old fellow-servant.

Fag. Excuse my glove, Thomas:—I'm devilish glad to see you, my lad. Why, my prince of charioteers, you look as hearty!—but who the deuce thought of seeing you in Bath?

* Pointing to Tragedy.

Thos. Sure, master. Madam Julia, Harry, Mrs. Kate, and the postillion, be all come.

Fag. Indeed!

Thos. Ay, master thought another fit of the gout was coming to make him a visit;—so he'd a mind to gi't the slip, and whip! we were all off at an hour's warning.

Fag. Ay, ay, hasty in every thing, or it would not be Sir Anthony Absolute!

Thos. But tell us, Mr. Fag, how does young master? Odd! Sir Anthony will stare to see the Captain here!

Fag. I do not serve Captain Absolute now.

Thos. Why sure!

Fag. At present I am employed by Ensign Beverley

Thos. I doubt, Mr. Fag, you ha'n't changed for the better

Fag. I have not changed, Thomas.

Thos. No! Why didn't you say you had left young master?

Fag. No.—Well, honest Thomas, I must puzzle you no farther:—briefly then—Captain Absolute and Ensign Beverley are one and the same person.

Thos. The devil they are!

Fag. So it is indeed, Thomas; and the ensign half of my master being on guard at present—the captain has nothing to do with me.

Thos. So, so!—What, this is some freak, I warrant!—Do tell us, Mr Fag, the meaning o't—you know I ha' trusted you.

Fag. You'll be secret, Thomas?

Thos. As a coach-horse.

Fag. Why then the cause of all this is—Love,—Love, Thomas, who (as you may get read to you) has been a masquerader ever since the days of Jupiter.

Thos. Ay, ay:—I guessed there was a lady in the case:—but pray, why does your master pass only for ensign?—Now if he had shammed general indeed——

Fag. Ah! Thomas, there lies the mystery o' the matter. Hark'ee, Thomas, my master is in love with a lady of a very singular taste: a lady who likes him better as a half pay ensign than if she knew he was son and heir to Sir Anthony Absolute, a baronet of three thousand a year.

Thos. That is an odd taste indeed!—But has she got the stuff, Mr. Fag? Is she rich, hey?

Fag. Rich!—Why, I believe she owns half the stocks!
Zounds! Thomas, she could pay the national debt as easily as
I could my washerwoman! She has a lapdog that eats out of
gold,—she feeds her parrot with small pearls,—and all her
thread-papers are made of bank-notes!

Thos. Bravo, faith!—Odd! I warrant she has a set of
thousands at least:—but does she draw kindly with the
captain?

Fag. As fond as pigeons.

Thos. May one hear her name?

Fag. Miss Lydia Languish.—But there is an old tough
aunt in the way; though, by the by, she has never seen my
master—for we got acquainted with miss while on a visit in
Gloucestershire.

Thos. Well—I wish they were once harnessed together in
matrimony.—But pray, Mr. Fag, what kind of a place is this
Bath?—I ha' heard a deal of it—here's a mort o' merry-
making, hey?

Fag. Pretty well, Thomas, pretty well—'tis a good lounge;
in the morning we go to the pump-room (though neither my
master nor I drink the waters); after breakfast we saunter on
the parades, or play a game at billiards; at night we dance;
but damn the place, I'm tired of it: their regular hours
stupify me—not a fiddle nor a card after eleven!—However,
Mr. Faulkland's gentleman and I keep it up a little in private
parties;—I'll introduce you there, Thomas—you'll like him
much.

Thos. Sure I know Mr. Du-Peigne—you know his master
is to marry Madam Julia.

Fag. I had forgot.—But, Thomas, you must polish a little
—indeed you must.—Here now—this wig!—What the devil
do you do with a wig, Thomas?—None of the London whips
of any degree of *ton* wear wigs now.

Thos. More's the pity! more's the pity! I say.—Odd's
life! when I heard how the lawyers and doctors had took to
their own hair, I thought how 'twould go next:—odd rabbit
it! when the fashion had got foot on the bar, I guessed
'twould mount to the box!—but 'tis all out of character,
believe me, Mr. Fag: and look'ee, I'll never gi' up mine—
the lawyers and doctors may do as they will.

Fag. Well, Thomas, we'll not quarrel about that.

Thos. Why, bless you, the gentlemen of the professions ben't all of a mind—for in our village now, thoff Jack Gauge, the exciseman, has ta'en to his carrots, there's little Dick the farrier swears he 'll never forsake his bob, though all the college should appear with their own heads!

Fag. Indeed! well said, Dick!—But hold—mark! mark! Thomas.

Thos. Zooks! 'tis the captain.—Is that the lady with him?

Fag. No, no, that is Madam Lucy, my master's mistress's maid. They lodge at that house—but I must after him to tell him the news.

Thos. Odd! he's giving her money!—Well, Mr. Fag——

Fag. Good-bye, Thomas. I have an appointment in Gyde's Porch this evening at eight; meet me there, and we 'll make a little party. [*Exeunt severally.*

SCENE II.—*A Dressing-room in* MRS. MALAPROP'S *Lodgings.*

LYDIA *sitting on a sofa, with a book in her hand.* LUCY, *as just returned from a message*

Lucy. Indeed, ma'am, I traversed half the town in search of it: I don't believe there's a circulating library in Bath I ha'n't been at.

Lyd. And could not you get *The Reward of Constancy?*

Lucy. No, indeed, ma'am.

Lyd. Nor *The Fatal Connexion?*

Lucy. No, indeed, ma'am.

Lyd. Nor *The Mistakes of the Heart?*

Lucy. Ma'am, as ill luck would have it, Mr. Bull said Miss Sukey Saunter had just fetched it away.

Lyd. Heigh-ho!—Did you inquire for *The Delicate Distress?*

Lucy. Or, *The Memoirs of Lady Woodford?* Yes, indeed, ma'am. I asked every where for it; and I might have brought it from Mr. Frederick's, but Lady Slattern Lounger, who had just sent it home, had so soiled and dog's-eared it, it wa'n't fit for a Christian to read.

Lyd. Heigh-ho!—Yes, I always know when Lady Slattern has been before me. She has a most observing thumb; and, I believe, cherishes her nails for the convenience of making marginal notes.—Well, child, what have you brought me?

Lucy. Oh! here, ma'am.—[*Taking books from under her cloak, and from her pockets.*] This is *The Gordian Knot,*—

and this *Peregrine Pickle*.   Here are *The Tears of Sensibility*, and *Humphrey Clinker*.   This is *The Memoirs of a Lady of Quality, written by herself*, and here the second volume of *The Sentimental Journey*.

Lyd. Heigh-ho!—What are those books by the glass?

Lucy. The great one is only *The Whole Duty of Man*, where I press a few blonds, ma'am.

Lyd. Very well—give me the sal volatile.

Lucy. Is it in a blue cover, ma'am?

Lyd. My smelling-bottle, you simpleton!

Lucy. Oh, the drops!—here, ma'am.

Lyd. Hold!—here's some one coming—quick, see who it is.—[*Exit* Lucy.]   Surely I heard my cousin Julia's voice.

Re-enter LUCY.

Lucy. Lud! ma'am, here is Miss Melville.

Lyd. Is it possible!—   [*Exit* Lucy

Enter JULIA.

Lyd. My dearest Julia, how delighted am I!—[*Embrace.*] How unexpected was this happiness!

Jul. True, Lydia—and our pleasure is the greater.—But what has been the matter?—you were denied to me at first!

Lyd. Ah, Julia, I have a thousand things to tell you!—But first inform me what has conjured you to Bath?—Is Sir Anthony here?

Jul. He is—we are arrived within this hour—and I suppose he will be here to wait on Mrs. Malaprop as soon as he is dressed.

Lyd. Then before we are interrupted, let me impart to you some of my distress!—I know your gentle nature will sympa-thize with me, though your prudence may condemn me!   My letters have informed you of my whole connection with Beverley; but I have lost him, Julia!   My aunt has dis-covered our intercourse by a note she intercepted, and has confined me ever since!   Yet, would you believe it? she has absolutely fallen in love with a tall Irish baronet she met one night since we have been here, at Lady Macshuffle's rout.

Jul. You jest, Lydia!

Lyd. No, upon my word.—She really carries on a kind of correspondence with him, under a feigned name though, till she chooses to be known to him;—but it is a Delia or a Celia, I assure you.

Jul. Then, surely, she is now more indulgent to her niece.

Lyd. Quite the contrary. Since she has discovered her own frailty, she is become more suspicious of mine. Then I must inform you of another plague!—That odius Acres is to be in Bath to-day; so that I protest I shall be teased out of all spirits!

Jul. Come, come, Lydia, hope for the best—Sir Anthony shall use his interest with Mrs. Malaprop.

Lyd. But you have not heard the worst. Unfortunately I had quarrelled with my poor Beverley, just before my aunt made the discovery, and I have not seen him since, to make it up.

Jul. What was his offence?

Lyd. Nothing at all!—But, I don't know how it was, as often as we had been together, we had never had a quarrel, and, somehow, I was afraid he would never give me an opportunity. So, last Thursday, I wrote a letter to myself, to inform myself that Beverley was at that time paying his addresses to another woman. I signed it *your friend unknown*, showed it to Beverley, charged him with his falsehood, put myself in a violent passion, and vowed I'd never see him more.

Jul. And you let him depart so, and have not seen him since?

Lyd. 'Twas the next day my aunt found the matter out. I intended only to have teased him three days and a half, and now I've lost him for ever.

Jul. If he is as deserving and sincere as you have represented him to me, he will never give you up so. Yet consider, Lydia, you tell me he is but an ensign, and you have thirty thousand pounds.

Lyd. But you know I lose most of my fortune if I marry without my aunt's consent, till of age; and that is what I have determined to do, ever since I knew the penalty. Nor could I love the man, who would wish to wait a day for the alternative.

Jul. Nay, this is caprice!

Lyd. What, does Julia tax me with caprice?—I thought her lover Faulkland had inured her to it.

Jul. I do not love even his faults.

Lyd. But apropos—you have sent to him, I suppose ?

Jul. Not yet, upon my word—nor has he the least idea of my being in Bath. Sir Anthony's resolution was so sudden, I could not inform him of it.

Lyd. Well, Julia, you are your own mistress, (though under the protection of Sir Anthony,) yet have you, for this long year, been a slave to the caprice, the whim, the jealousy of this ungrateful Faulkland, who will ever delay assuming the right of a husband, while you suffer him to be equally imperious as a lover.

Jul. Nay, you are wrong entirely. We were contracted before my father's death. That, and some consequent embarrassments, have delayed what I know to be my Faulkland's most ardent wish. He is too generous to trifle on such a point:—and for his character, you wrong him there too. No, Lydia, he is too proud, too noble to be jealous; if he is captious, 'tis without dissembling; if fretful, without rudeness. Unused to the fopperies of love, he is negligent of the little duties expected from a lover—but being unhackneyed in the passion, his affection is ardent and sincere; and as it engrosses his whole soul, he expects every thought and emotion of his mistress to move in unison with his. Yet, though his pride calls for this full return, his humility makes him undervalue those qualities in him which would entitle him to it; and not feeling why he should be loved to the degree he wishes, he still suspects that he is not loved enough. This temper, I must own, has cost me many unhappy hours ; but I have learned to think myself his debtor, for those imperfections which arise from the ardour of his attachment.

Lyd. Well, I cannot blame you for defending him. But tell me candidly, Julia, had he never saved your life, do you think you should have been attached to him as you are ?— Believe me, the rude blast that overset your boat was a prosperous gale of love to him.

Jul. Gratitude may have strengthened my attachment to Mr. Faulkland, but I loved him before he had preserved me; yet surely that alone were an obligation sufficient.

Lyd. Obligation! why a water spaniel would have done as much!—Well, I should never think of giving my heart to a man because he could swim.

Jul. Come, Lydia, you are too inconsiderate.

Lyd. Nay, I do but jest.—What's here?

Re-enter LUCY *in a hurry.*

Lucy. O ma'am, here is Sir Anthony Absolute just come home with your aunt.

Lyd. They'll not come here.—Lucy, do you watch.

[*Exit* LUCY.

Jul. Yet I must go. Sir Anthony does not know I am here, and if we meet, he'll detain me, to show me the town. I'll take another opportunity of paying my respects to Mrs. Malaprop, when she shall treat me, as long as she chooses, with her select words so ingeniously misapplied, without being mispronounced.

Re-enter LUCY.

Lucy. O Lud! ma'am, they are both coming up stairs.

Lyd. Well, I'll not detain you, coz.—Adieu, my dear Julia, I'm sure you are in haste to send to Faulkland.—There—through my room you'll find another staircase.

Jul. Adieu!   [*Embraces* LYDIA, *and exit.*

Lyd. Here, my dear Lucy, hide these books. Quick, quick.—*Fling Peregrine Pickle* under the toilet—throw *Roderick Random* into the closet—put *The Innocent Adultery* into *The Whole Duty of Man*—thrust *Lord Aimworth* under the sofa—cram *Ovid* behind the bolster—there—put *The Man of Feeling* into your pocket—so, so—now lay *Mrs. Chapone* in sight, and leave *Fordyce's Sermons* open on the table.

Lucy. O burn it, ma'am! the hair-dresser has torn away as far as *Proper Pride.*

Lyd. Never mind—open at *Sobriety.*—Fling me *Lord Chesterfield's Letters.*—Now for 'em.   [*Exit* LUCY.

Enter Mrs. MALAPROP, *and* Sir ANTHONY ABSOLUTE.

Mrs. Mal. There, Sir Anthony, there sits the deliberate simpleton who wants to disgrace her family, and lavish herself on a fellow not worth a shilling.

Lyd. Madam, I thought you once——

Mrs. Mal. You thought, miss! I don't know any business you have to think at all—thought does not become a young woman. But the point we would request of you is, that you will promise to forget this fellow—to illiterate him. I say, quite from your memory.

Lyd. Ah, madam! our memories are independent of our wills. It is not so easy to forget.

Mrs. Mal. But I say it is, miss; there is nothing on earth so easy as to forget, if a person chooses to set about it. I'm sure I have as much forgot your poor dear uncle as if he had never existed—and I thought it my duty so to do; and let me tell you, Lydia, these violent memories don't become a young woman.

Sir Anth. Why sure she won't pretend to remember what she's ordered not!—ay, this comes of her reading!

Lyd. What crime, madam, have I committed, to be treated thus?

Mrs. Mal. Now don't attempt to extirpate yourself from the matter; you know I have proof controvertible of it.—But tell me, will you promise to do as you're bid? Will you take a husband of your friends' choosing?

Lyd. Madam, I must tell you plainly, that had I no preference for any one else, the choice you have made would be my aversion.

Mrs. Mal. What business have you, miss, with preference and aversion? They don't become a young woman; and you ought to know, that as both always wear off, 'tis safest in matrimony to begin with a little aversion. I am sure I hated your poor dear uncle before marriage as if he'd been a blackamoor—and yet, miss, you are sensible what a wife I made!—and when it pleased Heaven to release me from him, 'tis unknown what tears I shed!—But suppose we were going to give you another choice, will you promise us to give up this Beverley?

Lyd. Could I belie my thoughts so far as to give that promise, my actions would certainly as far belie my words.

Mrs. Mal. Take yourself to your room.—You are fit company for nothing but your own ill-humours.

Lyd. Willingly, ma'am—I cannot change for the worse.

                                                    [*Exit.*

Mrs. Mal. There's a little intricate hussy for you!

Sir Anth. It is not to be wondered at, ma'am,—all this is

the natural consequence of teaching girls to read. Had I a thousand daughters, by Heaven! I'd as soon have them taught the black art as their alphabet!

Mrs. Mal. Nay, nay, Sir Anthony, you are an absolute misanthropy.

Sir Anth. In my way hither, Mrs. Malaprop, I observed your niece's maid coming forth from a circulating library!— She had a book in each hand—they were half-bound volumes, with marble covers!—From that moment I guessed how full of duty I should see her mistress!

Mrs. Mal. Those are vile places, indeed!

Sir Anth. Madam, a circulating library in a town is as an evergreen tree of diabolical knowledge! It blossoms through the year!—And depend on it, Mrs. Malaprop, that they who are so fond of handling the leaves, will long for the fruit at last.

Mrs. Mal. Fy, fy, Sir Anthony! you surely speak laconically.

Sir Anth. Why, Mrs. Malaprop, in moderation now, what would you have a woman know?

Mrs. Mal. Observe me, Sir Anthony. I would by no means wish a daughter of mine to be a progeny of learning; I don't think so much learning becomes a young woman; for instance, I would never let her meddle with Greek, or Hebrew, or algebra, or simony, or fluxions, or paradoxes, or such inflammatory branches of learning—neither would it be necessary for her to handle any of your mathematical, astronomical, diabolical instruments.—But, Sir Anthony, I would send her, at nine years old, to a boarding-school, in order to learn a little ingenuity and artifice. Then, sir, she should have a supercilious knowledge in accounts;—and as she grew up, I would have her instructed in geometry, that she might know something of the contagious countries;—but above all, Sir Anthony, she should be mistress of orthodoxy, that she might not misspell, and mis-pronounce words so shamefully as girls usually do; and likewise that she might reprehend the true meaning of what she is saying. This, Sir Anthony, is what I would have a woman know;—and I don't think there is a superstitious article in it.

Sir Anth. Well, well, Mrs. Malaprop, I will dispute the point no further with you; though I must confess, that you are a truly moderate and polite arguer, for almost every third word you say is on my side of the question.   But, Mrs. Malaprop, to the more important point in debate—you say you have no objection to my proposal?

Mrs. Mal. None, I assure you.   I am under no positive engagement with Mr. Acres, and as Lydia is so obstinate against him, perhaps your son may have better success.

Sir Anth. Well, madam, I will write for the boy directly. He knows not a syllable of this yet, though I have for some time had the proposal in my head.   He is at present with his regiment.

Mrs. Mal. We have never seen your son, Sir Anthony; but I hope no objection on his side.

Sir Anth. Objection!—let him object if he dare!—No, no, Mrs. Malaprop, Jack knows that the least demur puts me in a frenzy directly.   My process was always very simple—in their younger days, 'twas " Jack, do this ; "—if he demurred, I knocked him down—and if he grumbled at that, I always sent him out of the room.

Mrs. Mal. Ay, and the properest way, o' my conscience!— nothing is so conciliating to young people as severity.— Well, Sir Anthony, I shall give Mr. Acres his discharge, and prepare Lydia to receive your son's invocations :—and I hope you will represent her to the captain as an object not altogether illegible.

Sir Anth. Madam, I will handle the subject prudently.— Well, I must leave you ; and let me beg you, Mrs. Malaprop, to enforce this matter roundly to the girl.—Take my advice— keep a tight hand: if she rejects this proposal, clap her under lock and key ; and if you were just to let the servants forget to bring her dinner for three or four days, you can't conceive how she'd come about.   [*Exit.*

Mrs. Mal. Well, at any rate I shall be glad to get her from under my intuition. 'She has somehow discovered my partiality for Sir Lucius O'Trigger—sure, Lucy can't have betrayed me!—No, the girl is such a simpleton, I should have made her confess it.—Lucy!—Lucy!—[*Calls.*]   Had she been one of your artificial ones, I should never have trusted her.

Re-enter LUCY.

Lucy. Did you call, ma'am?

Mrs. Mal. Yes, girl.—Did you see Sir Lucius while you was out?

Lucy. No, indeed, ma'am, not a glimpse of him.

Mrs. Mal. You are sure, Lucy, that you never mentioned——

Lucy Oh gemini! I'd sooner cut my tongue out.

Mrs. Mal. Well, don't let your simplicity be imposed on.

Lucy. No, ma'am.

Mrs. Mal. So, come to me presently, and I'll give you another letter to Sir Lucius; but mind, Lucy—if ever you betray what you are entrusted with (unless it be other people's secrets to me), you forfeit my malevolence for ever; and your being a simpleton shall be no excuse for your locality. [*Exit.*

Lucy. Ha! ha! ha!—So, my dear Simplicity, let me give you a little respite.—[*Altering her manner.*] Let girls in my station be as fond as they please of appearing expert, and knowing in their trusts; commend me to a mask of silliness, and a pair of sharp eyes for my own interest under it!—Let me see to what account have I turned my simplicity lately.— [*Looks at a paper.*] For *abetting Miss Lydia Languish in a design of running away with an ensign!—in money, sundry times, twelve pound twelve; gowns, five; hats, ruffles, caps, &c. &c., numberless!—From the said ensign, within this last month, six guineas and a half.*—About a quarter's pay!— Item, *from Mrs. Malaprop, for betraying the young people to her*—when I found matters were likely to be discovered— *two guineas, and a black paduasoy.*—Item, *from Mr. Acres, for carrying divers letters*—which I never delivered—*two guineas, and a pair of buckles.*—Item, *from Sir Lucius O'Trigger, three crowns, two gold pocket-pieces, and a silver snuff-box!* —Well done, Simplicity!—Yet I was forced to make my Hibernian believe, that he was corresponding, not with the aunt, but with the niece: for though not over rich, I found he had too much pride and delicacy to sacrifice the feelings of a gentleman to the necessities of his fortune.　　　[*Exit.*

ACT II.

Scene I.—Captain Absolute's *Lodgings.*

Captain Absolute *and* Fag.

Fag. Sir, while I was there Sir Anthony came in: I told

him, you had sent me to inquire after his health, and to know if he was at leisure to see you.

Abs. And what did he say, on hearing I was at Bath?

Fag. Sir, in my life I never saw an elderly gentleman more astonished! He started back two or three paces, rapped out a dozen interjectural oaths, and asked, what the devil had brought you here.

Abs. Well, sir, and what did you say?

Fag. Oh, I lied, sir—I forget the precise lie; but you may depend on't, he got no truth from me. Yet, with submission, for fear of blunders in future, I should be glad to fix what has brought us to Bath; in order that we may lie a little consistently. Sir Anthony's servants were curious, sir, very curious indeed.

Abs. You have said nothing to them?

Fag. Oh, not a word, sir,—not a word! Mr. Thomas, indeed, the coachman (whom I take to be the discreetest of whips)——

Abs. 'Sdeath!—you rascal! you have not trusted him!

Fag. Oh, no, sir—no—no—not a syllable, upon my veracity!—He was, indeed, a little inquisitive; but I was sly, sir—devilish sly! My master (said I), honest Thomas, (you know, sir, one says honest to one's inferiors,) is come to Bath to recruit—Yes, sir, I said to recruit—and whether for men, money, or constitution, you know, sir, is nothing to him, nor any one else.

Abs. Well, recruit will do—let it be so.

Fag. Oh, sir, recruit will do surprisingly—indeed, to give the thing an air, I told Thomas, that your honour had already enlisted five disbanded chairmen, seven minority waiters, and thirteen billiard-markers.

Abs. You blockhead, never say more than is necessary.

Fag. I beg pardon, sir—I beg pardon—but, with submission, a lie is nothing unless one supports it. Sir, whenever I draw on my invention for a good current lie, I always forge indorsements as well as the bill.

Abs. Well, take care you don't hurt your credit, by offering too much security.—Is Mr. Faulkland returned?

Fag. He is above, sir, changing his dress.

Abs. Can you tell whether he has been informed of Sir Anthony and Miss Melville's arrival?

Fag. I fancy not, sir; he has seen no one since he came in but his gentleman, who was with him at Bristol.—I think, sir, I hear Mr. Faulkland coming down——

Abs. Go, tell him I am here.

Fag. Yes, sir.—[*Going.*] I beg pardon, sir, but should Sir Anthony call, you will do me the favour to remember that we are recruiting, if you please.

Abs. Well, well.

Fag. And, in tenderness to my character, if your honour could bring in the chairmen and waiters, I should esteem it as an obligation; for though I never scruple a lie to serve my master, yet it hurts one's conscience to be found out.

[*Exit.*

Abs. Now for my whimsical friend—if he does not know that his mistress is here, I'll tease him a little before I tell him—

Enter FAULKLAND.

Faulkland, you're welcome to Bath again; you are punctual in your return.

Faulk. Yes; I had nothing to detain me, when I had finished the business I went on. Well, what news since I left you? how stand matters between you and Lydia?

Abs. Faith, much as they were; I have not seen her since our quarrel; however, I expect to be recalled every hour.

Faulk. Why don't you persuade her to go off with you at once?

Abs. What, and lose two-thirds of her fortune? you forget that, my friend.—No, no, I could have brought her to that long ago.

Faulk. Nay then, you trifle too long—if you are sure of her, propose to the aunt in your own character, and write to Sir Anthony for his consent.

Abs. Softly, softly; for though I am convinced my little Lydia would elope with me as Ensign Beverley, yet am I by no means certain that she would take me with the impediment of our friends' consent, a regular humdrum wedding, and the reversion of a good fortune on my side: no, no; I must prepare her gradually for the discovery, and make myself necessary to her, before I risk it.—Well, but Faulkland, you'll dine with us to-day at the hotel?

Faulk. Indeed I cannot; I am not in spirits to be of such a party.

Abs. By heavens! I shall forswear your company. You are the most teasing, captious, incorrigible lover!—Do love like a man

Faulk. I own I am unfit for company.

Abs. Am not I a lover; ay, and a romantic one too? Yet do I carry every where with me such a confounded farrago of doubts, fears, hopes, wishes, and all the flimsy furniture of a country miss's brain!

Faulk. Ah! Jack, your heart and soul are not, like mine, fixed immutably on one only object. You throw for a large stake, but losing, you could stake and throw again:—but I have set my sum of happiness on this cast, and not to succeed, were to be stripped of all.

Abs. But, for Heaven's sake! what grounds for apprehension can your whimsical brain conjure up at present?

Faulk. What grounds for apprehension, did you say? Heavens! are there not a thousand! I fear for her spirits— her health—her life.—My absence may fret her; her anxiety for my return, her fears for me may oppress her gentle temper: and for her health, does not every hour bring me cause to be alarmed? If it rains, some shower may even then have chilled her delicate frame! If the wind be keen, some rude blast may have affected her! The heat of noon, the dews of the evening, may endanger the life of her, for whom only I value mine. O Jack! when delicate and feeling souls are separated, there is not a feature in the sky, not a movement of the elements, not an aspiration of the breeze, but hints some cause for a lover's apprehension!

Abs. Ay, but we may choose whether we will take the hint or not.—So, then, Faulkland, if you were convinced that Julia were well and in spirits, you would be entirely content?

Faulk. I should be happy beyond measure—I am anxious only for that.

Abs. Then to cure your anxiety at once—Miss Melville is in perfect health, and is at this moment in Bath.

Faulk. Nay, Jack—don't trifle with me.

Abs. She is arrived here with my father within this hour.

Faulk. Can you be serious?

Abs. I thought you knew Sir Anthony better than to be

surprised at a sudden whim of this kind.—Seriously, then, it is as I tell you—upon my honour.

Faulk. My dear friend!—Hollo, Du Peigne! my hat.—My dear Jack—now nothing on earth can give me a moment's uneasiness

Re-enter FAG.

Fag. Sir, Mr. Acres, just arrived, is below.

Abs. Stay, Faulkland, this Acres lives within a mile of Sir Anthony, and he shall tell you how your mistress has been ever since you left her.—Fag, show the gentleman up.

[*Exit* FAG.

Faulk. What, is he much acquainted in the family?

Abs. Oh, very intimate: I insist on your not going: besides, his character will divert you.

Faulk. Well, I should like to ask him a few questions.

Abs. He is likewise a rival of mine—that is, of my other self's, for he does not think his friend Captain Absolute ever saw the lady in question; and it is ridiculous enough to hear him complain to me of one Beverley, a concealed skulking rival, who——

Faulk. Hush!—he's here.

Enter ACRES.

Acres. Ha! my dear friend, noble captain, and honest Jack, how do'st thou? just arrived, faith, as you see.—Sir, your humble servant.—Warm work on the roads, Jack!—Odds whips and wheels! I've travelled like a comet, with a tail of dust all the way as long as the Mall.

Abs. Ah! Bob, you are indeed an eccentric planet, but we know your attraction hither.—Give me leave to introduce Mr. Faulkland to you; Mr. Faulkland, Mr. Acres.

Acres. Sir, I am most heartily glad to see you: sir, I solicit your connections.—Hey, Jack—what, this is Mr. Faulkland, who——

Abs. Ay, Bob, Miss Melville's Mr. Faulkland

Acres. Odso! she and your father can be but just arrived before me:—I suppose you have seen them. Ah! Mr. Faulkland, you are indeed a happy man.

Faulk. I have not seen Miss Melville, yet, sir;—I hope she enjoyed full health and spirits in Devonshire?

Acres. Never knew her better in my life, sir,—never better. Odds blushes and blooms! she has been as healthy as the German Spa.

Faulk. Indeed!—I did hear that she had been a little indisposed

Acres. False, false, sir—only said to vex you: quite the reverse, I assure you.

Faulk There, Jack, you see she has the advantage of me; I had almost fretted myself ill.

Abs. Now are you angry with your mistress for not having been sick?

Faulk. No, no, you misunderstand me: yet surely a little trifling indisposition is not an unnatural consequence of absence from those we love.—Now confess—isn't there something unkind in this violent, robust, unfeeling health?

Abs. Oh, it was very unkind of her to be well in your absence, to be sure!

Acres. Good apartments, Jack.

Faulk. Well, sir, but you was saying that Miss Melville has been so exceedingly well—what then she has been merry and gay, I suppose?—Always in spirits—hey?

Acres. Merry, odds crickets! she has been the belle and spirit of the company wherever she has been—so lively and entertaining! so full of wit and humour!

Faulk. There, Jack, there.—Oh, by my soul! there is an innate levity in woman, that nothing can overcome.—What! happy, and I away!

Abs. Have done.—How foolish this is! just now you were only apprehensive for your mistress' spirits.

Faulk. Why, Jack, have I been the joy and spirit of the company?

Abs. No indeed, you have not.

Faulk. Have I been lively and entertaining?

Abs. Oh, upon my word, I acquit you.

Faulk. Have I been full of wit and humour?

Abs. No, faith, to do you justice, you have been confoundedly stupid indeed.

Acres. What's the matter with the gentleman?

Abs. He is only expressing his great satisfaction at hearing that Julia has been so well and happy—that's all—hey, Faulkland?

Faulk. Oh! I am rejoiced to hear it—yes, yes, she has a happy disposition!

Acres. That she has indeed—then she is so accomplished—so sweet a voice—so expert at her harpsichord—such a mistress of flat and sharp, squallante, rumblante, and quiverante!—There was this time month—odds minims and crotchets! how she did chirrup at Mrs. Piano's concert!

Faulk. There again, what say you to this? you see she has been all mirth and song—not a thought of me!

Abs. Pho! man, is not music the food of love?

Faulk. Well, well, it may be so.—Pray, Mr. ——, what's his damned name?—Do you remember what songs Miss Melville sung?

Acres. Not I indeed.

Abs. Stay, now, they were some pretty melancholy purling-stream airs, I warrant; perhaps you may recollect;—did she sing, *When absent from my soul's delight?*

Acres. No, that wa'n't it.

Abs. Or, *Go, gentle gales!*   [*Sings.*

Acres. Oh, no! nothing like it.   Odds! now I recollect one of them—*My heart's my own, my will is free.*   [*Sings.*

Faulk. Fool! fool that I am! to fix all my happiness on such a trifler! 'Sdeath! to make herself the pipe and ballad-monger of a circle! to soothe her light heart with catches and glees!—What can you say to this, sir?

Abs. Why, that I should be glad to hear my mistress had been so merry, sir.

Faulk. Nay, nay, nay—I'm not sorry that she has been happy—no, no, I am glad of that—I would not have had her sad or sick—yet surely a sympathetic heart would have shown itself even in the choice of a song—she might have been temperately healthy, and somehow, plaintively gay;—but she has been dancing too, I doubt not!

Acres. What does the gentleman say about dancing?

Abs. He says the lady we speak of dances as well as she sings.

Acres. Ay, truly, does she—there was at our last race ball——

Faulk. Hell and the devil! There!—there—I told you so! I told you so! Oh! she thrives in my absence!—Dancing! but her whole feelings have been in opposition with mine;—I have been anxious, silent, pensive, sedentary—my days have been hours of care, my nights of watchfulness.—She has been all health! spirit! laugh! song! dance!—Oh! damned, damned levity!

Abs. For Heaven's sake, Faulkland, don't expose yourself so!—Suppose she has danced, what then?—does not the ceremony of society often oblige ——

Faulk. Well, well, I'll contain myself—perhaps as you say—for form sake.—What, Mr. Acres, you were praising Miss Melville's manner of dancing a minuet—hey?

Acres. Oh, I dare insure her for that—but what I was going to speak of was her country-dancing. Odds swimmings! she has such an air with her!

Faulk. Now disappointment on her!—Defend this, Absolute; why don't you defend this?—Country-dances! jigs and reels! am I to blame now? A minuet I could have forgiven—I should not have minded that—I say I should not have regarded a minuet—but country-dances!—Zounds! had she made one in a cotillion—I believe I could have forgiven even that—but to be monkey-led for a night!—to run the gauntlet through a string of amorous palming puppies! to show paces like a managed filly!—Oh, Jack, there never can be but one man in the world whom a truly modest and delicate woman ought to pair with in a country-dance; and, even then, the rest of the couples should be her great-uncles and aunts!

Abs. Ay, to be sure!—grandfathers and grandmothers!

Faulk. If there be but one vicious mind in the set, 'twill spread like a contagion—the action of their pulse beats to the lascivious movement of the jig—their quivering, warm-breathed sighs impregnate the very air—the atmosphere becomes electrical to love, and each amorous spark darts through every link of the chain!—I must leave you—I own I am somewhat flurried—and that confounded looby has perceived it.   [*Going.*

Abs. Nay, but stay, Faulkland, and thank Mr. Acres for his good news.

Faulk. Damn his news!   [*Exit.*

Abs. Ha! ha! ha! poor Faulkland five minutes since—"nothing on earth could give him a moment's uneasiness!"

Acres. The gentleman wa'n't angry at my praising his mistress, was he?

Abs. A little jealous, I believe, Bob.

Acres. You don't say so? Ha! ha! jealous of me—that's a good joke.

Abs. There's nothing strange in that, Bob; let me tell you, that sprightly grace and insinuating manner of yours will do some mischief among the girls here.

Acres. Ah! you joke—ha! ha! mischief—ha! ha! but you know I am not my own property, my dear Lydia has forestalled me. She could never abide me in the country, because I used to dress so badly—but odds frogs and tambours! I shan't take matters so here, now ancient madam has no voice in it: I'll make my old clothes know who's master. I shall straight-way cashier the hunting-frock, and render my leather breeches incapable. My hair has been in training some time.

Abs. Indeed!

Acres. Ay—and tho'ff the side curls are a little restive, my hind-part takes it very kindly.

Abs. Oh, you'll polish, I doubt not.

Acres. Absolutely I propose so—then if I can find out this Ensign Beverley, odds triggers and flints! I'll make him know the difference o't.

Abs. Spoke like a man! But pray, Bob, I observe you have got an odd kind of a new method of swearing——

Acres. Ha! ha! you've taken notice of it—'tis genteel, isn't it!—I didn't invent it myself though; but a commander in our militia, a great scholar, I assure you, says that there is no meaning in the common oaths, and that nothing but their antiquity makes them respectable;—because, he says, the ancients would never stick to an oath or two, but would say, by Jove! or by Bacchus! or by Mars! or by Venus! or by Pallas, according to the sentiment: so that to swear with propriety, says my little major, the oath should be an echo to the sense; and this we call the *oath referential* or *sentimental swearing*— ha! ha! 'tis genteel, isn't it?

Abs. Very genteel, and very new, indeed!—and I dare say will supplant all other figures of imprecation.

Acres. Ay, ay, the best terms will grow obsolete.—Damns have had their day.

Re-enter FAG.

Fag. Sir, there is a gentleman below desires to see you.— Shall I show him into the parlour?

Abs. Ay—you may.

Acres. Well, I must be gone——

Abs. Stay; who is it, Fag?

Fag. Your father, sir.

Abs. You puppy, why didn't you show him up directly?

[*Exit* FAG

Acres. You have business with Sir Anthony.—I expect a message from Mrs. Malaprop at my lodgings. I have sent also to my dear friend Sir Lucius O'Trigger. Adieu, Jack! we must meet at night, when you shall give me a dozen bumpers to little Lydia.

Abs. That I will with all my heart.—[*Exit* ACRES.] Now for a parental lecture—I hope he has heard nothing of the business that has brought me here—I wish the gout had held him fast in Devonshire, with all my soul!

Enter Sir ANTHONY ABSOLUTE.

Sir, I am delighted to see you here; looking so well! your sudden arrival at Bath made me apprehensive for your health.

Sir Anth. Very apprehensive, I dare say, Jack.—What, you are recruiting here, hey?

Abs. Yes, sir, I am on duty.

Sir Anth. Well, Jack, I am glad to see you, though I did not expect it, for I was going to write to you on a little matter of business.—Jack, I have been considering that I grow old and infirm, and shall probably not trouble you long.

Abs. Pardon me, sir, I never saw you look more strong and hearty; and I pray frequently that you may continue so.

Sir Anth. I hope your prayers may be heard, with all my heart. Well then, Jack, I have been considering that I am so strong and hearty I may continue to plague you a long time. Now, Jack, I am sensible that the income of your commission, and what I have hitherto allowed you, is but a small pittance for a lad of your spirit.

Abs. Sir, you are very good.

Sir Anth. And it is my wish, while yet I live, to have my boy make some figure in the world. I have resolved, therefore, to fix you at once in a noble independence.

Abs. Sir, your kindness overpowers me—such generosity makes the gratitude of reason more lively than the sensations even of filial affection.

Sir Anth. I am glad you are so sensible of my attention—and you shall be master of a large estate in a few weeks.

Abs. Let my future life, sir, speak my gratitude; I cannot express the sense I have of your munificence.—Yet, sir, I presume you would not wish me to quit the army?

Sir Anth. Oh, that shall be as your wife chooses.

Abs. My wife, sir!

Sir Anth. Ay, ay, settle that between you—settle that between you.

Abs. A wife, sir, did you say?

Sir Anth. Ay, a wife—why, did not I mention her before?

Abs. Not a word of her, sir.

Sir Anth. Odd so!—I mustn't forget her though.—Yes, Jack, the independence I was talking of is by a marriage—the fortune is saddled with a wife—but I suppose that makes no difference.

Abs. Sir! sir!—you amaze me!

Sir Anth. Why, what the devil's the matter with the fool? Just now you were all gratitude and duty.

Abs. I was, sir,—you talked to me of independence and a fortune, but not a word of a wife.

Sir Anth. Why—what difference does that make? Odds life, sir! if you have the estate, you must take it with the live stock on it, as it stands.

Abs. If my happiness is to be the price, I must beg leave to decline the purchase.—Pray, sir, who is the lady?

Sir Anth. What's that to you, sir?—Come, give me your promise to love, and to marry her directly.

Abs. Sure, sir, this is not very reasonable, to summon my affections for a lady I know nothing of!

Sir Anth. I am sure, sir, 'tis more unreasonable in you to object to a lady you know nothing of.

Abs. Then, sir, I must tell you plainly that my inclinations are fixed on another—my heart is engaged to an angel.

Sir Anth. Then pray let it send an excuse. It is very sorry—but business prevents its waiting on her.

Abs. But my vows are pledged to her.

Sir Anth. Let her foreclose, Jack; let her foreclose; they are not worth redeeming; besides, you have the angel's vows in exchange, I suppose; so there can be no loss there.

Abs. You must excuse me, sir, if I tell you, oncé for all, that in this point I cannot obey you.

Sir Anth. Hark'ee, Jack;—I have heard you for some time with patience—I have been cool—quite cool; but take care— you know I am compliance itself—when I am not thwarted; —no one more easily led—when I have my own way;—but don't put me in a frenzy.

Abs. Sir, I must repeat it—in this I cannot obey you.

Sir Anth. Now damn me! if ever I call you Jack again while I live!

Abs. Nay, sir, but hear me.

Sir Anth. Sir, I won't hear a word—not a word! not one word! so give me your promise by a nod—and I 'll tell you what, Jack—I mean, you dog—if you don't, by——

Abs. What, sir, promise to link myself to some mass of ugliness! to——

Sir Anth. Zounds! sirrah! the lady shall be as ugly as I choose: she shall have a hump on each shoulder; she shall be as crooked as the crescent; her one eye shall roll like the bull's in Cox's Museum; she shall have a skin like a mummy, and the beard of a Jew—she shall be all this, sirrah!—yet I will make you ogle her all day, and sit up all night to write sonnets on her beauty.

Abs. This is reason and moderation indeed!

Sir Anth. None of your sneering, puppy! no grinning, jackanapes!

Abs. Indeed, sir, I never was in a worse humour for mirth in my life.

Sir Anth. 'Tis false, sir, I know you are laughing in your sleeve; I know you 'll grin when I am gone, sirrah!

Abs. Sir, I hope I know my duty better.

Sir Anth. None of your passion, sir! none of your violence, if you please!—It won't do with me, I promise you.

Abs. Indeed, sir, I never was cooler in my life.

Sir Anth. 'Tis a confounded lie!—I know you are in a passion in your heart; I know you are, you hypocritical young dog! but it won't do.

Abs. Nay, sir, upon my word——

Sir Anth. So you will fly out! can't you be cool like me? What the devil good can passion do?—Passion is of no service, you impudent, insolent, overbearing reprobate!—There, you sneer again! don't provoke me!—but you rely upon the mildness of my temper—you do, you dog! you play upon the meekness of my disposition!—Yet take care—the patience of a saint may be overcome at last!—but mark! I give you six hours and a half to consider of this: if you then agree, without any condition, to do every thing on earth that I choose, why—confound you! I may in time forgive you.—If not, zounds! don't enter the same hemisphere with me! don't dare to breathe the same air, or use the same light with me; but get an atmosphere and a sun of your own! I'll strip you of your commission; I'll lodge a five-and-threepence in the hands of trustees, and you shall live on the interest.—I'll disown you, I'll disinherit you, I'll unget you! and damn me! if ever I call you Jack again!   [*Exit.*

Abs. Mild, gentle, considerate father—I kiss your hands! —What a tender method of giving his opinion in these matters Sir Anthony has! I dare not trust him with the truth. —I wonder what old wealthy hag it is that he wants to bestow on me!—Yet he married himself for love! and was in his youth a bold intriguer, and a gay companion!

Re-enter FAG.

Fag. Assuredly, sir, your father is wrath to a degree; he comes down stairs eight or ten steps at a time—muttering, growling, and thumping the banisters all the way: I and the cook's dog stand bowing at the door—rap! he gives me a stroke on the head with his cane; bids me carry that to my master; then kicking the poor turnspit into the area, damns us all, for a puppy triumvirate!—Upon my credit, sir, were I in your place, and found my father such very bad company, I should certainly drop his acquaintance.

Abs. Cease your impertinence, sir, at present.—Did you come in for nothing more?—Stand out of the way!
                              [*Pushes him aside, and exit.*

Fag. So! Sir Anthony trims my master: he is afraid to reply to his father—then vents his spleen on poor Fag!—When one is vexed by one person, to revenge one's self on another, who happens to come in the way, is the vilest injustice! Ah! it shows the worst temper—the basest——

Enter BOY.

Boy. Mr. Fag! Mr. Fag! your master calls you.

Fag. Well, you little dirty puppy, you need not bawl so!—
The meanest disposition! the——

Boy. Quick, quick, Mr. Fag!

Fag. Quick! quick! you impudent jackanapes! am I to
be commanded by you too? you little impertinent, insolent,
kitchen-bred——   [*Exit kicking and beating him.*

SCENE II.—*The North Parade.*

Enter LUCY.

Lucy. So—I shall have another rival to add to my mistress's
list—Captain Absolute. However, I shall not enter his name
till my purse has received notice in form. Poor Acres is dismissed!—Well, I have done him a last friendly office, in
letting him know that Beverley was here before him.—Sir
Lucius is generally more punctual, when he expects to hear
from his *dear Dalia*, as he calls her: I wonder he's not here!
—I have a little scruple of conscience from this deceit;
though I should not be paid so well, if my hero knew that Delia
was near fifty, and her own mistress.

Enter SIR LUCIUS O'TRIGGER.

Sir Luc. Ha! my little ambassadress—upon my conscience,
I have been looking for you; I have been on the South Parade
this half hour.

Lucy. [*Speaking simply.*] O gemini! and I have been
waiting for your worship here on the North.

Sir Luc. Faith!—may be that was the reason we did not
meet; and it is very comical too, how you could go out and I
not see you—for I was only taking a nap at the Parade Coffee-
house, and I chose the window on purpose that I might not
miss you.

Lucy. My stars! Now I'd wager a sixpence I went by
while you were asleep.

Sir Luc. Sure enough it must have been so—and I never
dreamt it was so late, till I waked. Well, but my little girl,
have you got nothing for me?

Lucy. Yes, but I have—I've got a letter for you in my
pocket.

Sir Luc. O faith! I guessed you weren't come empty-handed
—Well—let me see what the dear creature says.

Lucy. There, Sir Lucius. [*Gives him a letter.*

Sir Luc. [Reads.] *Sir—there is often a sudden incentive
impulse in love, that has a greater induction than years of
domestic combination: such was the commotion I felt at the
first superfluous view of Sir Lucius O'Trigger.*—Very pretty,
upon my word.—*Female punctuation forbids me to say more;
yet let me add, that it will give me joy infallible to find Sir
Lucius worthy the last criterion of my affections.* DELIA.
Upon my conscience! Lucy, your lady is a great mistress of
language. Faith, she's quite the queen of the dictionary!—
for the devil a word dare refuse coming at her call—though
one would think it was quite out of hearing.

Lucy. Ay, sir, a lady of her experience——

Sir Luc. Experience! what, at seventeen?

Lucy. O true, sir—but then she reads so—my stars! how
she will read off hand!

Sir Luc. Faith, she must be very deep read to write this
way—though she is rather an arbitrary writer too—for here
are a great many poor words pressed into the service of this
note, that would get their *habeas corpus* from any court in
Christendom.

Lucy. Ah! Sir Lucius, if you were to hear how she talks
of you!

Sir Luc. Oh, tell her I'll make her the best husband in
the world, and Lady O'Trigger into the bargain!—But we
must get the old gentlewoman's consent—and do every thing
fairly.

Lucy. Nay, Sir Lucius, I thought you wa'n't rich enough
to be so nice!

Sir Luc. Upon my word, young woman, you have hit it:—
I am so poor, that I can't afford to do a dirty action.—If I
did not want money, I'd steal your mistress and her fortune
with a great deal of pleasure.—However, my pretty girl,
[*Gives her money.*] here's a little something to buy you a
ribbon; and meet me in the evening, and I'll give you an
answer to this. So, hussy, take a kiss beforehand to put you
in mind. [*Kisses her.*

Lucy. O Lud! Sir Lucius—I never seed such a gemman!
My lady won't like you if you're so impudent.

Sir Luc. Faith she will, Lucy!—That same—pho! what's the name of it?—modesty—is a quality in a lover more praised by the women than liked; so, if your mistress asks you whether Sir Lucius ever gave you a kiss, tell her fifty—my dear.

Lucy. What, would you have me tell her a lie?

Sir Luc. Ah, then, you baggage! I'll make it a truth presently.

Lucy. For shame now! here is some one coming.

Sir Luc. Oh, faith, I'll quiet your conscience!

[*Exit, humming a tune*

Enter FAG.

Fag. So, so, ma'am! I humbly beg pardon.

Lucy. O Lud! now, Mr. Fag—you flurry one so.

Fag. Come, come, Lucy, here's no one by—so a little less simplicity, with a grain or two more sincerity, if you please.—You play false with us, madam.—I saw you give the baronet a letter.—My master shall know this—and if he don't call him out, I will.

Lucy. Ha! ha! ha! you gentlemen's gentlemen are so hasty.—That letter was from Mrs. Malaprop, simpleton.—She is taken with Sir Lucius's address.

Fag. How! what tastes some people have!—Why, I suppose I have walked by her window a hundred times.—But what says our young lady? any message to my master?

Lucy. Sad news, Mr. Fag.—A worse rival than Acres! Sir Anthony Absolute has proposed his son.

Fag. What, Captain Absolute?

Lucy. Even so—I overheard it all.

Fag. Ha! ha! ha! very good, faith. Good bye, Lucy, I must away with this news.

Lucy. Well, you may laugh—but it is true, I assure you.—[*Going.*] But, Mr. Fag, tell your master not to be cast down by this.

Fag. Oh, he'll be so disconsolate!

Lucy. And charge him not to think of quarrelling with young Absolute.

Fag. Never fear! never fear!

Lucy. Be sure—bid him keep up his spirits.

Fag. We will—we will.   [*Exeunt severally*

ACT III.

SCENE I.—*The North Parade*

Enter CAPTAIN ABSOLUTE.

Abs. 'Tis just as Fag told me, indeed. Whimsical enough, faith! My father wants to force me to marry the very girl I am plotting to run away with! He must not know of my connection with her yet awhile. He has too summary a method of proceeding in these matters. However, I'll read my recantation instantly. My conversion is something sudden, indeed—but I can assure him it is very sincere. So, so—here he comes. He looks plaguy gruff.   [*Steps aside*

Enter Sir ANTHONY ABSOLUTE.

Sir Anth. No! I'll die sooner than forgive him. Die, did I say? I'll live these fifty years to plague him. At our last meeting, his impudence had almost put me out of temper. An obstinate, passionate, self-willed boy! Who can he take after? This is my return for getting him before all his brothers and sisters! for putting him, at twelve years old, into a marching regiment, and allowing him fifty pounds a year, besides his pay, ever since! But I have done with him; he's anybody's son for me. I never will see him more, never—never—never.

Abs. [*Aside, coming forward.*] Now for a penitential face.

Sir Anth. Fellow, get out of my way!

Abs. Sir, you see a penitent before you.

Sir Anth. I see an impudent scoundrel before me.

Abs. A sincere penitent. I am come, sir, to acknowledge my error, and to submit entirely to your will.

Sir Anth. What's that?

Abs. I have been revolving, and reflecting, and considering on your past goodness, and kindness, and condescension to me.

Sir Anth. Well, sir?

Abs. I have been likewise weighing and balancing what you were pleased to mention concerning duty, and obedience, and authority.

Sir Anth. Well, puppy?

Abs. Why then, sir, the result of my reflections is—a resolution to sacrifice every inclination of my own to your satisfaction.

Sir Anth. Why now you talk sense—absolute sense—I never heard any thing more sensible in my life. Confound you! you shall be Jack again.

Abs. I am happy in the appellation.

Sir Anth. Why then, Jack, my dear Jack, I will now inform you who the lady really is. Nothing but your passion and violence, you silly fellow, prevented my telling you at first. Prepare, Jack, for wonder and rapture—prepare. What think you of Miss Lydia Languish?

Abs. Languish! What, the Languishes of Worcestershire?

Sir Anth. Worcestershire! no. Did you never meet Mrs. Malaprop and her niece, Miss Languish, who came into our country just before you were last ordered to your regiment?

Abs. Malaprop! Languish! I don't remember ever to have heard the names before. Yet, stay—I think I do recollect something. Languish! Languish! She squints, don't she? A little red-haired girl?

Sir Anth. Squints! A red-haired girl! Zounds! no.

Abs. Then I must have forgot; it can't be the same person.

Sir Anth. Jack! Jack! what think you of blooming, love-breathing seventeen?

Abs. As to that, sir, I am quite indifferent. If I can please you in the matter, 'tis all I desire.

Sir Anth. Nay, but Jack, such eyes! such eyes! so innocently wild! so bashfully irresolute! not a glance but speaks and kindles some thought of love! Then, Jack, her cheeks! her cheeks, Jack! so deeply blushing at the insinuations of her tell-tale eyes! Then, Jack, her lips! O Jack, lips smiling at their own discretion; and if not smiling, more sweetly pouting; more lovely in sullenness!

Abs. That's she indeed. Well done, old gentleman. [*Aside.*

Sir Anth. Then, Jack, her neck! O Jack! Jack!

Abs. And which is to be mine, sir, the niece, or the aunt?

Sir Anth. Why, you unfeeling, insensible puppy, I despise you! When I was of your age, such a description would have made me fly like a rocket! The aunt indeed! Odds life! When I ran away with your mother, I would not have touched any thing old or ugly to gain an empire.

Abs. Not to please your father, sir?

Sir Anth. To please my father! zounds! not to please—Oh, my father—odd so!—yes—yes; if my father indeed had

Jul. Must I never cease to tax my Faulkland with this teasing minute caprice? Can the idle reports of a silly boor weigh in your breast against my tried affection?

Faulk. They have no weight with me, Julia: No, no—I am happy if you have been so—yet only say, that you did not sing with mirth—say that you thought of Faulkland in the dance.

Jul. I never can be happy in your absence. If I wear a countenance of content, it is to show that my mind holds no doubt of my Faulkland's truth. If I seemed sad, it were to make malice triumph; and say, that I had fixed my heart on one, who left me to lament his roving, and my own credulity. Believe me, Faulkland, I mean not to upbraid you, when I say, that I have often dressed sorrow in smiles, lest my friends should guess whose unkindness had caused my tears.

Faulk. You were ever all goodness to me. Oh, I am a brute, when I but admit a doubt of your true constancy!

Jul. If ever without such cause from you, as I will not suppose possible, you find my affections veering but a point, may I become a proverbial scoff for levity and base ingratitude.

Faulk. Ah! Julia, that last word is grating to me. I would I had no title to your gratitude! Search your heart, Julia; perhaps what you have mistaken for love, is but the warm effusion of a too thankful heart.

Jul. For what quality must I love you?

Faulk. For no quality! To regard me for any quality of mind or understanding, were only to esteem me. And for person—I have often wished myself deformed, to be convinced that I owed no obligation there for any part of your affection.

Jul. Where nature has bestowed a show of nice attention in the features of a man, he should laugh at it as misplaced. I have seen men, who in this vain article, perhaps, might rank above you; but my heart has never asked my eyes if it were so or not.

Faulk. Now this is not well from you, Julia—I despise person in a man—yet if you loved me as I wish, though I were an Æthiop, you 'd think none so fair.

Jul. I see you are determined to be unkind! The contract which my poor father bound us in gives you more than a lover's privilege.

Faulk. Again, Julia, you raise ideas that feed and justify my doubts. I would not have been more free—no—I am proud of my restraint. Yet—yet—perhaps your high respect alone for this solemn compact has fettered your inclinations, which else had made a worthier choice. How shall I be sure, had you remained unbound in thought and promise, that I should still have been the object of your persevering love?

Jul. Then try me now. Let us be free as strangers as to what is past: my heart will not feel more liberty!

Faulk. There now! so hasty, Julia! so anxious to be free! If your love for me were fixed and ardent, you would not lose your hold, even though I wished it!

Jul. Oh! you torture me to the heart! I cannot bear it.

Faulk. I do not mean to distress you. If I loved you less I should never give you an uneasy moment. But hear me. All my fretful doubts arise from this. Women are not used to weigh and separate the motives of their affections: the cold dictates of prudence, gratitude, or filial duty, may sometimes be mistaken for the pleadings of the heart. I would not boast; —yet let me say, that I have neither age, person, nor character, to found dislike on; my fortune such as few ladies could be charged with indiscretion in the match. O Julia! when love receives such countenance from prudence, nice minds will be suspicious of its birth.

Jul. I know not whither your insinuations would tend:— but as they seem pressing to insult me, I will spare you the regret of having done so.—I have given you no cause for this!

[*Exit in tears.*

Faulk. In tears! Stay, Julia: stay but for a moment.— The door is fastened!—Julia!—my soul—but for one moment! —I hear her sobbing!—'Sdeath! what a brute am I to use her thus! Yet stay.—Ay—she is coming now:—how little resolution there is in woman!—how a few soft words can turn them!—No, faith!—she is not coming either.—Why, Julia— my love—say but that you forgive me—come but to tell me that—now this is being too resentful. Stay! she is coming too—I thought she would—no steadiness in any thing: her going away must have been a mere trick then—she sha'nt see that I was hurt by it.—I'll affect indifference—[*Hums a tune: then listens.*] No—zounds! she's not coming!—nor don't intend it, I suppose.—This is not steadiness, but obstinacy Yet I deserve it.—What, after so long an absence to quarre with her tenderness!—'twas barbarous and unmanly!—; should be ashamed to see her now.—-I 'll wait till her just re sentment is abated—and when I distress her so again, may I lose her for ever! and be linked instead to some antique virago, whose gnawing passions, and long hoarded spleen, shall make me curse my folly half the day and all the night.

[*Exit.*

SCENE III.—MRS. MALAPROP's *Lodgings.*

MRS. MALAPROP, *with a letter in her hand,* and CAPTAIN ABSOLUTE

Mrs. Mal. Your being Sir Anthony's son, captain, would itself be a sufficient accommodation; but from the ingenuity of your appearance, I am convinced you deserve the character here given of you.

Abs. Permit me to say, madam, that as I never yet have had the pleasure of seeing Miss Languish, my principal inducement in this affair at present is the honour of being allied to Mrs. Malaprop; of whose intellectual accomplishments, elegant manners, and unaffected learning, no tongue is silent.

Mrs. Mal. Sir, you do me infinite honour! I beg, captain, you 'll be seated.—[*They sit.*] Ah! few gentlemen, now-a-days, know how to value the ineffectual qualities in a woman! few think how a little knowledge becomes a gentlewoman!— Men have no sense now but for the worthless flower of beauty!

Abs. It is but too true, indeed, ma'am;—yet I fear our ladies should share the blame—they think our admiration of beauty so great, that knowledge in them would be superfluous. Thus, like garden-trees, they seldom show fruit, till time has robbed them of the more specious blossom.—Few, like Mrs. Malaprop and the orange-tree, are rich in both at once!

Mrs. Mal. Sir, you overpower me with good-breeding.— He is the very pine-apple of politeness!—You are not ignorant, captain, that this giddy girl has somehow contrived to fix her affections on a beggarly, strolling, eaves-dropping ensign, whom none of us have seen, and nobody knows anything of.

Abs. Oh, I have heard the silly affair before.—I 'm not at all prejudiced against her on that account.

Mrs. Mal. You are very good and very considerate, captain

I am sure I have done every thing in my power since I exploded the affair; long ago I laid my positive conjunctions on her, never to think on the fellow again;—I have since laid Sir Anthony's preposition before her; but, I am sorry to say, she seems resolved to decline every particle that I enjoin her

Abs. It must be very distressing, indeed, ma'am.

Mrs. Mal. Oh! it gives me the hydrostatics to such a degree.—I thought she had persisted from corresponding with him; but, behold, this very day, I have interceded another letter from the fellow; I believe I have it in my pocket.

Abs. Oh, the devil! my last note. [*Aside.*

Mrs. Mal. Ay, here it is.

Abs. Ay, my note indeed! O the little traitress Lucy.
[*Aside.*

Mrs. Mal. There, perhaps you may know the writing.
[*Gives him the letter.*

Abs. I think I have seen the hand before—yes, I certainly must have seen this hand before—

Mrs. Mal. Nay, but read it, captain.

Abs. [Reads.] *My soul's idol, my adored Lydia!*—Very tender indeed!

Mrs. Mal. Tender! ay, and profane too, o' my conscience.

Abs. [Reads.] *I am excessively alarmed at the intelligence you send me, the more so as my new rival*——

Mrs. Mal. That's you, sir.

Abs. [Reads.] *Has universally the character of being an accomplished gentleman and a man of honour.*—Well, that's handsome enough.

Mrs. Mal. Oh, the fellow has some design in writing so.

Abs. That he had, I'll answer for him, ma'am.

Mrs. Mal. But go on, sir—you'll see presently.

Abs. [Reads.] *As for the old weather-beaten she-dragon who guards you*—Who can he mean by that?

Mrs. Mal. Me, sir!—me!—he means me!—There—what do you think now?—but go on a little further.

Abs. Impudent scoundrel!—[Reads.] *it shall go hard but I will elude her vigilance, as I am told that the same ridiculous vanity, which makes her dress up her coarse features, and deck her dull chat with hard words which she don't understand*——

Mrs. Mal. There, sir, an attack upon my language! what do you think of that?—an <u>aspersion</u> upon my parts of speech! was ever such a brute! Sure, if I reprehend any thing in this world, it is the use of my oracular tongue, and a nice derangement of epitaphs!

Abs. He deserves to be hanged and quartered! let me see —[Reads.] *same ridiculous vanity——*

Mrs. Mal. You need not read it again, sir.

Abs. I beg pardon, ma'am.—[Reads.] *does also lay her open to the grossest deceptions from flattery and pretended ad miration—an impudent coxcomb!—so that I have a scheme to see you shortly with the old <u>harridan's</u> consent, and even to make her a go-between in our <u>interview.</u>*—Was ever such assurance!

Mrs. Mal. Did you ever hear any thing like it?—he 'll elude my vigilance, will he—yes, yes! ha! ha! he 's very likely to enter these doors;—we 'll try who can plot best!

Abs. So we will, ma'am—so we will! Ha! ha! ha! a conceited puppy, ha! ha! ha!—Well, but Mrs. Malaprop, as the girl seems so infatuated by this fellow, suppose you were to wink at her corresponding with him for a little time—let her even plot an elopement with him—then do you connive at her escape—while I, just in the nick, will have the fellow laid by the heels, and fairly contrive to carry her off in his stead.

Mrs. Mal. I am delighted with the scheme; never was anything better <u>perpetrated</u>!

Abs. But, pray, could not I see the lady for a few minutes now?—I should like to try her temper a little.

Mrs. Mal. Why, I don't know—I doubt she is not prepared for a visit of this kind. There is a decorum in these matters.

Abs. O Lord! she won't mind me—only tell her Bever ley——

Mrs. Mal. Sir!

Abs. Gently, good tongue.　　　　　　　　　　[*Aside.*

Mrs. Mal. What did you say of Beverley?

Abs. Oh, I was going to propose that you should tell her, by way of jest, that it was Beverley who was below; she 'd come down fast enough then—ha! ha! ha!

Mrs. Mal. 'Twould be a trick she well deserves; besides

you know the fellow tells her he'll get my consent to see her—ha! ha! Let him if he can, I say again. Lydia, come down here!—[*Calling.*] He'll make me a go-between in their interviews!—ha! ha! ha! Come down, I say, Lydia! I don't wonder at your laughing, ha! ha! ha! his impudence is truly ridiculous.

Abs. 'Tis very ridiculous, upon my soul, ma'am, ha! ha! ha!

Mrs. Mal. The little hussy won't hear. Well, I'll go and tell her at once who it is—she shall know that Captain Absolute is come to wait on her. And I'll make her behave as becomes a young woman.

Abs. As you please, ma'am.

Mrs. Mal. For the present, captain, your servant. Ah! you've not done laughing yet, I see—elude my vigilance; yes, yes; ha! ha! ha!   [*Exit.*

Abs. Ha! ha! ha! one would think now that I might throw off all disguise at once, and seize my prize with security; but such is Lydia's caprice, that to undeceive were probably to lose her. I'll see whether she knows me.

[*Walks aside, and seems engaged in looking at the pictures.*

Enter LYDIA.

Lyd. What a scene am I now to go through! surely nothing can be more dreadful than to be obliged to listen to the loathsome addresses of a stranger to one's heart. I have heard of girls persecuted as I am, who have appealed in behalf of their favoured lover to the generosity of his rival suppose I were to try it—there stands the hated rival—an officer too!—but oh, how unlike my Beverley! I wonder he don't begin—truly he seems a very negligent wooer!—quite at his ease, upon my word!—I'll speak first—Mr. Absolute.

Abs. Ma'am.   [*Turns round.*

Lyd. O heavens! Beverley!

Abs. Hush!—hush, my life! softly! be not surprised!

Lyd. I am so astonished! and so terrified! and so overjoyed!—for Heaven's sake! how came you here?

Abs. Briefly, I have deceived your aunt—I was informed that my new rival was to visit here this evening, and contriving to have him kept away, have passed myself on her for Captain Absolute.

Lyd. O charming! And she really takes you for young Absolute?

Abs. Oh, she's convinced of it.

Lyd. Ha! ha! ha! I can't forbear laughing to think how her sagacity is overreached!

Abs. But we trifle with our precious moments—such another opportunity may not occur; then let me now conjure my kind, my condescending angel, to fix the time when I may rescue her from undeserving persecution, and with a licensed warmth plead for my reward.

Lyd. Will you then, Beverley, consent to forfeit that portion of my paltry wealth?—that burden on the wings of love?

Abs. Oh, come to me—rich only thus—in loveliness! Bring no portion to me but thy love—'twill be generous in you, Lydia—for well you know, it is the only dower your poor Beverley can repay.

Lyd. How persuasive are his words!—how charming will poverty be with him!   [*Aside.*

Abs. Ah! my soul, what a life will we then live! Love shall be our idol and support! we will worship him with a monastic strictness; abjuring all worldly toys, to centre every thought and action there. Proud of calamity, we will enjoy the wreck of wealth; while the surrounding gloom of adversity shall make the flame of our pure love show doubly bright. By Heavens! I would fling all goods of fortune from me with a prodigal hand, to enjoy the scene where I might clasp my Lydia to my bosom, and say, the world affords no smile to me but here—[*Embracing her.*] If she holds out now, the devil is in it!   [*Aside.*

Lyd. Now could I fly with him to the antipodes! but my persecution is not yet come to a crisis.   [*Aside.*

Re-enter MRS. MALAPROP, *listening.*

Mrs. Mal. I am impatient to know how the little hussy deports herself.   [*Aside*

Abs. So pensive, Lydia!—is then your warmth abated?

Mrs. Mal. Warmth abated!—so!—she has been in a passion, I suppose.   [*Aside*

Lyd. No—nor ever can while I have life.

Mrs. Mal. An ill tempered little devil! She'll be in a passion all her life—will she?   [*Aside.*

Lyd. Think not the idle threats of my ridiculous aunt can ever have any weight with me.

Mrs. Mal. Very dutiful, upon my word!   [*Aside.*

Lyd. Let her choice be Captain Absolute, but Beverley is mine.

Mrs. Mal. I am astonished at her assurance!—to his face —this is to his face!   [*Aside*

Abs. Thus then let me enforce my suit.   [*Kneeling.*

Mrs. Mal. [*Aside.*] Ay, poor young man!—down on his knees entreating for pity!—I can contain no longer.—[*Coming for ward.*] Why, thou vixen!—I have overheard you.

Abs. Oh, confound her vigilance!   [*Aside*

Mrs. Mal. Captain Absolute, I know not how to apologize for her shocking rudeness.

Abs. [*Aside.*] So all's safe, I find.—[*Aloud.*] I have hopes, madam, that time will bring the young lady——

Mrs. Mal. Oh, there's nothing to be hoped for from her! she's as headstrong as an allegory on the banks of Nile.

Lyd. Nay, madam, what do you charge me with now?

Mrs. Mal. Why, thou unblushing rebel—didn't you tell this gentleman to his face that you loved another better? —didn't you say you never would be his?

Lyd. No, madam—I did not.

Mrs. Mal. Good Heavens! what assurance!—Lydia, Lydia, you ought to know that lying don't become a young woman! —Didn't you boast that Beverley, that stroller Beverley, possessed your heart?—Tell me that, I say.

Lyd. 'Tis true, ma'am, and none but Beverley——

Mrs. Mal. Hold!—hold, Assurance!—you shall not be so rude.

Abs. Nay, pray, Mrs. Malaprop, don't stop the young lady's speech: she's very welcome to talk thus—it does not hurt me in the least, I assure you.

Mrs. Mal. You are too good, captain—too amiably patient— but come with me, miss.—Let us see you again soon, captain— remember what we have fixed.

Abs. I shall ma'am.

Mrs. Mal. Come, take a graceful leave of the gentleman

Lyd. May every blessing wait on my Beverley, my loved Bev——

Mrs. Mal. Hussy! I'll choke the word in your throat!—come along—come along.

> [*Exeunt severally;* CAPTAIN ABSOLUTE *kissing his hand to* LYDIA—Mrs. MALAPROP *stopping her from speaking.*

SCENE IV.—ACRES' *Lodgings.*

ACRES, *as just dressed, and* DAVID.

Acres. Indeed, David—do you think I become it so?

Dav. You are quite another creature, believe me, master, by the mass! an' we've any luck we shall see the Devon mon kerony in all the print-shops in Bath!

Acres. Dress does make a difference, David.

Dav. 'Tis all in all, I think.—Difference! why, an' you were to go now to Clod-hall, I am certain the old lady wouldn't know you: master Butler wouldn't believe his own eyes, and Mrs. Pickle would cry, Lard presarve me! our dairy-maid would come giggling to the door, and I warrant Dolly Tester, your honour's favourite, would blush like my waistcoat.—Oons! I'll hold a gallon, there an't a dog in the house but would bark, and I question whether Phillis would wag a hair of her tail!

Acres. Ay, David, there's nothing like polishing.

Dav. So I says of your honour's boots; but the boy never heeds me!

Acres. But, David, has Mr. De-la-grace been here? I must rub up my balancing, and chasing, and boring.

Dav. I'll call again, sir.

Acres. Do—and see if there are any letters for me at the post-office

Dav. I will.—By the mass, I can't help looking at your head!—if I hadn't been by at the cooking, I wish I may die if I should have known the dish again myself! [*Exit.*

Acres. [*Practising a dancing-step.*] Sink, slide—coupee.—Confound the first inventors of cotillons! say I—they are as bad as algebra to us country gentlemen—I can walk a minuet easy enough when I am forced!—and I have been accounted a good stick in a country-dance.—Odds jigs and tabors! I never valued your cross-over to couple—figure in—right and left—and I'd foot it with e'er a captain in the county!—but

these-outlandish heathen allemandes and cotillons are quite
beyond me!—I shall never prosper at 'em, that's sure—mine
are true-born English legs—they don't understand their curst
French lingo!—their *pas* this, and *pas* that, and *pas* t'other!
—damn me! my.feet don't like to be called paws! no, 'tis
certain I have most Antigallican toes!

Enter SERVANT.

Serv. Here is Sir Lucius O'Trigger to wait on you, sir.
Acres. Show him in.   [*Exit* SERVANT.

Enter SIR LUCIUS O'TRIGGER.

Sir Luc. Mr. Acres, I am delighted to embrace you.
Acres. My dear Sir Lucius, I kiss your hands.
Sir Luc. Pray, my friend, what has brought you so suddenly to Bath?
Acres. Faith! I have followed Cupid's Jack-a-lantern, and
find myself in a quagmire at last.—In short, I have been very
ill used, Sir Lucius.—I don't choose to mention names, but
look on me as on a very ill-used gentleman.
Sir Luc. Pray what is the case?—I ask no names.
Acres. Mark me, Sir Lucius, I fall as deep as need be in
love with a young lady—her friends take my part—I follow
her to Bath—send word of my arrival; and receive answer,
that the lady is to be otherwise disposed of.—This, Sir Lucius, I call being ill used.
Sir Luc. Very ill, upon my conscience.—Pray, can you divine the cause of it?
Acres. Why, there's the matter; she has another lover,
one Beverley, who, I am told, is now in Bath.—Odds slanders
and lies! he must be at the bottom of it.
Sir Luc. A rival in the case, is there?—and you think he
has supplanted you unfairly?
Acres. Unfairly! to be sure he has.   He never could have
done it fairly.
Sir Luc. Then sure you know what is to be done!
Acres. Not I, upon my soul!
Sir Luc. We wear no swords here, but you understand me.
Acres. What! fight him!
Sir Luc. Ay, to be sure: what can I mean else?
Acres. But he has given me no provocation.
Sir Luc. Now, I think he has given you the greatest pro

vocation in the world.   Can a man commit a more heinous offence against another than to fall in love with the same woman?   Oh, by my soul! it is the most unpardonable breach of friendship.

Acres. Breach of friendship! ay, ay; but I have no acquaintance with this man.   I never saw him in my life.

Sir Luc. That's no argument at all—he has the less right then to take such a liberty.

Acres. Gad, that's true—I grow full of anger, Sir Lucius! —I fire apace!   Odds hilts and blades! I find a man may have a deal of valour in him, and not know it!   But couldn't I contrive to have a little right of my side?

Sir Luc. What the devil signifies right, when your honour is concerned?   Do you think Achilles, or my little Alexander the Great, ever inquired where the right lay?   No, by my soul, they drew their broad-swords, and left the lazy sons of peace to settle the justice of it.

Acres. Your words are a grenadier's march to my heart! I believe courage must be catching!   I certainly do feel a kind of valour rising as it were—a kind of courage, as I may say.—Odds flints, pans, and triggers! I 'll challenge him directly.

Sir Luc. Ah, my little friend, if I had Blunderbuss Hall here, I could show you a range of ancestry, in the O'Trigger line, that would furnish the new room; every one of whom had killed his man!—For though the mansion-house and dirty acres have slipped through my fingers, I thank heaven our honour and the family-pictures are as fresh as ever.

Acres. O, Sir Lucius! I have had ancestors too!—every man of 'em colonel or captain in the militia!—Odds balls and barrels! say no more—I 'm braced for it.   The thunder of your words has soured the milk of human kindness in my breast;—Zounds! as the man in the play says, *I could do such deeds!*

Sir Luc. Come, come, there must be no passion at all in the case—these things should always be done civilly.

Acres. I must be in a passion, Sir Lucius—I must be in a rage.—Dear Sir Lucius, let me be in a rage, if you love me. Come, here 's pen and paper.—[*Sits down to write.*] I would the ink were red!—Indite, I say indite!—How shall I be-

gin?   Odds bullets and blades! I'll write a good bold hand,
however.

Sir Luc. Pray compose yourself.

Acres. Come—now, shall I begin with an oath?   Do, Sir
Lucius, let me begin with a damme.

Sir Luc. Pho! pho! do the thing decently, and like a
Christian.   Begin now—*Sir*——

Acres. That's too civil by half.

Sir Luc. To prevent the confusion that might arise——

Acres. Well——

Sir Luc. From our both addressing the same lady——

Acres. Ay, there's the reason—*same lady*—well——

Sir Luc. I shall expect the honour of your company——

Acres. Zounds! I'm not asking him to dinner.

Sir Luc. Pray be easy.

Acres. Well then, *honour of your company*——

Sir Luc. To settle our pretensions——

Acres. Well.

Sir Luc. Let me see, ay, King's-Mead-Field will do—*in
King's-Mead-Fields.*

Acres. So, that's done—Well, I'll fold it up presently;
my own crest—a hand and dagger shall be the seal.

Sir Luc. You see now this little explanation will put a stop
at once to all confusion or misunderstanding that might arise
between you.

Acres. Ay, we fight to prevent any misunderstanding.

Sir Luc. Now, I'll leave you to fix your own time.—Take
my advice, and you'll decide it this evening if you can; then
let the worst come of it, 'twill be off your mind to-morrow.

Acres. Very true.

Sir Luc. So I shall see nothing more of you, unless it be by
letter, till the evening.—I would do myself the honour to
carry your message; but, to tell you a secret, I believe I shall
have just such another affair on my own hands.   There is a
gay captain here, who put a jest on me lately, at the expense
of my country, and I only want to fall in with the gentleman,
to call him out.

Acres. By my valour, I should like to see you fight first!
Odds life! I should like to see you kill him, if it was only
to get a little lesson.

Sir Luc. I shall be very proud of instructing you.—Well for the present—but remember now, when you meet your antagonist, do everything in a mild and agreeable manner.— Let your courage be as keen, but at the same time as polished, as your sword.   [*Exeunt severally.*

ACT IV.

Scene I.—Acres' *Lodgings.*
Acres *and* David.

Dav. Then, by the mass, sir! I would do no such thing —ne'er a Sir Lucius O'Trigger in the kingdom should make me fight, when I wa'n't so minded. Oons! what will the old lady say, when she hears o't?

Acres. Ah! David, if you had heard Sir Lucius!—Odds sparks and flames! he would have roused your valour.

Dav. Not he, indeed. I hate such bloodthirsty cormorants. Look'ee, master, if you'd wanted a bout at boxing, quarter-staff, or short-staff, I should never be the man to bid you cry off: but for your curst sharps and snaps, I never knew any good come of 'em.

Acres. But my honour, David, my honour! I must be very careful of my honour.

Dav. Ay, by the mass! and I would be very careful of it; and I think in return my honour couldn't do less than to be very careful of me.

Acres. Odds blades! David, no gentleman will ever risk the loss of his honour!

Dav. I say then, it would be but civil in honour never to risk the loss of a gentleman.—Look'ee, master, this honour seems to me to be a marvellous false friend: ay, truly, a very courtier-like servant.—Put the case, I was a gentleman (which, thank God, no one can say of me;) well—my honour makes me quarrel with another gentleman of my acquaintance.—So —we fight. (Pleasant enough that!) Boh!—I kill him— (the more's my luck!) now, pray who gets the profit of it?— Why, my honour. But put the case that he kills me!—by the mass! I go to the worms, and my honour whips over to my enemy.

Acres. No, David—in that case!—Odds crowns and laurels! your honour follows you to the grave.

Dav. Now, that's just the place where I could make a shift to do without it.

Acres. Zounds! David, you are a coward!—It doesn't become my valour to listen to you.—What, shall I disgrace my ancestors?—Think of that, David—think what it would be to disgrace my ancestors!

Dav. Under favour, the surest way of not disgracing them, is to keep as long as you can out of their company. Look'ee now, master, to go to them in such haste—with an ounce of lead in your brains—I should think might as well be let alone. Our ancestors are very good kind of folks; but they are the last people I should choose to have a visiting acquaintance with.

Acres. But, David, now, you don't think there is such very, very, very great danger, hey?—Odds life! people often fight without any mischief done!

Dav. By the mass, I think 'tis ten to one against you!—Oons! here to meet some lion-headed fellow, I warrant, with his damned double-barrelled swords, and cut-and-thrust pistols!—Lord bless us! it makes me tremble to think o't!—Those be such desperate bloody-minded weapons! Well, I never could abide 'em—from a child I never could fancy 'em!—I suppose there a'nt been so merciless a beast in the world as your loaded pistol!

Acres. Zounds! I won't be afraid!—Odds fire and fury! you shan't make me afraid.—Here is the challenge, and I have sent for my dear friend Jack Absolute to carry it for me.

Dav. Ay, i'the name of mischief, let him be the messenger.—For my part, I wouldn't lend a hand to it for the best horse in your stable. By the mass! it don't look like another letter! It is, as I may say, a designing and malicious-looking letter; and I warrant smells of gunpowder like a soldier's pouch!—Oons! I wouldn't swear it mayn't go off!

Acres. Out, you poltroon! you ha'nt the valour of a grasshopper.

Dav. Well, I say no more—'twill be sad news, to be sure, at Clod-Hall! but I ha' done.—How Phillis will howl when she hears of it!—Ay, poor bitch, she little thinks what shooting her master's going after! And I warrant old Crop, who has carried your honour, field and road, these ten years, will curse the hour he was born   [*Whimpering.*

Acres. It won't do, David—I am determined to fight—so get along you coward, while I'm in the mind.

Enter SERVANT.

Ser. Captain Absolute, sir.

Acres. Oh! show him up.   [*Exit* SERVANT.

Dav. Well, Heaven send we be all alive this time to-morrow.

Acres. What's that?—Don't provoke me, David!

Dav. Good-bye, master.   [*Whimpering.*

Acres. Get along, you cowardly, dastardly, croaking raven!
          [*Exit* DAVID.

Enter CAPTAIN ABSOLUTE.

Abs. What's the matter, Bob?

Acres. A vile, sheep-hearted blockhead! If I hadn't the valour of St. George and the dragon to boot——

Abs. But what did you want with me, Bob?

Acres. Oh!—There——   [*Gives him the challenge.*

Abs. [*Aside.*] *To Ensign Beverley.*—So, what's going on now!—[*Aloud.*] Well, what's this?

Acres. A challenge!

Abs. Indeed! Why, you won't fight him; will you, Bob?

Acres. Egad, but I will, Jack. Sir Lucius has wrought me to it. He has left me full of rage—and I'll fight this evening, that so much good passion mayn't be wasted.

Abs. But what have I to do with this?

Acres. Why, as I think you know something of this fellow, I want you to find him out for me, and give him this mortal defiance.

Abs. Well, give it to me, and trust me he gets it.

Acres. Thank you, my dear friend, my dear Jack; but it is giving you a great deal of trouble.

Abs. Not in the least—I beg you won't mention it.—No trouble in the world, I assure you.

Acres. You are very kind.—What it is to have a friend!—You couldn't be my second, could you, Jack?

Abs. Why no, Bob—not in this affair—it would not be quite so proper.

Acres. Well, then, I must get my friend Sir Lucius. I shall have your good wishes, however, Jack?

Abs. Whenever he meets you, believe me.

Re-enter SERVANT.

Ser. Sir Anthony Absolute is below, inquiring for the captain.

Abs. I 'll come instantly.—[*Exit* SERVANT.] Well, my little hero, success attend you.   [*Going.*

Acres.—Stay—stay, Jack.—If Beverley should ask you what kind of a man your friend Acres is, do tell him I am a devil of a fellow—will you, Jack?

Abs. To be sure I shall. I 'll say you are a determined dog—hey, Bob!

Acres. Ay, do, do—and if that frightens him, egad, per haps he mayn't come. So tell him I generally kill a man a week; will you, Jack?

Abs. I will, I will; I 'll say you are called in the country Fighting Bob.

Acres. Right—right—'tis all to prevent mischief; for I don't want to take his life if I clear my honour.

Abs. No!—that 's very kind of you.

Acres. Why, you don't wish me to kill him—do you, Jack?

Abs. No, upon my soul, I do not. But a devil of a fellow, hey?   [*Going.*

Acres. True, true—but stay—stay, Jack—you may add, that you never saw me in such a rage before—a most devouring rage!

Abs. I will, I will.

Acres. Remember, Jack—a determined dog!

Abs. Ay, ay, Fighting Bob!   [*Exeunt severally.*

SCENE. II.—MRS. MALAPROP'S *Lodgings.*

MRS. MALAPROP *and* LYDIA.

Mrs. Mal. Why, thou perverse one!—tell me what you can object to him? Isn't he a handsome man?—tell me that. A genteel man? a pretty figure of a man?

Lyd. [*Aside.*] She little thinks whom she is praising!— [*Aloud.*] So is Beverley, ma'am.

Mrs Mal. No caparisons, miss, if you please. Caparisons don't become a young woman. No! Captain Absolute is indeed a fine gentleman!

Lyd. Ay, the Captain Absolute you have seen. [*Aside.*

Mrs. Mal. Then he's so well bred;—so full of alacrity, and adulation!—and has so much to say for himself:—in such good language too! His physiognomy so grammatical! Then his presence is so noble! I protest, when I saw him, I thought of what Hamlet says in the play :—

> "Hesperian curls —the front of Job himself!—
> An eye, like March, to threaten at command !—
> A station, like Harry Mercury, new—"

Something about kissing—on a hill—however, the similitude struck me directly.

Lyd. How enraged she'll be presently, when she discovers her mistake! [*Aside.*

Enter SERVANT.

Ser. Sir Anthony and Captain Absolute are below, ma'am.

Mrs. Mal. Show them up here.—[*Exit* SERVANT.] Now, Lydia, I insist on your behaving as becomes a young woman. Show your good breeding, at least, though you have forgot your duty.

Lyd. Madam, I have told you my resolution!—I shall not only give him no encouragement, but I won't even speak to, or look at him.

[*Flings herself into a chair, with her face from the door.*

Enter SIR ANTHONY ABSOLUTE *and* CAPTAIN ABSOLUTE.

Sir Anth. Here we are, Mrs. Malaprop; come to mitigate the frowns of unrelenting beauty,—and difficulty enough I had to bring this fellow.—I don't know what's the matter; but if I had not held him by force, he'd have given me the slip.

Mrs. Mal. You have infinite trouble, Sir Anthony, in the affair. I am ashamed for the cause!—[*Aside to* LYDIA.] Lydia, Lydia, rise, I beseech you!—pay your respects!

Sir Anth. I hope, madam, that Miss Languish has reflected on the worth of this gentleman, and the regard due to her aunt's choice, and my alliance.—[*Aside to* CAPTAIN ABSOLUTE.] Now, Jack, speak to her.

Abs. [*Aside.*] What the devil shall I do!—[*Aside to* SIR ANTHONY.] You see, sir, she won't even look at me whilst

s 2

you are here. I knew she wouldn't! I told you so. Let me entreat you, sir, to leave us together!

[*Seems to expostulate with his father.*

Lyd. [*Aside.*] I wonder I ha'n't heard my aunt exclaim yet! sure she can't have looked at him!—perhaps their regimentals are alike, and she is something blind.

Sir Anth. I say, sir, I won't stir a foot yet!

Mrs. Mal. I am sorry to say, Sir Anthony, that my affluence over my niece is very small.—[*Aside to* LYDIA.] Turn round, Lydia: I blush for you!

Sir Anth. May I not flatter myself, that Miss Languish will assign what cause of dislike she can have to my son!—[*Aside to* CAPTAIN ABSOLUTE.] Why don't you begin, Jack?—Speak, you puppy—speak!

Mrs. Mal. It is impossible, Sir Anthony, she can have any. She will not say she has.—[*Aside to* LYDIA.] Answer, hussy! why don't you answer?

Sir Anth. Then, madam, I trust that a childish and hasty predilection will be no bar to Jack's happiness.—[*Aside to* CAPTAIN ABSOLUTE.]—Zounds! sirrah! why don't you speak!

Lyd. [*Aside.*] I think my lover seems as little inclined to conversation as myself.—How strangely blind my aunt must be!

Abs. Hem! hem! madam—hem!—[*Attempts to speak, then returns to* SIR ANTHONY.] Faith! sir, I am so confounded!—and—so—so—confused!—I told you I should be so, sir—I knew it.—The—the—tremor of my passion entirely takes away my presence of mind.

Sir Anth. But it don't take away your voice, fool, does it?—Go up, and speak to her directly!

[CAPTAIN ABSOLUTE *makes signs to* MRS. MALAPROP *to leave them together.*

Mrs. Mal. Sir Anthony, shall we leave them together?—[*Aside to* LYDIA.] Ah! you stubborn little vixen!

Sir Anth. Not yet, ma'am, not yet!—[*Aside to* CAPTAIN ABSOLUTE.] What the devil are you at? unlock your jaws, sirrah, or——

Abs. [*Aside.*] Now Heaven send she may be too sullen to look round!—I must disguise my voice.—[*Draws near* LYDIA, *and speaks in a low hoarse tone.*] Will not Miss Languish lend an ear to the mild accents of true love? Will not——

Sir Anth. What the devil ails the fellow? Why don't you speak out?—not stand croaking like a frog in a quinsy!

Abs. The—the—excess of my awe, and my—my—my modesty, quite choke me!

Sir Anth. Ah! your modesty again!—I 'll tell you what, Jack; if you don't speak out directly, and glibly too, I shall be in such a rage!—Mrs. Malaprop, I wish the lady would favour us with something more than a side-front.

[MRS. MALAPROP *seems to chide* LYDIA.

Abs. [*Aside*] So all will out, I see!—[*Goes up to* LYDIA, *speaks softly.*] Be not surprised, my Lydia, suppress all supprise at present.

Lyd. [*Aside.*] Heavens! 'tis Beverley's voice! Sure he can't have imposed on Sir Anthony too!—[*Looks round by degrees, then starts up.*] Is this possible!—my Beverley!—how can this be?—my Beverley?

Abs. Ah! 'tis all over.   [*Aside.*

Sir Anth. Beverley!—the devil—Beverley!—What can the girl mean?—This is my son, Jack Absolute.

Mrs. Mal. For shame, hussy! for shame! your head runs so on that fellow, that you have him always in your eyes!—beg Captain Absolute's pardon directly.

Lyd. I see no Captain Absolute, but my loved Beverley!

Sir Anth. Zounds! the girl's mad!—her brain 's turned by reading.

Mrs. Mal. O' my conscience, I believe so!—What do you mean by Beverley, hussy?—You saw Captain Absolute before to-day; there he is—your husband that shall be.

Lyd. With all my soul, ma'am—when I refuse my Beverley——

Sir Anth. Oh! she 's as mad as Bedlam!—or has this fellow been playing us a rogue's trick!—Come here, sirrah, who the devil are you?

Abs. Faith, sir, I am not quite clear myself; but I 'll endeavour to recollect.

Sir Anth. Are you my son or not?—answer for your mother, you dog, if you won't for me.

Mrs. Mal. Ay, sir, who are you? O mercy! I begin to suspect!—

Abs. [*Aside.*] Ye powers of impudence, befriend me!—[*Aloud.*] Sir Anthony, most assuredly I am your wife's son.

and that I sincerely believe myself to be your's also, I hope my duty has always shown.—Mrs. Malaprop, I am your most respectful admirer, and shall be proud to add affectionate nephew.—I need not tell my Lydia, that she sees her faithful Beverley, who, knowing the singular generosity of her temper, assumed that name and station, which has proved a test of the most disinterested love, which he now hopes to enjoy in a more elevated character.

Lyd. So!—there will be no elopement after all! [*Sullenly.*

Sir Anth. Upon my soul, Jack, thou art a very impudent fellow! to do you justice, I think I never saw a piece of more consummate assurance!

Abs. Oh, you flatter me, sir—you compliment—'tis my modesty you know, sir,—my modesty that has stood in my way.

Sir Anth. Well, I am glad you are not the dull, insensible varlet you pretended to be, however!—I'm glad you have made a fool of your father, you dog—I am. So this was your *penitence,* your *duty* and *obedience!*—I thought it was damned sudden!—*You never heard their names before,* not you!—*what the Languishes of Worcestershire,* hey?—*if you could please me in the affair it was all you desired!*—Ah! you dissembling villain!—What!—[*Pointing to* LYDIA] *she squints, don't she?* —*a little red-haired girl!*—hey?—Why, you hypocritical young rascal!—I wonder you an't ashamed to hold up your head!

Abs. 'Tis with difficulty, sir.—I am confused—very much confused, as you must perceive.

Mrs. Mal. O Lud! Sir Anthony!—a new light breaks in upon me!—hey!—how! what! captain, did you write the letters then?—What—am I to thank you for the elegant com-pilation of *an old weather-beaten she-dragon*—hey!—O mercy! —was it you that reflected on my parts of speech?

Abs. Dear sir! my modesty will be overpowered at last, if you don't assist me—I shall certainly not be able to stand it!

Sir Anth. Come, come, Mrs. Malaprop, we must forget and forgive;—odds life! matters have taken so clever a turn all of a sudden, that I could find in my heart to be so good-humoured! and so gallant! hey! Mrs. Malaprop!

Mrs. Mal. Well, sir Anthony, since you desire it, we will

not anticipate the past!—so mind, young people—our retrospection will be all to the future.

Sir Anth. Come, we must leave them together; Mrs. Malaprop, they long to fly into each other's arms, I warrant!—Jack—isn't the cheek as I said, hey?—and the eye, you rogue!—and the lip—hey? Come, Mrs. Malaprop, we'll not disturb their tenderness—theirs is the time of life for happiness!—*Youth's the season made for joy*—[*Sings*]—hey!—Odds life! I'm in such spirits,—I don't know what I could not do!—Permit me, ma'am—[*Gives his hand to* Mrs. MALAPROP.] Tol-de-rol—'gad, I should like to have a little fooling myself—Tol-de-rol! de-rol.

[*Exit, singing and handing* Mrs. MALAPROP.—LYDIA *sits sullenly in her chair.*

Abs. [*Aside.*] So much thought bodes me no good.—[*Aloud.*] So grave, Lydia!

Lyd. Sir!

Abs. [*Aside.*] So!—egad! I thought as much!—that damned monosyllable has froze me!—[*Aloud.*] What, Lydia, now that we are as happy in our friends' consent, as in our mutual vows——

Lyd. Friends' consent indeed!　　　　　　　　[*Peevishly.*

Abs. Come, come, we must lay aside some of our romance—a little wealth and comfort may be endured after all. And for your fortune, the lawyers shall make such settlements as——

Lyd. Lawyers! I hate lawyers!

Abs. Nay, then, we will not wait for their lingering forms, but instantly procure the licence, and——

Lyd. The licence!—I hate licence!

Abs. Oh my love! be not so unkind!—thus let me entreat—— 　　　　　　　　　　　　　　　　　　[*Kneeling.*

Lyd. Psha!—what signifies kneeling, when you know I must have you?

Abs. [*Rising.*] Nay, madam, there shall be no constraint upon your inclinations, I promise you.—If I have lost your heart—I resign the rest—[*Aside.*] 'Gad, I must try what a little spirit will do.

Lyd. [*Rising.*] Then, sir, let me tell you, the interest you had there was acquired by a mean, unmanly imposition, and deserves the punishment of fraud.—What, you have been treating me like a child!—humouring my romance! and laughing, I suppose, at your success!

Abs. You wrong me, Lydia, you wrong me—only hear——

Lyd. So, while I fondly imagined we were deceiving my relations, and flattered myself that I should outwit and incense them all—behold my hopes are to be crushed at once, by my aunt's consent and approbation—and I am myself the only dupe at last!—[*Walking about in a heat.*]   But here, sir, here is the picture—Beverley's picture! [*taking a miniature from her bosom*] which I have worn, night and day, in spite of threats and entreaties!—There, sir; [*flings it to him*] and be assured I throw the original from my heart as easily.

Abs. Nay, nay, ma'am, we will not differ as to that.—Here, [*taking out a picture*] here is Miss Lydia Languish.—What a difference!—ay, there is the heavenly assenting smile that first gave soul and spirit to my hopes!—those are the lips which sealed a vow, as yet scarce dry in Cupid's calendar! and there the half-resentful blush, that would have checked the ardour of my thanks!—Well, all that's past!—all over indeed!—There, madam—in beauty, that copy is not equal to you, but in my mind its merit over the original, in being still the same, is such—that—I cannot find in my heart to part with it.   [*Puts it up again.*

Lyd. [*Softening.*] 'Tis your own doing, sir—I, I, I suppose you are perfectly satisfied.

Abs. O, most certainly—sure, now, this is much better than being in love!—ha! ha! ha!—there's some spirit in this!— What signifies breaking some scores of solemn promises:—all that's of no consequence, you know.—To be sure people will say, that miss don't know her own mind—but never mind that! Or, perhaps, they may be ill-natured enough to hint, that the gentleman grew tired of the lady and forsook her— but don't let that fret you.

Lyd. There is no bearing his insolence. [*Bursts into tears.*

Re-enter MRS. MALAPROP *and* SIR ANTHONY ABSOLUTE.

Mrs. Mal. Come, we must interrupt your billing and cooing awhile.

Lyd. This is worse than your treachery and deceit, you base ingrate!   [*Sobbing.*

Sir Anth. What the devil's the matter now!—Zounds!

Mrs. Malaprop, this is the oddest billing and cooing I ever heard!—but what the deuce is the meaning of it?—I am quite astonished!

Abs. Ask the lady, sir.

Mrs. Mal. Oh mercy!—I'm quite analysed, for my part! —Why, Lydia, what is the reason of this?

Lyd. Ask the gentleman, ma'am.

Sir Anth. Zounds! I shall be in a frenzy!—Why, Jack, you are not come out to be any one else, are you?

Mrs. Mal. Ay, sir, there's no more trick, is there?—you are not like Cerberus, three gentlemen at once, are you?

Abs. You'll not let me speak—I say the lady can account for this much better than I can.

Lyd. Ma'am, you once commanded me never to think of Beverley again—there is the man—I now obey you: for, from this moment, I renounce him for ever.   [*Exit.*

Mrs. Mal. O mercy! and miracles! what a turn here is—why sure, captain, you haven't behaved disrespectfully to my niece.

Sir Anth. Ha! ha! ha!—ha! ha! ha!—now I see it. Ha! ha! ha!—now I see it—you have been too lively, Jack.

Abs. Nay, sir, upon my word——

Sir Anth. Come, no lying, Jack—I'm sure 'twas so.

Mrs. Mal. O Lud! Sir Anthony!—O fy, captain!

Abs. Upon my soul, ma'am——

Sir Anth. Come, no excuses, Jack; why, your father, you rogue, was so before you:—the blood of the Absolutes was always impatient.—Ha! ha! ha! poor little Lydia! why, you've frightened her, you dog, you have.

Abs. By all that's good, sir——

Sir Anth. Zounds! say no more, I tell you—Mrs. Malaprop shall make your peace.—You must make his peace, Mrs. Malaprop:—you must tell her 'tis Jack's way—tell her 'tis all our ways—it runs in the blood of our family!—Come away, Jack —Ha! ha! ha! Mrs. Malaprop—a young villain!

[*Pushing him out.*

Mrs. Mal. O! Sir Anthony!—O fy, captain!

[*Exeunt severally.*

SCENE III.—*The North Parade.*

Enter SIR LUCIUS O'TRIGGER.

Sir Luc I wonder where this Captain Absolute hides him

self! Upon my conscience! these officers are always in one's way in love affairs :—I remember I might have married lady Dorothy Carmine, if it had not been for a little rogue of a major, who ran away with her before she could get a sight of me! And I wonder too what it is the ladies can see in them to be so fond of them—unless it be a touch of the old serpent in 'em, that makes the little creatures be caught, like vipers, with a bit of red cloth. Ha! isn't this the captain coming?—faith it is!—There is a probability of succeeding about that fellow, that is mighty provoking! Who the devil is he talking to?   [Steps aside.

Enter CAPTAIN ABSOLUTE.

Abs. [*Aside.*] To what fine purpose I have been plotting! a noble reward for all my schemes, upon my soul!—a little gipsy!—I did not think her romance could have made her so damned absurd either. 'Sdeath, I never was in a worse humour in my life!—I could cut my own throat, or any other person's, with the greatest pleasure in the world!

Sir Luc. Oh, faith! I'm in the luck of it. I never could have found him in a sweeter temper for my purpose—to be sure I'm just come in the nick! Now to enter into conversation with him, and so quarrel genteelly.—[*Goes up to* CAPTAIN ABSOLUTE.] With regard to that matter, captain, I must beg leave to differ in opinion with you.

Abs. Upon my word, then, you must be a very subtle disputant:—because, sir, I happened just then to be giving no opinion at all.

Sir Luc. That's no reason. For give me leave to tell you, a man may think an untruth as well as speak one.

Abs. Very true, sir; but if a man never utters his thoughts, I should think they might stand a chance of escaping controversy.

Sir Luc. Then, sir, you differ in opinion with me, which amounts to the same thing.

Abs. Hark'ee, Sir Lucius; if I had not before known you to be a gentleman, upon my soul, I should not have discovered it at this interview: for what you can drive at, unless you mean to quarrel with me, I cannot conceive!

Sir Luc. I humbly thank you, sir, for the quickness of your apprehension.—[*Bowing.*] You have named the very thing I would be at.

Abs. Very well, sir ; I shall certainly not balk your inclina
tions.—But I should be glad you would please to explain
your motives.

Sir Luc. Pray sir, be easy; the quarrel is a very pretty
quarrel as it stands ; we should.only spoil it by trying to explain it. However, your memory is very short, or you could
not have forgot an affront you passed on me within this week.
So, no more, but name your time and place.

Abs. Well, sir, since you are so bent on it, the sooner the
better; let it be this evening—here, by the Spring Gardens.
We shall scarcely be interrupted.

Sir Luc. Faith! that same interruption in affairs of this
nature shows very great ill-breeding. I don't know what's
the reason, but in England, if a thing of this kind gets
wind, people make such a pother, that a gentleman can never
fight in peace and quietness. However, if it's the same to
you, captain, I should take it as a particular kindness if you'd
let us meet in King's-Mead-Fields, as a little business will
call me there about six o'clock, and I may despatch both matters at once.

Abs. 'Tis the same to me exactly. A little after six, then,
we will discuss this matter more seriously.

Sir Luc. If you please, sir; there will be very pretty small-
sword light, though it won't do for a long shot. So that matter's settled, and my mind's at ease! [*Exit.*

Enter FAULKLAND.

Abs. Well met! I was going to look for you. O Faulkland! all the demons of spite and disappointment have conspired against me! I'm so vexed, that if I had not the
prospect of a resource in being knocked o' the head by-and-
by, I should scarce have spirits to tell you the cause.

Faulk. What can you mean?—Has Lydia changed her
mind?—I should have thought her duty and inclination would
now have pointed to the same object.

Abs. Ay, just as the eyes do of a person who squints:
when her love-eye was fixed on me, t'other, her eye of duty,
was finely obliqued: but when duty bid her point that the
same way, off t'other turned on a swivel, and secured its retreat with a frown!

Faulk. But what's the resource you——

Abs. Oh, to wind up the whole, a good-natured Irishman here has—[*Mimicking* SIR LUCIUS]— begged leave to have the pleasure of cutting my throat; and I mean to indulge him—that's all.

Faulk. Prithee, be serious!

Abs. 'Tis fact, upon my soul! Sir Lucius O'Trigger—you know him by sight—for some affront, which I am sure I never intended, has obliged me to meet him this evening at six o'clock: 'tis on that account I wished to see you; you must go with me.

Faulk. Nay, there must be some mistake, sure. Sir Lucius shall explain himself, and I dare say matters may be accommodated. But this evening did you say? I wish it had been any other time.

Abs. Why? there will be light enough: there will (as Sir Lucius says) be very pretty small-sword light, though it will not do for a long shot. Confound his long shots.

Faulk. But I am myself a good deal ruffled by a difference I have had with Julia. My vile tormenting temper has made me treat her so cruelly, that I shall not be myself till we are reconciled.

Abs. By heavens! Faulkland, you don't deserve her!

Enter SERVANT, *gives* FAULKLAND *a letter, and exit.*

Faulk. Oh, Jack! this is from Julia. I dread to open it! I fear it may be to take a last leave!—perhaps to bid me return her letters, and restore——Oh, how I suffer for my folly!

Abs. Here, let me see.—[*Takes the letter and opens it.*] Ay, a final sentence, indeed!—'tis all over with you, faith!

Faulk. Nay, Jack, don't keep me in suspense!

Abs. Hear then.—[Reads.] *As I am convinced that my dear Faulkland's own reflections have already upbraided him for his last unkindness to me, I will not add a word on the subject. I wish to speak with you as soon as possible. Yours ever and truly,* JULIA. There's stubbornness and resentment for you!—[*Gives him the letter.*] Why, man, you don't seem one whit the happier at this!

Faulk. O yes, I am; but—but——

Abs. Confound your buts! you never hear any thing that

would make another man bless himself, but you immediately damn it with a but!

Faulk.. Now, Jack, as you are my friend, own honestly—don't you think there is something forward, something indelicate, in this haste to forgive? Women should never sue for reconciliation: that should always come from us. They should retain their coldness till wooed to kindness; and their pardon, like their love, should " not unsought be won."

Abs. I have not patience to listen to you! thou 'rt incorrigible! so say no more on the subject. I must go to settle a few matters. Let me see you before six, remember, at my lodgings. A poor industrious devil like me, who have toiled, and drudged, and plotted to gain my ends, and am at last disappointed by other people's folly, may in pity be allowed to swear and grumble a little; but a captious sceptic in love, a slave to fretfulness and whim, who has no difficulties but of his own creating, is a subject more fit for ridicule than compassion!   [*Exit.*

Faulk. I feel his reproaches; yet I would not change this too exquisite nicety for the gross content with which he tramples on the thorns of love! His engaging me in this duel has started an idea in my head, which I will instantly pursue. I 'll use it as the touchstone of Julia's sincerity and disinterestedness. If her love prove pure and sterling ore, my name will rest on it with honour; and once I 've stamped it there, I lay aside my doubts for ever! But if the dross of selfishness, the alloy of pride, predominate, 'twill be best to leave her as a toy for some less cautious fool to sigh for!
                                                        [*Exit.*

ACT V.

Scene I.—Julia's *Dressing-Room.*

Julia *discovered alone.*

Jul How this message has alarmed me! what dreadful accident can he mean? why such charge to be alone?—O Faulkland!—how many unhappy moments—how many tears have you cost me.

Enter FAULKLAND.

Jul. What means this?—why this caution, Faulkland?

Faulk. Alas! Julia, I am come to take a long farewell.

Jul. Heavens! what do you mean?

Faulk. You see before you a wretch, whose life is forfeited. Nay, start not!—the infirmity of my temper has drawn all this misery on me. I left you fretful and passionate—an untoward accident drew me into a quarrel—the event is, that I must fly this kingdom instantly. O Julia, had I been so fortunate as to have called you mine entirely, before this mischance had fallen on me, I should not so deeply dread my banishment!

Jul. My soul is oppressed with sorrow at the nature of your misfortune: had these adverse circumstances arisen from a less fatal cause, I should have felt strong comfort in the thought that I could now chase from your bosom every doubt of the warm sincerity of my love. My heart has long known no other guardian—I now entrust my person to your honour —we will fly together. When safe from pursuit, my father's will may be fulfilled—and I receive a legal claim to be the partner of your sorrows, and tenderest comforter. Then on the bosom of your wedded Julia, you may lull your keen regret to slumbering; while virtuous love, with a cherub's hand, shall smooth the brow of upbraiding thought, and pluck the thorn from compunction.

Faulk. O Julia! I am bankrupt in gratitude! but the time is so pressing, it calls on you for so hasty a resolution.— Would you not wish some hours to weigh the advantages you forego, and what little compensation poor Faulkland can make you beside his solitary love?

Jul. I ask not a moment. No, Faulkland, I have loved you for yourself: and if I now, more than ever, prize the solemn engagement which so long has pledged us to each other, it is because it leaves no room for hard aspersions on my fame, and puts the seal of duty to an act of love. But let us not linger. Perhaps this delay——

Faulk. 'Twill be better I should not venture out again till dark. Yet am I grieved to think what numberless distresses will press heavy on your gentle disposition!

Jul. Perhaps your fortune 'may be forfeited by this unhappy act.—I know not whether 'tis so; but sure that alone can never make us unhappy. The little I have will be sufficient to support us; and exile never should be splendid.

Faulk. Ay, but in such an abject state of Life, my wounded pride perhaps may increase the natural fretfulness of my temper, till I become a rude, morose companion, beyond your patience to endure. Perhaps the recollection of a deed my conscience cannot justify may haunt me in such gloomy and unsocial fits, that I shall hate the tenderness that would relieve me, break from your arms, and quarrel with your fondness!

Jul. If your thoughts should assume so unhappy a bent, you will the more want some mild and affectionate spirit to watch over and console you: one who, by bearing your infirmities with gentleness and resignation, may teach you so to bear the evils of your fortune.

Faulk. Julia, I have proved you to the quick! and with this useless device I throw away all my doubts. How shall I plead to be forgiven this last unworthy effect of my restless, unsatisfied disposition?

Jul. Has no such disaster happened as you related?

Faulk. I am ashamed to own that it was pretended; yet in pity, Julia, do not kill me with resenting a fault which never can be repeated: but sealing, this once, my pardon, let me to-morrow, in the face of Heaven, receive my future guide and monitress, and expiate my past folly by years of tender adoration.

Jul. Hold, Faulkland!—that you are free from a crime, which I before feared to name, Heaven knows how sincerely I rejoice! These are tears of thankfulness for that! But that your cruel doubts should have urged you to an imposition that has wrung my heart, gives me now a pang more keen than I can express!

Faulk. By Heavens! Julia——

Jul. Yet hear me.—My father loved you, Faulkland! and you preserved the life that tender parent gave me; in his presence I pledged my hand—joyfully pledged it—where before I had given my heart. When, soon after, I lost that parent, it seemed to me that Providence had, in Faulkland, shown me whither to transfer without a pause, my grateful duty, as well as my affection : hence I have been content to bear from you what pride and delicacy would have forbid me from another. I will not upbraid you, by repeating how you have trifled with my sincerity——

Faulk. I confess it all! yet hear——

Jul. After such a year of trial, I might have flattered myself that I should not have been insulted with a new probation of my sincerity, as cruel as unnecessary! I now see it is not in your nature to be content or confident in love. With this conviction—I never will be yours. While I had hopes that my persevering attention, and unreproaching kindness, might in time reform your temper, I should have been happy to have gained a dearer influence over you; but I will not furnish you with a licensed power to keep alive an incorrigible fault, at the expense of one who never would contend with you.

Faulk. Nay, but, Julia, by my soul and honour, if after this——

Jul. But one word more.—As my faith has once been given to you, I never will barter it with another.—I shall pray for your happiness with the truest sincerity; and the dearest blessing I can ask of Heaven to send you will be to charm you from that unhappy temper, which alone has prevented the performance of our solemn engagement. All I request of you is, that you will yourself reflect upon this infirmity, and when you number up the many true delights it has deprived you of, let it not be your least regret, that it lost you the love of one who would have followed you in beggary through the world!   [*Exit.*

Faulk. She's gone—for ever!—There was an awful resolution in her manner, that riveted me to my place.—O fool!—dolt!—barbarian! Cursed as I am, with more imperfections than my fellow wretches, kind Fortune sent a heaven-gifted cherub to my aid, and, like a ruffian, I have driven her from my side!—I must now haste to my appointment. Well, my mind is tuned for such a scene. I shall wish only to become a principal in it, and reverse the tale my cursed folly put me upon forging here.—O Love!—tormentor!—fiend!—whose influence, like the moon's, acting on men of dull souls, makes idiots of them, but meeting subtler spirits, betrays their course, and urges sensibility to madness!   [*Exit.*

Enter LYDIA *and* MAID.

Maid. My mistress, ma'am, I know, was here just now—perhaps she is only in the next room.   [*Exit.*

Lyd. Heigh-ho! Though he has used me so, this fellow runs strangely in my head. I believe one lecture from my grave cousin will make me recall him. [*Re-enter* JULIA.] O Julia, I am come to you with such an appetite for consolation.—Lud! child, what's the matter with you? You have been crying!—I 'll be hanged if that Faulkland has not been tormenting you!

Jul. You mistake the cause of my uneasiness!—Something has flurried me a little. Nothing that you can guess at.— [*Aside.*] I would not accuse Faulkland to a sister!

Lyd. Ah! whatever vexations you may have, I can assure you mine surpass them. You know who Beverley proves to be?

Jul. I will now own to you, Lydia, that Mr. Faulkland had before informed me of the whole affair. Had young Absolute been the person you took him for, I should not have accepted your confidence on the subject, without a serious endeavour to counteract your caprice.

Lyd. So, then, I see I have been deceived by every one! But I don't care—I 'll never have him.

Jul. Nay, Lydia——

Lyd. Why, is it not provoking? when I thought we were coming to the prettiest distress imaginable, to find myself made a mere Smithfield bargain of at last! There, had I projected one of the most sentimental elopements!—so becoming a disguise!—so amiable a ladder of ropes!—Conscious moon—four horses—Scotch parson—with such surprise to Mrs. Malaprop—and such paragraphs in the newspapers!— Oh, I shall die with disappointment!

Jul. I don't wonder at it!

Lyd. Now—sad reverse!—what have I to expect, but, after a deal of flimsy preparation with a bishop's licence, and my aunt's blessing, to go simpering up to the altar; or perhaps be cried three times in a country church, and have an unmannerly fat clerk ask the consent of every butcher in the parish to join John Absolute and Lydia Languish, spinster! Oh that I should live to hear myself called spinster!

Jul. Melancholy indeed!

Lyd. How mortifying, to remember the dear delicious shifts I used to be put to, to gain half a minute's conversation with this fellow! How often have I stole forth, in the coldest night in January, and found him in the garden, stuck like a dripping statue! There would he kneel to me in the snow, and sneeze and cough so pathetically! he shivering with cold and I with apprehension! and while the freezing blast numbed our joints, how warmly would he press me to pity his flame, and glow with mutual ardour!—Ah, Julia, that was something like being in love.

Jul. If I were in spirits, Lydia, I should chide you only by laughing heartily at you; but it suits more the situation of my mind, at present, earnestly to entreat you not to let a man, who loves you with sincerity, suffer that unhappiness from your caprice, which I know too well caprice can inflict.

Lyd. O Lud! what has brought my aunt here?

Enter MRS MALAPROP, FAG, *and* DAVID.

Mrs. Mal. So! so! here's fine work!—here's fine suicide, parricide, and simulation, going on in the fields! and Sir Anthony not to be found to prevent the antistrophe!

Jul. For Heaven's sake, madam, what's the meaning of this?

Mrs. Mal. That gentleman can tell you—'twas he enveloped the affair to me.

Lyd. Do, sir, will you, inform us? [*To* FAG.

Fag. Ma'am, I should hold myself very deficient in every requisite that forms the man of breeding, if I delayed a moment to give all the information in my power to a lady so deeply interested in the affair as you are.

Lyd. But quick! quick sir!

Fag. True, ma'am, as you say, one should be quick in divulging matters of this nature; for should we be tedious, perhaps while we are flourishing on the subject, two or three lives may be lost!

Lyd. O patience!—Do, ma'am, for Heaven's sake! tell us what is the matter?

Mrs. Mal. Why, murder's the matter! slaughter's the matter! killing's the matter!—but he can tell you the perpendiculars.

Lyd. Then, prithee, sir, be brief.

Fag. Why then, ma'am, as to murder—I cannot take upon me to say—and as to slaughter, or manslaughter, that will be as the jury finds it.

Lyd. But who, sir—who are engaged in this?

Fag. Faith, ma'am, one is a young gentleman whom I should be very sorry any thing was to happen to—a very pretty behaved gentleman! We have lived much together, and always on terms.

Lyd. But who is this? who! who! who?

Fag. My master, ma'am—my master—I speak of my master.

Lyd. Heavens! What, Captain Absolute!

Mrs. Mal. Oh, to be sure, you are frightened now!

Jul. But who are with him, sir?

Fag. As to the rest, ma'am, this gentleman can inform you better than I.

Jul. Do speak, friend.　　　　　　　　[*To* DAVID.

Dav. Look'ee, my lady—by the mass! there's mischief going on. Folks don't use to meet for amusement with firearms, firelocks, fire-engines, fire-screens, fire-office, and the devil knows what other crackers beside!—This, my lady, I say, has an angry favour.

Jul. But who is there beside Captain Absolute, friend?

Dav. My poor master—under favour for mentioning him first. You know me, my lady—I am David—and my master of course is, or was, Squire Acres. Then comes Squire Faulkland.

Jul. Do, ma'am, let us instantly endeavour to prevent mischief.

Mrs. Mal. O fy!—it would be very inelegant in us:—we should only participate things.

Dav. Ah! do, Mrs. Aunt, save a few lives—they are desperately given, believe me.—Above all, there is that bloodthirsty Philistine, Sir Lucius O'Trigger.

Mrs. Mal. Sir Lucius O'Trigger? O mercy! have they drawn poor little dear Sir Lucius into the scrape?—Why, how you stand, girl! you have no more feeling than one of the Derbyshire petrifactions!

Lyd. What are we to do, madam?

Mrs. Mal. Why fly with the utmost felicity, to be sure, to prevent mischief!—Here, friend, you can show us the place?

Fag. If you please, ma'am, I will conduct you.—David, do you look for Sir Anthony.　　　　　　*[Exit David.*

Mrs. Mal. Come, girls! this gentleman will exhort us.—Come, sir, you 're our envoy—lead the way, and we 'll precede.

Fag. Not a step before the ladies for the world!

Mrs. Mal. You 're sure you know the spot?

Fag. I think I can find it, ma'am; and one good thing is, we shall hear the report of the pistols as we draw near, so we can't well miss them;—never fear, ma'am, never fear.

　　　　　　　　　　　[Exeunt, he talking.

Scene II.—*The South Parade.*

Enter Captain Absolute, *putting his sword under his great coat.*

Abs. A sword seen in the streets of Bath would raise as great an alarm as a mad dog.—How provoking this is in Faulkland!—never punctual! I shall be obliged to go without him at last.—Oh, the devil! here 's Sir Anthony! how shall I escape him?

　　　　　[Muffles up his face, and takes a circle to go off.

Enter Sir Anthony Absolute.

Sir. Anth. How one may be deceived at a little distance! only that I see he don't know me, I could have sworn that was Jack!—Hey! Gad's life! it is.—Why, Jack, what are you afraid of? hey!—sure I 'm right.—Why Jack, Jack Absolute!

　　　　　　　　　　　[Goes up to him.

Abs. Really, sir, you have the advantage of me:—I don't remember ever to have had the honour—my name is Saunderson, at your service.

Sir. Anth. Sir, I beg your pardon—I took you—hey?—why, zounds! it is—Stay—[*Looks up to his face.*] So, so—your humble servant, Mr. Saunderson! Why, you scoundrel, what tricks are you after now?

Abs. Oh, a joke, sir, a joke! I came here on purpose to look for you, sir.

Sir. Anth. You did! well, I am glad you were so lucky:—but what are you muffled up so for?—what 's this for?—hey!

Abs. 'Tis cool, sir; isn't?—rather chilly somehow:—but I shall be late—I have a particular engagement.

Sir Anth. Stay!—Why, I thought you were looking for me?—Pray, Jack, where is 't you are going?

Abs. Going, sir!

Sir Anth. Ay, where are you going?

Abs. Where am I going?

Sir Anth. You unmannerly puppy!

Abs. I was going, sir, to—to—to—to Lydia—sir, to Lydia—to make matters up if I could;—and I was looking for you, sir, to—to—

Sir Anth. To go with you, I suppose.—Well, come along.

Abs. Oh! zounds! no, sir, not for the world!—I wished to meet with you, sir,—to—to—to—You find it cool, I'm sure, sir—you'd better not stay out.

Sir Anth. Cool!—not at all.—Well, Jack—and what will you say to Lydia?

Abs. Oh, sir, beg her pardon, humour her—promise and vow: but I detain you, sir—consider the cold air on your gout.

Sir Anth. Oh, not at all!—not at all! I'm in no hurry.—Ah! Jack, you youngsters, when once you are wounded here [*Putting his hand to* CAPTAIN ABSOLUTE'S *breast.*] Hey! what the deuce have you got here?

Abs. Nothing, sir—nothing;

Sir Anth. What's this?—here's something damned hard.

Abs. Oh, trinkets, sir! trinkets!—a bauble for Lydia!

Sir Anth. Nay, let me see your taste.—[*Pulls his coat open, the sword falls.*] Trinkets!—a bauble for Lydia!—Zounds! sirrah, you are not going to cut her throat, are you?

Abs. Ha! ha! ha!—I thought it would divert you, sir, though I didn't mean to tell you till afterwards.

Sir Anth. You didn't?—Yes, this is a very diverting trinket, truly!

Abs. Sir, I'll explain to you.—You know, sir, Lydia is romantic, devilish romantic, and very absurd of course: now, sir, I intend, if she refuses to forgive me, to unsheath this sword, and swear—I'll fall upon its point, and expire at her feet!

Sir Anth. Fall upon a fiddlestick's end!—why, I suppose it is the very thing that would please her.—Get along, you fool!

Abs. Well, sir, you shall hear of my success—you shall hear.—*O Lydia!—forgive me, or this pointed steel*—says I.

Sir Anth. O, booby! *stab away and welcome*—says she.— Get along! and damn your trinkets! [*Exit* CAPTAIN ABSOLUTE.

Enter DAVID, *running.*

Dav. Stop him! stop him! Murder! Thief! Fire!— Stop fire! Stop fire!—O Sir Anthony—call! call! bid 'm stop! Murder! Fire!

Sir Anth. Fire! Murder!—Where?

Dav. Oons! he's out of sight! and I'm out of breath! for my part! O Sir Anthony, why didn't you stop him? why didn't you stop him?

Sir Anth. Zounds! the fellow's mad!—Stop whom? stop Jack?

Dav. Ay, the captain, sir!—there's murder and slaughter——

Sir Anth. Murder!

Dav. Ay, please you, Sir Anthony, there's all kinds of murder, all sorts of slaughter to be seen in the fields: there's fighting going on, sir—bloody sword-and-gun fighting!

Sir Anth. Who are going to fight, dunce?

Dav. Every body that I know of, Sir Anthony:—every body is going to fight, my poor master, Sir Lucius O'Trigger, your son, the captain——

Sir Anth. Oh, the dog! I see his tricks.—Do you know the place?

Dav. King's-Mead-Fields.

Sir Anth. You know the way?

Dav. Not an inch; but I'll call the mayor—aldermen— constables—churchwardens—and beadles—we can't be too many to part them.

Sir Anth. Come along—give me your shoulder! we'll get assistance as we go—the lying villain!—Well, I shall be in such a frenzy!—So—this was the history of his trinkets! I'll bauble him! [*Exeunt.*

SCENE III.—*King's-Mead-Fields.*

Enter Sir LUCIUS O'TRIGGER *and* ACRES, *with pistols.*

Acres. By my valour! then, Sir Lucius, forty yards is a good distance. Odds levels and aims!—I say it is a good distance.

Sir Luc. Is it for muskets or small field-pieces? Upon my conscience, Mr. Acres, you must leave those things to me.—Stay now—I 'll show you.—[*Measures paces along the stage.*] There now, that is a very pretty distance—a pretty gentleman's distance.

Acres. Zounds! we might as well fight in a sentry-box! I tell you, Sir Lucius, the farther he is off, the cooler I shall take my aim.

Sir Luc. Faith! then I suppose you would aim at him best of all if he was out of sight!

Acres. No, Sir Lucius; but I should think forty or eight-and-thirty yards——

Sir Luc. Pho! pho! nonsense! three or four feet between the mouths of your pistols is as good as a mile.

Acres. Odds bullets, no!—by my valour! there is no merit in killing him so near: do, my dear Sir Lucius, let me bring him down at a long shot:—a long shot, Sir Lucius, if you love me!

Sir Luc. Well, the gentleman's friend and I must settle that.—But tell me now, Mr. Acres, in case of an accident, is there any little will or commission I could execute for you?

Acres. I am much obliged to you, Sir Lucius—but I don't understand——

Sir Luc. Why, you may think there's no being shot at without a little risk—and if an unlucky bullet should carry a quietus with it—I say it will be no time then to be bothering you about family matters.

Acres. A quietus!

Sir Luc. For instance, now—if that should be the case—would you choose to be pickled and sent home?—or would it be the same to you to lie here in the Abbey?—I 'm told there is very snug lying in the Abbey.

Acres. Pickled!—Snug lying in the Abbey!—Odds tremors! Sir Lucius, don't talk so!

Sir Luc. I suppose, Mr. Acres, you never were engaged in an affair of this kind before?

Acres. No, Sir Lucius, never before.

Sir Luc. Ah! that's a pity!—there's nothing like being used to a thing.—Pray now, how would you receive the gentleman's shot?

Acres. Odds files!—I 've practised that—there, Sir Lucius

—there.—[*Puts himself in an attitude.*]   A side-front, hey? Odd! I 'll make myself small enough: I 'll stand edgeways.

Sir Luc. Now—you 're quite out—for if you stand so when I take my aim——   [*Levelling at him.*

Acres. Zounds! Sir Lucius—are you sure it is not cocked?

Sir Luc. Never fear.

Acres. But—but—you don't know—it may go off of its own head!

Sir Luc. Pho! be easy.—Well, now if I hit you in the body, my bullet has a double chance—for if it misses a vital part of your right side—'twill be very hard if it don't succeed on the left!

Acres. A vital part!

Sir Luc. But, there—fix yourself so—[*Placing him*]—let him see the broad-side of your full front—there—now a ball or two may pass clean through your body, and never do any harm at all.

Acres. Clean through me!—a ball or two clean through me!

Sir Luc. Ay—may they—and it is much the genteelest attitude into the bargain.

Acres. Look'ee! Sir Lucius— I 'd just as lieve be shot in an awkward posture as a genteel one; so, by my valour! I will stand edgeways.

Sir Luc. [*Looking at his watch.*]   Sure they don't mean to disappoint us—Hah!—no, faith—I think I see them coming.

Acres. Hey!—what!—coming!——

Sir Luc. Ay.—Who are those yonder getting over the stile?

Acres. There are two of them indeed!—well—let them come.—hey, Sir Lucius!—we—we—we—we—won't run.

Sir Luc. Run!

Acres. No—I say—we won't run, by my valour!

Sir Luc. What the devil 's the matter with you?

Acres. Nothing—nothing—my dear friend—my dear Sir Lucius—but I—I—I don't feel quite so bold, somehow, as I did.

Sir Luc. O fy!—consider your honour.

Acres. Ay—true—my honour. Do, Sir Lucius, edge in a word or two every now and then about my honour.

Sir Luc. Well, here they 're coming.   [*Looking.*

Acres. Sir Lucius—if I wa'n't with you, I should almost

think I was afraid.—If my valour should leave me!—Valour will come and go.

Sir Luc. Then pray keep it fast, while you have it.

Acres. Sir Lucius—I doubt it is going—yes—my valour is certainly going!—it is sneaking off!—I feel it oozing out as it were at the palms of my hands!

Sir Luc. Your honour—your honour.—Here they are.

Acres. O mercy!—now—that I was safe at Clod-Hall! or could be shot before I was aware!

Enter FAULKLAND *and* CAPTAIN ABSOLUTE.

Sir Luc. Gentlemen, your most obedient. — Hah!—what, Captain Absolute!—So, I suppose, sir, you are come here, just like myself—to do a kind office, first for your friend – then to proceed to business on your own account.

Acres. What, Jack!—my dear Jack!—my dear friend!

Abs. Hark'ee, Bob, Beverley's at hand.

Sir Luc. Well, Mr. Acres—I don't blame your saluting the gentleman civilly.—[*To* FAULKLAND.] So, Mr. Beverley, if you'll choose your weapons, the captain and I will measure the ground.

Faulk. My weapons, sir!

Acres. Odds life! Sir Lucius, I'm not going to fight Mr. Faulkland; these are my particular friends.

Sir Luc. What, sir, did you not come here to fight Mr. Acres?

Faulk. Not I, upon my word, sir.

Sir Luc. Well, now, that's mighty provoking! But I hope, Mr. Faulkland, as there are three of us come on purpose for the game, you won't be so cantanckerous as to spoil the party by sitting out.

Abs. O pray, Faulkland, fight to oblige Sir Lucius.

Faulk. Nay, if Mr. Acres is so bent on the matter——

Acres. No, no, Mr. Faulkland;—I'll bear my disappointment like a Christian.—Look'ee, Sir Lucius, there's no occasion at all for me to fight; and if it is the same to you, I'd as lieve let it alone.

Sir Luc. Observe me, Mr. Acres—I must not be trifled with. You have certainly challenged somebody—and you came here to fight him. Now, if that gentleman is willing to represent him—I can't see, for my soul, why it isn't just the same thing.

Acres. Why no—Sir Lucius—I tell you, 'tis one Beverley
I've challenged—a fellow, you see, that dare not show his
face!—If he were here, I'd make him give up his pretensions
directly!

Abs. Hold, Bob—let me set you right—there is no such man
as Beverley in the case.—The person who assumed that name
is before you; and as his pretensions are the same in both
characters, he is ready to support them in whatever way you
please.

Sir Luc. Well, this is lucky.—Now you have an opportunity——

Acres What, quarrel with my dear friend Jack Absolute?—
not if he were fifty Beverleys! Zounds! Sir Lucius, you would
not have me so unnatural.

Sir Luc. Upon my conscience, Mr. Acres, your valour has
oozed away with a vengeance!

Acres. Not in the least! Odds backs and abettors! I'll be
your second with all my heart—and if you should get a quietus,
you may command me entirely. I'll get you snug lying in
the Abbey here; or pickle you, and send you over to Blun-
derbuss-hall, or any thing of the kind, with the greatest
pleasure.

Sir Luc. Pho! pho! you are little better than a coward.

Acres. Mind, gentlemen, he calls me a coward; coward was
the word, by my valour!

Sir Luc. Well, sir?

Acres. Look 'ee, Sir Lucius, 'tisn't that I mind the word
coward—coward may be said in joke—But if you had called
me a poltroon, odds daggers and balls——

Sir Luc. Well, sir?

Acres. I should have thought you a very ill-bred man.

Sir Luc. Pho! you are beneath my notice.

Abs. Nay, Sir Lucius, you can't have a better second than
my friend Acres—He is a most determined dog—called in
the country, Fighting Bob.—He generally kills a man a week
—don't you, Bob?

Acres. Ay—at home!

Sir Luc. Well, then, captain, 'tis we must begin—so come
out, my little counsellor—[*Draws his sword*]—and ask the gentleman, whether he will resign the lady, without forcing you
to proceed against him?

Abs. Come on then, sir—[*Draws*] ; since you won't let it be an amicable suit, here 's my reply.

Enter SIR ANTHONY ABSOLUTE, DAVID, MRS. MALAPROP, LYDIA, *and* JULIA.

Dav. Knock 'em all down, sweet Sir Anthony; knock down my master in particular; and bind his hands over to their good behaviour !

Sir Anth. Put up, Jack, put up, or I shall be in a frenzy— how came you in a duel, sir?

Abs. Faith, sir, that gentleman can tell you better than I ; 'twas he called on me, and you know, sir, I serve his majesty.

Sir Anth. Here 's a pretty fellow ; I catch him going to cut a man's throat, and he tells me, he serves his majesty!—Zounds ! sirrah, then how durst you draw the king's sword against one of his subjects ?

Abs. Sir, I tell you! that gentleman called me out, without explaining his reasons.

Sir Anth. Gad! sir, how came you to call my son out, without explaining your reasons?

Sir Luc. Your son, sir, insulted me in a manner which my honour could not brook.

Sir Anth. Zounds! Jack, how durst you insult the gentleman in a manner which his honour could not brook?

Mrs. Mal. Come, come, let 's have no honour before ladies —Captain Absolute, come here—How could you intimidate us so?—Here 's Lydia has been terrified to death for you.

Abs. For fear I should be killed, or escape, ma'am?

Mrs. Mal. Nay, no delusions to the past—Lydia is convinced; speak, child.

Sir Luc. With your leave, ma'am, I must put in a word here : I believe I could interpret the young lady's silence. Now mark——

Lyd. What is it you mean, sir ?

Sir Luc. Come, come, Delia, we must be serious now—this is no time for trifling.

Lyd. 'Tis true, sir ; and your reproof bids me offer this gentleman my hand, and solicit the return of his affections.

Abs. O! my little angel, say you so !—Sir Lucius—I perceive there must be some mistake here, with regard to the affront which you affirm I have given you. I can only say, that it could not have been intentional. And as you must be convinced, that I should not fear to support a real injury—you shall now see that I am not ashamed to atone for an inadvertency—I ask your pardon.—But for this lady, while honoured with her approbation, I will support my claim against any man whatever.

Sir Anth. Well said, Jack, and I 'll stand by you, my boy.

Acres. Mind, I give up all my claim—I make no pretensions to any thing in the world ; and if I can't get a wife without fighting for her, by my valour! I 'll live a bachelor.

Sir Luc. Captain, give me your hand: an affront handsomely acknowledged becomes an obligation; and as for the lady, if she chooses to deny her own hand-writing, here——

[Takes out letters.

Mrs. Mal. O, he will dissolve my mystery!—Sir Lucius, perhaps there 's some mistake—perhaps I can illuminate——

Sir Luc. Pray, old gentlewoman, do'nt interfere where you have no business.—Miss Languish, are you my Delia, or not?

Lyd. Indeed, Sir Lucius, I am not.

[Walks aside with CAPTAIN ABSOLUTE.

Mrs. Mal. Sir Lucius O'Trigger—ungrateful as you are—I own the soft impeachment—pardon my blushes, I am Delia.

Sir Luc. You Delia—pho! pho! be easy.

Mrs. Mal. Why, thou barbarous Vandyke—those letters are mine—When you are more sensible of my benignity—perhaps I may be brought to encourage your addresses.

Sir Luc. Mrs. Malaprop, I am extremely sensible of your condescension ; and whether you or Lucy have put this trick on me, I am equally beholden to you.—And, to show you I am not ungrateful, Captain Absolute, since you have taken that lady from me, I 'll give you my Delia into the bargain.

Abs. I am much obliged to you, Sir Lucius ; but here 's my friend, Fighting Bob, unprovided for.

Sir Luc. Hah! little Valour—here, will you make your fortune?

Acres. Odds wrinkles! No.—But give me your hand, Sir Lucius, forget and forgive ; but if ever I give you a chance of picking me again, say Bob Acres is a dunce, that 's all.

Sir Anth. Come, Mrs. Malaprop, don't be cast down—you are in your bloom yet.

Mrs. Mal. O Sir Anthony—men are all barbarians.

[All retire but JULIA *and* FAULKLAND

Jul. [*Aside.*] He seems dejected and unhappy—not sullen; there was some foundation, however, for the tale he told me—O woman! how true should be your judgment, when your resolution is so weak!

Faulk. Julia!—how can I sue for what I so little deserve? I dare not presume—yet Hope is the child of Penitence.

Jul. Oh! Faulkland, you have not been more faulty in your unkind treatment of me, than I am now in wanting inclination to resent it. As my heart honestly bids me place my weakness to the account of love, I should be ungenerous not to admit the same plea for yours.

Faulk. Now I shall be blest indeed!

Sir Anth. [*Coming forward.*] What's going on here?—So you have been quarrelling too, I warrant! Come, Julia, I never interfered before; but let me have a hand in the matter at last.—All the faults I have ever seen in my friend Faulkland seemed to proceed from what he calls the delicacy and warmth of his affection for you—There, marry him directly, Julia; you'll find he'll mend surprisingly!

[*The rest come forward.*

Sir Luc. Come, now, I hope there is no dissatisfied person, but what is content; for as I have been disappointed myself, it will be very hard if I have not the satisfaction of seeing other people succeed better.

Acres. You are right, Sir Lucius.—So Jack, I wish you joy—Mr. Faulkland the same.—Ladies,—come now, to show you I'm neither vexed nor angry, odds tabors and pipes! I'll order the fiddles in half an hour to the New Rooms—and I insist on your all meeting me there.

Sir Anth. 'Gad! sir, I like your spirit; and at night we single lads will drink a health to the young couples, and a husband to Mrs. Malaprop.

Faulk. Our partners are stolen from us, Jack—I hope to be congratulated by each other—yours for having checked in time the errors of an ill-directed imagination, which might have betrayed an innocent heart; and mine, for having, by her gentleness and candour, reformed the unhappy temper of one, who by it made wretched whom he loved most, and tortured the heart he ought to have adored.

Abs. Well, Jack, we have both tasted the bitters, as well as the sweets of love; with this difference only, that you always prepared the bitter cup for yourself, while I——

Lyd. Was always obliged to me for it, hey! Mr. Modesty?

——But, come, no more of that—our happiness is now as unalloyed as general.

Jul. Then let us study to preserve it so : and while Hope pictures to us a flattering scene of future bliss, let us deny its pencil those colours which are too bright to be lasting.—When hearts deserving happiness would unite their fortunes, Virtue would crown them with an unfading garland of modest hurtless flowers; but ill-judging Passion will force the gaudier rose into the wreath, whose thorn offends them when its leaves are dropped!   [*Exeunt omnes.*

EPILOGUE.

BY THE AUTHOR.

SPOKEN BY MRS. BULKLEY.

LADIES, for you—I heard our poet say—
He 'd try to coax some moral from his play:
" One moral's plain," cried I, " without more fuss ;
Man's social happiness all rests on us :
Through all the drama—whether damn'd or not—
Love gilds the scene, and women guide the plot.
From every rank obedience is our due—
D'ye doubt?—The world's great stage shall prove it true."
    The cit, well skill'd to shun domestic strife,
Will sup abroad; but first he 'll ask his wife :
John Trot, his friend, for once will do the same,
But then—he 'll just step home to tell his dame.
    The surly squire at noon resolves to rule,
And half the day—Zounds! madam is a fool!
Convinced at night, the vanquish'd victor says,
Ah, Kate! you women have such coaxing ways
    The jolly toper chides each tardy blade,
Till reeling Bacchus calls on Love for aid :
Then with each toast he sees fair bumpers swim,
And kisses Chloe on the sparkling brim!

Nay, I have heard that statesmen—great and wise—
Will sometimes counsel with a lady's eyes!
The servile suitors watch her various face,
She smiles preferment, or she frowns disgrace,
Curtsies a pension here—there nods a place.
  Nor with less awe, in scenes of humbler life,
Is view'd the mistress, or is heard the wife.
The poorest peasant of the poorest soil,
The child of poverty, and heir to toil,
Early from radiant Love's impartial light
Steals one small spark to cheer this world of night:
Dear spark! that oft through winter's chilling woes
Is all the warmth his little cottage knows!
  The wandering tar, who not for years has press'd,
The widow'd partner of his day of rest,
On the cold deck, far from her arms removed,
Still hums the ditty which his Susan loved;
And while around the cadence rude is blown,
The boatswain whistles in a softer tone.
  The soldier, fairly proud of wounds and toil,
Pants for the triumph of his Nancy's smile;
But ere the battle should he list her cries,
The lover trembles—and the hero dies!
That heart, by war and honour steel'd to fear,
Droops on a sigh, and sickens at a tear!
  But ye more cautious, ye nice-judging few,
Who give to beauty only beauty's due,
Though friends to love—ye view with deep regret
Our conquests marr'd, our triumphs incomplete,
Till polish'd wit more lasting charms disclose,
And judgment fix the darts which beauty throws!
In female breasts did sense and merit rule,
The lover's mind would ask no other school;
Shamed into sense, the scholars of our eyes,
Our beaux from gallantry would soon be wise;
Would gladly light, their homage to improve,
The lamp of knowledge at the torch of love!

ST. PATRICK'S DAY;

OR,

THE SCHEMING LIEUTENANT.

A FARCE.

DRAMATIS PERSONÆ

AS ORIGINALLY ACTED AT COVENT-GARDEN THEATRE IN 1775.

LIEUTENANT O'CONNOR *Mr. Clinch.* | LAURETTA . . . . *Mrs. Caryill.*
DOCTOR ROSY . . *Mr. Quick.* | MRS. BRIDGET CRE-} *Mrs. Pitt.*
JUSTICE CREDULOUS . *Mr. Lee Lewes.* | DULOUS. }
SERJEANT TROUNCE . *Mr. Booth.* | Drummer, Soldiers, Countrymen, *and*
CORPORAL FLINT . | Servant.

SCENE.—A TOWN IN ENGLAND.

ACT I.

SCENE I.—LIEUTENANT O'CONNOR'S *Lodgings.*
Enter SERJEANT TROUNCE, CORPORAL FLINT, *and four*
SOLDIERS.

1 *Sol.* I say you are wrong; we should all speak together, each for himself, and all at once, that we may be heard the better.

2 *Sol.* Right, Jack, we'll argue in platoons.

3 *Sol.* Ay, ay, let him have our grievances in a volley, and if we be to have a spokesman, there's the corporal is the lieutenant's countryman, and knows his humour.

Flint. Let me alone for that. I served three years, within a bit, under his honour, in the Royal Inniskillions, and I never will see a sweeter tempered gentleman, nor one more free with his purse. I put a great shammock in his hat this morning, and I'll be bound for him he'll wear it, was it as big as Steven's Green.

4 *Sol.* I say again then you talk like youngsters, like raw striplings: there's a discipline, look'ee, in all things, whereof the serjeant must be our guide; he's a gentleman of words; he understands your foreign lingo, your figures, and such like auxiliaries in scoring. Confess now for a reckoning, whether in chalk or writing, ben't he your only man?

Flint. Why the serjeant is a scholar to be sure, and has the gift of reading.

Trounce. Good soldiers, and fellow gentlemen, if you make

me your spokesman, you will show the more judgment; and let me alone for the argument. I'll be as loud as a drum, and point blank from the purpose.

All. Agreed, agreed.

Flint. Oh, fait! here comes the lieutenant.—Now, serjeant.

Trounce. So then, to order.—Put on your mutiny looks; every man grumble a little to himself, and some of you hum the Deserter's March.

Enter LIEUTENANT O'CONNOR.

O'Con. Well, honest lads, what is it you have to complain of?

Sol. Ahem! hem!

Trounce. So please your honour; the very grievance of the matter is this:—ever since your honour differed with Justice Credulous, our inn-keepers use us most scurvily. By my halbert, their treatment is such, that if your spirit was willing to put up with it, flesh and blood could by no means agree; so we humbly petition that your honour would make an end of the matter at once, by running away with the justice's daughter, or else get us fresh quarters,—hem! hem!

O'Con. Indeed! Pray which of the houses use you ill?.

1 Sol. There's the Red Lion an't half the civility of the old Red Lion.

2 Sol. There's the White Horse, if he wasn't casehardened, ought to be ashamed to show his face.

O'Con. Very well; the Horse and the Lion shall answer for it at the quarter sessions.

Trounce. The two Magpies are civil enough; but the Angel uses us like devils, and the Rising Sun refuses us light to go to bed by.

O'Con. Then, upon my word, I'll have the Rising Sun put down, and the Angel shall give security for his good behaviour; but are you sure you do nothing to quit scores with them?

Flint. Nothing at all, your honour, unless now and then we happen to fling a cartridge into the kitchen fire, or put a spatterdash or so into the soup; and sometimes Ned drums up and down stairs a little of a night.

O'Con. Oh, all that's fair; but hark'ee lads, I must have no grumbling on St. Patrick's day; so here, take this, and divide it amongst you. But observe me now,—show yourselves men of spirit, and don't spend sixpence of it in drink.

Trounce. Nay, hang it, your honour, soldiers should never bear malice; we must drink St. Patrick's and your honour's health.

All. Oh, damn malice! St. Patrick's and his honour's by all means.

Flint. Come away, then, lads, and first we 'll parade round the Market-cross, for the honour of King George.

1 *Sol.* Thank your honour.—Come along; St. Patrick, his honour, and strong beer for ever! [*Exeunt* SOLDIERS.

O'Con. Get along, you thoughtless vagabonds! yet, upon my conscience, 'tis very hard these poor fellows should scarcely have bread from the soil they would die to defend.

Enter DOCTOR ROSY.

Ah, my little Dr. Rosy, my Galen a-bridge, what's the news?

Rosy. All things are as they were, my Alexander; the justice is as violent as ever: I felt his pulse on the matter again, and, thinking his rage began to intermit, I wanted to throw in the bark of good advice, but it would not do. He says you and your cut-throats have a plot upon his life, and swears he had rather see his daughter in a scarlet fever than in the arms of a soldier.

O'Con. Upon my word the army is very much obliged to him. Well, then, I must marry the girl first, and ask his consent afterwards.

Rosy. So, then, the case of her fortune is desperate, hey?

O'Con. Oh, hang fortune,—let that take its chance; there is a beauty in Lauretta's simplicity, so pure a bloom upon her charms.

Rosy. So there is, so there is. You are for beauty as nature made her, hey! No artificial graces, no cosmetic varnish, no beauty in grain, hey!

O'Con. Upon my word, doctor, you are right; the London ladies were always too handsome for me; then they are so defended, such a circumvallation of hoop, with a breast-work of whalebone that would turn a pistol-bullet, much less Cupid's arrows,—then turret on turret on top, with stores of concealed weapons, under pretence of black pins,—and above all, a standard of feathers that would do honour to a knight of the

Bath. Upon my conscience, I could as soon embrace an Amazon, armed at all points.

Rosy. Right, right, my Alexander! my taste to a tittle.

O'Con. Then, doctor, though I admire modesty in women, I like to see their faces. I am for the changeable rose; but with one of these quality Amazons, if their midnight dissipations had left them blood enough to raise a blush, they have not room enough in their cheeks to show it. To be sure, bashfulness is a very pretty thing; but, in my mind, there is nothing on earth so impudent as an everlasting blush

Rosy. My taste, my taste!—Well, Lauretta is none of these. Ah! I never see her but she puts me in mind of my poor dear wife.

O'Con. Ay, faith; in my opinion she can't do a worse thing. Now he is going to bother me about an old hag that has been dead these six years!   [*Aside.*

Rosy. Oh, poor Dolly! I never shall see her like again; such an arm for a bandage—veins that seemed to invite the lancet. Then her skin, smooth and white as a gallipot; her mouth as round and not larger than the mouth of a penny phial; her lips conserve of roses; and then her teeth —none of your sturdy fixtures—ache as they would, it was but a small pull, and out they came. I believe I have drawn half a score of her poor dear pearls—[*weeps*]—But what avails her beauty? Death has no consideration—one must die as well as another.

O'Con. [*Aside.*] Oh, if he begins to moralize——

[*Takes out his snuff-box.*

Rosy. Fair and ugly, crooked or straight, rich or poor—flesh is grass—flowers fade!

O'Con. Here, doctor, take a pinch, and keep up your spirits.

Rosy. True, true, my friend; grief can't mend the matter —all's for the best; but such a woman was a great loss, lieutenant.

O'Con. To be sure, for doubtless she had mental accomplishments equal to her beauty.

Rosy. Mental accomplishments! she would have stuffed an alligator, or pickled a lizard, with any apothecary's wife in the kingdom. Why, she could decipher a prescription, and invent the ingredients, almost as well as myself: then she was such a hand at making foreign waters!—for Seltzer, Pyrmont,

Islington, or Chalybeate, she never had her equal; and her Bath and Bristol springs exceeded the originals.—Ah, poor Dolly! she fell a martyr to her own discoveries.

O'Con. How so, pray?

Rosy. Poor soul! her illness was occasioned by her zeal in trying an improvement on the Spa-water, by an infusion of rum and acid.

O'Con. Ay, ay, spirits never agree with water-drinkers.

Rosy. No, no, you mistake. Rum agreed with her well enough; it was not the rum that killed the poor dear creature, for she died of a dropsy. Well, she is gone never to return, and has left no pledge of our loves behind. No little babe, to hang like a label round papa's neck. Well, well, we are all mortal—sooner or later—flesh is grass—flowers fade.

O'Con. Oh, the devil!—again!   [*Aside.*

Rosy. Life's a shadow—the world a stage—we strut an hour.

O'Con. Here, doctor.   [*Offers snuff.*

Rosy. True, true, my friend: well, high grief can't cure it. All's for the best, hey! my little Alexander.

O'Con. Right, right; an apothecary should never be out of spirits. But come, faith, 'tis time honest Humphrey should wait on the justice; that must be our first scheme.

Rosy. True, true; you should be ready: the clothes are at my house, and I have given you such a character that he is impatient to have you: he swears you shall be his body-guard. Well, I honour the army, or I should never do so much to serve you.

O'Con. Indeed I am bound to you for ever, doctor; and when once I'm possessed of my dear Lauretta, I will endeavour to make work for you as fast as possible.

Rosy. Now you put me in mind of my poor wife again.

O'Con. Ah, pray forget her a little: we shall be too late.

Rosy. Poor Dolly!

O'Con. 'Tis past twelve.

Rosy. Inhuman dropsy!

O'Con. The justice will wait.

Rosy. Cropped in her prime!

O'Con. For Heaven's sake, come!

Rosy. Well, flesh is grass.

O'Con. O, the devil!

Rosy. We must all die——

O'Con, Doctor!

Rosy. Kings, lords, and common whores——

[*Exeunt,* LIEUTENANT O'CONNOR *forcing* ROSY *off.*

SCENE II.—*A Room in* JUSTICE CREDULOUS' *House.*

Enter LAURETTA *and* MRS. BRIDGET CREDULOUS.

Lau. I repeat it again, mamma, officers are the prettiest men in the world, and Lieutenant O'Connor is the prettiest officer I ever saw.

Mrs. Bri. For shame, Laura! how can you talk so?—or if you must have a military man, there's Lieutenant Plow, or Captain Haycock, or Major Dray, the brewer, are all your admirers; and though they are peaceable, good kind of men, they have as large cockades, and become scarlet as well as the fighting folks.

Lau. Psha! you know, mamma, I hate militia officers; a set of dunghill cocks with spurs on—heroes scratched off a church door—clowns in military masquerade, wearing the dress without supporting the character. No, give me the bold upright youth, who makes love to-day, and his head shot off to-morrow. Dear! to think how the sweet fellows sleep on the ground, and fight in silk stockings and lace ruffles.

Mrs. Bri. Oh, barbarous! to want a husband that may wed you to-day, and be sent the Lord knows where before night; then in a twelvemonth perhaps to have him come like a Colossus, with one leg at New York and the other at Chelsea Hospital.

Lau. Then I'll be his crutch, mamma.

Mrs. Bri. No, give me a husband that knows where his limbs are, though he want the use of them:—and if he should take you with him, to sleep in a baggage-cart, and stroll about the camp like a gipsy, with a knapsack and two children at your back;—then, by way of entertainment in the evening, to make a party with the serjeant's wife to drink bohea tea, and play at all-fours on a drumhead:—'tis a precious life, to be sure!

Lau. Nay, mamma, you shouldn't be against my lieutenant, for I heard him say you were the best natured and best looking woman in the world.

Mrs. Bri. Why, child, I never said but that Lieutenant

O'Connor was a very well-bred and discerning young man; 'tis your papa is so violent against him.

Lau. Why, Cousin Sophy married an officer.

Mrs. Bri. Ay, Laury, an officer in the militia.

Lau. No, indeed, mamma, a marching regiment.

Mrs. Bri. No, child, I tell you he was major of militia.

Lau. Indeed, mamma, it wasn't.

Enter JUSTICE CREDULOUS.

Just. Bridget, my love. I have had a message

Lau. It was Cousin Sophy told me so.

Just. I have had a message, love——

Mrs. Bri. No, child, she would say no such thing.

Just. A message, I say.

Lau. How could he be in the militia, when he was ordered abroad?

Mrs. Bri. Ay, girl, hold your tongue!—Well, my dear.

Just. I have had a message from Doctor Rosy.

Mrs. Bri. He ordered abroad! He went abroad for his health.

Just. Why, Bridget!——

Mrs. Bri. Well, deary.—Now hold your tongue, miss.

Just. A message from Dr. Rosy, and Doctor Rosy says——

Lau. I'm sure, mamma, his regimentals——

Just. Damn his regimentals!—Why don't you listen?

Mrs. Bri. Ay, girl, how durst you interrupt your papa?

Lau. Well, papa.

Just. Doctor Rosy says he'll bring——

Lau. Were blue turned up with red, mamma.

Just. Laury!—says he will bring the young man——

Mrs. Bri. Red! yellow, if you please, miss.

Just. Bridget!—the young man that is to be hired——

Mrs. Bri. Besides, miss, it is very unbecoming in you to want to have the last word with your mamma; you should know——

Just. Why, zounds! will you hear me or no?

Mrs. Bri. I am listening, my love—I am listening!—But what signifies my silence, what good is my not speaking a word, if this girl will interrupt and let nobody speak but herself?—Ay, I don't wonder, my life, at your impatience; your poor dear lips quiver to speak; but I suppose she'll run on, and not let you put in a word.—You may very well be angry; there is nothing, sure, so provoking as a chattering, talking——

Lau. Nay, I'm sure, mamma, it is you will not let papa speak now.

Mrs. Bri. Why, you little provoking minx——

Just. Get out of the room directly, both of you—get out!

Mrs. Bri. Ay, go, girl.

Just. Go, Bridget, you are worse than she, you old hag. I wish you were both up to the neck in the canal, to argue there till I took you out.

Enter SERVANT.

Ser. Doctor Rosy, sir.

Just. Show him up.　　　　　　　　　　[*Exit* SERVANT.

Lau. Then you own, mamma, it was a marching regiment?

Mrs. Bri. You're an obstinate fool, I tell you; for if that had been the case——

Just. You won't go?

Mrs. Bri. We are going, Mr. Surly.—If that had been the case, I say, how could——

Lau. Nay, mamma, one proof——

Mrs. Bri. How could Major——

Lau. And a full proof——

[JUSTICE CREDULOUS *drives them off.*

Just. There they go, ding dong in for the day. Good lack! a fluent tongue is the only thing a mother don't like her daughter to resemble her in.

Enter DOCTOR ROSY.

Well, doctor, where's the lad—where's Trusty?

Rosy. At hand; he'll be here in a minute, I'll answer for 't. He's such a one as you an't met with,—brave as a lion, gentle as a saline draught.

Just. Ah, he comes in the place of a rogue, a dog that was corrupted by the lieutenant. But this is a sturdy fellow, is he, doctor?

Rosy. As Hercules; and the best back-sword in the country. Egad, he'll make the red-coats keep their distance.

Just. O the villains! this is St. Patrick's day, and the rascals have been parading my house all the morning. I know they have a design upon me; but I have taken all precautions: I have magazines of arms, and if this fellow does but prove faithful, I shall be more at ease.

Rosy. Doubtless he 'll be a comfort to you.

Re-enter SERVANT.

Ser. There is a man below, sir, inquires for Doctor Rosy.

Rosy. Show him up.

Just. Hold! a little caution—How does he look?

Ser. A country-looking fellow, your worship.

Just. Oh, well, well, for Doctor Rosy; these rascals try all ways to get in here.

Ser. Yes, please your worship; there was one here this morning wanted to speak to you: he said his name was Corporal Breakbones.

Just. Corporal Breakbones!

Ser. And drummer Crackskull came again.

Just. Ay! did you ever hear of such a damned confounded crew? Well, show the lad in here!   [*Exit* SERVANT.

Rosy. Ay, he 'll be your porter; he 'll give the rogues an answer.

Enter LIEUTENANT O'CONNOR, *disguised.*

Just. So, a tall—Efacks! what! has lost an eye?

Rosy. Only a bruise he got in taking seven or eight high-waymen.

Just. He has a damned wicked leer somehow with the other.

Rosy. Oh, no, he 's bashful—a sheepish look——

Just. Well, my lad, what 's your name?

O'Con. Humphrey Hum.

Just. Hum—I don't like Hum!

O'Con. But I be mostly called honest Humphrey——

Rosy. There, I told you so, of noted honesty.

Just. Well, honest Humphrey, the doctor has told you my terms, and you are willing to serve, hey?

O'Con. And please your worship I shall be well content.

Just. Well, then, hark'ye, honest Humphrey,—you are sure now you will never be a rogue—never take a bribe, hey, honest Humphrey?

O'Con. A bribe! What 's that?

Just. A very ignorant fellow indeed!

Rosy. His worship hopes you will never part with your honesty for money.

O'Con. Noa, noa.

Just. Well said, Humphrey—my chief business with you is to watch the motions of a rake-helly fellow here, one Lieutenant O'Connor.

Rosy. Ay, you don't value the soldiers, do you, Humphrey?

O'Con. Not I; they are but zwaggerers, and you 'll see they 'll be as much afraid of me as they would of their captain.

Just. And i'faith, Humphrey, you have a pretty cudgel there!

O'Con. Ay, the zwitch is better than nothing, but I should be glad of a stouter: ha' you got such a thing in the house as an old coach-pole, or a spare bed-post?

Just. Oons! what a dragon it is!—Well, Humphrey, come with me.—I 'll just show him to Bridget, doctor, and we 'll agree.—Come along, honest Humphrey.   [*Exit.*

O'Con. My dear doctor, now remember to bring the justice presently to the walk: I have a scheme to get into his confidence at once.

Rosy. I will, I will.   [*They shake hands.*

Re-enter JUSTICE CREDULOUS.

Just. Why, honest Humphrey, hey! what the devil are you at?

Rosy. I was just giving him a little advice.—Well, I must go for the present.—Good morning to your worship—you need not fear the lieutenant while he is in your house.

Just. Well, get in, Humphrey. Good morning to you, doctor.—[*Exit* DOCTOR ROSY.] Come along, Humphrey.—Now I think I am a match for the lieutenant and all his gang.   [*Exeunt.*

ACT II.

SCENE I.—*A Street.*

Enter SERJEANT TROUNCE, DRUMMER, *and* SOLDIERS.

Trounce. Come, silence your drum—there is no valour stirring to day. I thought St. Patrick would have given us a recruit or two to-day.

Sol. Mark, serjeant!

Enter two COUNTRYMEN.

Trounce. Oh! these are the lads I was looking for; they have the looks of gentlemen.—A'n't you single, my lads?

1 *Coun.* Yes, an please you, I be quite single: my relations be all dead, thank heavens, more or less. I have but one poor mother left in the world, and she 's an helpless woman.

Trounce. Indeed! a very extraordinary case—quite your own master then—the fitter to serve his Majesty.—Can you read?

1 *Coun.* Noa, I was always too lively to take to learning; but John here is main clever at it.

Trounce. So, what you 're a scholar, friend?

2 *Coun.* I was born so, measter. Feyther kept grammar-school.

Trounce. Lucky man—in a campaign or two put yourself down chaplain to the regiment. And I warrant you have read of warriors and heroes?

2 *Coun.* Yes, that I have: I have read of Jack the Giant-killer, and the Dragon of Wantly, and the—Noa, I believe that's all in the hero way, except once about a comet.

Trounce. Wonderful knowledge!—Well, my heroes, I 'll write word to the king of your good intentions, and meet me half an hour hence at the Two Magpies.

Coun. We will, your honour, we will.

Trounce. But stay; for fear I shouldn't see you again in the crowd, clap these little bits of ribbon into your hats.

1 *Coun.* Our hats are none of the best,

Trounce. Well, meet me at the Magpies, and I 'll give you money to buy new ones.

Coun. Bless your honour, thank your honour.   [*Exeunt.*

Trounce. [*Winking at* SOLDIERS.] Jack! [*Exeunt* SOLDIERS.

Enter LIEUTENANT O'CONNOR.

So, here comes one would make a grenadier—Stop, friend, will you list?

O'Con. Who shall I serve under?

Trounce. Under me, to be sure.

O'Con. Isn't Lieutenant O'Connor your officer?

Trounce. He is; and I am commander over him.

O'Con. What! be your serjeants greater than your captains?

Trounce. To be sure, we are; 'tis our business to keep them

in order   For instance now, the general writes to me, dear
Serjeant, or dear Trounce, or dear Serjeant Trounce, according
to his hurry, if your lieutenant does not demean himself accordingly, let me know.—Yours, General Deluge.

O'Con. And do you complain of him often?

Trounce. No, hang him, the lad is good-natured at bottom,
so I pass over small things.   But hark'ee, between ourselves,
he is most confoundedly given to wenching.

Enter CORPORAL FLINT.

Flint. Please your honour, the doctor is coming this way
with his worship—We are all ready, and have our cues. [*Exit.*

O'Con. Then, my dear Trounce, or my dear Serjeant, or my
dear Serjeant Trounce, take yourself away.

Trounce. Zounds! the lieutenant—I smell of the black
hole already.   [*Exit*

Enter JUSTICE CREDULOUS *and* DOCTOR ROSY.

Just. I thought I saw some of the cut-throats.

Rosy. I fancy not; there's no one but honest Humphrey.
Ha! Odds life, here come some of them—we'll stay by these
trees, and let them pass.

Just. Oh, the bloody-looking dogs!

[*Walks aside with* DOCTOR ROSY

Re-enter CORPORAL FLINT *and two* SOLDIERS.

Flint. Halloa, friend! do you serve Justice Credulous?

O'Con. I do.

Flint. Are you rich?

O'Con. Noa.

Flint. Nor ever will be with that old stingy booby.   Look
here—take it.   ·   [*Gives him a purse.*

O'Con. What must I do for this?

Flint. Mark me, our lieutenant is in love with the old
rogue's daughter: help us to break his worship's bones, and
carry off the girl, and you are a made man.

O'Con. I'll see you hanged first, you pack of skurry villains!   [*Throws away the purse.*

Flint. What, sirrah, do you mutiny?   Lay hold of him.

O'Con. Nay then, I'll try your armour for you. [*Beats them.*

All. Oh! oh!—quarter! quarter!

[*Exeunt* CORPORAL FLINT *and* SOLDIERS

Just. [*Coming forward.*] Trim them, trounce them, break their bones, honest Humphrey —What a spirit he has!

Rosy. Aquafortis.

O'Con. Betray your master!

Rosy. What a miracle of fidelity!

Just. Ay, and it shall not go unrewarded—I'll give him sixpence on the spot. Here, honest Humphrey, there's for yourself : as for this bribe, [*takes up the purse.*] such trash is best in the hands of justice. Now then, doctor. I think I may trust him to guard the women : while he is with them I may go out with safety.

Rosy. Doubtless you may—I'll answer for the lieutenant's behaviour whilst honest Humphrey is with your daughter.

Just. Ay, ay, she shall go nowhere without him. Come along, honest Humphrey. How rare it is to meet with such a servant!   [*Exeunt.*

SCENE II.—*A Garden.*

LAURETTA *discovered.* *Enter* JUSTICE CREDULOUS *and* LIEUTENANT O'CONNOR.

Just. Why, you little truant, how durst you wander so far from the house without my leave? Do you want to invite that scoundrel lieutenant to scale the walls and carry you off?

Lau. Lud, papa, you are so apprehensive for nothing.

Just. Why, hussy——

Lau. Well then, I can't bear to be shut up all day so like a nun. I am sure it is enough to make one wish to be run away with—and I wish I was run away with—I do—and I wish the lieutenant knew it.

Just. You do, do you, hussy? Well, I think I'll take pretty good care of you. Here, Humphrey, I leave this lady in your care. Now you may walk about the garden, Miss Pert; but Humphrey shall go with you wherever you go. So mind, honest Humphrey, I am obliged to go abroad for a little while; let no one but yourself come near her; don't be shame-faced, you booby, but keep close to her. And now, miss, let your lieutenant or any of his crew come near you if they can.

                                                        [*Exit.*

Lau. How this booby stares after him! [*Sits down and sings.*

O'Con. Lauretta!

Lau. Not so free, fellow!

                                                        [*Sings*

O'Con. Lauretta! look on me.

Lau. Not so free, fellow!

O'Con. No recollection!

Lau. Honest Humphrey, be quiet.

O'Con. Have you forgot your faithful soldier?

Lau. Ah! Oh preserve me!

O'Con. 'Tis, my soul! your truest slave, passing on your father in this disguise.

Lau. Well now; I declare this is charming—you are so disguised, my dear lieutenant, and you look so delightfully ugly. I am sure no one will find you out, ha! ha! ha!—You know I am under your protection; papa charged you to keep close to me.

O'Con. True, my angel, and thus let me fulfil——

Lau. O pray now, dear Humphrey——

O'Con. Nay, 'tis but what old Mittimus commanded

[*Offers to kiss her*

Re-enter JUSTICE CREDULOUS.

Just. Laury, my—hey! what the devil's here?

Lau. Well now, one kiss, and be quiet.

Just. Your very humble servant, honest Humphrey! Don't let me—pray don't let me interrupt you!

Lau. Lud, papa! Now that's so good-natured—indeed there's no harm. You did not mean any rudeness, did you, Humphrey?

O'Con. No, indeed, miss; his worship knows it is not in me.

Just. I know that you are a lying, canting, hypocritical scoundrel; and if you don't take yourself out of my sight——

Lau. Indeed, papa, now I'll tell you how it was. I was sometime taken with a sudden giddiness, and Humphrey seeing me beginning to totter, ran to my assistance, quite frightened, poor fellow, and took me in his arms.

Just. Oh! was that all—nothing but a little giddiness, hey!

O'Con. That's all, indeed, your worship; for seeing miss change colour, I ran up instantly.

Just. Oh, 'twas very kind in you!

O'Con. And luckily recovered her.

Just. And who made you a doctor, you impudent rascal, hey? Get out of my sight, I say, this instant, or by all the statutes——

Lau. Oh now, papa, you frighten me, and I am giddy again!
—Oh, help!

O'Con. O dear lady, she 'll fall! [*Takes her into his arms.*

Just. Zounds! what before my face—why then, thou miracle
of impudence!—[*Lays hold of him and discovers him.*]—Mercy
on me, who have we here?—Murder! Robbery! Fire! Rape!
Gunpowder! Soldiers! John! Susan! Bridget!

O'Con. Good sir, don't be alarmed; I mean you no harm

Just. Thieves! Robbers! Soldiers!

O'Con. You know my love for your daughter——

Just. Fire! Cut-throats!

O'Con. And that alone——

Just. Treason! Gunpowder!

Enter a SERVANT *with a blunderbuss.*

Now, scoundrel! let her go this instant.

Lau. O papa, you 'll kill me!

Just. Honest Humphrey, be advised. Ay, miss, this way,
if you please.

O'Con. Nay, sir, but hear me——

Just. I 'll shoot.

O'Con. And you 'll be convinced——

Just. I 'll shoot.

O'Con. How injurious——

Just. I 'll shoot—and so your very humble servant, honest
Humphrey Hum. [*Exeunt separately.*

SCENE III.—*A Walk.*

Enter DOCTOR ROSY.

Rosy. Well, I think my friend is now in a fair way of succeeding. Ah! I warrant he is full of hope and fear, doubt
and anxiety; truly he has the fever of love strong upon him,
faint, peevish, languishing all day, with burning, restless
nights. Ah! just my case when I pined for my poor dear
Dolly! when she used to have her daily colics, and her little
doctor be sent for. Then would I interpret the language of
her pulse—declare my own sufferings in my receipt for her—
send her a pearl necklace in a pill-box, or a cordial draught
with an acrostic on the label. Well, those days are over: no
happiness lasting: all is vanity—now sunshine, now cloudy—
we are, as it were, king and beggar—then what avails——

Enter Lieutenant O'Connor.

O'Con. O doctor! ruined and undone.

Rosy. The pride of beauty——

O'Con. I am discovered, and——

Rosy. The gaudy palace——

O'Con. The justice is——

Rosy. The pompous wig——

O'Con. Is more enraged than ever.

Rosy. The gilded cane——

O'Con. Why, doctor!   [*Slapping him on the shoulder.*

Rosy. Hey!

O'Con. Confound your morals! I tell you I am discovered, discomfited, disappointed.

Rosy. Indeed! Good lack, good lack, to think of the instability of human affairs! Nothing certain in this world— most deceived when most confident—fools of fortune all.

O'Con. My dear doctor, I want at present a little practical wisdom. I am resolved this instant to try the scheme we were going to put in execution last week. I have the letter ready, and only want your assistance to recover my ground.

Rosy. With all my heart—I 'll warrant you I 'll bear a part in it: but how the deuce were you discovered?

O'Con. I 'll tell you as we go; there 's not a moment to be lost.

Rosy. Heaven send we succeed better!—but there 's no knowing.

O'Con. Very true.

Rosy. We may, and we may not.

O'Con. Right.

Rosy. Time must show.

O'Con. Certainly.

Rosy. We are but blind guessers

O'Con. Nothing more.

Rosy. Thick-sighted mortals.

O'Con. Remarkably.

Rosy. Wandering in error

O'Con. Even so.

Rosy. Futurity is dark.

O'Con. As a cellar.

Rosy. Men are moles

            [*Exeunt,* Lieutenant O'Connor *forcing out* Rosy

SCENE IV.—*A Room in* JUSTICE CREDULOUS' *House.*

Enter JUSTICE CREDULOUS *and* MRS. BRIDGET CREDULOUS.

Just. Odds life, Bridget, you are enough to make one mad!
I tell you he would have deceived a chief justice: the dog
seemed as ignorant as my clerk, and talked of honesty as if
he had been a churchwarden.

Mrs. Bri. Pho! nonsense, honesty!—what had you to do,
pray, with honesty? A fine business you have made of it with
your Humphrey Hum; and miss, too, she must have been
privy to it. Lauretta! ay, you would have her called so; but
for my part I never knew any good come of giving girls these
heathen christian names: if you had called her Deborah, or
Tabitha, or Ruth, or Rebecca, or Joan, nothing of this had
ever happened; but I always knew Lauretta was a runaway
name.

Just. Psha, you're a fool!

Mrs. Bri. No, Mr. Credulous, it is you who are a fool, and
no one but such a simpleton would be so imposed on.

Just. Why, zounds, madam, how durst you talk so? If
you have no respect for your husband, I should think *unus
quorum* might command a little deference.

Mrs. Bri. Don't tell me!—Unus fiddlestick! you ought to
be ashamed to show your face at the sessions: you'll be a
laughing-stock to the whole bench, and a byword with all the
pig-tailed lawyers and bag-wigged attorneys about town.

Just. Is this language for his majesty's representative? By
the statutes, it's high treason and petty treason, both at once!

Enter SERVANT.

Ser. A letter for your worship.

Just. Who brought it?

Ser. A soldier.

Just. Take it away and burn it.

Mrs. Bri. Stay!—Now you're in such a hurry—it is some
canting scrawl from the lieutenant, I suppose.—[*Takes the
letter.—Exit* SERVANT.] Let me see:—ay, 'tis signed O'Con
nor.

Just. Well, come read it out.

Mrs. Bri. [Reads.] *Revenge is sweet.*

Just. It begins so, does it? I'm glad of that; I'll let the
dog know I'm of his opinion.

Mrs. Bri. [Reads.] *And though disappointed of my designs upon your daughter, I have still the satisfaction of knowing I am revenged on her unnatural father; for this morning, in your chocolate, I had the pleasure to administer to you a dose of poison.*—Mercy on us!

Just. No tricks, Bridget; come, you know it is not so ; you know it is a lie.

Mrs. Bri. Read it yourself.

Just. [Reads.] *Pleasure to administer a dose of poison!*— Oh, horrible! Cut-throat villain!—Bridget!

Mrs. Bri. Lovee, stay, here's a postcript.—[Reads.] *N.B. 'Tis not in the power of medicine to save you.*

Just. Odds my life, Bridget! why don't you call for help? I've lost my voice.—My brain is giddy—I shall burst, and no assistance.—John!—Laury!—John!

Mrs. Bri. You see, lovee, what you have brought on yourself.

Re-enter SERVANT.

Ser. Your worship!

Just. Stay, John; did you perceive any thing in my chocolate cup this morning?

Ser. Nothing, your worship, unless it was a little grounds.

Just. What colour were they?

Ser. Blackish, your worship.

Just. Ay, arsenic, black arsenic!—Why don't you run for Doctor Rosy, you rascal?

Ser. Now, sir?

Mrs. Bri. Oh lovee, you may be sure it is in vain : let him run for the lawyer to witness your will, my life.

Just. Zounds! go for the doctor, you scoundrel. You are all confederate murderers.

Ser. Oh, here he is, your worship.　　　　　[*Exit.*

Just. Now, Bridget, hold your tongue, and let me see if my horrid situation be apparent.

Enter DOCTOR ROSY.

Rosy. I have but just called to inform—hey! bless me, what's the matter with your worship? '

Just. There, he sees it already!—Poison in my face, in capitals! Yes, yes, I'm a sure job for the undertakers indeed!

Mrs. Bri. Oh! oh! alas, doctor!

x

Just. Peace, Bridget!—Why doctor, my dear old friend, do you really see any change in me?

Rosy. Change! never was man so altered: how came these black spots on your nose?

Just. Spots on my nose!

Rosy. And that wild stare in your right eye!

Just. In my right eye!

Rosy. Ay, and alack, alack, how you are swelled!

Just. Swelled!

Rosy. Ay, don't you think he is, madam?

Mrs. Bri. Oh, 'tis in vain to conceal it!—Indeed, lovee, you are as big again as you were this morning.

Just. Yes, I feel it now—I'm poisoned!—Doctor, help me, for the love of justice! Give me life to see my murderer hanged.

Rosy. What?

Just. I'm poisoned, I say!

Rosy. Speak out!

Just. What! can't you hear me?

Rosy. Your voice is so low and hollow, as it were, I can't hear a word you say.

Just. I'm gone then!—*Hic jacet*, many years one of his majesty's justices!

Mrs. Bri. Read, doctor!—Ah, lovee, the will!—Consider, my life, how soon you will be dead.

Just. No, Bridget, I shall die by inches.

Rosy. I never heard such monstrous iniquity.—Oh, you are gone indeed, my friend! the mortgage of your little bit of clay is out, and the sexton has nothing to do but to close. We must all go, sooner or later—high and low—Death's a debt; his mandamus binds all alike—no bail, no demurrer.

Just. Silence, Doctor Croaker! will you cure me or will you not?

Rosy. Alas! my dear friend, it is not in my power, but I'll certainly see justice done on your murderer.

Just. I thank you, my dear friend, but I had rather see it myself.

Rosy. Ay, but if you recover, the villain will escape.

Mrs. Bri. Will he? then indeed it would be a pity you should recover. I am so enraged against the villain, I can't bear the thought of his escaping the halter.

Just. That's very kind in you, my dear; but if it's the same thing to you, my dear, I had as soon recover, notwithstanding. ——What, doctor, no assistance!

Rosy. Efacks, I can do nothing, but there's the German quack, whom you wanted to send from town; I met him at the next door, and I know he has antidotes for all poisons.

Just. Fetch him, my dear friend, fetch him! I'll get him a diploma if he cures me.

Rosy. Well, there's no time to be lost; you continue to swell immensely.   [*Exit.*

Mrs. Bri. What, my dear, will you submit to be cured by a quack nostrum-monger? For my part, as much as I love you, I had rather follow you to your grave than see you owe your life to any but a regular-bred physician.

Just. I'm sensible of your affection, dearest; and be assured nothing consoles me in my melancholy situation so much as the thoughts of leaving you behind.

Re-enter DOCTOR ROSY, *with* LIEUTENANT O'CONNOR *disguised*

Rosy. Great lŭck; met him passing by the door.

O'Con. Metto dowsei pulsum.

Rosy. He desires me to feel your pulse.

Just. Can't he speak English?

Rosy. Not a word.

O'Con. Palio vivem mortem soonem.

Rosy. He says you have not six hours to live.

Just. O mercy! does he know my distemper?

Rosy. I believe not.

Just. Tell him 'tis black arsenic they have given me

Rosy. Geneable illi arsnecca.

O'Con. Pisonatus.

Just. What does he say?

Rosy. He says you are poisoned.

Just. We know that; but what will be the effect?

Rosy. Quid effectum?

O'Con. Diable tutellum.

Rosy. He says you'll die presently.

Just. Oh horrible! What, no antidote?

O'Con. Curum benakere bono fullum.

Just. What, does he say I must row in a boat to Fulham?

Rosy. He says he'll undertake to cure you for three thousand pounds.

Mrs. Bri. Three thousand pounds! three thousand halters!
—No, lovee, you shall never submit to such impositions; die
at once, and be a customer to none of them.

Just. I won't die, Bridget—I don't like death.

Mrs. Bri. Psha! there is nothing in it: a moment, and it
is over.

Just. Ay, but it leaves a numbness behind that lasts a
plaguy long time.

Mrs. Bri. O my dear, pray consider the will.

Enter LAURETTA.

Lau. O my father, what is this I hear?

O'Con. Quiddam seomriam deos tollam rosnm

Rosy. The doctor is astonished at the sight of your fair
daughter.

Just. How so?

O'Con. Damsellum livivum suvum rislibani.

Rosy. He says that he has lost his heart to her, and that if
you will give him leave to pay his addresses to the young lady,
and promise your consent to the union, if he should gain her
affections, he will on those conditions cure you instantly, without fee or reward.

Just. The devil! did he say all that in so few words? What
a fine language it is! Well, I agree, if he can prevail on the
girl.—[*Aside.*] And that I am sure he never will.

Rosy. Greal.

O'Con. Writhum bothum.

Rosy. He says you must give this under your hand, while
he writes you a miraculous receipt.

                              [*Both sit down to write.*

Lau. Do, mamma, tell me the meaning of this.

Mrs. Bri. Don't speak to me, girl.—Unnatural parent!

Just. There, doctor; there's what he requires.

Rosy. And here's your receipt: read it yourself.

Just. Hey! what's here? plain English!

Rosy. Read it out; a wondrous nostrum, I'll answer for it.

Just. [*Reads.*] *In reading this you are cured, by your affectionate son-in-law,* O'CONNOR.—Who, in the name of Beelzebub, sirrah, who are you?

O'Con. Your affectionate son-in-law, O'Connor, and your
very humble servant, Humphrey Hum.

Just. 'Tis false, you dog! you are not my son-in-law; for

I 'll be poison'd again, and you shall be hanged.—I 'll die, sirrah, and leave Bridget my estate.

Mrs. Bri. Ay, pray do, my dear, leave me your estate : I 'm sure he deserves to be hanged.

Just. He does, you say!—Hark'ee, Bridget, you showed such a tender concern for me when you thought me poisoned, that for the future I am resolved never to take your advice again in any thing.—[*To* LIEUTENANT O'CONNOR.] So, do you hear, sir, you are an Irishman and a soldier, an't you?

O'Con. I am, sir, and proud of both.

Just. The two things on earth I most hate ; so I 'll tell you what—renounce your country and sell your commission, and I 'll forgive you.

O'Con. Hark'ee, Mr. Justice—if you were not the father of my Lauretta, I would pull your nose for asking the first, and break your bones for desiring the second.

Rosy. Ay, ay, you 're right.

Just. Is he? then I 'm sure I must be wrong.—Here, sir, I give my daughter to you, who are the most impudent dog I ever saw in my life.

O'Con. Oh, sir, say what you please ; with such a gift as Lauretta, every word is a compliment.

Mrs. Bri. Well, my lovee, I think this will be a good subject for us to quarrel about the rest of our lives.

Just. Why, truly, my dear, I think so, though we are seldom at a loss for that.

Rosy. This is all as it should be.—My Alexander, I give you joy, and you, my little god-daughter ; and now my sincere wish is, that you may make just such a wife as my poor dear Dolly.   *[Exeunt omnes*

THE DUENNA.
A COMIC OPERA.

DRAMATIS PERSONÆ.

AS ORIGINALLY ACTED AT COVENT GARDEN THEATRE, NOV. 21, 1775.

Don Ferdinand	. *Mr. Mattocks.*	Lopez	*Mr. Wewitzer.*
Don Jerome .	. *Mr. Wilson.*		
Don Antonio .	. *Mr. DubellLamy.*	Donna Louisa .	. *Mrs. Mattocks.*
Don Carlos .	. *Mr. Leoni.*	Donna Clara .	. *Mrs. Cargill.*
Isaac Mendoza .	. *Mr. Quick.*	The Duenna .	. *Mrs. Green.*
Father Paul .	. *Mr. Mahon.*		
Father Francis	. *Mr. Fox.*	Masquemders, Friars, Porter, Maid,
Father Augustine	*Mr. Baker.*	and Servants.

SCENE.—SEVILLE.

ACT I.

SCENE I. —*The Street before* Don Jerome's *House.*

Enter Lopez, *with a dark lantern.*

Lop. Past three o'clock!—So! a notable hour for one of my regular disposition, to be strolling like a bravo through the streets of Seville! Well, of all services, to serve a young lover is the hardest.—Not that I am an enemy to love; but my love and my master's differ strangely.—Don Ferdinand is much too gallant to eat, drink, or sleep :—now, my love gives me an appetite—then I am fond of dreaming of my mistress, and I love dearly to toast her.—This cannot be done without good sleep and good liquor: hence my partiality to a feather-bed and a bottle. What a pity, now, that I have not further time for reflections! but my master expects thee, honest Lopez, to . . secure his retreat from Donna Clara's window, as I guess.—[*Music without.*] Hey! sure, I heard music! So, so! who have we here? Oh, Don Antonio, my master's friend, come from the masquerade, to serenade my young mistress, Donna Louisa, I suppose : so! we shall have the old gentleman up presently.—Lest he should miss his son, I had best lose no time in getting to my post. [*Exit*

Enter DON ANTONIO, *with* MASQUERADERS *and music.*

SONG.—*Don Ant.*

Tell me, my lute, can thy soft strain
　So gently speak thy master's pain?
So softly sing, so humbly sigh,
　That, though my sleeping love shall know
　Who sings—who sighs below,
Her rosy slumbers shall not fly!
　Thus, may some vision whisper more
　Than ever I dare speak before.

1 *Mas.* Antonio, your mistress will never wake, while you sing so dolefully; love, like a cradled infant, is lulled by a sad melody.

Don Ant. I do not wish to disturb her rest.

1 *Mas.* The reason is, because you know she does not regard you enough to appear, if you awaked her

Don Ant. Nay, then, I'll convince you.　　　[*Sings.*

The breath of morn bids hence the night,
　Unveil those beauteous eyes, my fair;
For till the dawn of love is there,
　I feel no day, I own no light.

DONNA LOUISA—*replies from a window.*

Waking, I heard thy numbers chide,
　Waking, the dawn did bless my sight;
'Tis Phœbus sure that woos, I cried,
　Who speaks in song, who moves in light.

DON JEROME—*from a window.*

What vagabonds are these, I hear,
　Fiddling, fluting, rhyming, ranting,
　Piping, scraping, whining, canting,
Fly, scurvy minstrels, fly!

TRIO.

Don. Louisa. Nay, prithee, father, why so rough?
Don Ant. . . An humble lover I.
Don Jer. . . How durst you, daughter, lend an ear
　　　To such deceitful stuff?
　　　Quick, from the window fly!
Don. Louisa. Adieu, Antonio!
Don Ant. . . Must you go?
Don. Louisa⎱ We soon, perhaps, may meet again.
Don Ant. .⎰　For though hard fortune is our foe,
　　　The god of love will fight for us.
Don Jer. . . Reach me the blunderbuss.
Don Ant.⎱
Don. Louisa⎰ The god of love, who knows our pain—
Don Jer. Hence, or these slugs are through your brain.
　　　　　　　　　　'[*Exeunt severally.*

SCENE II.—*A Piazza.*

Enter DON FERDINAND *and* LOPEZ.

Lop. Truly, sir, I think that a little sleep once in a week or so——

Don Ferd. Peace, fool! don't mention sleep to me.

Lop. No, no, sir, I don't mention your lowbred, vulgar, sound sleep; but I can't help thinking that a gentle slumber, or half an hour's dozing, if it were only for the novelty of the thing——

Don Ferd. Peace, booby, I say!—Oh Clara, dear, cruel disturber of my rest!

Lop. And of mine too.   [*Aside.*

Don Ferd. 'Sdeath, to trifle with me at such a juncture as this!—now to stand on punctilios!—Love me! I don't believe she ever did.

Lop. Nor I either.   [*Aside.*

Don Ferd. Or is it, that her sex never know their desires for an hour together?

Lop. Ah, they know them oftener than they'll own them.
                                                           [*Aside.*

Don Ferd. Is there, in the world, so inconstant a creature as Clara?

Lop. I could name one.   [*Aside.*

Don Ferd. Yes; the tame fool who submits to her caprice.

Lop. I thought he could'nt miss it.   [*Aside.*

Don Ferd. Is she not capricious, teasing, tyrannical, obstinate, perverse, absurd? ay, a wilderness of faults and follies; her looks are scorn, and her very smiles—'Sdeath! I wish I hadn't mentioned her smiles; for she does smile such beaming loveliness, such fascinating brightness—Oh, death and madness! I shall die if I lose her.

Lop. Oh, those damned smiles have undone all!   [*Aside.*

AIR.—*Don Ferd.*

Could I her faults remember,
  Forgetting every charm,
Soon would impartial reason
  The tyrant love disarm:
But when enraged I number
  Each failing of her mind,
Love still suggests each beauty,
  And sees—while reason's blind.

Lop. Here comes Don Antonio, sir.

Don Ferd. Well, go you home—I shall be there presently

Lop. Ah, those cursed smiles!　　　　　　　[*Exit .*

Enter Don Antonio.

Don Ferd. Antonio, Lopez tells me he left you chanting before our door—was my father waked?

Don Ant. Yes, yes; he has a singular affection for music, so I left him roaring at his barred window, like the print of Bajazet in the cage. And what brings you out so early?

Don Ferd. I believe I told you, that to-morrow was the day fixed by Don Pedro and Clara's unnatural stepmother, for her to enter a convent; in order that her brat might possess her fortune : made desperate by this, I procured a key to the door, and bribed Clara's maid to leave it unbolted; at two this morning, I entered, unperceived, and stole to her chamber—I found her waking and weeping.

Don Ant. Happy Ferdinand!

Don Ferd. 'Sdeath! hear the conclusion.—I was rated as the most confident ruffian, for daring to approach her room at that hour of night..

Don Ant. Ay, ay, this was at first.

Don Ferd. No such thing! she would not hear a word from me, but threatened to raise her mother, if I did not instantly leave her.

Don Ant. Well, but at last?——

Don Ferd. At last! why I was forced to leave the house as I came in.

Don Ant. And did you do nothing to offend her?

Don Ferd. Nothing, as I hope to be saved!—I believe, I might snatch a dozen or two of kisses.

Don. Ant. Was that all? well, I think, I never heard of such assurance!

Don Ferd. Zounds! I tell you I behaved with the utmost respect.

Don Ant. O Lord! I don't mean you, but in her. But, hark ye, Ferdinand, did you leave your key with them?

Don. Ferd. Yes; the maid, who saw me out, took it from the door.

Don. Ant. Then, my life for it, her mistress elopes after you.

Don Ferd. Ay, to bless my rival, perhaps. I am in a humour to suspect every body.—You loved her once, and thought her an angel, as I do now.

Don. Ant. Yes, I loved her, till I found she wouldn't love me, and then I discovered that she hadn't a good feature in her face.

AIR.

I ne'er could any lustre see
In eyes that would not look on me;
I ne'er saw nectar on a lip,
But where my own did hope to sip.
Has the maid who seeks my heart
Cheeks of rose, untouch'd by art?
I will own the colour true,
When yielding blushes aid their hue.

Is her hand so soft and pure?
I must press it, to be sure;
Nor can I be certain then,
Till it, grateful, press again.
Must I, with attentive eye,
Watch her heaving bosom sigh?
I will do so, when I see
That heaving bosom sigh for me.

Besides, Ferdinand, you have full security in my love for your sister; help me there, and I can never disturb you with Clara.

Don Ferd. As far as I can, consistently with the honour of our family, you know I will ; but there must be no eloping.

Don Ant. And yet, now, you would carry off Clara?

Don Ferd. Ay, that's a different case!—we never mean that others should act to our sisters and wives as we do to others'.—But, to-morrow, Clara is to be forced into a convent.

Don Ant. Well, and am not I so unfortunately circumstanced? To-morrow, your father forces Louisa to marry Isaac, the Portuguese—but come with me, and we'll devise something, I warrant.

Don Ferd. I must go home.

Don Ant. Well, adieu!

Don Ferd. But, Antonio, if you did not love my sister, you have too much honour and friendship to supplant me with Clara?——

AIR.—*Don Ant.*

Friendship is the bond of reason;
But if beauty disapprove,
Heaven dissolves all other treason
In the heart that's true to love.

The faith which to my friend I swore,
    As a civil oath I view;
But to the charms which I adore,
    'Tis religion to be true.   [*Exit.*

Don Ferd. There is always a levity in Antonio's manner of replying to me on this subject that is very alarming.—'Sdeath! if Clara should love him after all!

SONG.

Though cause for suspicion appears,
    Yet proofs of her love, too, are strong;
I'm a wretch if I'm right in my fears,
    And unworthy of bliss if I'm wrong.
What heart-breaking torments from jealousy flow,
Ah! none but the jealous—the jealous can know!

When blest with the smiles of my fair,
    I know not how much I adore:
These smiles let another but share,
    And I wonder I prized them no more!
Then whence can I hope a relief from my woe,
When the falser she seems, still the fonder I grow!   [*Exit.*

SCENE III.—*A Room in* DON JEROME'S *House.*

Enter DONNA LOUISA *and* DUENNA.

Don. Louisa. But, my dear Margaret, my charming Duenna, do you think we shall succeed?

Duen. I tell you again, I have no doubt on't; but it must be instantly put to the trial. Every thing is prepared in your room, and for the rest we must trust to fortune.

Don. Louisa. My father's oath was, never to see me till I had consented to——

Duen. 'Twas thus I overheard him say to his friend, Don Guzman,—*I will demand of her to-morrow, once for all, whether she will consent to marry Isaac Mendoza; if she hesitates, I will make a solemn oath never to see or speak to her till she returns to her duty.*—These were his words.

Don. Louisa. And on his known obstinate adherence to what he has once said, you have formed this plan for my escape. ——But have you secured my maid in our interest?

Duen. She is a party in the whole; but remember, if we succeed, you resign all right and title in little Isaac, the Jew, over to me.

Don. Louisa. That I do with all my soul; get him, if you can, and I shall wish you joy, most heartily. He is twenty times as rich as my poor Antonio.

AIR.

Thou canst not boast of fortune's store,
  My love, while me they wealthy call:
But I was glad to find thee poor—
  For with my heart I'd give thee all.
    And then the grateful youth shall own
    I loved him for himself alone.

But when his worth my hand shall gain,
  No word or look of mine shall show
That I the smallest thought retain
  Of what my bounty did bestow :
    Yet still his grateful heart shall own
    I loved him for himself alone.

Duen. I hear Don Jerome coming.—Quick, give me the last letter I brought you from Antonio—you know that is to be the ground of my dismission—I must slip out to seal it up, as undelivered.   [*Exit.*

Enter DON JEROME *and* DON FERDINAND.

Don Jer. What, I suppose you have been serenading too! Eh, disturbing some peaceable neighbourhood with villanous catgut and lascivious piping! Out on't! you set your sister, here, a vile example; but I come to tell you, madam, that I'll suffer no more of these midnight incantations—these amorous orgies, that steal the senses in the hearing; as, they say, Egyptian embalmers serve mummies, extracting the brain through the ears. However, there's an end of your frolics—Isaac Mendoza will be here presently, and to-morrow you shall marry him.

Don. Louisa. Never, while I have life!

Don Ferd. Indeed, sir, I wonder how you can think of such a man for a son-in-law.

Don Jer. Sir, you are very kind to favour me with your sentiments—and pray, what is your objection to him?

Don Ferd. He is a Portuguese, in the first place.

Don Jer. No such thing, boy; he has forsworn his country

Don. Louisa. He is a Jew.

Don Jer. Another mistake: he has been a Christian these six weeks.

Don Ferd. Ay, he left his old religion for an estate, and has not had time to get a new one.

Don. Louisa. But stands like a dead wall between church and synagogue, or like the blank leaves between the Old and New Testament.

Don Jer. Any thing more?

Don Ferd. But the most remarkable part of his character is his passion for deceit and tricks of cunning

Don. Louisa. Though at the same time the fool predominates so much over the knave, that I am told he is generally the dupe of his own art.

Don Ferd. True; like an unskilful gunner, he usually misses his aim, and is hurt by the recoil of his own piece.

Don Jer. Any thing more?

Don. Louisa. To sum up all, he has the worst fault a husband can have—he 's not my choice.

Don Jer. But you are his; and choice on one side is sufficient—two lovers should never meet in marriage—be you sour as you please, he is sweet tempered; and for your good fruit, there 's nothing like ingrafting on a crab.

Don. Louisa. I detest him as a lover, and shall ten times more as a husband.

Don Jer. I don't know that—marriage generally makes a great change—but, to cut the matter short, will you have him or not?

Don. Louisa. There is nothing else I could disobey you in.

Don Jer. Do you value your father's peace?

Don. Louisa. So much, that I will not fasten on him the regret of making an only daughter wretched.

Don Jer. Very well, ma'am, then mark me—never more will I see or converse with you till you return to your duty—no reply—this and your chamber shall be your apartments; I never will stir out without leaving you under lock and key, and when I 'm at home no creature can approach you but through my library: we 'll try who can be most obstinate. Out of my sight!—there remain till you know your duty.

[*Pushes her out.*

Don Ferd. Surely, sir, my sister's inclinations should be consulted in a matter of this kind, and some regard paid to Don Antonio, being my particular friend.

Don. Jer. That, doubtless, is a very great recommendation!—I certainly have not paid sufficient respect to it.

Don Ferd. There is not a man living I would sooner choose for a brother-in-law.

Don Jer. Very possible; and if you happen to have e'er a sister, who is not at the same time a daughter of mine, I 'm sure I shall have no objection to the relationship; but at present, if you please, we'll drop the subject.

Don Ferd. Nay, sir, 'tis only my regard for my sister makes me speak.

Don Jer. Then, pray, sir, in future, let your regard for your father make you hold your tongue.

Don Ferd. I have done, sir. I shall only add a wish that you would reflect what at our age you would have felt, had you been crossed in your affection for the mother of her you are so severe to.

Don Jer. Why, I must confess I had a great affection for your mother's ducats, but that was all, boy. I married her for her fortune, and she took me in obedience to her father, and a very happy couple we were. We never expected any love from one another, and so we were never disappointed. If we grumbled a little now and then, it was soon over, for we were never fond enough to quarrel; and when the good woman died, why, why,—I had as lieve she had lived, and I wish every widower in Seville could say the same. I shall now go and get the key of this dressing-room—so, good son, if you have any lecture in support of disobedience to give your sister, it must be brief; so make the best of your time, d'ye hear?
[*Exit.*

Don Ferd. I fear, indeed, my friend Antonio has little to hope for; however, Louisa has firmness, and my father's anger will probably only increase her affection.—In our intercourse with the world, it is natural for us to dislike those who are innocently the cause of our distress; but in the heart's attachment a woman never likes a man with ardour till she has suffered for his sake—[*Noise.*] so! What bustle is here! between my father and the Duenna too—I'll e'en get out of the way.
[*Exit.*

Re-enter DON JEROME *with a letter, pulling in* DUENNA.

Don Jer. I'm astonished! I'm thunder-struck! here's treachery and conspiracy with a vengeance! You, Antonio's creature, and chief manager of this plot for my daughter's eloping!—you, that I placed here as a scarecrow?

Duen. What?

Don Jer. A scarecrow—to prove a decoy-duck! What have you to say for yourself?

Duen. Well sir, since you have forced that letter from me, and discovered my real sentiments, I scorn to renounce them. —I am Antonio's friend, and it was my intention that your daughter should have served you as all such old tyrannical sots should be served—I delight in the tender passions, and would befriend all under their influence.

Don Jer. The tender passions ! yes, they would become those impenetrable features ! Why, thou deceitful hag ! I placed thee as a guard to the rich blossoms of my daughter's beauty. I thought that dragon's front of thine would cry aloof to the sons of gallantry : steel traps and spring guns seemed writ in every wrinkle of it.—But you shall quit my house this instant. The tender passions, indeed ! go, thou wanton sibyl, thou amorous woman of Endor, go !

Duen. You base, scurrilous, old—but I won't demean myself by naming what you are.—Yes, savage, I'll leave your den ; but I suppose you don't mean to detain my apparel—I may have my things, I presume ?

Don Jer. I took you, mistress, with your wardrobe on— what have you pilfered, eh ?

Duen. Sir, I must take leave of my mistress ; she has valuables of mine : besides, my cardinal and veil are in her room.

Don Jer. Your veil, forsooth ! what, do you dread being gazed at ? or are you afraid of your complexion ? Well, go take your leave, and get your veil and cardinal ! so ! you quit the house within these five minutes.—In—in—quick !—[*Exit* DUENNA.] Here was a precious plot of mischief !—these are the comforts daughters bring us !

AIR.

If a daughter you have, she's the plague of your life,
No peace shall you know, though you've buried your wife !
At twenty she mocks at the duty you taught her—
Oh, what a plague is an obstinate daughter !
    Sighing and whining,
    Dying and pining,
Oh, what a plague is an obstinate daughter !

When scarce in their teens, they have wit to perplex us,
With letters and lovers for ever they vex us ;
While each still rejects the fair suitor you've brought her ;
Oh, what a plague is an obstinate daughter !
    Wrangling and jangling,
    Flouting and pouting,
Oh, what a plague is an obstinate daughter !

Re-enter DONNA LOUISA, *dressed as* DUENNA, *with cardinal and veil, seeming to cry.*

This way, mistress, this way.—What, I warrant, a tender parting; so! tears of turpentine down those deal cheeks.— Ay, you may well hide your head—yes, whine till your heart breaks; but I 'll not hear one word of excuse—so you are right to be dumb.   This way, this way.   [*Exeunt*

Re-enter DUENNA.

Duen. So, speed you well, sagacious Don Jerome!   Oh, rare effects of passion and obstinacy!   Now shall I try whether I can't play the fine lady as well as my mistress, and if I suc-ceed, I may be a fine lady for the rest of my life—I 'll lose no time to equip myself.   [*Exit.*

SCENE IV.—*The Court before* DON JEROME'S *House.*

Enter DON JEROME *and* DONNA LOUISA.

Don Jer. Come, mistress, there is your way—the world lies before you, so troop, thou antiquated Eve, thou original sin!   Hold, yonder is some fellow skulking; perhaps it is Antonio—go to him, d'ye hear, and tell him to make you amends, and as he has got you turned away, tell him I say it is but just he should take you himself; go.—[*Exit* DONNA LOUISA.]   So! I am rid of her, thank heaven! and now I shall be able to keep my oath, and confine my daughter with better security.   [*Exit.*

SCENE V.—*The Piazza.*

Enter DONNA CLARA *and* MAID.

Maid. But where, madam, is it you intend to go?

Don. Clara. Any where to avoid the selfish violence of my mother-in-law, and Ferdinand's insolent importunity.

Maid. Indeed, ma'am, since we have profited by Don Fer-dinand's key, in making our escape, I think we had best find him, if it were only to thank him.

Don. Clara. No—he has offended me exceedingly. [*Retire*

Enter DONNA LOUISA.

Don. Louisa. So I have succeeded in being turned out of doors—but how shall I find Antonio?   I dare not inquire for him, for fear of being discovered; I would send to my friend Clara, but that I doubt her prudery would condemn me.

Maid. Then suppose, ma'am, you were to try if your friend Donna Louisa would not receive you?

Don. Clara. No, her notions of filial duty are so severe, she would certainly betray me.

Don. Louisa. Clara is of a cold temper, and would think this step of mine highly forward.

Don. Clara. Louisa's respect for her father is so great, she would not credit the unkindness of mine.

[DONNA LOUISA *turns, and sees* DONNA CLARA *and* MAID.

Don. Louisa. Ha! who are those? sure one is Clara—if it be, I'll trust her.　Clara!　　　　　　　　　[*Advances.*

Don. Clara. Louisa! and in masquerade too!

Don. Louisa. You will be more surprised when I tell you, that I have run away from my father.

Don. Clara. Surprised indeed! and I should certainly chide you most horridly, only that I have just run away from mine.

Don. Louisa. My dear Clara!　　　　　・　　　　[*Embrace*

Don. Clara. Dear sister truant! and whither are you going?

Don. Louisa. To find the man I love, to be sure: and, I presume, you would have no aversion to meet with my brother?

Don. Clara. Indeed I should: he has behaved so ill to me, I don't believe I shall ever forgive him.

AIR.

When sable night, each drooping plant restoring,
　Wept o'er the flowers her breath did cheer,
As some sad widow o'er her babe deploring,
　Wakes its beauty with a tear;
When all did sleep whose weary hearts did borrow
　One hour from love and care to rest,
Lo! as I press'd my couch in silent sorrow,
　My lover caught me to his breast!
　　He vow'd he came to save me
　　From those who would enslave me!
　　　Then kneeling,
　　　Kisses stealing,
　　Endless faith he swore;
　　　But soon I chid him thence,
　　　For had his fond pretence
　　　Obtain'd one favour then,
　　　And he had press'd again,
　I fear'd my treacherous heart might grant him more.

Don. Louisa. Well, for all this, I would have sent him to plead his pardon, but that I would not yet a while have him know of my flight. And where do you hope to find protection?

Y

Don. Clara. The Lady Abbess of the convent of St. Catharine is a relation and kind friend of mine—I shall be secure with her, and you had best go thither with me.

Don. Louisa. No; I am determined to find Antonio first; and, as I live, here comes the very man I will employ to seek him for me.

Don. Clara. Who is he? he's a strange figure!

Don. Louisa. Yes; that sweet creature is the man whom my father has fixed on for my husband.

Don. Clara. And will you speak to him? are you mad?

Don. Louisa. He is the fittest man in the world for my purpose; for, though I was to have married him to-morrow, he is the only man in Seville, who, I am sure, never saw me in his life.

Don. Clara. And how do you know him?

Don. Louisa. He arrived but yesterday, and he was shown to me from the window, as he visited my father.

Don. Clara. Well, I'll begone.

Don. Louisa. Hold, my dear Clara—a thought has struck me: will you give me leave to borrow your name, as I see occasion?

Don. Clara. It will but disgrace you; but use it as you please: I dare not stay.—[*Going.*]—But, Louisa, if you should see your brother, be sure you don't inform him that I have taken refuge with the Dame Prior of the convent of St. Catharine, on the left hand side of the piazza, which leads to the church of St. Anthony.

Don. Louisa. Ha! ha! ha! I'll be very particular in my directions where he may not find you.—[*Exeunt* DONNA CLARA *and* MAID.]—So! my swain, yonder, has done admiring himself, and draws nearer.   [*Retires.*

Enter ISAAC *and* DON CARLOS.

Isaac. [*Looking in a pocket-glass.*] I tell you, friend Carlos, I will please myself in the habit of my chin.

Don Car. But, my dear friend, how can you think to please a lady with such a face?

Isaac. Why, what's the matter with the face! I think it is a very engaging face; and, I am sure, a lady must have very little taste who could dislike my beard.—[*Sees* DONNA LOUISA.] —See now! I'll die if here is not a little damsel struck with it already.

Don. Louisa. Signor, are you disposed to oblige a lady who greatly wants your assistance?   [*Unveils.*

Isaac. Egad, a very pretty black-eyed girl! she has certainly taken a fancy to me, Carlos. First, ma'am, I must beg the favour of your name.

Don. Louisa. [*Aside.*] So! it's well I am provided.— [*Aloud.*]—My name, sir, is Donna Clara d'Almanza.

Isaac. What? Don Guzman's daughter? I'faith, I just now heard she was missing.

Don. Louisa. But sure, sir, you have too much gallantry and honour to betray me, whose fault is love?

Isaac. So! a passion for me! poor girl! Why, ma'am, as for betraying you, I don't see how I could get any thing by it; so, you may rely on my honour; but as for your love, I am sorry your case is so desperate.

Don. Louisa. Why so, signor?

Isaac. Because I am positively engaged to another—an't I, Carlos?

Don. Louisa. Nay, but hear me.

Isaac. No, no; what should I hear for? It is impossible for me to court you in an honourable way; and for any thing else, if I were to comply now, I suppose you have some un grateful brother, or cousin, who would want to cut my throat for my civility—so, truly, you had best go home again.

Don. Louisa. [*Aside.*] Odious wretch!—[*Aloud.*]—But, good signor, it is Antonio d'Ercilla, on whose account I have eloped.

Isaac. How! what! it is not with me, then, that you are in love?

Don. Louisa. No, indeed, it is not.

Isaac. Then you are a forward, impertinent simpleton! and I shall certainly acquaint your father.

Don. Louisa. Is this your gallantry?

Isaac. Yet hold—Antonio d'Ercilla, did you say? egad, I may make something of this—Antonio d'Ercilla?

Don. Louisa. Yes; and, if ever you hope to prosper in love, you will bring me to him.

Isaac. By St. Iago and I will too!—Carlos, this Antonio is one who rivals me (as I have heard) with Louisa—now, if I could hamper him with this girl, I should have the field to myself; hey, Carlos! A lucky thought, isn't it?

Don Car. Yes, very good—very good!

Isaac. Ah! this little brain is never at a loss—cunning

Isaac! cunning rogue! Donna Clara, will you trust yourself
awhile to my friend's direction?

Don. Louisa. May I rely on you, good signor?

Don Car. Lady, it is impossible I should deceive you.

AIR.

Had I a heart for falsehood framed,
    I ne'er could injure you;
For though your tongue no promise claim'd,
    Your charms would make me true.
To you no soul shall bear deceit,
    No stranger offer wrong;
But friends in all the aged you'll meet,
    And lovers in the young.

But when they learn that you have blest
    Another with your heart,
They'll bid aspiring passion rest,
    And act a brother's part:
Then, lady, dread not here deceit,
    Nor fear to suffer wrong;
For friends in all the aged you'll meet,
    And brothers in the young.

Isaac. Conduct the lady to my lodgings, Carlos; I must
haste to Don Jerome. Perhaps you know Louisa, ma'am.
She's divinely handsome, isn't she?

Don. Louisa. You must excuse me not joining with you.

Isaac. Why, I have heard it on all hands.

Don. Louisa. Her father is uncommonly partial to her; but
I believe you will find she has rather a matronly air.

Isaac. Carlos, this is all envy.—You pretty girls never speak
well of one another.—[*To* DON CARLOS.] Hark ye, find out
Antonio, and I'll saddle him with this scrape, I warrant.
Oh, 'twas the luckiest thought! Donna Clara, your very obedient. Carlos to your post.

DUET.

Isaac. . . . My mistress expects me, and I must go to her,
    Or how can I hope for a smile?
Don. Louisa. Soon may you return a prosperous wooer,
    But think what I suffer the while!
    Alone, and away from the man whom I love,
    In strangers I'm forced to confide.
Isaac. . . . Dear lady, my friend you may trust, and he'll prove
    Your servant, protector, and guide.

AIR.

Don Car. . . Gentle maid, ah! why suspect me?
    Let me serve thee—then reject me.

Canst thou trust, and I deceive thee?
Art thou sad, and shall I grieve thee?
Gentle maid, ah! why suspect me?
Let me serve thee—then reject me.

TRIO.

Don. Louisa.　　Never mayst thou happy be,
　　　　　　　　If in aught thou 'rt false to me.
Isaac. . .　　Never may he happy be,
　　　　　　　　If in aught he 's false to thee.
Don Car. .　　Never may I happy be,
　　　　　　　　If in aught I 'm false to thee.
Don. Louisa.　　Never mayst thou, &c.
Isaac. . . .　　Never may he, &c.
Don Car. .　　Never may I, &c.　　　　　　*[Exeunt.*

ACT II.

SCENE I.—*A Library in* DON JEROME'S *House.*

Enter DON JEROME *and* ISAAC.

Don Jer. Ha! ha! ha! run away from her father! has she given him the slip? Ha! ha! ha! poor Don Guzman!

Isaac. Ay; and I am to conduct her to Antonio; by which means you see I shall hamper him so that he can give me no disturbance with your daughter—this is trap, isn't it? a nice stroke of cunning, hey?

Don Jer. Excellent! excellent! yes, yes, carry her to him, hamper him by all means, ha! ha! ha! poor Don Guzman! an old fool! imposed on by a girl!

Isaac. Nay, they have the cunning of serpents, that 's the truth on 't.

Don Jer. Psha! they are cunning only when they have fools to deal with. Why don't my girl play me such a trick —let her cunning over-reach my caution, I say—hey, little Isaac!

Isaac. True, true; or let me see any of the sex make a fool of me!—No, no, egad! little Solomon (as my aunt used to call me) understands tricking a little too well.

Don Jer. Ay, but such a driveller as Don Guzman!

Isaac. And such a dupe as Antonio!

Don Jer. True; never were seen such a couple of credulous simpletons! But come, 'tis time you should see my daughter —you must carry on the siege by yourself, friend Isaac.

Isaac. Sir, you 'll introduce——

Don Jer. No—I have sworn a solemn oath not to see or

speak to her till she renounces her disobedience; win her to that, and she gains a father and a husband at once.

Isaac. Gad, I shall never be able to deal with her alone; nothing keeps me in such awe as perfect beauty—now there is something consoling and encouraging in ugliness.

SONG.

Give Isaac the nymph who no beauty can boast,
But health and good humour to make her his toast;
If straight, I don't mind whether slender or fat,
And six feet or four—we'll ne'er quarrel for that.

Whate'er her complexion, I vow I don't care;
If brown, it is lasting—more pleasing, if fair:
And though in her face I no dimples should see,
Let her smile—and each dell is a dimple to me.

Let her locks be the reddest that ever were seen,
And her eyes may be e'en any colour but green;
For in eyes, though so various the lustre and hue,
I swear I've no choice—only let her have two.

'Tis true I'd dispense with a throne on her back,
And white teeth, I own, are genteeler than black;
A little round chin too 's a beauty, I've heard;
But I only desire she mayn't have a beard.

Don Jer. You will change your note, my friend, when you've seen Louisa.

Isaac. Oh, Don Jerome, the honour of your alliance——

Don Jer. Ay, but her beauty will affect you—she is, though I say it, who am her father, a very prodigy. There you will see features with an eye like mine—yes, i' faith, there is a kind of wicked sparkling—something of a roguish brightness, that shows her to be my own.

Isaac. Pretty rogue!

Don Jer. Then, when she smiles, you'll see a little dimple in one cheek only; a beauty it is certainly, yet you shall not say which is prettiest, the cheek with the dimple, or the cheek without.

Isaac. Pretty rogue!

Don Jer. Then the roses on those cheeks are shaded with a sort of velvet down, that gives a delicacy to the glow of health.

Isaac. Pretty rogue!

Don Jer. Her skin pure dimity, yet more fair, being spangled here and there with a golden freckle.

Isaac. Charming pretty rogue! pray how is the tone of her voice?

Don Jer. Remarkably pleasing—but if you could prevail on her to sing, you would be enchanted—she is a nightingale— a Virginia nightingale! But come, come; her maid shall conduct you to her antechamber.

Isaac. Well, egad, I'll pluck up resolution, and meet her frowns intrepidly.

Don Jer. Ay! woo her briskly—win her, and give me a proof of your address, my little Solomon.

Isaac. But hold—I expect my friend Carlos to call on me here. If he comes, will you send him to me?

Don Jer. I will. Lauretta!—[*Calls.*]—Come—she'll show you to the room. What! do you droop? here's a mournful face to make love with! [*Exeunt.*

SCENE II.—DONNA LOUISA'S *Dressing Room.*

Enter ISAAC *and* MAID.

Maid. Sir, my mistress will wait on you presently.

[*Goes to the door.*

Isaac. When she's at leisure—don't hurry her.—[*Exit* MAID.]—I wish I had ever practised a love-scene—I doubt I shall make a poor figure—I couldn't be more afraid if I was going before the Inquisition. So, the door opens—yes, she's coming—the very rustling of her silk has a disdainful sound.

Enter DUENNA, *dressed as* DONNA LOUISA.

Now dar'n't I look round for the soul of me—her beauty will certainly strike me dumb if I do. I wish she'd speak first.

Duen. Sir, I attend your pleasure.

Isaac. [*Aside.*] So! the ice is broke, and a pretty civil beginning too!—[*Aloud.*] Hem! madam—miss—I'm all attention.

Duen. Nay, sir, 'tis I who should listen, and you propose.

Isaac. [*Aside.*] Egad, this isn't so disdainful neither—I believe I may venture to look. No—I dar'n't—one glance of those roguish sparklers would fix me again.

Duen. You seem thoughtful, sir. Let me persuade you to sit down.

Isaac. [*Aside.*] So, so; she mollifies apace—she's struck with my figure! this attitude has had its effect.

Duen. Come, sir, here's a chair.

Isaac. Madam, the greatness of your goodness overpowers me—that a lady so lovely should deign to turn her beauteous eyes on me so.   [*She takes his hand, he turns and sees her.*

Duen. You seem surprised at my condescension.

Isaac. Why, yes, madam, I am a little surprised at it.— [*Aside.*] Zounds! this can never be Louisa—she's as old as my mother!

Duen. But former prepossessions give way to my father's commands.

Isaac. [*Aside.*] Her father! Yes, 'tis she then.—Lord, Lord; how blind some parents are!

Duen. Signor Isaac!

Isaac. [*Aside.*] Truly, the little damsel was right—she has rather a matronly air, indeed! ah! 'tis well my affections are fixed on her fortune, and not her person.

Duen. Signor, won't you sit?   [*She sits.*

Isaac. Pardon me, madam, I have scarce recovered my astonishment at — your condescension, madam. —[*Aside.*] She has the devil's own dimples, to be sure!

Duen. I do not wonder, sir, that you are surprised at my affability—I own, signor, that I was vastly prepossessed against you, and, being teased by my father, I did give some encouragement to Antonio; but then, sir, you were described to me as quite a different person.

Isaac. Ay, and so you were to me, upon my soul, madam.

Duen. But when I saw you I was never more struck in my life.

Isaac. That was just my case too, madam: I was struck all on a heap, for my part.

Duen. Well, sir, I see our misapprehension has been mutual—you expected to find me haughty and averse, and I was taught to believe you a little black, snub-nosed fellow, without person, manners, or address.

Isaac. Egad, I wish she had answered her picture as well! [*Aside.*

Duen. But, sir, your air is noble—something so liberal in your carriage, with so penetrating an eye, and so bewitching a smile!

Isaac. Egad, now I look at her again, I don't think she is so ugly! [*Aside.*

Duen. So little like a Jew, and so much like a gentleman!

Isaac. Well, certainly, there is something pleasing in the tone of her voice.　　　　　　　　　　　　　　[*Aside.*

Duen. You will pardon this breach of decorum in praising you thus, but my joy at being so agreeably deceived has given me such a flow of spirits!

Isaac. Oh, dear lady, may I thank those dear lips for this goodness?—[*Kisses her.*]　Why she has a pretty sort of velvet down, that 's the truth on 't.　　　　　　　　[*Aside.*

Duen. O sir, you have the most insinuating manner, but indeed you should get rid of that odious beard—one might as well kiss a hedgehog.

Isaac. [*Aside.*] Yes, ma'am, the razor wouldn't be amiss— for either of us.—[*Aloud.*]　Could you favour me with a song?

Duen. Willingly, sir, though I am rather hoarse—ahem!

　　　　　　　　　　　　　　　　[*Begins to sing.*

Isaac. [*Aside.*] Very like a Virginia nightingale!—[*Aloud.*] Ma'am, I perceive you 're hoarse—I beg you will not distress——

Duen. Oh, not in the least distressed.　Now, sir.

SONG.

When a tender maid
Is first assay'd
By some admiring swain,
How her blushes rise
If she meet his eyes,
While he unfolds his pain!
If he takes her hand, she trembles quite!
Touch her lips, and she swoons outright!
While a pit-a-pat, &c.
Her heart avows her fright.

But in time appear
Fewer signs of fear;
The youth she boldly views :
If her hand he grasp,
Or her bosom clasp,
No mantling blush ensues !
Then to church well pleased the lovers move
While her smiles her contentment prove ;
And a-pit-a-pat, &c.
Her heart avows her love.

Isaac. Charming, ma'am! enchanting! and, 'truly,' your notes put me in mind of one that 's very dear to me—a lady, indeed, whom you greatly resemble!

Duen. How! is there, then, another so dear to you?

Isaac. Oh, no, ma'am, you mistake; it was my mother I meant.

Duen. Come, sir, I see you are amazed and confounded at my condescension, and know not what to say.

Isaac. It is very true, indeed, ma'am; but it is a judgment, I look on it as a judgment on me, for delaying to urge the time when you 'll permit me to complete my happiness, by acquainting Don Jerome with your condescension.

Duen. Sir, I must frankly own to you, that I can never be yours with my father's consent.

Isaac. Good lack! how so?

Duen. When my father, in his passion, swore he would never see me again till I acquiesced in his will, I also made a vow, that I would never take a husband from his hand; nothing shall make me break that oath: but, if you have spirit and contrivance enough to carry me off without his knowledge, I 'm yours.

Isaac. Hum!

Duen. Nay, sir, if you hesitate——

Isaac. [*Aside.*] I' faith, no bad whim this!—If I take her at her word, I shall secure her fortune, and avoid making any settlement in return; thus I shall not only cheat the lover, but the father too. Oh, cunning rogue, Isaac! ay, ay, let this little brain alone! Egad, I 'll take her in the mind!

Duen. Well, sir, what 's your determination?

Isaac. Madam, I was dumb only from rapture—I applaud your spirit, and joyfully close with your proposal; for which thus let me, on this lily hand, express my gratitude.

Duen. Well, sir, you must get my father's consent to walk with me in the garden. But by no means inform him of my kindness to you.

Isaac. No, to be sure, that would spoil all: but, trust me when tricking is the word—let me alone for a piece of cunning; this very day you shall be out of his power.

Duen. Well, I leave the management of it all to you; I perceive plainly, sir, that you are not one that can be easily outwitted.

Isaac. Egad, you 're right, madam—you 're right, i' faith.

Re-enter MAID.

Maid. Here 's a gentleman at the door, who begs permission to speak with Signor Isaac.

Isaac. A friend of mine, ma'am, and a trusty friend—let him come in—[*Exit* MAID.] He is one to be depended on, ma'am.

Enter DON CARLOS.

So, coz.   [*Talks apart with* DON CARLOS.

Don Car. I have left Donna Clara at your lodgings, but can nowhere find Antonio.

Isaac. Well, I will search him out myself. Carlos, you rogue, I thrive, I prosper!

Don Car. Where is your mistress?

Isaac. There, you booby, there she stands.

Don Car. Why, she's damned ugly!

Isaac. Hush!   [*Stops his mouth*

Duen. What is your friend saying, signor?

Isaac. Oh, ma'am, he is expressing his raptures at such charms as he never saw before. Eh, Carlos?

Don Car. Ay, such as I never saw before, indeed!

Duen. You are a very obliging gentleman. Well, signor Isaac, I believe we had better part for the present. Remember our plan.

Isaac. Oh, ma'am, it is written in my heart, fixed as the image of those divine beauties. Adieu, idol of my soul!—yet once more permit me——   [*Kisses her.*

Duen. Sweet, courteous sir, adieu!

Isaac. Your slave eternally! Come, Carlos, say something civil at taking leave.

Don Car. I' faith, Isaac, she is the hardest woman to compliment I ever saw; however, I'll try something I had studied for the occasion.

SONG.

Ah! sure a pair was never seen
　So justly form'd to meet by nature!
The youth excelling so in mien,
　The maid in ev'ry grace of feature.
Oh, how happy are such lovers,
　When kindred beauties each discovers!
　　For surely she
　　Was made for thee,
And thou to bless this lovely creature!

So mild your looks, your children thence
　Will early learn the task of duty—
The boys with all their father's sense,
　The girls with all their mother's beauty!

Oh, how happy to inherit
At once such graces and such spirit !
Thus while you live
May fortune give
Each blessing equal to your merit !   [*Exeunt.*

SCENE III.—*A Library in* DON JEROME'S *House.*

DON JEROME *and* DON FERDINAND *discovered.*

Don Jer. Object to Antonio ! I have said it. His poverty,
can you acquit him of that ?

Don Ferd. Sir, I own he is not over rich ; but he is of as
ancient and honourable a family as any in the kingdom.

Don Jer. Yes, I know the beggars are a very ancient family
in most kingdoms ; but never in great repute, boy.

Don Ferd. Antonio, sir, has many amiable qualities.

Don Jer. But he is poor ; can you clear him of that, I say ?
Is he not a gay, dissipated rake, who has squandered his
patrimony ?

Don Ferd. Sir, he inherited but little ; and that, his generosity, more than his profuseness, has stripped him of ; but he
has never sullied his honour, which, with his title, has outlived his means.

Don Jer. Psha ! you talk like a blockhead ! nobility, without an estate, is as ridiculous as gold lace on a frieze coat.

Don Ferd. This language, sir, would better become a Dutch
or English trader than a Spaniard.

Don Jer. Yes ; and those Dutch and English traders, as
you call them, are the wiser people. Why, booby, in England
they were formerly as nice, as to birth and family, as we are :
but they have long discovered what a wonderful purifier gold
is ; and now, no one there regards pedigree in any thing but
a horse. Oh, here comes Isaac ! I hope he has prospered in
his suit.

Don Ferd. Doubtless, that agreeable figure of his must
have helped his suit surprisingly.

Don Jer. How now?   [DON FERDINAND *walks aside*

Enter ISAAC.

Well, my friend, have you softened her ?

Isaac. Oh, yes ; I have softened her.

Don Jer. What, does she come to ?

Isaac. Why, truly, she was kinder than I expected to find
her.

Don Jer. And the dear little angel was civil, eh?

Isaac. Yes, the pretty little angel was very civil.

Don Jer. I'm transported to hear it! Well, and you were astonished at her beauty, hey?

Isaac. I was astonished, indeed! Pray, how old is miss?

Don Jer. How old! let me see—eight and twelve—she is twenty.

Isaac. Twenty?

Don Jer. Ay, to a month.

Isaac. Then, upon my soul, she is the oldest-looking girl of her age in Christendom!

Don Jer. Do you think so? But, I believe, you will not see a prettier girl.

Isaac. Here and there one.

Don Jer. Louisa has the family face.

Isaac. Yes, egad, I should have taken it for a family face, and one that has been in the family some time too.   [*Aside.*

Don Jer. She has her father's eyes.

Isaac. Truly, I should have guessed them to have been so! If she had her mother's spectacles, I believe she would not see the worse.   [*Aside.*

Don Jer. Her aunt Ursula's nose, and her grandmother's forehead, to a hair.

Isaac. Ay, 'faith, and her grandfather's chin, to a hair.

[*Aside.*

Don Jer. Well, if she was but as dutiful as she's handsome —and hark ye, friend Isaac, she is none of your made-up beauties—her charms are of the lasting kind.

Isaac. I'faith, so they should—for if she be but twenty now, she may double her age before her years will overtake her face.

Don Jer. Why, zounds, Master Isaac! you are not sneering, are you?

Isaac. Why now, seriously, Don Jerome, do you think your daughter handsome?

Don Jer. By this light, she's as handsome a girl as any in Seville.

Isaac. Then, by those eyes, I think her as plain a woman as ever I beheld.

Don Jer. By St. Iago! you must be blind.

Isaac. No, no; 'tis you are partial.

Don Jer. How! have I neither sense nor taste? If a fair skin, fine eyes, teeth of ivory, with a lovely bloom, and a deli-

cate shape—if these, with a heavenly voice, and a world of
grace, are not charms, I know not what you call beautiful.

Isaac. Good lack, with what eyes a father sees! As I have
life, she is the very reverse of all this : as for the dimity skin
you told me of, I swear 'tis a thorough nankeen as ever I saw!
for her eyes, their utmost merit is not squinting—for her
teeth, where there is one of ivory, its neighbour is pure ebony,
black and white alternately, just like the keys of a harpsichord.
Then, as to her singing, and heavenly voice—by this hand, she
has a shrill, cracked pipe, that sounds, for all the world, like a
child's trumpet.

Don Jer. Why, you little Hebrew scoundrel, do you mean
to insult me? Out of my house, I say!

Don Ferd. [*Coming forward.*] Dear sir, what's the matter?

Don Jer. Why, this Israelite here has the impudence to say
your sister's ugly.

Don Ferd. He must be either blind or insolent.

Isaac. So, I find they are all in a story. Egad, I believe I
have gone too far! [*Aside.*

Don Ferd. Sure, sir, there must be some mistake; it can't
be my sister whom he has seen.

Don Jer. 'Sdeath! you are as great a fool as he! What
mistake can there be? Did not I lock up Louisa, and haven't
I the key in my own pocket? and didn't her maid show him
into the dressing-room? and yet you talk of a mistake! No,
the Portuguese meant to insult me—and, but that this roof
protects him, old as I am, this sword should do me justice.

Isaac. I must get off as well as I can—her fortune is not
the less handsome [*Aside*

DUET.

Isaac.	Believe me, good sir, I ne'er meant to offend ;
	My mistress I love, and I value my friend :
	To win her and wed her is still my request,
	For better for worse—and I swear I don't jest.
Don Jer.	Zounds! you'd best not provoke me, my rage is so high!
Isaac.	Hold him fast, I beseech you, his rage is so high !
	Good sir, you're too hot, and this place I must fly.
Don Jer.	You're a knave and a sot, and this place you'd best fly.

Isaac. Don Jerome, come now, let us lay aside all joking,
and be serious.

Don Jer. How?

Isaac. Ha! ha! ha! I'll be hanged if you haven't taken
my abuse of your daughter seriously.

Don Jer. You meant it so, did not you?

Isaac. O mercy, no! a joke—just to try how angry it would make you,.

Don Jer. Was that all, i'faith? I didn't know you had been such a wag. Ha! ha! ha! By St. Iago! you made me very angry, though. Well, and you do think Louisa handsome?

Isaac. Handsome! Venus de Medicis was a sibyl to her.

Don Jer. Give me your hand, you little jocose rogue! Egad, I thought we had been all off.

Don Ferd. So! I was in hopes this would have been a quarrel; but I find the Jew is too cunning. [*Aside.*

Don Jer. Ay, this gust of passion has made me dry—I am seldom ruffled. Order some wine in the next room—let us drink the poor girl's health. Poor Louisa! ugly, eh! ha! ha! ha! 'twas a very good joke, indeed!

Isaac. And a very true one, for all that. [*Aside.*

Don Jer. And, Ferdinand, I insist upon your drinking success to my friend.

Don Ferd. Sir, I will drink success to my friend with all my heart.

Don Jer. Come, little Solomon, if any sparks of anger had remained, this would be the only way to quench them

TRIO

A bumper of good liquor
Will end a contest quicker
Than justice, judge, or vicar;
    So fill a cheerful glass,
    And let good humour pass.

But if more deep the quarrel,
Why, sooner drain the barrel
Than be the hateful fellow
That's crabbed when he's mellow.
    A bumper, &c. [*Exeunt.*

SCENE IV.—ISAAC'S *Lodgings.*

Enter DONNA LOUISA.

Don. Louisa. Was ever truant daughter so whimsically circumstanced as I am? I have sent my intended husband to look after my lover—the man of my father's choice is gone to bring me the man of my own: but how dispiriting is this interval of expectation!

SONG.

What bard, O Time, discover,
    With wings first made thee move!
Ah! sure it was some lover
    Who ne'er had left his love!
For who that once did prove
The pangs which absence brings,
    Though but one day
    He were away,
Could picture thee with wings?
    What bard, &c.

Enter DON CARLOS.

So, friend, is Antonio found?

Don Car. I could not meet with him, lady; but I doubt not my friend Isaac will be here with him presently.

Don. Louisa. Oh, shame! you have used no diligence. Is this your courtesy to a lady, who has trusted herself to your protection?

Don Car. Indeed, madam, I have not been remiss.

Don. Louisa. Well, well; but if either of you had known how each moment of delay weighs upon the heart of her who loves, and waits the object of her love, oh, ye would not then have trifled thus!

Don Car. Alas, I know it well!

Don. Louisa. Were you ever in love, then?

Don Car. I was, lady; but, while I have life, will never be again.

Don. Louisa. Was your mistress so cruel?

Don Car. If she had always been so, I should have been happier.

SONG.

Oh, had my love ne'er smiled on me,
    I ne'er had known such anguish;
But think how false, how cruel she,
    To bid me cease to languish;
To bid me hope her hand to gain,
    Breathe on a flame half perish'd;
And then, with cold and fix'd disdain,
    To kill the hope she cherish'd.

Not worse his fate, who on a wreck,
    That drove as winds did blow it,
Silent had left the shatter'd deck,
    To find a grave below it.
Then land was cried—no more resign'd,
    He glow'd with joy to hear it;
Not worse his fate, his woe, to find
    The wreck must sink ere near it!

Don Louisa. As I live, here is your friend coming with Antonio! I·ll retire for a moment to surprise him. [*Exit.*

Enter ISAAC *and* DON ANTONIO.

Don Ant. Indeed, my good friend, you must be mistaken. Clara d'Almanza in love with me, and employ you to bring me to meet her! It is impossible!

Isaac. That you shall see in an instant. Carlos, where is the lady?—[DON CARLOS *points to the door.*] In the next room, is she?

Don Ant. Nay, if that lady is really here, she certainly wants me to conduct her to a dear friend of mine, who has long been her lover.

Isaac. Psha! I tell you 'tis no such thing—you are the man she wants, and nobody but you. Here 's ado to persuade you to take a pretty girl that 's dying for you!

Don Ant. But I have no affection for this lady.

Isaac. And you have for Louisa, hey? But take my word for it, Antonio, you have no chance there—so you may as well secure the good that offers itself to you.

Don Ant. And could you reconcile it to your conscience to supplant your friend?

Isaac. Pish! Conscience has no more to do with gallantry than it has with politics. Why, you are no honest fellow if love can't make a rogue of you—so come, do go in and speak to her, at least.

Don Ant. Well, I have no objection to that.

Isaac. [*Opens the door.*] There—there she is—yonder by the window—get in, do.—[*Pushes him in, and half shuts the door.*] Now, Carlos, now I shall hamper him, I warrant! Stay, I 'll peep how they go on. Egad, he looks confoundedly posed! Now she 's coaxing him. See, Carlos, he begins to come to—ay, ay, he 'll soon forget his conscience.

Don Car. Look—now they are both laughing!

Isaac. Ay, so they are—yes, yes, they are laughing at that dear friend he talked of—ay, poor devil, they have outwitted him

Don Car. Now he 's kissing her hand.

Isaac. Yes, yes, 'faith, they 're agreed—he 's caught, he 's entangled. My dear Carlos, we have brought it about. Oh, this little cunning head! I 'm a Machiavel—a very Machiavel!

Don Car. I hear somebody inquiring for you—I 'll see who it is. [*Exit*

z

Re-enter DON ANTONIO *and* DONNA LOUISA.

Don Ant. Well, my good friend, this lady has so entirely convinced me of the certainty of your success at Don Jerome's, that I now resign my pretensions there.

Isaac. You never did a wiser thing, believe me; and, as for deceiving your friend, that's nothing at all—tricking is all fair in love, isn't it, ma'am?'

Don. Louisa. Certainly, sir; and I am particularly glad to find you are of that opinion.

Isaac. O lud! yes, ma'am—let any one outwit me that can, I say! But here, let me join your hands. There, you lucky rogue! I wish you happily married, from the bottom of my soul!

Don. Louisa. And I am sure, if you wish it, no one else should prevent it.

Isaac. Now, Antonio, we are rivals no more; so let us be friends, will you?

Don Ant. With all my heart, Isaac.

Isaac. It is not every man, let me tell you, that would have taken such pains, or been so generous to a rival.

Don Ant. No, 'faith, I don't believe there's another beside yourself in all Spain.

Isaac. Well, but you resign all pretensions to the other lady?

Don Ant. That I do, most sincerely.

Isaac. I doubt you have a little hankering there still.

Don Ant. None in the least, upon my soul.

Isaac. I mean after her fortune.

Don Ant. No, believe me. You are heartily welcome to every thing she has.

Isaac. Well, i' faith, you have the best of the bargain, as to beauty, twenty to one. Now I'll tell you a secret—I am to carry off Louisa this very evening.

Don. Louisa. Indeed!

Isaac. Yes, she has sworn not to take a husband from her father's hand—so I've persuaded him to trust her to walk with me in the garden, and then we shall give him the slip.

Don. Louisa. And is Don Jerome to know nothing of this?

Isaac. O Lud, no! there lies the jest. Don't you see that, by this step, I over-reach him? I shall be entitled to the girl's fortune, without settling a ducat on her. Ha! ha! ha! I'm a cunning dog, an't I? a sly little villain, eh?

Don Ant. Ha! ha! ha! you are indeed!

Isaac. Roguish, you'll say, but keen, hey? devilish keen?

Don Ant. So you are indeed—keen—very keen.

Isaac. And what a laugh we shall have at Don Jerome's when the truth comes out! hey?

Don. Louisa. Yes, I'll answer for it, we shall have a good laugh when the truth comes out. Ha! ha! ha!

Re-enter DON CARLOS.

Don Car. Here are the dancers come to practise the fandango you intended to have honoured Donna Louisa with.

Isaac. Oh, I shan't want them; but, as I must pay them, I'll see a caper for my money. Will you excuse me?

Don. Louisa. Willingly.

Isaac. Here's my friend, whom you may command for any service. Madam, your most obedient—Antonio, I wish you all happiness.—[*Aside.*] Oh, the easy blockhead! what a tool I have made of him!—This was a masterpiece! [*Exit.*

Don. Louisa. Carlos, will you be my guard again, and convey me to the convent of St. Catharine?

Don Ant. Why, Louisa—why should you go there?

Don. Louisa. I have my reasons, and you must not be seen to go with me; I shall write from thence to my father; perhaps, when he finds what he has driven me to, he may relent.

Don Ant. I have no hope from him. O Louisa! in these arms should be your sanctuary.

Don. Louisa. Be patient but for a little while—my father cannot force me from thence. But let me see you there before evening, and I will explain myself.

Don Ant. I shall obey.

Don. Louisa. Come, friend. Antonio, Carlos has been a lover himself.

Don Ant. Then he knows the value of his trust.

Don Car. You shall not find me unfaithful.

TRIO.

Soft pity never leaves the gentle breast
Where love has been received a welcome guest;
As wandering saints poor huts have sacred made,
He hallows every heart he once has sway'd,
And, when his presence we no longer share,
Still leaves compassion as a relic there. [*Exeunt.*

ACT III.

Scene I.—*A Library in* Don Jerome's *House.*

Enter Don Jerome *and* Servant.

Don Jer. Why, I never was so amazed in my life! Louisa gone off with Isaac Mendoza! What! steal away with the very man whom I wanted her to marry—elope with her own husband, as it were—it is impossible!

Ser. Her maid says, sir, they had your leave to walk in the garden while you were abroad. The door by the shrubbery was found open, and they have not been heard of since. [*Exit.*

Don Jer. Well, it is the most unaccountable affair! 'sdeath! there is certainly some infernal mystery in it I can't comprehend!

Enter Second Servant, *with a letter.*

Ser. Here is a letter, sir, from Signor Isaac. [*Exit.*

Don Jer. So, so, this will explain—ay, Isaac Mendoza—let me see—— [*Reads.*

Dearest Sir,

You must, doubtless, be much surprised at my flight with your daughter!—yes, 'faith, and well I may—*I had the happiness to gain her heart at our first interview.*—The devil you had!—*But, she having unfortunately made a vow not to receive a husband from your hands, I was obliged to comply with her whim!*—So, so!—*We shall shortly throw ourselves at your feet, and I hope you will have a blessing ready for one, who will then be your son-in-law,*   Isaac Mendoza.

A whim, hey? Why, the devil's in the girl, I think! This morning, she would die sooner than have him, and before evening she runs away with him! Well, well, my will's accomplished—let the motive be what it will—and the Portuguese, sure, will never deny to fulfil the rest of the article.

Re-enter Servant, *with another letter.*

Ser. Sir, here's a man below, who says he brought this from my young lady, Donna Louisa. [*Exit.*

Don Jer. How! yes, it's my daughter's hand, indeed! Lord, there was no occasion for them both to write; well, let's see what she says—— [*Reads.*

My dearest Father,

How shall I entreat your pardon for the rash step I have

taken--how confess the motive?—Pish! hasn't Isaac just told me the motive?---one would think they weren't together when they wrote.—*If I have a spirit too resentful of ill usage, I have also a heart as easily affected by kindness.*—So, so, here the whole matter comes out; her resentment for Antonio's ill usage has made her sensible of Isaac's kindness—yes, yes, it is all plain enough. Well.—*I am not married yet, though with a man, I am convinced, adores me.*—Yes, yes, I dare say Isaac is very fond of her.—*But I shall anxiously expect your answer, in which, should I be so fortunate as to receive your consent, you will make completely happy your ever affectionate daughter,*

LOUISA.

My consent! to be sure she shall have it! Egad, I was never better pleased--I have fulfilled my resolution—I knew I should. Oh, there's nothing like obstinacy! Lewis! [*Calls*

Re-enter SERVANT.

Let the man, who brought the last letter, wait; and get me a pen and ink below.—[*Exit* SERVANT.] I am impatient to set poor Louisa's heart at rest. Holloa! Lewis! Sancho! [*Calls.*

Enter SERVANTS.

See that there be a noble supper provided in the saloon to-night; serve up my best wines, and let me have music, d'ye hear?

Ser. Yes, sir.

Don Jer. And order all my doors to be thrown open; admit all guests, with masks or without masks.—[*Exeunt* SERVANTS.] I'faith, we'll have a night of it! and I'll let them see how merry an old man can be.

SONG.

Oh, the days when I was young,
　　When I laugh'd in fortune's spite;
Talk'd of love the whole day long,
　　And with nectar crown'd the night!
Then it was, old father Care,
　　Little reck'd I of thy frown;
Half thy malice youth could bear,
　　And the rest a bumper drown.

Truth, they say, lies in a well,
　　Why, I vow I ne'er could see;
Let the water-drinkers tell,
　　There it always lay for me.

For when sparkling wine went round,
    Never saw I falsehood's mask;
But still honest truth I found
    In the bottom of each flask.

True, at length my vigour's flown,
    I have years to bring decay;
Few the locks that now I own,
    And the few I have are grey.
Yet, old Jerome, thou mayst boast,
    While thy spirits do not tire;
Still beneath thy age's frost
    Glows a spark of youthful fire.   [*Exit.*

SCENE II.—*The New Piazza.*

Enter DON FERDINAND *and* LOPEZ.

Don Ferd. What, could you gather no tidings of her? nor guess where she was gone? O Clara! Clara!

Lop. In truth, sir, I could not. That she was run away from her father, was in everybody's mouth; and that Don Guzman was in pursuit of her, was also a very common report. Where she was gone, or what was become of her, no one could take upon them to say.

Don Ferd. 'Sdeath and fury, you blockhead! she can't be out of Seville.

Lop. So I said to myself, sir. 'Sdeath and fury, you blockhead, says I, she can't be out of Seville. Then some said, she had hanged herself for love; and others have it, Don Antonio had carried her off.

Don Ferd. 'Tis false, scoundrel! no one said that.

Lop. Then I misunderstood them, sir.

Don Ferd. Go, fool, get home! and never let me see you again till you bring me news of her.—[*Exit* LOPEZ.] Oh, how my fondness for this ungrateful girl has hurt my disposition.

Enter ISAAC.

Isaac. So, I have her safe, and have only to find a priest to marry us. Antonio now may marry Clara, or not, if he pleases.

Don Ferd. What! what was that you said of Clara?

Isaac. Oh, Ferdinand! my brother-in-law that shall be, who thought of meeting you?

Don Ferd. But what of Clara?

Isaac. I'faith, you shall hear. This morning, as I was

coming down, I met a pretty damsel, who told me her name was Clara d'Almanza, and begged my protection.

Don Ferd. How!

Isaac. She said she had eloped from her father, Don Guzman, but that love for a young gentleman in Seville was the cause.

Don Ferd. Oh, Heavens! did she confess it?

Isaac. Oh, yes, she confessed at once. But then, says she, my lover is not informed of my flight, nor suspects my intention.

Don Ferd. [*Aside.*] Dear creature! no more I did indeed! Oh, I am the happiest fellow!—[*Aloud.*] Well, Isaac?

Isaac. Why then she entreated me to find him out for her, and bring him to her.

Don Ferd. Good Heavens, how lucky! Well, come along, let's lose no time. [*Pulling him.*

Isaac. Zooks! where are we to go?

Don Ferd. Why, did any thing more pass?

Isaac. Any thing more! yes; the end on't was, that I was moved with her speeches, and complied with her desires.

Don Ferd. Well, and where is she?

Isaac. Where is she! why, don't I tell you? I complied with her request, and left her safe in the arms of her lover.

Don Ferd. 'Sdeath, you trifle with me!—I have never seen her.

Isaac. You! O Lud, no! how the devil should you? 'Twas Antonio she wanted; and with Antonio I left her.

Don Ferd. [*Aside.*] Hell and madness!—[*Aloud.*] What, Antonio d'Ercilla?

Isaac. Ay, ay, the very man; and the best part of it was, he was shy of taking her at first. He talked a good deal about honour, and conscience, and deceiving some dear friend; but, Lord, we soon overruled that!

Don Ferd. You did!

Isaac. Oh, yes, presently.—Such deceit! says he.—Pish! says the lady, tricking is all fair in love. But then, my friend, says he.—Psha! damn your friend, says I. So, poor wretch, he has no chance.—No, no; he may hang himself as soon as he pleases.

Don Ferd. I must go, or I shall betray myself. [*Aside.*

Isaac. But stay, Ferdinand, you ha'n't heard the best of the joke.

Don Ferd. Curse on your joke!

Isaac. Good lack! what's the matter now? I thought to have diverted you.

Don Ferd. Be racked! tortured! damned!

Isaac. Why, sure you are not the poor devil of a lover, are you?—I'faith, as sure as can be, he is! This is a better joke than t'other. Ha! ha! ha!

Don Ferd. What! do you laugh? you vile, mischievous varlet!—[*Collars him.*] But that you're beneath my anger, I'd tear your heart out!   [*Throws him from him.*

Isaac. O mercy! here's usage for a brother-in-law!

Don Ferd. But, hark ye, rascal! tell me directly where these false friends are gone, or, by my soul——   [*Draws.*

Isaac. For Heaven's sake, now, my dear brother-in-law, don't be in a rage! I'll recollect as well as I can.

Don Ferd. Be quick then!

Isaac. I will, I will!—but people's memories differ; some have a treacherous memory: now mine is a cowardly memory —it takes to its heels at sight of a drawn sword, it does, i'faith; and I could as soon fight as recollect.

Don Ferd. Zounds! tell me the truth, and I won't hurt you.

Isaac. No, no, I know you won't, my dear brother-in-law; but that ill-looking thing there——

Don Ferd. What, then, you won't tell me?

Isaac. Yes, yes, I will; I'll tell you all, upon my soul!— but why need you listen, sword in hand?

Don Ferd. Why, there.—[*Puts up.*] Now.

Isaac. Why, then, I believe they are gone to—that is, my friend Carlos told me, he had left Donna Clara—dear Ferdinand, keep your hands off—at the convent of St. Catharine.

Don Ferd. St. Catharine!

Isaac. Yes; and that Antonio was to come to her there

Don Ferd. Is this the truth?

Isaac. It is indeed; and all I know, as I hope for life!

Don Ferd. Well, coward, take your life! 'tis that false, dishonourable Antonio, who shall feel my vengeance.

Isaac. Ay, ay, kill him; cut his throat, and welcome.

Don Ferd. But, for Clara! infamy on her! she is not worth my resentment.

Isaac. No more she is, my dear brother-in-law. I'faith, I

would not be angry about her; she is not worth it, indeed.

Don Ferd. 'Tis false! she is worth the enmity of princes!

Isaac. True, true, so she is; and I pity you exceedingly for having lost her.

Don Ferd. 'Sdeath, you rascal! how durst you talk of pitying me?

Isaac. Oh, dear brother-in-law, I beg pardon! I don't pity you in the least, upon my soul!

Don Ferd. Get hence, fool, and provoke me no further; nothing but your insignificance saves you!

Isaac. [*Aside.*] I'faith, then, my insignificance is the best friend I have.—[*Aloud.*] I'm going, dear Ferdinand.—[*Aside.*] What a curst hot-headed bully it is!

[*Exeunt severally.*

SCENE III.—*The Garden of the Convent*

Enter DONNA LOUISA *and* DONNA CLARA.

Don. Louisa. And you really wish my brother may not find you out?

Don. Clara. Why else have I concealed myself under this disguise?

Don. Louisa. Why, perhaps, because the dress becomes you; for you certainly don't intend to be a nun for life.

Don. Clara. If, indeed, Ferdinand had not offended me so last night——

Don. Louisa. Come, come, it was his fear of losing you made him so rash.

Don. Clara. Well, you may think me cruel, but I swear, if he were here this instant, I believe I should forgive him.

SONG.

By him we love offended,
    How soon our anger flies!
One day apart, 'tis ended;
    Behold him, and it dies.

Last night, your roving brother,
    Enraged, I bade depart;
And sure his rude presumption
    Deserved to lose my heart.

Yet, were he now before me,
    In spite of injured pride,
I fear my eyes would pardon
    Before my tongue could chide.

Don. Louisa. I protest, Clara, I shall begin to think you are seriously resolved to enter on your probation.

Don. Clara. And, seriously, I very much doubt whether the character of a nun would not become me best.

Don. Louisa. Why, to be sure, the character of a nun is a very becoming one at a masquerade; but no pretty woman, in her senses, ever thought of taking the veil for above a night.

Don. Clara. Yonder I see your Antonio is returned—I shall only interrupt you; ah, Louisa, with what happy eagerness you turn to look for him!   [*Exit.*

Enter DON ANTONIO.

Don Ant. Well, my Louisa, any news since I left you?

Don. Louisa. None. The messenger is not yet returned from my father.

Don Ant. Well, I confess, I do not perceive what we are to expect from him.

Don. Louisa. I shall be easier, however, in having made the trial: I do not doubt your sincerity, Antonio; but there is a chilling air around poverty, that often kills affection, that was not nursed in it. If we would make love our household god, we had best secure him a comfortable roof.

SONG.—*Don Antonio.*

How oft, Louisa, hast thou told,
  (Nor wilt thou the fond boast disown,)
Thou wouldst not lose Antonio's love
  To reign the partner of a throne.
And by those lips, that spoke so kind,
  And by that hand, I've press'd to mine,
To be the lord of wealth and power,
  By Heavens, I would not part with thine!

Then how, my soul, can we be poor,
  Who own what kingdoms could not buy?
Of this true heart thou shalt be queen,
  In serving thee, a monarch I.
Thus uncontroll'd, in mutual bliss,
  I rich in love's exhaustless mine,
Do thou snatch treasures from my lips,
  And I'll take kingdoms back from thine!

Enter MAID, *with a letter.*

Don. Louisa. My father's answer, I suppose.

Don Ant. My dearest Louisa, you may be assured that it contains nothing but threats and reproaches.

Don. Louisa. Let us see, however.—[*Reads.*] *Dearest daughter, make your lover happy; you have my full consent to marry as your whim has chosen, but be sure come home and sup with your affectionate father.*

Don Ant. You jest, Louisa!

Don. Louisa. [*Gives him the letter.*]   Read! read!

Don Ant. 'Tis so, by Heavens!   Sure there must be some mistake; but that's none of our business.—Now, Louisa, you have no excuse for delay.

Don. Louisa. Shall we not then return and thank my father?

Don Ant. But first let the priest put it out of his power to recall his word.—I 'll fly to procure one.

Don. Louisa. Nay, if you part with me again, perhaps you may lose me.

Don Ant. Come then—there is a friar of a neighbouring convent is my friend; you have already been diverted by the manners of a nunnery; let us see whether there is less hypocrisy among the holy fathers.

Don. Louisa. I'm afraid not, Antonio—for in religion, as in friendship, they who profess most are ever the least sincere.

[*Exeunt.*

Re-enter DONNA CLARA.

Don. Clara. So, yonder they go, as happy as a mutual and confessed affection can make them, while I am left in solitude. Heigho! love may perhaps excuse the rashness of an elopement from one's friend, but I am sure nothing but the presence of the man we love can support it.   Ha! what do I see! Ferdinand, as I live, how could he gain admission?   By potent gold, I suppose, as Antonio did.   How eager and disturbed he seems!   He shall not know me as yet.

[*Lets down her veil*

Enter DON FERDINAND.

Don Ferd. Yes, those were certainly they—my information was right.   [*Going.*

Don. Clara. [*Stops him.*] Pray, signor, what is your business here?

Don Ferd. No matter—no matter!   Oh, they stop.—[*Looks out.*]   Yes, that is the perfidious Clara indeed!

Don. Clara. So, a jealous error—I'm glad to see him so moved.   [*Aside.*

Don Ferd Her disguise can't conceal her—no, no, I know her too well.

Don. Clara. [*Aside.*] Wonderful discernment!—[*Aloud.*] But, signor——

Don Ferd. Be quiet, good nun; don't tease me!—By Heavens, she leans upon his arm, hangs fondly on it! O woman, woman!

Don. Clara. But, signor, who is it you want?

Don Ferd. Not you, not you, so pr'ythee don't tease me. Yet pray stay—gentle nun, was it not Donna Clara d'Almanza just parted from you?

Don. Clara. Clara d'Almanza, signor, is not yet out of the garden.

Don Ferd. Ay, ay, I knew I was right! And pray is not that gentleman, now at the porch with her, Antonio d'Ercilla?

Don. Clara. It is indeed, signor.

Don Ferd. So, so; now but one question more—can you inform me for what purpose they have gone away?

Don. Clara. They are gone to be married, I believe.

Don Ferd. Very well—enough. Now if I don't mar their wedding!   [*Exit.*

Don. Clara. [*Unveils.*] I thought jealousy had made lovers quick-sighted, but it has made mine blind. Louisa's story accounts to me for this error, and I am glad to find I have power enough over him to make him so unhappy. But why should not I be present at his surprise when undeceived? When he's through the porch, I'll follow him; and, perhaps, Louisa shall not singly be a bride.

SONG.

Adieu, thou dreary pile, where never dies
The sullen echo of repentant sighs!
Ye sister mourners of each lonely cell,
Inured to hymns and sorrow, fare ye well!
For happier scenes I fly this darksome grove,
To saints a prison, but a tomb to love!   [*Exit*

SCENE IV.—*A Court before the Priory.*

Enter ISAAC, *crossing the stage,* DON ANTONIO *following.*

Don Ant. What, my friend Isaac!

Isaac. What, Antonio! wish me joy! I have Louisa safe

Don Ant. Have you? I wish you joy with all my soul.

Isaac. Yes, I am come here to procure a priest to marry us.

Don Ant. So, then, we are both on the same errand; I am come to look for Father Paul.

Isaac. Ha! I am glad on 't—but, i 'faith, he must tack me first; my love is waiting.

Don Ant. So is mine—I left her in the porch.

Isaac. Ay, but I am in haste to go back to Don Jerome

Don Ant. And so am I too.

Isaac. Well, perhaps he'll save time, and marry us both together—or I 'll be your father, and you shall be mine. Come along—but you 'ro obliged to me for all this.

Don Ant. Yes, yes.   [*Exeunt.*

SCENE V.—*A Room in the Priory.*

FATHER PAUL, FATHER FRANCIS, FATHER AUGUSTINE, *and other* FRIARS, *discovered at a table drinking.*

GLEE AND CHORUS.

This bottle's the sun of our table,
His beams are rosy wine:
We, planets, that are not able
Without his help to shine.
Let mirth and glee abound !
You 'll soon grow bright
With borrow'd light,
And shine as he goes round.

Paul. Brother Francis, toss the bottle about, and give me your toast.

Fran. Have we drunk the abbess of St. Ursuline?

Paul. Yes, yes; she was the last.

Fran. Then I 'll give you the blue-eyed nun of St. Catharine's.

Paul. With all my heart.—[*Drinks.*] Pray, brother Augustine, were there any benefactions left in my absence ?

Aug. Don Juan Corduba has left a hundred ducats, to remember him in our masses.

Paul. Has he? let them be paid to our wine-merchant, and we 'll remember him in our cups, which will do just as well.   Any thing more ?

Aug. Yes; Baptista, the rich miser, who died last week, has bequeathed us a thousand pistoles, and the silver lamp he used in his own chamber, to burn before the image of St. Anthony.

Paul. 'Twas well meant, but we 'll employ his money better

—Baptista's bounty shall light the living, not the dead. St.
Anthony is not afraid to be left in the dark, though he was.—
[*Knocking.*]   See who's there.

       [FATHER FRANCIS *goes to the door and opens it.*

            Enter PORTER.

  Port. Here's one without, in pressing haste to speak with
father Paul.

  Fran. Brother Paul!

      [FATHER PAUL *comes from behind a curtain, with a glass
       of wine, and in his hand a piece of cake.*

  Paul. Here! how durst you, fellow, thus abruptly break in
upon our devotions?

  Port. I thought they were finished.

  Paul. No, they were not—were they, brother Francis?

  Fran. Not by a bottle each.

  Paul. But neither you nor your fellows mark how the hours
go; no, you mind nothing but the gratifying of your appetites; ye eat and swill, and sleep, and gourmandise, and thrive,
while we are wasting in mortification.

  Port. We ask no more than nature craves.

  Paul. 'Tis false, ye have more appetites than hairs! and
your flushed, sleek, and pampered appearance is the disgrace
of our order—out on 't! If you are hungry, can't you be content with the wholesome roots of the earth? and, if you are
dry, isn't there the crystal spring?—[*Drinks.*]   Put this
away,—[*Gives the glass*] and show me where I'm wanted.—
[PORTER *drains the glass.*—PAUL, *going, turns.*] So, you would
have drunk it, if there had been any left! Ah, glutton!
glutton!   [*Exeunt.*

  SCENE VI.—*The Court before the Priory.*

    Enter ISAAC *and* DON ANTONIO.

  Isaac. A plaguy while coming, this same father Paul!—
He's detained at vespers, I suppose, poor fellow.

  Don Ant. No, here he comes.

      Enter FATHER PAUL.

Good father Paul, I crave your blessing.

  Isaac. Yes, good father Paul, we are come to beg a favour.

  Paul. What is it, pray?

  Isaac. To marry us, good father Paul; and in truth thou
dost look the very priest of Hymen.

Paul. In short, I may be called so; for I deal in repentance and mortification.

Isaac. No, no, thou seemest an officer of Hymen, because thy presence speaks content and good humour.

Paul. Alas! my appearance is deceitful. Bloated I am, indeed! for fasting is a windy recreation, and it hath swollen me like a bladder.

Don Ant. But thou hast a good fresh colour in thy face, father; rosy, i' faith!

Paul. Yes, I have blushed for mankind, till the hue of my shame is as fixed as their vices.

Isaac. Good man!,

Paul. And I have laboured too, but to what purpose? they continue to sin under my very nose.

Isaac. Efecks, father, I should have guessed as much, for your nose seems to be put to the blush more than any other part of your face.

Paul. Go, you're a wag!

Don Ant. But, to the purpose, father—will you officiate for us?

Paul. To join young people thus clandestinely is not safe: and, indeed, I have in my heart many weighty reasons against it.

Don Ant. And I have in my hand many weighty reasons for it. Isaac, haven't you an argument or two in our favour about you?

Isaac. Yes, yes; here is a most unanswerable purse.

Paul. For shame! you make me angry: you forget who I am, and when importunate people have forced their trash—ay, into this pocket, here—or into this—why, then the sin was theirs.—[*They put money into his pockets.*] Fie, now how you distress me! I would return it, but that I must touch it that way, and so wrong my oath.

Don Ant. Now then, come with us.

Isaac. Ay, now give us our title to joy and rapture.

Paul. Well, when your hour of repentance comes, don't blame me.

Don Ant. [*Aside.*] No bad caution to my friend Isaac.—[*Aloud.*] Well, well, father, do you do your part, and I'll abide the consequence.

Isaac. Ay, and so will I.

Enter DONNA LOUISA, *running.*

Don. Louisa. O Antonio, Ferdinand is at the porch, and inquiring for us.

Isaac. Who? Don Ferdinand! he's not inquiring for me, I hope.

Don Ant. Fear not, my love; I'll soon pacify him.

Isaac. Egad, you won't. Antonio, take my advice, and run away; this Ferdinand is the most unmerciful dog, and has the cursedest long sword!—and, upon my soul, he comes on purpose to cut your throat.

Don Ant. Never fear, never fear.

Isaac. Well, you may stay if you will; but I'll get some one to marry me; for, by St. Iago, he shall never meet me again, while I am master of a pair of heels.

[*Runs out.*—DONNA LOUISA *lets down her veil.*

Enter DON FERDINAND.

Don Ferd. So, sir, I have met with you at last.

Don Ant. Well, sir.

Don. Ferd. Base, treacherous man! whence can a false, deceitful soul, like yours, borrow confidence to look so steadily on the man you've injured?

Don. Ant. Ferdinand, you are too warm: 'tis true you find me on the point of wedding one I loved beyond my life; but no argument of mine prevailed on her to elope—I scorn deceit, as much as you. By heaven I knew not that she had left her father's till I saw her!

Don Ferd. What a mean excuse! You have wronged your friend, then, for one, whose wanton forwardness anticipated your treachery—of this, indeed, your Jew pander informed me; but let your conduct be consistent, and, since you have dared to do a wrong, follow me, and show you have a spirit to avow it.

Don. Louisa. Antonio, I perceive his mistake—leave him to me.

Paul. Friend, you are rude, to interrupt the union of two willing hearts.

Don Ferd. No, meddling priest! the hand he seeks is mine.

Paul. If so, I'll proceed no further. Lady, did you ever promise this youth your hand?

[*To* DONNA LOUISA, *who shakes her head*

Don Ferd. Clara, I thank you for your silence—I would not have heard your tongue avow such falsity; be 't your punishment to remember I have not reproached you.

Enter DONNA CLARA, *veiled.*

Don. Clara. What mockery is this?

Don Ferd. Antonio, you are protected now, but we shall meet

[*Going,* DONNA CLARA *holds one arm, and* DONNA LOUISA *the other.*

DUET.

> *Don. Louisa.* Turn thee round, I pray thee,
> Calm awhile thy rage.
> *Don. Clara.* I must help to stay thee,
> And thy wrath assunge.
> *Don. Louisa.* Couldst thou not discover
> One so dear to thee?
> *Don. Clara.* Canst thou be a lover,
> And thus fly from me? [*Both unveil.*

Don Ferd. How's this? My sister! Clara too—I'm confounded.

Don. Louisa. 'Tis even so, good brother.

Paul. How! what impiety? did the man want to marry his own sister?

Don. Louisa. And ar'n't you ashamed of yourself not to know your own sister?

Don. Clara. To drive away your own mistress——

Don. Louisa. Don't you see how jealousy blinds people?

Don. Clara. Ay, and will you ever be jealous again?

Don Ferd. Never—never!—You, sister, I know will forgive me—but how, Clara, shall I presume——

Don. Clara. No, no, just now you told me not to tease you —"Who do you want, good signor?" "Not you, not you!"— Oh, you blind wretch! but swear never to be jealous again, and I 'll forgive you.

Don Ferd. By all——

Don. Clara. There, that will do—you 'll keep the oath just as well. [*Gives her hand.*

Don. Louisa. But, brother, here is one to whom some apology is due.

Don Ferd. Antonio, I am ashamed to think——

Don Ant. Not a word of excuse, Ferdinand—I have not

A A.

been in love myself without learning that a lover's anger should never be resented. But come—let us retire with this good father, and we'll explain to you the cause of this error.

GLEE AND CHORUS.

Oft does Hymen smile to hear
   Wordy vows of feign'd regard;
Well he knows when they're sincere,
   Never slow to give reward:
For his glory is to prove
Kind to those who wed for love.   [*Exeunt.*

SCENE VII.—*A Grand Saloon in* DON JEROME'S *House.*

Enter DON JEROME, LOPEZ, *and* SERVANTS.

Don Jer. Be sure, now, let every thing be in the best order —let all my servants have on their merriest faces: but tell them to get as little drunk as possible, till after supper.— [*Exeunt* SERVANTS.] So, Lopez, where's your master? sha'n't we have him at supper?

Lop. Indeed, I believe, not, sir—he's mad, I doubt! I'm sure he has frighted me from him.

Don Jer. Ay, ay, he's after some wench, I suppose: a young rake! Well, well, we'll be merry without him. [*Exit* LOPEZ.

Enter a SERVANT.

Ser. Sir, here is Signor Isaac.   [*Exit.*

Enter ISAAC.

Don Jer. So, my dear son-in-law—there, take my blessing and forgiveness. But where's my daughter? where's Louisa?

Isaac. She's without, impatient for a blessing, but almost afraid to enter.

Don Jer. Oh, fly and bring her in.—[*Exit* ISAAC.] Poor girl, I long to see her pretty face.

Isaac. [*Without.*] Come, my charmer! my trembling angel!

Re-enter ISAAC *with* DUENNA; DON JEROME *runs to meet them; she kneels.*

Don Jer. Come to my arms, my—[*Starts back.*] Why, who the devil have we here?

Isaac. Nay, Don Jerome, you promised her forgiveness; see how the dear creature droops!

Don Jer. Droops indeed! Why, Gad take me, this is old Margaret! But where 's my daughter? where 's Louisa?

Isaac. Why, here, before your eyes—nay, don't be abashed, my sweet wife!

Don Jer. Wife with a vengeance! Why, zounds, you have not married the Duenna!

Duen. [*Kneeling.*] Oh, dear papa! you 'll not disown me, sure !

Don Jer. Papa! papa! Why, zounds, your impudence is as great as your ugliness!

Isaac. Rise, my charmer, go throw your snowy arms about his neck, and convince him you are——

Duen. Oh, sir, forgive me!   [*Embraces him.*

Don Jer. Help! murder!

Enter SERVANTS.

Ser. What 's the matter, sir?

Don Jer. Why, here, this damned Jew has brought an old harridan to strangle me.

Isaac. Lord, it is his own daughter, and he is so hard-hearted he won't forgive her!

Enter DON ANTONIO *and* DONNA LOUISA; *they kneel.*

Don Jer. Zounds and fury! what 's here now? who sent for you, sir, and who the devil are you?

Don Ant. This lady's husband, sir.

Isaac. Ay, that he is, I 'll be sworn; for I left them with a priest, and was to have given her away.

Don Jer. You were?

Isaac. Ay; that 's my honest friend, Antonio; and that 's the little girl I told you I had hampered him with.

Don Jer. Why, you are either drunk or mad—this is my daughter.

Isaac. No, no; 'tis you are both drunk and mad, I think—here 's your daughter.

Don Jer. Hark ye, old iniquity! will you explain all this, or not?

Duen. Come then, Don Jerome, I will—though our habits might inform you all. Look on your daughter, there, and on me.

Isaac. What 's this I hear?

Duen. The truth is, that in your passion this morning you made a small mistake; for you turned your daughter out of doors, and locked up your humble servant.

A A 2

Isaac. O Lud! O Lud! here's a pretty fellow, to turn his daughter out of doors, instead of an old Duenna!

Don Jer. And, O Lud! O Lud! here's a pretty fellow, to marry an old Duenna instead of my daughter! But how came the rest about?

Duen. I have only to add, that I remained in your daughter's place, and had the good fortune to engage the affections of my sweet husband here.

Isaac. Her husband! why, you old witch, do you think I'll be your husband now? This is a trick, a cheat! and you ought all to be ashamed of yourselves.

Don Ant. Hark ye, Isaac, do you dare to complain of tricking? Don Jerome, I give you my word, this cunning Portuguese has brought all this upon himself, by endeavouring to over-reach you, by getting your daughter's fortune, without making any settlement in return.

Don Jer. Over-reach me!

Don. Louisa. 'Tis so, indeed, sir, and we can prove it to you.

Don Jer. Why, Gad take me, it must be so, or he could never have put up with such a face as Margaret's—so, little Solomon, I wish you joy of your wife, with all my soul.

Don. Louisa. Isaac, tricking is all fair in love—let you alone for the plot!

Don Ant. A cunning dog, ar'n't you? A sly little villain, eh?

Don. Louisa. Roguish, perhaps; but keen, devilish keen!

Don Jer. Yes, yes; his aunt always called him little Solomon.

Isaac. Why, the plagues of Egypt upon you all!—but do you think I'll submit to such an imposition?

Don Ant. Isaac, one serious word—you'd better be content as you are; for, believe me, you will find that, in the opinion of the world, there is not a fairer subject for contempt and ridicule than a knave become the dupe of his own art.

Isaac. I don't care—I'll not endure this. Don Jerome, 'tis you have done this—you would be so cursed positive about the beauty of her you locked up, and all the time I told you she was as old as my mother, and as ugly as the devil.

Duen. Why, you little insignificant reptile!——

Don Jer. That's right!—attack him, Margaret.

Duen. Dare such a thing as you pretend to talk of beauty?

—A walking rouleau!—a body that seems to owe all its con
sequence to the dropsy!—a pair of eyes like two dead beetles
in a wad of brown dough!—a beard like an artichoke, with
dry shrivelled jaws, that would disgrace the mummy of a
monkey!

Don Jer. Well done, Margaret!

Duen. But you shall know that I have a brother who wears
a sword—and, if you don't do me justice——

Isaac. Fire seize your brother, and you too! I'll fly to
Jerusalem to avoid you!

Duen. Fly where you will, I 'll follow you.

Don Jer. Throw your snowy arms about him, Margaret.—
[*Exeunt* ISAAC *and* DUENNA,] But, Louisa, are you really married to this modest gentleman?

Don. Louisa. Sir, in obedience to your commands, I gave
him my hand within this hour.

Don Jer. My commands!

Don Ant. Yes, sir; here is your consent, under your own hand.

Don Jer. How! would you rob me of my child by a trick,
a false pretence? and do you think to get her fortune by the
same means? Why, 'slife, you are as great a rogue as Isaac!

Don Ant. No, Don Jerome; though I have profited by this
paper in gaining your daughter's hand, I scorn to obtain her
fortune by deceit. There, sir.—[*Gives a letter.*] Now give
her your blessing for a dower, and all the little I possess shall
be settled on her in return. Had you wedded her to a prince,
he could do no more.

Don Jer. Why, Gad take me, but you are a very extraordinary fellow! But have you the impudence to suppose no
one can do a generous action but yourself? Here, Louisa,
tell this proud fool of yours that he 's the only man I know
that would renounce your fortune; and, by my soul, he 's the
only man in Spain that 's worthy of it. There, bless you
both: I 'm an obstinate old fellow when I 'm in the wrong;
but you shall now find me as steady in the right.

Enter DON FERDINAND *and* DONNA CLARA.

Another wonder still! Why, sirrah! Ferdinand, you have not
stole a nun, have you?

Don Ferd. She is a nun in nothing but her habit, sir—look
nearer, and you will perceive 'tis Clara d'Almanza, Don Guz-

man's daughter; and, with pardon for stealing a wedding, she is also my wife.

Don Jer. Gadsbud, and a great fortune! Ferdinand, you are a prudent young rogue, and I forgive you: and, ifecks, you are a pretty little damsel. Give your father-in-law a kiss, you smiling rogue!

Don. Clara. There, old gentleman; and now mind you behave well to us.

Don Jer. Ifecks, those lips ha'n't been chilled by kissing beads! Egad, I believe I shall grow the best-humoured fellow in Spain. Lewis! Sancho! Carlos! d'ye hear? are all my doors thrown open? Our children's weddings are the only holidays our age can boast; and then we drain, with pleasure, the little stock of spirits time has left us.—[*Music within.*] But see, here come our friends and neighbours!

Enter MASQUERADERS.

And, i' faith, we'll make a night on't, with wine, and dance, and catches—then old and young shall join us.

FINALE.

Don Jer. . . .	Come now for jest and smiling,
	Both old and young beguiling,
	Let us laugh and play, so blithe and gay,
	Till we banish care away.
Don. Louisa .	Thus crown'd with dance and song,
	The hours shall glide along,
	With a heart at ease, merry, merry glees
	Can never fail to please.
Don Ferd. .	Each bride with blushes glowing,
	Our wine as rosy flowing,
	Let us laugh and play, so blithe and gay,
	Till we banish care away.
Don Ant. .	Then healths to every friend
	The night's repast shall end,
	With a heart at ease, merry, merry glees
	Can never fail to please.
Don. Clara .	Nor, while we are so joyous,
	Shall anxious fear annoy us;
	Let us laugh and play, so blithe and gay,
	Till we banish care away.
Don Jer. . . .	For generous guests like these
	Accept the wish to please,
	So we'll laugh and play, so blithe and gay,
	Your smiles drive care away. [*Exeunt omnes.*

THE SCHOOL FOR SCANDAL.

A COMEDY.

DRAMATIS PERSONÆ.

AS ORIGINALLY ACTED AT DRURY-LANE THEATRE IN 1777.

Sir Peter Teazle	. *Mr. King.*	Crabtree . . .	. *Mr. Parsons.*
Sir Oliver Surface	*Mr. Yates.*	Rowley . .	. *Mr. Aickin.*
Sir Harry Bumper	. *Mr. Gawdry.*	Moses	. *Mr. Baddeley.*
Sir Benjamin Back-bite	} *Mr. Dodd.*	Trip	. *Mr. Lamash.*
		Lady Teazle	. *Mrs. Abington.*
Joseph Surface	. *Mr. Palmer.*	Lady Sneerwell	*Miss Sherry.*
Charles Surface	. *Mr. Smith.*	Mrs. Candour	. *Miss Pope.*
Careless	. *Mr. Farren.*	Maria . . .	. *Miss P. Hopkins.*
Snake	. *Mr. Packer.*	Gentlemen, Maid, *and* Servants.	

SCENE.—London.

A PORTRAIT;

ADDRESSED TO MRS. CREWE, WITH THE COMEDY OF THE SCHOOL FOR SCANDAL.

BY R. B. SHERIDAN, ESQ.

Tell me, ye prim adepts in Scandal's school,
Who rail by precept, and detract by rule,
Lives there no character, so tried, so known,
So deck'd with grace, and so unlike your own,
That even you assist her fame to raise,
Approve by envy, and by silence praise !
Attend !—a model shall attract your view—
Daughters of calumny, I summon you !
You shall decide if this a portrait prove,
Or fond creation of the Muse and Love.
Attend, ye virgin critics, shrewd and sage,
Ye matron censors of this childish age,
Whose peering eye and wrinkled front declare
A fix'd antipathy to young and fair ;
By cunning, cautious ; or by nature, cold,
In maiden madness, virulently bold !—
Attend, ye skill'd to coin the precious tale,
Creating proof, where innuendos fail !
Whose practised memories, cruelly exact,
Omit no circumstance, except the fact !—
Attend, all ye who boast,—or old or young,—
The living libel of a slanderous tongue !

So shall my theme as far contrasted be,
As saints by fiends, or hymns by calumny.
Come, gentle Amoret (for 'neath that name
In worthier verse is sung thy beauty's fame);
Come—for but thee who seeks the Muse? and while
Celestial blushes check thy conscious' smile,
With timid grace, and hesitating eye
The perfect model, which I boast, supply:—
Vain Muse! couldst thou the humblest sketch create
Of her, or slightest charm couldst imitate—
Could thy blest strain in kindred colours trace
The faintest wonder of her form and face—
Poets would study the immortal line,
And Reynolds own his art subdued by thine;
That art, which well might added lustre give
To Nature's best, and Heaven's superlative:
On Granby's cheek might bid new glories rise,
Or point a purer beam from Devon's eyes!
Hard is the task to shape that beauty's praise,
Whose judgment scorns the homage flattery pays!
But praising Amoret we cannot err,
No tongue o'ervalues Heaven, or flatters her!
Yet she by fate's perverseness—she alone
Would doubt our truth, nor deem such praise her own
Adorning fashion, unadorn'd by dress,
Simple from taste, and not from carelessness;
Discreet in gesture, in deportment mild,
Not stiff with prudence, nor uncouthly wild:
No state has Amoret; no studied mien;
She frowns no goddess, and she moves no queen.
The softer charm that in her manner lies
Is framed to captivate, yet not surprise;
It justly suits the expression of her face,—
'Tis less than dignity, and more than grace!
On her pure cheek the native hue is such,
That, form'd by Heaven to be admired so much,
The hand divine, with a less partial care,
Might well have fix'd a fainter crimson there,
And bade the gentle inmate of her breast—
Inshrined Modesty—supply the rest.
But who the peril of her lips shall paint?
Strip them of smiles—still, still all words are faint!
But moving Love himself appears to teach
Their action, though denied to rule her speech;
And thou who seest her speak, and dost not hear,
Mourn not her distant accents 'scape thine ear;
Viewing those lips, thou still may'st make pretence
To judge of what she says, and swear 'tis sense:
Clothed with such grace, with such expression fraught,
They move in meaning, and they pause in thought!

But dost thou farther watch, with charm'd surprise,
The mild irresolution of her eyes,
Curious to mark how frequent they repose,
In brief eclipse and momentary close—
Ah! seest thou not an ambush'd Cupid there,
Too tim'rous of his charge, with jealous care
Veils and unveils those beams of heavenly light,
Too full, too fatal else, for mortal sight?
Nor yet, such pleasing vengeance fond to meet,
In pard'ning dimples hope a safe retreat.
What though her peaceful breast should ne'er allow
Subduing frowns to arm her alter'd brow,
By Love, I swear, and by his gentle wiles,
More fatal still the mercy of her smiles!
Thus lovely, thus adorn'd, possessing all
Of bright or fair that can to woman fall,
The height of vanity might well be thought
Prerogative in her, and Nature's fault.
Yet gentle Amoret, in mind supreme
As well as charms, rejects the vainer theme;
And, half mistrustful of her beauty's store,
She barbs with wit those darts too keen before:—
Read in all knowledge that her sex should reach,
Though Greville, or the Muse, should deign to teach,
Fond to improve, nor timorous to discern
How far it is a woman's grace to learn;
In Millar's dialect she would not prove
Apollo's priestess, but Apollo's love,
Graced by those signs which truth delights to own,
The timid blush, and mild submitted tone:
Whate'er she says, though sense appear throughout,
Displays the tender hue of female doubt;
Deck'd with that charm, how lovely wit appears,
How graceful science, when that robe she wears!
Such too her talents, and her bent of mind,
As speak a sprightly heart by thought refined:
A taste for mirth, by contemplation school'd,
A turn for ridicule, by candour ruled,
A scorn of folly, which she tries to hide;
An awe of talent, which she owns with pride!

   Peace, idle Muse! no more thy strain prolong,
But yield a theme, thy warmest praises wrong;
Just to her merit, though thou canst not raise
Thy feeble verse, behold th' acknowledged praise
Has spread conviction through the envious train,
And cast a fatal gloom o'er Scandal's reign!
And lo! each pallid hag, with blister'd tongue,
Mutters assent to all thy zeal has sung—
Owns all the colours just—the outline true;
Thee my inspirer, and my model—CREWE!

PROLOGUE.

WRITTEN BY MR. GARRICK.

A School for Scandal! tell me, I beseech you,
Needs there a school this modish art to teach you?
No need of lessons now, the knowing think;
We might as well be taught to eat and drink.
Caused by a dearth of scandal, should the vapours
Distress our fair ones—let them read the papers;
Their powerful mixtures such disorders hit;
Crave what you will—there's *quantum sufficit.*
" Lord!" cries my Lady Wormwood (who loves tattle,
And puts much salt and pepper in her prattle),
Just risen at noon, all night at cards when threshing
Strong tea and scandal—"Bless me, how refreshing!
Give me the papers, Lisp—how bold and free! [*Sips.*
Last night Lord L. [Sips] was caught with Lady D.
For aching heads what charming *sal volatile!* [*Sips.*
If Mrs. B. will still continue flirting,
We hope she'll DRAW, *or we'll* UNDRAW *the curtain.*
Fine satire, poz—in public all abuse it,
But, by ourselves [*Sips*], our praise we can't refuse it.
Now, Lisp, read you—there, at that dash and star:"
" Yes, ma'am—*A certain lord had best beware,*
Who lives not twenty miles from Grosvenor Square;
For, should he Lady W. find willing,
Wormwood is bitter"——" Oh! that's me! the villain!
Throw it behind the fire, and never more
Let that vile paper come within my door."
Thus at our friends we laugh, who feel the dart;
To reach our feelings, we ourselves must smart.
Is our young bard so young, to think that he
Can stop the full spring-tide of calumny?
Knows he the world so little, and its trade?
Alas! the devil's sooner raised than laid.
So strong, so swift, the monster there's no gagging:
Cut Scandal's head off, still the tongue is wagging.
Proud of your smiles once lavishly bestow'd,
Again our young Don Quixote takes the road;
To show his gratitude he draws his pen,
And seeks this hydra, Scandal, in his den.
For your applause all perils he would through—
He'll fight—that's write—a cavalliero true,
Till every drop of blood—that's ink—is spilt for you.

ACT I.

SCENE I.—LADY SNEERWELL's *Dressing-room*.

LADY SNEERWELL *discovered at her toilet*; SNAKE *drinking chocolate.*

Lady Sneer. The paragraphs, you say, Mr. Snake, were all inserted?

Snake. They were, madam; and, as I copied them myself in a feigned hand, there can be no suspicion whence they came.

Lady Sneer. Did you circulate the report of Lady Brittle's intrigue with Captain Boastall?

Snake. That's in as fine a train as your ladyship could wish. In the common course of things, I think it must reach Mrs. Clackitt's ears within four-and-twenty hours; and then, you know, the business is as good as done.

Lady Sneer. Why, truly, Mrs. Clackitt has a very pretty talent, and a great deal of industry.

Snake. True, madam, and has been tolerably successful in her day. To my knowledge, she has been the cause of six matches being broken off, and three sons being disinherited; of four forced elopements, and as many close confinements; nine separate maintenances, and two divorces. Nay, I have more than once traced her causing a *tête-à-tête* in the "Town and Country Magazine," when the parties, perhaps, had never seen each other's face before in the course of their lives.

Lady Sneer. She certainly has talents, but her manner is gross.

Snake. 'Tis very true. She generally designs well, has a free tongue and a bold invention; but her colouring is too dark, and her outlines often extravagant. She wants that delicacy of tint, and mellowness of sneer, which distinguish your ladyship's scandal.

Lady Sneer. You are partial, Snake.

Snake. Not in the least; every body allows that Lady Sneerwell can do more with a word or look than many can with the most laboured detail, even when they happen to have a little truth on their side to support it.

Lady Sneer. Yes, my dear Snake; and I am no hypocrite to deny the satisfaction I reap from the success of my efforts. Wounded myself, in the early part of my life, by the envenomed tongue of slander, I confess I have since known no pleasure equal to the reducing others to the level of my own reputation.

Snake. Nothing can be more natural. But, Lady Sneerwell, there is one affair in which you have lately employed me, wherein, I confess, I am at a loss to guess your motives.

Lady Sneer. I conceive you mean with respect to my neighbour, Sir Peter Teazle, and his family?

Snake. I do. Here are two young men, to whom Sir Peter has acted as a kind of guardian since their father's death; the eldest possessing the most amiable character, and universally well spoken of—the youngest, the most dissipated and extravagant young fellow in the kingdom, without friends or character: the former an avowed admirer of your ladyship, and apparently your favourite; the latter attached to Maria, Sir Peter's ward, and confessedly beloved by her. Now, on the face of these circumstances, it is utterly unaccountable to me, why you, the widow of a city knight, with a good jointure, should not close with the passion of a man of such character and expectations as Mr. Surface; and more so why you should be so uncommonly earnest to destroy the mutual attachment subsisting between his brother Charles and Maria.

Lady Sneer. Then, at once to unravel this mystery, I must inform you that love has no share whatever in the intercourse between Mr. Surface and me.

Snake. No!

Lady Sneer. His real attachment is to Maria, or her fortune; but, finding in his brother a favoured rival, he has been obliged to mask his pretensions, and profit by my assistance.

Snake. Yet still I am more puzzled why you should interest yourself in his success.

Lady Sneer. Heavens! how dull you are! Cannot you surmise the weakness which I hitherto, through shame, have concealed even from you? Must I confess that Charles—that libertine, that extravagant, that bankrupt in fortune and reputation—that he it is for whom I am thus anxious and malicious, and to gain whom I would sacrifice every thing?

Snake. Now, indeed, your conduct appears consistent: but how came you and Mr. Surface so confidential?

Lady Sneer. For our mutual interest. I have found him out a long time since. I know him to be artful, selfish, and malicious—in short, a sentimental knave; while with Sir Peter, and indeed with all his acquaintance, he passes for a youthful miracle of prudence, good sense, and benevolence.

Snake. Yes; yet Sir Peter vows he has not his equal in England; and, above all, he praises him as a man of sentiment.

Lady Sneer. True; and with the assistance of his sentiment and hypocrisy he has brought Sir Peter entirely into his interest with regard to Maria; while poor Charles has no friend in the house—though, I fear, he has a powerful one in Maria's heart, against whom we must direct our schemes.

Enter SERVANT.

Ser. Mr. Surface.

Lady Sneer. Show him up. [*Exit* SERVANT.] He generally calls about this time. I don't wonder at people giving him to me for a lover.

Enter JOSEPH SURFACE.

Jos. Surf. My dear Lady Sneerwell, how do you do to-day? Mr. Snake, your most obedient.

Lady Sneer. Snake has just been rallying me on our mutual attachment: but I have informed him of our real views. You know how useful he has been to us; and, believe me, the confidence is not ill placed.

Jos. Surf. Madam, it is impossible for me to suspect a man of Mr. Snake's sensibility and discernment.

Lady Sneer. Well, well, no compliments now; but tell me when you saw your mistress, Maria—or, what is more material to me, your brother.

Jos. Surf. I have not seen either since I left you; but I can inform you that they never meet. Some of your stories have taken a good effect on Maria.

Lady Sneer. Ah, my dear Snake! the merit of this belongs to you. But do your brother's distresses increase?

Jos. Surf. Every hour. I am told he has had another execution in the house yesterday. In short, his dissipation and extravagance exceed any thing I have ever heard of.

Lady Sneer. Poor Charles!

Jos. Surf. True, madam; notwithstanding his vices, one can't help feeling for him. Poor Charles! I'm sure I wish it were in my power to be of any essential service to him; for the man who does not share in the distresses of a brother, even though merited by his own misconduct, deserves——

Lady Sneer. O Lud! you are going to be moral, and forget that you are among friends.

Jos. Surf. Egad, that's true! I'll keep that sentiment till I see Sir Peter. However, it is certainly a charity to rescue Maria from such a libertine, who, if he is to be reclaimed, can be so only by a person of your ladyship's superior accomplishments and understanding.

Snake. I believe, Lady Sneerwell, here's company coming: I'll go and copy the letter I mentioned to you. Mr. Surface, your most obedient.

Jos. Surf. Sir, your very devoted.—[*Exit* SNAKE.] Lady Sneerwell, I am very sorry you have put any further confidence in that fellow.

Lady Sneer. Why so?

Jos. Surf. I have lately detected him in frequent conference with old Rowley, who was formerly my father's steward, and has never, you know, been a friend of mine.

Lady Sneer. And do you think he would betray us?

Jos. Surf. Nothing more likely: take my word for 't, Lady Sneerwell, that fellow hasn't virtue enough to be faithful even to his own villany. Ah, Maria!

Enter MARIA.

Lady Sneer. Maria, my dear, how do you do? What's the matter?

Mar. Oh! there's that disagreeable lover of mine, Sir Benjamin Backbite, has just called at my guardian's, with his odious uncle, Crabtree; so I slipped out, and ran hither to avoid them.

Lady Sneer. Is that all?

Jos. Surf. If my brother Charles had been of the party, madam, perhaps you would not have been so much alarmed.

Lady Sneer. Nay, now you are severe; for I dare swear the truth of the matter is, Maria heard you were here. But, my dear, what has Sir Benjamin done, that you should avoid him so?

Mar. Oh, he has done nothing—but 'tis for what he has said: his conversation is a perpetual libel on all his acquaintance.

Jos. Surf. Ay, and the worst of it is, there is no advantage in not knowing him; for he 'll abuse a stranger just as soon as his best friend: and his uncle 's as bad.

Lady Sneer. Nay, but we should make allowance; Sir Benjamin is a wit and a poet.

Mar. For my part, I own, madam, wit loses its respect with me, when I see it in company with malice. What do you think, Mr. Surface?

Jos. Surf. Certainly, madam; to smile at the jest which plants a thorn in another's breast is to become a principal in the mischief.

Lady Sneer. Psha! there's no possibility of being witty without a little ill nature: the malice of a good thing is the barb that makes it stick. What's your opinion, Mr. Surface?

Jos. Surf. To be sure, madam; that conversation, where the spirit of raillery is suppressed, will ever appear tedious and insipid.

Mar. Well, I'll not debate how far scandal may be allowable; but in a man, I am sure, it is always contemptible. We have pride, envy, rivalship, and a thousand motives to depreciate each other; but the male slanderer must have the cowardice of a woman before he can traduce one.

Re-enter SERVANT.

Ser. Madam, Mrs. Candour is below, and, if your ladyship's at leisure, will leave her carriage.

Lady Sneer. Beg her to walk in.—[*Exit* SERVANT.]   Now, Maria, here is a character to your taste; for, though Mrs. Candour is a little talkative, every body allows her to be the best natured and best sort of woman.

Mar. Yes, with a very gross affectation of good nature and benevolence, she does more mischief than the direct malice of old Crabtree.

Jos. Surf. I' faith that's true, Lady Sneerwell: whenever I hear the current running against the characters of my friends, I never think them in such danger as when Candour undertakes their defence.

Lady Sneer. Hush!—here she is!

Enter MRS. CANDOUR.

Mrs. Can. My dear Lady Sneerwell, how have you been this century?—Mr. Surface, what news do you hear?—though indeed it is no matter, for I think one hears nothing else but scandal.

Jos. Surf. Just so, indeed, ma'am.

Mrs Can. Oh, Maria! child,—what, is the whole affair

off between you and Charles? His extravagance, I presume —the town talks of nothing else.

Mar. I am very sorry, ma'am, the town has so little to do.

Mrs. Can. True, true, child: but there's no stopping people's tongues. I own I was hurt to hear it, as I indeed was to learn, from the same quarter, that your guardian, Sir Peter, and Lady Teazle have not agreed lately as well as could be wished.

Mar. 'Tis strangely impertinent for people to busy themselves so.

Mrs. Can. Very true, child: but what's to be done? People will talk—there's no preventing it. Why, it was but yesterday I was told that Miss Gadabout had eloped with Sir Filigree Flirt. But, Lord! there's no minding what one hears; though, to be sure, I had this from very good authority.

Mar. Such reports are highly scandalous.

Mrs. Can. So they are, child—shameful, shameful! But the world is so censorious, no character escapes. Lord, now who would have suspected your friend, Miss Prim, of an indiscretion? Yet such is the ill nature of people, that they say her uncle stopped her last week, just as she was stepping into the York Mail with her dancing-master.

Mar. I'll answer for't there are no grounds for that report.

Mrs. Can. Ah, no foundation in the world, I dare swear: no more, probably, than for the story circulated last month, of Mrs. Festino's affair with Colonel Cassino—though, to be sure, that matter was never rightly cleared up.

Jos. Surf. The licence of invention some people take is monstrous indeed.

Mar. 'Tis so; but, in my opinion, those who report such things are equally culpable.

Mrs. Can. To be sure they are; tale-bearers are as bad as the tale-makers—'tis an old observation, and a very true one; but what's to be done, as I said before? how will you prevent people from talking? To-day, Mrs. Clackitt assured me, Mr. and Mrs. Honeymoon were at last become mere man and wife, like the rest of their acquaintance. She likewise hinted that a certain widow, in the next street, had got rid of her dropsy and recovered her shape in a most surprising manner. And at the same time Miss Tattle, who was by, affirmed, that Lord Buffalo had discovered his lady at a house of no extraordinary fame; and that Sir Harry Bouquet and Tom Saunter were to measure swords on a similar provocation. But, Lord, do you think I would report these things! No, no! tale-bearers, as I said before, are just as bad as the tale-makers.

Jos. Surf. Ah! Mrs. Candour, if every body had your forbearance and good nature!

Mrs. Can. I confess, Mr. Surface, I cannot bear to hear people attacked behind their backs; and when ugly circumstances come out against our acquaintance I own I always love to think the best. By the by, I hope 'tis not true that your brother is absolutely ruined?

Jos. Surf. I am afraid his circumstances are very bad indeed, ma'am.

Mrs. Can. Ah! I heard so—but you must tell him to keep up his spirits; every body almost is in the same way: Lord Spindle, Sir Thomas Splint, Captain Quinze, and Mr. Nickit —all up, I hear, within this week; so, if Charles is undone, he'll find half his acquaintance ruined too, and that, you know, is a consolation.

Jos. Surf. Doubtless, ma'am—a very great one.

Re-enter SERVANT.

Ser. Mr. Crabtree and Sir Benjamin Backbite. [*Exit.*

Lady Sneer. So, Maria, you see your lover pursues you; positively you sha'n't escape.

Enter CRABTREE *and* SIR BENJAMIN BACKBITE.

Crab. Lady Sneerwell, I kiss your hand. Mrs. Candour, I don't believe you are acquainted with my nephew, Sir Benjamin Backbite? Egad, ma'am, he has a pretty wit, and is a pretty poet too. Isn't he, Lady Sneerwell?

Sir Ben. Oh, fie, uncle!

Crab. Nay, egad it's true; I back him at a rebus or a charade against the best rhymer in the kingdom. Has your ladyship heard the epigram he wrote last week on Lady Frizzle's feather catching fire?—Do, Benjamin, repeat it, or the charade you made last night extempore at Mrs. Drowzie's conversazione. Come now; your first is the name of a fish, your second a great naval commander, and——

Sir Ben. Uncle, now—pr'ythee——

Crab. I' faith, ma'am, 'twould surprise you to hear how ready he is at all these sort of things.

Lady Sneer. I wonder, Sir Benjamin, you never publish any thing.

Sir Ben. To say truth, ma'am, 'tis very vulgar to print; and, as my little productions are mostly satires and lampoons on particular people, I find they circulate more by giving copies in confidence to the friends of the parties. However, I have some love elegies, which, when favoured with the lady's smiles, I mean to give the public.   [*Pointing to* MARIA.

Crab. [*To* MARIA.] 'Fore heaven, ma'am, they 'll immortalize you!—you will be handed down to posterity, like Petrarch's Laura, or Waller's Sacharissa.

Sir Ben. [*To* MARIA.]   Yes, madam, I think you will like them, when you shall see them on a beautiful quarto page, where a neat rivulet of text shall meander through a meadow of margin. 'Fore Gad they will be the most elegant things of their kind!

Crab. But, ladies, that 's true—have you heard the news?

Mrs. Can. What, sir, do you mean the report of——

Crab. No, ma'am, that 's not it.—Miss Nicely is going to be married to her own footman.

Mrs. Can. Impossible.

Crab. Ask Sir Benjamin.

Sir Ben. 'Tis very true, ma'am: every thing is fixed, and the wedding liveries bespoke.

Crab. Yes—and they do say there were pressing reasons for it.

Lady Sneer. Why, I have heard something of this before.

Mrs. Can. It can't be—and I wonder any one should believe such a story of so prudent a lady as Miss Nicely.

Sir Ben. O Lud! ma'am, that 's the very reason 'twas believed at once. She has always been so cautious and so reserved, that every body was sure there was some reason for it at bottom.

Mrs. Can. Why, to be sure, a tale of scandal is as fatal to the credit of a prudent lady of her stamp as a fever is generally to those of the strongest constitutions. But there is a sort of puny sickly reputation, that is always ailing, yet will outlive the robuster characters of a hundred prudes.

Sir Ben. True, madam, there are valetudinarians in reputation as well as constitution, who, being conscious of their weak part, avoid the least breath of air, and supply their want of stamina by care and circumspection.

Mrs. Can. Well, but this may be all a mistake. You know, Sir Benjamin, very trifling circumstances often give rise to the most injurious tales.

Crab. That they do, I'll be sworn, ma'am. Did you ever hear how Miss Piper came to lose her lover and her character last summer at Tunbridge?—Sir Benjamin, you remember it?

Sir Ben. Oh, to be sure!—the most whimsical circumstance.

Lady Sneer. How was it, pray?

Crab. Why, one evening, at Mrs. Ponto's assembly, the conversation happened to turn on the breeding Nova Scotia sheep in this country. Says a young lady in company, I have known instances of it; for Miss Letitia Piper, a first cousin of mine, had a Nova Scotia sheep that produced her twins. "What!" cries the Lady Dowager Dundizzy (who you know is as deaf as a post), "has Miss Piper had twins?" This mistake, as you may imagine, threw the whole company into a fit of laughter. However, 'twas the next morning every where reported, and in a few days believed by the whole town, that Miss Letitia Piper had actually been brought to bed of a fine boy and a girl: and in less than a week there were some people who could name the father, and the farm-house where the babies were put to nurse.

Lady Sneer. Strange, indeed!

Crab. Matter of fact, I assure you. O Lud! Mr. Surface, pray is it true that your uncle, Sir Oliver, is coming home?

Jos. Surf. Not that I know of, indeed, sir.

Crab. He has been in the East Indies a long time. You can scarcely remember him, I believe? Sad comfort, whenever he returns, to hear how your brother has gone on!

Jos. Surf. Charles has been imprudent, sir, to be sure; but I hope no busy people have already prejudiced Sir Oliver against him. He may reform.

Sir Ben. To be sure he may: for my part, I never believed him to be so utterly void of principle as people say; and, though he has lost all his friends, I am told nobody is better spoken of by the Jews.

Crab. That's true, egad, nephew. If the Old Jewry was a ward, I believe Charles would be an alderman: no man more popular there, 'fore Gad! I hear he pays as many annuities as the Irish tontine; and that, whenever he is sick,

B B 2

they have prayers for the recovery of his health in all the synagogues.

Sir Ben. Yet no man lives in greater splendour. They tell me, when he entertains his friends he will sit down to dinner with a dozen of his own securities ; have a score of tradesmen waiting in the antechamber, and an officer behind every guest's chair.

Jos. Surf. This may be entertainment to you, gentlemen, but you pay very little regard to the feelings of a brother.

Mar. [*Aside.*] Their malice is intolerable !—[*Aloud.*] Lady Sneerwell, I must wish you a good morning : I 'm not very well. [*Exit*

Mrs. Can. O dear ! she changes colour very much.

Lady Sneer. Do, Mrs. Candour, follow her : she may want your assistance.

Mrs. Can. That I will, with all my soul, ma'am.— Poor dear girl, who knows what her situation may be ! [*Exit.*

Lady Sneer. 'Twas nothing but that she could not bear to hear Charles reflected on, notwithstanding their difference.

Sir Ben. The young lady's *penchant* is obvious.

Crab. But, Benjamin, you must not give up the pursuit for that : follow her, and put her into good humour. Repeat her some of your own verses. Come, I 'll assist you.

Sir Ben. Mr. Surface, I did not mean to hurt you ; but depend on 't your brother is utterly undone.

Crab. O Lud, ay ! undone as ever man was—can't raise a guinea !

Sir Ben. And every thing sold, I 'm told, that was movable.

Crab. I have seen one that was at his house. Not a thing left but some empty bottles that were overlooked, and the family pictures, which I believe are framed in the wainscots.

Sir Ben. And I 'm very sorry also to hear some bad stories against him. [*Going.*

Crab. Oh, he has done many mean things, that 's certain.

Sir Ben. But, however, as he 's your brother—— [*Going.*

Crab. We 'll tell you all another opportunity.

[*Exeunt* CRABTREE *and* SIR BENJAMIN.

Lady Sneer. Ha ! ha ! 'tis very hard for them to leave a subject they have not quite run down.

Jos. Surf. And I believe the abuse was no more acceptable to your ladyship than Maria.

Lady Sneer. I doubt her affections are farther engaged than we imagine. But the family are to be here this evening, so you may as well dine where you are, and we shall have an opportunity of observing farther; in the meantime, I'll go and plot mischief, and you shall study sentiment.　　*[Exeunt*

SCENE II.—*A Room in* SIR PETER TEAZLE's *House.*

Enter SIR PETER TEAZLE

Sir Pet. When an old bachelor marries a young wife, what is he to expect? 'Tis now six months since Lady Teazle made me the happiest of men—and I have been the most miserable dog ever since! We tift a little going to church, and fairly quarrelled before the bells had done ringing, I was more than once nearly choked with gall during the honeymoon, and had lost all comfort in life before my friends had done wishing me joy. Yet I chose with caution—a girl bred wholly in the country, who never knew luxury beyond one silk gown, nor dissipation above the annual gala of a race ball. Yet she now plays her part in all the extravagant fopperies of fashion and the town, with as ready a grace as if she never had seen a bush or a grass-plot out of Grosvenor Square! I am sneered at by all my acquaintance, and paragraphed in the newspapers. She dissipates my fortune, and contradicts all my humours; yet the worst of it is, I doubt I love her, or I should never bear all this. However, I'll never be weak enough to own it.

Enter ROWLEY.

Row. Oh! Sir Peter, your servant: how is it with you, sir?

Sir Pet. Very bad, Master Rowley, very bad. I meet with nothing but crosses and vexations.

Row. What can have happened since yesterday?

Sir Pet. A good question to a married man!

Row. Nay, I'm sure, Sir Peter, your lady can't be the cause of your uneasiness.

Sir Pet. Why, has any body told you she was dead?

Row. Come, come, Sir Peter you love her, notwithstanding your tempers don't exactly agree.

Sir Pet. But the fault is entirely hers, Master Rowley. I am, myself, the sweetest-tempered man alive, and hate a teasing temper; and so I tell her a hundred times a day.

Row. Indeed!

Sir Pet. Ay; and what is very extraordinary, in all our disputes she is always in the wrong! But Lady Sneerwell, and the set she meets at her house, encourage the perverseness of her disposition. Then, to complete my vexation, Maria, my ward, whom I ought to have the power of a father over, is determined to turn rebel too, and absolutely refuses the man whom I have long resolved on for her husband; meaning, I suppose, to bestow herself on his profligate brother.

Row. You know, Sir Peter, I have always taken the liberty to differ with you on the subject of these two young gentlemen. I only wish you may not be deceived in your opinion of the elder. For Charles, my life on 't! he will retrieve his errors yet. Their worthy father, once my honoured master, was, at his years, nearly as wild a spark; yet, when he died, he did not leave a more benevolent heart to lament his loss.

Sir Pet. You are wrong, Master Rowley. On their father's death, you know, I acted as a kind of guardian to them both, till their uncle Sir Oliver's liberality gave them an early independence: of course, no person could have more opportunities of judging of their hearts, and I was never mistaken in my life. Joseph is indeed a model for the young men of the age. He is a man of sentiment, and acts up to the sentiments he professes; but, for the other, take my word for 't, if he had any grain of virtue by descent, he has dissipated it with the rest of his inheritance. Ah! my old friend, Sir Oliver, will be deeply mortified when he finds how part of his bounty has been misapplied.

Row. I am sorry to find you so violent against the young man, because this may be the most critical period of his fortune. I came hither with news that will surprise you.

Sir Pet. What! let me hear.

Row. Sir Oliver is arrived, and at this moment in town.

Sir Pet. How! you astonish me! I thought you did not expect him this month.

Row. I did not: but his passage has been remarkably quick.

Sir Pet. Egad, I shall rejoice to see my old friend. 'Tis sixteen years since we met. We have had many a day together:—but does he still enjoin us not to inform his nephews of his arrival?

Row. Most strictly. He means, before it is known, to make some trial of their dispositions.

Sir Pet. Ah! there needs no art to discover their merits

—however he shall have his way; but, pray, does he know I am married?

Row. Yes, and will soon wish you joy.

Sir Pet. What, as we drink health to a friend in a consumption! Ah! Oliver will laugh at me. We used to rail at matrimony together, but he has been steady to his text. Well, he must be soon at my house, though—I 'll instantly give orders for his reception. But, Master Rowley, don't drop a word that Lady Teazle and I ever disagree.

Row. By no means.

Sir Pet. For I should never be able to stand Noll's jokes; so I 'll have him think, Lord forgive me! that we are a very happy couple.

Row. I understand you :—but then you must be very careful not to differ while he is in the house with you.

Sir Pet. Egad, and so we must—and that 's impossible. Ah! Master Rowley, when an old bachelor marries a young wife, he deserves—no— the crime carries its punishment along with it   [*Exeunt*

ACT II.

SCENE I.—*A Room in* SIR PETER TEAZLE'S *House.*

Enter SIR PETER *and* LADY TEAZLE.

Sir Pet. Lady Teazle, Lady Teazle, I 'll not bear it!

Lady Teaz. Sir Peter, Sir Peter, you may bear it or not, as you please; but I ought to have my own way in every thing, and, what 's more, I will too. What! though I was educated in the country, I know very well that women of fashion in London are accountable to nobody after they are married.

Sir Pet. Very well, ma'am, very well; so a husband is to have no influence, no authority?

Lady Teaz. Authority! No, to be sure :—if you wanted authority over me, you should have adopted me, and not married me: I am sure you were old enough.

Sir Pet. Old enough!—ay, there it is. Well, well, Lady Teazle, though my life may be made unhappy by your temper, I 'll not be ruined by your extravagance!

Lady Teaz. My extravagance! I 'm sure I 'm not more extravagant than a woman of fashion ought to be.

Sir Pet. No, no, madam, you shall throw away no more sums on such unmeaning luxury. 'Slife! to spend as much to furnish your dressing-room with flowers in winter as would suffice to turn the Pantheon into a greenhouse, and give a *fête champêtre* at Christmas.

Lady Teaz. And am I to blame, Sir Peter, because flowers are dear in cold weather? You should find fault with the climate, and not with me. For my part, I'm sure I wish it was spring all the year round, and that roses grew under our feet!

Sir Pet. Oons! madam—if you had been born to this, I should'nt wonder at your talking thus; but you forget what your situation was when I married you.

Lady Teaz. No, no, I don't; 'twas a very disagreeable one, or I should never have married you.

Sir Pet. Yes, yes, madam, you were then in somewhat a humbler style—the daughter of a plain country squire. Recollect, Lady Teazle, when I saw you first sitting at your tambour, in a pretty figured linen gown, with a bunch of keys at your side, your hair combed smooth over a roll, and your apartment hung round with fruits in worsted, of your own working.

Lady Teaz. Oh, yes! I remember it very well, and a curious life I led. My daily occupation to inspect the dairy, superintend the poultry, make extracts from the family receipt-book, and comb my aunt Deborah's lap-dog.

Sir Pet. Yes, yes, ma'am, 'twas so indeed.

Lady Teaz. And then you know, my evening amusements! To draw patterns for ruffles, which I had not materials to make up; to play Pope Joan with the curate; to read a sermon to my aunt; or to be stuck down to an old spinet to strum my father to sleep after a fox-chase.

Sir Pet. I am glad you have so good a memory. Yes, madam, these were the re-creations I took you from; but now you must have your coach—*vis-à-vis*—and three powdered footmen before your chair; and, in the summer, a pair of white cats to draw you to Kensington Gardens. No recollection, I suppose, when you were content to ride double, behind the butler, on a docked coach-horse.

Lady Teaz. No—I swear I never did that: I deny the butler and the coach-horse.

Sir Pet. This, madam, was your situation; and what have I done for you? I have made you a woman of fashion, of fortune, of rank—in short, I have made you my wife.

Lady Teaz. Well, then, and there is but one thing more you can make me to add to the obligation, that is——

Sir Pet. My widow, I suppose?

Lady Teaz. Hem! hem!

Sir Pet. I thank you, madam—but don't flatter yourself; for, though your ill conduct may disturb my peace of mind, it shall never break my heart, I promise you: however, I am equally obliged to you for the hint.

Lady Teaz. Then why will you endeavour to make yourself so disagreeable to me, and thwart me in every little elegant expense?

Sir Pet. 'Slife, madam, I say, had you any of these little elegant expenses when you married me?

Lady Teaz. Lud, Sir Peter! would you have me be out of the fashion?

Sir Pet. The fashion, indeed! what had you to do with the fashion before you married me?

Lady Teaz. For my part, I should think you would like to have your wife thought a woman of taste.

Sir Pet. Ay—there again—taste! Zounds! madam, you had no taste when you married me!

Lady Teaz. That's very true, indeed, Sir Peter! and, after having married you, I should never pretend to taste again, I allow. But now, Sir Peter, since we have finished our daily jangle, I presume I may go to my engagement at Lady Sneerwell's.

Sir Pet. Ay, there's another precious circumstance—a charming set of acquaintance you have made there!

Lady Teaz. Nay, Sir Peter, they are all people of rank and fortune, and remarkably tenacious of reputation.

Sir Pet. Yes, egad, they are tenacious of reputation with a vengeance; for they don't choose anybody should have a character but themselves! Such a crew! Ah! many a wretch has rid on a hurdle who has done less mischief than these utterers of forged tales, coiners of scandal, and clippers of reputation.

Lady Teaz. What, would you restrain the freedom of speech?

Sir Pet. Ah! they have made you just as bad as any one of the society.

Lady Teaz. Why, I believe I do bear a part with a tolerable grace.

Sir Pet. Grace indeed!

Lady Teaz. But I vow I bear no malice against the people I abuse: when I say an ill-natured thing, 'tis out of pure good humour; and I take it for granted they deal exactly in the same manner with me. But, Sir Peter, you know you promised to come to Lady Sneerwell's too.

Sir Pet. Well, well, I 'll call in, just to look after my own character.

Lady Teaz. Then, indeed, you must make haste after me, or you 'll be too late. So good by to ye.   [*Exit.*

Sir Pet. So—I have gained much by my intended expostulation ! Yet with what a charming air she contradicts every thing I say, and how pleasantly she shows her contempt for my authority ! Well, though I can't make her love me, there is great satisfaction in quarrelling with her; and I think she never appears to such advantage as when she is doing every thing in her power to plague me.   [*Exit.*

SCENE II.—*A Room in* LADY SNEERWELL'S *House.*

LADY SNEERWELL, MRS. CANDOUR, CRABTREE, SIR BENJAMIN BACKBITE, *and* JOSEPH SURFACE, *discovered.*

Lady Sneer. Nay, positively, we will hear it.

Jos. Surf. Yes, yes, the epigram, by all means.

Sir Ben. O plague on 't, uncle ! 'tis mere nonsense.

Crab. No, no; 'fore Gad, very clever for an extempore !

Sir Ben. But, ladies, you should be acquainted with the circumstance. You must know, that one day last week, as Lady Betty Curricle was taking the dust in Hyde Park, in a sort of duodecimo phaeton, she desired me to write some verses on her ponies ; upon which, I took out my pocket-book, and in one moment produced the following :—

> Sure never were seen two such beautiful ponies ;
> Other horses are clowns, but these macaronies :
> To give them this title I 'm sure can't be wrong,
> Their legs are so slim, and their tails are so long.

Crab. There, ladies, done in the smack of a whip, and on horseback too.

Jos. Surf. A very Phœbus, mounted—indeed, Sir Benjamin !

Sir Ben. Oh dear, sir ! trifles—trifles.

Enter LADY TEAZLE *and* MARIA.

Mrs. Can. I must have a copy.

Lady Sneer. Lady Teazle, I hope we shall see Sir Peter?

Lady Teaz. I believe he 'll wait on your ladyship presently.

Lady Sneer. Maria, my love, you look grave. Come, you shall sit down to piquet with Mr. Surface.

Mar. I take very little pleasure in cards—however, I 'll do as your ladyship pleases

Lady Teaz. I am surprised Mr. Surface should sit down with her; I thought he would have embraced this opportunity of speaking to me before Sir Peter came.   [*Aside.*

Mrs. Can. Now, I'll die; but you are so scandalous, I'll forswear your society.

Lady Teaz. What's the matter, Mrs. Candour?

Mrs. Can. They'll not allow our friend Miss Vermilion to be handsome.

Lady Sneer. Oh, surely she is a pretty woman

Crab. I am very glad you think so, ma'am.

Mrs. Can. She has a charming fresh colour.

Lady Teaz. Yes, when it is fresh put on.

Mrs. Can. Oh, fie! I'll swear her colour is natural: I have seen it come and go!

Lady Teaz. I dare swear you have, ma'am: it goes off at night, and comes again in the morning.

Sir Ben. True, ma'am, it not only comes and goes; but, what's more, egad, her maid can fetch and carry it!

Mrs. Can. Ha! ha! ha! how I hate to hear you talk so! But surely, now, her sister is, or was, very handsome.

Crab. Who? Mrs. Evergreen? O Lord! she's six-and-fifty if she's an hour!

Mrs. Can. Now positively you wrong her; fifty-two or fifty-three is the utmost—and I don't think she looks more.

Sir Ben. Ah! there's no judging by her looks, unless one could see her face.

Lady Sneer. Well, well, if Mrs. Evergreen does take some pains to repair the ravages of time, you must allow she effects it with great ingenuity; and surely that's better than the careless manner in which the widow Ochre caulks her wrinkles.

Sir Ben. Nay, now, Lady Sneerwell, you are severe upon the widow. Come, come, 'tis not that she paints so ill—but, when she has finished her face, she joins it on so badly to her neck, that she looks like a mended statue, in which the connoisseur may see at once that the head is modern, though the trunk's antique.

Crab. Ha! ha! ha! Well said, nephew!

Mrs. Can. Ha! ha! ha! Well, you make me laugh; but I vow I hate you for it. What do you think of Miss Simper?

Sir Ben. Why, she has very pretty teeth.

Lady Teaz. Yes; and on that account, when she is neither

speaking nor laughing (which very seldom happens), she never
absolutely shuts her mouth, but leaves it always on a-jar, as it
were—thus.   [*Shows her teeth.*

Mrs. Can. How can you be so ill-natured?

Lady Teaz. Nay, I allow even that's better than the pains
Mrs. Prim takes to conceal her losses in front. She draws her
mouth till it positively resembles the aperture of a poor's-box,
and all her words appear to slide out edgewise, as it were—
thus: *How do you do, madam? Yes, madam.*   [*Mimics.*

Lady Sneer. Very well, Lady Teazle; I see you can be a
little severe.

Lady Teaz. In defence of a friend it is but justice. But
here comes Sir Peter to spoil our pleasantry.

Enter SIR PETER TEAZLE.

Sir Pet. Ladies, your most obedient.—[*Aside.*] Mercy on
me, here is the whole set! a character dead at every word, I
suppose.

Mrs. Can. I am rejoiced you are come, Sir Peter. They
have been so censorious—and Lady Teazle as bad as any
one.

Sir Pet. That must be very distressing to you, indeed,
Mrs. Candour.

Mrs. Can. Oh, they will allow good qualities to nobody;
not even good nature to our friend Mrs. Pursy.

Lady Teaz. What, the fat dowager who was at Mrs. Qua-
drille's last night?

Mrs. Can. Nay, her bulk is her misfortune; and, when she
takes so much pains to get rid of it, you ought not to reflect
on her.

Lady Sneer. That's very true, indeed.

Lady Teaz. Yes, I know she almost lives on acids and small
whey; laces herself by pulleys; and often, in the hottest noon
in summer, you may see her on a little squat pony, with her
hair plaited up behind like a drummer's and puffing round the
Ring on a full trot.

Mrs. Can. I thank you, Lady Teazle, for defending her.

Sir Pet. Yes, a good defence, truly.

Mrs. Can. Truly, Lady Teazle is as censorious as Miss
Sallow.

Crab. Yes, and she is a curious being to pretend to be censorious—an awkward gawky, without any one good point under heaven.

Mrs. Can. Positively you shall not be so very severe. Miss Sallow is a near relation of mine by marriage, and, as for her person, great allowance is to be made; for, let me tell you, a woman labours under many disadvantages who tries to pass for a girl of six-and-thirty.

Lady Sneer. Though, surely, she is handsome still—and for the weakness in her eyes, considering how much she reads by candlelight, it is not to be wondered at.

Mrs. Can True, and then as to her manner; upon my word I think it is particularly graceful, considering she never had the least education: for you know her mother was a Welsh milliner, and her father a sugar-baker at Bristol.

Sir Ben. Ah! you are both of you too good-natured!

Sir Pet. Yes, damned good-natured! This their own relation! mercy on me!   [*Aside.*

Mrs. Can. For my part, I own I cannot bear to hear a friend ill spoken of.

Sir Pet. No, to be sure!

Sir Ben. Oh! you are of a moral turn. Mrs. Candour and I can sit for an hour and hear Lady Stucco talk sentiment.

Lady Teaz. Nay, I vow Lady Stucco is very well with the dessert after dinner; for she 's just like the French fruit one cracks for mottoes—made up of paint and proverb.

Mrs. Can. Well, I will never join in ridiculing a friend; and so I constantly tell my cousin Ogle, and you all know what pretensions she has to be critical on beauty.

Crab. Oh, to be sure! she has herself the oddest countenance that ever was seen; 'tis a collection of features from all the different countries of the globe.

Sir Ben. So she has, indeed—an Irish front——

Crab. Caledonian locks——

Sir Ben. Dutch nose——

Crab. Austrian lips——

Sir Ben. Complexion of a Spaniard——

Crab. And teeth *à la Chinoise*——

Sir Ben. In short, her face resembles a *table d'hôte* at Spa —where no two guests are of a nation——

Crab. Or a congress at the close of a general war—wherein all the members, even to her eyes, appear to have a different interest, and her nose and chin are the only parties likely to join issue.

Mrs. Can. Ha! ha! ha!

Sir Pet. Mercy on my life!—a person they dine with twice a week!   [*Aside.*

Mrs. Can. Nay, but I vow you shall not carry the laugh off so—for give me leave to say, that Mrs. Ogle——

Sir Pet. Madam, madam, I beg your pardon—there's no stopping these good gentlemen's tongues. But when I tell you, Mrs. Candour, that the lady they are abusing is a particular friend of mine, I hope you'll not take her part.

Lady Sneer. Ha! ha! ha! well said, Sir Peter! but you are a cruel creature—too phlegmatic yourself for a jest, and too peevish to allow wit in others.

Sir Pet. Ah, madam, true wit is more nearly allied to good nature than your ladyship is aware of.

Lady Teaz. True, Sir Peter: I believe they are so near akin that they can never be united.

Sir Ben. Or rather, suppose them man and wife, because one seldom sees them together.

Lady Teaz. But Sir Peter is such an enemy to scandal, I believe he would have it put down by parliament.

Sir Pet. 'Fore heaven, madam, if they were to consider the sporting with reputation of as much importance as poaching on manors, and pass an act for the preservation of fame, as well as game, I believe many would thank them for the bill.

Lady Sneer. O Lud! Sir Peter; would you deprive us of our privileges?

Sir Pet. Ay, madam; and then no person should be permitted to kill characters and run down reputations, but qualified old maids and disappointed widows.

Lady Sneer. Go, you monster!

Mrs. Can. But, surely, you would not be quite so severe on those who only report what they hear?

Sir Pet. Yes, madam, I would have law merchant for them too; and in all cases of slander currency, whenever the drawer of the lie was not to be found, the injured parties should have a right to come on any of the indorsers.

Crab. Well, for my part, I believe there never was a scandalous tale without some foundation.

Lady Sneer. Come, ladies, shall we sit down to cards in the next room?

Enter SERVANT, *who whispers* SIR PETER.

Sir Pet. I'll be with them directly.—[*Exit* SERVANT.] I'll get away unperceived. [*Aside.*

Lady Sneer. Sir Peter, you are not going to leave us?

Sir Pet. Your ladyship must excuse me; I'm called away by particular business. But I leave my character behind me. [*Exit.*

Sir Ben. Well—certainly, Lady Teazle, that lord of yours is a strange being: I could tell you some storie of him would make you laugh heartily if he were not your husband.

Lady Teaz. Oh, pray don't mind that; come, do let's hear them. [*Exeunt all but* JOSEPH SURFACE *and* MARIA.

Jos. Surf. Maria, I see you have no satisfaction in this society.

Mar. How is it possible I should? If to raise malicious smiles at the infirmities or misfortunes of those who have never injured us be the province of wit or humour, Heaven grant me a double portion of dulness!

Jos. Surf. Yet they appear more ill-natured than they are; they have no malice at heart.

Mar. Then is their conduct still more contemptible; for, in my opinion, nothing could excuse the intemperance of their tongues but a natural and uncontrollable bitterness of mind.

Jos. Surf. Undoubtedly, madam; and it has always been a sentiment of mine, that to propagate a malicious truth wantonly is more despicable than to falsify from revenge. But can you, Maria, feel thus for others, and be unkind to me alone? Is hope to be denied the tenderest passion?

Mar. Why will you distress me by renewing this subject?

Jos. Surf. Ah, Maria! you would not treat me thus, and oppose your guardian, Sir Peter's will, but that I see that profligate Charles is still a favoured rival.

Mar. Ungenerously urged! But, whatever my sentiments are for that unfortunate young man, be assured I shall not feel more bound to give him up, because his distresses have lost him the regard even of a brother.

Jos. Surf. Nay, but, Maria, do not leave me with a frown: by all that's honest, I swear—— [*Kneels*

Re-enter LADY TEAZLE *behind.*

[*Aside.*] Gad's life, here 's Lady Teazle.—[*Aloud to* MARIA.] You must not—no, you shall not—for, though I have the greatest regard for Lady Teazle——

Mar. Lady Teazle!

Jos. Surf. Yet were Sir Peter to suspect——

Lady Teaz. [*Coming forward.*] What is this, pray? Does he take her for me?—Child, you are wanted in the next room.—[*Exit* MARIA.] What is all this, pray?

Jos. Surf. Oh, the most unlucky circumstance in nature! Maria has somehow suspected the tender concern I have for your happiness, and threatened to acquaint Sir Peter with her suspicions, and I was just endeavouring to reason with her when you came in.

Lady Teaz. Indeed! but you seemed to adopt a very tender mode of reasoning—do you usually argue on your knees?

Jos. Surf. Oh, she 's a child, and I thought a little bombast——But, Lady Teazle, when are you to give me your judgment on my library, as you promised?

Lady Teaz. No, no; I begin to think it would be imprudent, and you know I admit you as a lover no farther than fashion requires.

Jos. Surf. True—a mere Platonic cicisbeo, what every wife is entitled to.

Lady Teaz. Certainly, one must not be out of the fashion. However, I have so many of my country prejudices left, that, though Sir Peter's ill humour may vex me ever so, it never shall provoke me to——

Jos. Surf. The only revenge in your power. Well, I applaud your moderation.

Lady Teaz. Go—you are an insinuating wretch! But we shall be missed—let us join the company.

Jos. Surf. But we had best not return together.

Lady Teaz. Well, don't stay; for Maria sha'n't come to hear any more of your reasoning, I promise you. [*Exit.*

Jos. Surf. A curious dilemma, truly, my politics have run me into! I wanted, at first, only to ingratiate myself with Lady Teazle, that she might not be my enemy with Maria; and I have, I don't know how, become her serious lover. Sincerely I begin to wish I had never made such a point of gaining so very good a character, for it has led me into so many cursed rogueries that I doubt I shall be exposed at last.   [*Exit.*

SCENE III.—*A Room in* SIR PETER TEAZLE's *House.*

Enter SIR OLIVER SURFACE *and* ROWLEY.

Sir Oliv. Ha! ha! ha! so my old friend is married, hey? —a young wife out of the country. Ha! ha! ha! that he should have stood bluff to old bachelor so long, and sink into a husband at last!

Row. But you must not rally him on the subject, Sir Oliver; 'tis a tender point, I assure you, though he has been married only seven months.

Sir Oliv. Then he has been just half a year on the stool of repentance!—Poor Peter! But you say he has entirely given up Charles—never sees him, hey?

Row. His prejudice against him is astonishing, and I am sure greatly increased by a jealousy of him with Lady Teazle, which he has industriously been led into by a scandalous society in the neighbourhood, who have contributed not a little to Charles's ill name. Whereas the truth is, I believe, if the lady is partial to either of them, his brother is the favourite.

Sir Oliv. Ay, I know there are a set of malicious, prating, prudent gossips, both male and female, who murder characters to kill time, and will rob a young fellow of his good name before he has years to know the value of it. But I am not to be prejudiced against my nephew by such, I promise you! No, no; if Charles has done nothing false or mean, I shall compound for his extravagance.

Row. Then, my life on 't, you will reclaim him. Ah, sir, it gives me new life to find that your heart is not turned against him, and that the son of my good old master has one friend, however, left.

Sir Oliv. What! shall I forget, Master Rowley, when I was at his years myself? Egad, my brother and I were neither of us very prudent youths; and yet, I believe, you have not seen many better men than your old master was?

Row. Sir, 'tis this reflection gives me assurance that Charles may yet be a credit to his family. But here comes Sir Peter.

Sir Oliv. Egad, so he does! Mercy on me! he's greatly

altered, and seems to have a settled married look! One may read husband in his face at this distance!

Enter SIR PETER TEAZLE.

Sir Pet. Ha! Sir Oliver—my old friend! Welcome to England a thousand times!

Sir Oliv. Thank you, thank you, Sir Peter! and i' faith I am glad to find you well, believe me!

Sir Pet. Oh! 'tis a long time since we met—fifteen years, I doubt, Sir Oliver, and many a cross accident in the time.

Sir Oliv. Ay, I have had my share. But, what! I find you are married, hey, my old boy? Well, well, it can't be helped; and so—I wish you joy with all my heart!

Sir Pet. Thank you, thank you, Sir Oliver.—Yes, I have entered into—the happy state; but we 'll not talk of that now.

Sir Oliv. True, true, Sir Peter; old friends should not begin on grievances at first meeting. No, no, no.

Row. [*Aside to* SIR OLIVER.] Take care, pray, sir.

Sir Oliv. Well, so one of my nephews is a wild rogue, hey?

Sir Pet. Wild! Ah! my old friend, I grieve for your disappointment there; he 's a lost young man, indeed. However, his brother will make you amends; Joseph is, indeed, what a youth should be—every body in the world speaks well of him.

Sir Oliv. I am sorry to hear it; he has too good a character to be an honest fellow. Every body speaks well of him! Psha! then he has bowed as low to knaves and fools as to the honest dignity of genius and virtue.

Sir Pet. What, Sir Oliver! do you blame him for not making enemies?

Sir Oliv. Yes, if he has merit enough to deserve them.

Sir Pet. Well, well—you 'll be convinced when you know him. 'Tis edification to hear him converse; he professes the noblest sentiments.

Sir Oliv. Oh, plague of his sentiments! If he salutes me with a scrap of morality in his mouth, I shall be sick directly. But, however, don't mistake me, Sir Peter; I don't mean to defend Charles's errors: but, before I form my judgment of either of them, I intend to make a trial of their hearts;

and my friend Rowley and I have planned something for the purpose.

Row. And Sir Peter shall own for once he has been mistaken.

Sir Pet. Oh, my life on Joseph's honour!

Sir Oliv. Well—come, give us a bottle of good wine, and we'll drink the lads' health, and tell you our scheme.

Sir Pet. Allons, then!

Sir Oliv. And don't, Sir Peter, be so severe against your old friend's son.   Odds my life! I am not sorry that he has run out of the course a little: for my part, I hate to see prudence clinging to the green suckers of youth; 'tis like ivy round a sapling, and spoils the growth of the tree.

[*Exeunt.*

ACT III.

Scene I.—*A Room in* Sir Peter Teazle's *House.*

Enter Sir Peter Teazle, Sir Oliver Surface, *and* Rowley

Sir Pet. Well, then, we will see this fellow first, and have our wine afterwards But how is this. Master Rowley? I don't see the jet of your scheme.

Row. Why, sir, this Mr. Stanley, whom I was speaking of, is nearly related to them by their mother.   He was once a merchant in Dublin, but has been ruined by a series of undeserved misfortunes.   He has applied, by letter, since his confinement, both to Mr. Surface and Charles: from the former he has received nothing but evasive promises of future service, while Charles has done all that his extravagance has left him power to do; and he is, at this time, endeavouring to raise a sum of money, part of which, in the midst of his own distresses, I know he intends for the service of poor Stanley.

Sir Oliv. Ah! he is my brother's son.

Sir Pet. Well, but how is Sir Oliver personally to——

Row. Why, sir, I will inform Charles and his brother that Stanley has obtained permission to apply personally to his friends; and, as they have neither of them ever seen him, let Sir Oliver assume his character, and he will have a fair opportunity of judging, at least, of the benevolence of their dispositions: and believe me, sir, you will find in the youngest

brother one who, in the midst of folly and dissipation, ha:
still, as our immortal bard expresses it,—

> "a heart to pity, and a hand,
> Open as day, for melting charity."

Sir Pet. Psha! What signifies his having an open hand or
purse either, when he has nothing left to give? Well, well,
make the trial, if you please. But where is the fellow whom
you brought for Sir Oliver to examine, relative to Charles's
affairs?

Row. Below, waiting his commands, and no one can give
him better intelligence.—This, Sir Oliver, is a friendly Jew,
who, to do him justice, has done every thing in his power to
bring your nephew to a proper sense of his extravagance.

Sir Pet. Pray let us have him in.

Row. Desire Mr. Moses to walk up stairs.

[*Calls to* SERVANT.

Sir Pet. But, pray, why should you suppose he will speak
the truth?

Row. Oh, I have convinced him that he has no chance of
recovering certain sums advanced to Charles but through the
bounty of Sir Oliver, who he knows is arrived; so that you
may depend on his fidelity to his own interests. I have also
another evidence in my power, one Snake, whom I have detected in a matter little short of forgery, and shall shortly
produce to remove some of your prejudices, Sir Peter, relative
to Charles and Lady Teazle.

Sir Pet. I have heard too much on that subject.

Row. Here comes the honest Israelite.

Enter MOSES.

—This is Sir Oliver.

Sir Oliv. Sir, I understand you have lately had great dealings with my nephew Charles.

Mos. Yes, Sir Oliver, I have done all I could for him; but
he was ruined before he came to me for assistance.

Sir Oliv. That was unlucky, truly; for you have had no
opportunity of showing your talents.

Mos. None at all; I hadn't the pleasure of knowing his
distresses till he was some thousands worse than nothing.

Sir Oliv. Unfortunate, indeed! But I suppose you have
done all in your power for him, honest Moses?

Mos. Yes, he knows that. This very evening I was to have

brought him a gentleman from the city, who does not know him, and will, I believe, advance him some money.

Sir Pet. What, one Charles has never had money from before?

Mos. Yes, Mr. Premium, of Crutched Friars, formerly a broker.

Sir Pet. Egad, Sir Oliver, a thought strikes me!—Charles, you say, does not know Mr. Premium?

Mos. Not at all.

Sir Pet. Now then, Sir Oliver, you may have a better opportunity of satisfying yourself than by an old romancing tale of a poor relation: go with my friend Moses, and represent Premium, and then, I'll answer for it, you'll see your nephew in all his glory.

Sir Oliv. Egad, I like this idea better than the other, and I may visit Joseph afterwards as old Stanley.

Sir Pet. True—so you may.

Row. Well, this is taking Charles rather at a disadvantage, to be sure. However, Moses, you understand Sir Peter, and will be faithful?

Mos. You may depend upon me.—[*Looks at his watch.*] This is near the time I was to have gone.

Sir Oliv. I'll accompany you as soon as you please, Moses ———But hold! I have forgot one thing—how the plague shall I be able to pass for a Jew?

Mos. There's no need—the principal is Christian.

Sir Oliv. Is he? I'm very sorry to hear it. But, then again, an't I rather too smartly dressed to look like a money lender?

Sir Pet. Not at all; 'twould not be out of character, if you went in your own carriage—would it, Moses?

Mos. Not in the least.

Sir Oliv. Well, but how must I talk? there's certainly some cant of usury and mode of treating that I ought to know

Sir Pet. Oh, there's not much to learn. The great point, as I take it, is to be exorbitant enough in your demands. Hey, Moses?

Mos. Yes, that's a very great point.

Sir Oliv. I'll answer for 't I'll not be wanting in that. I'll ask him eight or ten per cent. on the loan, at least.

Mos. If you ask him no more than that, you'll be discovered immediately.

Sir Oliv. Hey! what, the plague! how much then?

Mos. That depends upon the circumstances. If he appears not very anxious for the supply, you should require only forty or fifty per cent.; but if you find him in great distress, and want the moneys very bad, you may ask double.

Sir Pet. A good honest trade you're learning, Sir Oliver!

Sir Oliv. Truly, I think so—and not unprofitable.

Mos. Then, you know, you haven't the moneys yourself, but are forced to borrow them for him of a friend.

Sir Oliv. Oh! I borrow it of a friend, do I?

Mos. And your friend is an unconscionable dog: but you can't help that.

Sir Oliv. My friend an unconscionable dog, is he?

Mos. Yes, and he himself has not the moneys by him, but is forced to sell stock at a great loss.

Sir Oliv. He is forced to sell stock at a great loss, is he? Well, that's very kind of him.

Sir Pet. I' faith, Sir Oliver—Mr. Premium, I mean—you 'll soon be master of the trade. But, Moses! would not you have him run out a little against the annuity bill? That would be in character, I should think.

Mos. Very much.

Row. And lament that a young man now must be at years of discretion before he is suffered to ruin himself?

Mos. Ay, great pity!

Sir Pet. And abuse the public for allowing merit to an act whose only object is to snatch misfortune and imprudence from the rapacious gripe of usury, and give the minor a chance of inheriting his estate without being undone by coming into possession.

Sir Oliv. So, so—Moses shall give me farther instructions as we go together.

Sir Pet. You will not have much time, for your nephew lives hard by.

Sir Oliv. Oh, never fear! my tutor appears so able, that though Charles lived in the next street, it must be my own fault if I am not a complete rogue before I turn the corner.

[*Exit with* MOSES.

Sir Pet. So, now, I think Sir Oliver will be convinced: you are partial, Rowley, and would have prepared Charles for the other plot.

Row. No, upon my word, Sir Peter.

Sir Pet. Well, go bring me this Snake, and I 'll hear wha he has to say presently. I see Maria, and want to speak with her.—[*Exit* ROWLEY.] I should be glad to be convinced my suspicions of Lady Teazle and Charles were unjust. I have never yet opened my mind on this subject to my friend Joseph —I am determined I will do it—he will give me his opinion sincerely.

Enter MARIA.

So, child, has Mr. Surface returned with you?

Mar. No, sir; he was engaged.

Sir Pet. Well, Maria, do you not reflect, the more you converse with that amiable young man, what return his partiality for you deserves?

Mar. Indeed, Sir Peter, your frequent importunity on this subject distresses me extremely—you compel me to declare, that I know no man who has ever paid me a particular attention whom I would not prefer to Mr. Surface.

Sir Pet. So—here's perverseness! No, no, Maria, 'tis Charles only whom you would prefer. 'Tis evident his vices and follies have won your heart.

Mar. This is unkind, sir. You know I have obeyed you in neither seeing nor corresponding with him: I have heard enough to convince me that he is unworthy my regard. Yet I cannot think it culpable, if, while my understanding severely condemns his vices, my heart suggests some pity for his distresses.

Sir Pet. Well, well, pity him as much as you please; but give your heart and hand to a worthier object.

Mar. Never to his brother!

Sir Pet. Go, perverse and obstinate! But take care, madam; you have never yet known what the authority of a guardian is: don't compel me to inform you of it.

Mar. I can only say, you shall not have just reason. 'Tis true, by my father's will, I am for a short period bound to regard you as his substitute; but must cease to think you so, when you would compel me to be miserable. [*Exit.*

Sir Pet. Was ever man so crossed as I am, every thing conspiring to fret me! I had not been involved in matrimony a fortnight, before her father, a hale and hearty man, died, on purpose, I believe, for the pleasure of plaguing me with the care of his daughter.—[*Lady Teazle sings without.*] But here comes my helpmate! She appears in great good humour

How happy I should be if I could tease her into loving me, though but a little!

Enter LADY TEAZLE.

Lady Teaz. Lud! Sir Peter, I hope you haven't been quarrelling with Maria? It is not using me well to be ill-humoured when I am not by.

Sir Pet. Ah, Lady Teazle, you might have the power to make me good humoured at all times.

Lady Teaz. I am sure I wish I had; for I want you to be in a charming sweet temper at this moment. Do be good humoured now, and let me have two hundred pounds, will you?

Sir Pet. Two hundred pounds; what an't I to be in a good humour without paying for it! But speak to me thus, and i' faith there's nothing I could refuse you. You shall have it; but seal me a bond for the repayment.

Lady Teaz. Oh, no—there—my note of hand will do as well.

[*Offering her hand.*

Sir Pet. And you shall no longer reproach me with not giving you an independent settlement. I mean shortly to surprise you: but shall we always live thus, hey?

Lady Teaz. If you please. I'm sure I don't care how soon we leave off quarrelling, provided you'll own you were tired first.

Sir Pet. Well—then let our future contest be, who shall be most obliging.

Lady Teaz. I assure you, Sir Peter, good nature becomes you. You look now as you did before we were married, when you used to walk with me under the elms, and tell me stories of what a gallant you were in your youth, and chuck me under the chin, you would; and ask me if I thought I could love an old fellow, who would deny me nothing—didn't you?

Sir Pet. Yes, yes, and you were as kind and attentive——

Lady Teaz. Ay, so I was, and would always take your part, when my acquaintance used to abuse you, and turn you into ridicule.

Sir Pet. Indeed!

Lady Teaz. Ay, and when my cousin Sophy has called you a stiff, peevish old bachelor, and laughed at me for thinking of marrying one who might be my father, I have always defended you, and said, I didn't think you so ugly by any means.

Sir Pet. Thank you.

Lady Teaz. And I dared say you'd make a very good sort of a husband.

Sir Pet. And you prophesied right; and we shall now be the happiest couple——

Lady Teaz. And never differ again?

Sir Pet. No, never!—though at the same time, indeed, my dear Lady Teazle, you must watch your temper very seriously; for in all our little quarrels, my dear, if you recollect, my love, you always began first.

Lady Teaz. I beg your pardon, my dear Sir Peter: indeed, you always gave the provocation.

Sir Pet. Now see, my angel! take care—contradicting isn't the way to keep friends.

Lady Teaz. Then don't you begin it, my love!

Sir Pet. There, now! you—you are going on. You don't perceive, my life, that you are just doing the very thing which you know always makes me angry.

Lady Teaz. Nay, you know if you will be angry without any reason, my dear——

Sir Pet. There! now you want to quarrel again.

Lady Teaz. No, I 'm sure I don't: but, if you will be so peevish——

Sir Pet. There now! who begins first?

Lady Teaz. Why, you, to be sure. I said nothing—but there 's no bearing your temper.

Sir Pet. No, no, madam: the fault 's in your own temper.

Lady Teaz. Ay, you are just what my cousin Sophy said you would be.

Sir Pet. Your cousin Sophy is a forward, impertinent gipsy.

Lady Teaz. You are a great bear, I 'm sure, to abuse my relations.

Sir Pet. Now may all the plagues of marriage be doubled on me, if ever I try to be friends with you any more!

Lady Teaz. So much the better.

Sir Pet. No, no, madam: 'tis evident you never cared a pin for me, and I was a madman to marry you—a pert, rural coquette, that had refused half the honest 'squires in the neighbourhood!

Lady Teaz. And I am sure I was a fool to marry you—an old dangling bachelor, who was single at fifty, only because he never could meet with any one who would have him.

Sir Pet. Ay, ay, madam; but you were pleased enough to listen to me: you never had such an offer before.

Lady Teaz. No! didn't I refuse Sir Tivy Terrier, who every body said would have been a better match? for his estate is just as good as yours, and he has broke his neck since we have been married.

Sir Pet. I have done with you, madam! You are an unfeeling, ungrateful—but there's an end of everything. I believe you capable of everything that is bad. Yes, madam, I now believe the reports relative to you and Charles, madam. Yes, madam, you and Charles are, not without grounds——

Lady Teaz. Take care, Sir Peter! you had better not insinuate any such thing! I'll not be suspected without cause, I promise you.

Sir Pet. Very well, madam! very well! A separate maintenance as soon as you please. Yes, madam, or a divorce! I'll make an example of myself for the benefit of all old bachelors. Let us separate, madam.

Lady Teaz. Agreed! agreed! And now, my dear Sir Peter, we are of a mind once more, we may be the happiest couple, and never differ again, you know: ha! ha! ha! Well, you are going to be in a passion, I see, and I shall only interrupt you—so, bye! bye!   *Exit.*

Sir Pet. Plagues and tortures! can't I make her angry either! Oh, I am the most miserable fellow! But I'll not bear her presuming to keep her temper: no! she may break my heart, but she shan't keep her temper.   [*Exit*

SCENE II.—*A Room in* CHARLES SURFACE'*s House.*

Enter TRIP, MOSES, *and* SIR OLIVER SURFACE.

Trip. Here, Master Moses! if you'll stay a moment, I'll try whether—what's the gentleman's name?

Sir Oliv. Mr. Moses, what is my name? [*Aside to* MOSES.

Mos. Mr. Premium.

Trip. Premium—very well.   [*Exit, taking snuff.*

Sir Oliv. To judge by the servants, one wouldn't believe the master was ruined. But what!—sure, this was my brother's house?

Mos. Yes, sir; Mr. Charles bought it of Mr. Joseph, with the furniture, pictures, &c., just as the old gentleman left it. Sir Peter thought it a piece of extravagance in him.

Sir Oliv. In my mind, the other's economy in selling it to him was more reprehensible by half.

Re-enter TRIP.

Trip. My master says you must wait, gentlemen: he has company, and can't speak with you yet.

Sir Oliv. If he knew who it was wanted to see him, perhaps he would not send such a message?

Trip. Yes, yes, sir; he knows you are here—I did not forget little Premium: no, no, no.

Sir Oliv. Very well; and I pray, sir, what may be your name?

Trip. Trip, sir; my name is Trip, at your ser: S

Sir Oliv. Well, then, Mr. Trip, you have a pleasant sort of place here, I guess?

Trip. Why, yes—here are three or four of us pass our time agreeably enough; but then our wages are sometimes a little in arrear—and not very great either—but fifty pounds a year, and find our own bags and bouquets.

Sir Oliv. Bags and bouquets! halters and bastinadoes!

　　　　　　　　　　　　　　　　　　　　　[*Aside.*

Trip. And *à propos*, Moses, have you been able to get me that little bill discounted?

Sir Oliv. Wants to raise money too!—mercy on me! Has his distresses too, I warrant, like a lord, and affects creditors and duns.　　　　　　　　　　　　　　　　　　[*Aside.*

Mos. 'Twas not to be done, indeed, Mr. Trip.

Trip. Good lack, you surprise me! My friend Brush has indorsed it, and I thought when he put his name at the back of a bill 'twas the same as cash.

Mos. No, 'twouldn't do.

Trip. A small sum—but twenty pounds. Hark'ee, Moses, do you think you couldn't get it me by way of annuity?

Sir Oliv. An annuity! ha! ha! a footman raise money by way of annuity! Well done, luxury, egad!　　　[*Aside.*

Mos. Well, but you must insure your place.

Trip. Oh, with all my heart! I'll insure my place, and my life too, if you please.

Sir Oliv. It's more than I would your neck.　　　[*Aside.*

Mos. But is there nothing you could deposit?

Trip. Why, nothing capital of my master's wardrobe has dropped lately; but I could give you a mortgage on some of his winter clothes, with equity of redemption before November —or you shall have the reversion of the French velvet, or a post-obit on the blue and silver;—these, I should think, Moses, with a few pair of point ruffles, as a collateral security—hey, my little fellow?

Mos. Well, well.   [*Bell rings.*

Trip. Egad, I heard the bell! I believe, gentlemen, I can now introduce you. Don't forget the annuity, little Moses! This way, gentlemen, I 'll insure my place, you know.

Sir Oliv. [*Aside.*] If the man be a shadow of the master, this is the temple of dissipation indeed!   [*Exeunt.*

SCENE III.—*Another Room in the same.*

CHARLES SURFACE, SIR HARRY BUMPER, CARELESS, *and* GEN-
TLEMEN, *discovered drinking.*

Chas. Surf. 'Fore heaven, 'tis true!—there 's the great de-
generacy of the age. Many of our acquaintance have taste, spirit, and politeness; but, plague on't, they won't drink.

Care. It is so, indeed, Charles! they give into all the sub-
stantial luxuries of the table, and abstain from nothing but wine and wit. Oh, certainly society suffers by it intolerably! for now, instead of the social spirit of raillery that used to mantle over a glass of bright Burgundy, their conversation is become just like the Spa-water they drink, which has all the pert-
ness and flatulency of champagne, without its spirit or flavour.

1 Gent. But what are they to do who love play better than wine?

Care. True! there 's Sir Harry diets himself for gaming, and is now under a hazard regimen.

Chas. Surf. Then he 'll have the worst of it. What! you wouldn't train a horse for the course by keeping him from corn? For my part, egad, I am never so successful as when I am a little merry: let me throw on a bottle of champagne, and I never lose.

All. Hey, what?

Care. At least I never feel my losses, which is exactly the same thing.

2 Gent. Ay, that I believe.

Chas. Surf. And then, what man can pretend to be a be-
liever in love, who is an abjurer of wine? 'Tis the test by which the lover knows his own heart. Fill a dozen bumpers to a dozen beauties, and she that floats at the top is the maid that has bewitched you.

Care. Now then, Charles, be honest, and give us your real favourite.

Chas. Surf. Why, I have withheld her only in compassion

to you.   If I toast her, you must give a round of her peers, which is impossible—on earth.

Care. Oh! then we 'll find some canonised vestals or heathen goddesses that will do, I warrant!

Chas. Surf. Here then, bumpers, you rogues! bumpers! Maria! Maria!——

Sir Har. Maria who?

Chas. Surf. Oh, damn the surname!—'tis too formal to be registered in Love's calendar—Maria!

All. Maria!

Chas. Surf. But now, Sir Harry, beware, we must have beauty superlative.

Care. Nay, never study, Sir Harry: we 'll stand to the toast, though your mistress should want an eye, and you know you have a song will excuse you.

Sir Har. Egad, so I have! and I 'll give him the song instead of the lady.   [*Sings.*

    Here 's to the maiden of bashful fifteen;
      Here 's to the widow of fifty;
    Here 's to the flaunting extravagant quean,
      And here 's to the housewife that 's thrifty.

Chorus. Let the toast pass,—
      Drink to the lass,
    I 'll warrant she 'll prove an excuse for the glass.
    Here 's to the charmer whose dimples we prize;
      Now to the maid who has none, sir:
    Here 's to the girl with a pair of blue eyes,
      And here 's to the nymph with but one, sir.

Chorus. Let the toast pass, &c.

    Here 's to the maid with a bosom of snow:
      Now to her that 's as brown as a berry:
    • Here 's to the wife with a face full of woe,
      And now to the damsel that 's merry.

Chorus. Let the toast pass, &c.

    For let 'em be clumsy, or let 'em be slim,
      Young or ancient, I care not a feather;
    So fill a pint bumper quite up to the brim,
    So fill up your glasses, nay, fill to the brim,
      And let us e'en toast them together.

Chorus. Let the toast pass, &c.

All. Bravo! bravo!

Enter TRIP, *and whispers* CHARLES SURFACE.

Chas. Surf. Gentlemen, you must excuse me a little.— Careless, take the chair, will you?

Care. Nay, pr'ythee, Charles, what now? This is one of your peerless beauties, I suppose, has dropped in by chance?

Chas. Surf. No, faith! To tell you the truth, 'tis a Jew and a broker, who are come by appointment.

Care. Oh, damn it! let's have the Jew in.

1 Gent. Ay, and the broker too, by all means.

2 Gent. Yes, yes, the Jew and the broker.

Chas. Surf. Egad, with all my heart!—Trip, bid the gen-tlemen walk in.—[*Exit* TRIP.] Though there's one of them a stranger, I can tell you.

Care. Charles, let us give them some generous Burgundy, and perhaps they'll grow conscientious.

Chas. Surf. Oh, hang 'em, no! wine does but draw forth a man's natural qualities; and to make them drink would only be to whet their knavery.

Re-enter TRIP, *with* SIR OLIVER SURFACE *and* MOSES.

Chas. Surf. So, honest Moses; walk in, pray; Mr. Premium —that's the gentleman's name, isn't it, Moses?

Mos. Yes, sir.

Chas. Surf. Set chairs, Trip.—Sit down, Mr. Premium.— Glasses, Trip.—[TRIP *gives chairs and glasses, and exit.*] Sit down, Moses.—Come, Mr. Premium, I'll give you a senti-ment; here's *Success to usury!*—Moses, fill the gentleman a bumper.

Mos. Success to usury!   [*Drinks*

Care. Right, Moses—usury is prudence and industry, and deserves to succeed.

Sir Oliv. Then here's—All the success it deserves! [*Drinks.*

Care. No, no, that won't do! Mr. Premium, you have demurred at the toast, and must drink it in a pint bumper.

1 Gent. A pint bumper, at least.

Mos. Oh, pray, sir, consider—Mr. Premium's a gentleman

Care. And therefore loves good wine.

2 Gent. Give Moses a quart glass—this is mutiny, and a high contempt for the chair.

Care. Here, now for 't! I'll see justice done, to the last drop of my bottle.

Sir Oliv. Nay, pray, gentlemen—I did not expect this usage.

Chas. Surf. No, hang it, you shan't; Mr. Premium's a stranger.

Sir Oliv. Odd! I wish I was well out of their company.

[*Aside*

Care. Plague on 'em then! if they won't drink, we 'll not sit down with them. Come, Harry, the dice are in the next room.—Charles, you 'll join us when you have finished your business with the gentlemen?

Chas. Surf. I will! I will!—[*Exeunt* Sir Harry Bumper *and* Gentlemen; Careless *following.*] Careless!

Care. [*Returning.*] Well!

Chas. Surf. Perhaps I may want you.

Care. Oh, you know I am always ready: word. note, or bond, 'tis all the same to me.   [*Exit.*

Mos. Sir, this is Mr. Premium, a gentleman of the strictest honour and secrecy; and always performs what he undertakes. Mr. Premium, this is——

Chas. Surf. Psha! have done. Sir, my friend Moses is a very honest fellow, but a little slow at expression: he 'll be an hour giving us our titles. Mr. Premium, the plain state of the matter is this: I am an extravagant young fellow who wants to borrow money; you I take to be a prudent old fellow, who have got money to lend. I am blockhead enough to give fifty per cent. sooner than not have it; and you, I presume, are rogue enough to take a hundred if you can get it. Now, sir, you see we are acquainted at once, and may proceed to business without farther ceremony.

Sir Oliv. Exceeding frank, upon my word. I see, sir, you are not a man of many compliments.

Chas. Surf. Oh, no, sir! plain dealing in business I always think best.

Sir Oliv. Sir, I like you the better for it. However, you are mistaken in one thing; I have no money to lend, but I believe I could procure some of a friend; but then he 's an unconscionable dog. Isn't he, Moses? And must sell stock to accommodate you. Mustn't he, Moses?

Mos. Yes, indeed! You know I always speak the truth, and scorn to tell a lie!

Chas. Surf. Right. People that speak truth generally do. But these are trifles, Mr. Premium. What! I know money isn't to be bought without paying for 't!

Sir Oliv. Well, but what security could you give? You have no land, I suppose?

Chas. Surf. Not a mole-hill, nor a twig, but what 's in the bough-pots out of the window!

Sir Oliv. Nor any stock, I presume?

Chas. Surf. Nothing but live stock—and that's only a few pointers and ponies. But pray, Mr. Premium, are you acquainted at all with any of my connexions?

Sir Oliv. Why, to say truth, I am.

Chas. Surf. Then you must know that I have a devilish rich uncle in the East Indies, Sir Oliver Surface, from whom I have the greatest expectations?

Sir Oliv. That you have a wealthy uncle, I have heard; but how your expectations will turn out is more, I believe, than you can tell.

Chas. Surf. Oh, no!—there can be no doubt. They tell me I'm a prodigious favourite, and that he talks of leaving me every thing.

Sir Oliv. Indeed! this is the first I've heard of it.

Chas. Surf. Yes, yes, 'tis just so. Moses knows 'tis true; don't you, Moses?

Mos. Oh, yes! I'll swear to 't.

Sir Oliv. Egad, they'll persuade me presently I'm at Bengal.   *[Aside.*

Chas. Surf. Now I propose, Mr. Premium, if it's agreeable to you, a post-obit on Sir Oliver's life: though at the same time the old fellow has been so liberal to me, that I give you my word, I should be very sorry to hear that any thing had happened to him.

Sir Oliv. Not more than I should, I assure you. But the bond you mention happens to be just the worst security you could offer me—for I might live to a hundred and never see the principal.

Chas. Surf. Oh, yes, you would! the moment Sir Oliver dies, you know, you would come on me for the money.

Sir Oliv. Then I believe I should be the most unwelcome dun you ever had in your life.

Chas. Surf. What! I suppose you're afraid that Sir Oliver is too good a life?

Sir Oliv. No, indeed I am not; though I have heard he is as hale and healthy as any man of his years in Christendom.

Chas. Surf. There again, now, you are misinformed. No, no, the climate has hurt him considerably, poor uncle Oliver. Yes, yes, he breaks apace, I'm told—and is so much altered lately that his nearest relations would not know him

Sir Oliv. No! Ha! ha! ha! so much altered lately that his nearest relations would not know him! Ha! ha! ha! egad—ha! ha! ha!

Chas. Surf. Ha! ha!—you're glad to hear that, little Premium?

Sir Oliv. No, no, I'm not.

Chas. Surf. Yes, yes, you are—ha! ha! ha!—you know that mends your chance.

Sir Oliv. But I'm told Sir Oliver is coming over; nay, some say he is actually arrived.

Chas. Surf. Psha! sure I must know better than you whether he's come or not. No, no, rely on't he's at this moment at Calcutta. Isn't he, Moses?

Mos. Oh, yes, certainly.

Sir Oliv. Very true, as you say, you must know better than I, though I have it from pretty good authority. Haven't I, Moses?

Mos. Yes, most undoubted!

Sir Oliv. But, sir, as I understand you want a few hundreds immediately, is there nothing you could dispose of?

Chas. Surf. How do you mean?

Sir Oliv. For instance, now, I have heard that your father left behind him a great quantity of massy old plate.

Chas. Surf. O Lud! that's gone long ago. Moses can tell you how better than I can.

Sir Oliv. [*Aside.*] Good lack! all the family race-cups and corporation-bowls!—[*Aloud.*] Then it was also supposed that his library was one of the most valuable and compact.

Chas. Surf. Yes, yes, so it was—vastly too much so for a private gentleman. For my part, I was always of a communicative disposition, so I thought it a shame to keep so much knowledge to myself.

Sir Oliv. [*Aside.*] Mercy upon me! learning that had run in the family like an heir-loom!—[*Aloud.*] Pray, what are become of the books?

Chas. Surf. You must inquire of the auctioneer, Master Premium, for I don't believe even Moses can direct you.

Mos. I know nothing of books.

Sir Oliv. So, so, nothing of the family property left, I suppose?

Chas. Surf. Not much, indeed; unless you have a mind to the family pictures. I have got a room full of ancestors above: and if you have a taste for old paintings, egad, you shall have 'em a bargain!

Sir Oliv. Hey! what the devil! sure, you wouldn't sell your forefathers, would you?

Chas. Surf. Every man of them, to the best bidder.

Sir Oliv. What! your great-uncles and aunts?

Chas. Surf. Ay, and my great-grandfathers and grandmothers too.

Sir Oliv. [*Aside.*] Now I give him up!—[*Aloud.*] What the plague, have you no bowels for your own kindred? Odd's life! do you take me for Shylock in the play, that you would raise money of me on your own flesh and blood?

Chas. Surf. Nay, my little broker, don't be angry: what need you care, if you have your money's worth?

Sir Oliv. Well, I'll be the purchaser: I think I can dispose of the family canvas.—[*Aside.*] Oh, I'll never forgive him this! never!

Re-enter CARELESS.

Care. Come, Charles, what keeps you?

Chas. Surf. I can't come yet. I'faith, we are going to have a sale above stairs; here's little Premium will buy all my ancestors!

Care. Oh, burn your ancestors!

Chas. Surf. No, he may do that afterwards, if he pleases. Stay, Careless, we want you: egad, you shall be auctioneer— so come along with us.

Care. Oh, have with you, if that's the case. I can handle a hammer as well as a dice-box! Going! going!

Sir Oliv. Oh, the profligates!   [*Aside.*

Chas. Surf. Come, Moses, you shall be appraiser, if we want one. Gad's life, little Premium, you don't seem to like the business?

Sir Oliv. Oh, yes, I do, vastly! Ha! ha! ha! yes, yes, I think it a rare joke to sell one's family by auction—ha! ha!— [*Aside.*] Oh, the prodigal!

Chas. Surf. To be sure! when a man wants money, where the plague should he get assistance, if he can't make free with his own relations?   [*Exeunt.*

Sir Oliv. I'll never forgive him; never! never!

ACT IV.

SCENE I.—*A Picture Room in* CHARLES SURFACE'S *House.*

Enter CHARLES SURFACE, SIR OLIVER SURFACE, MOSES, *and* CARELESS.

Chas. Surf. Walk in, gentlemen, pray walk in;—here they are, the family of the Surfaces, up to the Conquest.

Sir Oliv. And, in my opinion, a goodly collection.

Chas. Surf. Ay, ay, these are done in the true spirit of portrait-painting; no *volontière grace* or expression. Not like the works of your modern Raphaels, who give you the strongest resemblance, yet contrive to make your portrait independent of you; so that you may sink the original and not hurt the picture. No, no; the merit of these is the inveterate likeness—all still and awkward as the originals, and like nothing in human nature besides.

Sir Oliv. Ah! we shall never see such figures of men again.

Chas. Surf. I hope not. Well, you see, Master Premium, what a domestic character I am; here I sit of an evening surrounded by my family. But come, get to your pulpit, Mr. Auctioneer; here 's an old gouty chair of my grandfather's will answer the purpose.

Care. Ay, ay, this will do. But, Charles, I haven't a hammer; and what 's an auctioneer without his hammer?

Chas. Surf. Egad, that 's true. What parchment have we here? Oh, our genealogy in full. [*Taking pedigree down.*] Here, Careless, you shall have no common bit of mahogany, here 's the family tree for you, you rogue! This shall be your hammer, and now you may knock down my ancestors with their own pedigree.

Sir Oliv. What an unnatural rogue!—an *ex post facto* parricide!   [*Aside.*

Care. Yes, yes, here 's a list of your generation indeed;—faith, Charles, this is the most convenient thing you could have found for the business, for 'twill not only serve as a hammer, but a catalogue into the bargain. Come, begin—A-going, a-going, a-going!

Chas. Surf. Bravo, Careless! Well, here 's my great-uncle, Sir Richard Raveline, a marvellous good general in his day, I assure you. He served in all the Duke of Marlborough's wars, and got that cut over his eye at the battle of Malplaquet. What say you, Mr. Premium? ,look at him—there 's a

D D 2

hero! not cut out of his feathers. as your modern clipped captains are, but enveloped in wig and regimentals, as a general should be. What do you bid?

Sir Oliv. [*Aside to Moses.*] Bid him speak.

Mos. Mr. Premium would have you speak.

Chas. Surf. Why, then, he shall have him for ten pounds, and I'm sure that's not dear for a staff-officer.

Sir Oliv. [*Aside.*] Heaven deliver me! his famous uncle Richard for ten pounds!—[*Aloud.*] Very well, sir, I take him at that.

Chas. Surf. Careless, knock down my uncle Richard.—Here, now, is a maiden sister of his, my great-aunt Deborah, done by Kneller, in his best manner, and esteemed a very formidable likeness. There she is, you see, a shepherdess feeding her flock. You shall have her for five pounds ten—the sheep are worth the money.

Sir Oliv. [*Aside.*] Ah! poor Deborah! a woman who set such a value on herself!—[*Aloud.*] Five pounds ten—she's mine.

Chas. Surf. Knock down my aunt Deborah! Here, now, are two that were a sort of cousins of theirs.—You see, Moses, these pictures were done some time ago, when beaux wore wigs, and the ladies their own hair.

Sir Oliv. Yes, truly, head-dresses appear to have been a little lower in those days.

Chas. Surf. Well, take that couple for the same.

Mos. 'Tis a good bargain.

Chas. Surf. Careless!—This, now, is a grandfather of my mother's, a learned judge, well known on the western circuit.—What do you rate him at, Moses?

Mos. Four guineas.

Chas. Surf. Four guineas! Gad's life, you don't bid me the price of his wig.—Mr. Premium, you have more respect for the woolsack; do let us knock his lordship down at fifteen.

Sir Oliv. By all means.

Care. Gone!

Chas. Surf. And there are two brothers of his, William and Walter Blunt, Esquires, both members of parliament; and noted speakers; and, what's very extraordinary, I believe, this is the first time they were ever bought or sold.

Sir Oliv. That is very extraordinary, indeed! I'll take them at your own price, for the honour of parliament.

Care. Well said, little Premium! I'll knock them down at forty.

Chas. Surf. Here's a jolly fellow—I don't know what relation, but he was mayor of Norwich: take him at eight pounds.

Sir Oliv. No, no; six will do for the mayor.

Chas. Surf. Come, make it guineas, and I'll throw you the two aldermen there into the bargain.

Sir Oliv. They're mine.

Chas. Surf. Careless, knock down the mayor and alder men. But, plague on 't! we shall be all day retailing in this manner; do let us deal wholesale: what say you, little Premium? Give me three hundred pounds for the rest of the family in the lump.

Care. Ay, ay, that will be the best way.

Sir Oliv. Well, well, any thing to accommodate you; they are mine. But there is one portrait which you have always passed over.

Care. What, that ill-looking little fellow over the settee?

Sir Oliv. Yes, sir, I mean that; though I don't think him so ill-looking a little fellow, by any means.

Chas. Surf. What, that? Oh; that's my uncle Oliver! 'twas done before he went to India.

Care. Your uncle Oliver! Gad, then you'll never be friends, Charles. That, now, to me, is as stern a looking rogue as ever I saw; an unforgiving eye, and a damned disinheriting countenance! an inveterate knave, depend on 't. Don't you think so, little Premium?

Sir Oliv. Upon my soul, sir, I do not; I think it is as honest a looking face as any in the room, dead or alive. But I suppose uncle Oliver goes with the rest of the lumber?

Chas. Surf. No, hang it! I'll not part with poor Noll. The old fellow has been very good to me, and, egad, I'll keep his picture while I've a room to put it in.

Sir Oliv. [*Aside.*] The rogue's my nephew after all!— [*Aloud.*] But, sir, I have somehow taken a fancy to that picture.

Chas. Surf. I'm sorry for 't, for you certainly will not have it. Oons, haven't you got enough of them?

Sir Oliv. [*Aside.*] I forgive him every thing!—[*Aloud.*] But, sir, when I take a whim in my head, I don't value money. I'll give you as much for that as for all the rest.

Chas. Surf. Don't tease me, master broker; I tell you I'll not part with it, and there's an end of it.

Sir Oliv. [*Aside.*] How like his father the dog is!—[*Aloud.*] Well, well, I have done.—[*Aside.*] I did not perceive it before, but I think I never saw such a striking resemblance.—[*Aloud.*] Here is a draught for your sum.

Chas. Surf. Why, 'tis for eight hundred pounds!

Sir Oliv. You will not let Sir Oliver go?

Chas. Surf. Zounds! no! I tell you, once more.

Sir Oliv. Then never mind the difference, we'll balance that another time. But give me your hand on the bargain; you are an honest fellow, Charles—I beg pardon, sir, for being so free.—Come, Moses.

Chas. Surf. Egad, this is a whimsical old fellow!—But hark'ee, Premium, you'll prepare lodgings for these gentlemen.

Sir Oliv. Yes, yes, I'll send for them in a day or two.

Chas. Surf. But hold; do now send a genteel conveyance for them, for, I assure you, they were most of them used to ride in their own carriages.

Sir Oliv. I will, I will—for all but Oliver.

Chas. Surf. Ay, all but the little nabob.

Sir Oliv. You're fixed on that?

Chas. Surf. Peremptorily.

Sir Oliv. [*Aside.*] A dear extravagant rogue!—[*Aloud.*] Good day!—Come, Moses.—[*Aside.*] Let me hear now who dares call him profligate! [*Exit with Moses.*]

Care. Why, this is the oddest genius of the sort I ever met with!

Chas. Surf. Egad, he's the prince of brokers, I think. I wonder how the devil Moses got acquainted with so honest a fellow.—Ha! here's Rowley.—Do, Careless, say I'll join the company in a few moments.

Care. I will—but don't let that old blockhead persuade you to squander any of that money on old musty debts, or any such nonsense; for tradesmen, Charles, are the most exorbitant fellows.

Chas. Surf. Very true, and paying them is only encouraging them.

Care. Nothing else.

Chas. Surf. Ay, ay, never fear.—[*Exit* CARELESS.] So! this was an odd old fellow, indeed. Let me see, two-thirds of these five hundred and thirty odd pounds are mine by right. 'Fore Heaven! I find one's ancestors are more valuable relations than I took them for!—Ladies and gentlemen, your most obedient and very grateful servant.

[*Bows ceremoniously to the pictures.*

Enter ROWLEY.

Ha! old Rowley! egad, you are just come in time to take leave of your old acquaintance.

Row. Yes, I heard they were a-going. But I wonder you can have such spirits under so many distresses.

Chas. Surf. Why, there's the point! my distresses are so many, that I can't afford to part with my spirits; but I shall be rich and splenetic, all in good time. However, I suppose you are surprised that I am not more sorrowful at parting with so many near relations; to be sure, 'tis very affecting: but you see they never move a muscle, so why should I?

Row. There's no making you serious a moment.

Chas. Surf. Yes, faith, I am so now. Here, my honest Rowley, here, get me this changed directly, and take a hundred pounds of it immediately to old Stanley.

Row. A hundred pounds! Consider only——

Chas. Surf. Gad's life, don't talk about it! poor Stanley's wants are pressing, and, if you don't make haste, we shall have some one call that has a better right to the money.

Row. Ah! there's the point! I never will cease dunning you with the old proverb——

Chas. Surf. Be just before you're generous.—Why, so I would if I could; but Justice is an old, hobbling beldame, and I can't get her to keep pace with Generosity, for the soul of me.

Row. Yet, Charles, believe me, one hour's reflection——

Chas. Surf. Ay, ay, it's very true; but, hark'ee, Rowley, while I have, by Heaven I'll give; so, damn your economy! and now for hazard. [*Exeunt*

SCENE II.—*Another room in the same.*

Enter SIR OLIVER SURFACE *and* MOSES.

Mos. Well, sir, I think, as Sir Peter said, you have seen Mr. Charles in high glory; 'tis great pity he's so extravagant.

Sir Oliv. True, but he would not sell my picture.

Mos. And loves wine and women so much.

Sir Oliv. But he would not sell my picture.

Mos. And games so deep.

Sir Oliv. But he would not sell my picture.   Oh, here 's Rowley.

Enter ROWLEY.

Row. So, Sir Oliver, I find you have made a purchase——

Sir Oliv. Yes, yes, our young rake has parted with his ancestors like old tapestry.

Row. And here has he commissioned me to re-deliver you part of the purchase money—I mean, though, in your necessitous character of old Stanley.

Mos. Ah! there is the pity of all; he is so damned charitable.

Row. And I left a hosier and two tailors in the hall, who, I 'm sure, won't be paid, and this hundred would satisfy them.

Sir Oliv. Well, well, I 'll pay his debts, and his benevolence too.   But now I am no more a broker, and you shall introduce me to the elder brother as old Stanley.

Row. Not yet awhile; Sir Peter, I know, means to call there about this time.

Enter TRIP.

Trip. Oh, gentlemen, I beg pardon for not showing you out; this way—Moses, a word.   [*Exit with* MOSES.

Sir Oliv. There 's a fellow for you!   Would you believe it, that puppy intercepted the Jew on our coming, and wanted to raise money before he got to his master!

Row. Indeed!

Sir Oliv. Yes, they are now planning an annuity business. Ah, Master Rowley, in my days servants were content with the follies of their masters, when they were worn a little threadbare; but now they have their vices, like their birthday clothes, with the gloss on.   [*Exeunt.*

SCENE III.—*A Library in* JOSEPH SURFACE'S *House.*

Enter JOSEPH SURFACE *and* SERVANT.

Jos. Surf. No letter from Lady Teazle?

Ser. No, sir.

Jos. Surf. [*Aside.*] I am surprised she has not sent, if she is prevented from coming.   Sir Peter certainly does not suspect me.   Yet I wish I may not lose the heiress, through the scrape I have drawn myself into with the wife; however, Charles's imprudence and bad character are great points in my favour.   [*Knocking without.*

Ser. Sir, I believe that must be Lady Teazle.

Jos. Surf. Hold! See whether it is or not, before you go to the door: I have a particular message for you if it should be my brother.

Ser. 'Tis her ladyship, sir; she always leaves her chair at the milliner's in the next street.

Jos. Surf. Stay, stay; draw that screen before the window ——that will do;—my opposite neighbour is a maiden lady of so curious a temper.—[SERVANT *draws the screen, and exit.*] I have a difficult hand to play in this affair. Lady Teazle has lately suspected my views on Maria; but she must by no means be let into that secret,—at least, till I have her more in my power.

Enter LADY TEAZLE.

Lady Teaz. What, sentiment in soliloquy now? Have you been very impatient? O Lud! don't pretend to look grave. I vow I couldn't come before.

Jos. Surf. O madam, punctuality is a species of constancy very unfashionable in a lady of quality.

               [*Places chairs, and sits after* LADY TEAZLE *is seated.*

Lady Teaz. Upon my word, you ought to pity me. Do you know Sir Peter is grown so ill-natured to me of late, and so jealous of Charles too—that's the best of the story, isn't it?

Jos. Surf. I am glad my scandalous friends keep that up.
                                               [*Aside.*

Lady Teaz. I am sure I wish he would let Maria marry him, and then perhaps he would be convinced; don't you, Mr. Surface?

Jos. Surf. [*Aside.*] Indeed I do not.—[*Aloud.*] Oh, certainly I do! for then my dear Lady Teazle would also be convinced how wrong her suspicions were of my having any design on the silly girl.

Lady Teaz. Well, well, I'm inclined to believe you. But isn't it provoking, to have the most ill-natured things said of one? And there's my friend Lady Sneerwell has circulated I don't know how many scandalous tales of me, and all without any foundation too; that's what vexes me.

Jos. Surf. Ay, madam, to be sure, that is the provoking

circumstance — without foundation; yes, yes, there's the mortification, indeed; for, when a scandalous story is believed against one, there certainly is no comfort like the consciousness of having deserved it.

Lady Teaz. No, to be sure, then I'd forgive their malice; but to attack me, who am really so innocent, and who never say an ill-natured thing of anybody—that is, of any friend; and then Sir Peter, too, to have him so peevish, and so suspicious, when I know the integrity of my own heart—indeed 'tis monstrous!

Jos. Surf. But, my dear Lady Teazle, 'tis your own fault if you suffer it. When a husband entertains a groundless suspicion of his wife, and withdraws his confidence from her, the original compact is broken, and she owes it to the honour of her sex to endeavour to outwit him.

Lady Teaz. Indeed! So that, if he suspects me without cause, it follows, that the best way of curing his jealousy is to give him reason for't?

Jos. Surf. Undoubtedly—for your husband should never be deceived in you: and in that case it becomes you to be frail in compliment to his discernment.

Lady Teaz. To be sure, what you say is very reasonable, and when the consciousness of my innocence——

Jos. Surf. Ah, my dear madam, there is the great mistake! 'tis this very conscious innocence that is of the greatest prejudice to you. What is it makes you negligent of forms, and careless of the world's opinion? why, the consciousness of your own innocence. What makes you thoughtless in your conduct, and apt to run into a thousand little imprudences? why, the consciousness of your own innocence. What makes you impatient of Sir Peter's temper, and outrageous at his suspicions? why, the consciousness of your innocence.

Lady Teaz. 'Tis very true!

Jos. Surf. Now, my dear Lady Teazle, if you would but once make a trifling *faux pas*, you can't conceive how cautious you would grow, and how ready to humour and agree with your husband.

Lady Teaz. Do you think so?

Jos. Surf. Oh, I am sure on't; and then you would find all scandal would cease at once, for—in short, your character at present is like a person in a plethora, absolutely dying from too much health.

Lady Teaz. So, so; then I perceive your prescription is, that I must sin in my own defence, and part with my virtue to preserve my reputation?

Jos. Surf. Exactly so, upon my credit, ma'am.

Lady Teaz. Well, certainly this is the oddest doctrine, and the newest receipt for avoiding calumny!

Jos. Surf. An infallible one, believe me. Prudence, like experience, must be paid for.

Lady Teaz. Why, if my understanding were once convinced——

Jos. Surf. Oh, certainly, madam, your understanding should be convinced. Yes, yes—Heaven forbid I should persuade you to do any thing you thought wrong. No, no, I have too much honour to desire it.

Lady Teaz. Don't you think we may as well leave honour out of the argument? ·   [*Rises.*

Jos. Surf. Ah, the ill effects of your country education, I see, still remain with you.

Lady Teaz. I doubt they do indeed; and I will fairly own to you, that if I could be persuaded to do wrong, it would be by Sir Peter's ill usage sooner than your honourable logic, after all.

Jos. Surf. Then, by this hand, which he is unworthy of——

               [*Taking her hand.*

Re-enter SERVANT.

'Sdeath, you blockhead—what do you want?

Ser. I beg your pardon, sir, but I thought you would not choose Sir Peter to come up without announcing him.

Jos. Surf. Sir Peter!—Oons—the devil!

Lady Teaz. Sir Peter! O Lud! I'm ruined! I'm ruined!

Ser. Sir, 'twasn't I let him in.

Lady Teaz. Oh! I'm quite undone! What will become of me? Now, Mr. Logic—Oh! mercy, sir, he's on the stairs— I'll get behind here—and if ever I'm so imprudent again——

               [*Goes behind the screen.*

Jos. Surf. Give me that book.

      [*Sits down.* SERVANT *pretends to adjust his chair.*

Enter SIR PETER TEAZLE.

Sir Pet. Ay, ever improving himself—Mr. Surface, Mr. Surface——   [*Pats* JOSEPH *on the shoulder.*

Jos. Surf. Oh, my dear Sir Peter, I beg your pardon.—

[*Gaping, throws away the book.*] I have been dozing over a stupid book. Well, I am much obliged to you for this call. You haven't been here, I believe, since I fitted up this room. Books, you know, are the only things I am a coxcomb in.

Sir Pet. 'Tis very neat indeed. Well, well, that 's proper; and you can make even your screen a source of knowledge—hung, I perceive, with maps.

Jos. Surf. Oh, yes, I find great use in that screen.

Sir Pet. I dare say you must, certainly, when you want to find any thing in a hurry.

Jos. Surf. Ay, or to hide any thing in a hurry either.
                                                    [*Aside.*

Sir Pet. Well, I have a little private business——

Jos. Surf. You need not stay.   [*To* SERVANT.

Ser. No, sir.   [*Exit.*

Jos. Surf. Here 's a chair, Sir Peter—I beg——

Sir Pet. Well, now we are alone, there is a subject, my dear friend, on which I wish to unburden my mind to you—a point of the greatest moment to my peace; in short, my good friend, Lady Teazle's conduct of late has made me very unhappy.

Jos. Surf. Indeed! I am very sorry to hear it.

Sir Pet. Yes, 'tis but too plain she has not the least regard for me; but, what 's worse, I have pretty good authority to suppose she has formed an attachment to another.

Jos. Surf. Indeed! you astonish me!

Sir Pet. Yes! and, between ourselves, I think I 've discovered the person.

Jos. Surf. How! you alarm me exceedingly.

Sir Pet. Ay, my dear friend, I knew you would sympathise with me!

Jos. Surf. Yes, believe me, Sir Peter, such a discovery would hurt me just as much as it would you.

Sir Pet. I am convinced of it. Ah! it is a happiness to have a friend whom we can trust even with one's family secrets. But have you no guess who I mean?

Jos. Surf. I haven't the most distant idea. It can't be Sir Benjamin Backbite!

Sir Pet. Oh, no! What say you to Charles?

Jos. Surf. My brother! impossible!

Sir Pet. Oh, my dear friend, the goodness of your own heart misleads you. You judge of others by yourself.

Jos. Surf. Certainly, Sir Peter, the heart that is conscious of its own integrity is ever slow to credit another's treachery.

Sir Pet. True ; but your brother has no sentiment—you never hear him talk so.

Jos. Surf. Yet I can't but think Lady Teazle herself has too much principle.

Sir Pet. Ay ; but what is principle against the flattery of a handsome, lively young fellow?

Jos. Surf. That's very true.

Sir Pet. And then, you know, the difference of our ages makes it very improbable that she should have any great affection for me ; and if she were to be frail, and I were to make it public, why the town would only laugh at me, the foolish old bachelor, who had married a girl.

Jos. Surf. That's true, to be sure—they would laugh.

Sir Pet. Laugh! ay, and make ballads, and paragraphs, and the devil knows what of me.

Jos. Surf. No, you must never make it public.

Sir Pet. But then again—that the nephew of my old friend, Sir Oliver, should be the person to attempt such a wrong, hurts me more nearly.

Jos. Surf. Ay, there's the point. When ingratitude barbs the dart of injury, the wound has double danger in it.

Sir Pet. Ay—I, that was, in a manner, left his guardian ; in whose house he had been so often entertained ; who never in my life denied him—my advice!

Jos. Surf. Oh, 'tis not to be credited! There may be a man capable of such baseness, to be sure ; but, for my part, till you can give me positive proofs, I cannot but doubt it. However, if it should be proved on him, he is no longer a brother of mine—I disclaim kindred with him : for the man who can break the laws of hospitality, and tempt the wife of his friend, deserves to be branded as the pest of society.

Sir Pet. What a difference there is between you! What noble sentiments!

Jos. Surf. Yet I cannot suspect Lady Teazle's honour.

Sir Pet. I am sure I wish to think well of her, and to remove all ground of quarrel between us. She has lately reproached me more than once with having made no settlement on her ; and, in our last quarrel, she almost hinted that she should not break her heart if I was dead. Now, as we seem to differ in our ideas of expense, I have resolved she shall have her own way, and be her own mistress in that respect for the future; and, if I were to die, she will find I have not been inattentive to her interest while living. Here, my friend, are the drafts of two deeds, which I wish to have your opinion on. By one, she will enjoy eight hundred a year independent while I live; and, by the other, the bulk of my fortune at my death.

Jos. Surf. This conduct, Sir Peter, is indeed truly generous.——[*Aside.*] I wish it may not corrupt my pupil.

Sir Pet. Yes, I am determined she shall have no cause to complain, though I would not have her acquainted with the latter instance of my affection yet awhile.

Jos. Surf. Nor I, if I could help it.   [*Aside.*

Sir Pet. And now, my dear friend, if you please, we will talk over the situation of your hopes with Maria.

Jos. Surf. [*Softly.*] Oh, no, Sir Peter; another time, if you please.

Sir Pet. I am sensibly chagrined at the little progress you seem to make in her affections.

Jos. Surf. [*Softly.*] I beg you will not mention it. What are my disappointments when your happiness is in debate!—— [*Aside.*] 'Sdeath, I shall be ruined every way!

Sir Pet. And though you are averse to my acquainting Lady Teazle with your passion, I'm sure she 's not your enemy in the affair.

Jos. Surf. Pray, Sir Peter, now oblige me. I am really too much affected by the subject we have been speaking of to bestow a thought on my own concerns. The man who is entrusted with his friend's distresses can never——

Re-enter SERVANT.

Well, sir?

Ser. Your brother, sir, is speaking to a gentleman in the street, and says he knows you are within.

Jos. Surf. 'Sdeath, blockhead, I 'm not within—I 'm out for the day.

Sir Pet. Stay—hold—a thought has struck me:—you shall be at home.

Jos. Surf. Well, well, let him up.—[*Exit* SERVANT.] He 'll interrupt Sir Peter, however.   [*Aside.*

Sir Pet. Now, my good friend, oblige me, I entreat you. Before Charles comes, let me conceal myself somewhere, then do you tax him on the point we have been talking, and his answer may satisfy me at once.

Jos. Surf. Oh, fie, Sir Peter! would you have me join in so mean a trick?—to trepan my brother too?

Sir Pet. Nay, you tell me you are sure he is innocent; if so, you do him the greatest service by giving him an opportunity to clear himself, and you will set my heart at rest. Come, you shall not refuse me: [*Going up,*] here, behind the screen will be—Hey! what the devil! there seems to be one listener here already—I 'll swear I saw a petticoat!

Jos. Surf. Ha! ha! ha! Well, this is ridiculous enough. I 'll tell you, Sir Peter, though I hold a man of intrigue to be a most despicable character, yet, you know, it does not follow that one is to be an absolute Joseph either! Hark 'ee, 'tis a little French milliner, a silly rogue that plagues me; and having some character to lose, on your coming, sir, she ran behind the screen.

Sir Pet. Ah, Joseph! Joseph! Did I ever think that you——But, egad, she has overheard all I have been saying of my wife.

Jos. Surf. Oh, 'twill never go any farther, you may depend upon it!

Sir Pet. No! then, faith, let her hear it out.—Here's a closet will do as well.

Jos. Surf. Well, go in there.

Sir Pet. Sly, rogue! sly rogue!   [*Goes into the closet.*

Jos. Surf. A narrow escape, indeed! and a curious situation I 'm in, to part man and wife in this manner.

Lady Teaz. [*Peeping.*] Couldn't I steal off?

Jos. Surf. Keep close, my angel!

Sir Pet. [*Peeping.*] Joseph, tax him home.

Jos. Surf. Back, my dear friend!

Lady Teaz. [*Peeping.*] Couldn't you lock Sir Peter in?

Jos. Surf. Be still, my life!

Sir Pet. [*Peeping.*] You 're sure the little milliner won't blab?

Jos. Surf. In, in, my dear Sir Peter!—'Fore Gad, I wish I had a key to the door.

Enter CHARLES SURFACE.

Chas. Surf. Holla! brother, what has been the matter? Your fellow would not let me up at first. What! have you had a Jew or a wench with you?

Jos. Surf. Neither, brother, I assure you.

Chas. Surf. But what has made Sir Peter steal off? I thought he had been with you.

Jos. Surf. He was, brother; but, hearing you were coming, he did not choose to stay.

Chas. Surf. What! was the old gentleman afraid I wanted to borrow money of him?

Jos. Surf. No, sir: but I am sorry to find, Charles, you have lately given that worthy man grounds for great uneasiness.

Chas. Surf. Yes, they tell me I do that to a great many worthy men. But how so, pray?

Jos. Surf. To be plain with you, brother, he thinks you are endeavouring to gain Lady Teazle's affections from him.

Chas. Surf. Who, I? O Lud! not I, upon my word.— Ha! ha! ha! ha! so the old fellow has found out that he has got a young wife, has he?—or, what is worse, Lady Teazle has found out she has an old husband?

Jos. Surf. This is no subject to jest on, brother. He who can laugh——

Chas. Surf. True, true, as you were going to say—then, seriously, I never had the least idea of what you charge me with, upon my honour.

Jos. Surf. Well, it will give Sir Peter great satisfaction to hear this.   [*Raising his voice.*

Chas. Surf. To be sure, I once thought the lady seemed to have taken a fancy to me; but, upon my soul, I never gave her the least encouragement. Besides, you know my attachment to Maria.

Jos. Surf. But sure, brother, even if Lady Teazle had betrayed the fondest partiality for you——

Chas. Surf. Why, look'ee, Joseph, I hope I shall never deliberately do a dishonourable action; but if a pretty woman was purposely to throw herself in my way—and that pretty woman married to a man old enough to be her father——

Jos. Surf. Well!

Chas. Surf. Why, I believe I should be obliged to——

Jos. Surf. What?

Chas. Surf. To borrow a little of your morality, that's all. But, brother, do you know now that you surprise me exceedingly, by naming me with Lady Teazle; for, i'faith, I always understood you were her favourite.

Jos. Surf. Oh, for shame, Charles! This retort is foolish.

Chas. Surf. Nay, I swear I have seen you exchange such significant glances——

Jos. Surf. Nay, nay, sir, this is no jest.

Chas. Surf. Egad, I'm serious! Don't you remember one day, when I called here——

Jos. Surf. Nay, pr'ythee, Charles——

Chas. Surf. And found you together——

Jos. Surf. Zounds, sir, I insist——

Chas. Surf. And another time when your servant——

Jos. Surf. Brother, brother, a word with you!—[*Aside.*] Gad, I must stop him.

Chas. Surf. Informed, I say, that——

Jos. Surf. Hush! I beg your pardon, but Sir Peter has overheard all we have been saying. I knew you would clear yourself, or I should not have consented.

Chas. Surf. How, Sir Peter! Where is he?

Jos. Surf. Softly, there! [*Points to the closet.*

Chas. Surf. Oh, 'fore Heaven, I'll have him out. Sir Peter, come forth!

Jos. Surf. No, no——

Chas. Surf. I say, Sir Peter, come into court.—[*Pulls in* SIR PETER.] What! my old guardian!—What! turn inquisitor, and take evidence incog.? Oh, fie! Oh, fie!

Sir Pet. Give me your hand, Charles—I believe I have suspected you wrongfully; but you mustn't be angry with Joseph—'twas my plan!

Chas. Surf. Indeed!

Sir Pet. But I acquit you. I promise you I don't think near so ill of you as I did: what I have heard has given me great satisfaction.

Chas. Surf. Egad, then, 'twas lucky you didn't hear any more. Wasn't it, Joseph?

Sir Pet. Ah! you would have retorted on him.

Chas. Surf. Ah, ay, that was a joke.

Sir Pet. Yes, yes, I know his honour too well.

Chas. Surf. But you might as well have suspected him as me in this matter, for all that. Mightn't he, Joseph?

Sir Pet. Well, well, I believe you.

Jos. Surf. Would they were both out of the room! [*Aside*

Sir Pet. And in future, perhaps, we may not be such strangers.

E E

Re-enter SERVANT, *and whispers* JOSEPH SURFACE.

Serv. Lady Sneerwell is below, and says she will come up.

Jos. Surf. Lady Sneerwell! Gad's life! she must not come here. [*Exit* SERVANT.] Gentlemen, I beg pardon—I must wait on you down stairs: here is a person come on particular business.

Chas. Surf. Well, you can see him in another room. Sir Peter and I have not met a long time, and I have something to say to him.

Jos. Surf. [*Aside.*] They must not be left together.—[*Aloud.*] I'll send Lady Sneerwell away, and return directly.—[*Aside to* SIR PETER.] Sir Peter, not a word of the French milliner.

Sir Pet. [*Aside to* JOSEPH SURFACE.] I! not for the world! —[*Exit* JOSEPH SURFACE.] Ah, Charles, if you associated more with your brother, one might indeed hope for your reformation. He is a man of sentiment. Well, there is nothing in the world so noble as a man of sentiment.

Chas. Surf. Psha! he is too moral by half; and so apprehensive of his good name, as he calls it, that I suppose he would as soon let a priest into his house as a wench.

Sir Pet. No, no,—come, come,—you wrong him. No, no! Joseph is no rake, but he is no such saint either, in that respect.—[*Aside.*] I have a great mind to tell him—we should have such a laugh at Joseph.

Chas. Surf. Oh, hang him! he's a very anchorite, a young hermit!

Sir Pet. Hark'ee—you must not abuse him: he may chance to hear of it again, I promise you.

Chas. Surf. Why, you won't tell him?

Sir Pet. No—but—this way.—[*Aside.*] Egad, I'll tell him. —[*Aloud.*] Hark'ee—have you a mind to have a good laugh at Joseph?

Chas. Surf. I should like it of all things.

Sir Pet. Then, i'faith, we will! I'll be quit with him for discovering me. He had a girl with him when I called.

[*Whispers.*

Chas. Surf. What! Joseph? you jest.

Sir Pet. Hush!—a little French milliner—and the best of the jest is—she's in the room now.

Chas. Surf. The devil she is!

Sir Pet. Hush! I tell you. [*Points to the screen*

Chas. Surf. Behind the screen! 'Slife, let's unveil her!

Sir Pet. No, no, he's coming :—you sha'n't, indeed!

Chas. Surf. Oh, egad, we'll have a peep at the little milliner!

Sir Pet. Not for the world!—Joseph will never forgive me.

Chas. Surf. I'll stand by you——

Sir Pet. Odds, here he is!

·[CHARLES SURFACE *throws down the screen*

Re-enter JOSEPH SURFACE.

Chas. Surf. Lady Teazle, by all that's wonderful!

Sir Pet. Lady Teazle, by all that's damnable!

Chas. Surf. Sir Peter, this is one of the smartest French milliners I ever saw. Egad, you seem all to have been diverting yourselves here at hide and seek, and I don't see who is out of the secret. Shall I beg your ladyship to inform me? Not a word!—Brother, will you be pleased to explain this matter? What! is Morality dumb too?—Sir Peter, though I found you in the dark, perhaps you are not so now! All mute!—Well—though I can make nothing of the affair, I suppose you perfectly understand one another; so I'll leave you to yourselves.—[*Going.*] Brother, I'm sorry to find you have given that worthy man grounds for so much uneasiness. —Sir Peter! there's nothing in the world so noble as a man of sentiment! [*Exit.*

Jos. Surf. Sir Peter—notwithstanding—I confess—that appearances are against me—if you will afford me your patience—I make no doubt—but I shall explain every thing to your satisfaction.

Sir Pet. If you please, sir.

Jos. Surf. The fact is, sir, that Lady Teazle, knowing my pretensions to your ward Maria—I say, sir, Lady Teazle, being apprehensive of the jealousy of your temper—and knowing my friendship to the family—she, sir, I say—called here—in order that—I might explain these pretensions—but on your coming—being apprehensive—as I said—of your jealousy—she withdrew—and this, you may depend on it, is the whole truth of the matter.

Sir Pet. A very clear account, upon my word; and I dare swear the lady will vouch for every article of it.

Lady Teaz. For not one word of it, Sir Peter!

Sir Pet. How! don't you think it worth while to agree in the lie?

Lady Teaz. There is not one syllable of truth in what that gentleman has told you.

Sir Pet. I believe you, upon my soul, ma'am!

Jos. Surf. [*Aside to* LADY TEAZLE.] 'Sdeath, madam, will you betray me?

Lady Teaz. Good Mr. Hypocrite, by your leave, I'll speak for myself.

Sir Pet. Ay, let her alone, sir; you'll find she'll make out a better story than you, without prompting.

Lady Teaz. Hear me, Sir Peter!—I came here on no matter relating to your ward, and even ignorant of this gentleman's pretensions to her. But I came, seduced by his insidious arguments, at least to listen to his pretended passion, if not to sacrifice your honour to his baseness.

Sir Pet. Now, I believe, the truth is coming, indeed!

Jos. Surf. The woman's mad!

Lady Teaz. No, sir; she has recovered her senses, and your own arts have furnished her with the means.—Sir Peter, I do not expect you to credit me—but the tenderness you expressed for me, when I am sure you could not think I was a witness to it, has so penetrated to my heart, that had I left the place without the shame of this discovery, my future life should have spoken the sincerity of my gratitude. As for that smooth-tongued hypocrite, who would have seduced the wife of his too credulous friend, while he affected honourable addresses to his ward—I behold him now in a light so truly despicable, that I shall never again respect myself for having listened to him.   [*Exit.*

Jos. Surf. Notwithstanding all this, Sir Peter, Heaven knows——

Sir Pet. That you are a villain! and so I leave you to your conscience.

Jos. Surf. You are too rash, Sir Peter; you shall hear me. The man who shuts out conviction by refusing to——

Sir Pet. Oh, damn your sentiments!

[*Exeunt* SIR PETER *and* JOSEPH SURFACE, *talking.*

ACT V.

SCENE I.—*The Library in* JOSEPH SURFACE's *House.*

Enter JOSEPH SURFACE *and* SERVANT.

Jos. Surf. Mr. Stanley! and why should you think I would him? you must know he comes to ask something.

Ser. Sir, I should not have let him in, but that Mr. Rowley came to the door with him.

Jos. Surf. Psha! blockhead! to suppose that I should now be in a temper to receive visits from poor relations!—Well, why don't you show the fellow up?

Ser. I will, sir.—Why, sir, it was not my fault that Sir Peter discovered my lady——

Jos. Surf. Go, fool!—[*Exit* SERVANT.]   Sure Fortune never played a man of my policy such a trick before! My character with Sir Peter, my hopes with Maria, destroyed in a moment! I 'm in a rare humour to listen to other people's distresses! I sha'n't be able to bestow even a benevolent sentiment on Stanley.—So! here he comes, and Rowley with him. I must try to recover myself, and put a little charity into my face, however.   [*Exit.*

Enter SIR OLIVER SURFACE and ROWLEY.

Sir Oliv. What! does he avoid us? That was he, was it not?

Row. It was, sir. But I doubt you are come a little too abruptly. His nerves are so weak, that the sight of a poor relation may be too much for him. I should have gone first to break it to him.

Sir Oliv. Oh, plague of his nerves! Yet this is he whom Sir Peter extols as a man of the most benevolent way of thinking!

'Row. As to his way of thinking, I cannot pretend to decide; for, to do him justice, he appears to have as much speculative benevolence as any private gentleman in the kingdom, though he is seldom so sensual as to indulge himself in the exercise of it.

Sir Oliv. Yet he has a string of charitable sentiments at his fingers' ends.

Row. Or, rather, at his tongue's end, Sir Oliver; for I believe there is no sentiment he has such faith in as that *Charity begins at home.*

Sir Oliv. And his, I presume, is of that domestic sort which never stirs abroad at all.

Row. I doubt you 'll find it so;—but he 's coming. I mustn't seem to interrupt you; and you know, immediately as you leave him, I come in to announce your arrival in your real character.

Sir Oliv. True; and afterwards you 'll meet me at Sir Peter's.

Row. Without losing a moment.   [*Exit.*

Sir Oliv. I don't like the complaisance of his features.

Re-enter JOSEPH SURFACE.

Jos. Surf. Sir, I beg you ten thousand pardons for keeping you a moment waiting.—Mr. Stanley, I presume.

Sir Oliv. At your service.

Jos. Surf. Sir, I beg you will do me the honour to sit down —I entreat you, sir.

Sir Oliv. Dear sir—there's no occasion.—[*Aside.*] Too civil by half!

Jos. Surf. I have not the pleasure of knowing you, Mr. Stanley; but I am extremely happy to see you look so well. You were nearly related to my mother, I think, Mr. Stanley?

Sir Oliv. I was, sir; so nearly that my present poverty, I fear, may do discredit to her wealthy children, else I should not have presumed to trouble you.

Jos. Surf. Dear sir, there needs no apology;—he that is in distress, though a stranger, has a right to claim kindred with the wealthy. I am sure I wish I was one of that class, and had it in my power to offer you even a small relief.

Sir Oliv. If your uncle, Sir Oliver, were here, I should have a friend.

Jos. Surf. I wish he was, sir, with all my heart: you should not want an advocate with him, believe me, sir.

Sir Oliv. I should not need one—my distresses would recommend me. But I imagined his bounty would enable you to become the agent of his charity.

Jos. Surf. My dear sir, you were strangely misinformed. Sir Oliver is a worthy man, a very worthy man; but avarice, Mr. Stanley, is the vice of age. I will tell you, my good sir, in confidence, what he has done for me has been a mere nothing; though people, I know, have thought otherwise, and, for my part, I never chose to contradict the report.

Sir Oliv. What! has he never transmitted you bullion— rupees—pagodas?

Jos. Surf. Oh, dear sir, nothing of the kind! No, no; a few presents now and then—china, shawls, congou tea, avadavats, and Indian crackers—little more, believe me.

Sir Oliv. Here's gratitude for twelve thousand pounds!— Avadavats and Indian crackers! [*Aside.*

Jos. Surf. Then, my dear sir, you have heard, I doubt not, of the extravagance of my brother: there are very few would credit what I have done for that unfortunate young man.

Sir Oliv. Not I, for one!   ·   [*Aside.*

Jos. Surf. The sums I have lent him! Indeed I have been exceedingly to blame; it was an amiable weakness; however, I don't pretend to defend it—and now I feel it doubly culpable, since it has deprived me of the pleasure of serving you, Mr. Stanley, as my heart dictates.

Sir Oliv. [*Aside.*] Dissembler!—[*Aloud.*] Then, sir, you can't assist me?

Jos. Surf. At present, it grieves me to say, I cannot; but, whenever I have the ability, you may depend upon hearing from me.

Sir Oliv. I am extremely sorry——

Jos. Surf. Not more than I, believe me; to pity, without the power to relieve, is still more painful than to ask and be denied.

Sir Oliv. Kind sir, your most obedient humble servant.

Jos. Surf. You leave me deeply affected, Mr. Stanley.— William, be ready to open the door.   [*Calls to* SERVANT.

Sir. Oliv. Oh, dear sir, no ceremony.

Jos. Surf. Your very obedient.

Sir Oliv. Your most obsequious.

Jos. Surf. You may depend upon hearing from me, whenever I can be of service.

Sir Oliv. Sweet sir, you are too good!

Jos. Surf. In the meantime I wish you health and spirits.

Sir Oliv. Your ever grateful and perpetual humble servant

Jos. Surf. Sir, yours as sincerely.

Sir Oliv. [*Aside.*] Now I am satisfied.   [*Exit.*

Jos. Surf. This is one bad effect of a good character; it invites application from the unfortunate, and there needs no small degree of address to gain the reputation of benevolence without incurring the expense. The silver ore of pure charity is an expensive article in the catalogue of a man's good qualities; whereas the sentimental French plate I use instead of it makes just as good a show, and pays no tax.

Re-enter ROWLEY.

Row. Mr. Surface, your servant: I was apprehensive of interrupting you, though my business demands immediate attention, as this note will inform you.

Jos. Surf. Always happy to see Mr. Rowley,— a rascal.— [*Aside. Reads the letter.*] Sir Oliver Surface!—My uncle arrived!

Row. He is, indeed : we have just parted—quite well, after a speedy voyage, and impatient to embrace his worthy nephew.

Jos Surf. I am astonished!—William! stop Mr. Stanley, if he's not gone. [*Calls to* SERVANT.

Row. Oh! he's out of reach, I believe.

Jos. Surf. Why did you not let me know this when you came in together?

Row. I thought you had particular business. But I must be gone to inform your brother, and appoint him here to meet your uncle. He will be with you in a quarter of an hour.

Jos. Surf. So he says. Well, I am strangely overjoyed at his coming.—[*Aside.*] Never, to be sure, was any thing so damned unlucky!

Row. You will be delighted to see how well he looks.

Jos. Surf. Oh! I'm overjoyed to hear it.—[*Aside.*] Just at this time!

Row. I'll tell him how impatiently you expect him.

Jos. Surf. Do, do; pray give my best duty and affection. Indeed, I cannot express the sensations I feel at the thought of seeing him.—[*Exit* ROWLEY.] Certainly his coming just at this time is the cruellest piece of ill fortune. [*Exit.*

SCENE II.—*A Room in* SIR PETER TEAZLE's *House.*

Enter MRS. CANDOUR *and* MAID.

Maid. Indeed, ma'am, my lady will see nobody at present.

Mrs. Can. Did you tell her it was her friend Mrs. Candour?

Maid. Yes, ma'am; but she begs you will excuse her.

Mrs. Can. Do go again; I shall be glad to see her, if it be only for a moment, for I am sure she must be in great distress. —[*Exit* MAID.] Dear heart, how provoking! I'm not mistress of half the circumstances! We shall have the whole affair in the newspapers, with the names of the parties at length, before I have dropped the story at a dozen houses.

Enter SIR BENJAMIN BACKBITE.

Oh, dear Sir Benjamin! you have heard, I suppose——

Sir Ben. Of Lady Teazle and Mr. Surface——

Mrs. Can. And Sir Peter's discovery——

Sir Ben. Oh, the strangest piece of business, to be sure!

Mrs. Can. Well, I never was so surprised in my life. I am so sorry for all parties, indeed.

Sir Ben. Now, I don't pity Sir Peter at all: he was so extravagantly partial to Mr. Surface.

Mrs. Can. Mr. Surface! Why, 'twas with Charles Lady Teazle was detected.

Sir Ben. No, no, I tell you: Mr. Surface is the gallant.

Mrs. Can. No such thing! Charles is the man. 'Twas Mr. Surface brought Sir Peter on purpose to discover them.

Sir Ben. I tell you I had it from one——

Mrs. Can. And I have it from one——

Sir Ben. Who had it from one, who had it——

Mrs. Can. From one immediately. But here comes Lady Sneerwell; perhaps she knows the whole affair.

Enter LADY SNEERWELL.

Lady Sneer. So, my dear Mrs. Candour, here's a sad affair of our friend Lady Teazle!

Mrs. Can. Ay, my dear friend, who would have thought——

Lady Sneer. Well, there is no trusting appearances; though, indeed, she was always too lively for me.

Mrs. Can. To be sure, her manners were a little too free; but then she was so young!

Lady Sneer. And had, indeed, some good qualities.

Mrs. Can. So she had, indeed. But have you heard the particulars?

Lady Sneer. No; but every body says that Mr. Surface——

Sir Ben. Ay, there; I told you Mr. Surface was the man.

Mrs. Can. No, no: indeed the assignation was with Charles.

Lady Sneer. With Charles! You alarm me, Mrs. Candour!

Mrs. Can. Yes, yes; he was the lover. Mr. Surface, to do him justice, was only the informer.

Sir Ben. Well, I'll not dispute with you, Mrs. Candour; but, be it which it may, I hope that Sir Peter's wound will not——

Mrs. Can. Sir Peter's wound! Oh, mercy! I didn't hear a word of their fighting.

Lady Sneer. Nor I, a syllable.

Sir Ben. No! what, no mention of the duel?

Mrs. Can. Not a word.

Sir Ben. Oh, yes: they fought before they left the room

Lady Sneer. Pray, let us hear

Mrs. Can. Ay, do oblige us with the duel.

Sir Ben. "*Sir*," says Sir Peter, immediately after the discovery, "*you are a most ungrateful fellow.*"

Mrs. Can. Ay, to Charles——

Sir Ben. No, no—to Mr. Surface—*a most ungrateful fellow; and old as I am, sir,* says he, *I insist on immediate satisfaction.*

Mrs. Can. Ay, that must have been to Charles; for 'tis very unlikely Mr. Surface should fight in his own house.

Sir Ben. Gad's life, ma'am, not at all—*giving me immediate satisfaction.*—On this, ma'am, Lady Teazle, seeing Sir Peter in such danger, ran out of the room in strong hysterics, and Charles after her, calling out for hartshorn and water; then, madam, they began to fight with swords——

Enter CRABTREE.

Crab. With pistols, nephew—pistols! I have it from undoubted authority.

Mrs. Can. Oh, Mr. Crabtree, then it is all true!

Crab. Too true, indeed, madam, and Sir Peter is dangerously wounded——

Sir Ben. By a thrust in segoon quite through his left side——

Crab. By a bullet lodged in the thorax.

Mrs. Can. Mercy on me! Poor Sir Peter!

Crab. Yes, madam; though Charles would have avoided the matter, if he could.

Mrs. Can. I told you who it was; I knew Charles was the person.

Sir Ben. My uncle, I see, knows nothing of the matter.

Crab. But Sir Peter taxed him with the basest ingratitude——

Sir Ben. That I told you, you know——

Crab. Do, nephew, let me speak!—and insisted on immediate——

Sir Ben. Just as I said——

Crab. Odds life, nephew, allow others to know something too! A pair of pistols lay on the bureau (for Mr. Surface, it seems, had come home the night before late from Salthill, where he had been to see the Montem with a friend, who has a son at Eton), so, unluckily, the pistols were left charged.

Sir Ben. I heard nothing of this.

Crab. Sir Peter forced Charles to take one, and they fired, it seems, pretty nearly together.   Charles's shot took effect, as I tell you, and Sir Peter's missed; but, what is very extraordinary, the ball struck against a little bronze Shakspeare that stood over the fire-place, grazed out of the window at a right angle, and wounded the postman, who was just coming to the door with a double letter from Northamptonshire.

Sir Ben. My uncle's account is more circumstantial, I confess; but I believe mine is the true one, for all that.

Lady Sneer. [*Aside.*] I am more interested in this affair than they imagine, and must have better information. [*Exit.*

Sir Ben. Ah! Lady Sneerwell's alarm is very easily accounted for.

Crab. Yes, yes, they certainly do say—but that's neither here nor there.

Mrs. Can. But, pray, where is Sir Peter at present?

Crab. Oh! they brought him home, and he is now in the house, though the servants are ordered to deny him.

Mrs. Can. I believe so, and Lady Teazle, I suppose, attending him.

Crab. Yes, yes; and I saw one of the faculty enter just before me.

Sir Ben. Hey! who comes here?

Crab. Oh, this is he: the physician, depend on 't.

Mrs. Can. Oh, certainly! it must be the physician; and now we shall know.

Enter Sir Oliver Surface.

Crab. Well, doctor, what hopes?

Mrs. Can. Ay, doctor, how's your patient?

Sir Ben. Now, doctor, isn't it a wound with a small-sword?

Crab. A bullet lodged in the thorax, for a hundred!

Sir. Oliv. Doctor! a wound with a small-sword! and a bullet in the thorax!—Oons! are you mad, good people?

Sir Ben. Perhaps, sir, you are not a doctor?

Sir Oliv. Truly, I am to thank you for my degree, if I am.

Crab. Only a friend of Sir Peter's, then, I presume. But, sir, you must have heard of his accident?

Sir Oliv. Not a word!

Crab. Not of his being dangerously wounded?

Sir Oliv. The devil he is!

Sir Ben. Run through the body——

Crab. Shot in the breast——

Sir Ben. By one Mr. Surface——

Crab. Ay, the younger.

Sir Oliv. Hey! what the plague! you seem to differ strangely in your accounts: however, you agree that Sir Peter is dangerously wounded.

Sir Ben. Oh, yes, we agree in that.

Crab. Yes, yes, I believe there can be no doubt of that.

Sir Oliv. Then, upon my word, for a person in that situation, he is the most imprudent man alive; for here he comes, walking as if nothing at all was the matter.

Enter SIR PETER TEAZLE.

Odds heart, Sir Peter! you are come in good time, I promise you; for we had just given you over!

Sir Ben. [*Aside to* CRABTREE.] Egad, uncle, this is the most sudden recovery!

Sir Oliv. Why, man! what do you out of bed with a small-sword through your body, and a bullet lodged in your thorax?

Sir Pet. A small-sword and a bullet!

Sir Oliv. Ay; these gentlemen would have killed you without law or physic, and wanted to dub me a doctor, to make me an accomplice.

Sir Pet. Why, what is all this?

Sir Ben. We rejoice, Sir Peter, that the story of the duel is not true, and are sincerely sorry for your other misfortune.

Sir Pet. So, so; all over the town already!   [*Aside.*

Crab. Though, Sir Peter, you were certainly vastly to blame to marry at your years.

Sir Pet. Sir, what business is that of yours?

Mrs. Can. Though, indeed, as Sir Peter made so good a husband, he's very much to be pitied.

Sir Pet. Plague on your pity, ma'am! I desire none of it.

Sir Ben. However, Sir Peter, you must not mind the laughing and jests you will meet with on the occasion.

Sir Pet. Sir, sir! I desire to be master in my own house.

Crab. 'Tis no uncommon case, that's one comfort.

Sir Pet. I insist on being left to myself: without ceremony, I insist on your leaving my house directly!

Mrs. Can. Well, well, we are going; and depend on't, we'll make the best report of it we can.   [*Exit*

Sir Pet. Leave my house!

Crab. And tell how hardly you 've been treated. [*Exit.*

Sir Pet. Leave my house!

Sir Ben. And how patiently you bear it. [*Exit.*

Sir Pet. Fiends! vipers! furies! Oh! that their own venom would choke them!

Sir Oliv. They are very provoking indeed, Sir Peter.

Enter ROWLEY.

Row. I heard high words: what has ruffled you, sir?

Sir Pet. Psha! what signifies asking? Do I ever pass a day without my vexations?

Row. Well, I 'm not inquisitive

Sir Oliv. Well, Sir Peter, I have seen both my nephews in the manner we proposed.

Sir Pet. A precious couple they are!

Row. Yes, and Sir Oliver is convinced that your judgment was right, Sir Peter.

Sir Oliv. Yes, I find Joseph is indeed the man, after all.

Row. Ay, as Sir Peter says, he is a man of sentiment.

Sir Oliv. And acts up to the sentiments he professes.

Row. It certainly is edification to hear him talk.

Sir Oliv. Oh, he 's a model for the young men of the age! —But how 's this, Sir Peter? you don't join us in your friend Joseph's praise, as I expected.

Sir Pet. Sir Oliver, we live in a damned wicked world, and the fewer we praise the better.

Row. What! do you say so, Sir Peter, who were never mistaken in your life?

Sir Pet. Psha! plague on you both! I see by your sneering you have heard the whole affair. I shall go mad among you!

Row. Then, to fret you no longer, Sir Peter, we are indeed acquainted with it all. I met Lady Teazle coming from Mr. Surface's so humbled, that she deigned to request me to be her advocate with you.

Sir Pet. And does Sir Oliver know all this?

Sir Oliv. Every circumstance.

Sir Pet. What of the closet and the screen, hey?

Sir Oliv. Yes, yes, and the little French milliner. Oh, I have been vastly diverted with the story! ha! ha! ha!

Sir Pet. 'Twas very pleasant.

Sir Oliv. I never laughed more in my life, I assure you: ah! ah! ah!

Sir Pet. Oh, vastly diverting! ha! ha! ha!

Row. To be sure. Joseph with his sentiments! ha! ha! ha.

Sir Pet. Yes, yes his sentiments! ha! ha! ha! Hypocritical villain!

Sir Oliv. Ay, and that rogue Charles to pull Sir Peter out of the closet: ha! ha! ha!

Sir Pet. Ha! ha! 'twas devilish entertaining, to be sure!

Sir Oliv. Ha! ha! ha! Egad, Sir Peter, I should like to have seen your face when the screen was thrown down: ha! ha!

Sir Pet. Yes, yes, my face when the screen was thrown down: ha! ha! ha! Oh, I must never show my head again!

Sir Oliv. But come, come, it isn't fair to laugh at you neither, my old friend; though, upon my soul, I can't help it.

Sir Pet. Oh, pray don't restrain your mirth on my account: it does not hurt me at all! I laugh at the whole affair myself. Yes, yes, I think being a standing jest for all one's acquaintance a very happy situation. Oh, yes, and then of a morning to read the paragraphs about Mr. S——, Lady T——, and Sir P——, will be so entertaining!

Row. Without affectation, Sir Peter, you may despise the ridicule of fools. But I see Lady Teazle going towards the next room; I am sure you must desire a reconciliation as earnestly as she does.

Sir Oliv. Perhaps my being here prevents her coming to you. Well, I'll leave honest Rowley to mediate between you; but he must bring you all presently to Mr. Surface's, where I am now returning, if not to reclaim a libertine, at least to expose hypocrisy.

Sir Pet. Ah, I'll be present at your discovering yourself there with all my heart; though 'tis a vile unlucky place for discoveries.

Row. We'll follow.   [*Exit* SIR OLIVER SURFACE.

Sir Pet. She is not coming here, you see, Rowley.

Row. No, but she has left the door of that room open, you perceive. See, she is in tears.

Sir Pet. Certainly a little mortification appears very becoming in a wife. Don't you think it will do her good to let her pine a little?

Row. Oh, this is ungenerous in you!

Sir Pet. Well, I know not what to think. You remember the letter I found of hers evidently intended for Charles?

Row. A mere forgery, Sir Peter! laid in your way on purpose. This is one of the points which I intend Snake shall give you conviction of.

Sir Pet. I wish I were once satisfied of that. She looks this way. What a remarkably elegant turn of the head she has · Rowley, I'll go to her.

Row. Certainly.

Sir Pet. Though, when it is known that we are reconciled, people will laugh at me ten times more.

Row. Let them laugh, and retort their malice only by showing them you are happy in spite of it.

Sir Pet. I' faith, so I will! and, if I'm not mistaken, we may yet be the happiest couple in the country.

Row. Nay, Sir Peter, he who once lays aside suspicion——

Sir Pet. Hold, Master Rowley! if you have any regard for me, never let me hear you utter any thing like a sentiment: I have had enough of them to serve me the rest of my life.

[*Exeunt.*

SCENE III.—*The Library in* JOSEPH SURFACE'S *House.*

Enter JOSEPH SURFACE *and* LADY SNEERWELL.

Lady Sneer. Impossible! Will not Sir Peter immediately be reconciled to Charles, and of course no longer oppose his union with Maria? The thought is distraction to me.

Jos. Surf. Can passion furnish a remedy?

Lady Sneer. No, nor cunning either. Oh, I was a fool, an idiot, to league with such a blunderer!

Jos. Surf. Sure, Lady Sneerwell, I am the greatest sufferer; yet you see I bear the accident with calmness.

Lady Sneer. Because the disappointment doesn't reach your heart; your interest only attached you to Maria. Had you felt for her what I have for that ungrateful libertine, neither your temper nor hypocrisy could prevent your showing the sharpness of your vexation.

Jos. Surf. But why should your reproaches fall on me for this disappointment?

Lady Sneer. Are you not the cause of it? Had you not a sufficient field for your roguery in imposing upon Sir Peter.

and supplanting your brother, but you must endeavour to seduce his wife? I hate such an avarice of crimes; 'tis an unfair monopoly, and never prospers.

Jos. Surf. Well, I admit I have been to blame. I confess I deviated from the direct road of wrong, but I don't think we 're so totally defeated neither.

Lady Sneer. No!

Jos. Surf. You tell me you have made a trial of Snake since we met, and that you still believe him faithful to us?

Lady Sneer. I do believe so.

Jos. Surf. And that he has undertaken, should it be necessary, to swear and prove, that Charles is at this time contracted by vows and honour to your ladyship, which some of his former letters to you will serve to support?

Lady Sneer. This, indeed, might have assisted.

Jos. Surf. Come, come; it is not too late yet.—[*Knocking at the door.*] But hark! this is probably my uncle, Sir Oliver: retire to that room; we 'll consult farther when he is gone.

Lady Sneer. Well, but if he should find you out too?

Jos. Surf. Oh, I have no fear of that. Sir Peter will hold his tongue for his own credit's sake—and you may depend on it I shall soon discover Sir Oliver's weak side!

Lady Sneer. I have no diffidence of your abilities: only be constant to one roguery at a time.

Jos. Surf. I will, I will!—[*Exit* LADY SNEERWELL.] So! 'tis confounded hard, after such bad fortune, to be baited by one's confederate in evil. Well, at all events, my character is so much better than Charles's, that I certainly—hey!—what —this is not Sir Oliver, but old Stanley again. Plague on't that he should return to tease me just now! I shall have Sir Oliver come and find him here—and——

Enter SIR OLIVER SURFACE.

Gad's life, Mr. Stanley, why have you come back to plague me at this time? You must not stay now, upon my word.

Sir Oliv. Sir, I hear your uncle Oliver is expected here, and though he has been so penurious to you, I 'll try what he 'll do for me.

Jos. Surf. Sir, 'tis impossible for you to stay now, so I must beg——Come any other time, and I promise you, you shall be assisted.

Sir Oliv. No: Sir Oliver and I must be acquainted.

Jos. Surf. Zounds, sir! then I insist on your quitting the room directly   .——

Sir Oliv. Nay, sir——

Jos. Surf. Sir, I insist on't!—Here, William! show this gentleman out.   Since you compel me, sir, not one moment —this is such insolence.   [*Going to push him out.*

Enter CHARLES SURFACE.

Chas. Surf. Heyday! what's the matter now?   What the devil, have you got hold of my little broker here?   Zounds, brother, don't hurt little Premium.   What's the matter, my little fellow?

Jos. Surf. So! he has been with you too, has he?

Chas. Surf. To be sure, he has.   Why, he's as honest a little——But sure, Joseph, you have not been borrowing money too, have you?

Jos. Surf. Borrowing! no!   But, brother, you know we expect Sir Oliver here every——

Chas. Surf. O Gad, that's true!   Noll mustn't find the little broker here, to be sure.

Jos. Surf. Yet Mr. Stanley insists——

Chas. Surf. Stanley! why his name's Premium.

Jos. Surf. No, sir, Stanley.

Chas. Surf. No, no, Premium.

Jos. Surf. Well, no matter which—but——

Chas. Surf. Ay, ay, Stanley or Premium, 'tis the same thing, as you say; for I suppose he goes by half a hundred names, besides A. B. at the coffee-house.   [*Knocking.*

Jos. Surf. 'Sdeath! here's Sir Oliver at the door.—Now I beg, Mr. Stanley——

Chas. Surf. Ay, ay, and I beg, Mr. Premium——

Sir Oliv. Gentlemen——

Jos. Surf. Sir, by Heaven you shall go!

Chas. Surf. Ay, out with him, certainly!

Sir Oliv. This violence——

Jos. Surf. Sir, 'tis your own fault.

Chas. Surf. Out with him, to be sure.

[*Both forcing* SIR OLIVER *out*

Enter SIR PETER *and* LADY TEAZLE, MARIA, *and* ROWLEY.

Sir Pet. My old friend, Sir Oliver—hey!   What in the name of wonder—here are dutiful nephews—assault their uncle at first visit!

Lady Teaz. Indeed, Sir Oliver, 'twas well we came in to rescue you.

Row. Truly it was; for I perceive, Sir Oliver, the character of old Stanley was no protection to you.

Sir Oliv. Nor of Premium either : the necessities of the former could not extort a shilling from that benevolent gentletleman ; and with the other I stood a chance of faring worse than my ancestors, and being knocked down without being bid for.

Jos. Surf. Charles !

Chas. Surf. Joseph !

Jos. Surf. 'Tis now complete !

Chas. Surf. Very.

Sir Oliv. Sir Peter, my friend, and Rowley too—look on that elder nephew of mine. You know what he has already received from my bounty; and you also know how gladly I would have regarded half my fortune as held in trust for him: judge then my disappointment in discovering him to be destitute of truth, charity, and gratitude !

Sir Pet. Sir Oliver, I should be more surprised at this declaration, if I had not myself found him to be mean, treacherous, and hypocritical.

Lady Teaz. And if the gentleman pleads not guilty to these, pray let him call me to his character.

Sir Pet. Then, I believe, we need add no more: if he knows himself, he will consider it as the most perfect punishment, that he is known to the world.

Chas. Surf. If they talk this way to Honesty, what will they say to me, by and by ?   [*Aside.*

[SIR PETER, LADY TEAZLE, *and* MARIA *retire.*

Sir Oliv. As for that prodigal, his brother, there——

Chas. Surf. Ay, now comes my turn : the damned family pictures will ruin me !   [*Aside.*

Jos. Surf. Sir Oliver—uncle, will you honour me with a hearing ?

Chas. Surf. Now, if Joseph would make one of his long speeches, I might recollect myself a little.   [*Aside.*

Sir Oliv. I suppose you would undertake to justify yourself ?   [*To* JOSEPH SURFACE.

Jos. Surf. I trust I could.

Sir Oliv. [*To* CHARLES SURFACE.] Well, sir !—and you would justify yourself too, I suppose ?

Chas. Surf. Not that I know of, Sir Oliver.

Sir Oliv. What!—Little Premium has been let too much into the secret, I suppose?

Chas. Surf. True, sir; but they were family secrets, and should not be mentioned again, you know.

Row. Come, Sir Oliver, I know you cannot speak of Charles's follies with anger.

Sir Oliv. Odd's heart, no more I can; nor with gravity either. Sir Peter, do you know the rogue bargained with me for all his ancestors; sold me judges and generals by the foot, and maiden aunts as cheap as broken china.

Chas. Surf. To be sure, Sir Oliver, I did make a little free with the family canvas, that's the truth on't. My ancestors may rise in judgment against me, there's no denying it; but believe me sincere when I tell you—and upon my soul I would not say so if I was not—that if I do not appear mortified at the exposure of my follies, it is because I feel at this moment the warmest satisfaction in seeing you, my liberal benefactor.

Sir Oliv. Charles, I believe you. Give me your hand again: the ill-looking little fellow over the settee has made your peace.

Chas. Surf. Then, sir, my gratitude to the original is still increased.

Lady Teaz. [*Advancing.*] Yet, I believe, Sir Oliver, here is one whom Charles is still more anxious to be reconciled to.

[*Pointing to* Maria.

Sir Oliv. Oh, I have heard of his attachment there; and, with the young lady's pardon, if I construe right—that blush——

Sir Pet. Well, child, speak your sentiments!

Mar. Sir, I have little to say, but that I shall rejoice to hear that he is happy; for me, whatever claim I had to his attention, I willingly resign to one who has a better title.

Chas. Surf. How, Maria!

Sir Pet. Heyday! what's the mystery now? While he appeared an incorrigible rake, you would give your hand to no one else; and now that he is likely to reform I'll warrant you won't have him!

Mar. His own heart and Lady Sneerwell know the cause.

Chas. Surf. Lady Sneerwell!

Jos. Surf. Brother, it is with great concern I am obliged to speak on this point, but my regard to justice compels me, and Lady Sneerwell's injuries can no longer be concealed.

[*Opens the door.*

Enter LADY SNEERWELL.

Sir Pet. So! another French milliner! Egad, he has one in every room in the house, I suppose!

Lady Sneer. Ungrateful Charles! Well may you be surprised, and feel for the indelicate situation your perfidy has forced me into.

Chas. Surf. Pray, uncle, is this another plot of yours? For, as I have life, I don't understand it.

Jos. Surf. I believe, sir, there is but the evidence of one person more necessary to make it extremely clear.

Sir Pet. And that person, I imagine, is Mr. Snake.—Rowley, you were perfectly right to bring him with us, and pray let him appear.

Row. Walk in, Mr. Snake.

Enter SNAKE.

I thought his testimony might be wanted: however, it happens unluckily, that he comes to confront Lady Sneerwell, not to support her.

Lady Sneer. A villain! Treacherous to me at last! Speak, fellow, have you too conspired against me!

Snake. I beg your ladyship ten thousand pardons: you paid me extremely liberally for the lie in question; but I unfortunately have been offered double to speak the truth.

Sir Pet. Plot and counter-plot, egad! I wish your ladyship joy of your negociation.

Lady Sneer. The torments of shame and disappointment on you all!   [*Going.*

Lady Teaz. Hold, Lady Sneerwell—before you go, let me thank you for the trouble you and that gentleman have taken, in writing letters from me to Charles, and answering them yourself; and let me also request you to make my respects to the scandalous college, of which you are president, and inform them, that Lady Teazle, licentiate, begs leave to return the diploma they granted her, as she leaves off practice, and kills characters no longer.

Lady Sneer. You too, madam!—provoking—insolent! May your husband live these fifty years!   [*Exit.*

Sir Pet. Oons! what a fury!

Lady Teaz. A malicious creature, indeed!

Sir Pet. What! not for her last wish?

Lady Teaz. Oh, no!

Sir Oliv. Well, sir, and what have you to say now?

Jos. Surf. Sir, I am so confounded, to find that Lady Sneerwell could be guilty of suborning Mr. Snake in this manner, to impose on us all, that I know not what to say: however, lest her revengeful spirit should prompt her to injure my brother, I had certainly better follow her directly.   For the man who attempts to——   [*Exit.*

Sir Pet. Moral to the last!

Sir Oliv. Ay, and marry her, Joseph, if you can.   Oil and vinegar!—egad you 'll do very well together.

Row. I believe we have no more occasion for Mr. Snake at present?

Snake. Before I go, I beg pardon once for all, for whatever uneasiness I have been the humble instrument of causing to the parties present.

Sir Pet. Well, well, you have made atonement by a good deed at last.

Snake. But I must request of the company, that it shall never be known.

Sir Pet. Hey! what the plague! are you ashamed of having done a right thing once in your life?

Snake. Ah, sir, consider—I live by the badness of my character; and, if it were once known that I had been betrayed into an honest action, I should lose every friend I have in the world.

Sir Oliv. Well, well—we 'll not traduce you by saying any thing in your praise, never fear.   [*Exit* SNAKE.

Sir Pet. There 's a precious rogue!

Lady Teaz. See, Sir Oliver, there needs no persuasion now to reconcile your nephew and Maria.

Sir Oliv. Ay, ay, that 's as it should be, and, egad, we 'll have the wedding to-morrow morning.

Chas. Surf. Thank you, dear uncle.

Sir Pet. What, you rogue! don't you ask the girl's consent first?

Chas. Surf. Oh, I have done that a long time—a minute ago—and she has looked yes.

Mar. For shame, Charles!—I protest, Sir Peter, there has not been a word——

Sir Oliv. Well, then, the fewer the better; may your love for each other never know abatement.

Sir Pet. And may you live as happily together as Lady Teazle and I intend to do!

Chas. Surf. Rowley, my old friend, I am sure you congratulate me; and I suspect that I owe you much.

Sir Oliv. You do, indeed, Charles.

Sir Pet. Ay, honest Rowley always said you would reform.

Chas. Surf. Why, as to reforming, Sir Peter, I 'll make no
promises, and that I take to be a proof that I intend to set
about it. But here shall be my monitor—my gentle guide.—
Ah! can I leave the virtuous path those eyes illumine?

> Though thou, dear maid, shouldst waive thy beauty's sway,
> Thou still must rule, because I will obey:
> An humble fugitive from Folly view,
> No sanctuary near but Love and you :   [*To the audience.*
> You can, indeed, each anxious fear remove,
> For even Scandal dies, if you approve.   [*Exeunt omnes.*

EPILOGUE.

BY MR. COLMAN.

SPOKEN BY LADY TEAZLE.

> I, WHO was late so volatile and gay,
> Like a trade-wind must now blow all one way,
> Bend all my cares, my studies, and my vows,
> To one dull rusty weathercock—my spouse !
> So wills our virtuous bard—the motley Bayes
> Of crying epilogues and laughing plays !
> Old bachelors, who marry smart young wives,
> Learn from our play to regulate your lives :
> Each bring his dear to town, all faults upon her—
> London will prove the very source of honour.
> Plunged fairly in, like a cold bath it serves,
> When principles relax, to brace the nerves :
> Such is my case ; and yet I must deplore
> That the gay dream of dissipation 's o'er.
> And say, ye fair ! was ever lively wife,
> Born with a genius for the highest life,
> Like me untimely blasted in her bloom,
> Like me condemn'd to such a dismal doom ?
> Save money—when I just knew how to waste it !
> Leave London—just as I began to taste it !
> Must I then watch the early crowing cock,
> The melancholy ticking of a clock ;
> In a lone rustic hall for ever pounded,
> With dogs, cats, rats, and squalling brats surrounded

With humble curate can I now retire,
(While good Sir Peter boozes with the squire,)
And at backgammon mortify my soul,
That pants for loo, or flutters at a vole?
Seven 's the main! Dear sound that must expire,
Lost at hot cockles round a Christmas fire;
The transient hour of fashion too soon spent,
Farewell the tranquil mind, farewell content!
Farewell the plumèd head, the cushion'd tête,
That takes the cushion from its proper seat!
That spirit-stirring drum!—card drums I mean,
Spadille—odd trick—pam—basto—king and queen!
And you, ye knockers, that, with brazen throat,
The welcome visitors' approach denote;
Farewell all quality of high renown,
Pride, pomp, and circumstance of glorious town!
Farewell! your revels I partake no more,
And Lady Teazle's occupation 's o'er!
All this I told our bard; he smiled, and said 'twas clear,
I ought to play deep tragedy next year.
Meanwhile he drew wise morals from his play,
And in these solemn periods stalk'd away:—
" Bless'd were the fair like you; her faults who stopp'd,
And closed her follies when the curtain dropp'd!
No more in vice or error to engage,
Or play the fool at large on life's great stage."

THE CRITIC;

OR,

A TRAGEDY REHEARSED.

A DRAMATIC PIECE IN THREE ACTS.

TO MRS. GREVILLE.

MADAM,—In requesting your permission to address the following pages to you, which, as they aim themselves to be critical, require every protection and allowance that approving taste or friendly prejudice can give them, I yet ventured to mention no other motive than the gratification of private friendship and esteem. Had I suggested a hope that your implied approbation would give a sanction to their defects, your particular reserve, and dislike to the reputation of critical taste, as well as of poetical talent, would have made you refuse the protection of your name to such a purpose. However, I am not so ungrateful as now to attempt to combat this disposition in you. I shall not here presume to argue that the present state of poetry claims and expects every assistance that taste and example can afford it; nor endeavour to prove that a fastidious concealment of the most elegant productions of judgment and fancy is an ill return for the possession of those endowments. Continue to deceive yourself in the idea that you are known only to be eminently admired and regarded for the valuable qualities that attach private friendships, and the graceful talents that adorn conversation. Enough of what you have written has stolen into full public notice to answer my purpose; and you will, perhaps, be the only person, conversant in elegant literature, who shall read this address and not perceive that by publishing your particular approbation of the following drama, I have a more interested object than to boast the true respect and regard with which I have the honour to be, Madam, your very sincere and obedient humble servant,

R. B. SHERIDAN.

DRAMATIS PERSONÆ,

AS ORIGINALLY ACTED AT DRURY LANE THEATRE IN 1779.

SIR FRETFUL PLAGIARY	Mr. Parsons.	MR. HOPKINS	{ Mr. Hopkins.
PUFF	Mr. King.		
DANGLE	Mr. Dodd.	MRS. DANGLE	{ Mrs. Hopkins.
SNEER	Mr. Palmer.		
SIGNOR PASTICCIO RITORNELLO	Mr. Delpini.	SIGNORE PASTICCIO RITORNELLO	{ Miss Field and the Miss Abrams.
INTERPRETER	Mr. Baddeley.		
UNDER PROMPTER	Mr. Phillimore.	Scenemen, Musicians, and Servants.	

CHARACTERS OF THE TRAGEDY.

Lord Burleigh . .	Mr. Moody.	Justice	Mr. Packer
Governor of Tilbury Fort . .	Mr. Wrighten.	Son	Mr. Lamash.
		Constable . . .	Mr. Fawcett.
Earl of Leicester	Mr. Farren.	Thames	Mr. Gawdry.
		Tilburina	Miss Pope.
Sir Walter Raleigh	Mr. Burton.	Confidant . . .	Mrs. Bradshaw.
Sir Christopher Hatton . . .	Mr. Waldron.	Justice's Lady .	Mrs. Johnston.
		First Niece . .	Miss Collett.
Master of the Horse. . . .	Mr. Kenny.	Second Niece . .	Miss Kirby.
Don Ferolo Whiskerandos. . .	Mr. Bannister, jun.	Knights, Guards, Constables, Sentinels, Servants, Chorus, Rivers, Attendants, &c., &c.	
Beefeater . . .	Mr. Wright.		

Scene,—London: in Dangle's House during the First Act, and throughout the rest of the Play in Drury Lane Theatre.

PROLOGUE,

BY THE HONOURABLE RICHARD FITZPATRICK.

The sister muses, whom these realms obey,
Who o'er the drama hold divided sway,
Sometimes, by evil counsellers, 'tis said,
Like earth-born potentates have been misled.
In those gay days of wickedness and wit,
When Villiers criticised what Dryden writ,
The tragic queen, to please a tasteless crowd,
Had learn'd to bellow, rant, and roar so loud,
That frighten'd Nature, her best friend before,
The blustering beldam's company forswore;
Her comic sister, who had wit 'tis true,
With all her merits, had her failings too;
And would sometimes in mirthful moments use
A style too flippant for a well-bred muse;
Then female modesty abash'd began
To seek the friendly refuge of the fan,
Awhile behind that slight intrenchment stood,
Till driven from thence, she left the stage for good.
In our more pious, and far chaster times,
These sure no longer are the Muse's crimes!
But some complain that, former faults to shun,
The reformation to extremes has run.
The frantic hero's wild delirium past,
Now insipidity succeeds bombast;
So slow Melpomene's cold numbers creep,
Here dulness seems her drowsy court to keep,
And we are scarce awake, whilst you are fast asleep.

Thalia, once so ill-behaved and rude,
Reform'd, is now become an arrant prude;
Retailing nightly to the yawning pit
The purest morals, undefiled by wit!
Our author offers, in these motley scenes,
A slight remonstrance to the drama's queens:
Nor let the goddesses be over nice;
Free-spoken subjects give the best advice.
Although not quite a novice in his trade,
His cause to-night requires no common aid.
To this, a friendly, just, and powerful court,
I come ambassador to beg support.
Can he undaunted brave the critic's rage?
In civil broils with brother bards engage?
Hold forth their errors to the public eye,
Nay more, e'en newspapers themselves defy?
Say, must his single arm encounter all?
By numbers vanquish'd, e'en the brave may fall;
And though no leader should success distrust,
Whose troops are willing, and whose cause is just;
To bid such hosts of angry foes defiance,
His chief dependence must be, your alliance.

ACT I.

Scene I.—*A Room in* Dangle's *House.*

Mr. *and* Mrs. Dangle *discovered at breakfast, and reading newspapers.*

Dang. [Reading.] *Brutus to Lord North.—Letter the second on the State of the Army*—Psha! *To the first L dash D of the A dash Y.—Genuine extract of a Letter from St. Kitt's.—Coxheath Intelligence.—It is now confidently asserted that Sir Charles Hardy*—Psha! nothing but about the fleet and the nation!—and I hate all politics but theatrical politics.—Where's the Morning Chronicle?

Mrs. Dang. Yes, that's your Gazette

Dang. So, here we have it.—[Reads.] *Theatrical intelligence extraordinary.—We hear there is a new tragedy in rehearsal at Drury Lane Theatre, called the Spanish Armada, said to be written by Mr. Puff, a gentleman well known in the theatrical world. If we may allow ourselves to give credit to the report of the performers, who, truth to say, are in general but indifferent judges, this piece abounds with the most striking and received beauties of modern composition.*—So! I am very glad my friend Puff's tragedy is in such forwardness.—Mrs Dangle, my dear, you will be very glad. to hear that Puff's tragedy——

Mrs. Dang. Lord, Mr. Dangle, why will you plague me about such nonsense?—Now the plays are begun I shall have no peace.—Isn't it sufficient to make yourself ridiculous by your passion for the theatre, without continually teasing me to join you? Why can't you ride your hobby-horse without desiring to place me on a pillion behind you, Mr. Dangle?

Dang. Nay, my dear, I was only going to read——

Mrs. Dang. No, no; you will never read anything that's worth listening to. You hate to hear about your country; there are letters every day with Roman signatures, demonstrating the certainty of an invasion, and proving that the nation is utterly undone. But you never will read any thing to entertain one.

Dang. What has a woman to do with politics, Mrs. Dangle?

Mrs. Dang. And what have you to do with the theatre, Mr. Dangle? Why should you affect the character of a critic? I have no patience with you!—haven't you made yourself the jest of all your acquaintance by your interference in matters where you have no business? Are you not called a theatrical Quidnunc, and a mock Mæcenas to second-hand authors?

Dang. True; my power with the managers is pretty notorious. But is it no credit to have applications from all quarters for my interest—from lords to recommend fiddlers, from ladies to get boxes, from authors to get answers, and from actors to get engagements?

Mrs. Dang. Yes, truly; you have contrived to get a share in all the plague and trouble of theatrical property, without the profit, or even the credit of the abuse that attends it.

Dang. I am sure, Mrs. Dangle, you are no loser by it, however; you have all the advantages of it. Mightn't you, last winter, have had the reading of the new pantomime a fortnight previous to its performance? And doesn't Mr. Fosbrook let you take places for a play before it is advertised, and set you down for a box for every new piece through the season? And didn't my friend, Mr. Smatter, dedicate his last farce to you at my particular request, Mrs. Dangle?

Mrs. Dang. Yes; but wasn't the farce damned, Mr. Dangle? And to be sure it is extremely pleasant to have one's house made the motley rendezvous of all the lackeys of literature;

the very high 'Change of trading authors and jobbing critics?
—Yes, my drawing-room is an absolute register office for candidate actors, and poets without character.—Then to be continually alarmed with misses and ma'ams piping hysteric
changes on Juliets and Dorindas, Pollys, and Ophelias; and
the very furniture trembling at the probationary starts and
unprovoked rants of would-be Richards and Hamlets!—And
what is worse than all, now that the manager has monopolized
the Opera House, haven't we the signors and signoras calling
here, sliding their smooth semibreves, and gargling glib divisions in their outlandish throats—with foreign emissaries and
French spies, for aught I know, disguised like fiddlers and
figure-dancers?

Dang. Mercy! Mrs. Dangle!

Mrs. Dang. And to employ yourself so idly at such an
alarming crisis as this too—when, if you had the least spirit,
you would have been at the head of one of the Westminster
associations—or trailing a volunteer pike in the Artillery
Ground! But you—o' my conscience, I believe, if the French
were landed to-morrow, your first inquiry would be, whether
they had brought a theatrical troop with them.

Dang. Mrs. Dangle, it does not signify—I say the stage is
the Mirror of Nature, and the actors are *the Abstract and brief
Chronicles of the Time:* and pray what can a man of sense
study better?—Besides, you will not easily persuade me that
there is no credit or importance in being at the head of a band
of critics, who take upon them to decide for the whole town,
whose opinion and patronage all writers solicit, and whose recommendation no manager dares refuse.

Mrs. Dang. Ridiculous!—Both managers and authors of
the least merit laugh at your pretensions.—The public is their
critic—without whose fair approbation they know no play can
rest on the stage, and with whose applause they welcome such
attacks as yours, and laugh at the malice of them, where they
can't at the wit.

Dang. Very well, madam—very well!

Enter SERVANT.

Ser. Mr. Sneer, sir, to wait on you.

Dang. Oh, show Mr. Sneer up.—[*Exit* SERVANT.] Plague
on't, now we must appear loving and affectionate, or Sneer
will hitch us into a story.

Mrs. Dang. With all my heart; you can't be more ridiculous than you are.

Dang. You are enough to provoke——

Enter SNEER.

Ha! my dear Sneer, I am vastly glad to see you.—My dear, here 's Mr. Sneer.

Mrs. Dang. Good morning to you, sir.

Dang. Mrs. Dangle and I have been diverting ourselves with the papers. Pray, Sneer, won't you go to Drury Lane Theatre the first night of Puff's tragedy?

Sneer. Yes; but I suppose one shan't be able to get in, for on the first night of a new piece they always fill the house with orders to support it. But here, Dangle, I have brought you two pieces, one of which you must exert yourself to make the managers accept. I can tell you that; for 'tis written by a person of consequence.

Dang. So! now my plagues are beginning.

Sneer. Ay, I am glad of it, for now you 'll be happy. Why, my dear Dangle, it is a pleasure to see how you enjoy your volunteer fatigue, and your solicited solicitations.

Dang. It 's a great trouble—yet, egad, it 's pleasant too.— Why, sometimes of a morning I have a dozen people call on me at breakfast-time, whose faces I never saw before, nor ever desire to see again.

Sneer. That must be very pleasant indeed!

Dang. And not a week but I receive fifty letters, and not a line in them about any business of my own.

Sneer. An amusing correspondence!

Dang. [Reading.] *Bursts into tears, and exit.*—What, is this tragedy?

Sneer. No, that 's a genteel comedy, not a translation—only taken from the French: it is written in a style which they have lately tried to run down; the true sentimental, and nothing ridiculous in it from the beginning to the end.

Mrs. Dang. Well, if they had kept to that, I should not have been such an enemy to the stage; there was some edification to be got from those pieces, Mr. Sneer!

Sneer. I am quite of your opinion, Mrs. Dangle: the theatre, in proper hands, might certainly be made the school of morality; but now, I am sorry to say it, people seem to go there principally for their entertainment!

Mrs. Dang. It would have been more to the credit of the managers to have kept it in the other line.

Sneer. Undoubtedly, madam ; and hereafter perhaps to have had it recorded, that in the midst of a luxurious and dissipated age, they preserved two houses in the capital, where the conversation was always moral at least, if not entertaining!

Dang. Now, egad, I think the worst alteration is in the nicety of the audience!—No *double-entendre*, no smart innuendo admitted ; even Vanbrugh and Congreve obliged to undergo a bungling reformation!

Sneer. Yes, and our prudery in this respect is just on a par with the artificial bashfulness of a courtesan, who increases the blush upon her cheek in an exact proportion to the diminution of her modesty.

Dang. Sneer can't even give the public a good word! But what have we here?—This seems a very odd——

Sneer. Oh, that's a comedy, on a very new plan ; replete with wit and mirth, yet of a most serious moral! You see it is called *The Reformed House-breaker ;* where, by the mere force of humour, house-breaking is put into so ridiculous a light, that if the piece has its proper run, I have no doubt but that bolts and bars will be entirely useless by the end of the season.

Dang. Egad, this is new indeed!

Sneer. Yes ; it is written by a particular friend of mine, who has discovered that the follies and foibles of society are subjects unworthy the notice of the comic muse, who should be taught to stoop only at the greater vices and blacker crimes of humanity—gibbeting capital offences in five acts, and pillorying petty larcenies in two.—In short, his idea is to dramatise the penal laws, and make the stage a court of ease to the Old Bailey.

Dang. It is truly moral.

Re-enter SERVANT.

Ser. Sir Fretful Plagiary, sir.

Dang. Beg him to walk up.—[*Exit* SERVANT.] Now, Mrs. Dangle, Sir Fretful Plagiary is an author to your own taste.

Mrs. Dang. I confess he is a favourite of mine, because everybody else abuses him.

Sneer. Very much to the credit of your charity, madam, if not of your judgment

Dang. But, egad, he allows no merit to any author but himself, that's the truth on't—though he's my friend.

Sneer. Never.—He is as envious as an old maid verging on the desperation of six-and-thirty; and then the insidious humility with which he seduces you to give a free opinion on any of his works, can be exceeded only by the petulant arrogance with which he is sure to reject your observations.

Dang. Very true, egad—though he's my friend.

Sneer. Then his affected contempt of all newspaper strictures; though, at the same time, he is the sorest man alive, and shrinks like scorched parchment from the fiery ordeal of true criticism : yet is he so covetous of popularity, that he had rather be abused than not mentioned at all.

Dang. There's no denying it—though he is my friend.

Sneer. You have read the tragedy he has just finished, haven't you?

Dang. O yes ; he sent it to me yesterday.

Sneer. Well, and you think it execrable, don't you?

Dang. Why, between ourselves, egad, I must own—though he is my friend—that it is one of the most——He's here—[*Aside*]—finished and most admirable perform——

Sir Fret. [*Without.*] Mr. Sneer with him, did you say?

Enter SIR FRETFUL PLAGIARY.

Dang. Ah, my dear friend!—Egad, we were just speaking of your tragedy.—Admirable, Sir Fretful, admirable!

Sneer. You never did any thing beyond it, Sir Fretful—never in your life.

Sir Fret. You make me extremely happy ; for without a compliment, my dear Sneer, there isn't a man in the world whose judgment I value as I do yours and Mr. Dangle's.

Mrs. Dang. They are only laughing at you, Sir Fretful ; for it was but just now that——

Dang. Mrs. Dangle !—Ah, Sir Fretful, you know Mrs. Dangle.—My friend Sneer was rallying just now :—he knows how she admires you, and——

Sir Fret. O Lord, I am sure Mr. Sneer has more taste and sincerity than to——[*Aside*] A damned double-faced fellow!

Dang. Yes, yes—Sneer will jest—but a better humoured——

Sir Fret. Oh, I know——

Dang. He has a ready turn for ridicule—his wit costs him nothing.

Sir Fret. No, egad—or I should wonder how he came by it.   [*Aside.*

Mrs. Dang. Because his jest is always at the expense of his friend.   [*Aside.*

Dang. But, Sir Fretful, have you sent your play to the managers yet?—or can I be of any service to you?

Sir Fret. No, no, I thank you: I believe the piece had sufficient recommendation with it.—I thank you though.—I sent it to the manager of Covent Garden Theatre this morning.

Sneer. I should have thought now, that it might have been cast (as the actors call it) better at Drury Lane.

Sir Fret. O lud! no—never send a play there while I live—hark'ee!   [*Whispers* SNEER.

Sneer. Writes himself!—I know he does.

Sir Fret. I say nothing—I take away from no man's merit—am hurt at no man's good fortune—I say nothing.—But this I will say—through all my knowledge of life, I have observed—that there is not a passion so strongly rooted in the human heart as envy.

Sneer. I believe you have reason for what you say, indeed.

Sir Fret. Besides—I can tell you it is not always so safe to leave a play in the hands of those who write themselves.

Sneer. What, they may steal from them, hey, my dear Plagiary?

Sir Fret. Steal!—to be sure they may; and, egad, serve your best thoughts as gypsies do stolen children, disfigure them to make 'em pass for their own.

Sneer. But your present work is a sacrifice to Melpomene, and he, you know, never——

Sir Fret. That's no security: a dexterous plagiarist may do any thing. Why, sir, for aught I know, he might take out some of the best things in my tragedy, and put them into his own comedy.

Sneer. That might be done, I dare be sworn.

Sir Fret. And then, if such a person gives you the least hint or assistance, he is devilish apt to take the merit of the whole——

Dang. If it succeeds.

Sir Fret. Ay, but with regard to this piece, I think I can hit that gentleman, for I can safely swear he never read it.

Sneer. I'll tell you how you may hurt him more.

Sir Fret. How?

Sneer. Swear he wrote it.

Sir Fret. Plague on't now, Sneer, I shall take it ill!—I believe you want to take away my character as an author.

Sneer. Then I am sure you ought to be very much obliged to me.

Sir Fret. Hey!—sir!——

Dang. Oh, you know, he never means what he says.

Sir Fret. Sincerely then—you do like the piece?

Sneer. Wonderfully!

Sir Fret. But come now, there must be something that you think might be mended, hey?—Mr. Dangle, has nothing struck you?

Dang. Why, faith, it is but an ungracious thing, for the most part, to——

Sir Fret. With most authors it is just so indeed; they are in general strangely tenacious! But, for my part, I am never so well pleased as when a judicious critic points out any defect to me; for what is the purpose of showing a work to a friend, if you don't mean to profit by his opinion?

Sneer. Very true.—Why then, though I seriously admire the piece upon the whole, yet there is one small objection; which, if you'll give me leave, I'll mention.

Sir Fret. Sir, you can't oblige me more.

Sneer. I think it wants incident.

Sir Fret. Good God! you surprise me!—wants incident!

Sneer. Yes; I own I think the incidents are too few.

Sir Fret. Good God! Believe me, Mr. Sneer, there is no person for whose judgment I have a more implicit deference. But I protest to you, Mr. Sneer, I am only apprehensive that the incidents are too crowded.—My dear Dangle, how does it strike you?

Dang. Really I can't agree with my friend Sneer. I think the plot quite sufficient; and the four first acts by many degrees the best I ever read or saw in my life. If I might venture to suggest any thing, it is that the interest rather falls off in the fifth.

Sir Fret. Rises, I believe you mean, sir

Dang. No, I don't, upon my word.

Sir Fret. Yes, yes, you do, upon my soul!—it certainly don't fall off, I assure you.—No, no; it don't fall off.

Dang. Now, Mrs. Dangle, didn't you say it struck you in the same light?

Mrs. Dang. No, indeed, I did not—I did not see a fault in any part of the play, from the beginning to the end.

Sir Fret. Upon my soul, the women are the best judges after all !

Mrs. Dang. Or, if I made any objection, I am sure it was to nothing in the piece ; but that I was afraid it was, on the whole, a little too long.

Sir Fret. Pray, madam, do you speak as to duration of time ; or do you mean that the story is tediously spun out ?

Mrs. Dang. O lud ! no.—I speak only with reference to the usual length of acting plays.

Sir Fret. Then I am very happy—very happy indeed—because the play is a short play, a remarkably short play. I should not venture to differ with a lady on a point of taste ; but, on these occasions, the watch, you know, is the critic.

Mrs. Dang. Then, I suppose, it must have been Mr. Dangle's drawling manner of reading it to me.

Sir Fret. Oh, if Mr. Dangle read it, that's quite another affair !—But I assure you, Mrs. Dangle, the first evening you can spare me three hours and a half, I 'll undertake to read you the whole from beginning to end, with the prologue and epilogue, and allow time for the music between the acts.

Mrs. Dang. I hope to see it on the stage next.

Dang. Well, Sir Fretful, I wish you may be able to get rid as easily of the newspaper criticisms as you do of ours.

Sir Fret. The newspapers ! Sir, they are the most villanous — licentious — abominable — infernal — Not that I ever read them—no—I make it a rule never to look into a newspaper.

Dang. You are quite right ; for it certainly must hurt an author of delicate feelings to see the liberties they take.

Sir Fret. No, quite the contrary ! their abuse is, in fact, the best panegyric—I like it of all things. An author's reputation is only in danger from their support.

Sneer. Why that's true—and that attack, now, on you the other day——

Sir Fret. What ? where ?

Dang. Ay, you mean in a paper of Thursday : it was completely ill-natured, to be sure.

Sir Fret. Oh, so much the better.—Ha ! ha ! ha ! I wouldn't have it otherwise.

Dang. Certainly it is only to be laughed at ; for——

Sir Fret. You don't happen to recollect what the fellow said, do you?

Sneer. Pray, Dangle—Sir Fretful seems a little anxious——

Sir Fret. O lud, no!—anxious!—not I,—not the least.—I—but one may as well hear, you know.

Dang. Sneer, do you recollect?—[*Aside to* SNEER.] Make out something.

Sneer. [*Aside to* DANGLE.] I will.—[*Aloud.*] Yes, yes, I remember perfectly.

Sir Fret. Well, and pray now—not that it signifies—what might the gentleman say?

Sneer. Why, he roundly asserts that you have not the slightest invention or original genius whatever; though you are the greatest traducer of all other authors living.

Sir Fret. Ha! ha! ha!—very good!

Sneer. That as to comedy, you have not one idea of your own, he believes, even in your common-place-book—where stray jokes and pilfered witticisms are kept with as much method as the ledger of the lost and stolen office.

Sir Fret. Ha! ha! ha!—very pleasant!

Sneer. Nay, that you are so unlucky as not to have the skill even to steal with taste:—but that you glean from the refuse of obscure volumes, where more judicious plagiarists have been before you; so that the body of your work is a composition of dregs and sediments—like a bad tavern's worst wine.

Sir Fret. Ha! ha!

Sneer. In your more serious efforts, he says, your bombast would be less intolerable, if the thoughts were ever suited to the expression; but the homeliness of the sentiment stares through the fantastic encumbrance of its fine language, like a clown in one of the new uniforms!

Sir Fret. Ha! ha!

Sneer. That your occasional tropes and flowers suit the general coarseness of your style, as tambour sprigs would a ground of linsey-woolsey; while your imitations of Shakspeare resemble the mimicry of Falstaff's page, and are about as near the standard of the original.

Sir Fret. Ha!

Sneer. In short, that even the finest passages you steal are of no service to you; for the poverty of your own language prevents their assimilating; so that they lie on the surface like lumps of marl on a barren moor, encumbering what it is not in their power to fertilise!

Sir Fret. [*After great agitation.*] Now, another person would be vexed at this.

Sneer. Oh! but I wouldn't have told you—only to divert you.

Sir Fret. I know it—I am diverted.—Ha! ha! ha!—not the least invention!—Ha! ha! ha!—very good!—very good!

Sneer. Yes—no genius! ha! ha! ha!

Dang. A severe rogue! ha! ha! ha! But you are quite right, Sir Fretful, never to read such nonsense.

Sir Fret. To be sure—for if there is any thing to one's praise, it is a foolish vanity to be gratified at it; and, if it is abuse,—why one is always sure to hear of it from one damned good-natured friend or another!

Enter SERVANT

Ser. Sir, there is an Italian gentleman, with a French interpreter, and three young ladies, and a dozen musicians, who say they are sent by Lady Rondeau and Mrs. Fugue.

Dang. Gadso! they come by appointment!—Dear Mrs. Dangle, do let them know I'll see them directly.

Mrs. Dang. You know, Mr. Dangle, I shan't understand a word they say.

Dang. But you hear there's an interpreter.

Mrs. Dang. Well, I'll try to endure their complaisance till you come.   [*Exit.*

Ser. And Mr. Puff, sir, has sent word that the last rehearsal is to be this morning, and that he'll call on you presently.

Dang. That's true—I shall certainly be at home.—[*Exit* SERVANT.] Now, Sir Fretful, if you have a mind to have justice done you in the way of answer, egad, Mr. Puff's your man.

Sir Fret. Psha! Sir, why should I wish to have it answered, when I tell you I am pleased at it?

Dang. True, I had forgot that. But I hope you are not fretted at what Mr. Sneer——

Sir Fret. Zounds! no, Mr. Dangle; don't I tell you these things never fret me in the least?

Dang. Nay, I only thought——

Sir Fret. And let me tell you, Mr. Dangle, 'tis damned affronting in you to suppose that I am hurt when I tell you I am not.

Sneer. But why so warm, Sir Fretful?

Sir Fret. Gad's life! Mr. Sneer, you are as absurd as Dangle: how often must I repeat it to you, that nothing can vex me but your supposing it possible for me to mind the damned nonsense you have been repeating to me!—and, let me tell you, if you continue to believe this, you must mean to insult me, gentlemen—and, then, your disrespect will affect me no more than the newspaper criticisms—and I shall treat it with exactly the same calm indifference and philosophic contempt—and so your servant. [*Exit.*

Sneer. Ha! ha! ha! poor Sir Fretful! Now will he go and vent his philosophy in anonymous abuse of all modern critics and authors.—But, Dangle, you must get your friend Puff to take me to the rehearsal of his tragedy.

Dang. I'll answer for 't, he'll thank you for desiring it. But come and help me to judge of this musical family: they are recommended by people of consequence, I assure you.

Sneer. I am at your disposal the whole morning;—but I thought you had been a decided critic in music as well as in literature.

Dang. So I am—but I have a bad ear. I' faith, Sneer, though, I am afraid we were a little too severe on Sir Fretful —though he is my friend.

Sneer. Why, 'tis certain, that unnecessarily to mortify the vanity of any writer is a cruelty which mere dulness never can deserve; but where a base and personal malignity usurps the place of literary emulation, the aggressor deserves neither quarter nor pity.

Dang. That's true, egad!—though he 's my friend!

SCENE II.—*A Drawing-room in* DANGLE'S *House.*

MRS. DANGLE, SIGNOR PASTICCIO RITORNELLO, SIGNORE PAS-TICCIO RITORNELLO, INTERPRETER, *and* MUSICIANS, *discovered.*

Interp. Je dis, madame, j'ai l'honneur to introduce et de vous demander votre protection pour le signor Pasticcio Ritornello et pour sa charmante famille.

Signor Past. Ah! vosignoria, noi vi preghiamo di favoritevi colla vostra protezione.

1 *Signora Past.* Vosignoria fatevi questi grazie

2 *Signora Past.* Sì, signora.

Interp. Madame—me interpret.—C'est à dire—in English —qu'ils vous prient de leur faire l'honneur——

Mrs. Dang. I say again, gentleman, I don't understand a word you say.

Signor Past. Questo signore spiegherò——

Interp. Oui—me interpret.—Nous avons les lettres de recommendation pour monsieur Dangle de——

Mrs. Dang. Upon my word, sir, I don't understand you.

Signor Past. La contessa Rondeau è nostra padrona.

3 Signora Past. Si, padre, et miladi Fugue.

Interp. O!—me interpret.—Madame, ils disent—in English—Qu'ils ont l'honneur d'être protégés de ces dames.—You understand?

Mrs. Dang. No, sir,—no understand!

Enter DANGLE *and* SNEER.

Interp. Ah, voici monsieur Dangle!

All Italians. Ah! signor Dangle!

Mrs. Dang. Mr. Dangle, here are two very civil gentlemen trying to make themselves understood, and I don't know which is the interpreter.

Dang. Eh, bien!

[*The* INTERPRETER *and* SIGNOR PASTICCIO *here speak at the same time.*

Interp. Monsieur Dangle, le grand bruit de vos talens pour la critique, et de votre intérêt avec messieurs les directeurs à tous les théâtres——

Signor Past. Vosignoria siete si famoso par la vostra conoscenza, e vostra interessa colla le direttore da——

Dang. Egad, I think the interpreter is the hardest to be understood of the two!

Sneer. Why, I thought, Dangle, you had been an admirable linguist!

Dang. So I am, if they would not talk so damned fast.

Sneer. Well, I'll explain that—the less time we lose in hearing them the better—for that, I suppose, is what they are brought here for.

[*Speaks to* SIGNOR PASTICCIO—*they sing trios, &c.,* DANGLE *beating out of time.*

Enter SERVANT *and whispers* DANGLE.

Dang. Show him up.—[*Exit* SERVANT.] Bravo! admirable!

bravissimo! admirablissimo!—Ah! Sneer! where will you find voices such as these in England?

Sneer. Not easily.

Dang. But Puff is coming.—Signor and little signoras obligatissimo!—Sposa signora Danglena—Mrs. Dangle, shall I beg you to offer them some refreshments, and take their address in the next room.

[*Exit* MRS. DANGLE *with* SIGNOR PASTICCIO, SIGNORE PASTICCIO, MUSICIANS, *and* INTERPRETER, *ceremoniously.*

Re-enter SERVANT.

Ser. Mr. Puff, sir.　　　　　　　　　　　　　[*Exit.*

Enter PUFF.

Dang. My dear Puff!

Puff. My dear Dangle, how is it with you?

Dang. Mr. Sneer, give me leave to introduce Mr. Puff to you.

Puff. Mr. Sneer is this?—Sir, he is a gentleman whom I have long panted for the honour of knowing—a gentleman whose critical talents and transcendent judgment——

Sneer. Dear Sir——

Dang. Nay, don't be modest, Sneer; my friend Puff only talks to you in the style of his profession.

Sneer. His profession!

Puff. Yes, sir; I make no secret of the trade I follow: among friends and brother authors, Dangle knows I love to be frank on the subject, and to advertise myself *vivâ voce.*—I am, sir, a practitioner in panegyric, or, to speak more plainly, a professor of the art of puffing, at your service—or anybody else's.

Sneer. Sir, you are very obliging!—I believe, Mr. Puff, I have often admired your talents in the daily prints.

Puff. Yes, sir, I flatter myself I do as much business in that way as any six of the fraternity in town.—Devilish hard work all the summer, friend Dangle,—never worked harder! But, hark'ee,—the winter managers were a little sore, I believe.

Dang. No; I believe they took it all in good part.

Puff. Ay! then that must have been affectation in them; for, egad, there were some of the attacks which there was no laughing at!

Sneer. Ay, the humorous ones.—But I should think Mr.

Puff, that authors would in general be able to do this sort of work for themselves.

Puff. Why, yes—but in a clumsy way. Besides, we look on that as an encroachment, and so take the opposite side. I dare say, now, you conceive half the very civil paragraphs and advertisements you see to be written by the parties concerned, or their friends? No such thing: nine out of ten manufactured by me in the way of business.

Sneer. Indeed!

Puff. Even the auctioneers now—the auctioneers, I say—though the rogues have lately got some credit for their language—not an article of the merit theirs: take them out of their pulpits, and they are as dull as catalogues!—No, sir; 'twas I first enriched their style—'twas I first taught them to crowd their advertisements with panegyrical superlatives, each epithet rising above the other, like the bidders in their own auction-rooms! From me they learned to inlay their phraseology with variegated chips of exotic metaphor: by me too their inventive faculties were called forth:—yes, sir, by me they were instructed to clothe ideal walls with gratuitous fruits —to insinuate obsequious rivulets into visionary groves—to teach courteous shrubs to nod their approbation of the grateful soil; or on emergencies to raise upstart oaks, where there never had been an acorn; to create a delightful vicinage without the assistance of a neighbour; or fix the temple of Hygeia in the fens of Lincolnshire!

Dang. I am sure you have done them infinite service; for now, when a gentleman is ruined, he parts with his house with some credit.

Sneer. Service! if they had any gratitude, they would erect a statue to him; they would figure him as a presiding Mercury, the god of traffic and fiction, with a hammer in his hand instead of a caduceus.—But pray, Mr. Puff, what first put you on exercising your talents in this way?

Puff. Egad, sir, sheer necessity!—the proper parent of an art so nearly allied to invention. You must know, Mr. Sneer, that from the first time I tried my hand at an advertisement, my success was such, that for some time after I led a most extraordinary life indeed!

Sneer. How, pray.

Puff. Sir, I supported myself two years entirely by my misfortunes

Sneer. By your misfortunes!

Puff. Yes, sir, assisted by long sickness, and other occasional disorders; and a very comfortable living I had of it.

Sneer. From sickness and misfortunes! You practised as a doctor and an attorney at once?

Puff. No, egad; both maladies and miseries were my own.

Sneer. Hey! what the plague!

Dang. 'Tis true, i'faith.

Puff. Hark'ee!—By advertisements—*To the charitable and humane!* and *To those whom Providence hath blessed with affluence!*

Sneer. Oh, I understand you.

Puff. And, in truth, I deserved what I got; for I suppose never man went through such a series of calamities in the same space of time. Sir, I was five times made a bankrupt, and reduced from a state of affluence, by a train of unavoidable misfortunes: then, sir, though a very industrious tradesman, I was twice burned out, and lost my little all both times: I lived upon those fires a month. I soon after was confined by a most excruciating disorder, and lost the use of my limbs: that told very well; for I had the case strongly attested, and went about to collect the subscriptions myself.

Dang. Egad, I believe that was when you first called on me.

Puff. In November last?—O no; I was at that time a close prisoner in the Marshalsea, for a debt benevolently contracted to serve a friend. I was afterwards twice tapped for a dropsy, which declined into a very profitable consumption. I was then reduced to—O no—then, I became a widow with six helpless children, after having had eleven husbands pressed, and being left every time eight months gone with child, and without money to get me into an hospital!

Sneer. And you bore all with patience, I make no doubt?

Puff. Why, yes; though I made some occasional attempts at *felo de se;* but as I did not find those rash actions answer, I left off killing myself very soon. Well, sir, at last, what with bankruptcies, fires, gouts, dropsies, imprisonments, and other valuable calamities, having got together a pretty handsome sum, I determined to quit a business which had always gone rather against my conscience, and in a more liberal way still to indulge my talents for fiction and embellishment.

through my favourite channels of diurnal communication—and so, sir, you have my history.

Sneer. Most obligingly communicative indeed! and your confession, if published, might certainly serve the cause of true charity, by rescuing the most useful channels of appeal to benevolence from the cant of imposition. But surely, Mr. Puff, there is no great mystery in your present profession?

Puff. Mystery, sir! I will take upon me to say the matter was never scientifically treated nor reduced to rule before.

Sneer. Reduced to rule!

Puff. O lud, sir, you are very ignorant, I am afraid!—Yes, sir, puffing is of various sorts; the principal are, the puff direct, the puff preliminary, the puff collateral, the puff collusive, and the puff oblique, or puff by implication. These all assume, as circumstances require, the various forms of Letter to the Editor, Occasional Anecdote, Impartial Critique, Observation from Correspondent, or Advertisement from the Party.

Sneer. The puff direct, I can conceive——

Puff. O yes, that's simple enough! For instance,—a new comedy or farce is to be produced at one of the theatres (though by-the-by they don't bring out half what they ought to do)—the author, suppose Mr. Smatter, or Mr. Dapper, or any particular friend of mine—very well; the day before it is to be performed, I write an account of the manner in which it was received; I have the plot from the author, and only add —" characters strongly drawn—highly coloured—hand of a master—fund of genuine humour—mine of invention—neat dialogue—Attic salt." Then for the performance—" Mr. Dodd was astonishingly great in the character of Sir Harry. That universal and judicious actor, Mr. Palmer, perhaps never appeared to more advantage than in the colonel;—but it is not in the power of language to do justice to Mr. King: indeed he more than merited those repeated bursts of applause which he drew from a most brilliant and judicious audience. As to the scenery—the miraculous powers of Mr. De Loutherbourg's pencil are universally acknowledged. In short, we are at a loss which to admire most, the unrivalled genius of the author, the great attention and liberality of the managers, the wonderful abilities of the painter, or the incredible exertions of all the performers."

Sneer. That's pretty well indeed, sir.

Puff. Oh, cool!—quite cool!—to what I sometimes do.

Sneer. And do you think there are any who are influenced by this?

Puff. O lud, yes, sir! the number of those who undergo the fatigue of judging for themselves is very small indeed.

Sneer. Well, sir, the puff preliminary?

Puff. O, that, sir, does well in the form of a caution. In a matter of gallantry now—Sir Flimsy Gossamer wishes to be well with Lady Fanny Fete—he applies to me—I open trenches for him with a paragraph in the Morning Post.— " It is recommended to the beautiful and accomplished Lady F four stars F dash E to be on her guard against that dangerous character, Sir F dash G; who, however pleasing and insinuating his manners may be, is certainly not remarkable for the *constancy of his attachments!*"—in italics. Here, you see, Sir Flimsy Gossamer is introduced to the particular notice of Lady Fanny, who perhaps never thought of him before—she finds herself publicly cautioned to avoid him, which naturally makes her desirous of seeing him; the observation of their acquaintance causes a pretty kind of mutual embarrassment; this produces a sort of sympathy of interest, which if Sir Flimsy is unable to improve effectually, he at least gains the credit of having their names mentioned together, by a particular set, and in a particular way—which nine times out of ten is the full accomplishment of modern gallantry.

Dang. Egad, Sneer, you will be quite an adept in the business!

Puff. Now, sir, the puff collateral is much used as an appendage to advertisements, and may take the form of anecdote.—" Yesterday, as the celebrated George Bonmot was sauntering down St. James's Street, he met the lively Lady Mary Myrtle coming out of the park:—' Good God, Lady Mary, I'm surprised to meet you in a white jacket,—for I expected never to have seen you, but in a full-trimmed uniform and a light horseman's cap!'—' Heavens, George, where could you have learned that?'—' Why,' replied the wit, ' I just saw a print of you, in a new publication called the Camp Magazine; which, by the by, is a devilish clever thing, and is sold at No. 3, on the right hand of the way, two doors from the printing-office, the corner of Ivy Lane, Paternoster Row, price only one shilling.'"

Sneer. Very ingenious indeed!

Puff. But the puff collusive is the newest of any; for it
acts in the disguise of determined hostility. It is much used
by bold booksellers and enterprising poets.—" An indignant
correspondent observes, that the new poem called *Beelzebub's
Cotillon,* or *Proserpine's Fête Champêtre,* is one of the most
unjustifiable performances he ever read. The severity with
which certain characters are handled is quite shocking ; and
as there are many descriptions in it too warmly coloured for
female delicacy, the shameful avidity with which this piece is
bought by all people of fashion is a reproach on the taste of
the times, and a disgrace to the delicacy of the age." Here
you see the two strongest inducements are held forth;
first, that nobody ought to read it; and secondly, that everybody buys it: on the strength of which the publisher boldly
prints the tenth edition, before he had sold ten of the first;
and then establishes it by threatening himself with the pillory,
or absolutely indicting himself for *scan. mag.*

Dang. Ha! ha! ha;—'gad, I know it is so.

Puff. As to the puff oblique, or puff by implication, it is
too various and extensive to be illustrated by an instance : it
attracts in titles and presumes in patents ; it lurks in the li-
mitation of a subscription, and invites in the assurance of
crowd and incommodation at public places ; it delights to draw
forth concealed merit, with a most disinterested assiduity ;
and sometimes wears a countenance of smiling censure and
tender reproach. It has a wonderful memory for parliamentary debates, and will often give the whole speech of a favoured
member with the most flattering accuracy. But, above all, it
is a great dealer in reports and suppositions. It has the
earliest intelligence of intended preferments that will reflect
honour on the patrons ; and embryo promotions of modest gentlemen, who know nothing of the matter themselves. It can
hint a ribbon for implied services in the air of a common report ; and with the carelessness of a casual paragraph, suggest officers into commands, to which they have no pretension
but their wishes. This, sir, is the last principal class of the
art of puffing—an art which I hope you will now agree with
me is of the highest dignity, yielding a tablature of benevolence and public spirit ; befriending equally trade, gallantry,
criticism, and politics : the applause of genius—the register
of charity—the triumph of heroism—the self-defence of con-
tractors—the fame of orators—and the gazette of ministers.

Sneer. Sir, I am completely a convert both to the importance and ingenuity of your profession; and now, sir, there is
but one thing which can possibly increase my respect for you,
and that is, your permitting me to be present this morning at
the rehearsal of your new trage——

Puff. Hush, for heaven's sake!—*My* tragedy!—Egad,
Dangle, I take this very ill: you know how apprehensive I
am of being known to be the author.

Dang. I' faith I would not have told—but it 's in the papers,
and your name at length in the Morning Chronicle.

Puff. Ah! those damned editors never can keep a secret!
—Well, Mr. Sneer, no doubt you will do me great honour—
I shall be infinitely happy—highly flattered——

Dang. I believe it must be near the time—shall we go together?

Puff. No; it will not be yet this hour, for they are always
late at that theatre: besides, I must meet you there, for I
have some little matters here to send to the papers, and a few
paragraphs to scribble before I go.—[*Looking at memorandums.*] Here is *A conscientious Baker, on the subject of the
Army Bread;* and *A Detester of visible Brickwork, in favour
of the new-invented Stucco;* both in the style of Junius, and
promised for to-morrow. The Thames navigation too is at
a stand. Misomud or Anti-shoal must go to work again directly.—Here too are some political memorandums—I see;
ay—*To take Paul Jones, and get the Indiamen out of the
Shannon—reinforce Byron—compel the Dutch to—so!—I*
must do that in the evening papers, or reserve it for the
Morning Herald; for I know that I have undertaken to mor-
row, besides, to establish the unanimity of the fleet in the Public Advertiser, and to shoot Charles Fox in the Morning
Post.—So, egad, I ha'n't a moment to lose!

Dang. Well, we 'll meet in the Green Room.

[*Exeunt severally.*

ACT II.

SCENE I.—*The Theatre, before the Curtain.*

Enter DANGLE, PUFF, *and* SNEER.

Puff. No, no, sir; what Shakspeare says of actors may be
better applied to the purpose of plays; they ought to be the

abstract and brief chronicles of the time. Therefore when history, and particularly the history of our own country, furnishes any thing like a case in point, to the time in which an author writes, if he knows his own interest, he will take advantage of it; so, sir, I call my tragedy *The Spanish Armada;* and have laid the scene before Tilbury Fort

Sneer. A most happy thought, certainly!

Dang. Egad it was—I told you so. But pray now, I don't understand how you have contrived to introduce any love into it.

Puff. Love! oh, nothing so easy! for it is a received point among poets, that where history gives you a good heroic outline for a play, you may fill up with a little love at your own discretion: in doing which, nine times out of ten, you only make up a deficiency in the private history of the times. Now I rather think I have done this with some success.

Sneer. No scandal about Queen Elizabeth, I hope?

Puff. O lud! no, no;—I only suppose the governor of Tilbury Fort's daughter to be in love with the son of the Spanish admiral.

Sneer. Oh, is that all!

Dang. Excellent, i' faith! I see at once. But won't this appear rather improbable?

Puff. To be sure it will—but what the plague! a play is not to show occurrences that happen every day, but things just so strange, that though they never did, they might happen.

Sneer. Certainly nothing is unnatural, that is not physically impossible.

Puff. Very true—and for that matter Don Ferolo Whiskerandos, for that's the lover's name, might have been over here in the train of the Spanish Ambassador; or Tilburina, for that is the lady's name, might have been in love with him, from having heard his character, or seen his picture; or from knowing that he was the last man in the world she ought to be in love with—or for any other good female reason.—However, sir, the fact is, that though she is but a knight's daughter, egad! she is in love like any princess!

Dang. Poor young lady! I feel for her already! for I can conceive how great the conflict must be between her passion and her duty; her love for her country, and her love for Don Ferolo Whiskerandos!

Puff. Oh, amazing!—her poor susceptible heart is swayed to and fro by contending passions like——

Enter UNDER PROMPTER.

Und. Promp. Sir, the scene is set, and every thing is ready
to begin, if you please.

Puff. Egad, then we 'll lose no time.

Und Promp. Though, I believe, sir, you will find it very
short, for all the performers have profited by the kind permission you granted them.

Puff. Hey! what?

Und. Promp. You know, sir, you gave them leave to cut
out or omit whatever they found heavy or unnecessary to the
plot, and I must own they have taken very liberal advantage
of your indulgence.

Puff. Well, well.—They are in general very good judges,
and I know I am luxuriant.—Now, Mr. Hopkins, as soon as
you please.

Und. Promp. [*To the* Orchestra.] Gentlemen, will you play
a few bars of something, just to——

Puff. Ay, that's right; for as we have the scenes and
dresses, egad, we 'll go to 't, as if it was the first night's performance;—but you need not mind stopping between the acts
—[*Exit* UNDER PROMPTER.—Orchestra *play—then the bell
rings.*] So! stand clear, gentlemen. Now you know there
will be a cry of Down! down!—Hats off!—Silence!—Then
up curtain, and let us see what our painters have done for us.

[*Curtain rises.*

SCENE II.—*Tilbury Fort.*

" *Two* SENTINELS *discovered asleep.*"

Dang. Tilbury Fort!—very fine indeed!

Puff. Now, what do you think I open with?

Sneer. Faith, I can't guess——

Puff. A clock.—Hark!—[*Clock strikes.*] I open with a clock
striking, to beget an awful attention in the audience : it also
marks the time, which is four o'clock in the morning, and saves
a description of the rising sun, and a great deal about gilding
the eastern hemisphere.

Dang. But pray, are the sentinels to be asleep?

Puff. Fast as watchmen.

Sneer. Isn't that odd though at such an alarming crisis?

Puff. To be sure it is,—but smaller things must give way
to a striking scene at the opening; that's a rule. And the
case is, that two great men are coming to this very spot to be

gin the piece : now, it is not to be supposed they would open their lips, if these fellows were watching them ; so, egad, I must either have sent them off their posts, or set them asleep.

Sneer. Oh, that accounts for it.—But tell us, who are these coming?

Puff. These are they—Sir Walter Raleigh, and Sir Christopher Hatton. You 'll know Sir Christopher by his turning out his toes—famous, you know, for his dancing. I like to preserve all the little traits of character.—Now attend.

"*Enter* SIR WALTER RALEIGH *and* SIR CHRISTOPHER HATTON.
Sir Christ. True, gallant Raleigh!"—

Dang. What, they had been talking before?

Puff. O yes; all the way as they came along.—[*To the* Actors.] I beg pardon, gentlemen, but these are particular friends of mine, whose remarks may be of great service to us. —[*To* SNEER *and* DANGLE.] Don't mind interrupting them whenever any thing strikes you.

"*Sir Christ.* True, gallant Raleigh !
But oh, thou champion of thy country's fame,
There is a question which I yet must ask :
A question which I never ask'd before—
What mean these mighty armaments?
This general muster? and this throng of chiefs?"

Sneer. Pray, Mr. Puff, how came Sir Christopher Hatton never to ask that question before?

Puff. What, before the play began?—how the plague could he?

Dang. That 's true, i' faith !

Puff. But you will hear what he thinks of the matter

"*Sir Christ.* Alas ! my noble friend, when I behold
Yon tented plains in martial symmetry
Array'd; when I count o'er yon glittering lines
Of crested warriors, where the proud steeds neigh,
And valour-breathing trumpet's shrill appeal,
Responsive vibrate on my listening ear;
When virgin majesty herself I view,
Like her protecting Pallas, veil'd in steel,
With graceful confidence exhort to arms !
When, briefly, all I hear or see bears stamp
Of martial vigilance and stern defence,
I cannot but surmise—forgive, my friend,
If the conjecture's rash—I cannot but
Surmise the state some danger apprehends !"

Sneer. A very cautious conjecture that.

Puff. Yes, that's his character; not to give an opinion but
on secure grounds.—Now then.

" *Sir Walt.* O most accomplish'd Christopher!"——

Puff. He calls him by his christian name, to show that they
are on the most familiar terms

" *Sir Walt.* O most accomplish'd Christopher! I find
　　　　Thy staunch sagacity still tracks the future,
　　　　In the fresh print of the o'ertaken past."

Puff. Figurative!

" *Sir Walt.* Thy fears are just.
Sir Christ. But where? whence? when? and what
　　　　The danger is,—methinks I fain would learn.
Sir Walt. You know, my friend, scarce two revolving suns,
　　　　And three revolving moons, have closed their course,
　　　　Since haughty Philip, in despite of peace,
　　　　With hostile hand hath struck at England's trade.
Sir Christ. I know it well.
Sir Walt. Philip, you know, is proud Iberia's king!
Sir Christ. He is.
Sir Walt. 　　　　His subjects in base bigotry
　　　　And Catholic oppression held;—while we,
　　　　You know, the Protestant persuasion hold.
Sir Christ. We do.
Sir Walt. You know, beside, his boasted armament,
　　　　The famed Armada, by the Pope baptized,
　　　　With purpose to invade these realms——
Sir Christ. 　　　　　　　　　　Is sail'd,
　　　　Our last advices so report.
Sir Walt. While the Iberian admiral's chief hope,
　　　　His darling son——
Sir Christ. 　　　　Ferolo Whiskerandos hight——
Sir Walt. The same—by chance a prisoner hath been ta'en,
　　　　And in this fort of Tilbury——
Sir Christ. 　　　　　　　　Is now
　　　　Confined—'tis true, and oft from yon tall turret's top
　　　　I've mark'd the youthful Spaniard's haughty mien—
　　　　Unconquer'd, though in chains.
Sir Walt. 　　　　　　　　You also know"——

Dang. Mr. Puff, as he knows all this, why does Sir Walter
go on telling him?

Puff. But the audience are not supposed to know any thing
of the matter, are they?

Sneer. True; but I think you manage ill: for there certainly appears no reason why Sir Walter should be so communicative.

Puff. 'Fore Gad, now, that is one of the most ungrateful
observations I ever heard!—for the less inducement he has to

tell all this, the more, I think, you ought to be obliged to him; for I am sure you'd know nothing of the matter without it.

Dang. That's very true, upon my word.

Puff. But you will find he was not going on.

> "*Sir Christ.* Enough, enough—'tis plain—and I no more
>   Am in amazement lost!"——

Puff. Here, now you see, Sir Christopher did not in fact ask any one question for his own information.

Sneer. No, indeed: his has been a most disinterested curiosity!

Dang. Really, I find, we are very much obliged to them both.

Puff. To be sure you are. Now then for the commander-in-chief, the Earl of Leicester, who, you know, was no favourite but of the queen's.—We left off—*in amazement lost!*

> "*Sir Christ.*   Am in amazement lost.
>   But, see where noble Leicester comes! supreme
>   In honours and command.
> *Sir Walt.* .   And yet, methinks,
>   At such a time, so perilous, so fear'd,
>   That staff might well become an abler grasp.
> *Sir Christ.* . And so, by Heaven! think I; but soft, he's here!"

Puff. Ay, they envy him!

Sneer. But who are these with him?

Puff. Oh! very valiant knights: one is the governor of the fort, the other the master of the horse. And now, I think, you shall hear some better language: I was obliged to be plain and intelligible in the first scene, because there was so much matter of fact in it; but now, i'faith, you have trope, figure, and metaphor, as plenty as noun-substantives.

> "*Enter* EARL OF LEICESTER, GOVERNOR, MASTER OF THE HORSE,
>   KNIGHTS, &c.
> *Leic.* . . . How's this, my friends! is 't thus your new-fledged zeal
>   And plumèd valour moulds in roosted sloth?
>   Why dimly glimmers that heroic flame,
>   Whose reddening blaze, by patriot spirit fed,
>   Should be the beacon of a kindling realm?
>   Can the quick current of a patriot heart
>   Thus stagnate in a cold and weedy converse,
>   Or freeze in tideless inactivity?
>   No! rather let the fountain of your valour
>   Spring through each stream of enterprise,
>   Each petty channel of conducive daring,
>   Till the full torrent of your foaming wrath
>   O'erwhelm the flats of sunk hostility!'"

Puff. There it is—followed up !

"*Sir Walt.* No more !—the freshening breath of thy rebuke
Hath fill'd the swelling canvas of our souls !
And thus, though fate should cut the cable of
　　　　　　　　　　　　　　　　[*All take hands.*
　　　　Our topmost hopes, in friendship's closing line
　　　　We 'll grapple with despair, and if we fall,
　　　　We 'll fall in glory's wake !

Leic.　...　There spoke old England's genius !
　　　　Then, are we all resolved ?
All.　....　We are—all resolved.
Leic.　...　To conquer—or be free ?
All.　....　To conquer, or be free.
Leic.　...　All ?
All.　....　All."

Dang. Nem. con. egad !

Puff. O yes !—where they do agree on the stage, their unanimity is wonderful !

"*Leic.*　..　Then let 's embrace—and now——　　[*Kneels.*"

Sneer. What the plague, is he going to pray ?

Puff. Yes; hush !—in great emergencies, there is nothing like a prayer.

"*Leic.*　...　O mighty Mars !

Dang. But why should he pray to Mars ?

Puff. Hush !

"*Leic.*　...　　　　　If in thy homage bred,
　　　　Each point of discipline I 've still observed ;
　　　　Nor but by due promotion, and the right
　　　　Of service, to the rank of major-general
　　　　Have risen; assist thy votary now !
Gov.　...　Yet do not rise—hear me !　　　　　[*Kneels.*
Mast.　...　And me !　　　　　　　　　　　　[*Kneels.*
Knight.　..　And me !　　　　　　　　　　　[*Kneels.*
Sir Walt.　.　And me !　　　　　　　　　　　[*Kneels.*
Sir Christ.　And me !　　　　　　　　　　　[*Kneels.*"

Puff. Now pray altogether.

"*All.*　...　Behold thy votaries submissive beg,
　　　　That thou wilt deign to grant them all they ask ;
　　　　Assist them to accomplish all their ends,
　　　　And sanctify whatever means they use
　　　　To gain them !"

Sneer. A very orthodox quintetto !

Puff. Vastly well, gentlemen !—Is that well managed or not ?　Have you such a prayer as that on the stage ?

Sneer. Not exactly.

Leic. [*To* Puff.] But, sir, you haven't settled how we are to get off here.

Puff. You could not go off kneeling, could you?

Sir Walt. [*To* Puff.] O no, sir; impossible!

Puff. It would have a good effect, i'faith, if you could exeunt praying!—Yes, and would vary the established mode of springing off with a glance at the pit.

Sneer. Oh, never mind, so as you get them off!—I'll answer for it, the audience won't care how.

Puff. Well, then, repeat the last line standing, and go off the old way.

" *All* . . . And sanctify whatever means we use
          To gain them.   [*Exeunt.*"

Dang. Bravo! a fine exit

Sneer. Well, really, Mr. Puff——

Puff. Stay a moment!

          "*The* Sentinels *get up.*

1 *Sent.* . . All this shall to Lord Burleigh's ear.

2 *Sent.* . . 'Tis meet it should.   [*Exeunt.*"

Dang. Hey!—why, I thought those fellows had been asleep?

Puff. Only a pretence; there's the art of it: they were spies of Lord Burleigh's.

Sneer. But isn't it odd they never were taken notice of, not even by the commander-in-chief?

Puff. O lud, sir! if people, who want to listen or over-hear, were not always connived at in a tragedy, there would be no carrying on any plot in the world.

Dang. That's certain!

Puff. But take care, my dear Dangle! the morning-gun is going to fire.   [*Cannon fires.*

Dang. Well, that will have a fine effect!

Puff. I think so, and helps to realise the scene.—[*Cannon twice.*] What the plague! three morning guns! there never is but one!—Ay, this is always the way at the theatre: give these fellows a good thing, and they never know when to have done with it.—You have no more cannon to fire?

Und. Promp. [*Within.*] No, sir.

Puff. Now, then, for soft music.

Sneer. Pray what 's that for?

Puff. It shows that Tilburina is coming;—nothing intro-duces you a heroine like soft music. Here she comes!

Dang. And her confidant, I suppose?

Puff. To be sure! Here they are—inconsolable to the minuet in Ariadne!   [*Soft music*

"*Enter* TILBURINA *and* CONFIDANT.

Tilb.   .. Now has the whispering breath of gentle morn
Bid Nature's voice and Nature's beauty rise;
While orient Phœbus, with unborrow'd hues,
Clothes the waked loveliness which all night slept
In heavenly drapery!   Darkness is fled.
Now flowers unfold their beauties to the sun,
And, blushing, kiss the beam he sends to wake them—
The striped carnation, and the guarded rose,
The vulgar wallflower, and smart gillyflower,
The polyanthus mean—the dapper daisy,
Sweet-william, and sweet marjoram—and all
The tribe of single and of double pinks!
Now, too, the feather'd warblers tune their notes
Around, and charm the listening grove.   The lark!
The linnet! chaffinch! bullfinch! goldfinch! greenfinch!
But O, to me no joy can they afford!
Nor rose, nor wallflower, nor smart gillyflower,
Nor polyanthus mean, nor dapper daisy,
Nor William sweet, nor marjoram—nor lark,.
Linnet, nor all the finches of the grove!"

Puff. Your white handkerchief, madam!——

Tilb. I thought, sir, I wasn't to use that till *heart-rending woe.*

Puff. O yes, madam, at *the finches of the grove*, if you please

" *Tilb.* ....   Nor lark,
Linnet, nor all the finches of the grove! .   [*Weeps.*"

Puff. Vastly well, madam!

Dang. Vastly well, indeed!

" *Tilb.* .. For, O, too sure, heart-rending woe is now
The lot of wretched Tilburina!"

Dang. Oh!—'tis too much!

Sneer Oh!—it is indeed!

" *Con.* .. Be comforted, sweet lady; for who knows,
But Heaven has yet some milk-white day in store?

Tilb. ... Alas! my gentle Nora,
Thy tender youth as yet hath never mourn'd
Love's fatal dart.   Else wouldst thou know, that when
The soul is sunk in comfortless despair,
It cannot taste of merriment."

Dang. That's certain!

" *Con.* .... But see where your stern father comes:
It is not meet that he should find you thus."

Puff. Hey, what the plague!—what a cut is here! Why, what is become of the description of her first meeting with Don Whiskerandos—his gallant behaviour in the sea fight — and the simile of the canary-bird?

Tilb. Indeed, sir, you'll find they will not be missed.

Puff. Very well, very well!

Tilb. [*To* Confidant.] The cue, ma'am, if you please.

" *Con.* . . It is not meet that he should find you thus.
Tilb. . . . Thou counsel'st right; but 'tis no easy task
    For barefaced grief to wear a mask of joy.

Enter Governor.

Gov. . . . How's this!—in tears?—O Tilburina, shame!
    Is this a time for maudling tenderness,
    And Cupid's baby woes?—Hast thou not heard
    That haughty Spain's pope-consecrated fleet
    Advances to our shores, while England's fate,
    Like a clipp'd guinea, trembles in the scale?
Tilb. . . . Then is the crisis of my fate at hand!
    I see the fleets approach—I see——"

Puff. Now, pray, gentlemen, mind. This is one of the most useful figures we tragedy writers have, by which a hero or heroine, in consideration of their being often obliged to overlook things that are on the stage, is allowed to hear and see a number of things that are not.

Sneer. Yes; a kind of poetical second-sight!

Puff. Yes.—Now then, madam.

" *Tilb.* . . .   I see their decks
    Are clear'd!—I see the signal made!
    The line is form'd!—a cable's length asunder!—
    I see the frigates station'd in the rear;
    And now, I hear the thunder of the guns!
    I hear the victor's shouts!—I also hear
    The vanquish'd groan!—and now 'tis smoke—and now
    I see the loose sails shiver in the wind!
    I see—I see—what soon you'll see——
Gov. . . . Hold, daughter! peace! this love hath turn'd thy brain:
    The Spanish fleet thou canst not see—because
    —It is not yet in sight!"

Dang. Egad, though, the governor seems to make no allowance for this poetical figure you talk of.

Puff. No, a plain matter-of-fact man;—that's his character

" *Tilb.* . . But will you then refuse his offer?
Gov. . . . I must—I will—I can—I ought—I do.
Tilb. . . . Think what a noble price.
Gov. . . . No more—you urge in vain.
Tilb. . . . His liberty is all he asks."

Sneer. All who asks, Mr. Puff? Who is——

Puff. Egad, sir, I can't tell! Here has been such cutting and slashing, I don't know where they have got to myself.

Tilb. Indeed, sir, you will find it will connect very well.

" —And your reward secure."

Puff. Oh, if they hadn't been so devilish free with their cutting here, you would have found that Don Whiskerandos has been tampering for his liberty, and has persuaded Tilburina to make this proposal to her father. And now, pray observe the conciseness with which the argument is conducted. Egad, the *pro* and *con* goes as smart as hits in a fencing-match. It is indeed a sort of small-sword logic, which we have borrowed from the French.

" *Tilb.* . . . A retreat in Spain !
Gov. . . . Outlawry here !
Tilb. . . . Your daughter's prayer?
Gov. . . . Your father's oath.
Tilb. . . . My lover !
Gov. . . . My country !
Tilb. . . . Tilburina !
Gov. . . . . England !
Tilb. . . . A title !
Gov. . . . Honour !
Tilb. . . . . A pension !
Gov. . . . . Conscience !
Tilb. . . . . A thousand pounds !
Gov. . . . . Ha ! thou hast touch'd me nearly !"

Puff. There you see—she threw in *Tilburina*, Quick, parry quarte with *England!*—Ha! thrust in tierce *a title!*—parried by *honour.* Ha! *a pension* over the arm!—put by by *conscience.* Then flankonade with *a thousand pounds*—and a palpable hit, egad!

" *Tilb.* . . . Canst thou—
Reject the suppliant, and the daughter too
Gov. . . . . No more; I would not hear thee plead in vain:
The father softens—but the governor
Is fix'd!   [*Exit.*

Dang. Ay, that antithesis of persons is a most established figure.

" *Tilb.* . . . 'Tis well,—hence then, fond hopes,—fond passion, hence ;
Duty, behold I am all over thine——
Whisk. . . . [*Without.*] Where is my love—my——
Tilb. . . . Ha !

Enter DON FEROLO WHISKERANDOS.

Whisk. . . My beauteous enemy !——*

Puff. O dear, ma'am, you must start a great deal more than that! Consider, you had just determined in favour of duty—when, in a moment, the sound of his voice revives your passion—overthrows your resolution—destroys your obedience. If you don't express all that in your start, you do nothing at all

Tilb. Well, we'll try again!

Dang. Speaking from within has always a fine effect.

Sneer. Very.

" *Whisk.* . My conquering Tilburina! How! is 't thus
We meet! why are thy looks averse? what means
That falling tear—that frown of boding woe?
Ha! now indeed I am a prisoner!
Yes, now I feel the galling weight of these
Disgraceful chains—which, cruel Tilburina!
Thy doating captive gloried in before.—
But thou art false, and Whiskerandos is undone!

Tilb. . . . O no! how little dost thou know thy Tilburina!

Whisk. . . . Art thou then true?—Begone cares, doubts, and fears,
I make you all a present to the winds;
And if the winds reject you—try the waves."

Puff. The wind, you know, is the established receiver of all stolen sighs, and cast-off griefs and apprehensions

" *Tilb.* . . . Yet must we part!—stern duty seals our doom:
Though here I call yon conscious clouds to witness,
Could I pursue the bias of my soul,
All friends, all right of parents, I'd disclaim,
And thou, my Whiskerandos, shouldst be father
And mother, brother, cousin, uncle, aunt,
And friend to me!

Whisk. . . Oh, matchless excellence! and must we part?
Well, if—we must—we must—and in that case
The less is said the better."

Puff. Heyday! here's a cut!—What, are all the mutual protestations out?

Tilb. Now, pray, sir, don't interrupt us just here: you ruin our feelings.

Puff. Your feelings!—but zounds, my feelings, ma'am!

Sneer. No; pray don't interrupt them.

" *Whisk.* . One last embrace.
Tilb. . . . Now,—farewell, for ever.
Whisk. . . For ever!
Tilb. . . . Ay, for ever!   [*Going.*"

Puff. 'Sdeath and fury!—Gad's life!—sir! madam! if you go out without the parting look, you might as well dance out. Here, here!

Con. But pray, sir, how am I to get off here?

Puff. You! pshaw! what the devil signifies how you get off! edge away at the top, or where you will—[*Pushes the* CONFIDANT *off.*] Now, ma'am, you see——

Tilb. We understand you, sir.

" Ay, for ever.

Both. . . Oh! [*Turning back, and exeunt.—Scene closes.*"

Dang. Oh, charming!

Puff. Hey!—'tis pretty well, I believe : you see I don't attempt to strike out any thing new—but I take it I improve on the established modes,

Sneer. You do, indeed ! But pray is not Queen Elizabeth to appear?

Puff. No, not once—but she is to be talked of for ever; so that, egad, you'll think a hundred times that she is on the point of coming in.

Sneer. Hang it, I think it's a pity to keep her in the green-room all the night.

Puff. O no, that always has a fine effect—it keeps up expectation.

Dang. But are we not to have a battle?

Puff. Yes, yes, you will have a battle at last; but, egad, it's not to be by land, but by sea—and that is the only quite new thing in the piece.

Dang. What, Drake at the Armada, hey?

Puff. Yes, i'faith—fire-ships and all; then we shall end with the procession. Hey, that will do, I think?

Sneer. No, doubt on 't.

Puff. Come, we must not lose time; so now for the under-plot.

Sneer. What the plague, have you another plot?

Puff. O Lord, yes; ever while you live have two plots to your tragedy. The grand point in managing them is only to let your under-plot have as little connection with your main-plot as possible.—I flatter myself nothing can be more distinct than mine; for as in my chief plot the characters are all great people, I have laid my under-plot in low life; and as the former is to end in deep distress, I make the other end a-happy as a farce.—Now, Mr. Hopkins, as soon as you please.

Enter UNDER PROMPTER

Und. Promp. Sir, the carpenter says it is impossible you can go to the park scene yet.

Puff. The park scene! no! I mean the description scene here, in the wood.

Und. Promp. Sir, the performers have cut it out.

Puff. Cut it out!

Under Promp. Yes, sir.

Puff. What! the whole account of Queen Elizabeth?

Under Promp. Yes, sir.

Puff. And the description of her horse and side-saddle?

Under Promp. Yes, sir.

Puff. So, so; this is very fine indeed!—Mr. Hopkins, how the plague could you suffer this?

Mr. Hop. [*Within.*] Sir, indeed the pruning-knife——

Puff. The pruning-knife—zounds!—the axe! Why, here has been such lopping and topping, I shan't have the bare trunk of my play left presently!—Very well, sir—the performers must do as they please; but, upon my soul, I'll print it every word.

Sneer. That I would, indeed.

Puff. Very well, sir; then we must go on.—Zounds! I would not have parted with the description of the horse!—Well, sir, go on.—Sir, it was one of the finest and most laboured things.—Very well, sir; let them go on.—There you had him and his accoutrements, from the bit to the crupper. —Very well, sir; we must go to the park scene.

Under Promp. Sir, there is the point: the carpenters say, that unless there is some business put in here before the drop, they shan't have time to clear away the fort, or sink Gravesend and the river.

Puff. So! this is a pretty dilemma, truly!—Gentlemen, you must excuse me—these fellows will never be ready, unless I go and look after them myself.

Sneer. O dear, sir, these little things will happen.

Puff. To cut out this scene!—but I'll print it—egad, I'll print it every word!   [*Exeunt.*

ACT III.

SCENE I.—*The Theatre, before the Curtain.*

Enter PUFF, SNEER, *and* DANGLE.

Puff. Well, we are ready; now then for the justices.

[*Curtain rises*

" JUSTICES, CONSTABLES, &c., discovered."

Sneer. This, I suppose, is a sort of senate scene.

Puff. To be sure; there has not been one yet.

Dang. It is the under-plot, isn't it?

Puff. Yes.—What, gentlemen, do you mean to go at once to the discovery scene?

Just. If you please, sir.

Puff. Oh, very well!—Hark'ee, I don't choose to say any thing more; but, i' faith, they have mangled my play in a most shocking manner.

Dang. It's a great pity!

Puff. Now, then, Mr. Justice, if you please.

" *Just.* . . Are all the volunteers without?

Const. . . .   They are.
    Some ten in fetters, and some twenty drunk.

Just. . . . Attends the youth, whose most opprobrious fame
    And clear convicted crimes have stamp'd him soldier?

Const. . . . He waits your pleasure; eager to repay
    The blest reprieve that sends him to the fields
    Of glory, there to raise his branded hand
    In honour's cause.

Just. . . . .   'Tis well—'tis justice arms him!
    Oh! may he now defend his country's laws
    With half the spirit he has broke them all!
    If 'tis your worship's pleasure, bid him enter.

Const. . . . I fly, the herald of your will.   [*Exit.*"

Puff. Quick, sir.

Sneer. But, Mr. Puff, I think not only the Justice, but the clown seems to talk in as high a style as the first hero among them.

Puff. Heaven forbid they should not in a free country!— Sir, I am not for making slavish distinctions, and giving all the fine language to the upper sort of people.

Dang. That's very noble in you, indeed.

     " *Enter* JUSTICE'S LADY."

Puff. Now, pray mark this scene.

" *Lady.* . . Forgive this interruption, good my love;
    But as I just now pass'd a prisoner youth,
    Whom rude hands hither lead, strange bodings seized
    My fluttering heart, and to myself I said,
    An if our Tom had lived, he'd surely been
    This stripling's height!

Just. . . . . . Ha! sure some powerful sympathy directs
    Us both——

     Re-enter CONSTABLE *with* SON.
     What is thy name?

Son. . . . . . My name is Tom Jenkins—*alias* have I none—
    Though orphan'd, and without a friend!

Just. . . .   Thy parents?
Son. ` . . . My father dwelt in Rochester—and was,
                As I have heard—a fishmonger—no more."

Puff. What, sir, do you leave out the account of your birth,
parentage and education?

Son. They have settled it so, sir, here.

Puff. Oh! oh!

" *Lady.* . . How loudly nature whispers to my heart!
              Had he no other name?
Son. . . .   I've seen a bill
        Of his sign'd Tomkins, creditor.
Just. . . . . This does indeed confirm each circumstance
              The gipsy told!—Prepare!
Son. . . . .   I do.
Just. . . . . No orphan, nor without a friend art thou—
              I am thy father; here's thy mother; there
              Thy uncle—this thy first cousin, and those
              Are all your near relations!
Lady. . . . O ecstacy of bliss!
Son. . . . . . O most unlook'd for happiness!
Just. . . . . O wonderful event! [*They faint alternately in each other's arms."*]

Puff. There, you see relationship, like murder, will out.

" *Just.* . . Now let's revive—else were this joy too much!
              But come—and we'll unfold the rest within;
              And thou, my boy, must needs want rest and food.
              Hence may each orphan hope, as chance directs,
              To find a father—where he least expects!"   [*Exeunt."*]

Puff. What do you think of that?

Dang. One of the finest discovery-scenes I ever saw!—
Why, this under-plot would have made a tragedy itself.

Sneer. Ay, or a comedy either.

Puff. And keeps quite clear you see of the other.

            Enter SCENEMEN, *taking away the seats.*

Puff. The scene remains, does it?

Sceneman. Yes, sir.

Puff. You are to leave one chair, you know.—But it is always awkward in a tragedy, to have you fellows coming in in
your playhouse liveries to remove things.—I wish that could
be managed better.—So now for my mysterious yeoman.

            " *Enter* BEEFEATER.

Beef. . . . Perdition catch my soul, but I do love thee."

Sneer. Haven't I heard that line before?

Puff. No, I fancy not.—Where, pray?

Dang. Yes, I think there is something like it in Othello.

Puff. Gad! now you put me in mind on 't, I believe there is—but that 's of no consequence; all that can be said is, that two people happened to hit on the same thought—and Shakspeare made use of it first, that 's all.

Sneer. Very true.

Puff. Now, sir, your soliloquy—but speak more to the pit, if you please—the soliloquy always to the pit, that 's a rule

" *Beef.* . . Though hopeless love finds comfort in despair,
     It never can endure a rival's bliss !
     But soft—I am observed.   [*Exit.*"

Dang. That 's a very short soliloquy.

Puff. Yes—but it would have been a great deal longer if he had not been observed.

Sneer. A most sentimental Beefeater that, Mr. Puff !

Puff. Hark'ee—I would not have you be too sure that he is a Beefeater.

Sneer. What, a hero in disguise ?

Puff. No matter—I only give you a hint. But now for my principal character. Here he comes—Lord Burleigh in person ! Pray, gentlemen step this way—softly—I only hope the Lord High Treasurer is perfect—if he is but perfect !

" *Enter* LORD BURLEIGH, *goes slowly to a chair, and sits.*"

Sneer. Mr. Puff !

Puff. Hush !—Vastly well, sir ! vastly well ! a most interesting gravity !

Dang. What isn't he to speak at all ?

Puff. Egad, I thought you 'd ask me that !—Yes, it is a very likely thing—that a minister in his situation, with the whole affairs of the nation on his head, should have time to talk !—But hush ! or you 'll put him out.

Sneer. Put him out ! how the plague can that be, if he 's not going to say any thing !

Puff. There 's the reason ! why, his part is to think; and how the plague do you imagine he can think if you keep talking ?

Dang. That 's very true, upon my word !

" LORD BURLEIGH *comes forward, shakes his head, and exit.*"

Sneer. He is very perfect indeed ! Now, pray what did he mean by that ?

Puff. You don't take it ?

Sneer. No, I don't, upon my soul.

Puff. Why, by that shake of the head, he gave you to understand that even though they had more justice in their cause, and wisdom in their measures—yet, if there was not a greater spirit shown on the part of the people, the country would at last fall a sacrifice to the hostile ambition of the Spanish monarchy.

Sneer. The devil! did he mean all that by shaking his head?

Puff. Every word of it—if he shook his head as I taught him.

Dang. Ah! there certainly is a vast deal to be done on the stage by dumb show and expression of face; and a judicious author knows how much he may trust to it.

Sneer. Oh, here are some of our old acquaintance.

"*Enter* SIR CHRISTOPHER HATTON *and* SIR WALTER RALEIGH.

Sir Christ. My niece and your niece too!
By Heaven! there's witchcraft in 't.—He could not else
Have gain'd their hearts.—But see where they approach:
Some horrid purpose lowering on their brows!

Sir Walt. Let us withdraw and mark them.   [*They withdraw.*"

Sneer. What is all this?

Puff. Ah! here has been more pruning!—but the fact is, these two young ladies are also in love with Don Whiskerandos.—Now, gentlemen, this scene goes entirely for what we call situation and stage effect, by which the greatest applause may be obtained, without the assistance of language, sentiment, or character: pray mark!

"*Enter the two* NIECES.

1st Niece. . Ellena here!
She is his scorn as much as I—that is
Some comfort still!"

Puff. O dear, madam, you are not to say that to her face! —aside, ma'am, aside.—The whole scene is to be aside.

"*1st Niece.* She is his scorn as much as I—that is
Some comfort still.   [*Aside.*

2nd Niece. I know he prizes not Pollina's love;
But Tilburina lords it o'er his heart.   [*Aside.*

1st Niece. . But see the proud destroyer of my peace.
Revenge is all the good I've left.   [*Aside.*

2nd Niece. He comes, the false disturber of my quiet.
Now, vengeance do thy worst.   [*Aside*

Enter DON FEROLO WHISKERANDOS.

Whisk. .. O hateful liberty—if thus in vain
I seek my Tilburina!

Both Nieces. . . And ever shalt !

SIR CHRISTOPHER HATTON *and* SIR WALTER RALEIGH *come forward.*

Sir Christ. and Sir Walt. Hold ! we will avenge you.

Whisk. . . Hold you—or see your nieces bleed !

> [*The two* NIECES *draw their two daggers to strike* WHISKER-
> ANDOS : *the two* UNCLES *at the instant, with their two
> swords drawn, catch their two* NIECES' *arms, and turn
> the points of their swords to* WHISKERANDOS, *who imme-
> diately draws two daggers, and holds them to the two*
> NIECES' *bosoms.*"

Puff. There 's situation for you ! there 's an heroic group !
——You see the ladies can't stab Whiskerandos—he durst not
strike them, for fear of their uncles—the uncles durst not kill
him, because of their nieces—I have them all at a dead lock !
——for every one of them is afraid to let go first.

Sneer. Why, then they must stand there for ever !

Puff. So, they would, if I hadn't a very fine contrivance
for 't.—Now mind——

> " *Enter* BEEFEATER, *with his halberd.*

Beef. . . . In the queen's name I charge you all to drop
Your swords and daggers !

> [*They drop their swords and daggers.*"

Sneer. That is a contrivance indeed !

Puff. Ay—in the queen's name.

" *Sir Christ.* Come, niece !

Sir Walter. Come, niece !   [*Exeunt with the two* NIECES

Whisk. . . What 's he, who bids us thus renounce our guard?

Beef. . . . Thou must do more—renounce thy love !

Whisk. . . Thou liest—base Beefeater !

Beef.. . . . .   Ha ! hell ! the lie !
By Heaven thou 'st roused the lion in my heart !
Off, yeoman's habit !—base disguise ! off ! off !

> [*Discovers himself, by throwing off his upper dress, and ap-
> pearing in a very fine waistcoat.*

Am I a Beefeater now?
Or beams my crest as terrible as when
In Biscay's Bay I took thy captive sloop?"

Puff. There, egad ! he comes out to be the very captain of
the privateer who had taken Whiskerandos prisoner—and was
himself an old lover of Tilburina's.

Dang. Admirably managed, indeed !

Puff. Now, stand out of their way.

Whisk. . . . I thank thee, Fortune, that hast thus bestowed
A weapon to chastise this insolent. [*Takes up one of the swords*

Beef. . . . I take thy challenge, Spaniard, and I thank thee,
Fortune, too!   [*Takes up the other sword.*"

Dang. That's excellently contrived!—It seems as if the two uncles had left their swords on purpose for them.

Puff. No, egad, they could not help leaving them.

" *Whisk.* . Vengeance and Tilburina!
Beef.   Exactly so——
[*They fight—and after the usual number of rounds given,* WHISKERANDOS *falls.*

Whisk. . . O cursèd parry!—that last thrust in tierce
Was fatal.—Captain, thou hast fenced well!
And Whiskerandos quits this bustling scene
For all eter ——

Beef. . . .   ——nity—he would have added, but stern death
Cut short his being, and the noun at once!"

Puff. Oh, my dear sir, you are too slow: now mind me. —Sir, shall I trouble you to die again?

" *Whisk.* . And Whiskerandos quits this bustling scene
For all eter——

Beef. . . . .   ——nity—he would have added,——"

Puff. No, sir—that's not it—once more, if you please.

Whisk. I wish, sir, you would practise this without me—I can't stay dying here all night.

Puff. Very well; we'll go over it by-and-by.—[*Exit* WHIS-KERANDOS.] I must humour these gentlemen!

" *Beef.* . . Farewell, brave Spaniard! and when next"——

Puff. Dear sir, you needn't speak that speech, as the body has walked off.

Beef. That's true, sir—then I'll join the fleet.

Puff. If you please.—[*Exit* BEEFEATER.] Now, who comes on?

" *Enter* GOVERNOR, *with his hair properly disordered.*

Gov. . . . . . A hemisphere of evil planets reign!
And every planet sheds contagious frenzy!
My Spanish prisoner is slain! my daughter,
Meeting the dead corse borne along, has gone
Distract! .   [*A loud flourish of trumpets.*
But hark! I am summon'd to the fort:
Perhaps the fleets have met! amazing crisis!
O Tilburina! from thy aged father's beard
Thou'st pluck'd the few brown hairs which time had left!
[*Exit.*"

Sneer. Poor gentleman!

Puff. Yes—and no one to blame but his daughter!

Dang. And the planets——

Puff. True.—Now enter Tilburina!

Sneer. Egad, the business comes on quick here.

Puff. Yes, sir—now she comes in stark mad in white satin.

Sneer. Why in white satin?

Puff. O Lord, sir—when a heroine goes mad, she always goes into white satin.—Don't she, Dangle?

Dang. Always—it's a rule.

Puff. Yes—here it is—[*Looking at the book.*] "Enter Tilburina stark mad in white satin, and her confidant stark mad in white linen."

"*Enter* TILBURINA *and* CONFIDANT, *mad, according to custom.*"

Sneer. But, what the deuce, is the confidant to be mad too?

Puff. To be sure she is: the confidant is always to do whatever her mistress does; weep when she weeps, smile when she smiles, go mad when she goes mad.—Now, madam confidant—but keep your madness in the back-ground, if you please.

"*Tilb.* ... The wind whistles—the moon rises—see,
They have kill'd my squirrel in his cage;
Is this a grasshopper?—Ha! no; it is my
Whiskerandos—you shall not keep him—
I know you have him in your pocket—
An oyster may be cross'd in love!—Who says
A whale's a bird?—Ha! did you call, my love?—
He's here! he's there!—He's everywhere!
Ah me! he's nowhere!   [*Exit.*"

Puff. There, do you ever desire to see any body madder than that?

Sneer. Never, while I live!

Puff. You observed how she mangled the metre?

Dang. Yes—egad, it was the first thing made me suspect she was out of her senses!

Sneer. And pray what becomes of her?

Puff. She is gone to throw herself into the sea, to be sure—and that brings us at once to the scene of action, and so to my catastrophe— my sea-fight, I mean.

Sneer. What, you bring that in at last?

Puff. Yes, yes—you know my play is called *The Spanish Armada;* otherwise, egad, I have no occasion for the battle at

all.—Now then for my magnificence!—my battle!—my noise!
—and my procession!—You are all ready?

Und. Promp. [*Within.*] Yes, sir.

Puff. Is the Thames dressed?

"*Enter* THAMES *with two* ATTENDANTS."

Thames. Here I am, sir.

Puff. Very well, indeed!—See, gentlemen, there's a river
for you!—This is blending a little of the masque with my
tragedy—a new fancy, you know—and very useful in. my
case; for as there must be a procession, I suppose Thames,
and all his tributary rivers, to compliment Britannia with
a fête in honour of the victory.

Sneer. But pray, who are these gentlemen in green with
him?

Puff. Those?—those are his banks.

Sneer. His banks?

Puff. Yes, one crowned with alders, and the other with
a villa!—you take the allusions?—But hey! what the plague!
you have got both your banks on one side.—Here, sir, come
round.—Ever while you live, Thames, go between your
banks.—[*Bell rings.*] There, so! now for't!—Stand aside,
my dear friends!—Away, Thames!

[*Exit* THAMES *between his banks.*

[*Flourish of drums, trumpets, cannon, &c. &c. Scene
changes to the sea—the fleets engage—the music plays
"Britons strike home."—Spanish fleet destroyed by
fire-ships, &c.—English fleet advances—music plays
"Rule Britannia."—The procession of all the English
rivers, and their tributaries, with their emblems, &c.,
begins with Handel's water music, ends with a chorus,
to the march in Judas Maccabæus.—During this scene,*
PUFF *directs and applauds every thing—then*

Puff. Well, pretty well—but not quite perfect.—So, ladies
and gentlemen, if you please, we'll rehearse this piece again
to-morrow.   [*Curtain drops*

A TRIP TO SCARBOROUGH.
A COMEDY.

DRAMATIS PERSONÆ.

AS ORIGINALLY ACTED AT DRURY-LANE THEATRE IN 1777.

LORD FOPPINGTON .	Mr. Dodd.	SHOEMAKER . .	Mr. Carpenter.
SIR TUNBELLY CLUMSY	Mr. Moody.	TAILOR	Mr. Parker.
COLONEL TOWNLY .	Mr. Brereton.	AMANDA . . .	Mrs. Robinson.
LOVELESS . . .	Mr. Smith.	BERINTHIA . .	Miss Farren.
TOM FASHION . .	Mr. J. Palmer.	MISS HOYDEN . .	Mrs. Abington.
LA VAROLE . . .	Mr. Burton.	MRS. COUPLER .	Mrs. Booth.
LORY	Mr. Baddeley.	NURSE	Mrs. Bradshaw.
PROBE	Mr. Parsons.	SEMPSTRESS, POSTILION, MAID, and	
MENDLEGS . . .	Mr. Norris.	SERVANTS.	
JEWELLER . . .	Mr. Lamash.		

SCENE—SCARBOROUGH AND ITS NEIGHBOURHOOD.

PROLOGUE,

SPOKEN BY MR. KING.

WHAT various transformations we remark,
From east Whitechapel to the west Hyde Park !
Men, women, children, houses, signs, and fashions,
State, stage, trade, taste, the humours and the passions ;
The Exchange, 'Change Alley, wheresoe'er you 're ranging,
Court, city, country, all are changed or changing :
The streets, some time ago, were paved with stones,
Which, aided by a hackney-coach, half broke your bones.
The purest lovers then indulged in bliss ;
They run great hazard if they stole a kiss.
One chaste salute !—the damsel cried—Oh, fie !
As they approach'd—slap went the coach awry—
Poor Sylvia got a bump, and Damon a black eye.
    But now weak nerves in hackney-coaches roam,
And the cramm'd glutton snores, unjolted, home :
Of former times, that polish'd thing a beau,
Is metamorphosed now from top to toe ;
Then the full flaxen wig, spread o'er the shoulders,
Conceal'd the shallow head from the beholders !
But now the whole 's reversed—each fop appears,
Cropp'd and trimm'd up, exposing head and ears :
The buckle then its modest limits knew,
Now, like the ocean, dreadful to the view,
Hath broke its bounds, and swallows up the shoe ;

I I 2

The wearer's foot, like his once fine estate,
Is almost lost, the encumbrance is so great.
Ladies may smile—are they not in the plot?
The bounds of nature have not they forgot?
Were they design'd to be, when put together,
Made up, like shuttlecocks, of cork and feather?
Their pale-faced grandmammas appear'd with grace,
When dawning blushes rose upon the face;
No blushes now their once loved station seek;
The foe is in possession of the cheek!
No heads of old, too high in feather'd state,
Hinder'd the fair to pass the lowest gate;
A church to enter now, they must be bent,
If ever they should try the experiment.
   As change thus circulates throughout the nation,
Some plays may justly call for alteration;
At least to draw some slender covering o'er,
That *graceless wit* * which was too bare before:
Those writers well and wisely use their pens,
Who turn our wantons into Magdalens;
And howsoever wicked wits revile 'em,
We hope to find in you their stage asylum.

ACT I.

Scene I.—*The Hall of an Inn.*

Enter Tom Fashion *and* Lory, Postilion *following with a portmanteau.*

Fash. Lory, pay the postboy, and take the portmanteau.

Lory. [*Aside to* Tom Fashion.] Faith, sir, we had better let the postboy take the portmanteau and pay himself.

Fash. [*Aside to* Lory.] Why, sure, there 's something left in it!

Lory. Not a rag, upon my honour, sir! We eat the last of your wardrobe at Newmalton—and, if we had had twenty miles further to go, our next meal must have been of the cloak-bag.

Fash. Why, 'sdeath, it appears full!

Lory. Yes, sir—I made bold to stuff it with hay, to save appearances, and look like baggage.

Fash. [*Aside.*] What the devil shall I do?—[*Aloud.*] Hark'ee, boy, what's the chaise?

Post. Thirteen shillings, please your honour.

Fash. Can you give me change for a guinea?

Post. Oh, yes, sir.

Lory. [*Aside.*] So, what will he do now?—[*Aloud.*] Lord, sir, you had better let the boy be paid below.

Fash. Why, as you say, Lory, I believe it will be as well.

Lory. Yes, yes; I'll tell them to discharge you below, honest friend.

Post. Please your honour, there are the turnpikes too

Fash. Ay, ay, the turnpikes by all means.

Post. And I hope your honour will order me something for myself.

---

* " And *Van* want grace, who never wanted wit."—Pope.

Fash. To be sure; bid them give you a crown.

Lory. Yes, yes—my master doesn't care what you charge them—so get along, you——

Post. And there's the hostler, your honour.

Lory. Psha! damn the ostler!—would you impose upon the gentleman's generosity?—[*Pushes him out.*] A rascal, to be so cursed ready with his change!

Fash. Why, faith, Lory, he had nearly posed me.

Lory. Well, sir, we are arrived at Scarborough, not worth a guinea! I hope you'll own yourself a happy man—you have outlived all your cares.

Fash. How so, sir?

Lory. Why you have nothing left to take care of.

Fash. Yes, sirrah, I have myself and you to take care of still.

Lory. Sir, if you could prevail with somebody else to do that for you. I fancy we might both fare the better for it. But now, sir, for my Lord Foppington, your elder brother.

Fash. Damn my eldest brother!

Lory. With all my heart; but get him to redeem your annuity, however. Look you, sir, you must wheedle him, or you must starve.

Fash. Look you, sir, I will neither wheedle him nor starve.

Lory. Why, what will you do, then?

Fash. Cut his throat, or get some one to do it for me.

Lory. 'Gad so, sir, I'm glad to find I was not so well acquainted with the strength of your conscience as with the weakness of your purse.

Fash. Why, art thou so impenetrable a blockhead as to believe he'll help me with a farthing?

Lory. Not if you treat him *de haut en bas,* as you used to do.

Fash. Why, how wouldst have me treat him?

Lory. Like a trout—tickle him.

Fash. I can't flatter.

Lory. Can you starve?

Fash. Yes.

Lory. I can't—good by t' ye, sir.

Fash. Stay—thou 'lt distract me. But who comes here? My old friend, Colonel Townly.

Enter COLONEL TOWNLY.

My dear Colonel, I am rejoiced to meet you here.

Col. Town. Dear Tom, this is an unexpected pleasure! What, are you come to Scarborough to be present at your brother's wedding?

Lory. Ah, sir, if it had been his funeral, we should have come with pleasure.

Col Town. What, honest Lory, are you with your master still?

Lory. Yes, sir, I have been starving with him ever since I saw your honour last.

Fash. Why, Lory is an attached rogue—there's no getting rid of him.

Lory. True, sir, as my master says, there's no seducing me from his service.—[*Aside.*] Till he's able to pay me my wages.

Fash. Go, go, sir—and take care of the baggage.

Lory. Yes, sir—the baggage!—O Lord! [*Takes up the portmanteau.*] I suppose, sir, I must charge the landlord to be very particular where he stows this?

Fash. Get along, you rascal.—[*Exit* LORY, *with the portmanteau.*] But, Colonel, are you acquainted with my proposed sister-in-law?

Col. Town. Only by character—her father, Sir Tunbelly Clumsy, lives within a quarter of a mile of this place, in a lonely old house, which nobody comes near. She never goes abroad, nor sees company at home; to prevent all misfortunes, she has her breeding within doors; the parson of the parish teaches her to play upon the dulcimer, the clerk to sing, her nurse to dress, and her father to dance;—in short, nobody has free admission there but our old acquaintance, Mother Coupler, who has procured your brother this match, and is, I believe, a distant relation of Sir Tunbelly's.

Fash. But is her fortune so considerable?

Col. Town. Three thousand a year, and a good sum of money, independent of her father, beside.

Fash. 'Sdeath! that my old acquaintance, Dame Coupler, could not have thought of me, as well as my brother, for such a prize.

Col. Town. Egad, I wouldn't swear that you are too late—his lordship, I know, hasn't yet seen the lady—and, I believe, has quarrelled with his patroness.

Fash. My dear Colonel, what an idea have you started!

Col. Town. Pursue it, if you can, and I promise you you shall have my assistance; for, besides my natural contempt for his lordship, I have at present the enmity of a rival towards him.

Fash. What, has he been addressing your old flame, the widow Berinthia?

Col. Town. Faith, Tom, I am at present most whimsically circumstanced. I came here a month ago to meet the lady you mention; but she failing in her promise, I, partly from pique and partly from idleness, have been diverting my chagrin by offering up incense to the beauties of Amanda, our friend Loveless's wife.

Fash. I never have seen her, but have heard her spoken of as a youthful wonder of beauty and prudence.

Col. Town. She is so indeed; and, Loveless being too careless and insensible of the treasure he possesses, my lodging in the same house has given me a thousand opportunities of making my assiduities acceptable; so that, in less than a fortnight, I began to bear my disappointment from the widow with the most Christian resignation.

Fash. And Berinthia has never appeared?

Col. Town. Oh, there's the perplexity! for, just as I began not to care whether I ever saw her again or not, last night she arrived.

Fash. And instantly resumed her empire.

Col. Town. No, faith—we met—but, the lady not condescending to give me any serious reasons for having fooled me for a month, I left her in a huff.

Fash. Well, well, I'll answer for it she'll soon resume her power, especially as friendship will prevent your pursuing the other too far.—But my coxcomb of a brother is an admirer of Amanda's too, is he?

Col. Town. Yes, and I believe is most heartily despised by her. But come with me, and you shall see her and your old friend Loveless.

Fash. I must pay my respects to his lordship—perhaps you can direct me to his lodgings.

Col. Town. Come with me; I shall pass by it.

Fash. I wish you could pay this visit for me, or could tell me what I should say to him.

Col. Town. Say nothing to him—apply yourself to his bag, his sword, his feather, his snuff-box; and when you are well with them desire him to lend you a thousand pounds, and I'll engage you prosper.

Fash. 'Sdeath and furies! why was that coxcomb thrust into the world before me? O Fortune, Fortune, thou art a jilt, by Gad!   [*Exeunt.*

SCENE II.—LORD FOPPINGTON'S *Dressing-room.*

Enter LORD FOPPINGTON *in his nightgown, and* LA VAROLE.

Lord Fop. [*Aside.*] Well, 'tis an unspeakable pleasure to be a man of quality—strike me dumb! Even the boors of this northern spa have learned the respect due to a title.—[*Aloud.*] La Varole!

La Var. Milor——

Lord Fop. You han't yet been at Muddymoat Hall, to announce my arrival, have you?

La Var. Not yet, milor.

Lord Fop. Then you need not go till Saturday—[*Exit* LA VAROLE] as I am in no particular haste to view my intended sposa. I shall sacrifice a day or two more to the pursuit of my friend Loveless's wife. Amanda is a charming creature—strike me ugly! and, if I have any discernment in the world, she thinks no less of my Lord Foppington.

Re-enter LA VAROLE.

La Var. Milor, de shoemaker, de tailor, de hosier, de sempstress, de peru, be all ready, if your lordship please to dress.

Lord Fop. 'Tis well; admit them.

La Var. Hey, messieurs, entrez!

Enter TAILOR, SHOEMAKER, SEMPSTRESS, JEWELLER, *and* MENDLEGS.

Lord Fop. So, gentlemen, I hope you have all taken pains to show yourselves masters in your professions?

Tai. I think I may presume, sir——

La Var. Milor, you clown, you!

Tai. My lord—I ask your lordship's pardon, my lord. I hope, my lord, your lordship will be pleased to own I have brought your lordship as accomplished a suit of clothes as ever peer of England wore, my lord—will your lordship please to view 'em now?

Lord Fop. Ay; but let my people dispose the glasses so that I may see myself before and behind; for I love to see myself all round.
    [*Puts on his clothes.*

Enter TOM FASHION *and* LORY. *They remain behind, conversing apart.*

Fash. Heyday! what the devil have we here? Sure my gentleman's grown a favourite at court, he has got so many people at his levee.

Lory. Sir, these people come in order to make him a favourite at court—they are to establish him with the ladies.

Fash. Good Heaven! to what an ebb of taste are women fallen, that it should be in the power of a laced coat to recommend a gallant to them!

Lory. Sir, tailors and hair-dressers debauch all the women.

Fash. Thou sayest true. But now for my reception.

Lord Fop. [*To Tailor.*] Death and eternal tortures! Sir—I say the coat is too wide here by a foot.

Tai. My lord, if it had been tighter, 'twould neither have hooked nor buttoned.

Lord Fop. Rat the hooks and buttons, sir! Can any thing be worse than this? As Gad shall jedge me, it hangs on my shoulders like a chairman's surtout.

Tai. 'Tis not for me to dispute your lordship's fancy.

Lory. There, sir, observe what respect does.

Fash. Respect! damn him for a coxcomb!—But let's accost him.— [*Coming forward.*] Brother, I'm your humble servant.

Lord Fop. O Lard, Tam! I did not expect you in England brother, I'm glad to see you.—But what has brought you to Scarborough, Tam!—[*To the* TAILOR.] Look you, sir, I shall never be reconciled to this naus ous wrapping-gown, therefore pray get me another suit with all possible expedition; for this is my eternal aversion.—[*Exit* TAILOR.] Well but, Tam, you don't tell me what has driven you to Scarborough.—Mrs. Calico, are not you of my mind?

Semp. Directly, my lord.—I hope your lordship is pleased with your ruffles?

Lord Fop. In love with them, stap my vitals!—Bring my bill, you shall be paid to-morrow.

Semp. I humbly thank your lordship.   [*Exit.*

Lord. Fop. Hark thee, shoemaker, these shoes aren't ugly, but they don't fit me.

Shoe. My lord, I think they fit you very well.

Lord Fop. They hurt me just below the instep.

Shoe. [*Feels his foot.*] No, my lord, they don't hurt you there.

Lord Fop. I tell thee they pinch me execrahly.

Shoe. Why then, my lord, if those shoes pinch you, I'll be damned.

Lord Fop. Why, wilt thou undertake to persuade me I cannot eel?

Shoe. Your lordship may please to f el what you think fit, but that shoe does not hurt you—I think I understand my trade.

Lord Fop. Now, by all that's good and powerful, thou art an incomprehensive coxcomb!—but thou makest good shoes, and so I'll bear with thee.

Shoe. My lord, I have worked for half the people of quality in this town these twenty years, and 'tis very hard I shouldn't know when a shoe hurts, and when it don't.

Lord Fop. Well, pr'ythee be gone about thy business.—[*Exit* SHOEMAKER.] Mr. Mendlegs. a word with you.—The calves of these stockings are thickened a little too much; they make my legs look like a porter's.

Mend. My lord, methinks they look mighty well.

Lord Fop. Ay, but you are not so good a judge of those things as I am —I have studied them all my life—therefore pray let the next be the thickness of a crown-piece less.

Mend. Indeed, my lord, they are the same kind I had the honour to furnish your lordship with in town.

Lord Fop. Very possibly, Mr. Mendlegs; but that was in the beginning of the winter, and you should always remember, Mr. Hosier, that if you make a nobleman's spring legs as robust as his autumnal calves, you commit a manstrous impropriety, and make no allowance for the fatigues of the winter.   [*Exit* MENDLEGS.

Jewel. I hope, my lord, these buckles have had the unspeakable satisfaction of being honoured with your lordship's approbation?

Lord Fop. Why, they are of a pretty fancy; but don't you think them rather of the smallest?

Jewel. My lord, they could not well be larger, to keep on your lordship's shoe.

Lord Fop. My good sir, you forget that these matters are not as they used to be; formerly, indeed, the buckle was a sort of machine, intended to keep on the shoe; but the case is now quite reversed, and the shoe is of no earthly use, but to keep on the buckle.—Now give me my watches, [SERVANT *fetches the watches,*] my chapeau, [SERVANT *brings a dress hat,*] my handkerchief, [SERVANT *pours some scented liquor on a handkerchief and brings it,*] my snuff-box, [SERVANT *brings snuff-box.*] There, now the business of the morning is pretty well over. [*Exit* JEWELLER.

Fash. [*Aside to* LORY.] Well, Lory, what dost think on't?—a very friendly reception from a brother, after three years' absence!

Lory. [*Aside to* TOM FASHION.] Why, sir, 'tis your own fault—here you have stood ever since you came in, and have not commended any one thing that belongs to him. [SERVANTS *all go off.*

Fash. [*Aside to* LORY.] Nor ever shall, while they belong to a coxcomb. —[*To* LORD FOPPINGTON.] Now your people of business are gone, brother, I hope I may obtain a quarter of an hour's audience of you?

Lord Fop. Faith, Tam, I must beg you'll excuse me at this time, for I have an engagement which I would not break for the salvation of mankind. —Hey!—there!—is my carriage at the door?—You'll excuse me, brother.

[*Going.*

Fash. Shall you be back to dinner?

Lord Fop. As Gad shall jedge me, I can't tell; for it is passible I may dine with some friends at Donner's.

Fash. Shall I meet you there? for I must needs talk with you.

Lord Fop. That I'm afraid mayn't be quite so praper; for those I commonly eat with are people of nice conversation; and you know, Tam, your education has been a little at large.—But there are other ordinaries in town —very good beef ordinaries—I suppose, Tam, you can eat beef?—However, dear Tam, I'm glad to see thee in England, stap my vitals!

[*Exit,* LA VAROLE *following.*

Fash. Hell and furies! is this to be borne?

Lory. Faith, sir, I could almost have given him a knock o' the pate myself.

Fash. 'Tis enough; I will now show you the excess of my passion, by being very calm.—Come, Lory, lay your loggerhead to mine, and, in cold blood, let us contrive his destruction.

Lory. Here comes a head, sir, would contrive it better than both our loggerheads, if she would but join in the confederacy.

Fash. By this light, Madam Coupler! she seems dissatisfied at something: let us observe her.

Enter MRS. COUPLER.

Mrs. Coup. So! I am likely to be well rewarded for my services, truly; my suspicions. I find, were but too just.—What! refuse to advance me a petty sum, when I am upon the point of making him master of a galleon! But let him look to the consequences; an ungrateful narrow-minded coxcomb!

Fash. So he is, upon my soul, old lady; it must be my brother you speak of

Mrs. Coup. Ha! stripling, how came you here? What, hast spent all, eh? And art thou come to dun his lordship for assistance?

Fash. No, I want somebody's assistance to cut his lordship's throat, without the risk of being hanged for him.

Mrs Coup. Egad, sirrah, I could help thee to do him almost as good a turn, without the danger of being burned in the hand for 't.

Fash. How—how, old Mischief?

Mrs. Coup. Why, you must know I have done you the kindness to make up a match for your brother.

Fash. I am very much beholden to you, truly!

Mrs. Coup. You may before the wedding-day yet : the lady is a great heiress, the match is concluded, the writings are drawn, and his lordship is come hither to put the finishing hand to the business.

Fash. I understand as much.

Mrs. Coup. Now, you must know, stripling, your brother's a knave.

Fash. Good.

Mrs Coup. He has given me a bond of a thousand pounds for helping him to this fortune, and has promised me as much more, in ready money, upon the day of the marriage ; which, I understand by a friend, he never designs to pay me ; and his just now refusing to pay me a part is a proof of it. If, therefore, you will be a generous young rogue, and secure me five thousand pounds, I 'll help you to the lady.

Fash. And how the devil wilt thou do that?

Mrs. Coup. Without the devil's aid, I warrant thee. Thy brother's face not one of the family ever saw ; the whole business has been managed by me, and all his letters go through my hands. Sir Tunbelly Clumsy, my relation—for that 's the old gentleman's name—is apprised of his lordship's being down here, and expects him to-morrow to receive his daughter's hand ; but the peer, I find, means to bait here a few days longer, to recover the fatigue of his journey, I suppose. Now you shall go to Muddymoat Hall in his place.—I 'll give you a letter of introduction: and if you don't marry the girl before sunset, you deserve to be hanged before morning.

Fash. Agreed! agreed! and for thy reward——

Mrs. Coup. Well, well;—though I warrant thou hast not a farthing of money in thy pocket now—no—one may see it in thy face.

Fash. Not a sous, by Jupiter!

Mrs. Coup. Must I advance, then? Well, be at my lodgings, next door, this evening, and I 'll see what may be done—we 'll sign and seal, and when I have given thee some further instructions, thou shalt hoist sail and begone.
[*Exit.*

Fash. So, Lory, Fortune, thou seest, at last takes care of merit ! we are in a fair way to be great people.

Lory. Ay, sir, if the devil don't step between the cup and the lip, as he used to do.

Fash. Why, faith, he has played me many a damned trick to spoil my fortune ; and, egad, I am almost afraid he 's at work about it again now : but if I should tell thee how, thou 'dst wonder at me.

Lory. Indeed, sir, I should not.

Fash. How dost know?

Lory. Because, sir, I have wondered at you so often, I can wonder at you no more.

Fash. No! What wouldst thou say, if a qualm of conscience should spoil my design?

Lory. I would eat my words, and wonder more than ever.

Fash. Why faith, Lory, though I have played many a roguish trick, this is so full-grown a cheat, I find I must take pains to come up to 't—I have scruples.

Lory. They are strong symptoms of death. If you find they increase, sir, pray make your will.

Fash. No, my conscience shan't starve me neither : but thus far I 'll listen to it. Before I execute this project, I 'll try my brother to the bottom. If he has yet so much humanity about him as to assist me—though with a moderate aid—I 'll drop my project at his feet, and show him how I can do for him much more than what I 'd ask he 'd do for me. This one conclusive trial of him I resolve to make.—

Succeed or fail, still victory is my lot ;
If I subdue his heart, 'tis well—if not,
I will subdue my conscience to my plot.   [*Exeunt.*

ACT II.

Scene I.—Loveless's *Lodgings.*

Enter Loveless *and* Amanda.

Love. How do you like these lodgings, my dear? For my part, I am so pleased with them, I shall hardly remove whilst we stay here, if you are satisfied.

Aman. I am satisfied with every thing that pleases you, else I had not come to Scarborough at all.

Love. Oh, a little of the noise and folly of this place will sweeten the pleasures of our retreat ; we shall find the charms of our retirement doubled when we return to it.

Aman. That pleasing prospect will be my chiefest entertainment, whilst, much against my will, I engage in those empty pleasures which 'tis so much the fashion to be fond of.

Love. I own most of them are, indeed, but empty ; yet there are delights of which a private life is destitute, which may divert an honest man, and be a harmless entertainment to a virtuous woman : good music is one ; and truly (with some small allowance) the plays, I think, may be esteemed another.

Aman. Plays, I must confess, have some small charms. What do you think of that you saw last night?

Love. To say truth, I did not mind it much—my attention was for some time taken off to admire the workmanship of nature, in the face of a young lady who sat some distance from me, she was so exquisitely handsome.

Aman. So exquisitely handsome!

Love. Why do you repeat my words, my dear?

Aman. Because you seemed to speak them with such pleasure, I thought I might oblige you with their echo.

Love. Then, you are alarmed, Amanda?

Aman. It is my duty to be so when you are in danger.

Love. You are too quick in apprehending for me.   I viewed her with a world of admiration, but not one glance of love.

Aman. Take heed of trusting to such nice distinctions.   But were you eyes the only things that were inquisitive ? Had I been in your place, my tongue, I fancy, had been curious too.   I should have asked her where she lived—yet still without design—who was she, pray ?

Love. Indeed I cannot tell.

Aman. You will not tell.

Love. Upon my honour, then, I did not ask.

Aman. Nor do you know what company was with her?

Love. I do not.   But why are you so earnest ?

Aman. I thought I had cause.

Love. But you thought wrong, Amanda ; for turn the case, and let it be your story : should you come home and tell me you had seen a handsome man, should I grow jealous because you had eyes ?

Aman. But should I tell you he was exquisitely so, and that I had gazed on him with admiration, should you not think 'twere possible I might go one step further, and inquire his name ?

Love. [*Aside.*] She has reason on her side ; I have talked too much ; but I must turn off another way.—[*Aloud.*] Will you 'then make no difference, Amanda, between the language of our sex and yours ?   There is a modesty restrains your tongues, which makes you speak by halves when you commend ; but roving flattery gives a loose to ours, which makes us still speak double what we think.

Enter SERVANT.

Serv. Madam, there is a lady at the door in a chair desires to know whether your ladyship sees company ; her name is Berinthia.

Aman. Oh dear ! 'tis a relation I have not seen these five years ; pray her to walk in.—[*Exit* SERVANT.] Here 's another beauty for you ; she was, when I saw her last, reckoned extremely handsome.

Love. Don't be jealous now ; for I shall gaze upon her too.

Enter BERINTHIA.

Ha ! by heavens, the very woman !   [*Aside.*

Ber. [*Salutes* AMANDA.]   Dear Amanda, I did not expect to meet you in Scarborough.

Aman. Sweet cousin, I 'm overjoyed to see you.—Mr. Loveless, here 's a relation and a friend of mine, I desire you 'll be better acquainted with.

Love. [*Salutes* BERINTHIA.] If my wife never desires a harder thing, madam, her request will be easily granted.

Re-enter SERVANT.

Serv. Sir, my Lord Foppington presents his humble service to you, and desires to know how you do.   He 's at the next door ; and, if it be not inconvenient to you, he 'll come and wait upon you.

Love. Give my compliments to his lordship, and I shall be glad to see him.—[*Exit* SERVANT.] If you are not acquainted with his lordship, madam, you will be entertained with his character.

Aman. Now it moves my pity more than my mirth to see a man whom nature has made no fool be so very industrious to pass for an ass.

Love. No, there you are wrong, Amanda; you should never bestow your pity upon those who take pains for your contempt: pity those whom nature abuses, never those who abuse nature.

Enter LORD FOPPINGTON.

Lord Fop. Dear Loveless, I am your most humble servant.

Love. My lord, I 'm yours.

Lord Fop. Madam, your ladyship's very obedient slave.

Love. My lord, this lady is a relation of my wife's.

Lord Fop [*Salutes* BERINTHIA.] The beautifulest race of people upon earth, rat me! Dear Loveless, I am overjoyed that you think of continuing here: I am, stap my vitals!—[*To* AMANDA.] For Gad's sake, madam, how has your ladyship been able to subsist thus long, under the fatigue of a country life?

Aman. My life has been very far from that, my lord; it has been a very quiet one.

Lord Fop. Why, that's the fatigue I speak of, madam; for 'tis impossible to be quiet without thinking: now thinking is to me the greatest fatigue in the world.

Aman. Does not your lordship love reading, then?

Lord Fop. Oh, passionately, madam; but I never think of what I read. For example, madam, my life is a perpetual stream of pleasure, that glides through with such a variety of entertainments, I believe the wisest of our ancestors never had the least conception of any of 'em. I rise, madam, when in tawn, about twelve o'clock. I don't rise sooner, because it is the worst thing in the world for the complexion: nat that I pretend to be a beau; but a man must endeavour to look decent, lest he makes so odious a figure in the side-bax, the ladies should be compelled to turn their eyes upon the play. So at twelve o'clock, I say, I rise. Naw, if I find it is a good day, I resolve to take the exercise of riding; so drink my chocolate, and draw on my boots by two. On my return, I dress; and, after dinner, lounge perhaps to the opera.

Ber. Your lordship, I suppose, is fond of music?

Lord Fop. Oh, passionately, on Tuesdays and Saturdays; for then there is always the best company, and one is not expected to undergo the fatigue of listening.

Aman. Does your lordship think that the case at the opera?

Lord Fop. Most certainly, madam. There is my Lady Tattle, my Lady Prate, my Lady Titter, my Lady Sneer, my Lady Giggle, and my Lady Grin—these have boxes in the front, and while any favourite air is singing, are the prettiest company in the waurld, stap my vitals!—Mayn't we hope for the honour to see you added to our society, madam?

Aman. Alas! my lord, I am the worst company in the world at a concert, I'm so apt to attend to the music.

Lord Fop. Why, madam, that is very pardonable in the country or at church, but a monstrous inattention in a polite assembly. But I am afraid I tire the company?

Love. Not at all. Pray go on.

Lord Fop. Why then, ladies. there only remains to add, that I generally conclude the evening at one or other of the clubs; nat that I ever play deep;

indeed I have been for some time tied up from losing above five thousand pounds at a sitting.

Love. But isn't your lordship sometimes obliged to attend the weighty affairs of the nation?

Lord Fop. Sir, as to weighty affairs, I leave them to weighty heads; I never intend mine shall be a burden to my body.

Ber. Nay, my lord, but you are a pillar of the state.

Lord Fop. An ornamental pillar, madam; for sooner than undergo any part of the fatigue, rat me, but the whole building should fall plump to the ground!

Aman. But, my lord, a fine gentleman spends a great deal of his time in his intrigues; you have given us no account of them yet.

Lord Fop. [*Aside.*] So! she would inquire into my amours—that's jealousy, poor soul!—I see she's in love with me.—[*Aloud.*] O Lord, madam, I had like to have forgot a secret I must needs tell your ladyship.—Ned, you must not be so jealous now as to listen.

Love. [*Leading* BERINTHIA *up the stage.*] Not I, my lord; I am too fashionable a husband to pry into the secrets of my wife.

Lord Fop. [*Aside to* AMANDA, *squeezing her hand.*] I am in love with you to desperation, strike me speechless!

Aman. [*Strikes him on the ear.*] Then thus I return your passion.—An impudent fool!

Lord Fop. Gad's curse, madam, I am a peer of the realm!

Love. [*Hastily returning.*] Hey! what the devil, do you affront my wife, sir? Nay, then—— [*Draws. They fight.*

Aman. What has my folly done?—Help! murder! help! Part them, for Heaven's sake.

Lord Fop. [*Falls back and leans on his sword.*] Ah! quite through the body, stap my vitals!

Enter SERVANTS.

Love. [*Runs to* LORD FOPPINGTON.] I hope I han't killed the fool, however. Bear him up.—Call a surgeon there.

Lord Fop. Ay, pray make haste. [*Exit* SERVANT.

Love. This mischief you may thank yourself for.

Lord Fop. I may so; love's the devil indeed, Ned.

Re-enter SERVANT, *with* PROBE.

Ser. Here's Mr. Probe, sir, was just going by the door.

Lord Fop. He's the welcomest man alive.

Probe. Stand by, stand by, stand by; pray, gentlemen, stand by. Lord have mercy upon us, did you never see a man run through the body before?—Pray stand by.

Lord Fop. Ah, Mr. Probe, I'm a dead man.

Probe. A dead man, and I by! I should laugh to see that, egad.

Love. Pr'ythee don't stand prating, but look upon his wound.

Probe. Why, what if I won't look upon his wound this hour, sir?

Love. Why, then he'll bleed to death, sir.

Probe. Why, then I'll fetch him to life again, sir.

Love. 'Slife! he's run through the body, I tell thee.

Probe. I wish he was run through the heart, and I should get the by his cure. Now I hope you are satisfied? Come, now let me come at him—now let me come at him.—[*Viewing his wound.*] Oons! what a gash is here! why, sir, a man may drive a coach and six horses into your body.

Lord Fop. Oh!

Probe. Why, what the devil have you run the gentleman through with a scythe?—[*Aside.*] A little scratch between the skin and the ribs, that's all.

Love. Let me see his wound.

Probe. Then you shall dress it, sir; for if any body looks upon it I won't.

Love. Why thou art the veriest coxcomb I ever saw!

Probe. Sir, I am not master of my trade for nothing.

Lord Fop. Surgeon!

Probe. Sir.

Lord. Fop. Are there any hopes?

Probe. Hopes! I can't tell. What are you willing to give for a cure?

Lord Fop. Five hundred paunds with pleasure.

Probe. Why then perhaps there may be hopes; but we most avoid further delay.—Here, help the gentleman into a chair, and carry him to my house presently—that's the properest place—[*Aside*] to bubble him out of his money.—[*Aloud.*] Come, a chair—a chair quickly—there, in with him.

[SERVANTS *put* LORD FOPPINGTON *into a chair.*

Lord Fop. Dear Loveless, adieu! if I die, I forgive thee; and if I live, I hope thou wilt do as much by me. I am sorry you and I should quarrel, but I hope here's an end on't; for, if you are satisfied, I am.

Love. I shall hardly think it worth my prosecuting any further, so you may be at rest, sir.

Lord Fop. Thou art a generous fellow, strike me dumb!—[*Aside.*] But thou hast an impertinent wife, stap my vitals!

Probe. So—carry him off, carry him off!—We shall have him prate himself into a fever by-and-by.—Carry him off! [*Exit with* LORD FOPPINGTON.

Enter COLONEL TOWNLY.

Col. Town. So, so, I am glad to find you all alive—I met a wounded peer carrying off. For heaven's sake what was the matter?

Love. Oh, a trifle! he would have made love to my wife before my face, so she obliged him with a box o' the ear, and I run him through the body, that was all.

Col. Town. Bagatelle on all sides. But pray, madam, how long has this noble lord been an humble servant of yours?

Aman. This is the first I have heard on't—so, I suppose, 'tis his quality more than his love has brought him into this adventure. He thinks his title an authentic passport to every woman's heart below the degree of a peeress.

Col. Town. He's coxcomb enough to think any thing; but I would not have you brought into trouble for him. I hope there's no danger of his life?

Love. None at all. He's fallen into the hands of a roguish surgeon, who, I perceive, designs to frighten a little money out of him: but I saw his wound—'tis nothing: he may go to the ball to-night if he pleases.

Col. Town. I am glad you have corrected him without further mischief, or you might have deprived me of the pleasure of executing a plot against his lordship, which I have been contriving with an old acquaintance of yours.

Love. Explain.

Col. Town. His brother, Tom Fashion, is come down here, and we have it in contemplation to save him the trouble of his intended wedding ; but we want your assistance. Tom would have called, but he is preparing for his enterprise, so I promised to bring you to him—so sir, if these ladies can spare you ——

Love. I 'll go with you with all my heart.—[*Aside.*] Though I could wish, methinks, to stay and gaze a little longer on that creature. Good gods ! how engaging she is !—but what have I to do with beauty ? I have already had my portion, and must not covet more.

Aman. Mr. Loveless, pray one word with you before you go.

[Exit COLONEL TOWNLY.

Love. What would my dear ?

Aman. Only a woman's foolish question : how do you like my cousin here ?

Love. Jealous already, Amanda ?

Aman. Not at all : I ask you for another reason.

Love. [*Aside.*] Whate'er her reason be, I must not tell her true.—[*Aloud.*] Why, I confess, she 's handsome : but you must not think I slight your kinswoman, if I own to you, of all the women who may claim that character, she is the last that would triumph in my heart.

Aman. I 'm satisfied.

Love. Now tell me why you asked ?

Aman. At night I will—adieu !

Love. I 'm yours.   [*Kisses her, and exit.*

Aman. I 'm glad to find he does not like her, for I have a great mind to persuade her to come and live with me.   [*Aside.*

Ber. So ! I find my colonel continues in his airs : there must be something more at the bottom of this than the provocation he pretends from me.

[Aside.

Aman. For Heaven's sake, Berinthia, tell me what way I shall take to persuade you to come and live with me.

Ber. Why, one way in the world there is, and but one.

Aman. And pray what is that ?

Ber. It is to assure me—I shall be very welcome.

Aman. If that be all, you shall e'en sleep here to-night.

Ber. To-night !

Aman. Yes, to-night.

Ber. Why, the people where I lodge will think me mad.

Aman. Let 'em think what they please.

Ber. Say you so, Amanda ? Why, then, they shall think what they please : for I 'm a young widow, and I care not what any body thinks.— Ah, Amanda, it 's a delicious thing to be a young widow !

Aman. You 'll hardly make me think so.

Ber. Poh ! because you are in love with your husband.

Aman. Pray, 'tis with a world of innocence I would inquire whether you think those we call women of reputation do really escape all other men as they do those shadows of beaux ?

Ber. Oh no, Amanda ; there are a sort of men make dreadful work amongst 'em, men that may be called the beau's antipathy, for they agree in nothing but walking upon two legs. These have brains, the beau has none. These are in love with their mistress, the beau with himself.

They take care of their reputation, the beau is industrious to destroy it. They are decent, he's a fop; in short, they are men, he's an ass.

A man. If this be their character, I fancy we had here, e'en now, a pattern of 'em both.

Ber. His lordship and Colonel Townly?

A man. The same.

Ber. As for the lord, he is eminently so; and for the other, I can assure you there's not a man in town who has a better interest with the women, that are worth having an interest with.

A man. He answers the opinion I had ever of him.—[*Takes her hand.*] I must acquaint you with a secret—'tis not that fool alone has talked to me of love; Townly has been tampering too.

Ber. [*Aside.*] So, so! here the mystery comes out!—[*Aloud.*] Colonel Townly! impossible, my dear!

A man. 'Tis true, indeed; though he has done it in vain; nor do I think that all the merit of mankind combined could shake the tender love I bear my husband; yet I will own to you, Berinthia, I did not start at his addresses, as when they came from one whom I contemned.

Ber. [*Aside.*] Oh, this is better and better!—[*Aloud.*] Well said, Innocence! and you really think, my dear, that nothing could abate your constancy and attachment to your husband?

A man. Nothing, I am convinced.

Ber. What, if you found he loved another woman better?

A man. Well!

Ber. Well!—why, were I that thing they call a slighted wife, somebody should run the risk of being that thing they call—a husband. Don't I talk madly?

A man. Madly indeed!

Ber. Yet I'm very innocent.

A man. That I dare swear you are. I know how to make allowances for your humour: but you resolve then never to marry again?

Ber. Oh no! I resolve I will.

A man. How so?

Ber. That I never may.

A man. You banter me.

Ber. Indeed I don't: but I consider I'm a woman, and form my resolutions accordingly.

A man. Well, my opinion' is, form what resolution you will, matrimony will be the end on 't.

Ber. I doubt it—but a——Heavens! I have business at home, and am half an hour too late.

A man. As you are to return with me, I'll just give some orders, and walk with you.

Ber. Well, make haste, and we'll finish this subject as we go.—[*Exit* AMANDA.] Ah, poor Amanda! you have led a country life. Well, this discovery is lucky! Base Townly! at once false to me and treacherous to his friend!—And my innocent and demure cousin too! I have it in my power to be revenged on her, however. Her husband, if I have any skill in countenance, would be as happy in my smiles as Townly can hope to be in hers. I'll make the experiment, come what will on 't. The woman who can forgive the being robbed of a favoured lover, must be either an idiot or something worse. [*Exit.*

K K

ACT III.

Scene I.—Lord Foppington's *Lodgings.*

Enter Lord Foppington *and* La Varole.

Lord Fop. Hey, fellow, let my vis-à-vis come to the door.

La Var. Will your lordship venture so soon to expose yourself to the weather?

Lord Fop. Sir, I will venture as soon as I can to expose myself to the ladies.

La Var. I wish your lordship would please to keep house a little longer; I'm afraid your honour does not well consider your wound.

Lord Fop. My wound!—I would not be in eclipse another day, though I had as many wounds in my body as I have had in my heart. So mind, Varole, let these cards be left as directed; for this evening I shall wait on my future father-in-law, Sir Tunbelly, and I mean to commence my devoirs to the lady, by giving an entertainment at her father's expense; and hark thee, tell Mr. Loveless I request he and his company will honour me with their presence, or I shall think we are not friends.

La Var. I will be sure, milor.   [*Exit.*

Enter Tom Fashion.

Fash. Brother, your servant; how do you find yourself to-day?

Lord Fop. So well that I have ordered my coach to the door—so there's no danger of death this bout, Tam.

Fash. I'm very glad of it.

Lord Fop. [*Aside.*] That I believe's a lie.—[*Aloud.*] Pr'ythee, Tam, tell me one thing,—did not your heart cut a caper up to your mouth, when you heard I was run through the body?

Fash. Why do you think it should?

Lord Fop. Because I remember mine did so, when I heard my uncle was shot through the head.

Fash. It then did very ill.

Lord Fop. Pr'ythee, why so?

Fash. Because he used you very well.

Lord Fop. Well!—Naw, strike me dumb! he starved me; he has let me want a thausand women for want of a thausand paund.

Fash. Then he hindered you from making a great many ill bargains; for I think no woman worth money that will take money.

Lord Fop. If I was a younger brother I should think so too.

Fash. Then you are seldom much in love?

Lord Fop. Never, stap my vitals!

Fash. Why, then, did you make all this bustle about Amanda?

Lord Fop. Because she's a woman of insolent virtue, and I thought myself piqued, in honour, to debauch her.

Fash. Very well.—[*Aside.*] Here's a rare fellow for you, to have the spending of ten thousand pounds a year! But now for my business with him. [*Aloud.*] Brother, though I know to talk of any business (especially of money) is a theme not quite so entertaining to you as that of the ladies, my necessities are such, I hope you'll have patience to hear me.

Lord Fop. The greatness of your necessities, Tam, is the worst argument in the waurld for your being patiently heard. I do believe you are going to make a very good speech, but, strike me dumb! it has the worst beginning of any speech I have heard this twelvemonth.

Fash. I'm sorry you think so.

Lord Fop. I do believe thou art: but come, let's know the affair quickly.

Fash. Why then, my case in a word is this: the necessary expenses of my travels have so much exceeded the wretched income of my annuity, that I have been forced to mortgage it for five hundred pounds, which is spent. So, unless you are so kind as to assist me in redeeming it, I know no remedy but to take a purse.

Lord Fop. Why faith, Tam, to give you my sense of the thing, I do think taking a purse the best remedy in the waurld; for if you succeed, you are relieved that way, if you are taken, [*Drawing his hand round his neck,*] you are relieved t'other.

Fash. I'm glad to see you are in so pleasant a humour; I hope I shall find the effects on't.

Lord Fop. Why, do you then really think it a reasonable thing, that I should give you five hundred paunds?

Fash. I do not ask it as a due, brother; I am willing to receive it as a favour.

Lord Fop. Then thou art willing to receive it any how, strike me speechless! But these are damned times to give money in; taxes are so great, repairs so exorbitant, tenants such rogues, and bouquets so dear, that, the devil take me, I am reduced to that extremity in my cash, I have been forced to retrench in that one article of sweet pawder, till I have brought it down to five guineas a maunth—now judge, Tam, whether I can spare you five hundred paunds.

Fash. If you can't, I must starve, that's all.—[*Aside.*] Damn him!

Lord Fop. All I can say is, you should have been a better husband.

Fash. Ouns! if you can't live upon ten thousand a year, how do you think should do't upon two hundred?

Lord Fop. Don't be in a passion, Tam, for passion is the most unbecoming thing in the waurld—to the face. Look you, I don't love to say any thing to you to make you melancholy, but upon this occasion I must take leave to put you in mind that a running horse does require more attendance than a coach-horse. Nature has made some difference 'twixt you and me.

Fash. Yes—she has made you older.—[*Aside.*] Plague take her!

Lord Fop. That is not all, Tam.

Fash. Why, what is there else?

Lord Fop. [*Looks first on himself, and then on his brother.*] Ask the ladies.

Fash. Why, thou essence-bottle, thou musk-cat! dost thou then think thou hast any advantage over me but what Fortune has given thee?

Lord Fop. I do, stap my vitals!

Fash. Now, by all that's great and powerful, thou art the prince of coxcombs!

Lord Fop. Sir, I am proud at being at the head of so prevailing a party.

Fash. Will nothing provoke thee?—Draw, coward!

Lord Fop. Look you, Tam, you know I have always taken you for a mighty dull fellow, and here is one of the foolishest plats broke out that I have seen a long time. Your poverty makes life so burdensome to you, you would provoke me to a quarrel, in hopes either to slip through my lungs into my estate, or to get yourself run through the guts, to put an end to your pain. But I will disappoint you in both your designs; for with the temper of a philosopher, and the discretion of a statesman—I shall leave the room with my sword in the scabbard.   [*Exit.*

Fash. So! farewell, brother; and now, conscience, I defy thee. Lory !

Enter LORY.

Lory. Sir !

Fash. Here's rare news, Lory; his lordship has given me a pill has purged off all my scruples.

Lory. Then my heart's at ease again: for I have been in a lamentable fright, sir, ever since your conscience had the impudence to intrude into your company.

Fash. Be at peace; it will come there no more : my brother has given it a wring by the nose, and I have kicked it down stairs. So run away to the inn, get the chaise ready quickly, and bring it to Dame Coupler's without a moment's delay.

Lory. Then, sir, you are going straight about the fortune?

Fash. I am.—Away—fly, Lory !

Lory. The happiest day I ever saw. I'm upon the wing already. Now then I shall get my wages.   [*Exeunt.*

SCENE II.—*A Garden behind* LOVELESS'S *Lodgings.*

Enter LOVELESS *and* SERVANT.

Love. Is my wife within?

Serv. No, sir, she has gone out this half hour.

Love. Well, leave me.—[*Exit* SERVANT.] How strangely does my mind run on this widow !—Never was my heart so suddenly seized on before. That my wife should pick out her, of all womankind, to be her playfellow ! But what fate does, let fate answer for: I sought it not. So! by Heavens ! here she comes.

Enter BERINTHIA.

Ber. What makes you look so thoughtful, sir? I hope you are not ill.

Love. I was debating, madam, whether I was so or not, and that was it which made me look so thoughtful.

Ber. Is it then so hard a matter to decide? I thought all people were acquainted with their own bodies, though few people know their own minds.

Love. What if the distemper I suspect be in the mind?

Ber. Why then I'll undertake to prescribe you a cure.

Love. Alas! you undertake you know not what.

Ber. So far at least, then, you allow me to be a physician.

Love. Nay, I'll allow you to be so yet further; for I have reason to believe, should I put myself into your hands, you would increase my distemper.

Ber. How?

Love. Oh, you might betray me to my wife.

Ber. And so lose all my practice.

Love. Will you then keep my secret?

Ber. I will.

Love. Well—but swear it.

Ber. I swear by woman.

Love. Nay, that's swearing by my deity; swear by your own, and I shall believe you.

Ber. Well then, I swear by man!

Love. I'm satisfied. Now hear my symptoms, and give me your advice. The first were these; when I saw you at the play, a random glance you threw at first alarmed me. I could not turn my eyes from whence the danger came —I gazed upon you till my heart began to pant—nay, even now, on your approaching me, my illness is so increased that if you do not help me I shall, whilst you look on, consume to ashes.　　　*[Takes her hand.*

Ber. O Lord, let me go! 'tis the plague, and we shall be infected.
　　　　　　　　　　　　　　　　　　　[Breaking from him.

Love. Then we'll die together, my charming angel.

Ber. O Gad! the devil's in you! Lord, let me go!—here's somebody coming.

Re-enter SERVANT.

Serv. Sir, my lady's come home, and desires to speak with you.

Love. Tell her I'm coming.—[*Exit* SERVANT.] But before I go, one glass of nectar to drink her health.　　　　　　　　*[To* BERINTHIA.

Ber. Stand off, or I shall hate you, by Heavens!

Love. [*Kissing her.*] In matters of love, a woman's oath is no more to be minded than a man's.　　　　　　　　　　　　　　*[Exit.*

Ber. Um!

Enter COLONEL TOWNLY.

Col. Town. [*Aside.*] So! what's here—Berinthia and Loveless—and in such close conversation!—I cannot now wonder at her indifference in excusing herself to me!—O rare woman!—Well then, let Loveless look to his wife, 'twill be but the retort courteous on both sides.—[*Aloud.*] Your servant, madam; I need not ask you how you do, you have got so good a colour.

Ber. No better than I used to have, I suppose.

Col. Town. A little more blood in your cheeks.

Ber. I have been walking!

Col. Town. Is that all? Pray was it Mr. Loveless went from here just now?

Ber. O yes—he has been walking with me.

Col. Town. He has!

Ber. Upon my word I think he is a very agreeable man; and there is certainly something particularly insinuating in his address!

Col. Town. [*Aside.*] So, so! she hasn't even the modesty to dissemble! [*Aloud.*] Pray, madam, may I, without impertinence, trouble you with a few serious questions?

Ber. As many as you please; but pray let them be as little serious as possible.

Col. Town. Is it not near two years since I have presumed to address you?

Ber. I don't know exactly—but it has been a tedious long time.

Col. Town. Have I not, during that period, had every reason to believe that my assiduities were far from being unacceptable?

Ber. Why, to do you justice, you have been extremely troublesome—and I confess I have been more civil to you than you deserved.

Col. Town. Did I not come to this place at your express desire, and for no purpose but the honour of meeting you?—and after waiting a month in disappointment, have you condescended to explain, or in the slightest way apologise, for your conduct?

Ber. O heavens! apologise for my conduct!—apologise to you! O you barbarian! But pray now, my good serious colonel, have you any thing more to add?

Col. Town. Nothing, madam, but that after such behaviour I am less surprised at what I saw just now; it is not very wonderful that the woman who can trifle with the delicate addresses of an honourable lover should be found coquetting with the husband of her friend.

Ber. Very true: no more wonderful than it was for this honourable lover to divert himself in the absence of this coquette, with endeavouring to seduce his friend's wife! O colonel, colonel, don't talk of honour or your friend, for Heaven's sake!

Col. Town. [*Aside.*] 'Sdeath! how came she to suspect this!—[*Aloud.*] Really, madam, I don't understand you.

Ber. Nay, nay, you saw I did not pretend to misunderstand you.—But here comes the lady: perhaps you would be glad to be left with her for an explanation.

Col. Town. O madam, this recrimination is a poor resource; and to convince you how much you are mistaken, I beg leave to decline the happiness you propose me.—Madam, your servant.

Enter AMANDA. COLONEL TOWNLY *whispers* AMANDA, *and exit.*

Ber. [*Aside.*] He carries it off well, however; upon my word, very well! How tenderly they part!—[*Aloud.*] So, cousin; I hope you have not been chiding your admirer for being with me? I assure you we have been talking of you.

Aman. Fy, Berinthia!—my admirer! will you never learn to talk in earnest of any thing?

Ber. Why this shall be in earnest, if you please; for my part, I only tell you matter of fact.

Aman. I'm sure there's so much jest and earnest in what you say to me on this subject, I scarce know how to take it. I have just parted with Mr. Loveless; perhaps it is fancy, but I think there is an alteration in his manner which alarms me.

Ber. And so you are jealous! is that all?

Aman. That all! is jealousy, then, nothing?

Ber. It should be nothing, if I were in your case.

Aman. Why, what would you do?

Ber. I'd cure myself.

Aman. How?

Ber. Care as little for my husband as he did for me. Look you, Amanda, you may build castles in the air, and fume, and fret, and grow thin, and lean, and pale, and ugly, if you please; but I tell you, no man worth having is true to his wife, or ever was, or ever will be so.

Aman. Do you then really think he's false to me? for I did not suspect him.

Ber. Think so? I am sure of it.

Aman. You are sure on't?

Ber. Positively—he fell in love at the play.

Aman. Right—the very same! But who could have told you this?

Ber. Um!—Oh, Townly! I suppose your husband has made him his confidant.

Aman. O base Loveless! And what did Townly say on 't?

Ber. [*Aside.*] So, so! why should she ask that?—[*Aloud.*] Say! why he abused Loveless extremely, and said all the tender things of you in the world.

Aman. Did he?—Oh! my heart!—I'm very ill—dear Berinthia, don't leave me a moment.   [*Exeunt.*

SCENE III.—*Outside of* SIR TUNBELLY CLUMSY'S *House.*

Enter TOM FASHION *and* LORY.

Fash. So, here's our inheritance, Lory, if we can but get into possession. But methinks the seat of our family looks like Noah's ark, as if the chief part on 't were designed for the fowls of the air, and the beasts of the field.

Lory. Pray, sir, don't let your head run upon the orders of building here: get but the heiress, let the devil take the house.

Fash. Get but the house, let the devil take the heiress! I say.—But come, we have no time to squander; knock at the door.—[LORY *knocks two or three times at the gate.*] What the devil! have they got no ears in this house?—Knock harder.

Lory. Egad, sir, this will prove some enchanted castle; we shall have the giant come out, by-and-by, with his club, and beat our brains out.
                                                     [*Knocks again.*

Fash. Hush, they come.

Serv. [*Within.*] Who is there?

Lory. Open the door and see: is that your country breeding?

Serv. Ay, but two words to that bargain.—Tummas, is the blunderbuss primed?

Fash. Ouns! give 'em good words, Lory,—or we shall be shot here a fortune catching.

Lory. Egad, sir, I think you're in the right on't.—Ho! Mr. What-d'ye-call-'um, will you please to let us in? or are we to be left to grow like willows by your moat side?

SERVANT *appears at the window with a blunderbuss.*

Serv. Well naw, what's ya're business?

Fash. Nothing, sir, but to wait upon Sir Tunbelly, with your leave.

Serv. To weat upon Sir Tunbelly! why you'll find that's just as Sir Tunbelly pleases.

Fash. But will you do me the favour, sir, to know whether Sir Tunbelly pleases or not?

Serv. Why, look you, d'ye see, with good words much may be done.—Ralph, go thy ways, and ask Sir Tunbelly if he pleases to be waited upon—and dost hear, call to nurse, that she may lock up Miss Hoyden before the gates open.

Fash. D'ye hear that, Lory?

Enter SIR TUNBELLY CLUMSY, *with* SERVANTS, *armed with guns, clubs, pitchforks,* &c.

Lory. Oh! [*Runs behind his master.*] O Lord! O Lord! Lord! we are both dead men!

Fash. Fool! thy fear will ruin us.   [*Aside to* LORY.

Lory. My fear, sir! 'sdeath, sir, I fear nothing.—[*Aside.*] Would I were well up to the chin in a horsepond!

Sir Tun. Who is it here hath any business with me?

Fash. Sir, 'tis I, if your name be Sir Tunbelly Clumsy.

Sir Tun. Sir, my name is Sir Tunbelly Clumsy, whether you have any business with me or not.—So you see I am not ashamed of my name, nor my face either.

Fash. Sir, you have no cause that I know of.

Sir Tun. Sir, if you have no cause either, I desire to know who you are; for, till I know your name, I shan't ask you to come into my house: and when I do know your name, 'tis six to four I don't ask you then.

Fash. Sir, I hope you'll find this letter an authentic passport.

[*Gives him a letter.*

Sir Tun. Cod's my life, from Mrs. Coupler!—I ask your lordship's pardon ten thousand times.—[*To a* SERVANT.] Here, run in a-doors quickly; get a Scotch coal fire in the parlour, set all the Turkey work chairs in their places, get the brass candlesticks out, and be sure stick the socket full of laurel—run!—[*Turns to* TOM FASHION.] My lord, I ask your lordship's pardon.—[*To* SERVANT.] And, do you hear, run away to nurse; bid her let Miss Hoyden loose again.—[*Exit* SERVANT.] I hope your honour will excuse the disorder of my family. We are not used to receive men of your lordship's great quality every day. Pray where are your coaches and servants, my lord?

Fash. Sir, that I might give you and your daughter a proof how impatient I am to be nearer akin to you, I left my equipage to follow me, and came away post with only one servant.

Sir Tun. Your lordship does me too much honour—it was exposing your person to too much fatigue and danger, I protest it was; but my daughter shall endeavour to make you what amends she can; and, though I say it that should not say it, Hoyden has charms.

Fash. Sir, I am not a stranger to them, though I am to her; common fame has done her justice.

Sir Tun. My lord, I am common fame's very grateful, humble servant. My lord, my girl's young—Hoyden is young, my lord: but this I must say for her, what she wants in art she has in breeding; and what's wanting in her age, is made good in her constitution.—So pray, my lord, walk in; pray, my lord, walk in.

Fash. Sir, I wait upon you.   [*Exeunt.*

SCENE IV.—*A Room in* SIR TUNBELLY CLUMSY'S *House.*

MISS HOYDEN *discovered alone.*

Miss Hoyd. Sure, nobody was ever used as I am! I know well enough what other girls do, for all they think to make a fool o' me. It's well I have a husband a-coming, or ecod I'd marry the baker, I would so. Nobody can knock at the gate, but presently I must be locked up; and here's the young greyhound can run loose about the house all the day long, so she can.—'Tis very well!

Nurse. [*Without, opening the door.*] Miss Hoyden! miss, miss, miss! Miss Hoyden!

Enter NURSE.

Miss Hoyd. Well, what do you make such a noise for, ha? What do you din a body's ears for? Can't one be at quiet for you?

Nurse. What do I din your ears for? Here's one come will din your ears for you.

Miss Hoyd. What care I who's come? I care not a fig who comes, or who goes, so long as I must be locked up like the ale-cellar.

Nurse. That, miss, is for fear you should be drank before you are ripe.

Miss Hoyd. Oh, don't trouble your head about that; I'm as ripe as you, though not so mellow.

Nurse. Very well! Now I have a good mind to lock you up again, and not let you see my lord to-night.

Miss Hoyd. My lord: why, is my husband come?

Nurse. Yes, marry, is he; and a goodly person too.

Miss Hoyd. [*Hugs* NURSE.] Oh, my dear nurse, forgive me this once, and I'll never misuse you again; no, if I do, you shall give me three thumps on the back, and a great pinch by the cheek.

Nurse. Ah, the poor thing! see now it melts; it's as full of good-nature as an egg's full of meat.

Miss Hoyd. But, my dear nurse, don't lie now—is he come, by your troth?

Nurse. Yes, by my truly, is he.

Miss Hoyd. O Lord! I'll go and put on my laced tucker, though I'm locked up for a month for 't.

[*Exeunt.* MISS HOYDEN *goes off capering, and twirling her doll by its leg.*

ACT IV.

SCENE I.—*A Room in* SIR TUNBELLY CLUMSY'S *House.*

Enter MISS HOYDEN *and* NURSE.

Nurse. Well, miss, how do you like your husband that is to be?

Miss Hoyd. O Lord, nurse, I'm so overjoyed I can scarce contain myself!

Nurse. Oh, but you must have a care of being too fond; for men, now-adays, hate a woman that loves 'em.

Miss Hoyd. Love him! why, do you think I love him, nurse? Ecod, I would not care if he was hanged, so I were but once married to him. No, that which pleases me is to think what work I'll make when I get to London; for when I am a wife and a lady both, ecod, I'll flaunt it with the best of 'em. Ay, and I shall have money enough to do so too, nurse.

Nurse. Ah, there's no knowing that, miss; for though these lords have a power of wealth indeed, yet, as I have heard say, they give it all to their sluts and their trulls, who joggle it about in their coaches, with a murrain to em, whilst poor madam sits sighing and wishing, and has not a spare half-crown to buy her a Practice of Piety.

Miss Hoyd. Oh, but for that, don't deceive yourself, nurse; for this I must say of my lord, he's as free as an open house at Christmas; for this very morning he told me I should have six hundred a year to buy pins. Now if he gives me six hundred a year to buy pins, what do you think he'll give me to buy petticoats?

Nurse. Ah, my dearest, he deceives thee foully, and he's no better than a rogue for his pains! These Londoners have got a gibberish with 'em would confound a gipsy. That which they call pin-money, is to buy everything in the versal world, down to their very shoe-knots. Nay, I have heard some folks say that some ladies, if they'll have gallants as they call 'em, are forced to find them out of their pin-money too.—But look, look, if his honour be not coming to you!—Now, if I were sure you would behave yourself handsomely, and not disgrace me that have brought you up, I'd leave you alone together.

Miss Hoyd. That's my best nurse; do as you'd be done by. Trust us together this once, and if I don't show my breeding, I wish I may never be married, but die an old maid.

Nurse. Well, this once I'll venture you. But if you disparage me——

Miss Hoyd. Never fear.   [*Exit* NURSE.

Enter TOM FASHION.

Fash. Your servant, madam; I'm glad to find you alone, for I have something of importance to speak to you about.

Miss Hoyd. Sir (my lord, I meant), you may speak to me about what you please, I shall give you a civil answer.

Fash. You give so obliging an one, it encourages me to tell you in a few words what I think, both for your interest and mine. Your father, I suppose you know, has resolved to make me happy in being your husband; and I hope I may obtain your consent to perform what he desires.

Miss Hoyd. Sir, I never disobey my father in any thing but eating green gooseberries.

Fash. So good a daughter must needs be an admirable wife. I am therefore impatient till you are mine, and hope you will so far consider the violence of my love, that you won't have the cruelty to defer my happiness so long as your father designs it.

Miss Hoyd. Pray, my lord, how long is that?

Fash. Madam, a thousand years—a whole week.

Miss Hoyd. Why I thought it was to be to-morrow morning, as soon as I was up. I'm sure nurse told me so.

Fash. And it shall be to-morrow morning, if you'll consent.

Miss Hoyd. If I'll consent! Why I thought I was to obey you as my husband?

Fash. That's when we are married. Till then, I'm to obey you.

Miss Hoyd. Why then, if we are to take it by turns, it's the same thing. I'll obey you now, and when we are married, you shall obey me.

Fash. With all my heart. But I doubt we must get nurse on our side, or we shall hardly prevail with the chaplain.

Miss Hoyd: No more we shan't, indeed; for he loves her better than he loves his pulpit, and would always be a-preaching to her by his good will.

Fash. Why then, my dear, if you'll call her hither, we'll persuade her presently.

Miss Hoyd. O Lud! I'll tell you a way how to persuade her to any thing.

Fash. How's that?

Miss Hoyd. Why tell her she's a handsome comely woman, and give her half-a-crown.

Fash. Nay, if that will do, she shall have half a score of 'em.

Miss Hoyd. O gemini! for half that she'd marry you herself.—I'll run and call her.　　　　　　　　　　　　　　　　[*Exit.*

Fash. So! matters go on swimmingly. This is a rare girl, i'faith. I shall have a fine time on 't with her at London.

Enter LORY.

So, Lory, what's the matter?

Lory. Here, sir—an intercepted packet from the enemy; your brother's postillion brought it. I knew the livery, pretended to be a servant of Sir Tunbelly's, and so got possession of the letter.

Fash. [*Looks at the letter.*] Ouns! he tells Sir Tunbelly here that he will be with him this evening, with a large party to supper.—Egad, I must marry the girl directly.

Lory. Oh, zounds, sir, directly to be sure. . Here she comes.　　[*Exit.*

Fash. And the old Jezebel with her.

Re-enter MISS HOYDEN and NURSE.

How do you do, good Mrs. Nurse? I desired your young lady would give me leave to see you, that I might thank you for your extraordinary care and kind conduct in her education: pray accept of this small acknowledgment for it at present, and depend upon my further kindness when I shall be that happy thing her husband.　　　　　　　　　　　　　[*Gives her money.*

Nurse. [*Aside.*] Gold, by the maakins!—[*Aloud.*] Your honour's goodness is too great. Alas! all I can boast of is, I gave her pure good milk, and so your honour would have said, an you had seen how the poor thing thrived, and how it would look up in my face, and crow and laugh, it would.

Miss Hoyd. [*To* NURSE, *taking her angrily aside.*] Pray, one word with you. Pr'ythee, nurse, don't stand ripping up old stories, to make one ashamed before one's love. Do you think such a fine proper gentleman as he is cares for a fiddlecome tale of a child? If you have a mind to make him have a good opinion of a woman, don't tell him what one did then, tell him what one can do now.—[*To* TOM FASHION.] I hope your honour will excuse my mis-manners to whisper before you; it was only to give some orders about the family.

Fash. Oh, every thing, madam, is to give way to business; besides, good housewifery is a very commendable quality in a young lady.

Miss Hoyd. Pray, sir, are young ladies good housewives at London-town? Do they darn their own linen?

Fash. Oh no, they study how to spend money, not to save.

Miss Hoyd. Ecod, I don't know but that may be better sport, ha, nurse?

Fash. Well, you shall have your choice when you come there.

Miss Hoyd. Shall I? then, by my troth, I'll get there as fast as I can.—[*To* NURSE.] His honour desires you'll be so kind as to let us be married to-morrow.

Nurse. To-morrow, my dear madam?

Fash. Ay, faith, nurse, you may well be surprised at miss's wanting to put it off so long. To-morrow! no, no; 'tis now, this very hour, I would have the ceremony performed.

Miss Hoyd. Ecod, with all my heart.

Nurse. O mercy! worse and worse!

Fash. Yes, sweet nurse, now and privately; for all things being signed and sealed, why should Sir Tunbelly make us stay a week for a wedding-dinner?

Nurse. But if you should be married now, what will you do when Sir Tunbelly calls for you to be married?

Miss Hoyd. Why then we will be married again.

Nurse. What twice, my child?

Miss Hoyd. Ecod, I don't care how often I'm married, not I.

Nurse. Well, I'm such a tender-hearted fool, I find I can refuse you no-thing. So you shall e'en follow your own inventions.

Miss Hoyd. Shall I? O Lord, I could leap over the moon!

Fash. Dear nurse, this goodness of yours shall be still more rewarded. But now you must employ your power with the chaplain, that he may do his friendly office too, and then we shall be all happy. Do you think you can prevail with him?

Nurse. Prevail with him! or he shall never prevail with me, I can tell him that.

Fash. I'm glad to hear it; however, to strengthen your interest with him, you may let him know I have several fat livings in my gift, and that the first that falls shall be in your disposal.

Nurse. Nay, then, I'll make him marry more folks than one, I'll promise him!

Miss Hoyd. Faith, do, nurse, make him marry you too; I'm sure he'll do't for a fat living.

Fash. Well, nurse, while you go and settle matters with him, your lady and I will go and take a walk in the garden.—[*Exit* NURSE.] Come, madam, dare you venture yourself alone with me? [*Takes* MISS HOYDEN *by the hand.*

Miss Hoyd. Oh dear, yes, sir; I don't think you'll do any thing to me I need be afraid on.   [*Exeunt.*

SCENE II.—AMANDA'S *Dressing-room.*

Enter AMANDA, *followed by her* MAID.

Maid. If you please, madam, only to say whether you'll have me buy them or not?

Aman. Yes—no—Go, teaser; I care not what you do. Pr'ythee leave me.   [*Exit* MAID.

Enter BERINTHIA.

Ber. What, in the name of Jove, is the matter with you?

Aman. The matter, Berinthia! I'm almost mad; I'm plagued to death.

Ber. Who is it that plagues you?

Aman. Who do you think should plague a wife but her husband?

Ber. O, ho! is it come to that?—We shall have you wish yourself a widow, by-and-by.

Aman. Would I were any thing but what I am! A base, ungrateful man, to use me thus!

Ber. What has he given you fresh reason to suspect his wandering?

Aman. Every hour gives me reason.

Ber. And yet, Amanda, you perhaps at this moment cause in another's breast the same tormenting doubts and jealousies which you feel so sensibly yourself.

Aman. Heaven knows I would not.

Ber. Why, you can't tell but there may be some one as tenderly attached to Townly, whom you boast of as your conquest, as you can be to your husband?

Aman. I 'm sure I never encouraged his pretensions.

Ber. Psha! psha! no sensible man ever perseveres to love without encouragement. Why have you not treated him as you have Lord Foppington?

Aman. Because he presumed not so far. But let us drop the subject. Men, not women, are riddles. Mr. Loveless now follows some flirt for variety, whom I 'm sure he does not like so well as he does me.

Ber. That's more than you know, madam.

Aman. Why, do you know the ugly thing?

Ber. I think I can guess at the person; but she 's no such ugly thing neither.

Aman. Is she very handsome?

Ber. Truly I think so.

Aman. Whate'er she be, I 'm sure he does not like her well enough to bestow any thing more than a little outward gallantry upon her.

Ber. [*Aside.*] Outward gallantry! I can't bear this.—[*Aloud.*] Come, come, don't you be too secure, Amanda: while you suffer Townly to imagine that you do not detest him for his designs on you, you have no right to complain that your husband is engaged elsewhere. But here comes the person we were speaking of.

Enter COLONEL TOWNLY.

Col. Town. Ladies, as I come uninvited, I beg, if I intrude, you will use the same freedom in turning me out again.

Aman. I believe it is near the time Loveless said he would be at home. He talked of accepting of Lord Foppington's invitation to sup at Sir Tunbelly Clumsy's.

Col. Town. His lordship has done me the honour to invite me also. If you 'll let me escort you, I 'll let you into a mystery as we go, in which you must play a part when we arrive.

Aman. But we have two hours yet to spare; the carriages are not ordered till eight, and it is not a five minutes' drive. So, cousin, let us keep the colonel to play at piquet with us, till Mr. Loveless comes home.

Ber. As you please, madam; but you know I have a letter to write.

Col. Town. Madam, you know you may command me, though I am a very wretched gamester.

Aman. Oh, you play well enough to lose your money, and that 's all the ladies require; and so, without any more ceremony, let us go into the next room, and call for cards and candles.   [*Exeunt.*

SCENE III.—BERINTHIA'S *Dressing-room.*

Enter LOVELESS.

Love. So, thus far all 's well: I have got into her dressing-room, and it being dusk, I think nobody has perceived me steal into the house. I heard Berinthia tell my wife she had some particular letters to write this evening, before she went to Sir Tunbelly's, and here are the implements of correspondence.—How shall I muster up assurance to show myself when she comes? I think she has given me encouragement; and, to do my impudence justice, I have made the most of it.—I hear a door open, and some one coming. If it should be my wife, what the devil should I say? I believe she mistrusts me, and, by my life, I don't deserve her tenderness; however, I am determined to reform—though not yet. Ha! Berinthia!—So, I'll step in here, till I see what sort of humour she is in.   [*Goes into the closet.*

Enter BERINTHIA.

Ber. Was ever so provoking a situation! To think I should sit and hear him compliment Amanda to my face! I have lost all patience with them both! I would not for something have Loveless know what temper of mind they have piqued me into; yet I can't bear to leave them together. No, I'll put my papers away, and return to disappoint them.—[*Goes to the closet.*]—O Lord! a ghost! a ghost! a ghost!

Re-enter LOVELESS.

Love. Peace, my angel! it's no ghost, but one worth a hundred spirits.

Ber. How, sir, have you had the insolence to presume to —— run in again, here's somebody coming.   [LOVELESS *goes into the closet.*

Enter MAID.

Maid. O Lord, ma'am! what's the matter?

Ber. O Heavens! I'm almost frightened out of my wits! I thought verily I had seen a ghost, and 'twas nothing but a black hood pinned against the wall. You may go again; I am the fearfullest fool!   [*Exit* MAID.

Re-enter LOVELESS.

Love. Is the coast clear?

Ber. The coast clear! Upon my word, I wonder at your assurance!

Love. Why then you wonder before I have given you a proof of it. But where's my wife?

Ber. At cards.

Love. With whom?

Ber. With Townly.

Love. Then we are safe enough.

Ber. You are so! Some husbands would be of another mind, were he at cards with their wives.

Love. And they'd be in the right on't too; but I dare trust mine.

Ber. Indeed! and she, I doubt not, has the same confidence in you. Yet do you think she'd be content to come and find you here?

Love. Egad, as you say, that's true!—Then, for fear she should come, hadn't we better go into the next room, out of her way?

Ber. What, in the dark?

Love. Ay, or with a light, which you please.

Ber. You are certainly very impudent.

Love. Nay, then—let me conduct you, my angel!

Ber. Hold, hold! you are mistaken in your angel, I assure you.

Love. I hope not; for by this hand I swear ——

Ber. Come, come, let go my hand, or I shall hate you!—I'll cry out as I live!

Love. Impossible! you cannot be so cruel.

Ber. Ha! here's some one coming. Begone instantly!

Love. Will you promise to return, if I remain here?

Ber. Never trust myself in a room again with you while I live

Love. But I have something particular to communicate to you.

Ber. Well, well, before we go to Sir Tunbelly's, I'll walk upon the lawn. If you are fond of a moonlight evening, you'll find me there.

Love. I'faith, they're coming here now!—I take you at your word.

[*Exit into the closet.*

Ber. 'Tis Amanda, as I live! I hope she has not heard his voice; though I mean she should have her share of jealousy in her turn.

Enter AMANDA.

Aman. Berinthia, why did you leave me?

Ber. I thought I only spoiled your party.

Aman. Since you have been gone, Townly has attempted to renew his importunities. I must break with him—for I cannot venture to acquaint Mr. Loveless with his conduct.

Ber. Oh, no! Mr. Loveless mustn't know of it by any means.

Aman. Oh, not for the world!—I wish, Berinthia, you would undertake to speak to Townly on the subject.

Ber. Upon my word, it would be a very pleasant subject for me to talk upon! But, come, let us go back; and you may depend on't I'll not leave you together again, if I can help it.   [*Exeunt.*

Re-enter LOVELESS.

Love. So—so! a pretty piece of business I have overheard! Townly makes love to my wife, and I am not to know it for all the world. I must inquire into this—and, by Heaven, if I find that Amanda has, in the smallest degree—yet what have I been at here!—Oh, 'sdeath! that's no rule.

That wife alone unsullied credit wins,
Whose virtues can atone her husband's sins.
Thus, while the man has other nymphs in view,
It suits the woman to be doubly true.   [*Exit.*

ACT V.

SCENE I.—*The Garden behind* LOVELESS's *Lodgings.*

Enter LOVELESS.

Love. Now, does she mean to make a fool of me, or not! I shan't wait much longer, for my wife will soon be inquiring for me to set out on our supping party. Suspense is at all times the devil, but of all modes of suspense, the watching for a loitering mistress is the worst.—But let me accuse her no longer; she approaches with one smile to o'erpay the anxieties of a year.

Enter BERINTHIA.

O Berinthia, what a world of kindness are you in my debt! had you staid five minutes longer ——

Ber. You would have gone, I suppose?

Love. Egad, she's right enough.   [*Aside.*

Ber. And I assure you 'twas ten to one that I came at all. In short, I begin to think you are too dangerous a being to trifle with; and as I shall probably only make a fool of you at last, I believe we had better let matters rest as they are.

Love. You cannot mean it, sure?

Ber. What more would you have me give to a married man?

Love. How doubly cruel to remind me of my misfortunes!

Ber. A misfortune to be married to so charming a woman as Amanda?

Love. I grant all her merit, but——'sdeath! now see what you have done by talking of her—she's here, by all that's unlucky, and Townly with her. —I'll observe them.

Ber. O Gad, we had better get out of the way; for I should feel as awkward to meet her as you.

Love. Ay, if I mistake not, I see Townly coming this way also. I must see a little into this matter.   [*Steps aside.*

Ber. Oh, if that's your intention, I am no woman if I suffer myself to be outdone in curiosity.   [*Goes on the other side.*

Enter AMANDA.

Aman. Mr. Loveless come home, and walking on the lawn! I will not suffer him to walk so late, though perhaps it is to show his neglect of me.— Mr. Loveless, I must speak with you.—Ha! Townly again! How I am persecuted!

Enter COLONEL TOWNLY.

Col. Town. Madam, you seem disturbed.

Aman. Sir, I have reason.

Col. Town. Whatever be the cause, I would to Heaven it were in my power to bear the pain, or to remove the malady.

Aman. Your interference can only add to my distress.

Col. Town. Ah, madam, if it be the sting of unrequited love you suffer from, seek for your remedy in revenge: weigh well the strength and beauty of your charms, and rouse up that spirit a woman ought to bear. Disdain the false embraces of a husband. See at your feet a real lover; his zeal may give him title to your pity, although his merit cannot claim your love.

Love. So, so, very fine, i' faith!   [*Aside.*

Aman. Why do you presume to talk to me thus? Is this your friendship to Mr. Loveless? I perceive you will compel me at last to acquaint him with your treachery.

Col. Town. He could not upbraid me if you were.—He deserves it from me; for he has not been more false to you than faithless to me.

Aman. To you?

Col. Town. Yes, madam; the lady for whom he now deserts those charms which he was never worthy of, was mine by right; and, I imagined too, by inclination. Yes, madam, Berinthia, who now——

Aman. Berinthia! Impossible!

Col. Town. 'Tis true, or may I never merit your attention. She is the deceitful sorceress who now holds your husband's heart in bondage.

Aman. I will not believe it.

Col. Town. By the faith of a true lover, I speak from conviction. This very day I saw them together, and overheard——

Aman. Peace, sir! I will not even listen to such slander—this is a poor device to work on my resentment, to listen to your insidious addresses. No, sir, though Mr. Loveless may be capable of error, I am convinced I cannot be deceived so grossly in him, as to believe what you now report; and for Berinthia, you should have fixed on some more probable person for my rival than her who is my relation and my friend: for while I am myself free from guilt, I will never believe that love can beget injury, or confidence create ingratitude.

Col. Town. If I do not prove to you——

Aman. You never shall have an opportunity. From the artful manner in which you first showed yourself to me, I might have been led, as far as virtue permitted, to have thought you less criminal than unhappy; but this last unmanly artifice merits at once my resentment and contempt.   [*Exit.*

Col. Town. Sure there's divinity about her; and she has dispensed some portion of honour's light to me: yet can I bear to lose Berinthia without revenge or compensation? Perhaps she is not so culpable as I thought her. I was mistaken when I began to think lightly of Amanda's virtue, and may be in my censure of my Berinthia. Surely I love her still, for I feel I should be happy to find myself in the wrong.   [*Exit.*

Re-enter LOVELESS *and* BERINTHIA.

Ber. Your servant, Mr. Loveless.

Love. Your servant, madam.

Ber. Pray what do you think of this?

Love. Truly, I don't know what to say.

Ber. Don't you think we steal forth two contemptible creatures?

Love. Why tolerably so, I must confess.

Ber. And do you conceive it possible for you ever to give Amanda the least uneasiness again?

Love. No, I think we never should indeed.

Ber. Wel why, monster, you don't pretend that I ever entertained a thought?

Love. Why then, sincerely and honestly, Berinthia, there is something in my wife's conduct which strikes me so forcibly, that if it were not for shame, and the fear of hurting you in her opinion, I swear I would follow her, confess my error, and trust to her generosity for forgiveness.

Ber. Nay, pr'ythee, don't let your respect for me prevent you; for as my object in trifling with you was nothing more than to pique Townly, and as I perceive he has been actuated by a similar motive, you may depend on't I shall make no mystery of the matter to him.

Love. By no means inform him; for though I may choose to pass by his conduct without resentment, how will he presume to look me in the face again?

Ber. How will you presume to look him in the face again?

Love. He, who has dared to attempt the honour of my wife!

Ber. You, who have dared to attempt the honour of his mistress! Come, come, be ruled by me, who affect more levity than I have, and don't think of anger in this cause. A readiness to resent injuries is a virtue only in those who are slow to injure.

Love. Then I will be ruled by you; and when you shall think proper to undeceive Townly, may your good qualities make as sincere a convert of him as Amanda's have of me.—When truth's extorted from us, then we own the robe of virtue is a sacred habit.

> Could women but our secret counsels scan—
> Could they but reach the deep reserve of man—
> To keep our love they'd rate their virtue high,
> They live together, and together die.   [*Exeunt.*

SCENE II.—*A Room in* SIR TUNBELLY CLUMSY'S *House.*

Enter MISS HOYDEN, NURSE, *and* TOM FASHION.

Fash. This quick despatch of the chaplain's I take so kindly, it shall give him claim to my favour as long as I live, I assure you.

Miss Hoyd. And to mine too, I promise you.

Nurse. I most humbly thank your honours; and may your children swarm about you like bees about a honeycomb!

Miss Hoyd. Ecod, with all my heart—the more the merrier, I say—ha, nurse?

Enter LORY.

Lory. One word with you, for Heaven's sake.
       [*Taking* TOM FASHION *hastily aside.*

Fash. What the devil's the matter?

Lory. Sir, your fortune's ruined if you are not married. Yonder's your brother arrived, with two coaches and six horses, twenty footmen, and a coat worth fourscore pounds—so judge what will become of your lady's heart.

Fash. Is he in the house yet?

Lory. No, they are capitulating with him at the gate. Sir Tunbelly luckily takes him for an impostor; and I have told him that we have heard of this plot before.

Fash. That's right.—[*Turning to* MISS HOYDEN.] My dear, here's a troublesome business my man tells me of, but don't be frightened; we shall be too hard for the rogue. Here's an impudent fellow at the gate (not knowing I was come hither incognito) has taken my name upon him, in hopes to run away with you.

Miss Hoyd. Oh, the brazen-faced varlet! it's well we are married, or may be we might never have been so.

Fash. [*Aside.*] Egad, like enough.—[*Aloud.*] Pr'ythee, nurse, run to Sir Tunbelly, and stop him from going to the gate before I speak with him.

Nurse. An't please your honour, my lady and I had best lock ourselves up till the danger be over.

Fash. Do so, if you please.

Miss Hoyd. Not so fast; I won't be locked up any more, now I'm married.

Fash. Yes, pray, my dear, do, till we have seized this rascal.

Miss Hoyd. Nay, if you'll pray me, I'll do any thing. [*Exit with* NURSE.

Fash. Hark you, sirrah, things are better than you imagine. The wedding's over.

Lory. The devil it is, sir!   [*Capers about.*

Fash. Not a word—all's safe—but Sir Tunbelly don't know it, nor must not yet. So I am resolved to brazen the brunt of the business out, and have the pleasure of turning the impostor upon his lordship, which I believe may easily be done.

Enter SIR TUNBELLY CLUMSY.

Did you ever hear, sir, of so impudent an undertaking?

Sir Tun. Never, by the mass; but we'll tickle him, I'll warrant you.

Fash. They tell me, sir, he has a great many people with him, disguised like servants.

Sir Tun. Ay, ay, rogues enow, but we have mastered them. We only fired a few shot over their heads, and the regiment scoured in an instant.—Here, Tummas, bring in your prisoner.

Fash. If you please, Sir Tunbelly, it will be best for me not to confront the fellow yet, till you have heard how far his impudence will carry him.

Sir Tun. Egad, your lordship is an ingenious person. Your lordship then will please to step aside.

Lory. [*Aside.*] 'Fore heaven, I applaud my master's modesty!

[*Exit with* TOM FASHION.

Enter SERVANTS, *with* LORD FOPPINGTON *disarmed.*

Sir Tun. Come, bring him along, bring him along.

Lord Fop. What the plague do you mean, gentlemen? is it fair time, that you are all drunk before supper?

Sir Tun. Drunk, sirrah! here's an impudent rogue for you now. Drunk or sober, bully, I'm a justice o' the peace, and know how to deal with strollers.

Lord Fop. Strollers!

Sir Tun. Ay, strollers. Come, give an account of yourself. What's your name? where do you live? do you pay scot and lot? Come, are you a freeholder or a copyholder?

Lord Fop. And why dost thou ask me so many impertinent questions?

Sir Tun. Because I'll make you answer 'em, before I have done with you, you rascal you!

Lord Fop. Before Gad, all the answers I can make to them is, that you are a very extraordinary old fellow, stap my vitals!

Sir Tun. Nay, if thou art joking deputy lieutenants, we know how to deal with you.—Here, draw a warrant for him immediately.

Lord Fop. A warrant! What the devil is 't thou wouldst be at, old gentleman?

Sir Tun. I would be at you, sirrah, (if my hands were not tied as a magistrate,) and with these two double fists beat your teeth down your throat, you dog you!   [*Driving him.*

Lord Fop. And why wouldst thou spoil my face at that rate?

Sir Tun. For your design to rob me of my daughter, villain.

Lord Fop. Rob thee of thy daughter! Now do I begin to believe I am in bed and asleep, and that all this is but a dream. Pr'ythee, old father, wilt thou give me leave to ask thee one question?

Sir Tun. I can't tell whether I will or not, till I know what it is.

Lord Fop. Why, then, it is, whether thou didst not write to my Lord Foppington, to come down and marry thy daughter?

Sir Tun. Yes, marry, did I, and my Lord Foppington is come down, and shall marry my daughter before she's a day older.

Lord Fop. Now give me thy hand, old dad; I thought we should understand one another at last.

Sir Tun. The fellow's mad!—Here, bind him hand and foot.

[*They bind him.*

Lord Fop. Nay, pr'ythee, knight, leave fooling; thy jest begins to grow dull.

Sir Tun. Bind him, I say—he's mad: bread and water, a dark room, and a whip, may bring him to his senses again.

Lord Fop. Pr'ythee, Sir Tunbelly, why should you take such an aversion to the freedom of my address as to suffer the rascals thus to skewer down my arms like a rabbit!—[*Aside.*] Egad, if I don't awake, by all that I can see, this is like to prove one of the most impertinent dreams that ever I dreamt in my life.

Re-enter MISS HOYDEN *and* NURSE.

Miss Hoyd. [*Going up to* LORD FOPPINGTON.] Is this he that would have run—Fough, how he stinks of sweets!—Pray, father, let him be dragged through the horsepond.

Lord Fop. This must be my wife, by her natural inclination to her husband.   [*Aside.*

Miss Hoyd. Pray, father, what do you intend to do with him—hang him?

Sir Tun. That at least, child.

Nurse. Ay, and it's e'en too good for him too.

Lord Fop. Madame la gouvernante, I presume: hitherto this appears to me to be one of the most extraordinary families that ever man of quality matched into.   [*Aside*

Sir Tun. What's become of my lord, daughter?

Miss Hoyd. He's just coming, sir.

Lord Fop. My lord, what does he mean by that, now!   [*Aside.*

Re-enter TOM FASHION *and* LORY.

Stap my vitals, Tam, now the dream's out!   [*Runs.*

Fash. Is this the fellow, sir, that designed to trick me of your daughter?

Sir Tun. This is he, my lord; how do you like him; is not he a pretty fellow to get a fortune?

Fash. I find by his dress he thought your daughter might be taken with a beau.

Miss Hoyd. Oh, gemini! is this a beau! let me see him again. [*Surveys him.*] Ha! I find a beau is no such ugly thing, neither.

Fash. [*Aside.*] Egad, she'll be in love with him presently—I'll e'en have him sent away to jail.—[*To* LORD FOPPINGTON.] Sir, though your undertaking shows you a person of no extraordinary modesty, I suppose you han't confidence enough to expect much favour from me?

Lord Fop. Strike me dumb, Tam, thou art a very impudent fellow.

Nurse. Look, if the varlet has not the effrontery to call his lordship plain Thomas!

Lord Fop. My Lord Foppington, shall I beg one word with your lordship?

Nurse. Ho, ho, it's my lord with him now! See how afflictions will humble folks.

Miss Hoyd. Pray, my lord—[*To* FASHION]—don't let him whisper too close, lest he bite your ear off.

Lord Fop. I am not altogether so hungry as your ladyship is pleased to imagine.—[*Aside to* TOM FASHION.] Look you, Tam, I am sensible I have not been so kind to you as I ought, but I hope you'll forgive what's past, and accept of the five thousand pounds I offer—thou mayst live in extreme splendour with it, stap my vitals!

Fash. It's a much easier matter to prevent a disease than to cure it. A quarter of that sum would have secured your mistress, twice as much cannot redeem her.   [*Aside to* LORD FOPPINGTON.

Sir Tun. Well, what says he!

Fash. Only the rascal offered me a bribe to let him go.

Sir Tun. Ay, he shall go, with a plague to him!—Lead on, constable.

Enter SERVANT.

Serv. Sir, here is Muster Loveless, and Muster Colonel Townly, and some ladies to wait on you.   [*To* TOM FASHION.

Lory. [*Aside to* TOM FASHION.]   So, sir, what will you do now.

Fash. [*Aside to* LORY.]   Be quiet; they are in the plot.—[*Aloud.*]   Only a few friends, Sir Tunbelly, whom I wish to introduce to you.

Lord Fop. Thou art the most impudent fellow, Tam, that ever nature yet brought into the world.—Sir Tunbelly, strike me speechless, but these are my friends and acquaintance, and my guests, and they will soon inform thee whether I am the true Lord Foppington or not.

Enter LOVELESS, COLONEL TOWNLY, AMANDA, *and* BERINTHIA.—LORD FOP-PINGTON *accosts them as they pass, but none answer him.*

Fash. So, gentlemen, this is friendly; I rejoice to see you.

Col Town. My lord, we are fortunate to be the witnesses of your lordship's happiness.

Love. But your lordship will do us the honour to introduce us to Sir Tunbelly Clumsy?

Aman. And us to your lady.

Lord Fop. Gad take me, but they are all in a story!   [*Aside.*

Sir Tun. Gentlemen, you do me much honour; my Lord Foppington's friends will ever be welcome to me and mine.

Fash. My love, let me introduce you to these ladies.

Miss Hoyd. By goles, they look so fine and so stiff, I am almost ashamed to come nigh 'em.

Aman. A most engaging lady, indeed!

Miss Hoyd. Thank ye, ma'am.

Ber. And I doubt not will soon distinguish herself in the beau-monde.

Miss Hoyd. Where is that?

Fash. You'll soon learn, my dear.

Love. But Lord Foppington ——

Lord Fop. Sir!

Love. Sir! I was not addressing myself to you, sir!—Pray who is this gentleman? He seems rather in a singular predicament ——

Col. Town. For so well-dressed a person, a little oddly circumstanced, indeed.

Sir Tun. Ha! ha! ha!—So, these are your friends and your guests, ha, my adventurer?

Lord Fop. I am struck dumb with their impudence, and cannot positively say whether I shall ever speak again or not.

Sir Tun. Why, sir, this modest gentleman wanted to pass himself upon me as Lord Foppington, and carry off my daughter.

Love. A likely plot to succeed, truly, ha! ha!

Lord Fop. As Gad shall judge me, Loveless, I did not expect this from thee. Come, pr'ythee confess the joke; tell Sir Tunbelly that I am the real

Lord Foppington, who yesterday made love to thy wife; was honoured by her with a slap on the face, and afterwards pinked through the body by thee.

Sir Tun. A likely story, truly, that a peer would behave thus!

Love. A pretty fellow, indeed, that would scandalize the character he wants to assume; but what will you do with him, Sir Tunbelly?

Sir Tun. Commit him, certainly, unless the bride and bridegroom choose to pardon him.

Lord Fop. Bride and bridegroom! For Gad's sake, Sir Tunbelly, 'tis tarture to me to hear you call 'em so.

Miss Hoyd. Why, you ugly thing, what would you have him call us—dog and cat?

Lord Fop. By no means, miss; for that sounds ten times more like man and wife than t' other.

Sir Tun. A precious rogue this to come a-wooing!

Re-enter SERVANT.

Serv. There are some gentlefolks below to wait upon Lord Foppington.
[*Exit.*

Col. Town. 'Sdeath, Tom, what will you do now?
[*Aside to* TOM FASHION.

Lord Fop. Now, Sir Tunbelly, here are witnesses who I believe are not corrupted.

Sir Tun. Peace, fellow!—Would your lordship choose to have your guests shown here, or shall they wait till we come to 'em?

Fash. I believe, Sir Tunbelly, we had better not have these visitors here yet.—[*Aside.*] Egad, all must out.

Love. Confess, confess; we'll stand by you.   [*Aside to* TOM FASHION.

Lord Fop. Nay, Sir Tunbelly, I insist on your calling evidence on both sides—and if I do not prove that fellow an impostor——

Fash. Brother, I will save you the trouble, by now confessing that I am not what I have passed myself for.—Sir Tunbelly, I am a gentleman, and I flatter myself a man of character; but 'tis with great pride I assure you I am not Lord Foppington.

Sir Tun. Ouns!—what's this?—an impostor?—a cheat?—fire and faggots, sir, if you are not Lord Foppington, who the devil are you?

Fash. Sir, the best of my condition is, I am your son-in-law; and the worst of it is, I am brother to that noble peer.

Lord Fop. Impudent to the last, Gad dem me!

Sir Tun. My son-in-law! not yet, I hope.

Fash. Pardon me, sir; thanks to the goodness of your chaplain, and the kind offices of this gentlewoman.

Lory. 'Tis true, indeed, sir; I gave your daughter away, and Mrs. Nurse, here, was clerk.

Sir Tun. Knock that rascal down!—But speak, Jezebel, how's this?

Nurse. Alas! your honour, forgive me; I have been overreached in this business as well as you. Your worship knows, if the wedding-dinner had been ready, you would have given her away with your own hands.

Sir Tun. But how durst you do this without acquainting me!

Nurse. Alas! if your worship had seen how the poor thing begged and prayed, and clung and twined about me like ivy round an old wall, you would say, I who had nursed it, and reared it, must have had a heart like stone to refuse it.

Sir Tun. Ouns! I shall go mad! Unloose my lord there, you scoundrels!

Lord Fop. Why, when these gentlemen are at leisure, I should be glad to congratulate you on your son-in-law, with a little more freedom of address.

Miss Hoyd. Egad, though, I don't see which is to be my husband after all.

Love. Come, come, Sir Tunbelly, a man of your understanding must perceive, that an affair of this kind is not to be mended by anger and reproaches.

Col. Town. Take my word for it, Sir Tunbelly, you are only tricked into a son-in-law you may be proud of: my friend Tom Fashion is as honest a fellow as ever breathed.

Love. That he is, depend on 't; and will hunt or drink with you most affectionately: be generous, old boy, and forgive them——

Sir Tun. Never! the hussy!—when I had set my heart on getting her a title.

Lord Fop. Now, Sir Tunbelly, that I am untrussed—give me leave to thank thee for the very extraordinary reception I have met with in thy damned, execrable mansion; and at the same time to assure you, that of all the bumpkins and blockheads I have had the misfortune to meet with, thou art the most obstinate and egregious, strike me ugly!

Sir Tun. What 's this? I believe you are both rogues alike.

Lord Fop. No, Sir Tunbelly, thou wilt find to thy unspeakable mortification, that I am the real Lord Foppington, who was to have disgraced myself by an alliance with a clod; and that thou hast matched thy girl to a beggarly younger brother of mine, whose title-deeds might be contained in thy tobacco-box.

Sir Tun. Puppy! puppy!—I might prevent their being beggars, if I chose it; for I could give 'em as good a rent-roll as your lordship.

Lord Fop. Ay, old fellow, but you will not do that—for that would be acting like a Christian, and thou art a barbarian, stap my vitals.

Sir Tun. Udzookers! now six such words more, and I 'll forgive them directly.

Love. 'Slife, Sir Tunbelly, you should do it, and bless yourself—Ladies, what say you?

Aman. Good Sir Tunbelly, you must consent.

Ber. Come, you have been young yourself, Sir Tunbelly.

Sir Tun. Well then, if I must, I must; but turn—turn that sneering lord out, however, and let me be revenged on somebody. But first look whether I am a barbarian or not; there, children, I join your hands; and when I 'm in a better humour, I 'll give you my blessing.

Love. Nobly done, Sir Tunbelly! and we shall see you dance at a grandson's christening yet.

Miss Hoyd. By goles, though, I don't understand this! What, an't I to be a lady after all? only plain Mrs.——What 's my husband's name, nurse?

Nurse. Squire Fashion.

Miss Hoyd. Squire, is he?—Well, that 's better than nothing.

Lord Fop. [*Aside.*] Now I will put on a philosophic air, and show these people, that it is not possible to put a man of my quality out of countenance. —[*Aloud.*] Dear Tam, since things are fallen out, pr'ythee give me leave to wish thee joy; I do it *de bon cœur*, strike me dumb! You have married into a family of great politeness and uncommon elegance of manners, and your bride appears to be a lady beautiful in person, modest in her deportment, refined in her sentiments, and of nice morality, split my windpipe!

Miss Hoyd. By goles, husband, break his bones, if he calls me names!

Fash. Your lordship may keep up your spirits with your grimace, if you please; I shall support mine by Sir Tunbelly's favour, with this lady and three thousand pounds a year.

Lord Fop. Well, adieu, Tam!—Ladies, I kiss your hands.—Sir Tunbelly, I shall now quit this thy den; but while I retain the use of my arms, I shall ever remember thou art a demned horrid savage; Ged demn me!

[*Exit.*

Sir Tun. By the mass, 'tis well he's gone—for I should ha' been provoked, by-and-by, to ha' dun un a mischief. Well, if this is a lord, I think Hoyden has luck o' her side, in troth.

Col. Town. She has indeed, Sir Tunbelly.—But I hear the fiddles; his lordship, I know, had provided 'em.

Love. Oh, a dance and a bottle, Sir Tunbelly, by all means!

Sir Tun. I had forgot the company below; well—what—we must be merry then, ha? and dance and drink, ha? Well, 'fore George, you shan't say I do these things by halves. Son-in-law there looks like a hearty rogue, so we'll have a night on't: and which of these ladies will be the old man's partner, ha?—Ecod, I don't know how I came to be in so good a humour.

Ber. Well, Sir Tunbelly, my friend and I both will endeavour to keep you so: you have done a generous action, and are entitled to our attention. If you should be at a loss to divert your new guests, we will assist you to relate to them the plot of your daughter's marriage, and his lordship's deserved mortification; a subject which perhaps may afford no bad evening's entertainment.

Sir Tun. Ecod, with all my heart; though I am a main bungler at a long story.

Ber. Never fear; we will assist you, if the tale is judged worth being repeated; but of this you may be assured, that while the intention is evidently to please, British auditors will ever be indulgent to the errors of the performance.   [*Exeunt omnes.*

PIZARRO.

A TRAGEDY.

ADVERTISEMENT.

As the two translations which have been published of Kotzebue's "Spaniards in Peru" have, I understand, been very generally read, the public are in possession of all the materials necessary to form a judgment on the merits and defects of the Play performed at Drury-lane Theatre.

DEDICATION.

To her, whose approbation of this Drama, and whose peculiar delight in the applause it has received from the public, have been to *me* the highest gratification derived from its success—I dedicate this Play.

RICHARD BRINSLEY SHERIDAN.

DRAMATIS PERSONÆ.

AS ORIGINALLY ACTED AT DRURY-LANE THEATRE IN 1799.

ATALIBA	*Mr. Powell.*	OLD BLIND MAN	*Mr. Cory.*
ROLLA	*Mr. Kemble.*	BOY	*Master Chatterley.*
OROZEMBO	*Mr. Dowton.*	SENTINEL	*Mr. Holland.*
ORANO	*Mr. Archer.*	ATTENDANT	*Mr. Maddocks.*
ALONZO	*Mr. C. Kemble.*	CORA	*Mrs. Jordan.*
PIZARRO	*Mr. Barrymore.*	ELVIRA	*Mrs. Siddons.*
ALMAGRO	*Mr. Caulfield.*	ZULUGA	
GONZALO	*Mr. Wentworth.*	Peruvian Warriors, Women, and
DAVILLA	*Mr. Trueman.*	Children, High-priest, Priests, and
GOMEZ	*Mr. Surmount.*	Virgins of the Sun, Spanish Officers,
VALVERDE	*Mr. R. Palmer.*	Soldiers, Guards, &c. &c.
LAS-CASAS	*Mr. Aickin.*	

SCENE—PERU.

PROLOGUE,

WRITTEN BY RICHARD BRINSLEY SHERIDAN.

SPOKEN BY MR. KING.

CHILL'D by rude gales, while yet reluctant May
Withholds the beauties of the vernal day;
As some fond maid, whom matron frowns reprove,
Suspends the smile her heart devotes to love;

The season's pleasures too delay their hour,
And Winter revels with protracted power:
Then blame not, critics, if, thus late, we bring
A Winter Drama—but reproach—the Spring.
What prudent cit dares yet the season trust,
Bask in his whisky, and enjoy the dust?
Horsed in Cheapside, scarce yet the gayer spark
Achieves the Sunday triumph of the Park;
Scarce yet you see him, dreading to be late,
Scour the New Road, and dash through Grosvenor Gate:—
Anxious—yet timorous too—his steed to show,
The hack Bucephalus of Rotten Row.
Careless he seems, yet vigilantly sly,
Woos the gay glance of ladies passing by,
While his off heel, insidiously aside,
Provokes the caper which he seems to chide.
Scarce rural Kensington due honour gains;
The vulgar verdure of her walk remains!
Where night-robed misses amble two by two,
Nodding to booted beaux—"How'do, how'do?"
With generous questions that no answer wait,
"How vastly full!   An't you come vastly late?
Isn't it quite charming? When do you leave town?
An't you quite tired? Pray, can't we sit down?"
These suburb pleasures of a London May,
Imperfect yet, we hail the cold delay;
Should our Play please—and you 're indulgent ever—
Be your decree—"'Tis better late than never."

ACT I.

Scene I.—*A Pavilion near* Pizarro's *Tent.*

Elvira *discovered sleeping under a canopy.* Valverde *enters, gazes on* Elvira, *kneels, and attempts to kiss her hand ;* Elvira, *awakened, rises and looks at him with indignation.*

Elv. Audacious ! Whence is thy privilege to interrupt the few moments of repose my harassed mind can snatch amid the tumults of this noisy camp? Shall I inform thy master, Pizarro, of this presumptuous treachery?

Val. I am his servant, it is true—trusted by him—and I know him well; and therefore 'tis I ask, by what magic could Pizarro gain your heart? by what fatality still holds he your affection?

Elv. Hold! thou trusty secretary !

Val. Ignobly born ! in mind and manners rude, ferocious, and unpolished, though cool and crafty if occasion need—in youth audacious—till his first manhood—a licensed pirate—treating men as brutes, the world as booty; yet now the Spanish hero is he styled—the first of Spanish conquerors ! and, for a warrior so accomplished, 'tis fit Elvira should leave her noble family, her fame, her home, to share the dangers, humours, and the crimes, of such a lover as Pizarro !

Elv. What! Valverde moralising! But grant I am in error, what is my incentive? Passion, infatuation, call it as you will; but what attaches thee to this despised, unworthy leader? Base lucre is thy object, mean fraud thy means. Could you gain me, you only hope to win a higher interest in Pizarro. I know you.

Val. On my soul, you wrong me! What else my faults, I have none towards you. But indulge the scorn and levity of your nature; do it while yet the time permits; the gloomy hour, I fear, too soon approaches.

Elv. Valverde a prophet too!

Val. Hear me, Elvira. Shame from his late defeat, and burning wishes for revenge, again have brought Pizarro to Peru; but trust me, he overrates his strength, nor measures well the foe. Encamped in a strange country, where terror cannot force, nor corruption buy a single friend, what have we to hope? The army murmuring at increasing hardships, while Pizarro decorates with gaudy spoil the gay pavilion of his luxury, each day diminishes our force.

Elv. But are you not the heirs of those that fall?

Val. Are gain and plunder, then, our only purpose? Is this Elvira's heroism?

Elv. No, so save me Heaven! I abhor the motive, means, and end of your pursuits; but I will trust none of you. In your whole army there is not one of you that has a heart, or speaks ingenuously—aged Las-Casas, and he alone, excepted.

Val. He! an enthusiast in the opposite and worst extreme!

Elv. Oh! had I earlier known that virtuous man, how different might my lot have been!

Val. I will grant Pizarro could not then so easily have duped you: forgive me, but at that event I still must wonder.

Elv. Hear me, Valverde. When first my virgin fancy waked to love, Pizarro was my country's idol. Self-taught, self-raised, and self-supported, he became a hero; and I was formed to be won by glory and renown. 'Tis known that, when he left Panama in a slight vessel, his force was not a hundred men. Arrived at the island of Gallo, with his sword he drew a line upon the sands, and said, "Pass those who fear to die or conquer with their leader." Thirteen alone remained, and at the head of these the warrior speed his ground. Even at the moment when my ears first caught this tale, my heart exclaimed, "Pizarro is its lord!" What since I have perceived, or thought, or felt, you must have more worth to win the knowledge of.

Val. I press no further, still assured that, while Alonzo de Molina, our general's former friend and pupil, leads the enemy, Pizarro never more will be a conqueror. [*Trumpets without.*]

Elv. Silence! I hear him coming; look not perplexed. How mystery and fraud confound the countenance! Quick, put on an honest face, if thou canst.

Piz. [*Without.*] Chain and secure him; I will examine him myself.

Enter PIZARRO. VALVERDE *bows.*—ELVIRA *laughs.*

Piz. Why dost thou smile, Elvira?

Elv. To laugh or weep without a reason is one of the few privileges women have.

Piz. Elvira, I will know the cause, I am resolved!

Elv. I am glad of that, because I love resolution, and am resolved not to tell you. Now my resolution, I take it, is the better of the two, because it depends upon myself, and yours does not.

Piz. Psha! trifler!

Val. Elvira was laughing at my apprehensions that——

Piz. Apprehensions!

Val. Yes—that Alonzo's skill and genius should so have disciplined and informed the enemy, as to——

Piz. Alonzo! the traitor! How I once loved that man! His noble mother intrusted him, a boy, to my protection. [ELVIRA *walks about pensively in the background.*] At my table did he feast—in my tent did he repose. I had marked his early genius, and the valorous spirit that grew with it. Often had I talked to him of our first adventures—what storms we struggled with—what perils we surmounted! When landed with a slender host upon an unknown land—then, when I told how famine and fatigue, discord and toil, day by day, did thin our ranks amid close-pressing enemies— how still undaunted I endured and dared—maintained my purpose and my power in despite of growling mutiny or bold revolt, till with my faithful few remaining I became at last victorious!—when, I say, of these things I spoke, the youth Alonzo, with tears of wonder and delight, would throw him on my neck, and swear his soul's ambition owned no other leader.

Val. What could subdue attachment so begun?

Piz. Las-Casas.—He it was, with fascinating craft and canting precepts of humanity, raised in Alonzo's mind a new enthusiasm, which forced him, as the stripling termed it, to forego his country's claims for those of human nature.

Val. Yes, the traitor left you, joined the Peruvians, and became thy enemy, and Spain's.

Piz. But first with weariless remonstrance he sued to win me from my purpose, and untwine the sword from my determined grasp. Much he spoke of right, of justice, and humanity, calling the Peruvians our innocent and unoffending brethren.

Val. They! Obdurate heathens! They our brethren!

Piz. But, when he found that the soft folly of the pleading tears he dropped upon my bosom fell on marble, he flew and joined the foe: then, profiting by the lessons he had gained in wronged Pizarro's school, the youth so disciplined and led his new allies, that soon he forced me—ha! I burn with shame and fury while I own it!—in base retreat and foul discomfiture to quit the shore.

Val. But the hour of revenge is come.

Piz. It is; I am returned: my force is strengthened, and the audacious boy shall soon know that Pizarro lives, and has—a grateful recollection of the thanks he owes him.

Val. 'Tis doubted whether still Alonzo lives.

Piz. 'Tis certain that he does; one of his armour-bearers is just made prisoner: twelve thousand is their force, as he reports, led by Alonzo and Peruvian Rolla. This day they make a solemn sacrifice on their ungodly altars. We must profit by their security, and attack them unprepared—the sacrificers shall become the victims.

Elv. Wretched innocents! And their own blood shall bedew their altars!

Piz. Right!—[*Trumpets without.*] Elvira, retire!

Elv. Why should I retire?

Piz. Because men are to meet here, and on manly business.

Elv. O men! men! ungrateful and perverse! O woman! still affectionate though wronged! [VALVERDE *retires back.*] The beings to whose eyes you turn for animation, hope, and rapture, through the days of mirth and revelry; and on whose bosoms, in the hour of sore calamity, you seek for rest and consolation; them, when the pompous follies of your mean ambition are the question, you treat as playthings or as slaves!—I shall not retire.

Piz. Remain then; and, if thou canst, be silent.

Elv. They only babble who practise not reflection. I shall think—and thought is silence.

Piz. [*Aside.*] Ha! there's somewhat in her manner lately——

[*Looks sternly and suspiciously at* ELVIRA, *who meets his glance with a commanding and unaltered eye.*

Enter LAS-CASAS, ALMAGRO, GONZALO, DAVILLA, OFFICERS *and* SOLDIERS.— *Trumpets without.*

Las-Cas. Pizarro, we attend thy summons.

Piz. Welcome, venerable father!—My friends, most welcome!—Friends and fellow soldiers, at length the hour is arrived, which to Pizarro's hopes presents the full reward of our undaunted enterprise and long-enduring toils. Confident in security, this day the foe devotes to solemn sacrifice: if with bold surprise we strike on their solemnity—trust to your leader's word—we shall not fail.

Alm. Too long inactive have we been mouldering on the coast; our stores exhausted, and our soldiers murmuring. Battle! battle!—then death to the armed, and chains for the defenceless.

Dav. Death to the whole Peruvian race!

Las-Cas. Merciful Heaven!

Alm. Yes, general, the attack, and instantly! Then shall Alonzo, basking at his ease, soon cease to scoff our sufferings, and scorn our force.

Las-Cas. Alonzo!—scorn and presumption are not in his nature.

Alm. 'Tis fit Las-Casas should defend his pupil.

Piz. Speak not of the traitor! or hear his name but as the bloody summons to assault and vengeance. It appears we are agreed?

Alm. Dav. We are.

Gon. All.—Battle! battle!

Las-Cas. Is, then, the dreadful measure of your cruelty not yet complete? Battle! gracious Heaven! against whom? Against a king, in whose mild bosom your atrocious injuries even yet have not excited hate! but who, insulted or victorious, still sues for peace. Against a people who never wronged the living being their Creator formed: a people who, children of innocence! received you as cherished guests with eager hospitality and confiding kindness. Generously and freely did they share with you their comforts, their treasures, and their homes: you repaid them by fraud, oppression, and dishonour. These eyes have witnessed all I speak—as gods you were received; as fiends have you acted.

Piz. Las-Casas!

Las-Cas. Pizarro, hear me!—Hear me, chieftains!—And thou, all-powerful! whose thunders can shiver into sand the adamantine rock—whose lightnings can pierce to the core of the rived and quaking earth—oh! let thy power give effect to thy servant's words, as thy spirit gives courage to his will!—Do not, I implore you, chieftains—countrymen—do not, I implore you, renew the foul barbarities which your insatiate avarice has inflicted on this wretched, unoffending race!—But hush, my sighs!—fall not, drops of useless sorrow!—heart-breaking anguish, choke not my utterance!—All I entreat is, send me once more to those you call your enemies.—Oh! let me be the messenger of penitence from you; I shall return with blessings and with peace from them. —[*Turning to* ELVIRA.] Elvira, you weep!—Alas! and does this dreadful crisis move no heart but thine?

Alm. Because there are no women here but she and thou.

Piz. Close this idle war of words: time flies, and our opportunity will be lost. Chieftains, are ye for instant battle?

Alm. We are.

Las-Cas. Oh, men of blood!—[*Kneels.*] God! thou hast anointed me thy servant—not to curse, but to bless my countrymen: yet now my blessing on their force were blasphemy against thy goodness.—[*Rises.*] No! I curse your purpose, homicides! I curse the bond of blood by which you are united. May fell division, infamy, and rout, defeat your projects and rebuke your hopes! On you, and on your children, be the peril of the innocent blood which shall be shed this day! I leave you, and for ever! No longer shall these aged eyes be seared by the horrors they have witnessed. In caves, in forests, will I hide myself; with tigers and with savage beasts will I commune; and when at length we meet before the blessed tribunal of that Deity, whose mild doctrines and whose mercies ye have this day renounced, then shall you feel the agony and grief of soul which tear the bosom of your accuser now!   [*Going.*

Elv. [*Rises and takes the hand of* LAS-CASAS.] 'Las-Casas! Oh, take me with thee, Las-Casas!

Las-Cas. Stay! lost, abused lady! I alone am useless here. Perhaps thy loveliness may persuade to pity, where reason and religion plead in vain. Oh! save thy innocent fellow-creatures if thou canst: then shall thy frailty be redeemed, and thou wilt share the mercy thou bestowest.   [*Exit.*

Piz. How, Elvira! wouldst thou leave me?

Elv. I am bewildered, grown terrified! Your inhumanity—and that good Las-Casas—oh! he appeared to me just now something more than heavenly: and you! ye all looked worse than earthly.

Piz. Compassion sometimes becomes a beauty.

Elv. Humanity always becomes a conqueror.

Alm. Well! Heaven be praised, we are rid of the old moralist.

Gon. I hope he'll join his preaching pupil, Alonzo.

Piz. [*Turning to* ALMAGRO.] Now to prepare our muster and our march. At midday is the hour of the sacrifice. [ELVIRA *sits.*] Consulting with our guides, the route of your divisions shall be given to each commander. If we surprise, we conquer; and, if we conquer, the gates of Quito will be open to us.

Alm. And Pizarro then be monarch of Peru.

Piz. Not so fast—ambition for a time must take counsel from discretion. Ataliba still must hold the shadow of a sceptre in his hand—Pizarro still appear dependent upon Spain: while the pledge of future peace, his daughter's hand, [ELVIRA *rises much agitated,*] secures the proud succession to the crown I seek.

Alm. This is best. In Pizarro's plans observe the statesman's wisdom guides the warrior's valour.

Val. [*Aside to* ELVIRA.] You mark, Elvira?

Elv. Oh, yes—this is best—this is excellent!

Piz. You seem offended. Elvira still retains my heart. Think—a sceptre waves me on.

Elv. Offended?—no! Thou knowest thy glory is my idol; and this will be most glorious, most just and honourable.

Piz. What mean you?

Elv. Oh, nothing!—mere woman's prattle—a jealous whim, perhaps: but let it not impede the royal hero's course.—[*Trumpets without.*] The call of arms invites you.—Away! away! you, his brave, his worthy fellow-warriors.

Piz. And go you not with me?

Elv. Undoubtedly! I needs must be first to hail the future monarch of Peru.

Enter GOMEZ.

Alm. How, Gomez! what bringest thou?

Gom. On yonder hill, among the palm-trees, we have surprised an old cacique: escape by flight he could not, and we seized him and his attendant unresisting; yet his lips breathe nought but bitterness and scorn.

Piz. Drag him before us.—[ELVIRA *sits pensively.* GOMEZ *goes out and returns with* OROZEMBO *and* Attendant, *in chains, guarded.*] What art thou, stranger?

Oro. First tell me which among you is the captain of this band of robbers.

Piz. Ha!

Alm. Madman!—Tear out his tongue, or else——

Oro. Thou 'lt hear some truth.

Dav. [*Showing his poniard.*] Shall I not plunge this into his heart?

Oro. [*To* PIZARRO.] Does your army boast many such heroes as this?

Piz. Audacious! this insolence has sealed thy doom. Die thou shalt grey-headed ruffian. But first confess what thou knowest.

Oro. I know that which thou hast just assured me of—that I shall die.

Piz. Less audacity perhaps might have preserved thy life.

Oro. My life is as a withered tree; it is not worth preserving.

Piz. Hear me, old man. Even now we march against the Peruvian army. We know there is a secret path that leads to your stronghold among the rocks: guide us to that, and name thy reward. If wealth be thy wish——

Oro. Ha! ha! ha! ha!

Piz. Dost thou despise my offer?

Oro. Thee and thy offer! Wealth!—I have the wealth of two dear gallant sons—I have stored in heaven the riches which repay good actions here—and still my chiefest treasure do I bear about me.

Piz. What is that? inform me.

Oro. I will; for it never can be thine—the treasure of a pure, unsullied conscience. [ELVIRA *sits, still paying marked attention to* OROZEMBO.]

Piz. I believe there is no other Peruvian who dares speak as thou dost.

Oro. Would I could believe there is no other Spaniard who dares act as thou dost!

Gom. Obdurate Pagan! How numerous is your army?

Oro. Count the leaves of yonder forest.

Alm. Which is the weakest part of your camp?

Oro. It has no weak part; on every side 'tis fortified by justice.

Piz. Where have you concealed your wives and your children?

Oro. In the hearts of their husbands and their fathers.

Piz. Knowest thou Alonzo?

Oro. Know him! Alonzo! Know him! Our nation's benefactor! the guardian angel of Peru!

Piz. By what has he merited that title?

Oro. By not resembling thee.

Alm. Who is this Rolla, joined with Alonzo in command?

Oro. I will answer that; for I love to hear and to repeat the hero's name. Rolla, the kinsman of the king, is the idol of our army; in war a tiger, chafed by the hunter's spear; in peace more gentle than the unweaned lamb. Cora was once betrothed to him; but, finding she preferred Alonzo, he resigned his claim, and, I fear, his peace, to friendship and to Cora's happiness; yet still he loves her with a pure and holy fire.

Piz. Romantic savage!—I shall meet this Rolla soon.

Oro. Thou hadst better not! the terrors of his noble eye would strike thee dead.

Dav. Silence, or tremble!

Oro. Beardless robber! I never yet have trembled before God; why should I tremble before man? Why before thee, thou less than man?

Dav. Another word, audacious heathen, and I strike!

Oro. Strike, Christian! Then boast among thy fellows—I too have murdered a Peruvian!

Dav. Hell and vengeance seize thee!   [*Stabs him.*

Piz. Hold!

Dav. Couldst thou longer have endured his insults?

Piz. And therefore should he die untortured?

Oro. True! Observe, young man—[*To* DAVILLA,] Thy unthinking rashness has saved me from the rack; and thou thyself hast lost the opportunity of a useful lesson; thou mightst thyself have seen with what cruelty vengeance would have inflicted torments—and with what patience virtue would have borne them.

Elv. [*Supporting* OROZEMBO'S *head upon her bosom.*] Oh, ye are monsters all! Look up, thou martyred innocent—look up once more, and bless me ere thou diest. God! how I pity thee!

Oro. Pity me!—me! so near my happiness! Bless thee, lady!—Spaniards —Heaven turn your hearts, and pardon you as I do.

Piz. Away!—[OROZEMBO *is borne off dying.*] Away! Davilla! if thus rash a second time—

Dav. Forgive the hasty indignation which——

Piz. No more! Unbind that trembling wretch—let him depart: 'tis well he should report the mercy which we show to insolent defiance—Hark! our troops are moving.

Attend. [*On passing* ELVIRA.] If through your gentle means my master's poor remains might be preserved from insult——

Elv. I understand thee.

Attend. His sons may yet thank your charity, if not avenge their father's fate.   [*Exit.*

Piz. What says the slave?

Elv. A parting word to thank you for your mercy.

Piz. Our guards and guides approach.—[SOLDIERS *march through the tents.*] Follow me, friends—each shall have his post assigned, and ere Peruvia's god shall sink beneath the main, the Spanish banner, bathed in blood, shall float above the walls of vanquished Quito.

[*Exeunt all but* ELVIRA *and* VALVERDE.

Val. Is it now presumption that my hopes gain strength with the increasing horrors which I see appal Elvira's soul?

Elv. I am mad with terror and remorse! Would I could fly these dreadful scenes!

Val. Might not Valverde's true attachment be thy refuge?

Elv. What wouldst thou do to save or to avenge me?

Val. I dare do all thy injuries may demand—a word—and he lies bleeding at your feet.

Elv. Perhaps we will speak again of this. Now leave me.—[*Exit* VALVERDE.] No! not this revenge—no! not this instrument. Fie, Elvira! even for a moment to counsel with this unworthy traitor! Can a wretch, false to a confiding master, be true to any pledge of love or honour?—Pizarro will abandon me—yes; me—who, for his sake, have sacrificed—oh, God! what have I not sacrificed for him! Yet, curbing the avenging pride that swells this bosom, I still will further try him. Oh, men! ye who, wearied by the fond fidelity of virtuous love, seek in the wanton's flattery a new delight, oh, ye may insult and leave the hearts to which your faith was pledged, and, stifling self-reproach, may fear no other peril;—because such hearts, howe'er you injure and desert them, have yet the proud retreat of an unspotted fame —of unreproaching conscience. But beware the desperate libertine who forsakes the creature whom his arts have first deprived of all natural protection —of all self-consolation! What has he left her? Despair and vengeance!

[*Exit.*

ACT II.

SCENE I.—*A Bank surrounded by a wild wood, and rocks.*

CORA *is discovered playing with her* CHILD; ALONZO *hanging over them with delight.*

Cora. Now confess, does he resemble thee, or not?

Alon. Indeed he is liker thee—thy rosy softness, thy smiling gentleness.

Cora. But his auburn hair, the colour of his eyes, Alonzo.—Oh, my lord's image, and my heart's adored!' [*Presses the* CHILD *to her bosom.*

Alon. The little darling urchin robs me, I doubt, of some portion of thy love, my Cora. At least he shares caresses, which till his birth were only mine.

Cora. Oh no, Alonzo! a mother's love for her sweet babe is not a stealth from the dear father's store; it is a new delight that turns with quickened gratitude to Him, the author of her augmented bliss.

Alon. Could Cora think me serious?

Cora. I am sure he will speak soon: then will be the last of the three holidays allowed by Nature's sanction to the fond, anxious mother's heart.

Alon. What are those three?

Cora. The ecstasy of his birth I pass; that in part is selfish: but when

M M

first the white blossoms of his teeth appear, breaking the crimson buds that did incase them, that is a day of joy; next, when from his father's arms ne runs without support, and clings, laughing and delighted, to his mother's knees, that is the mother's heart's next holiday; and sweeter still the third, whene'er his little stammering tongue shall utter the grateful sound of father! mother!—Oh, that is the dearest joy of all!

Alon. Beloved Cora!

Cora. Oh, my Alonzo! daily, hourly, do I pour thanks to Heaven for the dear blessing I possess in him and thee.

Alon. To Heaven and Rolla!

Cora. Yes, to Heaven and Rolla: and art thou not grateful to them too, Alonzo? art thou not happy?

Alon. Can Cora ask that question?

Cora. Why then of late so restless on thy couch? Why to my waking, watching ear so often does the stillness of the night betray thy struggling sighs?

Alon. Must not I fight against my country, against my brethren?

Cora. Do they not seek our destruction? and are not all men brethren?

Alon. Should they prove victorious?

Cora. I will fly, and meet thee in the mountains.

Alon. Fly, with thy infant, Cora?

Cora. What! think you a mother, when she runs from danger, can feel the weight of her child?

Alon. Cora, my beloved, do you wish to set my heart at rest?

Cora. Oh yes! yes! yes!

Alon. Hasten then to the concealment in the mountains; where all our matrons and virgins, and our warriors' offspring, are allotted to await the issue of the war. Cora will not alone resist her husband's, her sisters', and her monarch's wish.

Cora. Alonzo, I cannot leave you. Oh! how in every moment's absence would my fancy paint you, wounded, alone, abandoned! No, no, I cannot leave you.

Alon. Rolla will be with me.

Cora. Yes, while the battle rages, and where it rages most, brave Rolla will be found. He may revenge, but cannot save thee. To follow danger, he will leave even thee. But I have sworn never to forsake thee but with life. Dear, dear Alonzo! canst thou wish that I should break my vow?

Alon. Then be it so. Oh! excellence in all that's great and lovely, in courage, gentleness, and truth; my pride, my content, my all! Can there on this earth be fools who seek for happiness, and pass by love in the pursuit?

Cora. Alonzo, I cannot thank thee: silence is the gratitude of true affection: who seeks to follow it by sound will miss the track.—[*Shouts without.*] Does the king approach?

Alon. No, 'tis the general placing the guard that will surround the temple during the sacrifice. 'Tis Rolla comes, the first and best of heroes.

[*Trumpets sound.*

Rol. [*Without.*] Then place them on the hill fronting the Spanish camp.

Enter ROLLA.

Cora. Rolla! my friend, my brother!

Alon. Rolla! my friend, my benefactor! how can our lives repay the obligations which we owe thee?

Rol. Pass them in peace and bliss. Let Rolla witness it, he is overpaid.

Cora. Look on this child. He is the life-blood of my heart; but, if ever he loves or reveres thee less than his own father, his mother's hate fall on him!

Rol. Oh, no more! What sacrifice have I made to merit gratitude? The object of my love was Cora's happiness. I see her happy. Is not my object gained, and am I not rewarded? Now, Cora, listen to a friend's advice. Thou must away; thou must seek the sacred caverns, the unprofaned recess, whither, after this day's sacrifice, our matrons, and e'en the virgins of the sun, retire.

Cora. Not secure with Alonzo and with thee, Rolla!

Rol. We have heard Pizarro's plan is to surprise us. Thy presence, Cora, cannot aid, but may impede our efforts.

Cora. Impede!

Rol. Yes, yes. Thou knowest how tenderly we love thee; we, thy husband and thy friend. Art thou near us? our thoughts, our valour—vengeance will not be our own. No advantage will be pursued that leads us from the spot where thou art placed; no succour will be given but for thy protection. The faithful lover dares not be all himself amid the war, until he knows that the beloved of his soul is absent from the peril of the fight.

Alon. Thanks to my friend! 'tis this I would have urged.

Cora. This timid excess of love, producing fear instead of valour, flatters, but does not convince me: the wife is incredulous.

Rol. And is the mother unbelieving too?

Cora. [*Kisses child.*] No more! do with me as you please. My friend, my husband! place me where you will.

Alon. My adored! we thank you both.—[*March without.*] Hark! the king approaches to the sacrifice. You, Rolla, spoke of rumours of surprise. A servant of mine, I hear, is missing; whether surprised or treacherous, I know not.

Rol. It matters not. We are every where prepared. Come, Cora, upon the altar 'mid the rocks thou 'lt implore a blessing on our cause. The pious supplication of the trembling wife, and mother's heart, rises to the throne of mercy, the most resistless prayer of human homage. [*Exeunt.*

SCENE II.—*The Temple of the Sun.*

The HIGH-PRIEST, PRIESTS, *and* VIRGINS *of the* SUN, *discovered. A solemn march.* ATALIBA *and the* PERUVIAN WARRIORS *enter on one side; on the other* ROLLA, ALONZO, *and* CORA *with the* CHILD.

Ata. Welcome, Alonzo!—[*To* ROLLA.] Kinsman, thy hand.—[*To* CORA.] Blessed be the object of the happy mother's love.

Cora. May the sun bless the father of his people!

Ata. In the welfare of his children lives the happiness of their king.— Friends, what is the temper of our soldiers?

Rol. Such as becomes the cause which they support; their cry is, Victory or death! our king! our country! and our God.

Ata. Thou, Rolla, in the hour of peril, hast been wont to animate the spirit of their leaders, ere we proceed to consecrate the banners which thy valour knows so well to guard.

M M 2

Rol. Yet never was the hour of peril near, when to inspire them word were so little needed. My brave associates—partners of my toil, my feelings, and my fame!—can Rolla's words add vigour to the virtuous energies which inspire your hearts? No! You have judged, as I have, the foulness of the crafty plea by which these bold invaders would delude you. Your generous spirit has compared, as mine has, the motives which, in a war like this, can animate their minds and ours. They, by a strange frenzy driven, fight for power, for plunder, and extended rule: we, for our country, our altars, and our homes. They follow an adventurer whom they fear, and obey a power which they hate: we serve a monarch whom we love—a God whom we adore. Whene'er they move in anger, desolation tracks their progress! Whene'er they pause in amity, affliction mourns their friendship. They boast they come but to improve our state, enlarge our thoughts, and free us from the yoke of error! Yes: they will give enlightened freedom to our minds! who are themselves the slaves of passion, avarice, and pride. They offer us their protection: yes, such protection as vultures give to lambs—covering and devouring them! They call on us to barter all of good we have inherited and proved, for the desperate chance of something better which they promise. Be our plain answer this:—The throne we honour is the people's choice; the laws we reverence are our brave father's legacy; the faith we follow teaches us to live in bonds of charity with all mankind, and die with hope of bliss beyond the grave. Tell your invaders this, and tell them too, we seek no change; and, least of all, such change as they would bring . us.   [*Loud shouts of the* PERUVIAN WARRIORS.

Ata. [*Embracing* ROLLA.] Now, holy friends, ever mindful of these sacred truths, begin the sacrifice.—[*A solemn procession commences. The* PRIESTS *and* VIRGINS *arrange themselves on either side of the altar, which the* HIGH-PRIEST *approaches, and the solemnity begins. The invocation of the* HIGH-PRIEST *is followed by the choruses of the* PRIESTS *and* VIRGINS. *Fire from above lights upon the altar. The whole assembly rise, and join in the thanksgiving.*] Our offering is accepted. Now to arms, my friends; prepare for battle.

Enter ORANO.

Ora. The enemy.

Ata. How near?

Ora. From the hill's brow, e'en now as I o'erlooked their force, suddenly I perceived the whole in motion: with eager haste they march towards our deserted camp, as if apprised of this most solemn sacrifice.

Rol. They must be met before they reach it.

Ata. And you my daughters, with your dear children, away to the appointed place of safety.

Cora. Oh, Alonzo!   [*Embracing him.*

Alon. We shall meet again.

Cora. Bless us once more ere you leave us.

Alon. Heaven protect and bless thee, my beloved; and thee, my innocent!

Ata. Haste, haste! each moment is precious!

Cora. Farewell, Alonzo! Remember thy life is mine.

Rol. [*As she is passing him.*] Not one farewell to Rolla?

Cora. [*Giving him her hand.*] Farewell! The god of war be with you: but bring me back Alonzo.   [*Exit with the* CHILD.

Ata. [*Draws his sword.*] Now, my brethren, my sons, my friends, I

ow your valour. Should ill success assail us, be despair the last feeling of
ur hearts. If successful, let mercy be the first.—Alonzo, to you I give to
'end the narrow passage of the mountains. On the right of the wood be
.lla's station. For me straight forwards will I march to meet them, and
ht until I see my people saved, or they behold their monarch fall. Be the
.rd of battle—God! and our native land. [*A march. Exeunt.*

SCENE III.—*A Wood between the Temple and the Camp.*

Enter ROLLA *and* ALONZO.

Rol. Here, my friend, we separate—soon, I trust, to meet again in triumph.
Alon. Or perhaps we part to meet no more.—Rolla, a moment's pause;
, are yet before our army's strength; one earnest word at parting.
Rol. There is in language now no word but battle.
Alon. Yes, one word—one—Cora!
Rol. Cora!—speak!
Alon. The next hour brings us——
Rol. Death or victory!
Alon. It may be victory to one—death to the other.
Rol. Or both may fall.
Alon. If so, my wife and child I bequeath to the protection of Heaven
d my king. But should I only fall, Rolla, be thou my heir.
Rol. How?
Alon. Be Cora thy wife—be thou a father to my child.
Rol. Rouse thee, Alonzo! banish these timid fancies.
Alon. Rolla! I have tried in vain, and cannot fly from the foreboding
hich oppresses me: thou knowest it will not shake me in the fight: but
ve me the promise I exact.
Rol. If it be Cora's will—yes—I promise. [*Gives his hand.*
Alon. Tell her it was my last wish; and bear to her and to my son my,
st blessing!
Rol. I will.—Now then to our posts, and let our swords speak for us.
[*They draw their swords.*

Alon. For the king and Cora!
Rol. For Cora and the king. [*Exeunt severally. Alarms without.*

SCENE IV.—*The Peruvian Camp.*

Enter an OLD BLIND MAN *and a* BOY.

Old Man. Have none returned to the camp?
Boy. One messenger alone. From the temple they all marched to meet
e foe.
Old Man. Hark! I hear the din of battle. Oh, had I still retained my
ght, I might now have grasped a sword, and died a soldier's death!—Are
e quite alone?
Boy. Yes!—I hope my father will be safe!
Old Man. He will do his duty. I am more anxious for thee, my child.
Boy. I can stay with you, dear grandfather.
Old Man. But, should the enemy come, they will drag thee from me, my
oy.
Boy. Impossible, grandfather! for they will see at once that you are old
nd blind, and cannot do without me.
Old Man. Poor child! thou little knowest the hearts of these inhuman men.

—[*Discharge of cannon heard.*] Hark! the noise is near. I hear the dreadful roaring of the fiery engines of these cruel strangers.—[*Shouts at a distance.*] At every shout, with involuntary haste I clench my hand, and fancy still it grasps a sword! Alas! I can only serve my country by my prayers. Heaven preserve the Inca and his gallant soldiers!

Boy. O father! there are soldiers running——

Old Man. Spaniards, boy?

Boy. No, Peruvians!

Old Man. How! and flying from the field!—It cannot be.

Enter two PERUVIAN SOLDIERS.

Oh, speak to them, boy?—whence come you! how goes the battle?

Sold. We may not stop; we are sent for the reserve behind the hill. The day's against us. [*Exeunt* SOLDIERS.

Old Man. Quick, then, quick.

Boy. I see the points of lances glittering in the light.

Old Man. Those are Peruvians. Do they bend this way?

Enter a PERUVIAN SOLDIER.

Boy. Soldier, speak to my blind father.

Sold. I'm sent to tell the helpless father to retreat among the rocks: all will be lost, I fear. The king is wounded.

Old Man. Quick, boy! Lead me to the hill, where thou mayst view the pl in. [*Alarms.*

Enter ATALIBA, *wounded, with* ORANO, OFFICERS, *and* SOLDIERS.

Ata. My wound is bound; believe me, the hurt is nothing: I may return to the fight.

Ora. Pardon your servant; but the allotted priest who attends the sacred banner has pronounced that, the Inca's blood once shed, no blessing can await the day until he leave the field.

Ata. Hard restraint! Oh my poor brave soldiers! Hard that I may no longer be a witness of their valour.—But haste you; return to your comrades; I will not keep one soldier from his post. Go, and avenge your fallen brethren.—[*Exeunt* ORANO, OFFICERS, *and* SOLDIERS.] I will not repine; my own fate is the last anxiety of my heart. It is for you, my people, that I feel and fear.

Old Man. [*Coming forward.*] Did I not hear the voice of an unfortunate? —Who is it complains thus?

Ata. One almost by hope forsaken.

Old Man. Is the king alive?

Ata. The king still lives.

Old Man. Then thou art not forsaken! Ataliba protects the meanest of his subjects.

Ata. And who shall protect Ataliba?

Old Man. The immortal powers, that protect the just. The virtues of our monarch alike secure to him the affection of his people and the benign regard of Heaven.

Ata. How impious, had I murmured! How wondrous, thou supreme Disposer, are thy acts! Even in this moment, which I had thought the bitterest trial of mortal suffering, thou hast infused the sweetest sensation of my life—it is the assurance of my people's love. [*Aside.*

Boy. [*Turning forward.*] O father!—Stranger! see those hideous men that rush upon us yonder!

Ata. Ha! Spaniards! and I Ataliba—ill-fated fugitive, without a sword even to try the ransom of a monarch's life.

Enter DAVILLA, ALMAGRO, *and* SPANISH SOLDIERS.

Dav. 'Tis he—our hopes are answered—I know him well—it is the king!

Alm. Away! Follow with your prize. Avoid those Peruvians, though in flight. This way we may regain our line.

[*Exeunt* DAVILLA, ALMAGRO, *and* SOLDIERS, *with* ATALIBA *prisoner.*

Old Man. The king!—wretched old man, that could not see his gracious form!—Boy, would thou hadst led me to the reach of those ruffians' swords!

Boy. Father! all our countrymen are flying here for refuge.

Old Man. No—to the rescue of their king—they never will desert him.

[*Alarms without.*

Enter PERUVIAN OFFICERS *and* SOLDIERS, *flying across the stage;* ORANO *following.*

Ora. Hold, I charge you! Rolla calls you.

Officer. We cannot combat with their dreadful engines.

Enter ROLLA.

Rol. Hold! recreants! cowards! What, fear ye death, and fear not shame? By my soul's fury, I cleave to the earth the first of you that stirs, or plunge your dastard swords into your leader's heart, that he no more may witness your disgrace. Where is the king?

Ora. From this old man and boy I learn that the detachment of the enemy, which you observed so suddenly to quit the field, have succeeded in surprising him; they are yet in sight.

Rol. And bear the Inca off a prisoner?—Hear this, ye base, disloyal rout! Look there! The dust you see hangs on the bloody Spaniards' track, dragging with ruffian taunts your king, your father—Ataliba in bondage! Now fly, and seek your own vile safety if you can.

Old Man. Bless the voice of Rolla—and bless the stroke I once lamented, but which now spares these extinguished eyes the shame of seeing the pale, trembling wretches who dare not follow Rolla, though to save their king!

Rol. Shrink ye from the thunder of the foe—and fall ye not at this rebuke? Oh! had ye each but one drop of the loyal blood which gushes to waste through the brave heart of this sightless veteran! Eternal shame pursue you, if you desert me now!—But do—alone I go—alone—to die with glory by my monarch's side!

Soldiers. Rolla! we'll follow thee.

[*Trumpets sound;* ROLLA *rushes out, followed by* ORANO, OFFICERS *and* SOLDIERS.

Old Man. O godlike Rolla!—And thou, sun, send from thy clouds avenging lightning to his aid! Haste, my boy; ascend some height, and tell to my impatient terror what thou seest.

Boy. I can climb this rock, and the tree above.—[*Ascends a rock, and from thence into the tree.*] Oh—now I see them—now—yes—and the Spaniards turning by the steep.

Old Man. Rolla follows them?

Boy. He does—he does—he moves like an arrow! Now he waves his arm to our soldiers.—[*Report of cannon heard.*] Now there is fire and smoke.

Old Man. Yes, fire is the weapon of those fiends.

Boy. The wind blows off the smoke: they are all mixed together.

Old Man. Seest thou the king?

Boy. Yes—Rolla is near him! His sword sheds fire as he strikes!

Old Man. Bless thee, Rolla! Spare not the monsters.

Boy. Father! father! the Spaniards fly!—Oh—now I see the king embracing Rolla.

[*Waves his cap for joy. Shouts of victory, flourish of trumpets, &c.*

Old Man. [*Falls on his knees.*] Fountain of life! how can my exhausted breath bear to thee thanks for this one moment of my life!—My boy, come down, and let me kiss thee—my strength is gone.

Boy. [*Running to the Old Man.*] Let me help you, father—you tremble so——

Old Man. 'Tis with transport, boy!

[BOY *leads the* OLD MAN *off. Shouts, flourish, &c.*

Re-enter ATALIBA, ROLLA, *and* PERUVIAN OFFICERS *and* SOLDIERS.

Ata. In the name of my people, the saviour of whose sovereign thou hast this day been, accept this emblem of his gratitude.—[*Giving* ROLLA *his sun of diamonds.*] The tear that falls upon it may for a moment dim its lustre, yet does it not impair the value of the gift.

Rol. It was the hand of Heaven, not mine, that saved my king.

Enter PERUVIAN OFFICER *and* SOLDIERS.

Rol. Now, soldier, from Alonzo?

Off. Alonzo's genius soon repaired the panic which early broke our ranks; but I fear we have to mourn Alonzo's loss: his eager spirit urged him too far in the pursuit!

Ata. How! Alonzo slain?

1st Sold. I saw him fall.

2nd Sold. Trust me, I beheld him up again and fighting—he was then surrounded and disarmed.

Ata. O victory, dearly purchased!

Rol. O Cora! who shall tell thee this?

Ata. Rolla, our friend is lost—our native country saved! Our private sorrows must yield to the public claim for triumph. Now go we to fulfil the first, the most sacred duty which belongs to victory—to dry the widowed and the orphaned tear of those whose brave protectors have perished in their country's cause.   [*Triumphant march, and exeunt.*

ACT III.

SCENE I.—*A wild Retreat among stupendous rocks.*

CORA *and her* CHILD, *with other* WIVES *and* CHILDREN *of the* PERUVIAN WARRIORS, *discovered. They sing alternately stanzas expressive of their situation, with a Chorus, in which all join.*

1st Wom. Zuluga, seest thou nothing yet?

Zul. Yes, two Peruvian soldiers—one on the hill, the other entering the thicket in the vale.

2nd Wom. One more has passed.—He comes—but pale and terrified.

Cora. My heart will start from my bosom.

Enter a PERUVIAN SOLDIER, *panting for breath.*

Wom. Well! joy or death?

Sold. The battle is against us.   The king is wounded and a prisoner.

Wom. Despair and misery!

Cora. [*In a faint voice.*] And Alonzo?

Sold. I have not seen him.

1st Wom. Oh! whither must we fly?

2nd Wom. Deeper into the forest.

Cora. I shall not move.

2nd Sold. [*Without.*] Victory! victory!

Enter another PERUVIAN SOLDIER.

2nd Sold. Rejoice! rejoice! we are victorious!

Wom. [*Springing up.*] Welcome! welcome, thou messenger of joy :—but the king!

2nd Sold. He leads the brave warriors who approach.

[*The triumphant march of the army is heard at a distance. The* WOMEN *and* CHILDREN *join in a strain expressive of anxiety and exultation.*

Enter the PERUVIAN WARRIORS, *singing the Song of Victory.* ATALIBA *and* ROLLA *follow, and are greeted with rapturous shouts.* CORA, *with her* CHILD *in her arms, runs through the ranks searching for* ALONZO.

Ata. Thanks, thanks, my children! I am well, believe it; the blood once stopped, my wound was nothing.

Cora. [*To* ROLLA] Where is Alonzo?—[ROLLA *turns away in silence.*] Give me my husband; give this child his father. [*Falls at* ATALIBA's *feet.*

Ata. I grieve that Alonzo is not here.

Cora. Hoped you to find him?

Ata. Most anxiously.

Cora. Ataliba! is he not dead?

Ata. No! the gods will have heard our prayers.

Cora. Is he not dead, Ataliba?

Ata. He lives—in my heart.

Cora. O king! torture me not thus! Speak out, is this child fatherless?

Ata. Dearest Cora! do not thus dash aside the little hope that still remains.

Cora. The little hope! yet still there is hope! [*Turns to* ROLLA.] Speak to me, Rolla: you are the friend of truth.

Rol. Alonzo has not been found.

Cora. Not found! what mean you? will not you, Rolla, tell me truth? Oh! let me not hear the thunder rolling at a distance; let the bolt fall and crush my brain at once. Say not that he is not found: say at once that he is dead.

Rol. Then should I say false.

Cora. False! Blessings on thee for that word! But snatch me from this terrible suspense.—[CORA *and* CHILD *kneel to* ROLLA.] Lift up thy little hands, my child; perhaps thy ignorance may plead better than thy mother's agony.

Rol. Alonzo is taken prisoner.

Cora. Prisoner! and by the Spaniards?—Pizarro's prisoner? Then is he dead.

Ata. Hope better—the richest ransom which our realm can yield, a herald shall this instant bear.

Peruv. Wom. Oh! for Alonzo's ransom—our gold, our gems!—all! all! Here, dear Cora—here! here!

[*The* PERUVIAN WOMEN *eagerly tear off all their ornaments, and offer them to* CORA.

Ata. Yes, for Alonzo's ransom they would give all!—I thank thee, Father, who has given me such hearts to rule over!

Cora. Now one boon more, beloved monarch. Let me go with the herald.

Ata. Remember, Cora, thou art not a wife only, but a mother too: hazard not your own honour, and the safety of your infant. Among these barbarians the sight of thy youth, thy loveliness, and innocence, would but rivet faster your Alonzo's chains, and rack his heart with added fears for thee. Wait, Cora, the return of the herald.

Cora. Teach me how to live till then.

Ata. Now we go to offer to the gods thanks for our victory, and prayers for our Alonzo's safety. [*March and procession. Exeunt.*

SCENE II.—*The Wood.*

Enter CORA *and* CHILD.

Cora. Mild innocence, what will become of thee?

Enter ROLLA.

Rol. Cora, I attend thy summons at the appointed spot.

Cora. O my child, my boy! hast thou still a father?

Rol. Cora, can thy child be fatherless, while Rolla lives?

Cora. Will he not soon want a mother too? For canst thou think I will survive Alonzo's loss?

Rol. Yes! for his child's sake. Yes, as thou didst love Alonzo, Cora, listen to Alonzo's friend.

Cora. You bid me listen to the world.—Who was not Alonzo's friend?

Rol. His parting words——

Cora. His parting words!—[*Wildly.*] Oh, speak!

Rol. Consigned to me two precious trusts—his blessing to his son, and a last request to thee.

Cora. His last request! his last!—Oh, name it!

Rol. If I fall, said he (and sad forebodings shook him while he spoke), promise to take my Cora for thy wife; be thou a father to my child.—I pledged my word to him, and we parted. Observe me, Cora, I repeat this only, as my faith to do so was given to Alonzo: for myself, I neither cherish claim nor hope.

Cora. Ha! does my reason fail me, or what is this horrid light that presses on my brain? O Alonzo! it may be thou hast fallen a victim to thy own guileless heart: hadst thou been silent, hadst thou not made a fatal legacy of these wretched charms——

Rol. Cora! what hateful suspicion has possessed thy mind?

Cora. Yes, yes, 'tis clear!—his spirit was ensnared; he was led to the fatal spot, where mortal valour could not front a host of murderers. He fell —in vain did he exclaim for help to Rolla. At a distance you looked on and smiled: you could have saved him—could—but did not.

Rol. Oh, glorious sun! can I have deserved this?—Cora, rather bid me strike this sword into my heart.

Cora. No!—live! live for love!—for that love thou seekest; whose blossoms are to shoot from the bleeding grave of thy betrayed and slaughtered friend! But thou hast borne to me the last words of my Alonzo! now hear mine: sooner shall this boy draw poison from this tortured breast—sooner would I link me to the pallid corse of the meanest wretch that perished with Alonzo, than he call Rolla father—than I call Rolla husband!

Rol. Yet call me what I am—thy friend, thy protector!

Cora. [*Distractedly.*] Away! I have no protector but my God! With this child in my arms will I hasten to the field of slaughter: there with these bands will I turn up to the light every mangled body, seeking, howe'er by death disfigured, the sweet smile of my Alonzo: with fearful cries I will shriek out his name till my veins snap! If the smallest spark of life remain, he will know the voice of his Cora, open for a moment his unshrouded eyes, and bless me with a last look. But if we find him not—oh! then, my boy, we will to the Spanish camp—that look of thine will win my passage through a thousand swords—they too are men. Is there a heart that could drive back the wife that seeks her bleeding husband; or the innocent babe that cries for his imprisoned father? No, no, my child, every where we shall be safe. A wretched mother, bearing a poor orphan in her arms, has nature's passport through the world. Yes, yes, my son, we'll go and seek thy father.

[*Exit with the* CHILD.

Rol. [*After a pause of agitation.*] Could I have merited one breath of thy reproaches, Cora, I should be the wretch I think I was not formed to be. Her safety must be my present purpose—then to convince her she has wronged me! [*Exit.*

SCENE III.—PIZARRO'S *Tent.*

PIZARRO *discovered, traversing the scene in gloomy and furious agitation.*

Piz. Well, capricious idol, Fortune, be my ruin thy work and boast. To myself I will still be true. Yet, ere I fall, grant me thy smile to prosper in one act of vengeance, and be that smile Alonzo's death.

Enter ELVIRA.

Who's there? who dares intrude? Why does my guard neglect their duty?

Elv. Your guard did what they could—but they knew their duty better than to enforce authority, when I refused obedience.

Piz. And what is it you desire?

Elv. To see how a hero bears misfortune. Thou, Pizarro, art not now collected—nor thyself.

Piz. Wouldst thou I should rejoice that the spears of the enemy, led by accursed Alonzo, have pierced the bravest hearts of my followers?

Elv. No! I would have thee cold and dark as the night that follows the departed storm; still and sullen as the awful pause that precedes nature's convulsion: yet I would have thee feel assured that a new morning shall arise, when the warrior's spirit shall stalk forth—nor fear the future, nor lament the past.

Piz. Woman! Elvira!—why had not all my men hearts like thine?

Elv. Then would thy brows have this day worn the crown of Quito.

Piz. Oh! hope fails me while that scourge of my life and fame, Alonzo, leads the enemy.

Elv. Pizarro, I am come to probe the hero farther: not now his courage, but his magnanimity—Alonzo is your prisoner.

Piz. How!

Elv. 'Tis certain; Valverde saw him even now dragged in chains within your camp. I chose to bring you the intelligence myself.

Piz. Bless thee, Elvira, for the news!—Alonzo in my power!—then I am the conqueror—the victory is mine!

Elv. Pizarro, this is savage and unmanly triumph. Believe me, you raise impatience in my mind to see the man whose valour and whose genius awe Pizarro; whose misfortunes are Pizarro's triumph; whose bondage is Pizarro's safety.

Piz. Guard!

· *Enter* GUARD.

Drag here the Spanish prisoner, Alonzo! Quick, bring the traitor here.

[*Exit* GUARD.

Elv. What shall be his fate?

Piz. Death! death! in lingering torments! protracted to the last stretch that burning vengeance can devise, and fainting life sustain.

Elv. Shame on thee! Wilt thou have it said that the Peruvians found Pizarro could not conquer till Alonzo felt that he could murder?

Piz. Be it said—I care not. His fate is sealed.

Elv. Follow then thy will: but mark me, if basely thou dost shed the blood of this brave youth, Elvira's lost to thee for ever.

Piz. Why this interest for a stranger? What is Alonzo's fate to thee?

Elv. His fate, nothing. thy glory, every thing! Thinkest thou I could love thee, stripped of fame, of honour, and a just renown? Know me better.

Piz. Thou shouldst have known me better. Thou shouldst have known, that, once provoked to hate, I am for ever fixed in vengeance.

Re-enter GUARD *with* ALONZO *in chains.*

Welcome, welcome, Don Alonzo de Molina! 'tis long since we have met: thy mended looks should speak a life of rural indolence. How is it that, amid the toils and cares of war, thou dost preserve the healthful bloom of careless ease? Tell me thy secret.

Alon. Thou wilt not profit by it. Whate'er the toils or cares of war, peace still is here.   [*Putting his hand to his heart.*

Piz. Sarcastic boy!

Elv. Thou art answered rightly. Why sport with the unfortunate?

Piz. And thou art wedded too, I hear; ay, and the father of a lovely boy —the heir, no doubt of all his father's loyalty, of all his mother's faith?

Alon. The heir, I trust, of all his father's scorn of fraud, oppression, and hypocrisy—the heir, I hope, of all his mother's virtue, gentleness, and truth —the heir, I am sure, to all Pizarro's hate.

Piz. Really! Now do I feel for this poor orphan; for fatherless to-morrow's sun shall see that child. Alonzo, thy hours are numbered.

Elv. Pizarro—no !

Piz. Hence—or dread my anger.

Elv. I will not hence; nor do I dread thy anger.

Alon. Generous loveliness ! spare thy unavailing pity. Seek not to thwart the tiger with the prey beneath his fangs.

Piz. Audacious rebel ! thou a renegado from thy monarch and thy God !

Alon. 'Tis false !

Piz. Art thou not, tell me, a deserter from thy country's legions—and, with vile heathens leagued, hast thou not warred against thy native land ?

Alon. No ! deserter I am none ! I was not born among robbers ! pirates ! murderers ! When those legions, lured by the abhorred lust of gold, and by thy foul ambition urged, forgot the honour of Castilians, and forsook the duties of humanity, they deserted me. I have not warred against my native land, but against those who have usurped its power. The banners of my country, when first I followed arms beneath them, were justice, faith, and mercy. If these are beaten down and trampled under foot, I have no country, nor exists the power entitled to reproach me with revolt.

Piz. The power to judge and punish thee at least exists.

Alon. Where are my judges ?

Piz. Thou wouldst appeal to the war council ?

Alon. If the good Las-Casas have yet a seat there, yes; if not, I appeal to Heaven !

Piz. And, to impose upon the folly of Las-Casas, what would be the excuses of thy treason ?

Elv. The folly of Las-Casas ! Such, doubtless, his mild precepts seem to thy hard-hearted wisdom ! Oh, would I might have lived as I will die, a sharer in the follies of Las-Casas !

Alon. To him I should not need to urge the foul barbarities which drove me from your side; but I would gently lead him by the hand through all the lovely fields of Quito; there, in many a spot where late was barrenness and waste, I would show him how now the opening blossom, blade, or perfumed bud, sweet bashful pledges of delicious harvest, wafting their incense to the ripening sun, give cheerful promise to the hope of industry. This, I would say, is my work ! Next I should tell how hurtful customs and superstitions, strange and sullen, would often scatter and dismay the credulous minds of these deluded innocents; and then would I point out to him where now, in clustered villages, they live like brethren, social and confiding, while through the burning day Content sits basking on the cheek of Toil, till laughing Pastime leads them to the hour of rest—this too is mine ! And prouder yet, at that still pause between exertion and repose, belonging not to pastime, labour, or to rest, but unto Him who sanctions and ordains them all, I would show him many an eye, and many a hand, by gentleness from error won, raised in pure devotion to the true and only God !—this too I could tell him is Alonzo's work ! Then would Las-Casas clasp me in his aged arms; from his uplifted eyes a tear of gracious thankfulness would fall upon my head, and that one blessed drop would be to me at once this world's best proof that I had acted rightly here, and surest hope of my Creator's mercy and reward hereafter.

Elv. Happy, virtuous Alonzo ! And thou, Pizarro, wouldst appal with fear of death a man who thinks and acts as he does !

Piz. Daring, obstinate enthusiast ! But know, the pious blessing of thy

preceptor's tears does not await thee here: he has fled like thee—like thee,
no doubt, to join the foes of Spain.   The perilous trial of the next reward
you hope is nearer than perhaps you 've thought; for, by my country's
wrongs, and by mine own, to-morrow's sun shall see thy death!

Elv. Hold! Pizarro, hear me: if not always justly, at least act always
greatly.   Name not thy country's wrongs; 'tis plain they have no share in
thy resentment. Thy fury 'gainst this youth is private hate, and deadly personal revenge; if this be so, and even now thy detected conscience in that
look avows it, profane not the name of justice or thy country's cause, but let
him arm, and bid him to the field on equal terms.

Piz. Officious advocate for treason—peace! Bear him hence; he knows
his sentence.   [*Retires back.*

Alon. Thy revenge is eager, and I 'm thankful for it—to me thy haste is
mercy.—[*To* ELVIRA.] For thee, sweet pleader in misfortune's cause, accept
my parting thanks.   This camp is not thy proper sphere.   Wert thou among
yon savages, as they are called thou 'dst find companions more congenial to
thy heart.

Piz. Yes; she shall bear the tidings of thy death to Cora.

Alon. Inhuman man! that pang, at least, might have been spared me;
but thy malice shall not shake my constancy.   I go to death—many shall
bless, and none will curse my memory.   Thou wilt still live, and still wilt
be—Pizarro.   [*Exit, guarded.*

Elv. Now, by the indignant scorn that burns upon my cheek, my soul is
shamed and sickened at the meanness of thy vengeance!

Piz. What has thy romantic folly aimed at? He is mine enemy, and in
my power.

Elv. He is in your power, and therefore is no more an enemy.   Pizarro,
I demand not of thee virtue, I ask not from thee nobleness of mind, I require
only just dealing to the fame thou hast acquired: be not the assassin of thine
own renown.   How often have you sworn, that the sacrifice which thy wondrous valour's high report had won you from subdued Elvira, was the proudest
triumph of your fame!   Thou knowest I bear a mind not cast in the common mould, not formed for tame sequestered love, content mid household
cares to prattle to an idle offspring, and wait the dull delight of an obscure
lover's kindness: no! my heart was framed to look up with awe and homage
to the object it adored; my ears to own no music but the thrilling records of
his praise; my lips to scorn all babbling but the tales of his achievements;
my brain to turn giddy with delight, reading the applauding tributes of his
monarch's and his country's gratitude; my every faculty to throb with transport, while I heard the shouts of acclamation which announced the coming of
my hero; my whole soul to love him with devotion! with enthusiasm! to see
no other object—to own no other tie—but to make him my world!   Thus to
love is at least no common weakness. Pizarro! was not such my love for thee

Piz. It was, Elvira!

Elv. Then do not make me hateful to myself, by tearing off the mask at
once, baring the hideous imposture that has undone me!   Do not an act
which, howe'er thy present power may gloss it to the world, will make thee
hateful to all future ages—accursed and scorned by posterity.

Piz. And, should posterity applaud my deeds, thinkest thou my mouldering bones would rattle then with transport in my tomb? This is renown for
visionary boys to dream of; I understand it not. The fame I value shall up-

lift my living estimation, o'erbear with popular support the envy of my foes, advance my purposes, and aid my power.

Elv. Each word thou speakest, each moment that I hear thee, dispels the fatal mist through which I 've judged thee. Thou man of mighty name but little soul, I see thou wert not born to feel what genuine fame and glory are. Go! prefer the flattery of thy own fleeting day to the bright circle of a deathless name—go! prefer to stare upon the grain of sand on which you trample, to musing on the starred canopy above thee. Fame, the sovereign deity of proud ambition, is not to be worshipped so: who seeks alone for living homage stands a mean canvasser in her temple's porch, wooing promiscuously, from the fickle breath of every wretch that passes, the brittle tribute of his praise. He dares not approach the sacred altar—no noble sacrifice of his is placed there, nor ever shall his worshipped image, fixed above, claim for his memory a glorious immortality.

Piz. Elvira, leave me!

Elv. Pizarro, you no longer love me.

Piz. It is not so, Elvira. But what might I not suspect—this wondrous interest for a stranger! Take back thy reproach.

Elv. No, Pizarro, as yet I am not lost to you; one string still remains, and binds me to your fate. Do not, I conjure you—do not, for mine own sake, tear it asunder—shed not Alonzo's blood!

Piz. My resolution 's fixed.

Elv. Even though that moment lost you Elvira for ever?

Piz. Even so.

Elv. Pizarro, if not to honour, if not to humanity, yet listen to affection; bear some memory of the sacrifices I have made for thy sake. Have I not for thee quitted my parents, my friends, my fame, my native land? When escaping, did I not risk, in rushing to thy arms, to bury myself in the bosom of the deep? Have I not shared all thy perils—heavy storms at sea, and frightful 'scapes on shore? Even on this dreadful day, amid the rout of battle, who remained firm and constant at Pizarro's side? Who presented her bosom as his shield to the assailing foe?

Piz. 'Tis truly spoken all. In love thou art thy sex's miracle, in war the soldier's pattern; and therefore my whole heart and half my acquisitions are thy right.

Elv. Convince me I possess the first; I exchange all title to the latter for —mercy to Alonzo.

Piz. No more! Had I intended to prolong his doom, each word thou utterest now would hasten on his fate.

Elv. Alonzo then at morn will die?

Piz. Thinkest thou yon sun will set? As surely at his rising shall Alonzo die.

Elv. Then be it done—the string is cracked—sundered for ever. But mark me—thou hast heretofore had cause, 'tis true, to doubt my resolution, howe'er offended; but mark me now—the lips which, cold and jeering, laughing revenge with rancorous mockery, can insult a fallen enemy, shall never more receive the pledge of love: the arm which, unshaken by its bloody purpose, shall assign to needless torture the victim who avows his heart, never more shall press the hand of faith! Pizarro, scorn not my words; beware you slight them not! I feel how noble are the motives which now animate my thoughts. Who could not feel as I do, I condemn: who, feeling so, yet would not act as I shall, I despise!

Piz. I have heard thee, Elvira, and know well the noble motives which inspire thee—fit advocate in virtue's cause! Believe me, I pity thy tender feelings for the youth Alonzo! He dies at sunrise! [*Exit.*

Elv. 'Tis well! 'tis just I should be humbled—I had forgot myself, and in the cause of innocence assumed the tone of virtue. 'Twas fit I should be rebuked—and by Pizarro. Fall, fall, ye few reluctant drops of weakness—the last these eyes shall ever shed. How a woman can love, Pizarro, thou hast known too well—how she can hate, thou hast yet to learn. Yes, thou undaunted!—thou, whom yet no mortal hazard has appalled—thou, who on Panama's brow didst make alliance with the raging elements that tore the silence of that horrid night, when thou didst follow, as thy pioneer, the crashing thunder's drift; and, stalking o'er the trembling earth, didst plant thy banner by the red volcano's mouth! thou, who when battling on the sea, and thy brave ship was blown to splinters, wast seen, as thou didst bestride a fragment of the smoking wreck, to wave thy glittering sword above thy head, as thou wouldst defy the world in that extremity!—come, fearless man! now meet the last and fellest peril of thy life; meet and survive—an injured woman's fury, if thou canst. [*Exit.*

ACT IV.

SCENE I.—*A Dungeon.*

ALONZO is discovered in chains. A SENTINEL *walking near.*

Alon. For the last time I have beheld the shadowed ocean close upon the light. For the last time, through my cleft dungeon's roof, I now behold the quivering lustre of the stars. For the last time, O sun! (and soon the hour) I shall behold thy rising, and thy level beams melting the pale mists of morn to glittering dew-drops. Then comes my death, and in the morning of my day I fall, which—no, Alonzo, date not the life which thou hast run by the mean reckoning of the hours and days which thou hast breathed: a life spent worthily should be measured by a nobler line—by deeds, not years. Then wouldst thou murmur not, but bless the Providence which in so short a span made thee the instrument of wide and spreading blessings to the helpless and oppressed. Though sinking in decrepit age, he prematurely falls, whose memory records no benefit conferred by him on man. They only have lived long, who have lived virtuously.

Enter a SOLDIER, *shows the* SENTINEL *a passport, who withdraws.*

Alon. What bear you there?

Sold. These refreshments I was ordered to leave in your dungeon.

Alon. By whom ordered?

Sold. By the Lady Elvira: she will be here herself before the dawn.

Alon. Bear back to her my humblest thanks; and take thou the refreshments, friend—I need them not.

Sold. I have served under you, Don Alonzo. Pardon my saying, that my heart pities you. [*Exit*

Alon. In Pizarro's camp, to pity the unfortunate, no doubt requires for giveness.—[*Looking out.*] Surely, even now, thin streaks of glimmering light steal on the darkness of the east. If so, my life is but one hour more. I will not watch the coming dawn; but in the darkness of my cell, my last prayer to thee, Power Supreme! shall be for my wife and child! Grant them to dwell in innocence and peace; grant health and purity of mind—all else is worthless. [*Retires into the dungeon.*

Sent. Who's there? answer quickly! who's there?

Rol. [*Without.*] A friar come to visit your prisoner.

Enter ROLLA, *disguised as a* MONK.

Rol. Inform me, friend—is not Alonzo, the Spanish prisoner, confined in this dungeon?

Sent. He is.

Rol. I must speak with him.

Sent. You must not. [*Stopping him with his spear.*

Rol. He is my friend.

Sent. Not if he were your brother.

Rol. What is to be his fate?

Sent. He dies at sunrise.

Rol. Ha! then I am come in time.

Sent. Just—to witness his death.

Rol. Soldier, I must speak with him.

Sent. Back, back! It is impossible!

Rol. I do entreat thee but for one moment!

Sent. You entreat in vain; my orders are most strict.

Rol. Even now, I saw a messenger go hence.

Sent. He brought a pass, which we are all accustomed to obey

Rol. Look on this wedge of massive gold—look on these precious gems. In thy own land they will be wealth for thee and thine beyond thy hope or wish. Take them—they are thine. Let me but pass one minute with Alonzo.

Sent. Away! wouldst thou corrupt me?—me! an old Castilian! I know my duty better.

Rol. Soldier! hast thou a wife?

Sent. I have.

Rol. Hast thou children?

Sent. Four—honest, lovely boys.

Rol. Where didst thou leave them?

Sent. In my native village—even in the cot where myself was born.

Rol. Dost thou love thy children and thy wife?

Sent. Do I love them! God knows my heart—I do.

Rol. Soldier!—imagine thou wert doomed to die a cruel death in this strange land; what would be thy last request?

Sent. That some of my comrades should carry my dying blessing to my wife and children.

Rol. Oh, but if that comrade was at thy prison gate—and should there be told—thy fellow-soldier dies at sunrise—yet thou shalt not for a moment see him—nor shalt thou bear his dying blessing to his poor children or his wretched wife—what wouldst thou think of him, who thus could drive thy comrade from the door?

Sent. How!

Rol. Alonzo has a wife and child—I am come but to receive for her and for her babe the last blessing of my friend.

Sent. Go in.   [*Retires.*

Rol. Oh, holy Nature! thou dost never plead in vain. There is not, of our earth, a creature bearing form, and life, human or savage, native of the forest wild or giddy air, around whose parent bosom thou hast not a cord entwined of power to tie them to their offspring's claims, and at thy will to draw them back to thee. On iron pinions borne, the blood-stained vulture cleaves the storm, yet is the plumage closest to her breast soft as the cygnet's down, and o'er her unshelled brood the murmuring ringdove sits not more gently! Yes, now he is beyond the porch, barring the outer gate!—Alonzo! Alonzo! my friend! Ha! in gentle sleep!—Alonzo! rise!

Re-enter ALONZO.

Alon. [*Within.*] How! is my hour elapsed? Well—[*Returning from the recess.*] I am ready.

Rol. Alonzo, know me?

Alon. What voice is that?

Rol. 'Tis Rolla's.   [*Takes off his disguise.*]

Alon. Rolla!—my friend!—[*Embraces him.*] Heavens! how couldst thou pass the guard? Did this habit——

Rol. There is not a moment to be lost in words. This disguise I tore from the dead body of a friar, as I passed our field of battle; it has gained me entrance to thy dungeon—now take it thou, and fly.

Alon. And Rolla——

Rol. Will remain here in thy place.

Alon. And die for me! No! rather eternal tortures rack me.

Rol. I shall not die, Alonzo. It is thy life Pizarro seeks, not Rolla's; and from my prison soon will thy arm deliver me. Or, should it be otherwise, I am as a blighted plantain, standing alone amid the sandy desert; nothing seeks or lives beneath my shelter. Thou art a husband, and a father; the being of a lovely wife and helpless infant hangs upon thy life. Go! go! Alonzo! go! to save not thyself, but Cora, and thy child!

Alon. Urge me not thus, my friend! I had prepared to die in peace.

Rol. To die in peace! devoting her thou'st sworn to live for, to madness, misery, and death! For, be assured, the state I left her in forbids all hope but from thy quick return.

Alon. Oh, God!

Rol. If thou art yet irresolute, Alonzo, now heed me well. I think thou hast not known that Rolla ever pledged his word, and shrunk from its fulfilment. And by the heart of truth I swear, if thou art proudly obstinate to deny thy friend the transport of preserving Cora's life, in thee, no power that sways the will of man shall stir me hence; and thou'lt but have the desperate triumph of seeing Rolla perish by thy side, with the assured conviction that Cora and thy child are lost for ever.

Alon. Oh, Rolla! you distract me!

Rol. Begone! A moment's further pause, and all is lost. The dawn approaches. Fear not for me—I will treat with Pizarro as for surrender and submission. I shall gain time, doubt not, while thou, with a chosen band, passing the secret way, mayst at night return, release thy friend, and bear him back in triumph.　Yes, hasten, dear Alonzo!　Even now I hear the frantic Cora call thee!　Haste! haste! haste!

Alon.　Rolla, I fear thy friendship drives me from honour, and from right.

Rol.　Did Rolla ever counsel dishonour to his friend?

Alon.　Oh! my preserver!　　　　　　　　　　　　　　　［*Embraces him.*

Rol.　I feel thy warm tears dropping on my cheek.　Go! I am rewarded. —［*Throws the* FRIAR's *garment over* ALONZO.］　There! conceal thy face; and, that they may not clank, hold fast thy chains.　Now—God be with thee!

Alon.　At night we meet again.　Then, so aid me Heaven! I return to save—or—perish with thee!　　　　　　　　　　　　　　　　［*Exit.*

Rol.　［*Looking after him.*］　He has passed the outer porch. He is safe! He will soon embrace his wife and child!—Now, Cora, didst thou not wrong me? This is the first time throughout my life I ever deceived man.　Forgive me, God of truth! if I am wrong.　Alonzo flatters himself that we shall meet again.　Yes—there!—［*Lifting his hands to heaven.*］　Assuredly, we shall meet again: there possess in peace the joys of everlasting love and friendship—on earth, imperfect and embittered.　I will retire, lest the guard return before Alonzo may have passed their lines.　　　［*Retires into the dungeon.*

Enter ELVIRA.

Elv.　No, not Pizarro's brutal taunts, not the glowing admiration which I feel for this noble youth, shall raise an interest in my harassed bosom which honour would not sanction.　If he reject the vengeance my heart has sworn against the tyrant, whose death alone can save this land, yet shall the delight be mine to restore him to his Cora's arms, to his dear child, and to the unoffending people, whom his virtues guide, and valour guards.—Alonzo, come forth!

Re-enter ROLLA.

Ha! who art thou? where is Alonzo?

Rol.　Alonzo's fled.

Elv.　Fled!

Rol.　Yes—and he must not be pursued.　Pardon this roughness,— ［*Seizing her hand.*］ but a moment's precious to Alonzo's flight.

Elv.　What if I call the guard?

Rol.　Do so—Alonzo still gains time.

Elv.　What if thus I free myself?　　　　　　　　　　［*Shows a dagger.*

Rol.　Strike it to my heart—still, with the convulsive grasp of death, I'll hold thee fast.

Elv.　Release me—I give my faith, I neither will alarm the guard, nor cause pursuit.

Rol.　At once I trust thy word: a feeling boldness in those eyes assures me that thy soul is noble.

Elv.　What is thy name?　Speak freely: by my order the guard is removed beyond the outer porch.

Rol.　My name is Rolla.

Elv.　The Peruvian leader?

Rol.　I was so yesterday: to-day, the Spaniards' captive.

Elv.　And friendship for Alonzo moved thee to this act?

Rol. Alonzo is my friend; I am prepared to die for him. Yet is the cause a motive stronger far than friendship.

Elv. One only passion else could urge such generous rashness.

Rol. And that is——

Elv. Love?

Rol. True!

Elv. Gallant, ingenuous Rolla! Know that my purpose here was thine; and were I to save thy friend——

Rol. How! a woman blessed with gentleness and courage, and yet not Cora!

Elv. Does Rolla think so meanly of all female hearts?

Rol. Not so—you are worse and better than we are!

Elv. Were I to save thee, Rolla, from the tyrant's vengeance, restore thee to thy native land, and thy native land to peace, wouldst thou not rank Elvira with the good?

Rol. To judge the action, I must know the means.

Elv. Take this dagger.

Rol. How to be used?

Elv. I will conduct thee to the tent where fell Pizarro sleeps—the scourge of innocence, the terror of thy race, the fiend that desolates thy afflicted country.

Rol. Have you not been injured by Pizarro?

Elv. Deeply as scorn and insult can infuse their deadly venom.

Rol. And you ask that I shall murder him in his sleep!

Elv. Would he not have murdered Alonzo in his chains? He that sleeps, and he that's bound, are equally defenceless. Hear me, Rolla—so may I prosper in this perilous act, as, searching my full heart, I have put by all rancorous motive of private vengeance there, and feel that I advance to my dread purpose in the cause of human nature and at the call of sacred justice.

Rol. The God of justice sanctifies no evil as a step towards good. Great actions cannot be achieved by wicked means.

Elv. Then, Peruvian! since thou dost feel so coldly for thy country's wrongs, this hand, though it revolt my soul, shall strike the blow.

Rol. Then is thy destruction certain, and for Peru thou perishest! Give me the dagger!

Elv. Now follow me. But first—and dreadful is the hard necessity—thou must strike down the guard.

Rol. The soldier who was on duty here?

Elv. Yes, him—else, seeing thee, the alarm will be instant.

Rol. And I must stab that soldier as I pass? Take back thy dagger.

Elv. Rolla!

Rol. That soldier, mark me, is a man. All are not men that bear the human form. He refused my prayers, refused my gold, denying to admit me, till his own feelings bribed him. For my nation's safety, I would not harm that man!

Elv. Then he must with us—I will answer for his safety.

Rol. Be that plainly understood between us: for, whate'er betide our enterprise, I will not risk a hair of that man's head, to save my heart-strings from consuming fire.   [*Exeunt.*

SCENE II.—PIZARRO's *Tent.*

PIZARRO *is discovered on a couch, in disturbed sleep.*

Piz. [*In his sleep.*] No mercy, traitor!—Now at his heart!—Stand off there, you!—Let me see him bleed!—Ha! ha! ha!—Let me hear that groan again.

Enter ROLLA *and* ELVIRA.

Elv. There! Now, lose not a moment.

Rol. You must leave me now. This scene of blood fits not a woman's presence.

Elv. But a moment's pause may——

Rol. Go, retire to your own tent, and return not here—I will come to you. Be thou not known in this business, I implore you!

Elv. I will withdraw the guard that waits.   [*Exit.*

Rol. Now have I in my power the accursed destroyer of my country's peace: yet tranquilly he rests. God! can this man sleep?

Piz. [*In his sleep.*] Away! away! hideous fiends! Tear not my bosom thus!

Rol. No: I was in error—the balm of sweet repose he never more can know. Look here, ambition's fools! ye, by whose inhuman pride the bleeding sacrifice of nations is held as nothing, behold the rest of the guilty!— He is at my mercy—and one blow!——No! my heart and hand refuse the act: Rolla cannot be an assassin! Yet Elvira must be saved!—[*Approaches the couch.*] Pizarro! awake!

Piz. [*Starts up.*] Who?—Guard!——

Rol. Speak not—another word is thy death. Call not for aid! this arm will be swifter than thy guard.

Piz. Who art thou? and what is thy will?

Rol. I am thine enemy! Peruvian Rolla! Thy death is not my will, or I could have slain thee sleeping.

Piz. Speak, what else?

Rol. Now thou art at my mercy, answer me! Did a Peruvian ever yet wrong or injure thee, or any of thy nation? Didst thou, or any of thy nation, ever yet show mercy to a Peruvian in thy power? Now shalt thou feel, and if thou hast a heart thou 'lt feel it keenly, a Peruvian's vengeance! —[*Drops the dagger at his feet.*] There!

Piz. Is it possible!   [*Walks aside confounded.*

Rol. Can Pizarro be surprised at this? I thought forgiveness of injuries had been the Christian's precept. Thou seest, at least, it is the Peruvian's practice.

Piz. Rolla, thou hast indeed surprised—subdued me.

[*Walks aside again as in irresolute thought.*

Re-enter ELVIRA, *not seeing* PIZARRO.

[*Elv.*] Is it done! Is he dead?—[*Sees* PIZARRO.] How! still living?! Then art lost! And for you, wretched Peruvians! mercy is no more! O treacherous, or cowardly?

[*Elv.*] How! can it be that——

Rol. Away!—Elvira speaks she knows not what!—[*To* ELVIRA.] Leave me, I conjure you, with Pizarro.

Elv. How! Rolla, dost thou think I shall retract? or that I meanly will deny, that in thy hand I placed a poniard to be plunged into that tyrant's heart? No: my sole regret is, that I trusted to thy weakness, and did not strike the blow myself. Too soon thou 'lt learn that mercy to that man is direct cruelty to all thy race!

Piz. Guard! quick! a guard, to seize this frantic woman.

Elv. Yes, a guard! I call them too! And soon I know they'll lead me to my death. But think not, Pizarro, the fury of thy flashing eyes shall awe me for a moment! Nor think that woman's anger, or the feelings of an injured heart, prompted me to this design. No! had I been only influenced so—thus failing, shame and remorse would weigh me down. But, though defeated and destroyed, as now I am, such is the greatness of the cause that urged me, I shall perish, glorying in the attempt, and my last breath of life shall speak the proud avowal of my purpose—to have rescued millions of innocents from the bloodthirsty tyranny of one—by ridding the insulted world of thee.

Rol. Had the act been noble as the motive, Rolla would not have shrunk from its performance.

Enter GUARDS.

Piz. Seize this discovered fiend, who sought to kill your leader.

Elv. Touch me not, at the peril of your souls; I am your prisoner, and will follow you. But thou, their triumphant leader, first shalt hear me. Yet, first—for thee, Rolla, accept my forgiveness; even had I been the victim of thy nobleness of heart, I should have admired thee for it. But 'twas myself provoked my doom—thou wouldst have shielded me. Let not thy contempt follow me to the grave. Didst thou but know the fiend-like arts by which this hypocrite first undermined the virtue of a guileless heart! how, even in the pious sanctuary wherein I dwelt, by corruption and by fraud he practised upon those in whom I most confided—till my distempered fancy led me, step by step, into the abyss of guilt——

Piz. Why am I not obeyed? Tear her hence!

Elv. 'Tis past—but didst thou know my story, Rolla, thou wouldst pity me.

Rol. From my soul I do pity thee!

Piz. Villains! drag her to the dungeon!—prepare the torture instantly.

Elv. Soldiers, but a moment more—'tis to applaud your general. It is to tell the astonished world that, for once, Pizarro's sentence is an act of justice: yes, rack me with the sharpest tortures that ever agonised the human frame, it will be justice. Yes, bid the minions of thy fury wrench forth the sinews of those arms that have caressed—and even have defended thee! Bid them pour burning metal into the bleeding cases of these eyes, that so oft—oh, God!—have hung with love and homage on thy looks—then approach me bound on the abhorred wheel—there glut thy savage eyes with the convulsive spasms of that dishonoured bosom which was once thy pillow!—yet will I bear it all; for it will be justice, all! and when thou shalt bid them tear me to my death, hoping that thy unshrinking ears may at last be feasted with the music of my cries, I will not utter one shriek or groan; but to the last gasp my body's patience shall deride thy vengeance, as my soul defies thy power.

Piz. Hearest thou the wretch whose hands were even now prepared for murder?

Rol. Yes! and, if her accusation's false, thou wilt not shrink from hearing her; if true, thy barbarity cannot make her suffer the pangs thy conscience will inflict on thee.

Elv. And now, farewell, world!—Rolla, farewell!—farewell, thou condemned of Heaven! [*To* PIZARRO] for repentance and remorse, I know, will never touch thy heart.—We shall meet again.—Ha! be it thy horror here to know that we shall meet hereafter! And when thy parting hour approaches—hark to the knell, whose dreadful beat will strike to thy despairing soul. Then will vibrate on thy ear the curses of the cloistered saint from whom thou stolest me. Then the last shrieks which burst from my mother's breaking heart, as she died, appealing to her God against the seducer of her child! Then the blood-stifled groan of my murdered brother—murdered by thee, fell monster!—seeking atonement for his sister's ruined honour. I hear them now! To me the recollection's madness! At such an hour—what will it be to thee?

Piz. A moment's more delay, and at the peril of your lives——

Elv. I have spoken—and the last mortal frailty of my heart is passed. And now, with an undaunted spirit and unshaken firmness, I go to meet my destiny. That I could not live nobly, has been Pizarro's act; that I will die nobly, shall be my own.   [*Exit guarded.*

Piz. Rolla, I would not thou, a warrior, valiant and renowned, shouldst credit the vile tales of this frantic woman. The cause of all this fury—oh! a wanton passion for the rebel youth Alonzo, now my prisoner.

Rol. Alonzo is not now thy prisoner.

Piz. How!

Rol. I came to rescue him—to deceive his guard. I have succeeded; I remain thy prisoner.

Piz. Alonzo fled! Is then the vengeance dearest to my heart never to be gratified?

Rol. Dismiss such passions from thy heart, then thou'lt consult its peace.

Piz. I can face all enemies that dare confront me—I cannot war against my nature.

Rol. Then, Pizarro, ask not to be deemed a hero: to triumph o'er ourselves is the only conquest where fortune makes no claim. In battle, chance may snatch the laurel from thee, or chance may place it on thy brow; but, in a contest with thyself, be resolute, and the virtuous impulse must be the victor.

Piz. Peruvian! thou shalt not find me to thee ungrateful or ungenerous. Return to your countrymen—you are at liberty.

Rol. Thou dost act in this as honour and as duty bid thee.

Piz. I cannot but admire thee, Rolla: I would we might be friends.

Rol. Farewell! pity Elvira! become the friend of virtue—and thou wilt be mine.   [*Exit.*

Piz. Ambition! tell me what is the phantom I have followed? where is the one delight which it has made my own? My fame is the mark of envy, my love the dupe of treachery, my glory eclipsed by the boy I taught, my revenge defeated and rebuked by the rude honour of a savage foe, before whose native dignity of soul I have sunk confounded and subdued! I would I could retrace my steps!—I cannot. Would I could evade my own reflections! No! thought and memory are my hell!   [*Exit.*

ACT V.

SCENE I.—*A Forest.   In the background a Hut.*

CORA *is discovered leaning over her* CHILD, *who is laid on a bed of leaves and moss.—A Storm, with thunder and lightning.*

Cora. O Nature! thou hast not the strength of love. My anxious spirit is untired in its march; my wearied shivering frame sinks under it. And for thee, my boy, when faint beneath thy lovely burden, could I refuse to give thy slumbers that poor bed of rest! O my child! were I assured thy father breathes no more, how quickly would I lay me down by thy dear side! —but down—down for ever!—[*Thunder and lightning.*] I ask thee not, unpitying storm! to abate thy rage in mercy to poor Cora's misery; nor while thy thunders spare his slumbers will I disturb my sleeping cherub; though Heaven knows I wish to hear the voice of life, and feel that life is near me.   But I will endure all while what I have of reason holds. [*Sings.*

> Yes, yes, be merciless, thou tempest dire;
> Unaw'd, unshelter'd, I thy fury brave:
> I'll bare my bosom to thy forked fire,
> Let it but guide me to Alonzo's grave!

> O'er his pale corse then, while thy lightnings glare,
> I'll press his clay-cold lips, and perish there.

> But thou wilt wake again, my boy,
> Again thou'lt rise to life and joy—
> Thy father never!—
> Thy laughing eyes will meet the light,
> Unconscious that eternal night
> Veils his for ever.

> On yon green bed of moss there lies my child,
> Oh! safer lies from these chill'd arms apart;
> He sleeps, sweet lamb! nor heeds the tempest wild,
> Oh! sweeter sleeps, than near this breaking heart.

> Alas! my babe, if thou wouldst peaceful rest,
> Thy cradle must not be thy mother's breast.

> Yet thou wilt wake again, my boy,
> Again thou'lt rise to life and joy—
> Thy father never!—
> Thy laughing eyes will meet the light,
> Unconscious that eternal night
> Veils his for ever.   [*Thunder and lightning.*

Still, still implacable! unfeeling elements! yet still dost thou sleep, my smiling innocent! O Death! when wilt thou grant to this babe's mother such repose? Sure I may shield thee better from the storm; my veil may——

[*While she is wrapping her mantle and her veil over him,* ALONZO'S
voice is heard in the distance.

Alon. Cora!
Cora. Ha!   [*Rises.*

Alon. Cora!

Cora. Oh, my heart! Sweet Heaven, deceive me not! Is it not Alonzo's voice?

Alon. [*Nearer.*] Cora!

Cora. It is—it is Alonzo!

Alon. [*Nearer still.*] Cora! my beloved!

Cora. Alonzo!—Here! here!—Alonzo!   [*Runs out.*

Enter two Spanish Soldiers.

1st Sold. I tell you we are near our out-posts, and the word we heard just now was the countersign.

2nd Sold. Well, in our escape from the enemy, to have discovered their secret passage through the rocks, will prove a lucky chance to us. Pizarro will reward us.

1st Sold. This way: the sun, though clouded, is on our left.—[*Perceives the* Child.] What have we here?—A child, as I'm a soldier!

2nd Sold. 'Tis a sweet little babe! Now would it be a great charity to take this infant from its pagan mother's power.

1st Sold. It would so: I have one at home shall play with it.—Come along.   [*Exeunt with the* Child.

Cora. [*Without.*] This way, dear Alonzo!

Re-enter Cora, *with* Alonzo.

Now am I right—there—there—under that tree. Was it possible the instinct of a mother's heart could mistake the spot? Now wilt thou look at him as he sleeps, or shall I bring him waking, with his full, blue, laughing eyes, to welcome you at once? Yes, yes! Stand thou there; I'll snatch him from his rosy slumber, blushing like the perfumed morn.

[*She runs up to the spot, and finding only the mantle and veil, which she tears from the ground, and the* Child *gone, shrieks.*

Alon. [*Running to her.*] Cora! my heart's beloved!

Cora. He is gone!

Alon. Eternal God!

Cora. He is gone!—my child! my child!

Alon. Where didst thou leave him?

Cora. [*Dashing herself on the spot.*] Here!

Alon. Be calm, beloved Cora; he has waked and crept to a little distance; we shall find him. Are you assured this was the spot you left him in?

Cora. Did not these hands make that bed and shelter for him? and is not this the veil that covered him?

Alon. Here is a hut yet unobserved.

Cora. Ha! yes, yes! there lives the savage that has robbed me of my child.—[*Beats at the door.*] Give me back my child! restore to me my boy!

Enter Las-Casas *from the hut.*

Las-Cas. Who calls me from my wretched solitude?

Cora. Give me back my child!—[*Goes into the hut and calls.*] Fernando!

Alon. Almighty powers! do my eyes deceive me! Las-Casas!

Las-Cas. Alonzo, my beloved young friend!

Alon. My revered instructor!   [*Embracing.*

Re-enter CORA.

Cora. Will you embrace this man before he restores my boy?

Alon. Alas, my friend! in what a moment of misery do we meet!

Cora. Yet his look is goodness and humanity. Good old man, have compassion on a wretched mother, and I will be your servant while I live. But do not—for pity's sake, do not say you have him not; do not say you have not seen him.   [*Runs into the wood.*

Las-Cas. What can this mean?

Alon. She is my wife. Just rescued from the Spaniards' prison, I learned she had fled to this wild forest. Hearing my voice, she left the child, and flew to meet me: he was left sleeping under yonder tree.

Re-enter CORA.

Las-Cas. How! did you leave him?

Cora. Oh, you are right! right! unnatural mother that I was! I left my child, I forsook my innocent! But I will fly to the earth's brink, but I will find him.   [*Runs out.*

Alon. Forgive me, Las-Casas, I must follow her; for at night I attempt brave Rolla's rescue.

Las-Cas. I will not leave thee, Alonzo. You must try to lead her to the right: that way lies your camp. Wait not my infirm steps: I follow thee, my friend.   [*Exeunt.*

SCENE II.—*The Outpost of the Spanish Camp. In the background a torrent, over which a bridge is formed by a felled tree. Trumpets sound without.*

Enter ALMAGRO, *followed by* SOLDIERS, *leading* ROLLA *in chains.*

Alm. Bear him along; his story must be false.

Rol. False! Rolla utter falsehood! I would I had thee in a desert with thy troop around thee, and I but with my sword in this unshackled hand!
                                        [*Trumpets without.*

Alm. Is it to be credited, that Rolla, the renowned Peruvian hero, should be detected, like a spy, skulking through our camp!

Rol. Skulking!

Alm. But answer to the general; he is here.

Enter PIZARRO.

Piz. What do I see? Rolla!

Rol. Oh, to thy surprise, no doubt!

Piz. And bound too!

Rol. So fast, thou needest not fear approaching me.

Alm. The guards surprised him passing our outpost.

Piz. Release him instantly! Believe me, I regret this insult.

Rol. You feel then as you ought.

Piz. Nor can I brook to see a warrior of Rolla's fame disarmed. Accept this, though it has been thy enemy's.—[*Gives a sword.*] The Spaniards know the courtesy that's due to valour.

Rol. And the Peruvians how to forget offence.

Piz. May not Rolla and Pizarro cease to be foes?

Rol. When the sea divides us; yes! May I now depart?

Piz. Freely.

Rol. And shall I not again be intercepted?

Piz. No! Let the word be given that Rolla passes freely.

Enter DAVILLA *and* SOLDIERS, *with* ALONZO'S CHILD.

Dav. Here are two soldiers, captured yesterday, who have escaped from the Peruvian hold—and by the secret way we have so long endeavoured to discover.

Piz. Silence, imprudent! Seest thou not—— [*Pointing to* ROLLA.

Dav. In their way, they found a Peruvian child, who seems——

Piz. What is the imp to me? Bid them toss it into the sea.

Rol. Gracious Heavens! it is Alonzo's child! Give it to me.

Piz. Ha! Alonzo's child!—[*Takes the* CHILD.] Welcome, thou pretty hostage. Now Alonzo is again my prisoner!

Rol. Thou wilt not keep the infant from its mother?

Piz. Will I not! What, when I shall meet Alonzo in the heat of the victorious fight, thinkest thou I shall not have a check upon the valour of his heart, when he is reminded that a word of mine is this child's death?

Rol. I do not understand thee.

Piz. My vengeance has a long arrear of hate to settle with Alonzo! and this pledge may help to settle the account. [*Gives the* CHILD *to a* SOLDIER.]

Rol. Man! Man! Art thou a man? Couldst thou hurt that innocent?— By Heaven! it 's smiling in thy face.

Piz. Tell me, does it resemble Cora?

Rol. Pizarro! thou hast set my heart on fire. If thou dost harm that child, think not his blood will sink into the barren sand. No! faithful to the eager hope that now trembles in this indignant heart, 'twill rise to the common God of nature and humanity, and cry aloud for vengeance on his accursed destroyer's head.

Piz. Be that peril mine.

Rol. [*Throwing himself at his feet.*] Behold me at thy feet—me, Rolla! —me, the preserver of thy life!—me, that have never yet bent or bowed before created man! In humble agony I sue to thee—prostrate I implore thee—but spare that child, and I will be thy slave.

Piz. Rolla! still art thou free to go—this boy remains with me.

Rol. Then was this sword Heaven's gift, not thine!—[*Seizes the* CHILD.] Who moves one step to follow me, dies upon the spot. [*Exit with the* CHILD.

Piz. Pursue him instantly—but spare his life.—[*Exeunt* DAVILLA *and* ALMAGRO *with* SOLDIERS.] With what fury he defends himself! Ha! he fells them to the ground—and now——

Re-enter ALMAGRO.

Alm. Three of your brave soldiers are already victims to your command to spare this madman's life; and if he once gain the thicket——

Piz. Spare him no longer.—[*Exit* ALMAGRO.] Their guns must reach him—he 'll yet escape—hollow to those horse—the Peruvian sees them— and now he turns among the rocks—then is his retreat cut off.—[ROLLA *crosses the wooden bridge over the cataract, pursued by the* SOLDIERS—*they fire at him—a shot strikes him.*] Now!—quick! quick! seize the child! [ROLLA *tears from the rock the tree which supports the bridge, and retreats by the background, bearing off the* CHILD.

Re-enter ALMAGRO *and* DAVILLA.

Alm. By hell! he has escaped!—and with the child unhurt.

Dav. No—he bears his death with him. Believe me, I saw him struck upon the side.

Piz. But the child is saved—Alonzo's child! Oh! the furies of disappointed vengeance!

Alm. Away with the revenge of words—let us to deeds! Forget not we have acquired the knowledge of the secret pass, which through the rocky cavern's gloom brings you at once to the stronghold, where are lodged their women and their treasures.

Piz. Right, Almagro! Swift as thy thought, draw forth a daring and a chosen band—I will not wait for numbers. Stay, Almagro! Valverde is informed Elvira dies to-day?

Alm. He is—and one request alone she——

Piz. I'll hear of none.

Alm. The boon is small—'tis but for the noviciate habit which you first beheld her in—she wishes not to suffer in the gaudy trappings which remind her of her shame.

Piz. Well, do as thou wilt—but tell Valverde, at our return, as his life shall answer it, to let me hear that she is dead. [*Exeunt severally.*

SCENE III.—ATALIBA'S *Tent.*

Enter ATALIBA, *followed by* CORA *and* ALONZO.

Cora. Oh! avoid me not, Ataliba! To whom, but to her king, is the wretched mother to address her griefs? The gods refuse to hear my prayers! Did not my Alonzo fight for thee? and will not my sweet boy, if thou'lt but restore him to me, one day fight thy battles too?

Alon. Oh! my suffering love—my poor·heart-broken Cora!—thou but wound'st our sovereign's feeling soul, and not reliev'st thy own.

Cora. Is he our sovereign, and has he not the power to give me back my child?

Ata. When I reward desert, or can relieve my people, I feel what is the real glory of a king—when I hear them suffer, and cannot aid them, I mourn the impotence of all mortal power.

Soldiers. [*Without.*] Rolla! Rolla! Rolla!

Enter ROLLA, *bleeding, with the* CHILD, *followed by* PERUVIAN SOLDIERS.

Rol. Thy child!   [*Gives the* CHILD *into* CORA'S *arms, and falls.*

Cora. Oh, God! there's blood upon him!

Rol. 'Tis my blood, Cora!

Alon. Rolla, thou diest!

Rol. For thee, and Cora.   [*Dies.*

Enter ORANO.

Ora. Treachery has revealed our asylum in the rocks. Even now the foe assails the peaceful band retired for protection there.

Alon. Lose not a moment! Soldiers, be quick! Your wives and children cry to you. Bear our loved hero's body in the van: 'twill raise the fury of our men to madness. Now, fell Pizarro! the death of one of us is near! Away! Be the word of assault, Revenge and Rolla!

                                                [*Exeunt. Charge.*

SCENE IV.—*A Recess among the Rocks.*

Enter PIZARRO, ALMAGRO, VALVERDE, *and* SPANISH SOLDIERS.

Piz. Well! if surrounded, we must perish in the centre of them. Where do Rolla and Alonzo hide their heads?

Enter ALONZO, ORANO, *and* PERUVIAN WARRIORS.

Alon. Alonzo answers thee, and Alonzo's sword shall speak for Rolla.

Piz. Thou knowest the advantage of thy numbers. Thou darest not singly face Pizarro.

Alon. Peruvians, stir not a man! Be this contest only ours.

Piz. Spaniards! observe ye the same.—[*Charge. They fight.* ALONZO'S *shield is broken, and he is beat down.*] Now, traitor, to thy heart!

[*At this moment* ELVIRA *enters, habited as when* PIZARRO *first beheld her.* PIZARRO, *appalled, staggers back.* ALONZO *renews the fight, and slays him. Loud shouts from the* PERUVIANS.

Enter ATALIBA.

Ata. My brave Alonzo!   [*Embraces* ALONZO.

Alm. Alonzo, we submit. Spare us! we will embark, and leave the coast.

Val. Elvira will confess I saved her life; she has saved thine.

Alon. Fear not. You are safe.   [SPANIARDS *lay down their arms.*

Elv. Valverde speaks the truth; nor could he think to meet me here. An awful impulse, which my soul could not resist, impelled me hither.

Alon. Noble Elvira! my preserver! How can I speak what I, Ataliba, and his rescued country, owe to thee! If amid this grateful nation thou wouldst remain——

Elv. Alonzo, no! the destination of my future life is fixed. Humbled in penitence, I will endeavour to atone the guilty errors, which, however masked by shallow cheerfulness, have long consumed my secret heart. When, by my sufferings purified and penitence sincere, my soul shall dare address the Throne of Mercy in behalf of others, for thee, Alonzo, for thy Cora, and thy child, for thee, thou virtuous monarch, and the innocent race thou reignest over, shall Elvira's prayers address the God of Nature.—Valverde, you have preserved my life. Cherish humanity, avoid the foul examples thou hast viewed.—Spaniards, returning to your native home, assure your rulers they mistake the road to glory or to power. Tell them that the pursuits of avarice, conquest, and ambition, never yet made a people happy, or a nation great.

[*Casts a look of agony on the dead body of* PIZARRO *as she passes, and exit. Flourish of trumpets.* VALVERDE, ALMAGRO, *and* SPANISH SOLDIERS, *exeunt, bearing off* PIZARRO'S *body.*

Alon. Ataliba! think not I wish to check the voice of triumph, when I entreat we first may pay the tribute due to our loved Rolla's memory.

[*A solemn march. Procession of Peruvian* SOLDIERS, *bearing* ROLLA'S *body on a bier, surrounded by* .... *The banners and* PRIESTESSES *attending chant* .... *the bier.* ALONZO *and* CORA *kneel on either side* .... ROLLA'S *hands in silent agony. The curtain* ....

EPILOGUE,

WRITTEN BY THE HON. WILLIAM LAMB.

SPOKEN BY MRS. JORDAN.

ERE yet suspense has still'd its throbbing fear,
Or melancholy wiped the grateful tear,
While e'en the miseries of a sinking state,
A monarch's danger, and a nation's fate,
Command not now your eyes with grief to flow,
Lost in a trembling mother's nearer wo;
What moral lay shall poetry rehearse,
Or how shall elocution pour the verse
So sweetly, that its music shall repay
The loved illusion which it drives away?
Mine is the task, to rigid custom due,
To me ungrateful as 'tis harsh to you,
To mar the work the tragic scene has wrought,
To rouse the mind that broods in pensive thought,
To scare reflection, which, in absent dreams,
Still lingers musing on the recent themes;
Attention, ere with contemplation tired,
To turn from all that pleased, from all that fired;
To weaken lessons strongly now impress'd,
And chill the interest glowing in the breast—
Mine is the task; and be it mine to spare
The souls that pant, the griefs they see, to share;
Let me with no unhallow'd jest deride
The sigh, that sweet compassion owns with pride—
The sigh of comfort, to affliction dear,
That kindness heaves, and virtue loves to hear.
E'en gay Thalia will not now refuse
This gentle homage to her sister-muse.
  O ye, who listen to the plaintive strain,
With strange enjoyment, and with rapturous pain,
Who erst have felt the Stranger's lone despair,
And Haller's settled, sad, remorseful care,
Does Rolla's pure affection less excite
The inexpressive anguish of delight?
Do Cora's fears, which beat without control,
With less solicitude engross the soul?
Ah, no! your minds with kindred zeal approve
Maternal feeling, and heroic love.
You must approve: where man exists below,
In temperate climes, or midst drear wastes of snow,
Or where the solar fires incessant flame,
Thy laws, all-powerful Nature, are the same:
Vainly the sophist boasts he can explain
The causes of thy universal reign—

More vainly would his cold presumptuous art
Disprove thy general empire o'er the heart:
A voice proclaims thee, that we must believe—
A voice, that surely speaks not to deceive;
That voice poor Cora heard, and closely press'd
Her darling infant to her fearful breast;
Distracted dared the bloody field to tread,
And sought Alonzo through the heaps of dead,
Eager to catch the music of his breath,
Though faltering in the agonies of death,
To touch his lips, though pale and cold, once more,
And clasp his bosom, though it stream'd with gore;
That voice too Rolla heard, and, greatly brave,
His Cora's dearest treasure died to save;
Gave to the hopeless parent's arms her child,
Beheld her transports, and, expiring, smiled.
That voice we hear—oh! be its will obey'd!
'Tis valour's impulse, and 'tis virtue's aid—
It prompts to all benevolence admires,
To all that heavenly piety inspires,
To all that praise repeats through lengthen'd years,
That honour sanctifies, and time reveres.

VERSES

MEMORY OF GARRICK.

SPOKEN AS A MONODY, AT THE THEATRE ROYAL IN DRURY LANE.

To the right honourable COUNTESS SPENCER, whose approbation an esteem were justly considered by MR. GARRICK as the highest panegyric his talents or conduct could acquire, this imperfect tribute to his memory is, with great deference, inscribed by her ladyship's most obedient humble servant,

March 25th, 1779.   RICHARD BRINSLEY SHERIDAN.

If dying excellence deserves a tear,
If fond remembrance still is cherish'd here,
Can we persist to bid your sorrows flow
For fabled suff'rers and delusive woe?
Or with quaint smiles dismiss the plaintive strain,
Point the quick jest—indulge the comic vein—
Ere yet to buried Roscius we assign
One kind regret—one tributary line!
    His fame requires we act a tenderer part:
His memory claims the tear you gave his art!
    The general voice, the meed of mournful verse,
The splendid sorrows that adorn'd his hearse,
The throng that mourn'd as their dead favourite passed,
The graced respect that claim'd him to the last,
While Shakespere's image from its hallow'd base
Seem'd to prescribe the grave, and point the place,—
Nor these,—nor all the sad regrets that flow
From fond fidelity's domestic woe,—
So much are Garrick's praise—so much his due—
As on this spot—one tear bestow'd by you.
    Amid the hearts which seek ingenuous fame,
Our toil attempts the most precarious claim!
To him whose mimic pencil wins the prize,
Obedient Fame immortal wreaths supplies:
Whate'er of wonder Reynolds now may raise,
Raphael still boasts contemporary praise:
Each dazzling light and gaudier bloom subdued,
With undiminish'd awe his works are view'd:
E'en Beauty's portrait wears a softer prime,
Touch'd by the tender hand of mellowing Time.

O O

The patient Sculptor owns an humbler part,
A ruder toil, and more mechanic-art;
Content with slow and timorous stroke to trace
The lingering line, and mould the tardy grace:
But once achieved—though barbarous wreck o'erthrow
The sacred fane, and lay its glories low,
Yet shall the sculptured ruin rise to day,
Graced by defect, and worshipp'd in decay;
Th' enduring record bears the artist's name,
Demands his honours, and asserts his fame.

  Superior hopes the Poet's bosom fire;
O proud distinction of the sacred lyre!
Wide as th' inspiring Phœbus darts his ray,
Diffusive splendour gilds his votary's lay.
Whether the song heroic woes rehearse,
With epic grandeur, and the pomp of verse;
Or, fondly gay, with unambitious guile,
Attempt no prize but favouring beauty's smile;
Or bear dejected to the lonely grove
The soft despair of unprevailing love,—
Whate'er the theme—through every age and clime
Congenial passions meet th' according rhyme;
The pride of glory—pity's sigh sincere—
Youth's earliest blush—and beauty's virgin tear.

  Such is their meed—their honours thus secure,
Whose arts yield objects, and whose works endure.
The Actor, only, shrinks from Time's award;
Feeble tradition is his memory's guard;
By whose faint breath his merits must abide,
Unvouch'd by proof—to substance unallied!
E'en matchless Garrick's art, to heav'n resign'd,
No fix'd effect, no model leaves behind!
The grace of action—the adapted mien,
Faithful as nature to the varied scene;
Th' expressive glance—whose subtle comment draw
Entranced attention, and a mute applause;
Gesture that marks, with force and feeling fraught,
A sense in silence, and a will in thought;
Harmonious speech, whose pure and liquid tone
Gives verse a music, scarce confess'd its own;
As light from gems assumes a brighter ray,
And clothed with orient hues, transcends the day!
Passion's wild break—and frown that awes the sense
And every charm of gentler eloquence—
All perishable! like th' electric fire,
But strike the frame—and as they strike expire;
Incense too pure a bodied flame to bear,
Its fragrance charms the sense, and blends with air.

  Where then—while sunk in cold decay he lies,
And pale eclipse for ever veils those eyes—

Where is the blest memorial that ensures
Our Garrick's fame! whose is the trust?—'Tis yours.
  And O! by every charm his art essay'd
To sooth your cares!—by every grief allay'd!
By the hush'd wonder which his accents drew!
By his last parting tear, repaid by you!
By all those thoughts, which many a distant night
Shall mark his memory with a sad delight!
Still in your hearts' dear record bear his name;
Cherish the keen regret that lifts his fame;
To you it is bequeath'd,—assert the trust,
And to his worth—'tis all you can—be just.
  What more is due from sanctifying Time,
To cheerful wit, and many a favour'd rhyme,
O'er his graced urn shall bloom, a deathless wreath,
Whose blossom'd sweets shall deck the mask beneath.
For these,—when Sculpture's votive toil shall rear
The due memorial of a loss so dear—
O loveliest mourner, gentle Muse! be thine
The pleasing woe to guard the laurell'd shrine.
As Fancy, oft by Superstition led
To roam the mansions of the sainted dead,
Has view'd, by shadowy eve's unfaithful gloom
A weeping cherub on a martyr's tomb—
So thou, sweet Muse, hang o'er his sculptured bier
With patient woe, that loves the lingering tear;
With thoughts that mourn—nor yet desire relief·
With meek regret, and fond enduring grief;
With looks that speak—He never shall return!
Chilling thy tender bosom, clasp his urn;
And with soft sighs disperse th' irreverend dust
Which Time may strew upon his sacred bust.